The Problem of Slavery
in the Age of Revolution
1770–1823

OTHER BOOKS BY DAVID BRION DAVIS

The Problem of Slavery in Western Culture (Cornell University Press)
The Slave Power Conspiracy and the Paranoid Style
Homicide in American Fiction, 1798–1860 (Cornell University Press)

EDITOR OF

*The Fear of Conspiracy: Images of Un-American Subversion from the
    Revolution to the Present* (Cornell University Press)
Ante-Bellum Reform

The Problem of Slavery
in the Age of Revolution
1770–1823

David Brion Davis

Cornell University Press
ITHACA AND LONDON

First published 1975 by Cornell University Press.
Published in the United Kingdom by Cornell University Press Ltd.,
2–4 Brook Street, London W1Y 1AA.

Second printing 1975
First printing, Cornell Paperbacks, 1975
Second printing 1977

International Standard Book Number (cloth) 0-8014-0888-1
International Standard Book Number (paperback) 0-8014-9156-8
Library of Congress Catalog Card Number 74-9214
Printed in the United States of America

TO SARAH BRION DAVIS

Contents

Preface

This book is a sequel to *The Problem of Slavery in Western Culture*. The earlier volume explored the cultural heritage that provided an intellectual and moral framework for the great struggles over Negro slavery in the late eighteenth and nineteenth centuries. It also tried to explain the significance of a profound transformation in moral perception, a transformation that led a growing number of Europeans and Americans to see the full horror of a social evil to which mankind had been blind for centuries. The present study extends the inquiry both in time and in the nature of the questions asked. In the broadest sense, it is an analysis of the historical contexts and consequences of a change in moral perception within the white enslaving culture, and also of some of the ways in which black responses, most dramatically the St. Domingue revolution, impinged on and altered white perceptions of the problem of slavery.

For a number of reasons I have limited myself to the period from 1770 to 1823, which I rather arbitrarily call "The Age of Revolution." In the New World, at least, the Latin American wars of independence were the culmination of a period dominated by the ideals and aspirations of the American and French Revolutions. In the United States the Missouri controversy finally shattered whatever lingering hopes there were that the Founding Fathers had doomed slavery to imminent extinction; it also marked the beginning, as many men of the time clearly sensed, of a conflict of new dimensions. By 1822, British abolitionists had become disheartened by the failure of British diplomacy to secure international suppression of the African slave trade. They had also come to realize that ending the trade to the British West Indies had not induced planters to ameliorate the condition of their slaves or to begin to prepare their slaves for freedom. Consequently, the year 1823 brought a fundamental shift in British antislavery strategy and expectations. Of course, the main reason historians choose any terminal date is to limit the scope of their subject. I have taken the liberty of moving occasionally well beyond 1823 when it seemed that mention of later developments would elucidate the question at hand.

The thematic scope of this book is considerably different from the outline I projected many years ago. For example, I originally intended to devote more space to biographical studies of leading abolitionists. I also planned to give more attention to controversies over slavery in Latin America and, especially, in France. I finally decided to concentrate on the Anglo-American experience, but to approach this subject, as it were, with a wide-angle lens. Accordingly, the geographic focus gradually narrows. As I probe more deeply into the consequences and implications of antislavery activity in Britain and America, the reader will at least have some notion of the very different consequences and implications in France and Latin America. Yet I have barely touched on the Latin American experience, and have intended even the more detailed excursions into French history to serve only as spotlights of comparison that help to illuminate the Anglo-American subject.

The first three chapters present the wider economic and political setting for the half-century of controversy over slavery. After reviewing the cultural and philosophic antecedents that helped to undermine traditional justifications for the institution, I turn to the strengths and vulnerabilities of slavery itself, asking, in effect, whether there were independent trends and forces which helped to make the ideal of universal emancipation a realistic possibility. In Chapters Two and Three I survey, in Britain, France, and North America, the political implications and consequences of challenging a long-accepted institution, as well as the connections between the issue of slavery and conflicts over representation, jurisdiction, and sovereignty. In Chapters Four and Five I move on to questions of a different kind. What effect did the ideals of the Enlightenment and of the evangelical revival have in plantation societies, especially in the American South? How did a social structure dominated by plantation slavery respond to antislavery ideals? Conversely, what social groups in England and in the North became involved in organized antislavery activity? What significance can we attach to the Quaker antislavery initiative? The purpose of Chapters Four and Five, in short, is to explore some of the social circumstances which either limited or reinforced the effect of anti-slavery doctrine.

Chapters Six through Nine form the core of the study and contain its principal themes. They are concerned, essentially, with the ideological functions and implications of the British and American antislavery movements. Since these functions and implications were very different in the two countries, and since I examine the subject in some detail, I have chosen to treat the countries separately, except for brief and periodic comparisons. The meaning of "ideological functions and implications" should become clearer as I proceed. For the moment it is sufficient to say that in these four chapters I move from the cultural dimension, as analyzed in *The Problem of Slavery in Western Culture,* to points of intersection between ideals and social action.

As I suggested in my earlier book, any serious challenge to slavery carried momentous implications precisely because slavery symbolized the most extreme model of treating men as exploitable objects. The justifications for slavery had long been interwoven with the justifications for more widely accepted forms of dominion and subordination. Hence an attack on Negro slavery might open Pandora's box, successively discrediting the cultural sanctions for every traditional form of exploitation; or, if contained, the attack might give at least temporary moral insulation to less visible modes of human bondage. After pursuing these questions in Chapters Six through Nine, I finally turn, in Chapters Ten and Eleven, to two testing points of Western culture: human and divine law. The final questions concern the impact of antislavery argument upon changing conceptions of the conflict of laws, and upon interpretations of the Bible as a guide for man.

Readers who look to history for messages of present "relevance" may find this book less than satisfying in at least two respects. First, I have not cast the early abolitionists in a heroic mold, perceiving them as part of a higher liberal or radical tradition, nor have I cast them as marginal misfits who failed to understand the complexities of slavery and whose moralism prevented effective political action. I am interested in trying to understand the past, not in offering possible solutions for the problems of the past and present. The debate on the pathology of reform, it seems to me, misses the point that virtually all significant moral change springs from people who are in some sense deviant, at least insofar as they are willing to suffer the risk of continuing unpopularity. Second, I have deliberately underplayed the question of race, which is, after all, what slavery supposedly was all about. In recent years Winthrop D. Jordan, George M. Fredrickson, and other scholars have written a number of exceptionally able and thorough studies of racial attitudes. What they have contributed can now be taken fairly well for granted. We need no further proof that racism was pervasive in North America, and was by no means uncommon in England, France, and Latin America. We may still have much to learn about the variations and intensities of Negrophobia in different societies; thus far no one has adequately explained why rather similar ethnic stereotypes should have had such different social outcomes. My own research has persuaded me that, so far as slavery is concerned, racist arguments often served as an excuse for motives that were less easy to acknowledge. Indeed, I would argue that there was a kind of unconscious collaboration even between abolitionists and their opponents in defining race as the ultimate "reality." If my suspicions are valid, then a preoccupation with racial conflict, as the ultimate reality, may only help to obscure more fundamental issues of ideology and power.

Since "ideology" is a treacherous concept, which has been used and misused in a variety of ways, I shall try to clarify a few of my assumptions without pretending to resolve all the problems the concept raises. I have used "ideology" to mean an integrated system of beliefs, assumptions, and values, not necessarily true or false, which reflects the needs and interests of a group or class at a particular time in history. By "interest" I mean anything that benefits or is thought to benefit a specific collective identity. Because ideologies are modes of consciousness, containing the criteria for interpreting social reality, they help to define as well as to legitimate collective needs and interests. Hence there is a continuous interaction between ideology and the material forces of history. The salient characteristic of an ideology is that, while it is taken for granted by people who have internalized it, it is never the eternal or absolute truth it claims to be. Ideologies focus attention on certain phenomena, but only by arbitrarily screening out other phenomena in patterns that are not without meaning.

The analysis of other people's ideologies has commonly been used as a weapon for discrediting their beliefs. By now, however, we should have moved beyond this rather naïve level of self-understanding. There is no reason that we should consider a moral judgment wrong simply because it was an artifact of history, and thus the product of a humanly fallible group or class. If one could demonstrate, for example, that antislavery movements were the product of historical circumstance and that they served various ulterior purposes and functions, the demonstration in no way implies that their indictment of slavery was wrong. Obviously this question goes far beyond the concept of ideology. If a particular truth or moral judgment can be invalidated by historical (or psychological) explanation, then what is to prevent the explanation itself from being invalidated by the same method? The reductionist argument, in short, leads to infinite reductionism. A sharp distinction must be drawn between, on the one hand, paternalizing the past for not knowing what we think we now know and, on the other, using all the tools and concepts at our disposal for understanding our own paternity. No doubt in the future our own mixtures of insight and blindness will be interpreted from that then-present perspective from which one tries to understand the past. We will then be perceived in ways that we cannot perceive ourselves. And only a proper respect for evidence will prevent reckless assaults upon our muteness by omniscient and all-embracing explanation.

Whatever the fallibilities of historical explanation, we have had recent and eloquent affirmations that an understanding of the origins of a new moral consciousness need not lead to an invalidation of new social truths. For example, Erik H. Erikson has attempted to use the psychological concept of "transference" as a means of explaining the origins of Gandhi's militant nonviolence. But, for Erikson, the movement from "experimental encounters with a selected cast of primary counterplayers: father, wife, and boyhood friend," to such "corporate counterplayers" as India, the Empire, and mankind, was "by no means a mere matter of 'transferring' infantile energies and goals onto a widening reality of concerns. A crank, a fanatic, a psychotic can 'transfer,' but only a political genius can master the minute and concrete interplay by which he succeeds in arousing from powerful collectivities responses fully as unique as those which he had established in a smaller circle at home."*

* Erik H. Erikson, *Gandhi's Truth: On the Origins of Militant Nonviolence* (New York, 1969), pp. 114–15.

Erikson's aim, it should be stressed, was not to lower Gandhi's achievement by showing that it emerged from the anguish of human will and responsibility—or in other words, from the same sources that have given rise to movements we generally regard as evil. Rather, he tries to assess the wider strengths and weaknesses of Gandhi's "truth."

This approach to history, including the use of concepts like "ideology" and "transference," does entail consequences which many people may not care to accept. Speaking only for myself, I am prepared to believe that nothing in history is absolute or clear-cut; that truth is always framed in ambiguity; that good and evil are always colored by human ambivalence; that all liberations are won at a cost; that all choice involves negation. I also think that history is filled with moral ironies, and that one can point to ironies but never prove them. Yet when all this is frankly acknowledged, there is something left that is primary and irreducible—something which Erikson tried to convey in his study of Gandhi. Whatever one believes about historical progress—or the lack of it—we are the beneficiaries of past struggles, of the new and often temporary sensitivities of a collective conscience, and of brave men who thought that the time was right not only for appealing to unfulfilled promises of the past, but for breaking the proprieties of the present—for saying, in new contexts and to new audiences, "How long? Not long!"

My research for this book has stretched over a period of some fifteen years, during which I have accumulated many more professional and intellectual debts that I can possibly acknowledge here. The historian's primary dependence, of course, is upon libraries and librarians. For many years I was extraordinarily fortunate in being able to benefit from the wisdom and kindness of Felix Reichmann, then Assistant Director of Cornell University Libraries. I am also grateful to Cornell University for providing funds for microfilms and research assistance. I must mention my special appreciation for the gracious hospitality of James Thorpe and Ray Allen Billington, of the Henry E. Huntington Library, San Marino, California, where I spent a most pleasant summer. My research into Quaker antislavery history would hardly have been possible without the knowledgeable aid of Edward H. Milligan, of Friends House Library, London. I am also grateful for the many courtesies extended by Joyce Godber, County Archivist at the Bedford County Record Office, England.

I owe much to the help and cooperation I received from the staffs of the following libraries and institutions: Historical Manuscripts Commission, National Register of Archives, London; the library of the British Museum; Bodleian Library, Oxford; Picton Library, Liverpool; the National Library of Wales, Aberystwyth; the British and Foreign Bible Society, London; Lambeth Palace Library, London; the West India Committee Archives, London; the John Rylands Library, Manchester; Surrey County Record Office; University of London Library; Wilberforce House, the Hull Museum; the Bibliothèque de l'Institut de France, Paris; the Bibliothèque de l'Arsenal, Paris; the Bibliothèque Nationale; the Library of Congress; the Library Company of Philadelphia, Ridgeway Branch; the Historical Society of Pennsylvania; Duke University Libraries; Alderman Library, University of Virginia; New York Public Library; the New-York Historical Society; Howard University Library; Rutgers University Library; the Boston Athenaeum; Boston Public Library; Yale University Libraries; Harvard University Libraries; Oberlin College Library; the Johns Hopkins University Libraries; the American Antiquarian Society; the Western Reserve Historical Society; the Rhode Island Historical Society; Haverford College Library; the Ohio Historical Society; Stanford University Libraries; and the University of California Libraries, Berkeley.

I owe a special debt of gratitude to John A. Woods, and also to Miss Lloyd Baker, of Hardwicke Court, Gloucester, for allowing me to make use of Woods' transcripts of the Granville Sharp papers, which are in the possession of Miss Baker. I also greatly appreciate the generosity and warm hospitality of C. E. Wrangham, who allowed me to study the Wilberforce papers at Rosemary House, Catterick. I should like to thank R. C. Hanbury for giving me access to the William Allen papers at Allen & Hanburys Ltd., Bethnal Green; Major-General E. H. Goulburn, for allowing transcripts to be made of papers at the Surrey County Record Office; and Major Simon Whitbread, J.P., for allowing transcripts to be made from the Whitbread papers at Bedford.

For a variety of leads, aids, and suggestions I am indebted to E. Martin Hunt, Maurice Hutt, Gabriel Debien, David Lowenthal, John Walsh, Sidney Mintz, John Lombardi, Stephen A. Marglin, and the late Allan Knight Chalmers. During the earlier stages of research, I was immensely aided by the assistance of Jean Laux and Catharine

McCalmon. During the final year of writing, Richard Fox helped me greatly with footnote checking and various bibliographical chores. Early drafts of chapters benefited enormously from the criticisms of Aileen Kraditor, James Walvin, Robert Dawidoff, C. Vann Woodward, Lewis Perry, Edmund S. Morgan, John A. Woods, Stanley N. Katz, Robert M. Cover, William Clebsch, and Sydney Ahlstrom. Michael Kammen, C. Duncan Rice, and Stanley L. Engerman generously read the entire manuscript and saved me from many errors and infelicities. There are two other scholars to whom I owe an incalculable debt. Roger Anstey, of the University of Kent, generously sent me the results of his own research into antislavery history, including transcripts of the Dropmore manuscripts, which he had made through the courtesy of the late W. B. Hamilton. Anstey and I also exchanged drafts of our own work, and engaged in lengthy discussions which I hope were as informative to him as they were to me. I have also exchanged drafts and have had extensive discussion with Eugene D. Genovese, who was completing his own massive study of Negro slavery while we were both fellows at the Center for Advanced Study in the Behavioral Sciences. My relationship with both Anstey and Genovese has shown me that the ideal of scholarly interaction can become a reality. For the scholar there can be no greater reward than the open exchange of ideas, information, and mutual criticism with others engaged in parallel endeavors. But needless to say, none of my early readers or critics is responsible for whatever errors or distortions may be found in this book.

The completion of this book was made possible by the award of a fellowship at the Center for Advanced Study in the Behavioral Sciences. Like others who have been blessed with a year at the Center, I am enormously obliged to O. Meredith Wilson, Preston Cutler, Jane A. Kielsmeier, and all other members of the staff. In addition to the Center's generosity and ideal working conditions, the 1972–1973 year presented extraordinary intellectual stimulation, particularly in an informal seminar on the general themes of dominance and submission. In this respect I should like particularly to thank Percy Cohen and Steven Marcus for numerous helpful ideas and suggestions. I am also much indebted to Nancy B. Helmy, who guided the manuscript through various stages of typing, always with patience and unfailing good humor, and to Jane Dieckmann, who prepared the index.

I delivered an earlier and much shorter version of Chapter Four as my Inaugural Lecture as Harmsworth Professor at Oxford. I should like to thank the Clarendon Press, Oxford, which printed the lecture in 1970, for permission to use some of the same material.

Finally, I know of no way to express sufficient gratitude for my children's continuing faith and encouragement, and above all, for the devotion of Toni, my wife, who insistently protected my working hours, even after the recent birth of our son, and who has proved to be my best critic, though she professes to know nothing about history.

DAVID BRION DAVIS

Stanford, California
August, 1973

Notes on Terms

In accordance with customary usage, I mean "Evangelical" to refer to the movement for personal devotion and piety within the Church of England; "evangelical" to refer to the broader revivalist movements, including Methodism, in both Britain and America.

There has long been considerable confusion over the terms "antislavery" and "abolition." British historians have customarily used "abolition" and "abolitionist" to refer to the movement to abolish the slave trade (1787 to 1808). For them "antislavery" is synonymous with the movement for slave emancipation (beginning in 1823). American historians, on the other hand, have generally used "abolitionist" to refer to the militant reformers who demanded immediate emancipation (beginning, roughly, in 1831); in American history, "antislavery" has designated a less specific and usually more moderate or even theoretical opposition to slavery or to the expansion of slavery into the western territories. Yet these customary distinctions present many problems, for the early and more moderate American antislavery societies were called "abolition" societies, and the later and more militant groups were "antislavery" societies. As we shall see in Chapter Nine, British reformers, too, were by no means consistent in distinguishing the slave trade from slavery. In England, "the abolition" always referred to the end of the slave trade; but many "abolitionists" favored emancipation, and "emancipationists" were also known as "abolitionists." The term "anti-slavist," used by Jeremy Bentham, never gained wide currency. For both British and American

21

reformers, "abolitionism" and "antislavery" were often interchange-
able terms.

Obviously, it is rather clumsy to speak of "antislavery proponents"
or "antislavery people." I see no reason to follow rigid and arbitrary
distinctions, which were not used by the reformers themselves and
which tend to conceal important ambiguities of purpose. Therefore,
when the context permits, I use the terms interchangeably. I have tried
to keep the context clear, so that a reader will know at one point
that an "abolitionist" is solely or primarily concerned with abolishing
the slave trade, and at another point that an "abolitionist" wants to
destroy all slavery, root and branch. Clearly "abolitionism" is a more
specific term than "antislavery," and is associated with the doctrine
that slavery or the slave trade must be abolished. "Abolitionism," in
short, is the more activist expression of "antislavery." For convenience,
and following the precedent of the abolitionists themselves, I will use
"antislavery" as a noun, notwithstanding the shudders of one close
friend.

A Calendar of Events Associated with Slavery, the Slave Trade, and Emancipation, 1770–1823

(Abbreviations: FR—France; GB—Great Britain, LA—Latin America; US—United States)

1770

FR Abbé Raynal's *Histoire philosophique et politique des établissemens et du commerce des Européens dans les deux Indes* calls for a "Black Spartacus" to arise in the New World to avenge the rights of nature.

1771

US A bill passed by the Massachusetts assembly to end slave importations fails to win the governor's assent.

1772

BR The Somerset decision is popularly interpreted as outlawing slavery in England. Correspondence between Granville Sharp and Anthony Benezet begins, opening the way for continuing communication between Anglo-American abolitionists.

US The Virginia House of Burgesses enacts a prohibitive duty on slave imports, and requests the crown to accept this curtailment of "a Trade of great Inhumanity"; the crown disallows the bill.

1773

US   Massachusetts blacks petition the legislature for relief from oppression; Leicester and other Massachusetts towns instruct their representatives to work for laws against both slavery and the slave trade. An increasing number of antislavery tracts are published, including two essays by Benjamin Rush; Samuel Hopkins and Ezra Stiles send a circular letter to New England churches, urging them to oppose the slave trade.

1774

US   The Continental Congress adopts a resolution banning slave importations and further American participation in the slave trade; resolutions adopted by Virginia counties condemn the slave trade, and the Virginia Association orders an end to further slave imports. Philadelphia Yearly Meeting of the Society of Friends adopts rules forbidding Quakers to buy or sell slaves, and requires Quakers to prepare their bondsmen for imminent emancipation.

1775

US   Lord Dunmore, the royal governor of Virginia, promises freedom to any slaves who desert rebellious masters and who serve in the king's forces, an offer taken up by some 800 blacks. Blacks serve in the colonial militia in the battles around Boston. Philadelphia Quakers help organize a Society for the Relief of Free Negroes Unlawfully Held in Bondage.

1776

US   The Second Continental Congress resolves simply "that no slaves be imported into any of the Thirteen United Colonies." Delaware's constitution prohibits the importation of slaves. Philadelphia Yearly Meeting directs local meetings of Friends to disown any Quaker who resists final pleas to manumit his slaves. Congress deletes from the Declaration of Independence Jefferson's clause accusing the king of waging "cruel war against human nature itself, violating its most sacred rights of life and liberty in the persons of a distant people who never offended him, captivating and carrying them into slavery in another hemisphere."

1777

FR   A royal decree prohibits the immigration of Negroes or mulattoes, whether slave or free.

US Vermont's constitution outlaws slavery. North Carolina re-enacts a colonial law prohibiting private manumissions except for meritorious service approved by a court.

1778

GB The House of Commons appoints a committee to investigate the state of the slave trade.

US Virginia prohibits the importation of slaves (by statute, not by constitution). Maryland Quakers make slaveholding an offense warranting disownment.

1779

GB Granville Sharp tries to persuade Anglican bishops to oppose the slave trade.

US As the war shifts to the Deep South, John Laurens of South Carolina proposes arming 3,000 slaves with the promise of freedom. Congress approves the proposal, but the South Carolina legislature rejects it.

1780

US Pennsylvania adopts a gradual emancipation law.

1782

US Virginia enacts a law allowing private manumissions.

1783

GB British Quakers form two committees to work against the slave trade, one an informal publicity group and the other an official committee of London Meeting for Sufferings. An official Quaker petition to end the slave trade is presented to Parliament; the Quakers print over 10,000 copies of *The Case of Our Fellow Creatures, the Oppressed Africans,* which are personally distributed among men of influence. Granville Sharp helps publicize the facts of the *Zong* case, in which 133 blacks had been thrown overboard at sea.

US American Quakers petition Congress to prohibit the slave trade. In Massachusetts, the case of Commonwealth *v.* Jennison is interpreted as removing any judicial sanctions for slavery.

1784

GB James Ramsay publishes his influential *Essay on the Treatment and*

Conversion of African Slaves; both Ramsay and Sharp cooperate with Quaker abolitionists.

US   Connecticut and Rhode Island enact gradual emancipation laws. Congress narrowly rejects Jefferson's proposal to exclude slavery from all the western territories after the year 1800. The Pennsylvania Abolition Society is formed. The Baltimore Conference of the Methodist Episcopal Church adopts rules requiring Methodists to begin manumitting their slaves or to face excommunication. Virginia Quakers require members to free their slaves.

1785

US   New York's Council of Revision fails to approve a bill for gradual emancipation because it would also deny political and civil rights to free blacks. The New York Manumission Society is organized. The General Committee of Virginia Baptists condemns slavery as "contrary to the word of God"; the Methodist Conference at Baltimore decides to suspend the rule requiring gradual manumission. Jefferson publishes *Notes on Virginia,* portraying slavery as an unmitigated evil but suggesting that blacks are inherently inferior to whites.

1786

GB   Thomas Clarkson publishes *An Essay on the Slavery and Commerce of the Human Species,* which in 1785 had won a prize at Cambridge University.

1787

GB   The Society for Effecting the Abolition of the Slave Trade is formed; the Society is really an extension of the unofficial Quaker slave-trade committee; Clarkson travels to collect evidence for the Society.

US   Constitutional Convention agrees to count three-fifths of a state's slave population in apportioning representation; to forbid Congress from ending the slave trade until 1808; to require that fugitive slaves who cross state lines be surrendered to their owners. The Continental Congress enacts the Northwest Ordinance, prohibiting slavery in the territories north of the Ohio and east of the Mississippi rivers. South Carolina enacts a temporary prohibition on slave imports. Rhode Island responds to Quaker petitioning and forbids its citizens from participating in the slave trade.

1788

FR   The Société des Amis des Noirs is formed; it enters into correspondence with the London, Philadelphia, and New York abolition societies.

GB The London Society helps to organize a national petition campaign against the slave trade. Parliament passes a law regulating the conditions of the slave trade. The Privy Council Committee for Trade and Plantations conducts an inquiry into British commercial relations with Africa. Provincial abolition societies organize.

US Connecticut, New York, Massachusetts, and Pennsylvania forbid their citizens from participating in the slave trade.

1789

FR With the calling of the Estates General, the *Amis des noirs* urge the nation to follow the illustrious example of the United States, and to free the slaves in the colonies. The *Amis* make their first goal, however, the abolition of the slave trade. Clarkson visits France, furnishing the *Amis* with evidence against the slave trade. French mulattoes appear before the bar of the National Assembly, futilely petitioning to be seated as colonial delegates. The Assembly accepts the representation of white colonists who, with their merchant allies, prevent debate on the slave trade.

GB In Parliament, William Wilberforce introduces twelve resolutions against the slave trade, a subject eloquently debated in the Commons; despite a flood of petitions, the Commons insists on hearing further evidence, after which it turns to other matters.

US Delaware forbids its citizens from engaging in the slave trade. The Providence (Rhode Island) Society for Abolishing the Slave Trade is formed.

1790

FR The Constituent Assembly accepts the report of the Committee on Colonies: the Assembly agrees not to interfere with the slave trade; the colonies will have the right to submit constitutions for approval; any attempts to incite the slaves will be treason. Royal troops disperse the rebellious assembly at St. Marc, in St. Domingue. The Constituent Assembly orders the dissolution of general assemblies in the colonies, but promises not to interfere "with the status of persons." Vincent Ogé leads a mulatto uprising in St. Domingue, but it is crushed and he is executed.

GB A Select Committee of the House of Commons examines witnesses on the slave trade.

US Both the Quakers and the Pennsylvania Abolition Society petition Congress to use its fullest Constitutional powers to discourage slavery and the slave trade; the petitions evoke angry debate and attacks on the Quakers by Congressmen from the Deep South. In Richmond the Virginia Abolition Society is organized.

1791

FR   The Assembly extends suffrage rights to all colonists, regardless of color, who are born of free parents and who meet property requirements. Civil war breaks out in St. Domingue, and the slaves of the North Province rise in mass insurrection. The Assembly backtracks and renounces its jurisdiction over the status of persons in the colonies.

GB   The Commons continues to examine witnesses and to debate the slave trade, but rejects a motion by Wilberforce to introduce an abolition bill. Parliament grants a charter to the Sierra Leone Company, which for four years has been promoting the colonization of British free Negroes in Africa. The Company commits itself to oppose the slave trade.

1792

FR   The new Legislative Assembly now decrees equal rights for all free blacks and mulattoes in the colonies, and appoints civil commissioners to enforce its decrees and to help suppress the slave revolt. St. Domingue is engulfed in complex racial and civil war.

GB   After much oratory, the Commons votes to terminate the slave trade in 1796, but the bill fails to win assent in the House of Lords, which adopts tactics of delay. A popular movement to boycott slave-grown sugar gains momentum, but domestic political conflict and repressive reaction begin to weaken the antislavery movement, especially in towns like Manchester. The Sierra Leone Company sends off a further fleet to Africa, carrying black refugees from the American Revolution, many of whom had first been taken to Nova Scotia.

US   An antislavery petition from the Quaker, Warner Mifflin, provokes angry words in Congress, which refuses to accept it. Kentucky is admitted as the first new slave state.

Denmark: A royal ordinance requires an end to slave imports in the Danish colonies by 1803.

1793

FR   France is now at war with England and Spain, both of which invade St. Domingue. Toussaint L'Ouverture and other black leaders fight for a time on the Spanish side; white planters welcome English troops and also try to appease mulattoes. The French civil com-

·missioners, who had been sent by the Legislative Assembly, along with a large army, become involved in the civil war. After Commissioner Léger-Felicité Sonthonax proclaims freedom to slaves of the North Province, to gain their military support, the commissioners issue a general emancipation decree.

GB Upper Canada enacts a gradual emancipation law. In the House of Commons, Wilberforce now loses by eight votes on a motion to introduce a slave-trade abolition bill. The Commons also rejects a bill outlawing the British slave trade to foreign markets. There is a marked decline in popular antislavery zeal and in the Abolition Committee's funds.

US Congress passes a fugitive-slave law, as authorized by the Constitution. Georgia excludes slave imports from the West Indies or Spanish Florida but is the only state still legally importing slaves from Africa. The General Committee of Virginia Baptists now decides that emancipation is a political issue that belongs in the legislature, not the church. The New Jersey Abolition Society is formed. The invention by Eli Whitney of the cotton gin opens the way for the cultivation of short-staple cotton through much of the South.

1794

FR The Convention outlaws slavery in all the French colonies and extends the rights of citizenship to all men regardless of color. Toussaint and his followers shift from the Spanish side and join the forces of the French Republic. The British capture Martinique, Guadeloupe, and St. Lucia, though the latter two colonies are eventually recaptured by French armies that include many former slaves.

US Congress prohibits Americans from engaging in the slave trade to foreign countries. The Connecticut assembly passes a bill for immediate emancipation requiring masters to care for old and disabled blacks and providing for the education of Negro children; the council refuses to give the bill its assent. In Philadelphia, the first meeting is held of the Convention of Delegates from the Abolition Societies.

1796

GB Wilberforce's bill for abolition of the slave trade is defeated by four votes in the House of Commons which in 1795 had rejected his motion by a wide margin.

1797

FR British troops continue to suffer heavy casualities in St. Domingue;

Toussaint, now allied with the mulatto General André Rigaud, continues to win victories. The Directory sends General Gabrîel-Marie Hédouville to take charge of St. Domingue. The British capture Trinidad from Spain, now an ally of France.

GB Parliament accepts proposals from Charles Rose Ellis, representing the planter interest, that the crown recommend to the colonial legislatures measures that would encourage a natural increase in slaves and thus eventually render the slave trade unnecessary.

1798

FR British forces begin final withdrawal from St. Domingue, having concluded a treaty with Toussaint; the struggle begins between mulattoes (led by Rigaud and encouraged by Hédouville) and blacks (led by Toussaint).

US Georgia prohibits further slave importations. Congress debates a motion to prohibit slavery from Mississippi Territory, and rejects it.

1799

US New York State adopts a law for gradual emancipation.

1800

FR Toussaint wins full control of St. Domingue, and appoints Jean Jacques Dessalines governor of the South Province where the mulattoes have been defeated.

US Gabriel Prosser's plot to seize Richmond with a large force of armed slaves is uncovered.

1801

FR Toussaint captures Spanish Santo Domingo, unifying the island, and publishes a constitution which prohibits slavery forever and also makes him governor for life. Impending peace with England allows Napoleon to send a large expeditionary force, under General Charles Leclerc, to restore French authority in St. Domingue.

1802

FR The French restore slavery in Guadeloupe. Martinique and other slave colonies are returned to France and her allies by treaty during the brief period of peace. Of her Caribbean conquests, Britain retains only Trinidad. The blacks and mulattoes of St. Domingue fight Napoleon's troops, but Toussaint is captured by treachery and is shipped to France.

US Governor William Henry Harrison, of Indiana Territory, calls a convention at Vincennes, at which appeals are made to Congress to suspend the Northwest Ordinance and allow slaves to be brought into the territory. A later indentured-servants act allows *de facto* slavery.

1803

FR Slavery and the color line are formally restored in the French colonies. Resumption of war with England serves to isolate the French army in St. Domingue, where it is now suffering heavy casualties both from guerrilla war and yellow fever. Dessalines finally forces the French army to withdraw and to surrender to an English fleet. Dessalines proclaims the independence of Haiti from France. Other French and Dutch colonies are seized by England.

US Louisiana Territory is purchased from France. South Carolina opens her ports to the African slave trade.

1804

FR Haiti is established as an independent nation; Dessalines is proclaimed Emperor Jacques the First.

GB A revival of anti-slave-trade agitation occurs. A bill for abolition, proposed by Wilberforce, is passed by the House of Commons, but William Pitt's cabinet postpones debate in the House of Lords, arguing that there is not sufficient time to hear evidence.

US Congress debates an act for the organization of Louisiana Territory, and decides to restrict incoming slaves to the bona-fide property of actual settlers, but rejects a motion to limit the bondage of such slaves to one year. In accordance with the treaty of purchase, the federal government recognizes the property rights of slaveholders who had been protected by French or Spanish law. New Jersey adopts an act for gradual emancipation.

1805

GB The House of Commons defeats a bill proposed by Wilberforce for abolishing the slave trade. Pitt issues an Order-in-Council stopping the African slave trade to foreign colonies conquered by Britain, and restricting the annual introduction of any slaves to those colonies to 3 per cent of the existing slave populations.

1806

FR Dessalines is assassinated in Haiti and is succeeded by Henri Christophe. A struggle begins between the blacks, led by Christophe, and the mulattoes, led by Alexandre Pétion.

GB Pitt's death leads to the Ministry of All the Talents, and to secret government collaboration with the abolitionists. Parliament passes a law ending the British slave trade to foreign countries as well as to captured or ceded colonies. Parliament also overwhelmingly approves a resolution by Charles James Fox that the entire slave trade should be abolished but no immediate action follows.

US President Jefferson urges Congress to prohibit the slave trade as soon as the Constitutional restriction expires (that is, after 1807). Virginia passes a law requiring all slaves who are manumitted to leave the state within a year of their manumission. President Jefferson secures an embargo against any trade with Haiti.

1807

GB Lord Grenville secures passage in the House of Lords of a bill abolishing the slave trade; the measure receives the crown's approval after passing by an overwhelming majority in the House of Commons. A proposal by Earl Percy for gradual emancipation in the colonies is defeated and is disavowed by the abolitionists. The African Institution is formed as an organization to seek enforcement of the abolition law as well as to further the civilization of Africa and the development of markets for commodities other than slaves. The government of Sierra Leone is transferred to the crown, after considerable controversy over the private Sierra Leone Company's management.

US Congress passes a law prohibiting Americans from participating in the African slave trade.

1808

GB Thomas Clarkson publishes his two-volume *History of the Rise, Progress and Accomplishment of the Abolition of the African Slave-Trade by the British Parliament.*

US The General Conference of the Methodist Episcopal Church decides to delete the rules on slavery from copies of its *Discipline* sent to the Deep South.

1810

LA The Supreme Junta of Caracas proclaims the abolition of the slave trade. In Mexico, Hidalgo issues an emancipation decree before his rebellious movement is crushed. Dom João, ruler of the Portuguese empire, submits to British pressure after earlier being escorted by the British from Lisbon to Rio de Janeiro; he agrees to restrict the slave trade to certain geographic zones and to cooperate in eventually suppressing the trade entirely.

1811

LA   Cuba remonstrates against proposals debated in the Spanish Cortes to prohibit the slave trade and to provide for gradual emancipation in the colonies.

GB   A law is passed making participation in the slave trade a felony.

1812

GB   A British Order-in-Council requires that Trinidad, captured from Spain in 1797 and denied a legislature of its own, set up a registry of slaves to help detect illegal importations.

1814

GB   Public pressure mounts in Great Britain to force France to abolish the slave trade, after the first Treaty of Paris sanctions a five-year postponement of French abolition. Other maritime nations either abolish the slave trade or make commitments to Britain.

1815

FR   Napoleon, during his one hundred days, decrees the abolition of the slave trade. The restored Bourbon government succumbs to British pressure and passes an ineffective law against slave trading.

GB   At the Congress of Vienna, British statesmen secure an abstract declaration condemning the slave trade. In Parliament, British abolitionists move for a law requiring a centralized registration of all West Indian slaves, a plan that provokes heated controversy.

1816

LA   Simón Bolívar secures arms and supplies from Haiti, after promising Pétion that he will promote the cause of emancipation in South America. In Venezuela, Bolívar offers freedom to slaves willing to fight the royalists. José de San Martín also offers freedom to blacks who join his army in the invasion of Chile.

US   The American Colonization Society is formed to promote the colonization of free blacks in Africa. The newly formed African Methodist Episcopal Church denies membership to slaveholders. George Bourne publishes *The Book and Slavery Irreconcilable,* the most radical abolitionist tract yet to appear in America.

1817

GB   A treaty is signed with Portugal prohibiting the slave trade north of the equator but sanctioning the Portuguese-Brazilian trade south of the line. A treaty is also signed with Spain prohibiting the trade north of the equator and providing for total abolition in 1820. Britain agrees to pay a fixed sum as compensation for Spain's expected financial losses.

US   New York State enacts a law, effective July 4, 1827, freeing all Negroes who would not have been freed before then by the gradual emancipation act of 1799. In Philadelphia, James Forten leads a protest meeting of 3,000 blacks against the American Colonization Society.

1818

GB   Britain fails at the Congress of Aix-la-Chapelle to secure international agreement on the right of search.

US   Illinois drafts a state constitution, and sharp conflict erupts over the question of slavery. In Congress, James Tallmadge, Jr., of New York, opposes admission of Illinois because its constitution does not contain a strong-enough prohibition of slavery.

1819

LA   The Congress of Angostura rejects Bolívar's pleas to ratify his military emancipation policies; the Congress commits itself to the principle of emancipation but affirms that blacks must first be prepared for freedom.

GB   Parliament passes a compromise measure for the registration of colonial slaves, but it falls far short of abolitionist demands. Courts of mixed commission are set up at Sierra Leone to adjudicate cases involving captured slave ships.

US   A law authorizes the President to send armed vessels to Africa to suppress the illegal American slave trade. Congressman John W. Taylor, of New York, proposes an amendment to a bill organizing Arkansas Territory, applying the principles of the Northwest Ordinance to Arkansas; the amendment is defeated in a close sectional vote. James Tallmadge, Jr., introduces an amendment to the Missouri statehood bill that would prohibit the further introduction of slaves and would provide for gradual emancipation in Missouri. The fuse is thus ignited for the bitter Missouri controversy.

1820

US   Congress defines the slave trade as piracy. The American Colonization Society sends an expedition to Africa to establish a settlement. The House and Senate are deadlocked over the question of admitting Missouri as a slave state, and there is some fear of civil war. As a compromise, Congress adopts an amendment that there shall be no restriction on slavery in Missouri, but that the institution will be prohibited from the unorganized Louisiana Territory north of 36°30′ latitude. There is continuing agitation to refuse Missouri admission unless the state provides for gradual emancipation.

1821

FR   The Société de la morale chrétienne is formed and appoints an anti-slave-trade committee. The Chamber of Deputies had earlier rejected a petition of Joseph Morénas against the slave trade.

LA   The Congress of Cucutá adopts a gradual emancipation act for Gran Colombia. In Peru, San Martín proclaims an end to the slave trade and provides for gradual emancipation.

US   Missouri is admitted to the Union after further controversy over the lack of an antislavery clause in the state constitution and over a clause restricting the entry of free blacks and mulattoes. Benjamin Lundy begins publishing his *Genius of Universal Emancipation*.

1822

GB   The Congress of Verona marks the final failure of British attempts to win sanction for an international maritime police to suppress the slave trade. Diplomatic pressure now focuses on Brazil, which declares her independence from Portugal and is thus free from previous treaty obligations. British abolitionists begin to turn their attention to West Indian emancipation, and plan organized action to secure total though gradual abolition of slavery.

US   A movement gets under way in Illinois to adopt a constitution legalizing slavery; the question leads to a heated political struggle and is not resolved until 1824. In South Carolina, Denmark Vesey's planned slave rebellion is uncovered, adding fuel to southern fears of abolitionism and slave insurrection.

1823

LA   Chile enacts a measure for general emancipation. In Brazil, José Bonifácio de Andrada e Silva resists British pressures for a definite commitment to abolish the slave trade. Though Bonifácio personally favors gradual emancipation and gives cautious expression to his

principles, he is forced out of office partly because of his moderate
antislavery views. Brazil fails to adopt a proposed constitution that
contains an article condemning slavery in principle.

BR   The Society for the Mitigation and Gradual Abolition of Slavery is
organized. The Commons approves George Canning's resolutions
for the amelioration of colonial slavery, and the government recom-
mends specific reforms to colonial governors.

The Problem of Slavery
in the Age of Revolution
1770–1823

One ⁓

What the Abolitionists
Were Up Against

"The Problem of Slavery in Western Culture":
The Argument Summarized

The concept of chattel slavery, which must be distinguished from historical varieties of servitude and dependence, has always embodied a profound though subtle contradiction. Since man has a remarkable capacity to imagine abstract states of perfection, he very early imagined a perfect form of subordination. Plato compared the slave to the human body, the master to the body's soul. Slaves incarnated the irrationality and chaos of the material universe, as distinct from the masterlike Demiurge. There was thus a cosmic justification behind Aristotle's dictum that "from the hour of their birth, some men are marked out for subjection, others for rule." The true slave, according to Aristotle, could have no will or interests of his own; he was merely a tool or instrument—the extension of his owner's physical nature.

But even metaphysics had to recognize the slave as a conscious being. Aristotle allowed the bondsman a lower form of virtue, consisting, as one might expect, in the perfect fulfillment of his assigned function. The slave could affirm his consciousness, in other words, by partaking of his master's consciousness and by becoming one with his master's desires. The perfect slave, therefore, would be a paradigm of that ideal submission never quite approximated by the most obedient children, wives, subjects, students, or patients: he would be the automatic agent of his creator's will (not an autonomous Adam free to disobey).

At this point we arrive at the root of the "problem" of slavery. The more perfect the slave, as Hegel later observed, the more enslaved becomes the master. For the master's identity depends on having a slave who recognizes him as master: the truth of the master's independent consciousness lies in the dependent and supposedly unessential consciousness of the bondsman.[1]

This psychological paradox was not unknown to the ancient world. "It would be absurd," Diogenes of Sinope reportedly said, when his own slave had run away, "if Manes can live wihtout Diogenes, but Diogenes cannot get on without Manes." When pirates captured Diogenes and took him to a slave market in Crete, he pointed to a spectator wearing rich purple robes, and said, "Sell me to this man; he needs a master."

There is no need here to review the history of slave systems or to discuss the sociological gradations between various forms of servitude. It is sufficient to make three brief points about the concept and reality of slavery. First, the ancient ideal of personal subordination was modified by Christianity but continued to influence medieval and early modern thought, even in countries where chattel bondage had disappeared. In medieval England, for example, Bracton identified villeins with Roman slaves, and carefully distinguished them from other kinds of dependent laborers whose rights were protected by the state. Second, insofar as actual forms of servitude approximated the concept of slavery, as elaborated, for example, in Roman law, they represented the extreme example of treating men as objects to be manipulated, humiliated, and exploited. Hence the term "slavery" continued to acquire metaphorical associations implying the ultimate in dependence, disability, powerlessness, sinfulness, and negation of autonomous self-consciousness. Third, the internal contradictions of slavery were not confined to theory, but arose ultimately from historical attempts to keep and govern slaves, a situation which always necessitated compromise. No lawgivers could forget that tools and instruments do not run away, rebel, commit crimes, or help protect the state

[1] G. W. F. Hegel, *The Phenomenology of Mind,* tr. by J. B. Baillie (2nd ed., New York, 1964), pp. 235–37. The other references upon which this section is based can be found in *The Problem of Slavery in Western Culture* (Ithaca, N.Y., 1966).

from external danger. No masters, whether in ancient Rome, medieval Tuscany, or seventeenth-century Brazil, could forget that the obsequious servant might also be a "domestic enemy" bent on theft, poisoning, or arson. Throughout history it has been said that slaves, if occasionally as loyal and faithful as good dogs, were for the most part lazy, irresponsible, cunning, rebellious, untrustworthy, and sexually promiscuous.

The institution of slavery, then, has always given rise to conflict, fear, and accommodation. The settlement of the New World magnified these liabilities, since the slaves now came from an alien and unfamiliar culture; they often outnumbered their European rulers; and many colonial settlements were vulnerable to military attack or close to wilderness areas that offered easy refuge. Accordingly, the introduction of Negro slavery to the Americas brought spasmodic cries of warning, anxiety, and racial repugnance. But the grandiose visions of New World wealth—once the Spanish had plundered the Aztecs and Incas —seemed always to require slave labor. The Negro slave thus became an intrinsic part of the American experience.

The economics of slavery have no bearing on the argument at this point. It is obvious that the various colonizing nations, whatever their domestic traditions of servitude, seized upon Africans as the cheapest and most expedient labor supply to meet the immediate demands of mining and tropical agriculture. The institution took on a variety of forms as a result of European cultural differences, the character of the work performed, geographic and ecological conditions, and a host of other variables. But Anglo-American slavery was not unique in defining the bondsman as chattel property endowed with elements of human personality. Nor was Anglo-American society unusual in having to accommodate the underlying contradictions of the master-slave relationship.

The diversities of New World slavery should not blind us to the central point. In the 1760s there was nothing unprecedented about chattel slavery, even the slavery of one ethnic group to another. What was unprecedented by the 1760s and early 1770s was the emergence of a widespread conviction that New World slavery symbolized all the forces that threatened the true destiny of man. How does one explain this remarkable shift in moral consciousness, if it was not a direct response to an innovation of unparalleled iniquity? Presumably men of the mid-eighteenth century were no more virtuous than men of earlier times, although something might have altered their perceptions of virtue. No doubt the new antislavery opinion drew on the misgivings and anxieties which slavery had always engendered, but which had been checked by the desire for independence and wealth. Yet the slave systems of the New World, far from being in decay, had never appeared so prosperous, so secure, or so full of promise.

The emergence of an international antislavery opinion represented a momentous turning point in the evolution of man's moral perception, and thus in man's image of himself. The continuing "evolution" did not spring from transcendent sources: as a historical artifact, it reflected the ideological needs of various groups and classes. The explanation must begin, however, with the heritage of religious, legal, and philosophical tensions associated with slavery—or in other words, with the ways in which Western culture had organized man's experience with lordship and bondage.

From antiquity slavery has embodied symbolic meanings connected with the condition and destiny of man. For the Greeks (as for Saint Augustine and other early Christian theologians) physical bondage was part of the cosmic hierarchy, of the divine scheme for ordering and governing the forces of evil and rebellion. For the ancient Hebrews, slavery could be a divine punishment; a time of trial and self-purification prior to deliverance; and the starting point for a historical mission. The literature of Hellenistic and early Christian times is saturated with the paradoxes of human bondage: man was a slave to sin or to his own passions; his incapacity for virtuous self-government justified his external bondage; yet he might escape his internal slavery by becoming the servant of universal reason—or of the Lord. Emancipation from one form of slavery depended on the acceptance of a higher and more righteous bondage.

If Plato and Aristotle provided an ideology for masters, the Cynics, Sophists, and Stoics provided an ideology for slaves. Externally, the servant might be the instrument of his master's will, but internally, in his own self-consciousness, he remained a free soul. And he could affirm the truth of this subjective reality by denying the importance of the world of flesh and human convention. Physical constraint could never bar a man from true virtue. Hence the master, imagining himself to be free and omnipotent, might well be the true slave—at least in the eyes of the slave.

This transvaluation had profound and enduring consequences when absorbed by Christian theology. The early Church Fathers, living in a slave society, accommodated the institution's contradictions by synthesizing Greek and Hebrew notions of freedom. No human master could usurp God's role and demand absolute and unconditional submission from another man. The only slavery that mattered was slavery to sin, from which no man was exempt. Christianity thus harbored a negative equalitarianism, proclaiming that God was no respecter of persons, that lords and servants were equally subject to His wrath and forgiveness. For masters, paradoxically, a submission to God could mean a lessening dependence on their slaves' acceptance of lordship. Christianity also recognized the grievances and longings of slaves, but sublimated them into another realm of time and space. Any man might become truly free, but only by becoming an unconditional slave to the only true Master. The lowliest slave could look forward to emancipation, but only in another life. In this life, "he that was called in the Lord being a bondservant, is the Lord's freeman: likewise he that was called being free, is Christ's bondservant." Slaves should therefore bear their worldly condition for the glory of God, obeying their masters "with fear and trembling, in a singleness of your heart, as unto Christ." In one sense, the Epistle to the Ephesians gave an ingenious solution to the problem posed by Aristotle: a slave could be virtuous by conforming to his master's will, but only if he served the master "as unto Christ."

The early Christian view of slavery was of central importance in reconciling the masses to the existing social order. It constituted the core of an ideology that encouraged hope, patience, endurance, and submission, while reminding the powerful of their own fallibility. It would be a mistake to think of an immanent Christian equalitarianism that was certain to develop, on the analogy of a seed or root, into an unequivocal denunciation of physical slavery. Christianity represented one means of responding to the contradictions of lordship and bondage, and it wove those contradictions into its fundamental views of man and the world. Thus Saint Thomas Aquinas could affirm that slavery was contrary to the first and highest intent of nature, and yet insist that it conformed to the second intent of nature, which was adjusted to man's limited capacities. He could therefore suggest that slavery was a necessary part of the governing pattern of the universe, speak of the slave as the physical instrument of his owner, and find scholastic justifications for the Roman rule that the child of a free man and bondwoman should be a slave. Neither Luther nor Calvin, one may note, had any notion that Christian liberty could alter the fact that some men are born free and others slaves. Indeed, as a result of the verdict of many centuries, one could not begin to assert the universal sinfulness of slavery without questioning the doctrine of original sin and challenging the entire network of rationalization for every form of subordination.

The first groups to denounce the principle of slavery, and all that it implied, were the perfectionist and millennialist sects who sought to live their lives free from sin. In essence, their ideal involved a form of mutual love and recognition that precluded treating men as objects, even as objects with souls. The sectarians, whatever their distinctive beliefs and practices, looked for a form of authentic service, or selflessness, which could not be used as a lever for exploitation. For us their importance does not lie in the transmission of ideas, but in their attempts to realize a mode of interpersonal life that was the precise antithesis of chattel slavery. To the social order, of course, the sectarians were an intolerable affront. They were thus either annihilated or reduced to spiritualistic withdrawal.

The notable exception was the Society of Friends, which early found the means of compromise and thus survival. The Quakers not only contained and stabilized their quest for a purified life, but institutionalized methods for bearing witness to their faith. In other words, the Quakers achieved a dynamic balance between the impulse to perfection and the "reality principle." They also acquired considerable economic and political power, and were the only sect to become deeply involved with Negro slavery.

At the outset, it appeared that the Quakers would accommodate the contradictions of slavery much as Catholics and Protestants had done before them. By the early eighteenth century there were Quaker planters in the West Indies and Quaker slave merchants in London, Philadelphia, and Newport. But partly because of the Friends' testimony against war, slaveholding occasioned moral tensions that were less common among other denominations. For critics and deviants within the sect, the wealthy masters and slave-trading merchants presented a flagrant symbol of worldly compromise and an ideal target for attack. For a variety of reasons the Seven Years' War brought a spiritual crisis for the Society of Friends, resulting in much soul-searching, attempts at self-purification, and a final commitment to disengage themselves, collectively, from the Atlantic slave system.

The Quakers' growing anguish coincided with four complex and interrelated developments in Western culture, particularly the culture of British Protestantism. First, the emergence of secular social philosophy necessitated a redefinition of the place of human bondage in the rational order of being. With the exception of Jean Bodin, the great political theorists of the sixteenth and seventeenth centuries all found justifications for chattel slavery. On the other hand, by appealing to utility and social order, and by divorcing the subject from theological conceptions of sin, they narrowed the grounds of sanction. Thomas Hobbes, for example, gave his blessings to a form of bondage so absolute that a master could kill his servant with impunity. But by reducing the relationship to fear, power, and self-interest, Hobbes removed any ethical basis for condemning a successful revolt. He also swept away traditional distinctions based on natural merit and assigned status, and thus undermined both the classical and Christian justifications for unquestioned dominion. Because John Locke celebrated the importance of natural liberty, he had to place slavery outside the social compact, which was designed to protect man's inalienable rights. Locke thus imagined slavery as *"the state of War continued, between a lawful Conquerour, and a Captive."* Even by the 1730s such arguments were beginning to appear absurd to a generation of English and French writers who had learned from Locke to take an irreverent view of past authority and to subject all questions to the test of reason. It was Montesquieu, more than any other thinker, who put the subject of Negro slavery on the agenda of the European Enlightenment, weighing the institution against the general laws or principles that promoted human happiness, and encouraging the imaginative experiment of a reversal of roles in a world turned upside down. And by the 1760s the arguments of Montesquieu and Francis Hutcheson were being repeated, developed, and propagated by the cognoscenti of the enlightened world. John Locke, the great enemy of all absolute and arbitrary power, was the last major philosopher to seek a justification for absolute and perpetual slavery.

A second and closely related transformation was the popularization of an ethic of benevolence, personified in the "man of feeling." This ideal first appeared as an answer to the Calvinist and Hobbesian views of man's incapacity for virtue. The insistence on man's inner goodness, identified with his power of sympathy, became part of a gradual secularizing tendency in British Protestantism, a tendency awkwardly designated as "latitudinarianism." Ultimately, this liberal spirit led in two directions, each described by the titles of Adam Smith's two books: *The Theory of Moral Sentiments* and *The Wealth of Nations*. If there were unresolved tensions between sympathetic benevolence and individual enterprise, both theories condemned slavery as an intolerable obstacle to human progress. The man of sensibility needed to objectify his virtue by relieving the sufferings of innocent victims. The economic man required a social order that allowed and morally vindicated the free play of individual self-interest. By definition, the slave was both innocent and a victim, since he could not be held responsible for his own condition. The Negro's enslavement, unlike the legitimate restraints of society, seemed wholly undeserved. He represented innocent nature, and hence corresponded, psychologically, to the natural and spontaneous impulses of the man of feeling. Accordingly, the key to progress lay in the controlled emancipation of innocent nature as found both in the objective slave and in the subjective affections of the reformer. The latter's compassion would evoke compassion in the slave, and the reciprocal love would slowly free the world from corruption and illicit self-seeking. The slave would be lifted to a level of independent action and social obligation. The reformer would be assured of the beneficence of his own self-interest by merging himself in a transcendent cause. These results, at least, were the expectation of philanthropists who increasingly transformed the quest for salvation from a sinful world into a mission to cleanse the world of sin.

A third source of the antislavery impulse was the evangelical faith in instantaneous conversion and demonstrative sanctification. One must hasten to add that many Methodists, Anglican Evangelicals, and American revivalists subscribed to the traditional Christian justifications for human bondage. Leading Anglican Evangelicals, like Bishop Beilby Porteus, came to see the African slave trade as an unmitigated sin but recoiled from condemning any form of servitude so clearly sanctioned by Scripture. Yet the evangelical movement, traditional in overall theology and world view, emphasized man's burden of personal responsibility, dramatized the dangers of moral complacency, and magnified the rewards for an authentic change of heart. And by 1774 John Wesley had not only made it clear that the sins of the world would soon be judged, but that every slaveholder, slave merchant, and investor in slave property was deeply stained with blood and guilt. John Newton, who as a sailor had seen the full horrors of slave ships and West Indian plantations, could testify that "inattention and interest" had so blinded him to sin that he had never doubted the legitimacy of Negro slavery even after his religious conversion. Newton's decision to denounce slavery as a crime and to confess his former depravity became a model, for his pious admirers, of authentic sanctification.

Evangelical religion also gave a new thrust to the ancient desire to Christianize human bondage by imbuing both master and servant with a spirit of charity and forbearance. It thus led to sincere and continuing efforts to teach slaves the Christian hopes and virtues, and to persuade their owners that neither profits nor security could be endangered by the true faith. Yet by 1770 the Quakers were not alone in concluding that the institution was invulnerable to reform and exempt from the laws of Christian progress. The Negro's cultural difference commonly served as the justification for his enslavement, reinforcing the myth that he had been rescued from heathen darkness and taken to a land of spiritual light. But to be validated, this argument ultimately required religious conversion and an assimilation of slavery to the Christian model of benign and paternalistic service. As John Woolman pointed out, no master was saintly enough to avoid the temptations of absolute power; slavery, instead of being ameliorated by Christianity, corrupted the wellsprings of true religion.

The Negro's cultural difference, which served as an excuse for the failures at Christianization, acquired a positive image at the hands of eighteenth-century primitivists who searched through travel accounts and descriptions of exotic lands for examples of man's inherent virtue and creativity. I can only touch on a few of the complexities of this fourth source of antislavery sentiment. For the most part, the "noble savage" was little more than a literary convention that conflated the Iroquois and South Sea islander with sable Venuses, dusky swains, and tear-bedewed daughters of "injur'd Afric." The convention did, however, modify Europe's arrogant ethnocentrism and provide expression for at least a momentary ambivalence toward the human costs of modern civilization. It also tended to counteract the many fears and prejudices that had long cut the Negro off from the normal mechanisms of sympathy and identification. There is no evidence that literary primitivism made Americans any more inclined to view blacks as autonomous human beings. But for many Europeans, as diverse as John Wesley and the Abbé Raynal, the African was an innocent child of nature whose enslavement in America betrayed the very notion of the New World as a land of natural innocence and new hope for mankind. By the early 1770s such writers portrayed the Negro slave as a man of natural virtue and sensitivity who was at once oppressed by the worst vices of civilization and yet capable of receiving its greatest benefits.

These cultural transformations by no means explain, by themselves, the appearance of organized efforts to rid the world of slavery. The secular Enlightenment, for example, contained countervailing tendencies which encouraged the defense of Negro slavery on grounds of utility, racial inferiority, ethical relativism, or the presumed rationality of wealth-giving institutions. Christianity, for the most part, continued to distinguish worldly subordination from spiritual freedom, although there were increasing strains in the balanced dualisms that gave sanction to hereditary bondage. I have not been concerned, however, with immediate causation but rather with the conditions which weakened the traditional screening mechanisms of Western culture; which removed slavery from the list of supposedly inevitable misfortunes of life; and which made it easier to perceive—in a moral sense—the inherent contradictions of human bondage.

By the eve of the American Revolution there was a remarkable convergence of cultural and intellectual developments which at once undercut traditional rationalizations for slavery and offered new modes of sensibility for identifying with its victims. It is at this point that *The Problem of Slavery in Western Culture* concludes: with a rash of antislavery books, sermons, poems, plays, pamphlets; with the economic reassessments of empire occasioned by the Seven Years' War; with the initiative taken by individual reformers in America, France, and England, whose international communication led to an awareness of shared concerns and expectations. But what were the more material considerations which helped both to shape the new moral consciousness and to define its historical effects? If the growth of antislavery opinion signified a profound cultural change, what difference did it make in the end?

There are two sides to such questions. One could take the institution of slavery for granted and look at the impulses behind the antislavery phenomenon, asking how they reflected, either consciously or unconsciously, the social orders from which they emerged. The new hostility to human bondage cannot be reduced simply to the needs and interests of particular classes. Yet the needs and interests of particular classes had much to do with a given society's receptivity to new ideas and thus to the ideas' historical impact. Much of this book will be concerned with the ideological functions and implications of attacking this symbol of the most extreme subordination, exploitation, and de-humanization, at a time when various enlightened elites were experimenting with internalized moral and cultural controls to establish or preserve their own hegemony.

But one cannot ignore a second aspect, which has to do with the strength or vulnerability of slavery itself. There were many planters in Virginia, Jamaica, and St. Domingue who were open to the spirit of the Enlightenment. They did not, however, decide to give up their slave property after reading Montesquieu, *The Virginia Gazette,* or *The Weekly Magazine or Edinburgh Amusement.* The question of abolishing slavery was ultimately a question of power. In the broadest outline, one therefore needs to know what the abolitionists were up against, in the more obvious meaning of the pun. The first antislavery movements arose in an era of war, revolution, and rapid economic change. In what ways did these forces undermine or strengthen the slave systems of the New World? In what ways did shifts in economic, political, or military power help to shape the consequences of moral condemnation?

Demographic and Economic Trends, 1770–1823

In July, 1822, Benjamin Lundy, the Quaker abolitionist, surveyed the progress of emancipation in the Western world. He began by noting that John Randolph, an apologist for slavery in the United States Congress, had courted popularity in England by condemning the slave trade in a speech to the philanthropic African Institution. If the speech revealed Randolph's hypocrisy, Lundy also took it as heartening evidence of the world-wide abhorrence of the African slave traffic. He reminded readers of his *Genius of Universal Emancipation* that only a few years had passed since the slave trade had found defenders in all parts of America. Surely slavery itself would soon arouse the same universal indignation, and men would be ashamed to justify it in public:

The march of the mind is rapid. THE ADVOCATES OF LIBERTY ARE SURE OF THEIR MARK. Let them steadily pursue their object, and there is no danger. The fiend of slavery in North America is surrounded. The free states of this Union are on the east, the north, and the west—Hayti and Colombia, on the south. The mighty force of *Public Opinion,* in the former; powerfully aided in its march, shall bear resistless down the majestic Mississippi, driving him before it; and arrested by the rising genius of the latter, his gorgon head will disappear amid the dark and stormy waves of the Mexican gulph.[2]

For all his apocalyptic imagery, which curiously anticipated the expansionist rhetoric of the era of Manifest Destiny, Lundy perceived the problem of slavery in hemispheric and transatlantic terms. He knew that if Missouri had recently been admitted as a new slave state, so too the new republic of Gran Colombia had enacted a gradual emancipation law. And surely if the spirit of revolution and independence had brought freedom to nearly one half-million blacks in Haiti, it would soon kill the "fiend" throughout South America. And Lundy doubtless knew that British abolitionists, who had been closely watching events in Latin America and the United States, had decided that the time had arrived for an avowed movement for West Indian emancipation.[3]

Lundy's hopes, like those of the British abolitionists, rested on an unquestioned faith that history was on their side, that New World slavery could never withstand the forces of moral and economic progress, and that the events of the previous half-century had already brought the institution to its dying stages.[4] Let us take a realistic assessment of these hopes, in view of our present knowledge, without becoming enmeshed either in technical disputes or in the controversies over the precise relationship of slavery to modern capitalism. It will simplify matters if we first view slavery as a declining institution, taking note of the circumstances and trends which appeared to

---

[2] *The Genius of Universal Emancipation,* II (July, 1822), 4.

[3] Zachary Macaulay to Selina Macaulay, May 31, 1822; Thomas Clarkson to Zachary Macaulay, Nov. 24, 1822, Macaulay papers, Henry E. Huntington Library; James Cropper to Thomas Clarkson, Aug. 5, 1822; Oct. 12, 1822; Cropper to Zachary Macaulay, Feb. 5, 1822; Oct. 21, 1822, Add. MSS 41267A, British Museum. Cropper was in close communication on the slavery issue with two American Quakers, Philip Evan Thomas and Elias Hicks.

[4] Lundy, however, was not always so sanguine as in the quotation I have given. He was among the most realistic and prescient of American abolitionists.

give substance to the abolitionists' hopes. We can then turn to evidence of a less promising kind.

The abolitionists' optimism drew its chief support from the history of the African slave trade and the sugar colonies it supplied. Since New World slavery originated in the sugar colonies, any weakening of the Caribbean–South Atlantic system seemed to doom the institution at its source. According to the best available estimates, between 60 and 70 per cent of all the Africans who survived the voyages to the New World were destined for Europe's sugar colonies.[5] It was Europe's increasing demand for sugar that fueled the Atlantic slave trade, depositing dense populations of black workers first in the Portuguese isles off the West African coast, then in northeastern Brazil, Barbados, the Leeward Islands, Jamaica, St. Domingue, and last of all Cuba, transforming them all into plantation societies. Plantation agriculture also expanded outward to areas unsuitable for sugar, such as the interior valleys and uplands of tropical regions, or the coastal lowlands of more distant and temperate zones. By the second half of the eighteenth century there were relatively large concentrations of black slaves not only in the sugar colonies but in the mining regions of Brazil and present-day Colombia, along the rice coast of South Carolina, and in the tobacco country surrounding Chesapeake Bay. Forming an outer orbit, so to speak, smaller numbers of slaves had been spun off to the towns and port cities, to the larger commercial farms and domestic industries. Yet only in certain limited regions did the plantation shape and then come to dominate the entire structure of a society. And if such societies showed evidence of a sudden loss of energy and wealth, it was not unreasonable to assume that the satellites of the slave system could not long survive.

From the very start, the immense profits of sugar cultivation had been won at a heavy social and economic cost. Given the Caribbean traditions of frontier lawlessness, piracy, and plunder, it was perhaps unlikely that any of the islands would develop balanced economies or attract settlers who would look to their colony's long-term welfare. Yet the first English settlers in Barbados were much like those in North America. It was the "sugar revolution" of the 1640s, as Richard S. Dunn has ably demonstrated, which soon created a strong and cohesive

[5] Robert William Fogel and Stanley L. Engerman, *Time on the Cross: The Economics of American Negro Slavery* (2 vols., Boston, 1974), I, 16.

planter class, which consolidated the best lands in the hands of a few wealthy proprietors, which led to the continuing emigration of both successful and unsuccessful whites, and which transformed Barbados into the richest English colony in the New World, but one from which most English settlers longed to escape. Barbados was the first English colony to gravitate toward the extreme model of speculative profits, absentee proprietorship, monoculture, soil exhaustion, a stunted institutional life, and a white population notorious for its vulgarity, alcoholism, and general improvidence. By 1712 the colony's white population was hardly half as large as it had been in 1655; in the same interval, as a result of heavy importations from Africa, the number of slaves had more than doubled.[6]

The famed opulence of the West Indian planters rested on a fragile base that would begin to disintegrate if sugar prices fell, if production costs rose, or if it became more difficult to purchase provisions, secure credit, or compete with rival colonies which contained expanses of undepleted soil. The sugar colonies were also extraordinarily vulnerable to natural disasters, such as hurricanes, as well as to easy devastation by wartime enemies. To some extent the imperial privileges of bounties and a protected market in Britain concealed the effects of rising production costs, an over-investment in slaves, heavy interest charges on debts, and a speculative concentration on sugar at the expense of foodstuffs and other tropical staples. The period between the end of the Seven Years' War, when England acquired new colonies in the Windward Islands, and the onset of the American Revolution, was a golden age for the British planter, who could look forward to high sugar prices, lowered transportation costs, and an ample supply of labor. The American Revolution, though, shattered the illusion of an eternal cornucopia.

Naval warfare brought a temporary halt to the slave trade and threatened the British islands with capture or anihilation. By curtailing

[6] Richard S. Dunn, *Sugar and Slaves: The Rise of the Planter Class in the English West Indies, 1624–1713* (Chapel Hill, 1972); Lowell Joseph Ragatz, *The Fall of the Planter Class in the British Caribbean, 1763–1833* (New York, 1928); Elsa V. Goveia, *Slave Society in the British Leeward Islands at the End of the Eighteenth Century* (New Haven, 1965); H. Hoetink, *The Two Variants in Caribbean Race Relations: A Contribution to the Sociology of Segmented Societies* (London, 1967); Orlando Patterson, *The Sociology of Slavery: An Analysis of the Origins, Development and Structure of Negro Slave Society in Jamaica* (London, 1967).

the flow of provisions from North America, the war also gave rise to famine and inflation in the British Caribbean, thereby increasing production costs at a time when Britain was obliged to obtain revenue from heavy duties on sugar and other colonial imports. As if nature were conspiring to punish the slave system with final ruin, a series of hurricanes lashed Jamaica and the Leeward Islands with unprecedented force; cane fields were blighted by drought and borers. American independence meant that the British islands lost their principal source of provisions as well as a valuable market for molasses and rum. Equally distressing, it meant that the United States could legally trade with the French West Indies, and thus contribute to St. Domingue's incredible expansion of the 1780s which flooded the European market with cheap sugar, cacao, cotton, and indigo.[7]

Outstripped by their rivals, the British planters also found their property increasingly mortgaged to English merchants, and their profits increasingly dependent on England's protected market. Yet in England the public grew restive over the artificially inflated price of sugar. In 1791 the East India Company began marketing Bengal sugar, which, though disadvantaged by a discriminatory duty, successfully competed with the West Indian product. In 1700, British planters had supplied nearly half the sugar consumed in Western Europe; by 1789, St. Domingue alone was exporting more than all the British colonies combined. But the revolutionary destruction of St.

[7] In addition to the sources already cited, my discussion of Caribbean history draws particularly on Richard Pares, *War and Trade in the West Indies, 1739–1763* (Oxford, 1936); Pares, *Yankees and Creoles: The Trade between North America and the West Indies before the American Revolution* (London, 1956); Gaston Martin, *Histoire de l'esclavage dans les colonies françaises* (Paris, 1948); J. Saintoyant, *La Colonisation française pendant la révolution* (2 vols., Paris, 1930); Michael Craton and James Walvin, *A Jamaican Plantation: The History of Worthy Park, 1670–1970* (Toronto, 1970); Noel Deerr, *The History of Sugar* (2 vols., London, 1949–1950); R. B. Sheridan, "The Wealth of Jamaica in the Eighteenth Century," *Economic History Review,* 2nd ser., XVIII (1965), 292–311; Eric Williams, *Capitalism and Slavery* (Chapel Hill, 1944); O. W. Thoms, "Slavery in the Leeward Islands in the Mid-Eighteenth Century: A Reappraisal," *Bulletin of the Institute of Historical Research,* XLII (1969), 76–85; Sidney W. Mintz, "Currency Problems in Eighteenth Century Jamaica and Gresham's Law," in Robert A. Manners, ed., *Process and Pattern in Culture* (Chicago, 1964), pp. 248–64; Antoine Gisler, *L'Esclave aux Antilles françaises, XVIIe-XIXe siècle* (Fribourg, 1965); Frank Wesley Pitman, *The Development of the British West Indies, 1700–1763* (New Haven, 1917); Pitman, "Slavery on British West India Plantations in the Eighteenth Century," *Journal of Negro History,* XI (Oct., 1926), 584–668.

Domingue, beginning in 1791, created a sudden and massive shortage in the world's supply of sugar; this occurrence, in turn, stimulated production in the British colonies as well as in Cuba and Brazil. But if the 1790s temporarily revived speculative hopes, the Napoleonic wars exposed the inflexibility of the British planter class—a class which had been created by purchasing slaves and monopolizing the choicest lands for sugar; which had equated success with a life of ease and luxury in the mother country; and which had always shown more interest in achieving independence from the Caribbean, with its hot and dingy towns, its hoards of Negroes, and its knavish class of overseers and managers, than in helping to build a viable society.[8]

For a time, British speculators rushed to the recently conquered territories, such as Trinidad and the Dutch Guianan colonies of Essequibo, Demerara, and Berbice, where virgin land offered new prospects for quick fortune and early retirement. But in the older colonies land values dropped and bankruptcies multiplied. From 1799 to 1807 sixty-five Jamaican plantations were abandoned, and dozens more were sold by court order to meet unsatisfied claims. By 1811 the inhabitants of Tobago complained that the selling price of sugar failed to equal the cost of production. As a result of the successful Parliamentary campaign to outlaw the slave trade, British planters increasingly saw themselves as the victims of economic and political persecution, and became

[8] The pattern of rapid boom and decline is well illustrated by the history of the small island of Tobago, which lies northeast of Trinidad. Although several nations had tried to settle Tobago in the seventeenth century, England and France finally came to a tacit agreement not to embark on a cor etitive development of the so-called neutral islands, which also included Dominica, St. Vincent, and St. Lucia. But in 1763 Tobago was ceded to England, and began a period of speculative development, especially after being reoccupied by the British in 1793 (the island had been captured by France in the American Revolution and was not restored to England in 1783). In 1799, Tobago exported more sugar than Barbados, St. Kitts, or Grenada, and one-eighth as much as Jamaica—or more sugar than was produced in any year prior to 1717 by Jamaica, Guadeloupe, or St. Domingue. But 1799 marked the high point of production, even though the slave population grew from 14,800 in 1805 to 17,000 in 1808, reflecting heavy imports in expectation of the ending of the slave trade. By 1834, at the time of emancipation, the slave population had declined to 11,500. The white population, which apparently reached a maximum of 2,397 in 1776, had dwindled to 1,397 in 1787 and to only 439 in 1808. At the time of emancipation there were fewer than 300 whites on the island (Ragatz, *Fall of the Planter Class*, pp. 30, 111–15; Deerr, *History of Sugar*, I, 151, 178–79, 202; II, 279; Pares, *War and Trade in the West Indies*, pp. 195–215; *The Scot's Magazine*, XXXIV [1772], 45–46).

convinced, not without reason, that oppression of the West Indies had somehow become the "road to popularity" in England. In 1822, Britain finally abandoned the mercantilist restrictions on West Indian trade and permitted her colonists direct imports from the United States and exports to Europe. But by 1822 the planters were chained by debt to English merchants and agents, and the price of sugar had fallen to a new low, a price which was below the production costs of many British plantations.[9]

The decline of the British West Indies, coupled with the explosive destruction of St. Domingue, seemed to support the view that New World slavery was well on the road to extinction. The history of the Atlantic slave trade gave mixed but generally confirming evidence. The demographic experience of slave societies depended on a number of variables that are not applicable here.[10] What does need emphasis

[9] Ragatz, *Fall of the Planter Class*, pp. 204–38, 289–330; Goveia, *Slave Society in the British Leeward Islands, passim; Journals of the Assembly of Jamaica*, XI (Jamaica, 1811), 219–21. There is growing evidence that Ragatz and Williams exaggerated the rapidity of the economic decline of the British West Indies. In the early nineteenth century, for example, Jamaica expanded coffee production and demonstrated some flexibility in diversifying crops. The optimism of planters in the newer expanding areas, such as Trinidad, helped to offset the cries of distress from the older and more exhausted colonies. Moreover, the price of sugar continued to fluctuate and rose sharply after the business cycle hit a trough in the first decade of the nineteenth century. Seymour Drescher, in a forthcoming study which I have not had the opportunity to read, contends that the British West Indies maintained their relative weight in the imperial economy until after the Napoleonic wars (*A Case of Econocide: Economic Development and the Abolition of the British Slave Trade* [Madison, Wisc., 1974]). But regardless of short-term fluctuations, there can be no doubt that by 1822 the West Indies were of far less value to Britain than they had been a half-century earlier. Nor can there be any doubt that even in the eighteenth century, Barbados and the Leeward Islands had become economically stagnant; or that the entire British Caribbean suffered a continuing exodus of white settlers; or that British abolitionists, along with the disciples of Adam Smith, anticipated the decline as the inevitable outcome of slavery and monopolistic privilege.

[10] See, for example, Richard B. Sheridan, "Africa and the Carribean in the Atlantic Slave Trade," *American Historical Review*, LXXVII (Feb., 1972), 15–35; Craton and Walvin, *A Jamaican Plantation;* Fogel and Engerman, *Time on the Cross*, I, 25–27. The complexities of the subject have been explored in a number of pioneering papers presented at the Mathematical Social Science Board (hereafter M.S.S.B.) Conference on Systems of Slavery, March, 1972, University of Rochester, and especially in Jack Ericson Eblen's "On the Natural Increase of Slave Populations." The papers will appear in Stanley L. Engerman and Eugene D. Genovese, eds., *Race and Slavery in the Western Hemisphere: Quantitative Studies* (Princeton, 1974).

is the salient characteristic of all sugar colonies: a net natural decrease of the labor force of from 2 to 5 per cent a year. The black population of Barbados did not become self-perpetuating until after Britain had outlawed the slave trade; in Jamaica the deficit lasted until after emancipation. Accordingly, the Caribbean and Brazilian economies required the continuing importation of African labor. Indeed, partly as a result of emancipation, the larger Caribbean colonies like Trinidad, British Guiana, and Surinam long depended on supposedly voluntary labor imported from West Africa, China, India, and Java— laborers who were forced to work on plantations under penal sanction, and whose original "recruitment" and transport often differed little from that of African slaves.[11]

Beginning in the early sixteenth century, slave imports from Africa rose gradually to a high plateau in the mid-eighteenth century, when the smaller sugar colonies had acquired sufficient stocks of labor and were mainly concerned with replenishing losses from population decrease. The plateau of slave imports sloped up to a peak in the 1790s, from which there was a gradual and then sudden drop, by the 1810s. As Philip D. Curtin has pointed out, the total New World slave imports began to decline, as a result of the disruptions of the Napoleonic wars, before either England or America had outlawed the slave trade.[12] Economic trends do not explain the politics of British abolition, which I shall discuss in detail in later chapters. It must be emphasized, however, that after England had prohibited her own subjects from selling or buying slaves from Africa, it was hardly in her interest to allow rival nations to stock their colonies with the surplus labor. Moreover, by 1811 England had seized a virtual monopoly of the world's tropical produce, having captured enemy colonies from Java and Mauritius to Cayenne and Martinique, and having assumed a kind of proprietorship over the Spanish colonies and Brazil. Yet as a result of Napoleon's Continental System, England's warehouses were bursting with tropical

[11] Fogel and Engerman, *Time on the Cross*, I, 25–26; Philip D. Curtin, *The Atlantic Slave Trade: A Census* (Madison, 1969), pp. 28–34, 73; W. Kloosterboer, *Involuntary Labour since the Abolition of Slavery: A Survey of Compulsory Labour throughout the World* (Leiden, 1960), chs. 1, 3; Alan H. Adamson, "The Reconstruction of Plantation Labor after Emancipation: The Case of British Guiana," paper presented at the M.S.S.B. Conference on Systems of Slavery.

[12] Curtin, *Atlantic Slave Trade*, pp. 142–54, 222.

produce (in 1812, sugar cost nine times as much in Paris as in London). Wholly apart from moral and ideological considerations, it only made sense for Britain to commit herself to the international suppression of the slave trade, the continuation of which could only augment the production of tropical staples, add to the glut outside Napoleon's domains, and provide neutrals with more goods to smuggle through the British blockade.[13]

There were, of course, moral and ideological considerations, which gave an aura of righteousness to England's continuing campaign to stamp out the slave trade. British efforts succeeded in increasing the costs and risks (and thus the profits) of the Atlantic traffic; no doubt many more slaves would have been imported into the New World had there been no suppression policy. Britain also succeeded in curbing the flow of slaves from her older settled colonies to the undeveloped lands of Trinidad and Guiana.[14] But total slave imports into the Americas rose again in the 1820s to an annual average of approximately 50,600, compared with 58,800 in the period from 1781 to 1810. The trade then dropped in the 1830s, revived slightly in the 1840s, and declined sharply during the following two decades.

It would appear that the decline of slave economies had much less to do with any inherent defects of slave labor than with such matters as markets, credit, competition, absentee proprietorship, and cheaper sources of labor. One may note that Mexico imported some 200,000 African slaves, mostly in the sixteenth and early seventeenth centuries. This immense population gradually disappeared as it was replaced by or absorbed into a much larger pool of cheap Indian and mestizo labor. Cuba, to take another Spanish colony, imported some 700,000 African slaves, mostly in the nineteenth century. This population became the essential ingredient for a highly organized and industrial

[13] Holland Rose, "The Struggle with Napoleon, 1803—1815," *The Cambridge History of the British Empire,* ed. by J. Holland Rose, *et al.* (Cambridge, 1940), II, 83–128. One should add that the British succeeded in exporting considerable quantities of their own tropical produce to the Continent, notwithstanding Napoleon's edicts.

[14] Phillip LeVeen, "A Quantitative Analysis of the Impact of British Suppression Policies on the Volume of the Nineteenth-Century Slave Trade," paper presented at the M.S.S.B. Conference on Systems of Slavery; D. Eltis, "The Traffic in Slaves between the British West Indian Colonies, 1807–1833," *Economic History Review,* XXV (Feb., 1972), 55–64.

form of plantation agriculture which by 1859 was producing 536,000 tons of sugar, or nearly ten times Jamaica's output in 1790.[15]

The abolitionists' optimism failed to make allowance for the flexibility and adaptability of Negro slavery as an institution.[16] The reformers took the British West Indies as the model for all slave societies, and presupposed that an end to slave imports would allow economic laws to work toward their inevitable end of freedom. Thus when the African Institution expressed surprise and alarm over the admission of Missouri as a slave state, the British directors imagined the worst result to be a new incentive for the American traders who illegally infested the African coast. Neither they nor many Americans could quite grasp the significance of the fact that the number of slaves in the United States had increased by 33 per cent in the first decade and by a further 29 per cent in the second decade of the nineteenth century.[17]

As Professor Curtin has shown, North America was never more than "a marginal recipient of slaves from Africa." It is true, of course, that North Americans adapted the plantation system to such crops as tobacco, rice, indigo, and finally, cotton. But when compared with the sugar colonies of the New World, the growth of North America's Negro population was something of a demographic anomaly. The best estimates indicate that over the entire history of the Atlantic slave trade, North America received no more than 6 per cent of the Africans imported into the New World. By 1825, however, according to

[15] David M. Davidson, "Negro Slave Control and Resistance in Colonial Mexico, 1519–1650," *Hispanic American Historical Review*, XLVI (Aug., 1966), 236; Curtin, *Atlantic Slave Trade, passim;* Frederick P. Bowser, "The Free Person of Color in Mexico City and Lima: Manumission and Opportunity, 1580–1650," paper presented at the M.S.S.B. Conference on Systems of Slavery; Franklin W. Knight, *Slave Society in Cuba during the Nineteenth Century* (Madison, 1970), *passim.*

[16] For different views which emphasize the variability and adaptability of Negro slavery, see Eugene D. Genovese, *The World the Slaveholders Made: Two Essays in Interpretation* (New York, 1969), Part One, and *Roll, Jordan, Roll* (New York, 1974); Fogel and Engerman, *Time on the Cross;* Engerman, "Some Considerations Relating to Property Rights in Man," *Journal of Economic History*, XXXIII (March, 1973), 43–65.

[17] *Fourteenth Report of the Directors of the African Institution* . . . (London, 1820), p. 35; *Bureau of the Census, Negro Population, 1790–1915* (Washington, 1928). One should add, however, that the census figures for 1820 brought considerable alarm to American abolitionists ("American Convention of Abolition Societies, Documents," *Journal of Negro History*, VI [July, 1921], 310–14).

the calculations of Professors Fogel and Engerman, the slave population of the United States represented 36 per cent of all the slaves in the Western Hemisphere. If they had suffered the same natural decrease as the slaves in the West Indies, their numbers in 1800 would have amounted to only 186,000 instead of slightly over one million.[18]

It was once morally reassuring to assume that this demographic anomaly was undesired. Benjamin Lundy, for example, traveled to Haiti in 1825 to lay the groundwork for a fantastic project to export 50,000 free Negroes a year, a scheme which would allow the "gradual abolition of slavery in the United States without danger or loss to the South." The conviction that the United States should be "a white man's country" had strengthened the move to outlaw slave imports from Africa; as Lundy well knew, racial prejudice also served as an excuse, even in the North, for resisting emancipation.[19] But if the natural increase in the black population freed the South from dependence on the African slave trade, the region never became an exporter of supposedly surplus labor. On the contrary, even in the period between the end of the Revolution and the beginning of the cotton boom, when slavery was thought to be an economic burden, the aggregate demand for slaves continued to rise. As Professors Fogel and Engerman have recently indicated, there was never a time after 1783 when investment in slaves failed to bring high returns, or when the demand curve failed to rise, even if a more rapidly increasing labor supply, in the mid-1790s, brought a temporary dip in slave prices. In short, racist protestations tended to conceal economic choices based on the immense profitability of slave labor.[20]

Despite the "march of the mind," as Lundy termed it in 1822, the progress of the previous half-century was less encouraging than he and most abolitionists assumed. Notwithstanding nominal emancipations in the northern states, in Haiti, and in some of the Spanish American republics, the number of slaves in the New World had more than doubled. Population statistics for the period are notoriously untrust-

[18] Curtin, *Atlantic Slave Trade*, p. 89; Fogel and Engerman, *Time on the Cross*, I, 15, 29; II (*Evidence and Methods—A Supplement*), 29–33.

[19] Merton L. Dillon, *Benjamin Lundy and the Struggle for Negro Freedom* (Urbana, Ill., 1966), pp. 91–103.

[20] Fogel and Engerman, *Time on the Cross*, I, 4–5, 24–25, 70–73, 86–89. A major landmark in economic history, *Time on the Cross* promises to change the entire character of future debates over slavery.

worthy, but one can be reasonably certain that the number of slaves had doubled in Brazil, tripled in the United States, and increased by sevenfold in Cuba.[21] In Cuba and Brazil, where there was virtually no abolitionist sentiment, the slave populations had grown more rapidly than the populations of free blacks. Cuba, having undergone an agricultural reorganization, stood on the threshold of a "sugar revolution" that would demand unprecedented importations of slaves. Brazil had similarly entered the first stages of a coffee boom that would stimulate continuing slave importations as well as an inter-provincial trade from the northeastern coastal regions to the interior valleys of the south. In the United States the population of free Negroes had grown from 1790 to 1810 at a faster rate than that of slaves. From 1810 to 1820, however, this trend had ominously been reversed. By 1820, there were already 10,000 slaves in Missouri and 69,000 in Louisiana—a mark of the speed of southwestern expansion. Moreover, by 1823, directly west of the "dark and stormy waves of the Mexican gulph," the new Mexican government had reluctantly decided that, for all practical purposes, Texas would be open to settlement by North American slaveholders.[22]

[21] In addition to the slave population statistics presented by Curtin, Deerr, and Knight, see: J. Potter, "The Growth of Population in America, 1700–1860," in *Population in History: Essays in Historical Demography*, ed. by D. V. Glass and D. E. C. Eversley (Chicago, 1965), pp. 637 ff; Stella H. Sutherland, *Population Distribution in Colonial America* (New York, 1936); Roberto C. Simonsen, *História econômica do Brasil* (São Paulo, 1962); Dauril Alden, "The Population of Brazil in the Late Eighteenth Century: A Preliminary Study," *Hispanic American Historical Review*, XLIII (May, 1963), 173–205; Angel Rosenblat, *La población indígena de América, desde 1492 hasta la actualidad* (Buenos Aires, 1945); Rolando Mellafe, *La esclavitude en Hispanoamérica* (Buenos Aires, 1964); Gisler, *L'Esclave aux Antilles françaises*, p. 34; Daniel Bellet, *Les Grandes Antilles: Etude de géographie économique* (Paris, 1909), p. 30.

[22] Knight, *Slave Society in Cuba*; Arthur F. Corwin, *Spain and the Abolition of Slavery in Cuba, 1817–1886* (Austin, Texas, 1967); Leslie Bethell, *The Abolition of the Brazilian Slave Trade: Britain, Brazil and the Slave Trade Question, 1807–1869* (Cambridge, England, 1970); Robert Conrad, *The Destruction of Brazilian Slavery, 1850–1888* (Berkeley, 1972); Sidney Mintz, "Labor and Sugar in Puerto Rico and in Jamaica, 1800–1850," *Comparative Studies in Society and History*, I (March, 1959), 273–81; George Lockhart Rives, *The United States and Mexico, 1821–1848* (New York, 1913), II, 38–41. It should be emphasized, however, that the proportion of free blacks and mulattoes was considerable larger in the populations of Cuba and Brazil than in that of the United States, and that their social and economic opportunities were much

The decline and stagnation of the British West Indies fostered the comforting illusion that slave labor itself was inefficient, unprofitable, and an impediment to economic growth. We now have evidence that slave labor was successfully applied to the cultivation of virtually every New World crop, to various forms of mining, to food processing, construction, transport, industry, and the most highly skilled services and artisan crafts. Slave labor proved viable in temperate as well as tropical climates, in cities and towns as well as rural areas.[23] But the actual relationship between slavery and economic progress may have been of less significance, in the long run, than the changing ideology which defined that relationship.

In actuality, the sugar colonies were probably overvalued even before the American Revolution. Even then a "second British empire" took shape in the minds of merchants and statesmen who pondered the rising exports of manufactured goods, who studied maps of the Orient, or who speculated on the possibility of civil wars that would open the rich markets of Latin America to British trade. Nevertheless, in 1750 few men doubted that the West Indies were the most valuable of colonial possessions, or that the Atlantic slave trade, as described by Malachy Postlethwayt, was "an inexhaustible Fund of Wealth and Naval Power to this Nation." England and France may have been misled by the highly visible wealth that flowed from the sugar islands,

---

greater (see Herbert S. Klein, "The Colored Freedmen in Brazilian Slave Society," *Journal of Social History*, III [Fall, 1969], 30–52).

[23] Fogel and Engerman, *Time on the Cross*, I, 4–6, 38–43, 94–106, 191–223; Edgar J. McManus, *Black Bondage in the North* (Syracuse, 1973), pp. 36–54; Marcus W. Jernegan, *Laboring and Dependent Classes in Colonial America, 1607–1783: Studies of the Economic, Educational, and Social Significance of Slaves, Servants, Apprentices, and Poor Folk* (Chicago, 1931), pp. 10–11, 13–14, 16–18; Mary Karasch, "From Porterage to Proprietorship: African Occupations in Rio de Janeiro, 1808–1850," paper presented to the M.S.S.B. Conference on Systems of Slavery; Genovese, *Roll, Jordan, Roll*. Skills and diverse occupations were by no means limited to town economies. In describing one of Jamaica's great sugar plantations of the eighteenth century, Craton and Walvin observe that "the head boilerman, presiding over the supreme mysteries of the craft of sugar production, was probably as important to the estate as anyone save the overseer and attorney" (*A Jamaican Plantation*, p. 106). One can argue that if it were not for racial distinctions, the very term "slavery" would become too blurred to be of use. For, given the gradations of other forms of dependent labor, how can one class the head boilerman or wage-receiving artisan with the oppressed field hand? The answer, of course, is that all were black, that all were theoretically subject to sale as field hands, and that Negro slavery, whatever its adaptability, was a product of the plantation system.

but they repeatedly chose to make the Caribbean a major theater of naval warfare. The squadrons that kept speeding westward to protect Jamaica or Guadeloupe proved that sugar was a crucial symbol of national power.[24]

The West Indies' decline thus appeared all the more dramatic. Sugar and slaves were not a source of opulence, one discovered, but of debt, wasted soil, decayed properties, and social depravity. The resident planter was not an entrepreneur, intent on thrift and social improvements, but a dissolute tyrant, the heir of buccaneers, ready to plunder absentee proprietors or to undermine British trade by conniving with American smugglers. In the popular view there was thus a total dissociation between the old empire of plantation slavery and the new imperial search for raw materials and world markets. The emergence of the second empire involved a repudiation of the first. The second might depend on millions of involuntary laborers, but it was, by definition, a "free world."

Thus James Cropper, a wealthy Quaker merchant and in 1822 a prime instigator of the British emancipation movement, saw East Indian sugar as "the means which an allwise Creator has in the nature of things appointed for the destruction of this abominable system whether of slave trade or slave cultivation." To the charge that Cropper had private interests in reducing the duties on East Indian sugar, the Quaker could confidently reply that anyone who regulated his own commercial transactions in accordance with God's rules should never be discouraged from defending his rights or from "asserting their accordance with the welfare of their country & of the world at large." The abolition of the expensive premium the public paid for slave-grown produce would simply "remove impediments out of the way of the free operation of the Laws which the Creator has fixed in the nature of things." The new science of political economy had shown that the Creator had not, after all, promised maximum profits to those Christians who rescued African savages by making them

[24] Vincent T. Harlow, *The Founding of the Second British Empire, 1763–1793* (2 vols., London, 1952), *passim;* E. A. Benians, "The Beginnings of the New Empire, 1783–1793," in *The Cambridge History of the British Empire,* II, 1–35; Stanley L. Engerman, "The Slave Trade and British Capital Formation in the Eighteenth Century: A Comment on the Williams Thesis," *Business History Review,* XLVI (Winter, 1972), 430–43; Pares, *War and Trade, passim;* Pares, *Yankees and Creoles, passim.*

American slaves.[25] On the other hand, if Britain had suddenly given free operation to the laws Cropper worshipped, the immediate result would have been starvation for many West Indian blacks and an accelerating exploitation of labor in India and South America. The rise of the new imperialism may not have required the destruction of West Indian slavery, but the negative image of West Indian slavery did give sanction to the contrasting and therefore positive values of capitalist ideology.

It would be difficult to maintain, however, that slavery declined as a direct result of the progressive forces of world capitalism. One may agree with Eric Williams that no abolitionist movement could have succeeded in the mid-eighteenth century, when all the forces of interest were on the other side, and still insist that the decline of mercantilism did not bring the automatic fall of slavery.[26] In 1822, British slave-holders not only refused to acknowledge their doom, but would long prove more than an equal match for the abolitionists. In 1840, British abolitionists discovered to their horror (although the point had been made in reply to Cropper) that there were more slaves in British India than had been emancipated in the British Caribbean. During the following decade, as the abolitionists divided over the question of free trade, they came also to realize that lowering duties on foreign sugar would greatly stimulate the demand for slaves in Cuba and Brazil. The equalization of duties, in 1846, evoked celebration in Havana and cries of anguish in the British West Indies, along with

[25] James Cropper to Zachary Macaulay, Feb. 5, 1822; July 12, 1822; Aug. 5, 1822, Add. MSS 41267A, British Museum; Cropper, *Letters Addressed to William Wilberforce, M.P., Recommending the Encouragement of the Cultivation of Sugar in Our Dominions in the East Indies, as the Natural and Certain Means of Effecting the Total and General Abolition of the Slave Trade* (Liverpool, 1822), p. vii. It should be added that Cropper's humanitarian conscience compromised his economic dogma. He favored a program of gradual emancipation, to be encouraged by removing bounties on exported sugar and by paying temporary direct bounties, as means of compensation, to slaveholders. His colleagues in the Liverpool East India Association were reluctant to link the economic question of East India trade with the slavery question (K. Charlton, "James Cropper and Liverpool's Contribution to the Anti-Slavery Movement," *Transactions of the Historic Society of Lancashire and Cheshire,* CXXIII [1972], 59, 61).

[26] Williams, *Capitalism and Slavery,* p. 136, and *passim.* For critiques, see Engerman, "The Slave Trade and British Capital Formation"; and Roger Anstey, " 'Capitalism and Slavery': A Critique," *The Economic History Review,* 2nd ser., XXI (1968), 307–20.

demands for more indentured laborers from Sierra Leone. Finally, it was North American cotton, as Frank Thistlethwaite has rather extravagantly argued, that determined "the entire thrust of the Atlantic economy. The demand of Lancashire for raw cotton settled the Southwest, and British commercial credits and investment capital underwrote the Cotton Kingdom."[27]

Earlier, one may add, North American ships had hastened the ruin of the British West Indies by carrying to Europe the slave-grown produce of the French, Dutch, and Spanish colonies. According to Douglass C. North, it was this carrying trade, during the Napoleonic wars, that helped accelerate the economic growth of the northern states. And after the decline of this trade, it was cotton, soon accounting for more than half the value of all American exports, that paid for American imports and that gave a major stimulus to northern shipping, banking, insurance, and manufactures.[28]

By the early 1820s southern slaveholders could reassure themselves, despite a recent and disastrous drop in cotton prices, that their produce was the force that moved fleets of ships between New York and Liverpool, that influenced the flow of investment capital and brought prosperity to English mill towns and Ohio farms. Yet they were also beginning to ponder a question that had earlier been faced by the planters of St. Domingue and Jamaica: How, in an age of revolutionary ferment, could a minority region, differentiated by an increasingly unpopular institution, maintain its political power and defend its interests against an alliance of hostile groups and factions?

The Shifting Interests of Slave-Trade Diplomacy

Since the African slave trade formed an integral part of the Atlantic

---

[27] Howard Temperley, *British Antislavery, 1833–1870* (London, 1972), pp. 93–110, 137–67; Frank Thistlethwaite, *The Anglo-American Connection in the Early Nineteenth Century* (Philadelphia, 1959), pp. 9–14. Even by 1800 the United States sent considerably more cotton to Britain than the total amount consumed by the British economy in 1783; in the period from 1816 to 1820 the United States accounted for nearly half of British cotton imports, and ten years later, for over 74 per cent (J. H. Clapham, "The Industrial Revolution and the Colonies, 1783–1822," in *The Cambridge History of the British Empire,* II, 225–26). By 1822 the value of Britain's exports of cotton yarn and cotton manufactures was £26,911,000; in 1771 it had been £311,000 (B. R. Mitchell, *Abstract of British Historical Statistics* [Cambridge, England, 1971], pp. 294–95).

[28] Douglass C. North, *The Economic Growth of the United States, 1790–1860* (Englewood Cliffs, N.J., 1961), pp. 24–25, 62–68.

imperial systems, it presented a possible target for rebellious colonists wishing to coerce or break ties with a mother country. A boycott on slave imports could at once be a blow to European merchants and creditors, an assertion of economic independence, a meaure for increasing domestic security, and a means of attaching the moral stigma of slavery on the parent country as proof of her systematic oppression.

In Chapters Two and Three, I shall discuss the attempts, during and after the American Revolution, to outlaw the slave trade to the United States. For now let me simply note that in 1774 North America's disavowal of the slave trade was a defiance of British authority. Ironically, after England had relinquished her world leadership in slave trafficking, she acquired the reverse role in the drama of New World independence. Thus in 1822, as the sovereigns of Europe brooded over the independence movements in Latin America, the Duke of Wellington had official instructions to assure the Congress of Verona that "no state in the New World will be recognized by Great Britain which has not frankly and completely abolished the trade in slaves." British officials saw no conflict between this policy and George Canning's exclamation of 1824: "Spanish America is free and if we do not mismanage our affairs sadly she is *English.*" Accordingly, British recognition of Buenos Aires, Mexico, and Colombia took the form of commercial treaties which embodied a prohibition of the slave trade.[29]

With respect to the complexities of slave-trade diplomacy and Britain's part in the Latin American struggles for independence, the briefest summary should indicate the ways in which shifting interests, during the Age of Revolution, shattered the older imperial systems and isolated the major slaveholding societies. During the eighteenth century, when England had hatched various schemes for dismembering the Spanish empire, she had also been happy to supply the Spanish colonies, legally or illegally, with slaves. But by 1808, when Britain's own abolition law went into effect, Latin America presented opportunities of a different kind.

One should not discount the humanitarian motives which enabled England to prohibit her own citizens from engaging in the slave trade, nor should one underestimate the effects of abolitionist pressure on

[29] James F. King, "The Latin American Republics and the Suppression of the Slave Trade," *Hispanic American Historical Review,* XXIV (1944), 391; John Gallagher and Ronald Robinson, "The Imperialism of Free Trade," *The Economic History Review,* 2nd ser., VI (1953), 8.

later British diplomacy.[30] But other circumstances raised suspicion and resistance in the minds of Spanish, Portuguese, and French statesmen. Most obviously, if the slave trade were simply diverted to new markets, the British West Indies would suffer a competitive disadvantage, and Britain's humanitarianism would bring no benefits to Africa. Thus in 1822 Canning frankly acknowledged that only a universal abolition could save the British colonies from "utter ruin," and added that "the slave trade can be abolished only through Brazil." On the other hand, attempts to impose abolitionism on a nation like Brazil could well jeopardize British commercial interests. The problem for England, which would perplex much of her later imperial history, was how to reconcile conflicts between the economic and moral, or in other words cultural, domination of supposedly backward nations.[31]

By coincidence, England outlawed her own slave trade at a crucial moment in Latin American history. It was late in 1807 that Napoleon determined to close Portugal's ports to English trade, and in 1808 that he established his brother Joseph on the Spanish throne, as part of his campaign to bar British goods from all of Europe. In response to the first move, England safely installed the Portuguese royal court in Brazil, thereby making Rio de Janeiro the capital of the empire. In forging this alliance with the hesitant Prince Regent, England had threatened to seize the Portuguese colonies and had extorted an agreement, as the price for her protection, that she would be given the most favorable trading privileges with Brazil. While securing a rich market for British commerce—at a time when the United States was threatening commercial war—England also informed Dom João, the Prince Regent, that Portugal should begin taking steps to withdraw from the slave trade. In 1810, virtually with an English pistol at his head, Dom João agreed to restrict the African slave trade to certain areas and to cooperate in bringing about its gradual abolition "throughout the whole of his dominions."[32]

Meanwhile, Napoleon's seizure of Spain opened the Spanish colonies both to rebellion and to British trade. When the creole, or native-born elites of various Spanish American cities declared their independence of Spanish rule, they often affirmed their idealism by outlawing the slave

[30] Betty Fladeland, "Abolitionist Pressures on the Concert of Europe, 1814–1822," *Journal of Modern History*, XXXVIII (Dec., 1966), 355–73.
[31] Bethell, *Abolition of the Brazilian Slave Trade*, p. 35 and *passim*.
[32] *Ibid.*, ch. 1.

trade. Thus in Venezuela, where slave imports had almost ceased by 1800, the Supreme Junta of Caracas prohibited the "vile traffic" in 1810. Two years later large numbers of slaves joined the Spanish forces marching on the capital and helped to subdue the first republic. The proclamations from Caracas, from Chile, and from Buenos Aires reflected the earlier ideals of the American Revolution and a contempt for the decadence and corruption of the mother country. They were also in tune with British policy.[33]

To complicate matters, England was officially Spain's ally, valiantly defending Cádiz and advancing to liberate the Peninsula from French tyranny. In 1811, as the slavery issue began to stir the Spanish colonies, British officials encouraged liberal deputies in the revolutionary Cortes of Cádiz to propose an immediate end to the slave trade. The news of such proposals, which included gradual emancipation, brought immediate alarm to Cuba, where planters had begun to consolidate landholdings and to concentrate on the production of sugar. Spanish officials, including the temporarily deposed king, had no desire to stifle the flow of Cuban sugar or to endorse reforms that might breed further rebellion in the colonies, leading perhaps to the horrors of a new Haiti. As British armies secured more Spanish ground, the Spanish grew more suspicious of British influence. Jamaica, the Spanish observed, had been given ample opportunity to stock her plantations prior to British abolition. Cuba was just beginning to develop as a major competitor in sugar and had been deprived by war of adequate slave importations. Thus began a long charade of negotiations, treaties, delays, and British bribes. For decades the slave traders would converge on Cuba, the only opulent colony that Spain retained. The wars of liberation virtually ended slave imports to the new republics which (with the exception of Uruguay), had long ceased to have a need for African labor.

Before returning to Brazil and to a concluding assessment, the failures of British diplomacy in the period from 1814 to 1822 should be briefly noted. By 1814 the British navy had suppressed much of the slave trade north of the equator; both abolitionists and diplomats hoped to convert wartime suspension into permanent international prohibition. But when Napoleon's initial downfall brought a restora-

[33] King, "Latin American Republics and the Suppression of the Slave Trade," p. 388; Guillermo Feliú Cruz, *La abolición de la esclavitud en Chile* (Santiago de Chile, 1942), pp. 52–54; Mellafe, *La esclavitud en Hispanoamérica*, pp. 94–98.

tion of Bourbon rule in France, it became apparent that neither Louis XVIII nor Prince Talleyrand was a zealous abolitionist. The French resented hints that the restoration of their colonies might hinge on their profession of the new faith. They were even suspicious of the offer of Trinidad as bait for agreeing to deprive their colonists of further supplies of slaves. Like the Spanish, they pointed out that the war had given the British colonies a favorable lead in acquiring planta-tion labor. And since the British navy was the only force that could suppress the African trade, a mutual agreement on the right of seizure would be tantamount to recognizing England as the constable of the seas.

French resistance evoked an astonishing upsurge of English public indignation. In 1814 the country was alive with public meetings; hundreds of petitions demanded the universal abolition of the slave trade. Reformers appealed to the humanitarian sentiments of the pope, of the czar of Russia, and of the treaty-making dignitaries of Europe. But at the Congress of Vienna, Castlereagh, the English statesman, could secure only a vague declaration condemning the slave trade. French suspicions were further aroused by English talk of an economic boycott of nations that refused to follow England's altruistic example. Then Napoleon, at the outset of his dramatic Hundred Days, issued a decree abolishing the French slave trade, apparently in a bid for English public support. This precedent forced the Bourbon govern-ment, whose survival had depended on English arms, to acquiesce to English demands for an abolition law. But since the French neglected to publish the new law, which provided for no enforcement and which failed to make slave trading a crime, ships continued to sail without disguise for West African markets.

Reformers could draw encouragement from the unflagging exer-tions of British diplomats and from the fact that the Holy Alliance piously endorsed the principle of abolition. Yet humanitarian prin-ciples, no matter how sincerely expressed, could not overcome nation-alistic jealousies and suspicions. Thus in the Treaty of Ghent the United States agreed to join Britain in a mutual condemnation of the slave trade. But because of sensitivity to the issue of search and seizure —which had helped bring on the War of 1812—the Americans re-fused to allow British patrols to stop their ships. Some years later when the British Minister at Washington asked John Quincy Adams whether he could think of any greater evil than the slave trade, Adams curtly answered that there was a greater evil: to grant the right of search "would be making slaves of ourselves." And since the United States failed to enforce her own laws, the American flag became for a time the main protection of Cuban and Brazilian slave traders. As a result of incessant pressure and massive bribes, England did obtain in 1817 a limited right of search from Spain and Portugal. Both countries assented to abolition north of the equator. Spain promised to terminate the entire trade in 1820; by vaguely renewing her commitment to total abolition at some future date, Portugal won recognition of the legality of her slave trade south of the equator.[34]

As we have seen, the British navy did succeed in reducing the volume of the African slave trade. But despite the treaties and despite the flow of noble pronouncements from the governments and congresses of Europe, twenty-six slave ships arrived safely in Havana during the first year of formal abolition. Cuban planters, many of them refugees from the newly independent Latin American republics, were contemptuous of Spain's commitments to their British competitors. As late as the 1850s the colony would illegally import some 123,000 slaves. In the 1820s Brazil absorbed an estimated 325,000 African slaves—a somewhat smaller number than she would import in the 1840s.[35]

Brazil's refusal to outlaw slave imports delayed British recognition of her independence from Portugal, which she asserted in 1822. Although Britain tried to use the slave-trade issue to mediate the conflict between Brazil and Portugal, the latter claimed to have supported the commerce out of a concern for her colonists, whereas the colonists replied that the mother country had done nothing to prepare them for a sudden labor shortage. Since Brazil achieved her independence in a

[34] The preceding summary draws particularly on Corwin, *Spain and the Abolition of Slavery in Cuba*, pp. 17–46; Charles K. Webster, ed., *Britain and the Independence of Latin America, 1812–1830; Select Documents from the Foreign Office Archives* (London, 1838), I, 219–25; Webster, *The Foreign Policy of Castlereagh, 1812–1815: Britain and the Reconstruction of Europe* (London, 1950), pp. 413–21; Fladeland, "Abolitionist Pressures," pp. 355–73; Fladeland, *Men and Brothers: Anglo-American Antislavery Cooperation* (Urbana, Ill., 1972), pp. 106–24; A. T. Milne, "The Slave Trade and Anglo-American Relations, 1807–1862," M.A. thesis, University of London, 1930. In 1824 the United States finally agreed to a modified right of search, but Canning rejected the compromise, partly in protest against the Senate's revisory powers.

[35] Corwin, *Spain and the Abolition of Slavery in Cuba*, p. 35; Curtin, *Atlantic Slave Trade*, p. 234. As Professor Curtin emphasizes, these figures must be taken as very rough estimates.

unique and relatively nonviolent way, she might appear as the exception that proves a rule: namely, that wars of independence led to a disengagement from the Atlantic slave-trading system. With the exception of Brazil, the only remaining markets for African slaves by the 1820s were the colonies of Spain, France, and Holland. On the other hand, one must remember that a legal slave trade continued to the United States for thirty-two years after independence, and for twenty years after the adoption of the Constitution. In 1827 Brazil won British recognition by giving in to demands for commercial privileges and by agreeing to abolish the slave trade in 1830. Although the abolition law proved to be unenforceable, and Brazil did not bring slave imports to an end until mid-century, the unfulfilled commitment was of approximately the same duration as that of the United States.

Obviously the similarity cannot be pressed. Unlike the United States, Brazil faced the diplomatic, economic, and naval coercions of a much stronger power. Her sugar and coffee plantations depended on a trade which, after 1830, was technically illegal. Yet the comparison highlights an important question of independence and external coercion. Although the planters of South Carolina and Georgia enjoyed the benefits of a naturally increasing slave population, they would presumably have continued to import slaves, at least intermittently, if they had remained within an imperial system that permitted them to do so. The independence of the United States required them ultimately to bow to the interests and ideology of their sister states. They could never pool their political resources with the planters of the British Caribbean, who similarly found themselves too weak to resist the abolitionist pressures on the home government. And even when the South finally seceded from the Union, the fear of antagonizing British and border-state opinion helped to defeat agitation at the Confederate Constitutional Convention for the reopening of the African trade.[36]

Cuban planters had considerably more influence on the policies of Spain, in part because of the weakness of the Spanish government, but mainly because the wars of liberation had removed colonial interests that were not tied to the slave trade and the plantation system. Cuba, as Arthur F. Corwin has written, "had replaced Mexico, with her

[36] For the movement to reopen African slave imports to the American South, see Ronald T. Takaki, *A Pro-Slavery Crusade: The Agitation to Reopen the African Slave Trade* (New York, 1971).

gold and silver pieces, as the pearl in the Spanish diadem."[37] For Brazilian planters, resistance to British pressure signified patriotism and a proud spirit of cultural independence; Cubans were able to make the slave trade's continuation a fundamental condition for allegiance to Spain.

Yet in Cuba and especially in the urban centers of Brazil there was a rising bourgeoisie that looked to England as a model of economic and moral progress. More cosmopolitan than the planters of the hinterlands, these groups sought ways to assimilate the commercial liberalism of the nineteenth century to their own traditional cultures. And for British diplomats and resident bankers, traders, and professional men, there could be no more convincing symbol of civilized liberalism than an avowed abhorrence of the slave trade. If Napoleon had failed to make the principles of the French Revolution a justification for his temporary domination of Europe, England had succeeded in using abolitionism as a moral validation of her triumphant commercial empire. If she failed in the international congresses of 1818 and 1822 to win approval for international maritime police, her continuing crusade won international applause from liberal minds, and thus helped to detach a "progressive" class of Brazilians, and eventually Cubans, from the interests of the plantation system. Ultimately, England made it clear that she would enforce treaty obligations with naval gunfire; in the meantime, however, she wisely insisted that the abolition of the slave trade should at least appear to be an act of free will—like the choosing of Christ.

In the long view, therefore, there was some ground for Benjamin Lundy's optimism, even in 1822. The Age of Revolution, culminating in the independence of Brazil and the Spanish American republics, had been a major turning point in the history of New World slavery. It had brought a shattering of empires and commercial systems. The great slave regions—the Antilles, Brazil, and the southern United States—had become increasingly isolated and politically defensive. What could be termed the fringe areas of the old slave system had taken divergent paths of economic development. They were now freer to emancipate their small numbers of slaves than they had been as parts of an empire. Instead of spreading outward from the Caribbean, slavery had become circumscribed and dependent, though of course

[37] Corwin, *Spain and the Abolition of Slavery in Cuba*, p. 54.

it would continue to expand into extensive areas of Brazil and the United States.

The institution had also been disavowed in principle by the revolutionary leaders of France, the United States, and Latin America; its originating commerce had been condemned by Britain and by the reactionary congresses of Europe. For abolitionists the period had brought an end to certain naïve hopes. A series of defeats and disappointments, culminating in the Missouri Compromise and the Congress of Verona, showed that more would be required than a simple appeal to rulers, begging them to choose the path of virtue. In Britain, especially, the path of political action had been successfully mapped. Above all, in most parts of the New World the Negroes themselves had been aroused to a new consciousness of their rights. Hundreds of thousands had won their freedom. After the traumatic lesson of Haiti, especially, slaveholders could never again be altogether comfortable with the notion that blacks actually preferred bondage to freedom.

War and Emancipation

The wars of the Age of Revolution necessarily shattered the fragile security of many slaveholding societies. Armies moved and fought through regions heavily populated with slaves, some of whom took up arms on opposing sides, while others seized the opportunity to escape. When the French Revolution spread to the Caribbean, it ignited a racial war that fulfilled the darkest prophecies of the preceding century, feeding slaveholders' nightmares for a century to come. Other West Indian colonies were seldom free from threat of invasion or insurrection. Even on the coast of West Africa the British found their position weakened by the American War of Independence; in 1806 traditional slaving patterns were further disrupted when an Ashanti army near Cape Coast annihilated England's Fanti allies.[38]

Many historians have understandably been captivated by the romantic notion of slaves liberating themselves by force of arms. The frequency of insurrection has commonly been taken as a reassuring index of slave discontent, as if no more subtle evidence were available,

[38] W. E. F. Ward, *A History of Ghana* (rev. 2nd ed., London, 1958), pp. 146–55. Unfortunately, the question of the effects of war on slavery has not received the detailed study it deserves, and has too often been omitted from discussions of slave insurrection. I can only touch on the question here.

and as if the main result of such occurrences was not always an increase in mass executions of blacks. The subject of slave accommodation and resistance has recently been studied in considerable depth, and need not concern us here.[39] But it is important to discuss the ways in which a military crisis could affect opportunities for emancipation.

In April, 1775, Lord Dunmore, the royal governor of Virginia, threatened that he would proclaim liberty to the slaves and reduce Williamsburg to ashes if the colonists resorted to force against British authority. In November, after Dunmore and his small armed force had sought refuge on board warships in Norfolk harbor, he promised freedom to all Negroes "appertaining to Rebels" if they were able and willing to join "His Majesty's Troops . . . for the more speedily reducing the Colony to a proper sense of their duty, to His Majesty's crown and dignity." Several hundred Negroes succeeded in joining Dunmore's small army, but their forays along the coast were generally unsuccessful. The fleet finally sailed off to more promising war theaters.[40]

In June, 1793, Léger-Félicité Sonthonax, one of the commissioners sent to St. Domingue by the French Legislative Assembly, found himself in a position somewhat similar to that of Lord Dunmore. The whites of Le Cap, the capital city of the North Province, refused to accept the commissioners' authority. Over one thousand white sailors became involved in a race riot against the free mulattoes, whose rights the commissioners had defended. Sonthonax and his party retired from the city under heavy fire and seemed to face extermination, until Sonthonax called for support from the rebellious slaves in the country-

---

[39] There is a large and recent literature on slave "docility and rebelliousness," much of it provoked by Stanley M. Elkins's seminal study, *Slavery: A Problem in American Institutional and Intellectual Life* (Chicago, 1959). An excellent guide to the shifting terms of the debate can be found in the special issue of *Civil War History*, XIII (Dec., 1967). However, it seems likely that the starting point for all future discussion will be Eugene Genovese's *Roll, Jordan, Roll*, which brilliantly treats accommodation and resistance as parts of a subtle dialectical process.

[40] Peter Force, comp., *American Archives: Consisting of a Collection of Authentick Records, State Papers, Debates, and Letters and Other Notices of Publick Affairs* . . . (4th ser., Washington, 1840), III, 1385–87; IV 184–85; Gerald W. Mullin, *Flight and Rebellion: Slave Resistance in Eighteenth-Century Virginia* (New York, 1972), pp. 131–32; Benjamin Quarles, *The Negro in the American Revolution* (Chapel Hill, 1961), pp. 19–32.

side. Some ten thousand blacks then stormed down upon Le Cap, and it was the pro-planter governor, accompanied by most of the surviving white residents, who fled by sea. Sonthonax soon issued a general emancipation proclamation, which was later validated by the French Convention.[41]

One can quickly think of reasons that help to account for the striking contrast. In 1775, Virginia had not undergone four years of revolutionary turmoil. The white population did not constitute a tiny minority, nor was white supremacy challenged by a powerful group of mulattoes of almost equal numbers. Above all, the slaves of Virginia had not been in armed rebellion for nearly two years. Nor had officials in London begun to conclude that preservation of the empire would depend on free blacks and mulattoes. It would be hazardous, however, to draw hasty conclusions from these two incidents, which were parts of larger and more complex sets of events. In 1793 the French government had no more intention of turning slaves against their masters than the English government had in 1775. Who can say what might have happened if the British, anticipating Abraham Lincoln, had issued a decree emancipating all slaves in rebel hands? Or if the Americans had followed Silas Deane's suggestion of inciting insurrections in Jamaica, where in 1776 a massive uprising in Hanover and St. James parishes resulted in more than thirty executions?[42]

Slaveholding colonists universally deplored the practice of arming blacks, whether slave or free, and often hoped that a sense of common peril would give force to an understood taboo. Yet throughout colonial history slaves frequently won their freedom by military service, without weakening the foundations of the institution. The precedents were firmest in the Caribbean and in seventeenth-century Brazil, where the whites were so few in number and the settlements so vulnerable that slaves held the key to military security as well as to disaster. During

---

[41] C. L. R. James, *The Black Jacobins: Toussaint L'Ouverture and the San Domingo Revolution* (2nd rev. ed., New York, 1963), pp. 126–29; James G. Leyburn, *The Haitian People* (New Haven, 1941), *passim;* Theodore Lothrop Stoddard, *The French Revolution in San Domingo* (Boston, 1914), *passim;* J. Saintoyant, *La Colonisation française pendant la révolution, passim.* For the politics of French emancipation, see Chapters Two and Three below.

[42] Ragatz, *Fall of the Planter Class*, p. 145; Patterson, *Sociology of Slavery*, p. 272. In 1760 over one thousand Jamaican slaves had become involved in a revolt aimed at "a total massacre of the whites and to make the island a Negro colony" (Patterson, p. 271). Ironically, in St. Domingue, unlike Jamaica, there had been few slave revolts prior to 1791.

the Portuguese struggles against Dutch and French encroachments in Brazil, all the combatants enlisted large numbers of slaves. In 1772, when racial war broke out in Surinam, and when Paramaribo was terrorized by armies of fugitives from the surrounding jungle, the Dutch finally armed some three hundred slaves, with promises of freedom, in order to save the colony from annihilation. Similarly, the Jamaicans used black troops to crush the rebellious Maroons of the interior, although the Maroons of Jamaica and other colonies sometimes collaborated with the whites in returning fugitives or suppressing slave revolts. When French warships roamed the Caribbean during the American Revolution, British colonists fearfully armed their more trusted slaves, after first mobilizing them as "pioneers" for work on fortifications.[43]

Even in North America some Negro slaves won their freedom by serving in the various imperial wars between England and France. But in North America the local laws forbidding this practice were more strictly enforced than in Brazil and the Caribbean. The difference, as Carl Degler has pointed out, had nothing to do with attitudes toward slavery but arose from the simple availability of white manpower. Prior to the American Revolution, the arming of slaves was never more than a question of military expedience, always undertaken with reluctance and with the aim of preserving the slave system. If black soldiers fought with the expectation of freedom, they also knew that if they were captured, they would not be treated as prisoners of war.

Moreover, the rules of war were firmer when it came to inciting foreign slaves against their masters. In 1759, for example, the British

[43] Henry G. Dalton, *The History of British Guiana* (London, 1855), I, 197–217; Louise Collis, *Soldier in Paradise: The Life of Captain John Stedman, 1744–1797* (New York, 1965), pp. 107–08; Ragatz, *Fall of the Planter Class*, pp. 32–33, 220–22, and *passim;* Goveia, *Slave Society in the British Leeward Islands*, p. 148; *Journals of the Assembly of Jamaica* (Jamaica, 1805), IX, 28, 248, 420–26; Pares, *War and Trade in the West Indies*, pp. 252–56. In 1795 the English government urged that slaves be enlisted in a special black corps for the defense of the British Caribbean, a proposal which outraged the white colonists. But by 1795 the French revolutionary army had employed former slaves for the reconquest of Guadeloupe and St. Lucia, and had also begun to incite the slaves and Carib Indians of St. Vincent and Grenada, resulting in brutal civil warfare that nearly overthrew British dominion. Accordingly, the British colonists reluctantly began to arm slaves for local defense, and also deported some five thousand Caribs, ultimately to Ruatan, an island in Honduras Bay.

overruled Commodore John Moore's plan of proclaiming freedom to any slaves in Guadeloupe who would desert or turn against the French. By 1791, French planters themselves were quick to forget traditional rivalries and appeal to Jamaicans as fellow slaveholders who would share a similar fate if St. Domingue were lost. Pleading for troops and money from Jamaica, the governor reported that two hundred plantations had been burned and that over 100,000 slaves were in revolt. In September, 1793, former St. Domingue officials accompanied a British expeditionary force from Jamaica that was welcomed by many of the remaining white colonists, notwithstanding the state of war between Britain and France.[44]

But revolution, and revolutionary ideology, transformed the question of arming slaves. At the outset of the American Revolution, blacks in the northern colonies petitioned the local legislatures, appealing to the principles of natural and inalienable rights. Some of Lord Dunmore's armed fugitives wore the emblem, "Liberty to Slaves." The thousands of blacks in the South who sought refuge behind British or French lines knew that a new era had dawned, that some deliverer might be at hand. In the Caribbean, British slaves sometimes imagined that their masters were resisting and suppressing the king's efforts to free them; in 1790 this conviction sparked a revolt in Tortola. It was said that slaves leading the great St. Domingue uprising carried royalist banners and fought to the cry of God and king. Many had also heard heated discussion of the rights of man. The vague and often confused idea of revolution continued to spread. In 1823 a group of slaves in Honduras addressed a memorial to the Constituent Assembly of Central America, asserting that human bondage was inconsistent with political liberty. The blacks of Boston had made the same point fifty years before.[45]

Obviously "revolution" meant something very different in the

[44] Carl Degler, *Neither Black Nor White: Slavery and Race Relations in Brazil and the United States* (New York, 1971), pp. 75–82; Pares, *War and Trade in the West Indies,* pp. 252–53; *Journals of the Assembly of Jamaica,* IX, 51–52.

[45] Goveia, *Slave Society in the British Leeward Islands,* p. 334; Harold A. Bierck, Jr., "The Struggle for Abolition in Gran Colombia," *Hispanic American Historical Review,* XXXIII (1953), 366; Gaston Martin, *Histoire de l'esclavage,* pp. 210–23; James, *Black Jacobins,* p. 95; Quarles, *Negro in the American Revolution,* pp. 28, 44; *Collections* of the Massachusetts Historical Society, 5th ser., III, 382ff, 432–37; "La libertad de los esclavos," *Boletín del archivo general del gobierno* [Guatemala], III (No. 2, Jan., 1938), 277–78.

United States, in St. Domingue, and in Spanish America. Even an edict of emancipation meant one thing in a context of social fluidity and relative freedom of opportunity, and something very different in a society that took some form of mass serfdom or peonage for granted.

In Mexico, for example, most of the population consisted of Indians and mestizos who were oppressed by the ancient tributes and restrictions of the colonial regime. In 1810, at the time of the Hidalgo revolt, there were fewer Negro slaves in Mexico than in the state of New York. The ideals of the Enlightenment had won some favor, despite rigid censorship, among the educated native-born, or *criollos,* who often resented the privileges of the Spanish governing elite. But Hidalgo, a parish priest who had once been a professor and who knew French, came to envision a social revolution that went far beyond the aims of Thomas Jefferson. Hidalgo's goals shifted, partly because of his immediate need to mobilize an army of peasants, miners, and urban laborers, once his conspiracy had been divulged. In addition to proclaiming the end of tribute for Indian *castas,* lower taxes on liquor, and other popular reforms, he announced that the glorious moment had arrived when his brave American nation could throw off the yoke of three centuries of oppression. He thus ordered all masters to free their slaves within ten days, upon pain of death. In another decree, before his rampaging mob sacked Guanajuato, Hidalgo declared that freed slaves should have full equality with Spaniards. After Hidalgo had been crushed, his successor, José María Morelos, also appealed for mass support through an edict of emancipation. But while many conservative *criollos* could share the rebels' hostility toward European dominion, especially toward a mother country that had become the supine mistress of France, they united to stamp out a movement that threatened to abolish not only the vestiges of Negro slavery but the traditional relations beween labor, property, and wealth.[46]

The leaders of the American Revolution were, in their own way, conservative *criollos,* which helps to explain why, for all the natural rights philosophy embellishing the first state constitutions, only that of

[46] Hugh M. Hamill, Jr., *The Hidalgo Revolt: Prelude to Mexican Independence* (Gainsville, Fla., 1966), *passim;* Miguel León-Portilla, *et al.,* eds., *Historia documental de México* (México, D.F., 1964), II, 49, 55–56; Juan N. Chávarri, *Historia de la guerra de independencia de 1810 a 1821* (México, D.F., 1960), pp. 73–75.

Vermont moved from a ringing statement that "all men are born equally free and independent, and have certain natural, inherent and inalienable rights," to a "therefore" that specifically prohibited slavery. It is true that the Revolution elicited other official antislavery pronouncements in areas where a zeal for liberty coincided with a small proportion of Negroes. Even the loyalists of Upper Canada finally proclaimed that it was unjust for a people who enjoyed freedom by law (unlike their rebellious brethren to the south) to encourage the introduction of slaves.

The crucial question, however, was whether the emergencies of war would require the arming of slaves. Negroes served with valor in the colonial militia at the battles of Lexington and Bunker Hill. But by November, 1775, Congress and the leading officers of the army had decided to exclude even free blacks from future enlistment, and to rely, as soon as possible, on an all-white army. This restrictive policy arose from a sensitivity to southern opinion, from a fear of British retaliation, and from a desire to make the rebellious forces as "respectable" as possible. It is conceivable that sensitivities would have been less acute in an ordinary war, fought for somewhat less exalted purposes, when blacks would have been less likely to echo all the fine phrases about the rights of man. In any event, General Washington soon became fearful that the black troops, "very much dissatisfied at being discarded," might seek employment in the British army. The news of Lord Dunmore's proclamation gave bite to the message. Accordingly, Congress decided to allow the re-enlistment of free Negroes who had served in the army at Cambridge.[47]

[47] *Vermont State Papers: Being a Collection of Records and Documents, Connected with the Assumption and Establishment of Government by the People of Vermont* . . . (Middlebury, Vt., 1823), p. 244; Quarles, *Negro in the American Revolution, passim;* Pete Maslowski, "National Policy toward the Use of Black Troops in the Revolution," *South Carolina Historical Magazine,* LXXIII (Jan., 1972), 1–17; William Renwick Riddell, "Slavery in Canada," *Journal of Negro History,* V. (July, 1920), 319. In Commonwealth *v.* Jennison (1783), Chief Justice William Cushing shied away from interpreting the "free and equal" clause in the Massachusetts constitution as an implicit abolition of slavery, but said that in his judgment slavery was "as effectively abolished as it can be by the granting of rights and privileges wholly incompatible and repugnant to its existence" (see John D. Cushing, "The Cushing Court and the Abolition of Slavery in Massachusetts: More Notes on the Quock Walker Case," *American Journal of Legal History,* V [1961], 118–44). In 1802, long after Pennsylvania had adopted a gradual emancipation act, the state's highest court

By 1778 a shortage of manpower had brought a remarkable shift in sentiment, at least in the North, where various states encouraged the emancipation of slaves for military service. Some blacks served as substitutes for their masters, others as mercenaries hired by committees charged with meeting local quotas. In contrast to St. Domingue and Spanish America, the relative availability of white manpower precluded the necessity of exploiting emancipation as an emergency war measure. Yet it would appear—and much research still needs to be done on the subject—that the pressures of war did much to undermine slavery in the northern states. Not only did Tories appeal to slave unrest, feeding rumors that spread panic among slaveholders in areas like the Hudson valley, but the disruptions of civil war and British occupation gave blacks plentiful opportunities for escape. Many slaves posed as freedmen when offering to enlist; others reaped multiple bounties through desertion and re-enlistment. As far south as Virginia, the law required masters to free any slave who had served as a substitute.[48]

But the major challenge arose when the British occupied Savannah, at the end of 1778, and when the theatre of war shifted to the Deep South. Even earlier, John Laurens, a young and idealistic South Carolinian, and an aide-de-camp to Washington, had dreamed of leading a corps of emancipated blacks in the defense of liberty. He and his father, Henry Laurens, finally helped to persuade Congress to approve, unanimously, a plan for recruiting an army of three thousand slave troops in South Carolina and Georgia. The federal government would fully compensate the slaves' owners, and each black, upon the end of the war, would be emancipated and receive a sum of fifty dollars. The plan won the full support of generals of the southern army, such as Benjamin Lincoln and Nathaniel Greene. It did not, however, win the necessary support from the South Carolina legislature, despite John Laurens's eloquent pleas. One can debate whether a slight change in circumstance, or in military fortune, might have led to a different outcome. In the world of might-have-beens, the implica-

---

ruled that slavery *was* compatible with the declaration of rights in the constitution.

[48] McManus, *Black Bondage in the North,* pp. 143–59; Donald L. Robinson, *Slavery in the Structure of American Politics, 1765–1820* (New York, 1971), pp. 98–130.

tions of arming thousands of slaves in the Deep South, in a Revolutionary war, are incalculable. As a result of the war, many southern slaves were in fact impressed into service as laborers, engineers, and teamsters; thousands were freed and evacuated with the British and French armies. Yet the war brought no major weakening of the slave system, except in the North. The legislators of South Carolina and Georgia, who had not yet heard of Toussaint L'Ouverture, understood the potentialities of revolution.

It might have been otherwise if the British government had approved Dunmore's proposal to conquer the South with an army of ten thousand blacks. In South America the Spanish royalist forces later showed similar reluctance, but discovered that black troops were indispensable for crushing the first independence movements. In response, as early as 1813, Juan del Corral saw that the patriots' cause would require the manumission of slaves; the following year, as temporary dictator, he secured a law for gradual emancipation in Antioquia. In Venezuela, Francisco Miranda promised freedom in 1812 to any slave who would fight the Spaniards for ten years. Similarly, when the Viceroy of Peru invaded Chile in 1814 to suppress rebellion, José Miguel Carrera decreed freedom for slaves joining in the resistance and tried to coerce support from both Negroes and their owners.[49]

With the example of Haiti before them, the Spanish rebels and royalists were if anything more fearful of arming slaves than their Anglo-American counterparts had been a generation before. Yet the struggles for independence were much more prolonged than the American Revolution, the rebels had smaller resources of free manpower, and no ally like France intervened to reinforce the patriot armies and limit the mother country's ability to send soldiers and supplies. For a time the rebels hoped to appeal to the English, as fellow slaveholders, to send troops to suppress "the bandits, and fugitive slaves who carry pillage, death, and desolation to many of the best settlements and haciendas." But by 1816 Simón Bolívar had found an ally in Haiti,

---

[49] Eduardo Zuleta, "Movimiento antiesclavista en Antioquia," *Boletín de historia y antigüedades*, X (No. 109, May, 1915), 35–37; Feliú Cruz, *La abolición de la esclavitud en Chile*, pp. 73–79; John V. Lombardi, *The Decline and Abolition of Negro Slavery in Venezuela, 1820–1854* (Westport, Conn., 1971), pp. 36–38.

and had concluded that slave emancipation provided the key to independence.[50]

Bolívar soon discovered, however, that few slaves yearned to die for the cause of their *criollo* masters, and that Venezuelan masters were no more eager than South Carolinians to see field hands transformed into soldiers. Fearing a second and perhaps bloodier St. Domingue, even the Liberator assured slaveholders that his policy arose from military necessity and should not be confused with a general emancipation. During 1819 and 1820 the patriot army in western New Granada enlisted nearly three thousand Negro slaves, but General Francisco de Paula Santander finally put an end to such recruitment and ordered all Negroes not needed by the army to return to the mines.[51]

It is difficult to assess the effects of war on Spanish American emancipation. When compared with the American Revolution, the wars of liberation brought greater social disruption and more directly undermined plantation discipline. Both rebels and royalists found themselves forced to make far greater use of black manpower. By 1821, both in Gran Colombia (including Venezuela and Ecuador) and Peru, republican congresses had committed themselves to a policy of gradual emancipation. Yet the proportion of slaves in the populations of these countries was no greater than in the northern United States at the time of the Revolution. The process of gradual emancipation took approximately as long in Venezuela and Peru as in New York. In various parts of the New World the need for troops brought freedom for thousands of slaves and in some areas helped to weaken the plantation system. But only in St. Domingue did revolution and independence lead to mass emancipation, and only in St. Domingue did blacks wrest power from the hands of whites.

And by 1823, unfortunately, the example of Haiti gave little encouragement to the antislavery cause. Constantly fearing reconquest by France, its independence unrecognized by other nations, the republic had suffered years of domestic turmoil, war, and economic quarantine. If Henri Christophe had brought a degree of recovery to the North Province, his system of regimented labor could not reverse the effects of revolution and counterrevolution, or restore the regime

---

[50] Lombardi, *Decline and Abolition of Negro Slavery in Venezuela, passim.*
[51] *Ibid.*, pp. 41–46; Bierck, "The Struggle for Abolition," pp. 367–70.

of unchallenged authority on which the plantation economy had depended. The economic disintegration of the South Province—and of
the entire nation when reunited under Jean-Pierre Boyer—gave the
island's rulers a continuing excuse to substitute coerced labor for the
slavery of the past. Yet for American reformers like Benjamin Lundy,
Haiti seemed to present the only promising refuge for North American freedmen who faced an unmistakable hardening of racial prejudice and a new rash of discriminatory laws. Even the idealistic Bolívar,
envisioning the nightmare of racial war, saw the problem as a "bot-
tomless pit" where reason disappeared on entrance.[52]

In summary, then, slavery has always embodied a fundamental
contradiction arising from the ultimately impossible attempt to define
and treat men as objects. Historically, the contradiction has generated
conflict, fear, and accommodation, but from antiquity it also became
interwoven with religious and philosophic rationalizations for authority
and subordination. Prior to the eighteenth century, Christians often
exhorted masters to treat their slaves with charity and forbearance;
humanitarians expressed compassion for the misfortune of individual
slaves; a few critics voiced doubts over the justice of the African slave
trade. But even a widespread practice like the use of galley slaves—
which persisted in the Mediterranean from antiquity to modern times
—went virtually unchallenged in principle. Attacks on the principle
of slavery were confined to perfectionist religious sects whose radical
visions could have no positive effect on public policy.

By the eighteenth century, however, profound social changes,
particularly those connected with the rise of new classes and new
economic interests in Britain and America, created an audience hospi-
table to antislavery ideology. This ideology emerged from a convergence of complex religious, intellectual, and literary trends—trends
which are by no means reducible to the economic interests of particular classes, but which must be understood as part of a larger transformation in attitudes toward labor, property, and individual responsibility.
By the 1770s English Quakers and Methodists found the principle of
slavery no less repugnant than did French *philosophes;* the institution's
traditional sanctions had been repudiated by leading philosophers,
political economists, and authorities on jurisprudence. Yet the con-

---

[52] Leyburn, *The Haitian People,* pp. 43–64; Bierck, "The Struggle for
Abolition," p. 379.

sequences of this shift in intellectual history would largely be shaped by the material conditions and circumstances of the subsequent half-century. In other words, once a few men committed themselves to the goal of promoting universal emancipation, their opportunities and strategies would be framed by economic and political events.

The Age of Revolution coincided with the economic decline of the older sugar colonies in the Caribbean. It also witnessed the peak and gradual decline of the African slave trade, a decline stimulated by the wars of the French Revolution and by the independence of the United States and the Latin American republics. After England had abolished her own slave trade, both self-interest and ideology encouraged continuing diplomatic pressure to secure international suppression of the remaining traffic. Meanwhile, the diffusion of revolutionary ideals put a new perspective on the traditional reluctance to arm slaves in times of war. During the American Revolution, slaves in the northern states appealed to the rebels' ideology of natural rights. In various ways the war helped to undermine slavery in the North. And though South Carolina successfully resisted moves to mobilize thousands of slaves, the war gave many blacks the opportunity to escape behind enemy lines or to win their freedom by fighting for the patriot cause. Black military power became far more decisive during the Latin American wars of independence and resulted in official commitments to the goal of gradual emancipation. Throughout the New World, slave-holders brooded over the portent of St. Domingue, where war and revolution had not only destroyed the richest of all plantation economies, but where slaves had actually won their freedom and independence by force of arms.

By 1823 the leaders of Brazil, Cuba, and the southern United States were clearly on the defensive. But though the Age of Revolution had intellectually isolated the major slaveholding regimes, it had also, with the exception of the British West Indies, increased their independent political power. Plantation slavery had done more than simply survive the disruptions of a half-century of war and revolution. The system had proved to be far more vigorous, adaptable, and expansive than critics had imagined. Slave-grown cotton had become indispensable for the industrial development of Lancashire as well as New England. And if slave labor itself seemed repugnant to capitalist ideology, there was little ground for the hope that the free play of market forces would soon undermine a supposedly wasteful, unproductive, and unprofitable system of labor.

Two ⌇

The Seats of Power, I

Prospects for Reform

A modern-minded reformer living in the 1770s might sum up the prospects for general emancipation somewhat as follows. In the absence of full-scale insurrection or civil war, there will be little likelihood of persuading governments to take positive steps toward emancipation in regions dominated by the plantation system and dependent on slave labor. Even where slavery is of marginal economic importance, it will be sheltered by a concern for the rights and security of private property. An era of revolution may have begun, but revolutionary assemblies will generally be in the hands of merchants or landed interests imbued with a commercial spirit. Such groups will be acutely sensitive to any precedent that might harm traders, investors, and property owners, or to any threatened tax increases for poor relief or for compensation payments to slaveholders. In many areas white workers will threaten violence if faced by the competition in free Negro laborers. And as Benjamin Franklin cautiously warned, "slavery is such an atrocious debasement of human nature, that its very extirpation, if not performed with solicitous care, may sometimes open a source of serious evils."[1]

On the other hand, human bondage seems to contradict the ideals of liberty and natural rights that are used to justify revolution. In almost any assembly or convention, some delegates will be deeply

[1] Quoted in Frederick Law Olmsted, *A Journey in the Seaboard Slave States, with Remarks on Their Economy* (New York, 1856), p. 125.

troubled by official tributes to liberty that disguise quiet sanctions for slavery. Others will view involuntary labor as a source of economic backwardness or of military insecurity. With sufficient skill, organization, and perseverance, such reformers might exploit their ideological advantage and achieve some form of gradual emancipation, at least in countries where the entire social and economic system has not been assimilated to slavery.

But even this realistic appraisal fails to convey the true complexity of the question. To understand the first great political struggles over slavery, one must move beyond a simple dichotomy of "economic motives" and "humanitarian ideals." In the broadest sense, there can be no doubt that differences in economic structure and development governed the political response to slavery. No representatives of a plantation regime took serious moves toward a general emancipation. No northeastern United States legislature contemplated a commercial boycott of the West Indies in order to disengage themselves from the slave system. Yet it is fruitless to debate whether the northern states abolished slavery out of economic interest or whether Virginia slaveholders were "sincere" in their professed belief in natural rights. In Virginia the hegemony of a planter class set definite boundaries to the most sincere idealism. In the North, where there were many slave owners but no distinct slaveholding class, idealism could serve a variety of purposes and mix freely with objectives unrelated to social justice or the future status of the Negro. If there is no convincing evidence that slavery was unprofitable in the northern states or was dying there from economic causes, the institution hardly meshed with the ideology of *Poor Richard's Almanac*. The emerging consensus ruled that slave labor stifled the progress of industry and the mechanical arts. And as John Adams shrewdly observed, the white workingman's hostility toward Negroes could find an outlet in opposition to slavery as well as in racial persecution.

Yet slavery was always a potentially explosive problem because it raised fundamental issues few leaders were prepared to face, even in a revolutionary age. Through much of American history the shadowy presence of the slave was an irrepressible reminder of the systematic violence and exploitation which underlay a society genuinely dedicated to individual freedom and equality of opportunity. The entire rhetoric of liberalism reassured individuals that their own true freedom could not run counter to the best interests of anyone else; but the connection between slavery and economic success dramatized contradictions in the very meaning of liberty. And because debates over slavery allowed conflicts in values to be fused to specific conflicts of interest, they gave a moral and ideological dimension to struggles for prestige, material advantage, and power. Especially in national conventions and congresses, made up of widely divergent interest groups, the question of slavery could become a testing ground for disputes over representation, jurisdiction, and the limitation of power. It could provide the basis for compromise or a vulnerable target for dissident and rebellious groups. In the United States a series of compromises on slavery became the fulcrum of an uneasy balance of power; in Britain the triumph of the anti-slave-trade movement signaled a redefinition of national interest; in France antislavery and anticolonialism became ideological weapons in the contest for revolutionary leadership.

Emancipation in Nonslave Societies

Chapters Two and Three are mainly concerned with the political implications of antislavery doctrine as embodied in the compromises and commitments of national law-making bodies. But virtually all the emancipation acts from the American Revolution to the Latin American wars of independence issued from local assemblies which subscribed to a liberal ideology but which also had some slaveholder representation. To put the national conflicts in proper perspective, it is well to look first at the difficulties and delays in securing emancipation even where slavery was unpopular and relatively insignificant.

Emancipation could never be the simple matter of a legislature decreeing that after a certain year all slaves should be free. The absurdity of this notion becomes clear as soon as one thinks of the obstacles any modern government would face if it decided to outlaw a long-accepted species of private property or of labor use (say even a declining practice like the employment of domestic servants). No New World government had experience in eradicating an institution, let alone the bureaucratic machinery to deal with the variety of legal and extralegal subterfuges that could prevent effective implementation of a manumission law. Successful enforcement would require the strongest support from public opinion. Yet even the Quakers, with the most powerful religious sanctions and the most delicate social instruments of persuasion, had a long and difficult time ridding their own sect of slaveholding.

On the assumption that the American Revolution brought a smooth and relatively unopposed end to slavery in the northern states, historians have sometimes asked whether, with a little additional effort, the line of freedom might have been extended to the border of South Carolina. Much has been made of the plans of men like Thomas Jefferson and St. George Tucker for the gradual emancipation and colonization of Negroes. This apparent liberalism has seemed more promising when coupled with Virginia's allowance in 1782 of voluntary manumission and with the bold struggle against the legalization of slavery in the Kentucky constitutional convention. But even if we disregard evidence of slavery's continuing and growing strength in the Upper South, such stirrings seem less hopeful when placed within a larger comparative setting.

Consider first the caution and conservatism of northern legislators. In 1780 the New Hampshire legislature debated and then postponed the apparently touchy question of manumitting a handful of slaves, after receiving an eloquent appeal from Negroes "that the name of slave may not more be heard in a land gloriously contending for the sweets of freedom." The constituent conventions of both New York and Massachusetts defeated attempts at constitutional emancipation. Again and again, the legislatures of New England, New York, and New Jersey rejected even the most cautious proposals for gradual abolition. Although by 1800 there seem to have been fewer than fifty slaves in the province of Lower Canada, its House of Assembly refused, as late as 1803, to pass bills for gradual emancipation.[2]

In 1780 a group of Pennsylvania radicals secured the first emancipation law in the New World. The Philadelphia radicals, though politically opposed to the Quakers, fulfilled the Quakers' goal as proof of their own revolutionary sincerity, as a means of winning divine favor, and as an expression of gratitude to God for the British evacua-

----

[2] For the opposition to emancipation in the northern states, see Arthur Zilversmit, *The First Emancipation: The Abolition of Slavery in the North* (Chicago, 1967); and Edgar J. McManus, *Black Bondage in the North* (Syracuse, N.Y., 1973). For Canada, see Marcel Trudel, *L'Esclavage au Canada français* (Quebec, 1960), pp. 295–97, 309–10; and Robin W. Winks, *The Blacks in Canada: A History* (New Haven, 1971), pp. 96–113. Gary B. Nash has recently demonstrated that the decline of slavery in Philadelphia from 1767 to 1775 had far less to do with private manumissions than with the ending of slave importations, the availability of white indentured servants, and the natural decrease of the slave population ("Slaves and Slaveowners in Colonial Philadelphia," *William and Mary Quarterly*, 3rd ser., XXX [April, 1973], 223–56).

tion from their city, an event which had incidentally led also to the exodus of many Negro slaves. The law applied only to future generations of Negroes. By postponing their emancipation to the age of twenty-eight, it promised to compensate owners by having young servants earn the cost of their own upbringing.[3] Even so, a rural faction within the radical party strenuously resisted the measure. The law's defenders succeeded in defeating attempts at repeal and emasculation, but were unable to accelerate progress with a subsequent act for total abolition.

The pattern was similar throughout much of the North. In the absence of legislative action, judicial decisions eroded the institution fairly rapidly in Massachuetts and New Hampshire, but at a slower pace in Lower Canada and the Maritime provinces. From 1784 to 1804 gradual emancipation acts won grudging assent in Connecticut, Rhode Island, Upper Canada, New York, and New Jersey. As one might expect, the legislative contest was easiest where the proportion of Negroes was small. Yet even in Upper Canada, where there were a few hundred slaves at most, the law of 1793 provided freedom only for postnati at the age of twenty-five. The House of Assembly, which contained loyalist slaveholders who had fled the United States, prohibited private manumissions unless a master could provide security against his Negro's becoming a public charge. Under New York's first emancipation act of 1799, all existing slaves were to remain in per-

---

[3] Robert William Fogel and Stanley L. Engerman have recently raised penetrating questions about the price of philanthropy, a subject that has hitherto been curiously ignored. Since even the most dedicated antislavery legislators had no wish to see an assault on one form of private property widen into a general redistribution of wealth, the central question was how to apportion the financial burden of emancipation. Fogel and Engerman show that the postnate emancipation laws were designed above all to relieve nonslaveholding free Northerners of most of the direct financial burden. In effect, the slaves and their children paid the major cost of gradual emancipation (Fogel and Engerman, *Time on the Cross: The Economics of American Negro Slavery* [2 vols., Boston, 1974], I, 35–36; II [*Evidence and Methods—A Supplement*], II, 33–37; Fogel and Engerman, "Philanthrophy at Bargain Prices: Notes on the Economics of Gradual Emancipation," unpublished paper). Not only did the burden thus fall on the poorest and most vulnerable group, but as Claudia Dale Golden has argued, the slaves' children "were probably worked harder than if their owners had property rights to their lifetime earnings streams" ("The Economics of Emancipation," *Journal of Economic History,* XXXIII [March, 1973], 70). An announced or anticipated gradual emancipation probably encouraged more intensive work as well as the sale of northern slaves in southern markets.

petual servitude; as an additional compensation for postnate emancipation, the law allowed masters to abandon bondsmen at any time and thus to transfer the cost of rearing Negro children to the towns and ultimately to the state. Only in 1817, and after a bitter legislative struggle, could Negroes born before 1799 look forward to the promise of freedom after enduring still another decade of slavery. New Jersey's abolition law of 1804 was so conservative and slow in operation that the state still contained slaves, euphemistically defined as apprentices, at the time of the Civil War.

The problems raised by freeing some 11,000 blacks in New Jersey seem insignificant when compared with those faced by the British government at the time it was drafting a plan for the emancipation of 780,000 colonial slaves (or by the Russian government in 1861, when emancipating 22,000,000 serfs). Moreover, during the last two decades of the eighteenth century many more slaves were voluntarily manumitted in Virginia and Maryland than were affected by the emancipation laws of states like Connecticut and Rhode Island. In some respects the laws may have made little difference. In Delaware, for example, where the legislature spurned a gradual emancipation bill in 1786, slavery declined much as it did in New Jersey, until, by 1860, free Negroes outnumbered slaves by ten to one.[4] In view of these considerations, the conservatism and continuing resistance in the northern states seem all the more striking. Yet even apart from racial prejudice, contemporary social values provided little justification for the rehabilitation of the ex-slave; in no state or colony were there effective institutions for the support or education of slave children. At a time when the rights and status of the free laborer were increasingly uncertain, the future role of the freedman could arouse only the gravest misgivings.

[4] Monte A. Calvert, "The Abolition Society of Delaware, 1801–1807," *Delaware History*, X (Oct., 1963), 295–320; Ulrich Bonnell Phillips, *American Negro Slavery* (Gloucester, Mass., reprint ed., 1959), p. 121. Claudia Golden thinks it possible that twice as many New York State slaves were sold to the slave states further south than were freed by abolitionist legislation ("The Economics of Emancipation," p. 70). Fogel and Engerman conclude that "it is probable that, to a substantial degree, the decline of slavery in the North was due not to emancipation but to the actions of northern slaveholders who were cashing in on capital gains by selling their chattel in southern markets" ("Philanthropy at Bargain Prices," p. 19. I am much indebted to Professors Fogel and Engerman for sending me the revised draft, Feb. 12, 1974, of this important paper).

And in Latin America, despite vast differences in social structure and cultural heritage, one finds the same story of slaveholder resistance, concern for property rights, and delay in implementing high-sounding pronouncements. As in North America, revolutionary ideals had more decisive effect where slaves were few in number. With less than four thousand Negro bondsmen, many of whom were employed as domestic servants, Chile can be roughly compared with a northeastern state. Yet in 1811 attempts at gradual emancipation met stiff opposition from both rebels and royalists. The constitution of 1822 declared all Chileans equal before the law, but it was not until the following year that the senate, after much debate on the possible threat to property rights, finally agreed to general emancipation.[5] In 1824 the National Assembly of the United Provinces of Central America also passed an immediate abolition act. But this celebrated law freed no more than one thousand slaves, and still aroused long preliminary dispute over compensation, legislative jurisdiction, and the danger of antagonizing Cuba, Jamaica, or independent slaveholding nations. The Mexican constitution of 1824 evaded the question of slavery, notwithstanding republican enthusiasm over recent military victories and an act by the constituent congress outlawing an already defunct slave trade. Mexico finally abolished slavery in 1829 by a decree of the dictator Vincente Guerrero, in the face of a Spanish invasion; and the government allowed Texans the subterfuge of classifying their slaves as indentured servants.[6]

Progress was considerably slower in Venezuela, where the proportion of slaves in the total population was slightly smaller than in New York (in 1786 slaves constituted 7.9 per cent of New York's population; in 1810 the number of Venezuela did not exceed 5 per cent). In Venezuela, as in New York, revolution led to stirring demands for slave emancipation; both patriots and loyalists exploited the grievances of Negroes; and independence brought to power a conservative, commercially oriented elite. There, however, the similarities end. If Vene-

[5] Guillermo Feliú Cruz, *La abolición de la esclavitud en Chile* (Santiago de Chile, 1942), pp. 51–61, 69–70, 87, 95–102, 155; Rolando Mellafe, *Le esclavitud en Hispano-América* (Buenos Aires, 1964), p. 102.

[6] "La libertad de los esclavos," *Boletín del archivo general de gobierno* [Guatemala], III (1937–1938), No. 2 (Jan. 1938), 277–95; Carlos Martínez Durán and Daniel Contreras, "La abolición de la esclavitud en Centroamérica," *Journal of Inter-American Studies*, IV (April, 1962), 227–32; George Lockhart Rives, *The United States and Mexico, 1821–1848* (New York, 1913), I, 184–85.

zuela had become less dependent on slave labor with the decline of its cacao-plantation economy in the eighteenth century, a coffee boom beginning by 1830 increased the demand for some form of involuntary servitude. Nor could the white elite ever forget that the mass of Venezuelans were nonwhite *pardos,* a lowly caste that shared much in common with the Negro slaves.[7]

There were local circumstances, then, that enabled a powerful proslavery faction to dominate the Congress of Angostura in 1819, defeating Simón Bolívar's pleas to implement earlier wartime promises of liberty. A decree of January, 1820, called for gradual instead of immediate emancipation, on the ground that it would be necessary "to make them men before making them citizens"; yet this pronouncement carried no enabling legislation. It was only after independence and prolonged debate at the Congress of Cucutá that an emancipation law finally emerged. And despite the noble rhetoric accompanying it, the 1821 Cucutá law carefully guarded security and property rights by requiring slave children to serve their mother's owner until maturity, by granting local boards the power to determine the freedmen's future occupation, and by making the emancipation of adults depend on monetary compensation to be raised by a special inheritance tax. Since this cumbersome measure was to be administered by local juntas, which were often not appointed, slaveholders faced no immediate menace. A succession of idealistic decrees failed to raise the taxes for compensation, to unsnarl litigation, or to subdue mounting public resistance. In the province of Bogotá (with Venezuela, part of Gran Colombia), only twenty-two manumissions were recorded in 1822 and only one in 1823. In LaGuaria the law freed seven slaves in 1823 and 1824. Although the numbers soon increased, the expansion of coffee plantations brought an increased demand for labor and even an illicit revival of the slave trade.[8]

---

[7] John V. Lombardi, *The Decline and Abolition of Negro Slavery in Venezuela, 1820–1854* (Westport, Conn., 1971), pp. 3–53; Lombardi, "Los esclavos negros en las guerras Venezolanas de la independencia," *Cultura Universitaria* [Caracas], XCIII (Oct.–Dec., 1966), 153–68; Harold A. Bierck, Jr., "The Struggle for Abolition in Gran Colombia," *Hispanic American Historical Review,* XXXIII (1953), 368–85.

[8] Bierck, "Struggle for Abolition," pp. 368–85; Lombardi, *Decline and Abolition of Negro Slavery,* pp. 46–72, and *passim.* Lombardi shows that slaves played a relatively small role in the coffee boom, since they were mostly concentrated in the older cacao and sugar regions along the coast (pp. 109–10).

Compared to the northern United States, the Latin American republics faced insuperable obstacles to effective abolitionist legislation. Long dependent on Spanish administrators and imperial institutions, they lacked the strong traditions of local government essential for carrying out legislative reforms. Moreover, soon after independence they became almost wholly preoccupied with domestic disorder and civil war. It is not surprising, therefore, that in Venezuela, as in Colombia, Argentina, Paraguay, and Peru, slavery remained legal until the mid-nineteenth century. Yet from a comparative view one is most struck by the approximately thirty-year duration of gradual emancipation in territories as economically and socially diverse as New York and Venezuela. Nor can the chronology of final emancipation be explained by either the number or concentration of slaves. Negro slavery was technically legal in Canada for seven years—and in Connecticut for twenty-one years—after it had been outlawed in New York. The institution endured in Pennsylvania, New Jersey, and most of the Latin American republics long after it had been abolished in Haiti and in the British West Indies. From a realistic viewpoint, it is perhaps absurd to speak of the slowness of gradual emancipation. From 1780 to 1850 the New World witnessed a remarkable expansion of "free soil" areas, leaving only Cuba, Brazil, and the southern United States as bastions of a once-universal system. Nevertheless, the history of this expansion suggests the magnitude of resistance to peaceful and gradual emancipation in the great plantation societies.

Petitioning and Representation

The fate of antislavery in the Age of Revolution hinged on the the debates and decisions of five great deliberative bodies: the British Parliament, the French Constituent and Legislative Assemblies, and the Constitutional Convention and Congress of the United States. Before these assemblies took up questions relating to Negro bondage, antislavery appeared to be one of the many harmless philanthropic fashions of the late Enlightenment—one which could even attract sympathy, on the level of abstract principle, from benevolent planters and hard-headed politicians. But in the brief period from 1787 to 1794 antislavery became linked with major controversies over petitioning, representation, governmental jurisdiction, and sovereignty. The commitments and compromises growing out of these struggles helped to define the channels and limits of future abolitionist activity.

Obviously, the great assemblies differed widely in their relationship to the people and in their responsiveness to public opinion. France had no tradition of government by consent of the governed. For at least a century, the British Parliament had been conceived as a supreme authority, independent of shifting public opinion but capable of governing in the general interest because of its indirect or "virtual" representation of particular interests. In the North American colonies, as Bernard Bailyn has pointed out, representatives had traditionally been thought of as "attorneys" of the people, continuously accountable to their constituents and obligated to follow public instructions for promoting and defending the interests of their localities.[9]

In the period from 1787 to 1794 the assemblies of France and America faced revolutionary crises and struggled to reformulate law and write constitutions in the face of hard demands from shifting groups and alliances. The American leaders succeeded in stabilizing their revolution and framed a constitution that satisfied large segments of a public that had had no part in drafting it. France was imperiled by counterrevolution and foreign invasion; under the mounting pressure of peasant uprisings and urban mob violence, her revolution moved rapidly from a parliamentary regime that would preserve vestiges of the past social order to a republican Convention theoretically based on the sovereignty of the people. Meanwhile, British politics moved sharply to the right, after flirtations in the 1780s with proposals for moderate Parliamentary reform and for amplifying the public's voice in government. By 1793 the official view held that any expression of political opinion through spontaneously formed associations was criminal and dangerous to the state. On any conventional scale of radicalism and conservatism, it would appear that antislavery would face far greater obstacles in Britain than in the United States, and would win easiest acceptance in France, which did, after all, succeed in abolishing serfdom, seigneurial rights, and the entire feudal system without compensation.

[9] Bernard Bailyn, *The Ideological Origins of the American Revolution* (Cambridge, Mass., 1967), pp. 160–75.

But conventional scales can be misleading. All five assemblies contained minorities that can be termed "antislavery" in the broad sense that they favored restricting the slave trade and laying the foundations for gradual emancipation. But since antislavery in this general sense amounted to little more than personal disposition, it cut across lines of party and faction, providing no basis for unity when other issues took precedence.[10] The five assemblies also contained influential members who directly profited from the slave trade or plantation agriculture. They too were divided by interest as well as faction. In France, for example, the "colonial interest" included royalists as well as Jacobins, merchants who insisted on retaining a French monopoly on colonial trade as well as absentee proprietors who sided with the colonists' complaints against the mercantilist system. On one issue, however, these various groups could unite, drawing support from more neutral factions that feared national ruin: no reforms could be allowed to weaken or undermine the slave-plantation system. And the more critical the domestic divisions, the more imperative that demand became.

In France antislavery literature had stirred the hearts of *philosophes,* journalists, and the more enlightened nobility, including such impos-

[10] In August, 1792, the very month of the storming of the Tuileries and the imprisonment of Louis XVI, the French Legislative Assembly bestowed honorary citizenship not only on Thomas Paine, the Satan of English politics, but on William Wilberforce, the conservative friend of Pitt and Parliamentary leader of the movement against the slave trade. The Assembly also granted citizenship to Alexander Hamilton, an officer of the New York Manumission Society, but not to Thomas Jefferson, who as United States Minister to France had recently rebuffed the *Amis des noirs.* There can be no doubt that Wilberforce was honored for his stand against the slave trade, but Hamilton was chiefly known, along with Madison, for his defense of the new American Constitution (the French Convention drew its name from the American Constitutional Convention). On the other hand, Brissot de Warville, founder of the *Amis des noirs* and the Girondin leader in the Legislative Assembly, admired Hamilton and had visited the New York Manumission Society; Brissot was also the recipient of Jefferson's letter which declined an invitation to become associated with the *Amis,* on the ground that as American Minister he was obliged not to make a public display of his genuine desire to see an abolition of both slavery and the slave trade (Claude Perroud, ed., *Correspondance et papiers de Brissot* [Paris, 1912], pp. 164–65). It is startling to think of an international antislavery society led by Paine, Wilberforce, Brissot, and Hamilton. Yet in 1788 Brissot and Lafayette had close personal connections with leading abolitionists in London, Philadelphia, and New York, and placed their hopes in the international cooperation of men of enlightenment and good will.

ing figures as the Marquis de Lafayette, the Duc de La Rochefoucauld d'Enville, and the Comte de Mirabeau—all members of the
Société des Amis des Noirs (familiarly known as the *Amis des noirs* or
the *Amis*).[11] But this philanthropic group, formed in 1788 upon
the urging of British Quakers and based on a literary idealization of
the Quakers of Pennsylvania, lacked the perseverance, the organizational ability, and the communications network of the British and
American Society of Friends. In 1788, British sanction seemed to be
an asset rather than a liability. Brissot de Warville, the Society's
principal founder, had first offered to serve as the French agent for
the London Abolition Committee, which had declined to give him
financial aid but had encouraged him to form his own organization.
Brissot continued to hope that the two societies could be officially
affiliated, in order to create a more favorable public opinion and
because of circumstances, which he dared not put in writing to his
British correspondents, arising from "l'ordre de choses où nous exis-
tons." In the summer of 1789 the London Committee did send Thomas Clarkson to Paris to help the *Amis des noirs,* but by then even
informal association was becoming an embarrassment to both parties.
On August 18, Etienne Clavière sent an urgent message to his friend
Brissot: "J'ai appris hier à Versailles que l'on avoit fait parvenir au
Gouvernement l'avis d'un complot, attribué aux deux Sociétés, dont
l'objet est de soulever les esclaves de Saint-Domingue."[12]

[11] Edward D. Seeber, *Anti-Slavery Opinion in France during the Second Half
of the Eighteenth Century* (Baltimore, 1937); David Brion Davis, *The Problem
of Slavery in Western Culture* (Ithaca, N.Y., 1966), pp. 391–493; Roger Mercier,
L'Afrique noire dans la littérature française: Les Premières Images (Dakar,
1962).

[12] MS Proceedings of the Committee for the Abolition of the Slave Trade,
1787–1819, I, 14, 18, British Museum Add. MSS 21254–21256; *Analyse des
papiers anglais,* No. XIX, pp. 473–76; Perroud, ed., *Correspondance,* pp. 168–
69; *Le Patriote français,* No. XIX (Aug. 18, 1789), 4; J. P. Brissot de Warville,
*An Oration upon the Necessity of Establishing at Paris, a Society to Promote the
Abolition of the Trade and Slavery of the Negroes* (Philadelphia, 1788), pp.
152–54. Brissot greatly exaggerated the progress of antislavery opinion in
England and America. He thought that Parliament was about to pass an act
"which prohibits the Negro trade, and liberates the English slaves." In America,
"such is the empire of reason, when it unfolds itself under the auspices of liberty;
that scarcely was the independence of the United States confirmed, than the
question concerning the slavery of the blacks was agitated in the southern states,
than their cause was embraced there, defended with warmth by the best
geniuses, by the most respectable personages" (*Oration,* pp. 140-41, 154).

The *Amis* suffered other weaknesses besides the suspicion of treason. They published an elaborate forty-six page preamble and constitution, which suggested, as later confirmed by Etienne Dumont, that their meetings would be formal and tedious, discouraging attendance through sheer boredom. [13] They could claim as members many nobles of high rank, men of the royal courts, bankers, farmers-general, society women, nominally even the king—people whose pre-Revolutionary "influence" did not help the later antislavery cause. Following the English example, the *Amis* originaly fastened their hopes on the good will of government Ministers like Loménie de Brienne and Jacques Necker. Lafayette, who seemed to be slated to become the French Wilberforce, succeeded in winning Brienne's qualified approval of the organization, but with the warning that the *Amis* should show the utmost prudence in their meetings and writings. No doubt the government would have suppressed the Society if it had formed auxiliaries in the provinces and had seriously agitated the Third Estate. In any event, though Lafayette and Mirabeau helped to free antislavery writing from censorship, the public remained profoundly ignorant of and indifferent toward colonial issues. [14]

If the calling of the Estates General had not presented new opportunities, the *Amis* might soon have faded into oblivion. Brissot, after organizing the Society, had sailed off to the United States with no intention of ever returning. [15] What brought him back was the news

[13] *Réglemens de la Société des Amis des Noirs,* reprinted in *La Révolution française et l'abolition de l'esclavage* (12 vols., Paris, n.d.), VI; Etienne Dumont to Samuel Romilly, May 22, 1789, *Memoirs of the Life of Sir Samuel Romilly,* ed. by his sons (2 vols., London, 1840), I, 348–49.

[14] MS 2867, Bibliothèque de l'Arsenal; "Extrait du registre de la Société des Amis Noirs, copie de Mme. O'Connor," MS 857, Condorcet papers, Bibliothéque de l'Institut de France; MS 9534, Roland papers, nouvelles aquisitions, Bibliothèque Nationale; Claude Perroud, "La Société française des Amis des Noirs," *La Révolution française,* LXIX (1916), 122–47; Léon Cahen, "La Société des Amis des Noirs et Condorcet," *La Révolution française,* L (1906), 481–511; Daniel P. Resnick, "The Société des Amis des Noirs and the Abolition of Slavery," *French Historical Studies,* VII (Fall, 1972), 558–69; J. P. Brissot, *Mémoires, publiés aves étude critique et notes par Cl. Perroud* (Paris, 1910), II, 77–78; Eloise Ellery, *Brissot de Warville: A Study in the History of the French Revolution* (Boston, 1915), pp. 182–90; Elizabeth L. Hickman, "Anti-Slavery Agitation in France during the Latter Half of the Eighteenth Century," Ph. D. thesis, Cornell University, 1930, *passim.*

[15] Brissot was an impetuous opportunist whose "concept of Americanism," in Durand Echeverria's phrase, included "the trinity of liberty, virtue, and a

of an exciting political crisis which offered the chance to lobby for a variety of reforms. Early in 1789, the Marquis de Condorcet wrote addresses on behalf of the *Amis* to all the *bailliages* of the realm and to the *corps électoral,* urging France to follow the noble example of the Americans, who had realized that they would debase their own cause of liberty if they sanctioned Negro slavery:

Aussi, l'abolition de l'esclavage des nègres fut-elle regardée par les différents Etats-Unis, et par le sénat commun qui les représente, non-seulement comme une opération que la saine politique conseillait, mais comme un acte de justice, prescrit par l'honneur autant que par l'humanité. En effet, comment oser, sans rougir, réclamer ces déclarations des droits, ces remparts inviolables de la liberté, de la sûreté des citoyens, si chaque jour on se permet d'en violer soi-même les articles les plus sacrés?[16]

Partly in response to the *Amis'* appeals, forty-nine of the some six hundred general *cahiers de doléances* called for abolition of the slave trade or for gradual emancipation. Twenty-nine of these came from the clergy or nobility. The antislavery *cahiers* represented most parts of the kingdom; by some mystery, Bagnères, a remote village in the Pyrenees, demanded a total eradication of colonial slavery. Yet this hardly amounted to an impressive upswell of antislavery opinion, nor were the *cahiers* reinforced by continuing public agitation. Indeed, by December, 1789, the provinces received a circular letter charging

---

good profit margin" (introduction to J. P. Brissot de Warville, *New Travels in the United States of America, 1788* [Cambridge, Mass., 1964], pp. xviii–xix). Brissot went to America as the agent for the Swiss banker Clavière and others interested in speculating in the American domestic debt. His ostensible purpose was to gather information on slavery for French and British abolitionists. Yet it is also clear that Brissot intended to settle permanently in the United States, which he imagined, after reading Crèvecoeur, as a new Arcadia. It was thus a bit disingenuous of him to accuse the *Amis des noirs* of slackening zeal during his long absence (see Ellery, *Brissot,* pp. 66–90; Brissot, *Mémoires,* II, 74).

[16] *Lettre écrite par la Société des Amis des Noirs en France, aux differens bailliages et districts ayant droit d'envoyer les deputés aux Etats-Generaux* (n.p., n.d.); "Au corps électoral, contre l'esclavage des noirs" (Feb. 3, 1789), reprinted in *La Révolution française et l'abolition de l'esclavage,* VI. Freely translated, the above quotation reads as follows: "Furthermore, the abolition of Negro slavery was considered by the several United States, and by the Congress which represents them, not only as a measure essential for a sound commonwealth, but as an act of justice, required by both honor and humanity. To be candid, how can we dare, without shame, to proclaim these declarations of rights, these inviolable bulwarks of freedom and of the security of all citizens, if every day we acquiesce in the destruction of these sacred principles?"

that the *Amis* had been instigated and financed by the English, and that they had already sent agents to the West Indies "pour y soulever des Nègres & y détruire les Blancs." In the first months of 1790, before the Assembly committed itself to a policy of noninterference, there were some twenty-four petitions supporting the slave trade; not a single French city asked for its abolition.[17]

Even if antislavery had won more popular support, there were powerful forces in favor of suppressing political discussion. The slave trade itself may have been peripheral to the French economy, confined to a few port cities and controlled largely by Protestants who had closer ties with Dutch financiers than with the *rentiers* and *propriétaires* of inland France.[18] Nevertheless, informed contemporaries agreed that the slave trade was more vital to France than it was to England, a belief which raised suspicions of English-backed philanthropies.[19] The merchants and artisans of the port cities also insisted that the colonial trade was the indispensible foundation of national prosperity. For ambitious young men, noble as well as bourgeois, a few years in the West Indies had long been an accepted route to fortune or a means of replenishing a family's diminishing estate. Despite their differences on other issues, a substantial number of merchants and colonial landowners sensed a common peril when *cahiers* demanded

[17] Beatrice Fry Hyslop, *French Nationalism in 1789 According to the General Cahiers* (New York, 1934), pp. 142, 276–77; Shelby T. McCloy, *The Humanitarian Movement in Eighteenth-Century France* (Lexington, Ky., 1957), p. 110; McCloy, "Further Notes on Negroes and Mulattoes in Eighteenth-Century France," *Journal of Negro History,* XXXIX (Oct., 1954), 291; *Lettre aux bailliages de France* (Dec. 1, 1789; signed, "Les intéressés au commerce, aux manufactures & aux colonies de France"); Valerie Quinney, "Decisions on Slavery, the Slave-Trade and Civil Rights for Negroes in the Early French Revolution, *Journal of Negro History,* LV (1970), 124.

[18] These remarks are suggested by Perry Viles, "The Slaving Interest in the Atlantic Ports, 1763–1792," *French Historical Studies,* VII (Fall, 1972), 529–43, and by a paper presented by Professor Roger Anstey, at the 1972 M.S.S.B. Conference on Systems of Slavery, University of Rochester. See also Stanley L. Engerman, "The Slave Trade and British Capital Formation in the Eighteenth Century: A Comment on the Williams Thesis," *The Business History Review,* XLVI (Winter, 1972), 430–43; Jean Meyer, "Le Commerce négrier nantais," *Annales, Economies, Sociétés, Civilisations,* I (1960), 120–29; George V. Taylor, "Noncapitalist Wealth and the Origins of the French Revolution," *American Historical Review,* LXXII (Jan., 1967), 469–96.

[19] See, for example, Geoffrey de Villeneuve to Thomas Clarkson, March 28, 1790, Clarkson papers, Henry E. Huntington Library.

interference with the slave system. In 1789, anonymous letters threatened that if the *Amis* did not disband, the members would all be stabbed to death. William Short wrote Thomas Jefferson that he had heard that the first member of the Asembly to make a motion against the slave trade would be promptly assassinated. The rumor had supposedly frightened Mirabeau.[20]

As it turned out, the proslavery factions had no need of terrorism. The Constituent Assembly refused to consider addresses against the slave trade submitted by the *Amis des noirs,* although the latter could claim at least seventeen nominal members in the Assembly. As lobbyists and propagandists the *Amis* were no match for the urban chambers of commerce or for the various organizations of merchants and planters whose members swamped Assembly delegates with petitions, pamphlets, and personal remonstrances. The main result of the *Amis'* petitioning was to convince their opponents that even disputes over colonial representation and multattoes' rights concealed secret designs to subvert the slave system.[21] These issues later became the first major battleground. But, for the moment, the Assembly's Committee on Colonies, under mounting pressure from proslavery lobbyists, decided to omit from its initial report any recommendation that the Assembly give future attention to slavery or the slave trade. In early March, 1790, Pétion de Villeneuve had prepared an extremely cautious speech asking that the Assembly appoint a committee to investigate the most prudent means of ending the slave trade and ameliorating the condition of colonial slaves. But on March 8 the Assembly approved the report of the Committee on Colonies, which affirmed that the government had no intention of furthering innovation in any branch of colonial trade, and which also outlawed any

[20] Gabriel Debien, *Les Colons de Saint-Domingue et la Révolution: Essai sur le club Massiac, Août 1789–Août 1792* (Paris, 1953), pp. 49–53, 58–112; Ellery, *Brissot,* p. 192; William Short to Thomas Jefferson, Dec. 25, 1789, Julian P. Boyd, ed., *The Papers of Thomas Jefferson* (Princeton, 1950—), XVI, 46.

[21] Debien, *Les Colons de Saint-Domingue,* pp. 67, 122–39; Quinney, "Decisions on Slavery," pp. 119–25. Despite their attempts at caution, the *Amis'* ambiguous goals gave grounds for suspicion. Thus in October, 1789, Brissot printed with approval the following quotation: "De plus, l'admission des Noirs libres dans l'Assemblée Nationale préparera l'abolition de l'esclavage dans nos colonies, comme la convocation des hommes libres dans nos anciens Etats-Généraux prépara l'abolition de la servitude féodale" (*Patriote français,* No. LXV [Oct. 9, 1789], 4). See also *Analyse des papiers anglais,* No. XIX (Jan.–Feb., 1788).

agitation that might endanger colonial property. Thenceforth the Committee refused to consider antislavery petitions; the Assembly barred the subject from floor debate. The *Amis* vainly protested that they were in the vanguard of the Revolution, "car, lorqu'il s'agit de rompre des chaînes, le despotisme est inexorable." But they faced a new despotism that was more repressive than the old.[22]

The right and practice of petitioning were more firmly established in the United States than in France; antislavery ideals aroused more widespread public support. But since the southern states were deeply committed to a labor system that had begun to disappear from the North, antislavery petitions provoked an ominously sectional conflict of interest. Southern delegates could argue persuasively that, given such marked sectional differences, loyalty to the Union should take precedence over the right to petition. There was, of course, no metropolitan center that could serve as a focal point for national agitation. The decision to move the capital south from Philadelphia underscored the sectional character of Pennsylvania's abolitionism. I shall postpone discussing the consequences of this dilemma, but may now point out that even Benjamin Franklin thought it prudent to suppress a strong antislavery memorial he had been asked to present to the Constitutional Convention, nearly half of whose members owned slaves.[23] A petition to the First Congress from the Pennsylvania Abolition Society, signed by Franklin as the Society's chairman, unleashed angry and uninhibited debate. In 1792, however, Congress returned to its clerk a mild abolitionist petition from the Quaker Warner

[22] Quinney, "Decisions on Slavery," pp. 118, 125–28; *Archives parlementaires,* première série, XI (Jan. 21, 1790), 273–77; *Journal des Etats Généraux,* XXV (May 11, 1791), 382; Pétion de Villeneuve, *Discours sur la traite des noirs* (Paris, 1790), p. 71; *Seconde Adresse à l'Assemblée Nationale, par la Société des Amis des Noirs, établie à Paris* (Paris, 1790), p. 2; J. P. Brissot, *Lettre de J. P. Brissot à M. Barnave, sur ses rapports concernant les colonies* . . . (Paris, 1790), *passim.* Even by January 8, 1790, Brissot was imploring his co-workers not to abandon the *Amis:* "Dussé-je être abandonné, dussé-je rester seul, je le jure à la face du Ciel qui m'entend, et qui lit dans tous nos coeurs, je n'abandonnerai jamais la défense des Noirs" (*Patriote français,* No. CLIII, supplément [Jan. 8, 1790], 6).

[23] Max Farrand, ed., *The Records of the Federal Convention of 1787* (4 vols., New Haven, 1937), III, 361. Out of fifty-five Convention delegates, twenty-five are known to have owned slaves; only sixteen of these, according to Clinton Rossiter, owned what could be called "productive slaves" (Rossiter, *1787: The Grand Convention* [New York, 1966]).

Mifflin, after Representative William Smith, a South Carolina Federalist, had warned that the right to petition could not justify the "mere rant and rhapsody of a meddling fanatic," the very reading of which would prove highly dangerous.[24]

In the British Parliament, defenders of the slave trade tried similar tactics, but were overwhelmed by a rising tide of petitions and an unprecedented arousal of middle-class opinion. In June, 1788, the Earl of Carlisle could express atonishment over the Lord Chancellor's sarcastic reference to "a five days' fit of philanthropy," when everyone knew the slave trade "had engrossed the attention of every part of the kingdom for above these twelve months." The British abolitionists' success in mobilizing public opinion was all the more striking because governments had not yet become seasoned to national petition campaigns, organized by pressure groups, as an alternative or supplement to persuasion through personal influence.[25]

When confronted by radical political agitation in the early 1790s, Parliament could contemptuously dismiss petitions for constitutional reform and attempt to suppress such supposedly subversive groups as the Manchester Constitution Society. In 1793 the Earl of Abingdon warned that the abolition movement also drew on "Tom Paine's *Rights of Man* for its chief and best support," and that it carried "seeds of other abolitions, different and distinct from that which it professes." Yet the opponents of the slave trade took pains to make their campaign "respectable"; they observed established procedures in gathering petitions, avoiding, for the most part, promiscuous public meetings. They did, it is true, adopt the radical step of publicly testing candidates for Parliament by their stand on the slave-trade issue. Sir William Young, a West Indian proprietor, complained that in counties with large electorates they induced "leading characters" to influence the multitude. He also charged that abolitionists exploited the rotten boroughs in procuring petitions. But Young himself represented the rotten borough of St. Mawes, in Cornwall. And the truth was that both the slave trade and slavery depended for support on the landed interest and the traditional system of representation which allowed the purchase of rank and political influence. Any abolitionist

[24] *Annals of the Congress of the United States*, 2nd Cong., 2nd Sess., 728–31.
[25] *Parliamentary History of England*, XXVII, 644. For significant shifts in the pattern of petitioning, see Peter Fraser, "Public Petitioning and Parliament before 1832," *History*, XLVI (Oct., 1961), 195–211.

movement, backed by organized public opinion, was an indirect attack on the unreformed Parliament.[26]

This fact helps to account for the abolitionists' continuing failures. The British political system was flexible enough to permit abolitionist controversy and yet to contain it within the boundaries of the existing order. In England the public clamor against the slave trade far surpassed the relatively faint antislavery stirrings in France and the United States. In Parliament, unlike the National Assembly and Congress, abolitionist petitions led to intensive investigations and continuing debate. The cause found eloquent champions among the leaders of opposing parties, including the prime minister, William Pitt, and his great Whig rival, Charles James Fox. Given this sanction, defenders of the slave trade could neither stifle discussion nor bury the question in a Committee on Colonies (though they did for a time bury it in the House of Lords). On the other hand, the antiabolitionists controlled the procedural routes to legislation. And since their numbers included some of Pitt's most powerful friends and supporters, they could prevent the cause from being advanced as a government measure.[27]

Although the West Indies had no formal representatives in Parliament, Charles Fox remarked in 1796 that if ever a region had been "virtually represented," it was the West Indies in the House of Commons. This truth did not mean there was a solid and invincible West Indian "interest" of merchants and planters; nor did the continuance of the slave trade depend on the votes of the relatively few members who drew personal profit from slave ships or West Indian estates. In the 1790s the loose antiabolitionist alliance included the king and royal family; the admirals of the navy; leading commercial interests in London, Liverpool, and Bristol; and above all, many landed pro-

[26] *Parliamentary History*, XXX, 657; XXXI, 467–70; XXXII, 742; Stephen Fuller, MS Letterpress Book, Duke University Library, *passim; Memoirs of Romilly*, I, 425. By 1832, West Indians complained that Parliamentary reform would deprive them of most of their remaining representatives in the House of Commons.

[27] This summary is based on information supplied by Lewis Namier and John Brooke, *The History of Parliament: The House of Commons, 1754–1790* (3 vols., London, 1964), supplemented by Dale H. Porter, *The Abolition of the Slave Trade in England, 1784–1807* ([Hamden, Conn.], 1970), and Patrick Cleburne Lipscomb, III, "William Pitt and the Abolition of the Slave Trade," Ph.D. thesis, University of Texas, 1960.

prietors who feared any innovation that might weaken the empire, raise taxes, or set a precedent for more dangerous reforms.[28]

In the long run, however, the system of virtual representation provided tenuous protection for the West Indies. The slaves were "represented" in Parliament only in the sense that as capital they gave added political power to absentee owners and commercial interests dependent on their produce. But this kind of representation would also diminish if the West Indies declined in their relative value to the British economy. Moreover, the custom of absentee ownership, which was the key to the islands' virtual representation, removed from local leadership the wealthiest and most successful planters. Many of the most influential spokesmen for the "West India interest" in England had never seen the West Indies. They were happy, of course, to draw income from slave plantations so long as profits were forthcoming and the plantations were not too heavily mortgaged. But unlike the resident slaveholding class, they were part of a larger social order and could easily assimilate the changing social norms of the English gentry. Meanwhile, the West Indian legislatures increasingly fell into the hands of small local merchants and members of the managerial class, men who lacked both power and prestige in the eyes of the British elite. Therefore, when the West Indians lost much of their supposed virtual representation in Parliament, they had no constitutional protection against newer and more vigorous interests, except for their vain appeals to the theories of plural sovereignty and limited Parliamentary jurisdiction—appeals which had originally been developed by their formal rivals on the North American continent.[29]

[28] *Parliamentary History,* XXXII, 987; Lillian M. Penson, *The Colonial Agents of the British West Indies* (London, 1924); Penson, "The London West India Interests in the Eighteenth Century," *English Historical Review,* XXXVI (July, 1921), 373–92; Roger Anstey, "A Re-interpretation of the Abolition of the British Slave Trade, 1806–1807," *English Historical Review,* LXXXVII (April, 1972), 304–32; Patrick Lipscomb, "William Pitt and the Abolition Question: A Review of an Historical Controversy," *Proceedings of the Leeds Philosophical and Literary Society, Literary and Historical Section,* XII (June, 1967), 87–120.

[29] Elsa V. Goveia, *Slave Society in the British Leeward Islands at the End of the Eighteenth Century* (New Haven, 1965), pp. 311–38; R. L. Schuyler, *Parliament and the British Empire* (New York, 1929), pp. 117–92; John Gallagher and Ronald Robinson, "The Imperialism of Free Trade," *Economic History Review,* 2nd ser., VI (1953), 1–15; D. J. Murray, *The West Indies and the Development of Colonial Government, 1801–1834* (Oxford, 1965), pp. 146–232.

Political independence gave southern slaveholders the chance to build permanent constitutional barriers against such an erosion of political power. Howard A. Ohline has recently pointed out that the agreement to count three-fifths of a state's slaves in apportioning its number of Congressmen and presidential electors "was the major instrument in uniting slave and nonslave states in a national legislature that represented a significant advance over the static form of English constitutional structure. Slavery and the fears of slaveholders acted to assure a more democratic political system for white men."[30] One should add that the use of slaves to augment the political power of an entire region also gave nonslaveholding Southerners a political stake in the slave system, while confirming their dependence on slaveholding leaders.

In the 1780s, slavery was by no means extinct in the Middle Atlantic states; yet 90 per cent of the nation's blacks lived south of Delaware. In only five of the original thirteen states was the institution of central economic importance. Accordingly, slaveholders might find themselves at a disadvantage in assemblies like the Continental Congress and later the Senate, where all states had an equal vote. But in 1790, and presumably earlier, the total population of the southern states was roughly equal to that of the northern states, and was thought to be increasing at a more rapid rate. If slaves had been counted as the equivalent of free men, the South could have claimed nearly 50 per cent of the seats in Congress. If slaves had not been counted at all, the South would have been entitled to only 41 per cent of the seats.[31]

As Ohline makes clear, virtually all the delegates at the Constitutional Convention assumed from the start that slaves would be counted in apportioning both taxes and representation. They differed on the political weight to be granted to small states and on whether Congress itself should have the power to set future formulas for representation as a means of protecting existing interests against

[30] Howard A. Ohline, "Republicanism and Slavery: Origins of the Three-Fifths Clause in the United States Constitution," *William and Mary Quarterly*, 3rd ser., XXVIII (Oct., 1971), 563–84. Donald L. Robinson downplays the importance of the conflict between large and small states, but presents a somewhat similar interpretation (*Slavery in the Structure of American Politics, 1765–1820* [New York, 1971], pp. 177–206).

[31] Robinson, *Slavery in the Structure of American Politics,* pp. 179–80. The five southern states had about 38 per cent of the seats in the old Congress.

geographic shifts in population and wealth. Once the Convention had rejected the principle of state equality for the lower house of the legislature, the question came down to *how* slaves should be counted in determining representation—whether implicitly, as property; or explicitly, as a fixed proportion of the population which the House of Representatives should directly mirror. "Paradoxically," Ohline writes,

it was the issue of how to count the slaves that became the means of assuring that representation would be regulated by a census beyond the control of the national legislature, because southerners came to fear, as the debate developed, that if Congress fixed the representation it might not use slaves to determine ratios in the future.[32]

There were complex maneuvers and alliances that led to this result. But the three-fifths rule, which had originally been used by Congress in 1783 in making requisitions for revenue, served the purposes of both Northerners and Southerners who wished to subordinate state sovereignty to a federal system of direct taxation and proportional representation based on population. It was James Wilson, a liberal Pennsylvanian, who used the three-fifths principle to win southern support against the conservative and small-state resistance to any radical transformation of the older Confederation.[33]

In actual practice the three-fifths ratio did not fulfill southern expectations. In 1790 the major slaveholding states had nearly 45 per cent of the House seats; by 1820, because of an unexpected population increase in the North and Northwest, the number had fallen to 42 per cent. Increasingly the South looked to the Senate and to the admission of new slave states as its major line of defense (coupled, of course, with the constitutional rights reserved to the states)'. Nevertheless, by linking slaveholding to political power, the three-fifths compromise provided far more substantial protection than the informal alliances which for a time shielded the British West Indies. It also presented a vulnerable target for political attack.[34]

[32] Ohline, "Republicanism and Slavery," pp. 563–84. See also, Robinson, *Slavery in the Structure of American Politics*, pp. 146–49, 154–58.

[33] Ironically, in 1783 the South had fought for a four-to-one or a three-to-one ratio in apportioning taxes; the committee of the Continental Congress proposed two-to-one, and Madison suggested the "federal" compromise of five-to-three (*Journals of the Continental Congress, 1774–1789*, XXV, 948–49).

[34] I do not mean to imply that sectionalism dominated American politics as a

Even during the Convention, the general acceptance of slave representation could not subdue sectional fears and jealousies, or disguise the deeper political implications of slavery. When delegates from the small-population states saw the rejection of safeguards for their own interests, they objected that the proposed Constitution would result in a kind of enslavement of the smaller states to the large. These complaints prompted Madison to suspend the pretense of sectional compromise and to observe bluntly that the really important divisions of interest resulted from the effects of "having or not having slaves." If Madison aimed his arguments against proposals for state equality in the Senate, his tactics presupposed that Southerners would agree that state sovereignty was insignificant compared to Constitutional protections for slavery. Following Madison's lead, Northerners like Rufus King merged the slavery issue with their own political interests, suggesting that the Northeast could not accept slave representation without concessions that would prevent a shift of political power to the southwestern interior. These intimations alarmed the Southerners and helped to convert South Carolina to the doctrine of representation by population. For a time the South Carolinians insisted that Negroes be counted equally with whites in apportioning representation, on the ground that "the labour of a slave in S. Carola. was as productive & valuable as that of a freeman in Massts., that as wealth was the great means of defense and utility to the Nation they were equally valuable to it with freemen." Pierce Butler warned that Southerners would not confederate without the security of knowing that their slaves could not be taken from them, as he thought some Northerners, either within or outside the Convention, had a mind to do. William R. Davie of North Carolina also flatly stated that without slave representation his state could not remain in the Union.[35]

The Founding Fathers may not have seen the three-fifths rule as a specific endorsement of slavery, but that was the clear interpretation of the more volatile southern speeches. The Georgians and Carolinians

---

continuous force. Indeed, the success of national politics depended in large measure on an avoidance of sectional conflict and, ultimately, on the coalition of local factions into two national parties whose discipline muted sectional issues.

[35] Farrand, ed., *Records*, I, 486, 601–5; Ohline, "Republicanism and Slavery," pp. 570–72. In 1861, a week before Lincoln's inauguration, Congress approved an irrepealable Constitutional amendment guaranteeing that the federal government would never interfere with slavery within the existing slaveholding states.

tested the boundaries of northern acquiescence and were satisfied with
the result. During the 1790s some northern papers questioned, usually
on political grounds, whether the Union was worth such a concession.
When confronted by the acquisition of Louisiana, Rufus King complained that slave representation, one of the greatest blemishes of the
Constitution, would never have been consented to if Northerners had
foreseen that indirect taxes would be sufficient for raising revenue.
The argument was questionable, but suggested a future alliance of
antislavery and changing economic interest. Yet unlike the planters
of the Caribbean, southern slaveholders held a fixed bastion within
the national government; their political power drew sanction from
the supreme law of the land.[36]

The calling of the French Estates General led to disputes over
representation somewhat similar to those in the United States; yet the
marginal position of the slaveholding colonies and their distance from
the metropolis made them more analogous to the British West Indies
than to the southern states. Aside from such abstract parallels, the
French Revolution and the peculiar social structure of the French
colonies soon gave conflicts over representation a character all their
own.

In the absence of a national parliament, the French slaveholding
and slave-trading interests had long had influence in the royal government, which had, for example, granted subsidies to the African slave
trade and given planters limited permission to import foodstuffs from
the United States.[37] After the Estates were summoned, the more
conservative absentee proprietors opposed the idea of colonial representation. We may imagine that if England had been struck by revolution, British merchants and absentee planters would have had similar
motives: a desire to keep the control of colonial legislation in the
hands of the crown, and to prevent the flame of revolution from
spreading to the Caribbean. Even in the colonies there was some
sentiment against sending delegates to the Estates General, where they

[36] *The Connecticut Courant* (Nov. 21, 1796), p. 29; Boreas, *Slave Representation, by Boreas. Awake! O Spirit of the North!* (n.p. [Boston], 1812);
Farrand, ed., *Records*, III, 399–400.

[37] For a detailed account of the French colonists' struggle for free ports, see
Dorothy Burne Goebel, "The 'New England Trade' and the French West Indies,
1763–1774: A Study in Trade Policies," *William and Mary Quarterly*, 3rd ser.,
XX (July, 1963), 332–72.

would be vastly outnumbered by a metropolitan majority that might be inclined toward commercial exploitation as well as interference with slavery. Some French planters, as potentially secessionist as many South Carolinians, favored creating an autonomous assembly responsible only to the king.[38]

But the ideas and watchwords of the Enlightenment had given an edge to the grievances of the divided colonial population. If the colonists had no feudal regime to overthrow, they had long resented mercantilist restrictions on trade and were well aware that the North Americans had not only freed themselves from similar restraints, but now offered attractive markets which the French government would be determined to limit. Like their North American counterparts, many French colonists detested the royal bureaucrats and functionaries who tried to enforce imperial policy and who, unlike the British officials, appealed for support, when crisis came, from the mulattoes or *sang-mêlés*. The latter, who almost approximated the whites in number, owned a sizeable number of slaves and some of the finest plantations in the French colonies. Yet they suffered the indignities and discriminations of an *under*-caste, and looked for whatever protection they could find against the racism and jealousy of the *petits-blancs*. The poorer whites not only coveted the property of the vulnerable mulattoes, but felt little deference for wealthy white planters who aped the manners of the French aristocracy. The slogans of liberty, equality, and fraternity would have quite different meanings for these fragmented groups. And they would have a meaning altogether distinct for the Negro slaves who listened to heated political discussion or who, in the person of Toussaint L'Ouverture, even pondered the stirring and inflammatory words of the Abbé Raynal.[39]

[38] Gabriel Debien, *Esprit colon et esprit d'autonomie, à Saint-Domingue au XVIIIᵉ siècle* (2nd ed., Paris, 1954), pp. 24–31, 36–43; Debien, *Les Colons de Saint-Domingue*, pp. 49–57, 235–61; Mitchell B. Garrett, *The French Colonial Question, 1789–1791* (Ann Arbor, 1916), pp. 10–16, 19–20; Theodore Lothrop Stoddard, *The French Revolution in San Domingo* (Boston, 1914), pp. 67–81; C. L. R. James, *The Black Jacobins: Toussaint L'Ouverture and the San Domingo Revolution* (2nd rev. ed., New York, 1963), pp. 27–61; J. Saintoyant, *La Colonisation française pendant le révolution, 1789–1799* (2 vols., Paris, 1930), I, 48–51.

[39] James, *Black Jacobins, passim;* Lucien Peytraud, *L'Esclavage aux Antilles françaises avant 1789* (Paris, 1897), *passim;* Gaston Martin, *Histoire de l'esclavage dans les colonies françaises* (Paris, 1948), *passim.*

At the outset of the Revolution, when deputies met in Martinique to elect representatives to the National Assembly and draw up *cahiers de doléances,* a bitter struggle erupted between planter and merchant factions. The planters, finding they would be outnumbered by their merchant creditors, demanded a new election in which five slaves would count as three citizens in apportioning representation! We are not told whether the Martinique planters, who resolved to secede from the union with the merchants, knew of the American compromise arrived at two years before.[40]

Unlike the southern delegates to the American Convention, the deputies elected to the Estates General by wealthy St. Domingue planters soon lost their mandate, as the *petits-blancs,* donning the red cockade, looked for a Bastille to storm, and as the mulattoes, *grands-blancs,* merchants, and royalist government all became embroiled in a struggle for power. But meanwhile, the arrival of the deputies in France raised questions that echoed some of those recently asked in the Philadelphia Convention. Rebuffed by the first two Estates, the colonists finaly won acceptance from the desperate Third, except for the sticky question of numbers.[41] Mirabeau asked the new Constituent Assembly why a small white colonial population should have so many representatives. He was surprised to hear that slaves were counted in apportioning representation, on the excuse they were instruments of wealth. If that argument were valid, why not count the horses and cattle of France? If wealth were the basis of representation, why should the delegations from the French cities be so small? Mirabeau also touched a point that would have been unthinkable at the American Constitutional Convention. St. Domingue, he pointed out, contained a large population of free mulattoes, including men who owned property and paid taxes. Since these *gens de couleur* were barred

[40] Garrett, *French Colonial Question,* pp. 40–41; Saintoyant, *La Colonisation française,* II, 182–88.

[41] *Journal des Etats Généraux,* I, 260–71; Beatrice Fry Hyslop, *A Guide to the General Cahiers of 1789* (New York, 1936), pp. 418–19; Charles Oscar Hardy, *The Negro Question in the French Revolution* (Menasha, Wisc., 1919), pp. 9–11; Paul Grunebaum-Ballin, *Henri Grégoire, l'ami des hommes de toutes les couleurs, la lutte pour la suppression de la traite [des noirs] et l'abolition de l'esclavage, 1789–1831* (Paris, 1948), pp. 15–17; Saintoyant, *La Colonisation française,* I, 59–64; Philip D. Curtin, "The Declaration of the Rights of Man in Saint-Domingue, 1788–1791," *Hispanic American Historical Review,* XXX (May, 1950), 162.

from voting, how could the white deputies claim to represent the colony?[42]

Although the Assembly admitted ten of the elected deputies, the debates on the colonies' relation to the central government gave momentary openings for attacks on slavery and talk of eventual emancipation. The colonial deputies expressed alarm over such rhetoric. For a time they considered schemes for by-passing the Constituent Assembly by encouraging their fellow colonists to submit independent consitutions to the crown. It soon became clear, however, that their safest course lay in an alliance with the Revolution and in working with other West Indian interests in a special Committee on Colonies.[43]

In many ways the Revolution widened the divisions of interest separating various groups of merchants and proprietors with West Indian ties. The colonial deputies backed the Revolution and supported most of the reforms of the Constituent Assembly; the Club Massiac, or Corresponding Society of French Colonists, tended to be royalist and opposed to working through the Assembly. Even Jacobin merchants insisted on retaining the mercantilist restrictions which nettled the planters. But all these factions could applaud the efforts of the Club Massiac to expose and thwart the designs of the *Amis des noirs;* and all could unite against any threat to the security of the slave colonies.

The issue precipitating this alliance seemed irrelevant to the slave system. Despite legal attempts to exclude them, many mulattoes lived in France. Some were wealthy; few, if any opposed slavery. But like Mirabeau, they saw no reason why colonial representation should be confined to the white race, or why the Declaration of the Rights of Man should not bring equal citizenship to free men of any color. A group of wealthy mulattoes first sought backing from the Club Massiac. Some of the absentee proprietors, putting wealth ahead of color, recognized that granting some concessions to mulattoes might help subdue the revolutionary forces in the Caribbean. Many slave merchants were indifferent to questions of race, so long as their own

[42] *Journal des Etats Généraux,* I, 324–31. Although the *gens de couleur* included a small number of free blacks, they were commonly thought of as mulattoes, and for convenience I shall use that term.

[43] Debien, *Les Colons de Saint-Domingue,* pp. 63–78, 140–52; *Patriote français,* No. XIV (Aug. 12, 1789), 2; Garrett, *French Colonial Question,* pp. 18–20; Stoddard, *French Revolution,* pp. 67–81; James, *Black Jacobins,* pp. 59–61, 69; Quinney, "Decisions on Slavery," pp. 119–23.

profits were secure. Yet most of the West Indians in France feared that any blurring of the color line would not only spark a white secessionist movement in the colonies, but would also seriously undermine the discipline and social controls of the slave system. The absentee proprietors therefore refused to heed the mulattoes' appeals.[44]

The colored delegates, encouraged by the Declaration of the Rights of Man and by the subsequent republican rhetoric, appeared before the bar of the National Assembly on October 22, 1789, petitioning to be seated as West Indian deputies. Although the *Amis des noirs* had originally confined their objectives to ending the slave trade and to gradual emancipation, they now followed the lead of the Abbé Grégoire in championing the mulattoes' cause.[45] Lafayette, Mirabeau, and Jérôme Pétion joined Grégoire in demanding that mulatto representation be the prerequisite for settling colonial problems. But the connection between the mulatto question and half-hidden antislavery purposes aroused the planters and merchants who were otherwise divided over navigation laws, colonial autonomy, and the wisdom of forming a Committee on Colonies. The *Amis* were shouted down, outmaneuvered, and then distracted and divided by the supervening disruptions of revolution.[46]

[44] *Précis des gémissemens des sang-mêlés dans les colonies françaises, par J.M.C. Américan, sang-mêle* (Paris, 1789); Vincent Ogé, *Motion faite par M. Vincent Ogé, jeune à assemblée des colons, habitans de S.-Domingue, à l'hotel de Massiac, Place des Victoires* (Paris, 1789); James, Black Jacobins, pp. 67–68; Debien, *Les Colons de Saint-Domingue,* pp. 154–70.

[45] Hippolyte Carnot, ed., *Mémoires de Grégoire, ancien évêque de Blois . . .* (2 vols., Paris, 1840), I, 390; Garrett, *French Colonial Question,* pp. 22–23, 33; Ruth F. Necheles, *The Abbé Grégoire, 1787–1831: The Odyssey of an Egalitarian* (Westport, Conn., 1971), pp. 59–66; Henri Grégoire, *Mémoire en faveur des gens de couleur ou sang-mêlés des Saint-Domingue, et des autres îles françaises de l'Amérique . . .* (Paris, 1789). It is significant that the decision to concentrate on the mulatto issue did not come at a meeting of the *Amis des noirs,* but at a private conference between Grégoire and the leading *Amis.* After the mulattoes had presented their petition, on October 22, 1789, Brissot still hoped that "la cause des Noirs esclaves sera accueillie: celle des Noirs libres a été plaidée ce matin" (*Patriote française,* No. LXXVII [Oct. 23, 1789], 3).

[46] "Extrait du registre," MS 857, Condorcet papers; Necheles, *Abbé Grégoire,* pp. 61–66. According to Necheles, Grégoire succeeded in temporarily blocking the formation of a Committee on Colonies, but his defense of mulatto rights was stigmatized by his earlier radical defense of the Jews and by "his chiliastic rhetoric" which included the desire to see "a general universal insurrection" (p. 64). He thus tended to divert attention from the *Amis'* original objectives, but mixed the mulattoes' cause with antislavery ideology.

The West Indian merchants and planters, supported by delegates from the great commercial centers, maintained a formidable alliance from the fall of 1789 to the spring of 1791. For a time they benefited from the mood of national crisis. If the mulattoes could brand racial discrimination as an indefensible violation of revolutionary decrees, Arthur Dillon, a deputy from Martinique, could warn the Assembly that the colonists would revolt within fifteen minutes after hearing that the colored deputation had been seated. This would mean, he said, the loss of the West Indies to England, in accordance with the designs of English conspirators who lurked behind the *Amis des noirs*.[47] During the same years, defenders of slavery used similar threats with similar effectiveness in the assemblies of Britain and the United States. And in all three countries disputes over petitions and representation soon led to fundamental questions of constitutional jurisdiction and sovereignty.

[47] Garrett, *French Colonial Question,* pp. 92–99.

Three ❧

The Seats of Power, II

The Testing of Parliamentary Supremacy

In England, as in France and America, planter representatives maintained that slave property was immune from any interference by the central government. Reminding their legislative colleagues of the recent precedent of 1776, they warned that the security of their property was an essential requirement for political union. And as one might expect, direct challenges to slavery within the national assemblies were neither frequent nor threatening. James Sloan's move in Congress for abolition of slavery in the District of Columbia was as futile as Philip Francis's proposal in Parliament for gradual emancipation in the West Indies. The Constituent Assembly similarly ignored a plea from La Rochefoucauld d'Enville, orginally elected as a deputy for the nobility of Paris, asking that the abolition of slavery be considered before the Assembly finished its work. On the critical night of August 4, 1789, when the Assembly stripped the nobility of most of their privileges, La Rochefoucauld made an impassioned speech on behalf of the slaves.[1] But even the organized abolitionists of the three countries prudently disavowed any desire to free slaves by the direct action of a national government.

Accordingly, the crucial contests over slavery involved questions of governmental sanction and jurisdiction, especially in the regulation of

---

[1] Apparently no record of the speech remains. See *Archives parlementaries,* première série, VIII (June 27, 1789), 165; *Patriote français,* No. XIV (Aug. 12, 1789), 2.

commerce and territorial expansion. Since these controversies some-times led to violent denunciations of the slave system, and did much to influence the subsequent development of antislavery thought, I shall examine them in some detail, beginning first with Great Britain.

No one doubted Parliament's authority to regulate imperial trade, but the West Indian interests were quick to point out that even regu-lations prescribing a maximum number of slaves per ship's ton would have far-reaching implications. Any weakening of the British slave trade would reduce the productive capacity of West Indian property and would thus violate a long-standing contractual agreement between government and colonists. The assurance of a continuing labor supply had been the basis for heavy capital investment. Moreover, the intent of any interference would be misunderstood by the slaves, who might be encouraged to rise in a universal massacre of the whites.[2] Such objections, sustained by petitions from the port cities, nearly blocked a cautious regulation bill of 1788 which promised compensation for losses and which required Pitt's personal influence to pass the House of Lords.[3] The next year, as the anti-slave-trade campaign really got underway, merchants complained that the regulation law put them at a disadvantage in competing with New Englanders, whose state laws theoretically bared them from such commerce altogether.[4]

The struggle to abolish the British slave trade was dominated from the start by the fear of foreign competition and by sensitivity to events in foreign countries, particularly France. In 1791, Sir William Young reminded the House of Commons that two years had passed since William Wilberforce had spoken confidently of other nations follow-ing in the footsteps of British philanthropy. Yet the French National Assembly had adopted by acclamation a promise that it had no in-tention of ever disrupting the commerce between France and her colonies; the result of the French investigation of the slave trade had

[2] *Parliamentary History of England,* XXVII, 646–47. For doubts about Par-liament's power, see D. J. Murray, *The West Indies and the Development of Colonial Government, 1801–1834* (Oxford, 1965), p. 4.

[3] For Pitt's influence, see Patrick Lipscomb, "William Pitt and the Abolition Question: A Review of an Historical Controversy," *Proceedings of the Leeds Philosophical and Literary Society, Literary and Historical Section,* XII (June, 1967), 243–44. For the petitions, see *Journals of the House of Lords,* XXXVIII, 243b and *passim.*

[4] Elizabeth Donnan, ed., *Documents Illustrative of the History of the Slave Trade to America* (4 vols., Washington, 1930–1935), III, 606.

been French gains on the West African coast. Spain had issued a royal edict which encouraged the slave trade with a bounty; Holland and the United States were poised waiting to capture whatever part of the trade England abandoned.[5]

The British abolitionists' cause suffered not only from the failure of the *Amis des noirs,* but also from the ramifying effects of revolution and war. Many English leaders responded as enthusiastically as Edmund Burke to Wilberforce's great speech of May 13, 1789, which initiated the abolitionist campaign. But by 1792 Burke's own attack on the French Revolution had helped nourish the fear of Jacobinism that was being used to smother all reform. Insinuations that abolition was part of a radical plot were supplemented by petitions from planters, merchants, mortgagees, and annuitants, who claimed that their own ruin would also mean the triumph of France in the West Indies. It was futile for Wilberforce to suggest in 1796 that if England had abolished the slave trade the islands would not have such an "accumulation of inflammable matter" for the French to ignite. Henry Dundas's reply was that abolition would simply make it easier for Victor Hugues and his revolutionary French army to incite insurrections.[6]

Nevertheless, even in 1792 prospects looked more promising in the House of Commons until Henry Dundas, a close ally of Pitt, secured an amendment substituting gradual for immediate abolition of the African trade. In point of fact, "gradual" simply meant postponement to a specified date—Dundas urged the year 1800, but the House finally agreed on 1796. The shortness of the interval tended to obscure the importance of the reasoning given for delay, which specifically linked commercial regulation with the internal affairs of the colonies. Dundas argued that enforcement of abolition would require the co-operation of West Indian legislatures; and that laws ameliorating the condition of the slaves, and thus encouraging their national increase, must precede the closing of the African trade. Abolitionist leaders had always known that the slave trade and West Indian slavery were intimately connected, but had assumed that by stopping the former,

[5] *Parliamentary History,* XXIX, 296–97.
[6] *Ibid.,* XXVIII, 68; XXX, 515, 652–60; XXXII, 739, 753; William Wilberforce, *Speech, on Wednesday, the 13th of May, 1789, on the Question of the Abolition of the Slave Trade* (London, n.d.), pp. 44–47; *Journals of the House of Lords,* XXXIX, 404a.

which was within the province of Parliament, West Indians could be forced to improve the condition of their Negroes. By making the abolition of the slave trade depend on colonial reforms, Dundas suggested possibilities for indefinite delay. In 1797, for example, a year after abolition should have gone into effect according to the resolutions of the Lower House, Charles Rose Ellis, a West Indian leader, persuaded Parliament to support recommendations to the colonial governors, to be circulated by the crown, for domestic legislation that would decrease the islands' dependence on the African trade. No effective reforms resulted from these recommendations, but they implied that the House of Commons had temporarily surrendered its jurisdiction over the slave system. Meanwhile, the House of Lords had slowly buried the Lower House's resolutions of 1792, which were said by the Lord Chancellor to be an "unprecedented" attempt by Parliament to regulate the internal affairs of the colonies.[7]

This abdication of previously claimed power met some resistance, especially from Pitt's political opponents. In March, 1796, Pitt spoke eloquently, but not in the capacity of prime minister, supporting Wilberforce's new bill for immediate abolition. When the measure lost by a mere four votes, a crushing disappointment for Wilberforce, Philip Francis openly questioned Pitt's sincerity. A few weeks later he offered a remarkable plan for the direct reformation of slavery and gradual emancipation of Negroes. Though Francis presented his proposals as a substitute for the apparently hopeless approach of stopping the slave trade, his plan required Parliament to exercise more authoritarian power than was later used by the United States government in the crisis of Civil War and Reconstruction. And Francis challenged anyone to deny Parliament's supreme right to make laws for the colonies: to argue that such powers should be reserved was to acknowledge the existence of such powers. Anticipating reminders of the American Revolution, he drew a sharp distinction between the tyranny of taxation without representation, and social legislation for the common good. Besides, the West Indies could never become independent since the islands lacked unity or any semblance of a common bond, except perhaps for their barbarous slave codes. "Renounce your office," Francis told the House, "or perform your duty." This appeal

    [7] *Parliamentary History,* XXIX, 359, 1204–25, 1280–93, 1349–55; Robert Isaac Wilberforce and Samuel Wilberforce, eds., *The Correspondence of William Wilberforce* (2 vols., London, 1840), II, 496–97.

was taken up by Fox, who said he would prefer West Indian independence to the stigma of retaining connections with the abominable system of slavery. But Pitt warned that "stirring a question of such a delicate nature . . . would only excite a spirit of jealousy, and defeat its own object"; and on the matter of jurisdiction, he affirmed that the House "had relinquished the power of making any alteration with respect to the property of the negroes."[8]

Even if the abolitionists had been more numerous and had induced more people to sign petitions, there was little hope of ending the slave trade unless philanthropy could be buttressed by other forces. I shall give more detailed attention to the politics of British abolition in later chapters, and now simply summarize some of the circumstances that made it possible for Lord Grenville's administration to achieve the previously impossible goal. Napoleon's restoration of colonial slavery in 1802 removed some of the stigma of Jacobinism from the abolitionists' cause, which could now become part of the patriotic war against despotism. More important, Napoleon's failure to subdue Haiti meant an end to the threat of French competition in the Caribbean. As Britain conquered one after another of the French, Spanish, and Dutch colonies, she acquired an increasing surplus of tropical produce, at a time of unstable world prices and of diminishing British access to European markets. In 1806 the abolitionists could convincingly appeal to national interest in ending the slave trade to foreign colonies or states, since this British-supplied labor merely served to enhance the power of competitors and to augment the production of tropical staples which American ships could smuggle to Napoleon's Europe. Finally, by early 1807 Grenville could point to the probability of America's ending the slave trade within the coming year. Since the British fleet had stopped most of the trade of other foreign rivals north of the equator, a total end of the slave traffic seemed in sight.[9]

Although Grenville quickly steered his abolition bill through the House of Lords, the West Indians rallied in the Commons for a desperate last fight. In addition to the usual complaints of breaking

---

[8] *Parliamentary History,* XXXII, 901, 944–50, 970–80, 983–90.

[9] *Parliamentary Debates,* VI, 597–98, 805, 917–18, 1021–25; VII, 580–86; [James Stephen], *The Crisis of the Sugar Colonies* (London, 1802), pp. 151–57; Alan M. Rees, "Pitt and the Achievement of Abolition," *Journal of Negro History,* XXXIX (July, 1954), 167–84; Roger Anstey, "A Re-interpretation of the Abolition of the British Slave Trade, 1806–1807," *English Historical Review,* LXXXVII (April, 1972), 320–32.

faith with investors, who would supposedly be ruined by land-value depreciation, there was much talk about the threat to slavery itself. Sounding much like the South Carolinians in Congress, the West Indians defended slavery by citing Biblical precedents and by philosophizing on original sin. Their opponents, particularly when faced with demands for monetary compensation, vilified West Indian society and the character of its slaveholders. In the crucial vote of February 23, 1807, the West Indians were overwhelmed 283 to 16. After hearing their forecasts of ruin and disaster, Lord Howick, who as Secretary of State had introduced the bill in the Commons, agreed to change the preamble; instead of referring to the injustice and inhumanity of the African trade, it would simply read that "it is expedient that the slave trade be abolished."[10]

Despite this gesture of accommodation, the bill's passage was a stunning defeat for West Indian interests. Had they not chosen to fight the bill as an antislavery measure, they might have been able to eliminate some of its antislavery implications. But uncompromising opposition deprived the West Indians of the chance to modify one of the law's most significant provisions: captured Negroes were to be forfeited to the government and eventually freed; they could be enlisted in the armed forces or bound out as apprentices, but not sold, even if they had been taken to the West Indies. This method of disposal greatly alarmed the Jamaican House of Assembly. The forfeited Negroes would be placed in a state of freedom not only repugnant to local laws but highly dangerous to the island's safety. Worst of all, in the Assembly's eyes, the provision was a flagrant violation of its own legislative authority and the rights of British subjects. The king in council had been empowered to make regulations for the disposal and protection of the Negroes after their apprenticeship terms had expired. In a series of resolutions adopted October 29, 1807, the Jamaican House of Assembly asserted its exclusive and absolute right to make all laws for the internal governing of the island; denied the right of Parliament to interfere in domestic concerns; claimed that no laws could be binding on those not represented in the parliament which enacted them; and recognized their duty to resist by all constitutional means any law that subverted the ancient principles of the British constitution. But the only outcome of this bold defiance was

[10] *Parliamentary Debates*, VIII, 257, 601–2, 613–14, 657–72, 678–83, 701–2, 718–19, 829–38, 945–95; IX, 63–64, 142–45.

a self-defeating proposal to deny pay, subsistence, and the use of public buildings to the king's troops, who were, after all, essential for the island's security.[11]

Sanction and Jurisdiction in the United States: "Migration and Importation"

If Jamaica had taken a similar stance in 1774 and had become an ally of the continental colonies, she might have had more voice in national deliberations on the African trade.[12] In the United States, where the issue aroused a struggle of contending interests within the Constitutional Convention, slaveholding delegates played a crucial part in the final decision and commitment.

Before turning to that decision, I will briefly review some of the conditions affecting regional differences in the demand for African slaves. In all plantation societies a cheap supply of slaves encouraged upward mobility for whites by widening the ranks of the slaveholding class. Yet unlimited expansion of the labor supply often clashed with public policy. Thus in Jamaica (as well as in North America) legislators had long tried to limit the ratio of blacks to whites and to regulate slave imports by duties which were sometimes disallowed, as in 1774, by the crown.[13] In contrast to the West Indies, however, the southern states had assurance that cutting ties with Africa would not result in a shrinking labor force.

When the first Continental Congress agreed in 1774 to prohibit the importation of slaves, along with more innocent commodities, high moral principle gave added thrust to economic retaliation. But questions of morality and sincerity have tended to obscure the fundamental demand on which most of the colonists could agree: the right of localities to control slave importation as part of their larger right to self-determination. This demand did not necessarily mean hostility

[11] *Ibid.*, IX, 168; *Journals of the Assembly of Jamaica* (Jamaica, 1807), IX, 574–75, 600; Murray, *The West Indies*, pp. 41–42.

[12] In fact, in 1774, Jamaica took a constitutional stand quite similar to that of the continental colonies (see R. L. Schuyler, *Parliament and the British Empire* [New York, 1929], p. 135; Edward Brathwaite, *The Development of Creole Society in Jamaica, 1770–1820* [Oxford, 1971], pp. 68–79). But at that time slavery was by no means threatened, and there was little likelihood of the British West Indies allying with the rebellious colonies to the north.

[13] David Brion Davis, *The Problem of Slavery in Western Culture* (Ithaca, N.Y., 1966), pp. 135–44.

toward the slave trade. In 1750, for example, the colonists of Georgia, having demonstrated that laws could not keep settlers from acquiring slaves, succeeded in reversing the original free-soil policy of the Trustees and the British government. Because of Georgia's late start as a plantation economy, in 1760 there were only 3,500 blacks in a population of 9,600. The demand soared during the following decade and remained strong in 1774, when Georgians vehemently opposed the Continental Association's boycott. As late as 1793, when alarmed by the St. Domingue revolution, Georgia chose to exclude only slaves from the West Indies and Florida, contagious areas that might pass on the insurrectionary fever. Otherwise, legal imports continued for five more years, supplemented by a growing migration of South Carolinians accompanied by their slaves.[14]

South Carolina complied more willingly with the nonimportation agreements, in part to reduce debts and allow local merchants, as one manifesto put it, "to settle their accounts, and be ready with the return of liberty to renew trade." Certainly the South Carolinians had no desire to see nonimportation become permanent national policy, nor did they wish to become dependent on Virginia's surplus supply of labor, which of course included Virginia's most unruly and dangerous blacks. Yet self-determination allowed for the legal suspension of slave imports as a means of conserving specie, restoring economic stability, and preventing optimistic debtors from purchasing Negroes instead of paying their creditors. South Carolina's law of 1787 suspending the slave trade for three years was, in fact, part of an act requiring the rapid recovery of debts.[15]

Patrick S. Brady has shown that the division between debtors and creditors was actually less important than the division between "low-country" and "up-country" in determining South Carolina's slave-trade policy. The planters of the rice coast, who were well-stocked

[14] *Ibid.*, pp. 144–50; Darold D. Wax, "Georgia and the Negro before the American Revolution," *Georgia Historical Quarterly,* LI (March, 1967), 63–75.

[15] Patrick S. Brady, "The Slave Trade and Sectionalism in South Carolina, 1787–1808," *Journal of Southern History,* XXXVIII (Nov., 1972), 601–20. Peter H. Wood has shown that even by 1720 blacks constituted more than one-half the population of South Carolina; in 1741 the colony enacted a temporary prohibitive duty on slave imports ("More like a Negro Country: Demographic Patterns in Colonial South Carolina, 1700–1740," paper given at 1972 M.S.S.B. Conference on Systems of Slavery, University of Rochester).

with slaves and who stood to gain by rising slave prices, not only favored continuing the suspension of imports from Africa but objected particularly to the domestic slave trade from Virginia and North Carolina. Well before the boom in short-staple cotton, triggered in 1793 by Eli Whitney's gin, the up-country regions surrounding Camden and Columbia had begun a burst of enormous population growth and were clamoring for more slaves than the low-country areas could supply. By 1787, to complicate matters further, the sea-island districts of Beaufort and Colleton had begun cultivating long-staple, luxury cotton; because of their isolation from the domestic slave trade, these planters looked to Africa for their labor.[16]

By 1792 the news from St. Domingue reinforced the position of the dominant rice planters and helped to prolong the ban on slave importation. It was not until 1803 that the demands of King Cotton, amplified by the opening of Louisiana, finally took precedence over fear of insurrection. Even then, the legislature voted to exclude any black who had ever been in the West Indies and, with apparently unintentional irony, required that slaves brought in from other states have "good character; and have not been concerned in any insurrection or rebellion."[17] To be a slave in South Carolina, one had to meet the highest moral standards. Nevertheless, to the dismay and anger of her sister states to the north, South Carolina legally imported, from 1803 to 1808, nearly 40,000 Africans—presumably all of "good character."

In Virginia the market for African-born slaves had long been confined to new or small planters, traders, speculators, or miscellaneous people who simply wanted a servant. Yet as Darold D. Wax has pointed out, "throughout the colonial period, whenever economic conditions permitted, Virginia planters willingly purchased freshly imported Negro slaves." Until the late 1760s, Virginia had been allowed considerable leeway in taxing imported Africans. In 1772, however, the House of Burgesses self-righteously requested the crown to accept a heavy duty on such "a Trade of great Inhumanity." When the crown disallowed the act, the Virginians could piously claim they had never really wanted Negro slaves but had been forced to accept them by the perfidious English. Patriotic edicts did not necessarily

[16] Brady, "Slave Trade and Sectionalism," pp. 601–20.
[17] *Ibid.*, p. 612.

mean effective enforcement. For example, in September, 1773, an American slaving captain wrote his Rhode Island employers from Fredericksburg, reporting that since no one had shown up at an emergency meeting of the Association, which was supposed to prevent importations, he had disposed of all but two of his slaves, receiving especially fine prices for the children.[18]

Nevertheless, Virginia took the lead in making a disavowal of the slave trade a part of Revolutionary ideology. Even though the commonwealth was happy to supply slaves to her neighbors, her public policy opposed any further growth of Negro population, whether slave or free.

To put the non-importation agreements in proper perspective, we should note that the best recent estimates indicate that the period from 1780 to 1810 represented the peak of the slave trade to North America. Moreover, in 1820 the slave population of the United States was approximately three times greater than it had been at the outset of the Revolution.[19] On the other hand, the increase might have been still larger if the Revolution had not disrupted previous patterns of trade, if ten of the rebellious states had not followed Virginia's ideological lead, and if planters in Mississippi Territory and Louisiana had later won their appeals for direct slave imports from Africa.

With this background in mind, the decisions of the Constitutional Convention become more meaningful. It was a Virginian, George Mason, who reminded the delegates that western settlers were already crying out for slaves, and that it would be futile for Virginia to cut off further importations of Africans if they could be shipped to the

---

[18] Darold D. Wax, "Negro Import Duties in Colonial Virginia: A Study of British Commerical Policy and Local Public Policy," *The Virginia Magazine,* LXXIX (Jan., 1971), 29–44; Robert McColley, *Slavery and Jeffersonian Virginia* (Urbana, Ill., 1964), pp. 163–67, and *passim;* "Slavery Miscellaneous," Box 1, D21, D35, New-York Historical Society.

[19] Robert William Fogel and Stanley L. Engerman, *Time on the Cross: The Economics of American Negro Slavery* (2 vols., Boston, 1974), I, 24, 86–89; II, 30–33; Stella H. Sutherland, *Population Distribution in Colonial America* (New York, 1936), p. 271; Bureau of the Census, *Negro Population, 1790–1915* (Washington, 1928), p. 53. Because of the natural increase in the slave population, new imports from Africa had a lessening impact both on the price and total population of slaves. But if Fogel and Engerman are right in their demographic estimates, the period of state prohibition coincided with the period of greatest slave imports.

West by way of South Carolina and Georgia. The central question was whether the expansion of slavery should be sanctioned or impeded, or in Mason's words, whether the general government would have power "to prevent the increase of slavery."[20]

On July 23, Charles Cotesworth Pinckney, a South Carolinian educated at Oxford and the Middle Temple, announced that he would vote against the Constitution if it lacked some security against the future emancipation of southern slaves. Three days later the Committee of Detail, chaired by another South Carolinian, John Rutledge, began working on a draft of the Constitution. Although many Southerners were ardent nationalists who wished to create a strong and vigorous central government, they also feared that the Congressional power "to regulate commerce among the several states" could be used as a weapon against slavery and as a device for exploiting the plantation economy. The Committee of Detail failed to adopt the explicit guarantee demanded by Pinckney, but agreed to restrict the commerce clause by adding two sections protecting the economic and social interests of the Deep South. One was the requirement of a two-thirds majority in both legislative houses for the passage of import duties and laws regulating foreign trade. The other stipulated that "no tax or duty shall be laid by the Legislature on articles exported from any State; nor on the migration or importation of such persons as the several States shall think proper to admit; nor shall such migration or importation be prohibited."[21]

Some northern delegates took alarm at the Deep South's bid for economic freedom. On August 8, two days after the submission of the draft, Rufus King lost patience with orderly procedure. He provocatively linked the issue of representation to the continuation of the slave trade and to the prohibition of taxes on exports. He could never agree, he said, to let slaves be imported without limitation, for augmenting the South's representation would bind the government to defend the region against insurrection, yet leave the government powerless to tax slave produce. Roger Sherman, of Connecticut, tried to separate the slave trade from the issue of representation, which he

---

[20] Max Farrand, ed., *The Records of the Federal Convention of 1787* (4 vols., New Haven, 1937), II, 370. For a detailed analysis of the subject, see Donald L. Robinson, *Slavery in the Structure of American Politics, 1765–1820* (New York, 1971), pp. 207–47.

[21] Farrand, ed., *Records*, II, 95, 183.

thought already settled. But Gouverneur Morris then expanded on King's sectional attack, delivering a sweeping indictment of the South's "nefarious institution" which had turned Virginia and Maryland into "barren wastes" of misery and poverty, and which now induced the Georgian and Carolinian to go to Africa, where, "in defiance of the most sacred laws of humanity," he "tears away his fellow creatures from their dearest connections & dam(n)s them to the most cruel bondage," only to be rewarded by "more votes in a Govt. instituted for the protection of the rights of mankind."[22]

Suggestions that the northern public found slavery morally repugnant gave a cutting edge to demands for economic concessions. But Morris's rhetoric also exploited the contradictions underlying American liberty and union, contradictions which the Convention had tried to forget. On August 21 and 22, when the delegates directly faced the slave-trade issue, there was danger of impasse and failure. Charles Pinckney informed the assembly that ancient Greece and Rome furnished illustrious precedents for South Carolina, and that in all ages one-half of mankind had been slaves. Although he added that the southern states, if left alone, would probably stop importations, his cousin Charles Cotesworth candidly explained that this meant "only stop them occasionally as she now does." The Deep South stood firm in threatening to reject the Constitution if the Committee's clause were rejected. Charles Cotesworth Pinckney accused the Virginians of favoring an end to the slave trade so they could monopolize the domestic supply of Negroes. In any event, as John Rutledge pointed out, the Convention had no business dealing with religion or morality; the only question was whether mutual interests would allow the southern states to be parties to the Union.[23]

Angry southern threats shifted the contest back from the high ground of abstract principle to the easier terrain of immediate interests and mutual concessions. Roger Sherman gave voice to the mood of accommodation when he said it would be better to allow the southern states to go on importing slaves than to have them leave the Union. Gouverneur Morris, having paid tribute to the sacred laws of

[22] *Ibid.*, II, 220–23, Morris added, with questionable sincerity, that he would sooner submit to a tax sufficient to emancipate all the slaves than saddle posterity with such a Constitution.

[23] *Ibid.*, II, 371, 373–74.

humanity, suggested that a bargain might be struck if a special committee considered the slave trade along with taxes on imports and exports.[24]

On August 24 this committee of eleven submitted its recommendations, which embodied one of the crucial compromises of the Convention. As explained by Charles Cotesworth Pinckney, it had been in South Carolina's interest to ally with Virginia and the former majority of states desiring restrictions on navigation acts; however, in view of the northeastern states' "liberal" attitude on the slave trade, he was willing to recognize the commercial losses the Northeast had suffered as a result of the Revolution, and withdrew his support for the requirement of a two-thirds legislative majority for import duties and other commercial regulations.[25]

The "liberal" attitude Pinckney had in mind was the agreement by northeastern delegates that there should be no prohibition on the importation of slaves prior to the year 1800. On the Convention floor Pinckney moved that the date be advanced to 1808, which won New England's support, though Madison predicted that twenty years would bring as much evil as an indefinite period of slave trading. Before the Convention finished its work, it placed the prohibition on interference with the slave trade beyond the power of Constitutional amendment. Only the equal suffrage of states in the Senate shared this high sanctuary of immunity. And as part of the package of northern concessions, Article IV, on full faith and credit, included the provision that no fugitive slave could be freed by the laws of any state into which he escaped, and that all fugitives were to be delivered to their rightful owners.[26]

During subsequent decades there would be endless and involved debate on whether the Constitution implicitly challenged or gave positive sanction to the South's peculiar institution. Many of the framers, including Madison, had scruples against openly acknowledging that human beings could be property. The use of the euphemism "persons" could not disguise the support given to slavery by the three-fifths compromise and the clause respecting fugitives. The slave-trade provi-

[24] *Ibid.*, II, 374.

[25] *Ibid.*, II, 400, 449–50.

[26] *Ibid.*, II, 415; Jonathan Elliot, ed., *The Debates in the Several State Conventions, on the Adoption of the Federal Constitution* (Philadelphia, 1876), I, 372–73.

sion was another matter, since in 1808 a restraint on Congress could suddenly become a delegated power; in Charles Pinckney's words, it was a *"negative pregnant,* restraining for twenty years, and giving the power after."[27]

There is some evidence that "migration" referred to what today would be called "immigration," a word whose modern implications Jeremy Belknap helped to popularize in the 1790s.[28] It is likely that northern members of the Committee of Detail were willing to accept a continuance of the slave trade so long as no national restrictions could be imposed on immigration from Europe. Such immigration would presumably keep the North from falling behind the South in population and political power. Oliver Ellsworth, who represented Connecticut on the Committee, reassured northern delegates that an increase in white population would provide a pool of cheap labor that would eventually render slaves useless. In a different context, Charles Pinckney feared that the absence of uniform rules on naturalization and citizenship would allow new states to encourage unrestricted immigration. If the words "migration" and "persons" were simply a concession to northern interests as well as sentiment, the Committee may have intended the clause to refer solely to the movement of Negroes and whites from other countries to the United States.[29]

On the other hand, the original purpose of the clause was to prevent the federal government from ever interfering with state regulations

[27] Farrand, ed., *Records,* III, 443.

[28] See "immigration," *Oxford English Dictionary.* At the Convention, Mason "was for opening a wide door for emigrants; but did not chuse to let foreigners and adventurers make laws for us & govern us" (Farrand, ed., *Records,* II, 216). Yet Rutledge could refer to "an emigrant from N. England to S.C. or Georgia" (*ibid.,* p. 217). No consistent distinction was then drawn between an "immigrant" and "emigrant," nor between an "emigrant" from abroad and one from another state.

[29] Farrand, ed., *Records,* II, 371; III, 120. Charles Pinckney was clearly wrong when he later argued that the word "migration" had been chosen because "it was supposed, that, without some express grant to them of power on the subject, Congress would not be authorized ever to touch the question of migration hither, or emigration to this country, however pressing or urgent the necessity of such a measure might be" (*ibid.,* III, 443). In the draft of the Committee of Detail, Congress could *never* have prohibited "the migration or importation of such persons as the several States shall think proper to admit." On the other hand, Pinckney may have been right in suggesting there was an understanding that the power to limit the importation of slaves should be linked with the power to limit white immigration.

regarding the migration or importation of persons. And as we have seen, both Virginia and South Carolina placed restrictions on the migration of slaves from other states, even when accompanied by their masters. In 1792, South Carolina suspended the domestic slave trade along with foreign importations.[30] Given the restrictive purpose of the clause, the word "migration" must have been all-inclusive.

After the Convention had agreed on the twenty-year limitation, Gouverneur Morris offered two reasons for changing the wording of what was to become Article I, Section 9: inclusion of "persons" and "migration" might lead to national restrictions on immigration after 1808; and also the Convention should show that it had tolerated the slave trade only in compliance to the wishes of three states. Accordingly, Morris proposed the substitute phrase—if acceptable to the states concerned—"importation of slaves into N. Carolina, S. Carolina & Georgia." George Mason said he had no objection to using the word "slaves," but thought that naming the three states might give offense. John Dickinson, still desiring to except states that had already permanently outlawed the slave trade, suggested the less specific wording: "the importation of Slaves into such of the States as shall permit the same shall not be prohibited by the Legislature of the U—— S—— until the year 1808." The Convention decided not to sanction slavery so openly, and thus kept the original phrase "such persons." But by retaining the word "migration" and inserting the qualifier "now existing" after "several States," the delegates opened the way for violently conflicting interpretations.[31]

In the Congressional debates over the Alien Law of 1798, Federalists ultimately conceded that until 1808 the migration clause gave states exclusive control over admitting (though not deporting) aliens. But Jonathan Dayton, who had been a Convention delegate from New Jersey, contended that "such persons" applied only to slaves, and that "the sole reason assigned" for not using "slaves" was "that it would

[30] McColley, *Slavery and Jeffersonian Virginia*, pp. 165–66; Brady, "Slave Trade and Sectionalism," p. 608.

[31] Farrand, ed., *Records*, II, 415–16. Whatever the meaning of "migration," its application to the territories was not affected by the twenty-year restriction on Congressional power, which pertained only to "the several States now existing." Although James Wilson and others thought that the authorized ten-dollar duty could apply only to "'importations," and thus to slaves, Luther Martin contended that the wording was ambiguous enough to authorize a duty on white immigrants (*ibid.*, III, 161, 210).

be better not to stain the Constitutional code with such a term." Abraham Baldwin, a former Georgia delegate who challenged Dayton in the House of Representatives, correctly remembered that some of the Convention members had observed "that this expression would extend to other persons besides slaves, which was not denied, but this did not produce any alteration of it." Baldwin also recalled, however, that the original phrase had "used the word 'slaves' *instead of* 'migration,' or 'importation,' of persons" (*my italics*). He thus implied that "migration" could have referred to slaves as well as immigrants, and to a mode of arrival distinguishable from "importation." Even Madison, who in 1819 hotly denied that the framers had intended to include interstate movement, did not deny that the word "migration" included slaves: the term, he wrote, allowed "those who were scrupulous of acknowledging expressly a property in human beings, to view *imported* persons as a species of emigrants, whilst others might apply the term to foreign malefactors sent or coming into the country."[32]

Yet both Morris and Dickinson had opposed the expansion of slavery and had omitted "migration" from their substitute motions. And as Madison later pointed out, if southern delegates had supposed that the word included internal movement between the states or into the territories, they would surely have avoided using it. In 1820, when the clause served as one of the justifications for barring slavery from Missouri, Charles Pinckney argued that it had been adopted as a potential check on immigration to the North, in order to balance the South's losses from closing the slave trade. He also asserted that the Convention had made a solemn compact: in exchange for the South's concessions on the slave trade, the North had agreed that Congress would have no power ever to touch the question of slavery.[33]

[32] James Morton Smith, *Freedom's Fetters: The Alien and Sedition Laws and American Civil Liberties* (Ithaca, N.Y., 1956), pp. 80–83; Ferrand, ed., *Records,* III, 376–79, 436–37. At the time of the Missouri controversy, Madison insisted that "the term 'migration' . . . referred, exclusively, to a migration or importation from other countries into the U. States," and added that the Northwest Ordinance, which had been intended to restrict the markets for African slaves, would probably not have been adopted if Congress had possessed the power to end the foreign slave trade (Gaillard Hunt, ed., *The Writings of James Madison* . . . [9 vols., New York, 1900–1910], IX, 5).

[33] Farrand, ed., *Records,* III, 443–44. Walter Berns, in a detailed and learned analysis of the migration clause, suggests duplicity on the part of Madison and others for later fostering the "traditional interpretation" that "such persons" referred to white immigrants as well as slaves, and that the term "migration"

But this solemn compact never became explicit law. The southern delegates apparently failed to recognize the subtle implications of adding a time limitation to the original wording of the Committee of Detail. They succeeded in removing export duties from the temporary prohibition of Article I, Section 9, but the other phrases, chosen to put maximum restrictions on the commerce clause, now carried the opposite implications. The power of regulating commerce, subject to broad or narrow interpretation, now specifically included the power of

---

thus had no internal operation ("The Constitution and the Migration of Slaves," *Yale Law Journal,* LXXVIII [1968], 198–228). I disagree with Berns's argument, though not with all his conclusions, for the following reasons: (1) He fails to consider the possibility that "such persons" could have been thought to include white immigrants and also to refer to interstate "migration," especially in the original restrictive version proposed by the Committee of Detail. (2) Nothing is proved by the expectation of some Northerners that the clause would eventually put an end to slavery, for there was widespread confusion of "slavery" with the "slave trade." Both American and British abolitionists assumed that an end to slave imports would lead automatically to the amelioration and gradual abolition of slavery. Berns offers no positive evidence that in 1787 anyone thought of the commerce clause, or of interstate movement, as the key to general emancipation. In any event, the clause applied only to the states then existing (3) Berns fails to distinguish the interstate slave trade from the interstate migration of slaves with their masters. In fact, most slaves who moved westward did so with their masters, and one could debate whether this constituted "commerce." (4) It is a bit misleading to take the Northwest Ordinance as a sweeping precedent, since it did not affect the slaves already living in the Northwest. Though Congress re-enacted the Ordinance, it also refused to adopt positive emancipation measures to give force to the proscription against slavery. Moreover, for a time, the Ordinance was interpreted in a way that allowed slaveholders to settle in Indiana and Illinois with their slaves. (5) Most important, Berns presupposes that in 1787 slavery was a declining institution and that "nearly everyone viewed slavery as an evil which must and would be abolished as soon as practicable" (p. 214, n. 52). Yet there is abundant evidence that in 1787 both the demand for slaves and the number of slaveholders were steadily increasing, even in Virginia. The relative lack of controversy raised by the migration clause in South Carolina, of which Berns makes much, simply shows that the most ardent defenders of slavery saw the Constitution as a strong bulwark for their peculiar institution. The terms under which the southwestern territories were ceded to the federal government suggest the clear expectation that slavery would expand westward without interference. One may agree that the language of Article I, Section 9, might reasonably be construed as granting Congress the power to prohibit the movement of any slaves into the territories or new states, and, after 1808, into the original states. But this construction necessarily turns on changing values and definitions, and above all, on a frank disavowal of slavery as a matter of public policy—since it would constitute a clear discrimination against slaveholding migrants. There is no reason to believe that the framers intended or could have agreed upon such a construction.

prohibiting the migration or importation of persons. Even the effect of Article V, removing the provision from the reach of Constitutional amendment, was necessarily limited to a twenty-year term.

The very vagueness of the wording could be used to widen the potentially antislavery powers granted by the Fifth Amendment and by the clauses concerning interstate commerce, the general welfare, and the need for republican state governments. The Constitution could thus be interpreted as granting Congress the power to manumit contraband slaves, to prohibit the coastal and interstate slave trade, to bar slavery from the territories, to enlist slaves in the armed forces, or to purchase Negroes and emancipate them. Moreover, the phrase "several States now existing" suggested that Congress did not have to wait twenty years to apply its powers to new states or territories. Even Madison conceded that Article I, Section 9, had given Congress immediate power to stop the importation of foreign slaves into new states.[34]

The "true" meaning of the Constitution's provisions on slavery cannot be known, precisely because they were the products of an uneasy bargain and were deliberately shrouded in ambiguity. Agreement on concrete economic issues, or in blunter terms, a deal, could not resolve an unnegotiable conflict over the future of American slavery. Delegates who returned to the New England and Pennsylvania ratifying conventions could encourage the assumption that the power to be granted Congress in 1808 would become the basis for eradicating slavery from the country. James Wilson, in a famous speech to the Pennsylvania convention, is supposed to have said there could never be another slave state. Yet Virginians, who had strongly favored an immediate end to the slave trade, were confident that the Constitution posed no threat to slavery itself. And in the South Carolina legislature, where there was some fear that the Constitution might be used as a tool for northern interference with slave property, delegates swore that they would never have agreed to confederate without winning agreement on the right to import slaves. They reassured skeptics that the Deep South would even be able to defend the slave trade after 1808, when its power and support in Congress would presumably be invincible.[35]

[34] Robinson, *Slavery in the Structure of American Politics,* pp. 227–28.

[35] Farrand, ed., *Records,* III, 334, 437; Elliot, ed., *Debates,* I, 123–24; II, 452; IV, 272–86. It is significant that while Congressman Elias Boudinot ac-

Northern and southern delegates could tell the people in their respective sections that slavery had been given a mortal wound or the most secure protection; but ultimately both sections had agreed to defer the question to the future. Unlike Parliament's resolutions of 1792, which called for a definite ending of the slave trade at a specified date, the Constitution was open-ended, stating simply that Congress could not prohibit the trade for twenty years. Both opponents and defenders of slavery had faith that time was on their side. And both sides, if disposed to place the Union above inflammatory sectional interests, had strongly implied that the continuance of the Union would depend on the fulfillment of their expectations.

Gestation of the "Negative Pregnant"

Since the House of Lords smothered the Commons' resolutions of 1792, and William Pitt informed Parliament that it had relinquished the power of making "any alteration with respect to the property of the Negroes," it is not surprising to learn that in the 1790s Congress also relinquished whatever broad powers the Constitution had granted for curbing the growth of slavery. Neither Britain's struggle against revolutionary France nor America's efforts to establish national unity was conducive to social experimentation. And since Southerners had far more political power than did the West Indians in Parliament, their threats of resistance were also more credible.

On February 11, 1790, Congress interrupted its deliberations on Hamilton's Report on Public Credit to hear a Quaker petition praying that the infinite Father of Spirits would inspire the new Congress to exert all its power against the licentious wickedness of the slave trade, notwithstanding "seeming impediments." When a Pennsylvania Congressman moved that Quaker petitions be referred to a committee, and when a Virginia Congressman observed that the Constitution at least gave authority to levy a tax on slave imports, the Georgians and South Carolinians exploded in anger. Sneering at the hollow patriotism and hypocrisy of the Quakers, James Jackson baldly claimed that

---

knowledged in 1790 that the Constitution prohibited the government from interfering with the importation of slaves until 1808, he specifically connected importation with the phrase, "or promoting the emancipation of them prior to that period." Boudinot was not alone in assuming that Congress would have a wide array of powers after 1808 for dealing with slavery, but these powers were usually unspecified (see *Annals of Congress,* 1st Cong., 2nd Sess., 1517).

slavery was not only allowed by the Savior but positively commended by the Bible. William Smith then defined the rule that would ultimately prevail: prior to 1808, it would be a betrayal of Constitutional agreement even to consider possible ways of restricting slave importations.[36]

Before the debates had run their course in March, 1790, both sides had taken more extreme positions than those advanced in the contemporary House of Commons. Whereas the British abolitionists denied having any interest in direct emancipation, Elbridge Gerry, representing Massachusetts, claimed that Congress had the Constitutional right to purchase all the slaves in the South, using as a means the national resource of western lands. The petition from the Pennsylvania Abolition Society, signed by Benjamin Franklin as chairman, expressed the hope that Congress would not only "step to the very verge of the power vested in you" for discouraging the slave trade, but "be pleased to countenance the restoration of liberty to those unhappy men, who alone, in this land of freedom are degraded into perpetual bondage."[37]

To this last declaration Thomas Tucker, of South Carolina, had a simple and conclusive answer: "Do these men expect a general emancipation of slaves by law? This would never be submitted to by the Southern States without a civil war." When a Pennsylvanian hinted that if he were a federal judge he might well free any slave who came to him claiming natural liberty, Jackson replied that in Georgia the very existence of such a judge would be in danger. The South Carolinians drew freely on the propaganda of British slave traders, citing the testimony given by Lord Rodney and Admiral Barrington on the benefits of the African trade and the mildness of West Indian slavery. But the Southerners also had an advantage over the West Indians in being able to exploit a national prejudice against Negroes. Northern Congressmen could give no convincing reply to the argument that even Quakers refused to associate or intermarry with Negroes, and that the two races could not coexist if both were free. Smith assured Congress that the very survival of the Union would depend on the North's willingness to refrain from any meddling with

[36] *Annals of Congress,* 1st Cong., 2nd Sess., 1224–30, 1239–42; Pennsylvania Abolition Society MSS, II, 30–40, Historical Society of Pennsylvania; Hilda Justice, *Life and Ancestry of Warner Mifflin, Friend—Philanthropist—Patriot* (Philadelphia, 1905), pp. 170–73.

[37] *Annals of Congress,* 1st Cong., 2nd Sess., 1239–42, 1244–47, 1501–23.

slavery: "The Northern States adopted us with our slaves, and we adopted them with their Quakers. There was an implied compact between the Northern and Southern people, that no step should be taken to injure the property of the latter, or to disturb their tranquillity."

In accordance with this doctrine of implied compact, the House devoted more attention to the restraints on its jurisdiction than to the Constitutional means by which it might promote "the principles of justice, humanity, and good policy," as recommended by a committee report. Paradoxically, the House considered a clause *denying* its authority to legislate concerning "the instruction of slaves in the principles of morality and religion," the provision of "comfortable clothing, accommodation and subsistence," "the regulation of their marriages, and the prevention of the violation of the rights thereof," "the separation of children from their parents," adequate maintenance "in the case of sickness, age, or infirmity," or "the seizure, transportation, or sale of free negroes." Though put in the negative, this detailed list specified the very evils attacked by the abolitionists, and concluded with an appeal to the humanity and wisdom of the southern state legislatures—much as the Ellis resolutions in Parliament would appeal to the West Indian legislatures. The list indicated precisely the path of action slaveholders most feared, and in fact anticipated the reforms the British government later imposed on the crown colonies. As finally adopted, the resolution simply stated that Congress had no authority to interfere in the treatment or emancipation of slaves, but acknowledged that the Constitution conferred the authority to prevent aliens from outfitting slave ships in the United States and to prohibit the American slave trade to foreign ports.[38]

This self-denying resolution was a clear victory for the South. And by 1793, with the passage of a fugitive-slave law, the government had embraced a double standard in defining its jurisdiction over the peculiar institution: national authority could be exercised for the recovery but not the protection of slaves. Through the succeeding

---

[38] *Ibid.*, pp. 1523–25. Without indicating a source, both Mary Stoughton Locke and Thomas Drake state that the committee's report was based on a memorandum written by Warner Mifflin (Drake, *Quakers and Slavery in America* [New Haven, 1950], p. 105; Locke, *Anti-Slavery in America from the Introduction of African Slaves to the Prohibition of the Slave Trade* [Boston, 1901], p. 140).

decade slaveholders won further recognition and support for their own state legislation (for example, Congress refused to receive a petition from manumitted blacks who had been seized under the fugitive-slave law, on the ground that a North Carolina law had retroactively revoked their manumissions). But though specifically authorized to impose a ten-dollar duty on imported Negroes, Congress refused to exercise this power even when South Carolina's reopening of the trade provoked a wave of national indignation.[39]

In Britain abolition of the slave trade had no chance of success until proposed by Lord Grenville and sanctioned by the majority of his Cabinet. The American government showed no sign of moving against the traffic until President Jefferson, in his annual message of December, 1806, condemned "those violations of human rights which have been so long continued on the unoffending inhabitants of Africa," and urged Congress to take advantage of the approaching end of Constitutional limitation.[40]

Unlike the West Indians in Parliament, the southern representatives in Congress were not divided by such issues as stopping the shipment of slaves to captured or foreign territories; nor were they ideologically committed to the African trade as a necessary prop to slavery. Virginians could join with South Carolinians in denouncing any proposal that either reflected upon the morality of slaveholding or posed a threat to the security of the slave system. On the other side, the most outspoken critics of slavery in Congress tended to be men of little political weight. Northern Federalists, having taken the lead in promoting emancipation in their own states, commanded the small vote of free blacks who saw the Republicans as the party of racism and oppression.[41] But by 1806 Federalists looked with icy suspicion upon any of Jefferson's proposals, particularly ones that might weaken commerce

[39] Annals of Congress, 4th Cong., 2nd Sess., 2015–24; 8th Cong., 1st Sess., 991–1014. Some of the legislators who opposed the import duty offered the excuse of not wanting to sanction the slave trade; however, that issue had presumably been resolved by the Constitutional Convention. If the scruples were sincere, they can be taken as an example of a fatal American ambivalence toward governmental power.

[40] *Ibid.*, 9th Cong., 2nd Sess., 14. A year earlier, Stephen Bradley had introduced an abolition bill in the Senate, but it had been postponed.

[41] Leon F. Litwack, *North of Slavery: The Negro in the Free States, 1790–1860* (Chicago, 1961), pp. 14, 80–83; Edgar J. McManus, *A History of Negro Slavery in New York* (Syracuse, N.Y., 1966), pp. 185–87.

or encroach upon the rights of states. The antislavery Republicans were isolated from their Federalist opponents and from the conservative Southerners of their own party. And if there were no Wilberforces among the Federalists, there were no Samuel Romillys among the Republicans. With the possible exception of Stephen Bradley in the Senate, they were, in Henry Adams's phrase, "ordinary representatives of an intellectual mediocrity": James Sloan, a Jeffersonian evangelical from New Jersey, was "the butt of the House"; Barnabas Bidwell of Massachusetts, who later fled to Canada after stealing public money, was dubbed by John Randolph as "the President's clerk of the water-closet."[42]

On December 17, 1806, Sloan raised the question that would soon be debated in Parliament and later evoke angry outcries from the Jamaican House of Assembly. The President's recommendation had been referred to a committee headed by Peter Early, of Georgia, who presented a bill stipulating that captured slaves would be forfeited to the government and sold. Sloan moved that all such slaves coming into the hands of the government should be emancipated. Early immediately pointed out that the law could never be enforced if the illegally imported slaves were set free: "The whole people will rise up against it." Besides, Congress had no jurisdiction over manumission, which was controlled by state law. Sloan, in a reply that would have raised eyebrows among the West Indians, asked whether Congress did not have power "as completely to prohibit this trade as the Parliament of Great Britain?" Early then expanded on the underlying issues at stake:

We are told it is cruel and disgraceful to keep them in slavery. There is no doubt of it. But would it not be more cruel to place them in a situation where we must in self-defence . . . get rid of them in some way? We must either get rid of them, or they of us. . . . I will speak out; it is not my practice to be mealy-mouthed on a subject of importance. Not one of them would be left alive in a year.[43]

The northern Republicans gagged at the thought of the federal

[42] Henry Adams, *History of the United States of America during the Second Administration of Thomas Jefferson* (New York, 1890), I, 366 and *passim*. Of course Adams was prejudiced, and his own grandfather was anything but a champion of antislavery principles in his early years in the Senate.

[43] *Annals of Congress*, 9th Cong., 2nd Sess., 167–74. In 1800, John Rutledge had said he thanked God that the blacks were held in slavery: "if they were not, dreadful would be the consequences" (*ibid.*, 6th Cong., 1st Sess., 230).

government's becoming a seller of slaves: "We punish the criminal, and then step into his place, and complete the crime which he had only begun. . . . We sell his victims as slaves, receive the price of their slavery, and put it into the public treasury." But talk of criminals only exacerbated the debates on the proper penalty for slave traders. On December 31, Early finally announced that many Southerners did not consider slavery a crime: "I will tell the truth. A large majority of people in the Southern States do not consider slavery as even an evil."

Northern Federalists, whose constituents included prominent ex-slave traders, could agree that the practice was at least not a felony. Nor was it sensible to quibble over the word "forfeiture" merely because it implied that men could legally be property. Showing impatience over Bidwell's abstract principles, Josiah Quincy, of Massachusetts, appealed to down-to-earth practicality: no one could deny that African princes did in fact sell their subjects; the title to such slaves found confirmation in the present laws of southern states; it would be too dangerous to allow forfeited Negroes to go free in the South. With these cold facts in mind, one should simply trust the government to devise means to make the Africans "useful members of society, without any infringement of the rights of man."[44]

The crucial vote came on January 7, 1807, on a proposal by Bidwell that no person should be sold as a result of the abolition law. Most southern Congressmen interpreted the amendment as an unacceptable encroachment on property rights; the majority of New York Representatives joined with the South to produce a tie vote. The Speaker, Nathaniel Macon of North Carolina, then cast the deciding vote against the measure.

On February 9 a compromise bill emerged from a new committee, providing that forfeited Negroes should be conveyed to states where slavery was not permitted or was being gradually abolished, and there indentured as apprentices. Early threatened that Southerners would resist such a challenge with their lives. As an amendment he proposed that federal marshals should deliver all forfeited Negroes to the officers of states or territories, where they could be sold in accordance with local law. "We want no civil wars," he warned, "no rebellions, no insurrections, no resistance to the authority of the Government." John

[44] *Ibid.*, 9th Cong., 2nd Sess., 200–3, 221–22, 238.

Smilie, of Pennsylvania, became infuriated by such words: "Sir, this is new doctrine. The gentleman must know that we are not to be terrified by a threat of civil war." Sloan spoke scornfully of the South's magnanimous concession: they would withdraw the demand that the federal government sell Negroes, so long as they could sell the slaves themselves. But such barbs did not alter the final law, which prescribed that slaves would be disposed of in accordance with the laws of the states or territories into which they were brought, and which also allowed their sale for the benefit of informers.[45]

This law was actually an amended version of a Senate bill introduced by Stephen Bradley. It contained one provision that survived all southern attempts at intimidation. To guard against smuggling from Florida or the West Indies, it prohibited the interstate coastal slave trade in vessels of under forty tons burden. John Randolph claimed that this provision could become an entering wedge for general emancipation, and would "blow up the Constitution in ruins." Hinting again at disunion and civil war, he proclaimed that he would rather lose all the laws passed since the government had been established than agree to such a dangerous measure. Randolph's defeat added a taste of bitterness to the southern victory. But in the last analysis, the abolition act gave indirect justification to slavery. It did not even bring immediate peril to American slave traders. Twelve years elapsed before Congress empowered the president to send out armed cruisers for the interception of slave ships. The West Indians might well have envied so successful an outcome.[46]

Jurisdiction in the French Revolution: The Formula for Loss of Control

French planters, whether in the metropolis or in the colonies, were no less sensitive than Georgians or South Carolinians to the threat of governmental meddling with slavery. In 1789, however, their prospects could hardly have seemed more favorable. There was little likelihood that the metropolis, so preoccupied with domestic reform, would seriously interfere with societies three thousand miles across the sea. The doctrines of the early Revolution gave sanction to self-government and the rights of private property. In November, when St. Domingue

[45] *Ibid.,* pp. 265–67, 270–72.
[46] *Ibid.,* p. 626

colonists became panicked by rumors that agents of the *Amis des noirs* were roaming the island, they threatened to follow the example of the United States if the Revolution should lead to any tampering with slavery. Even the assembly of the North Province, led by merchants and lawyers closely tied to France, repeated the warning and symbolically separated the colony's "general will" from that of the mother country. By March, 1790, separatism became more explicit in the rival assembly at St. Marc, in the West Province, which drafted an unauthorized constitution and declared that the colony's internal affairs were beyond the jurisdiction of the Constituent Assembly.[47]

If these rumblings disturbed French merchants and absentee proprietors, they were also politically useful in helping to smother antislavery rhetoric and to win constitutional autonomy for the islands' domestic governance. Ordinarily, one might have expected to find the strongest antislavery sentiment among the middle-class delegates from the great port cities, where the spirit of the Enlightenment had been absorbed and had nourished a progressive, cosmopolitan, and tolerant frame of mind, often institutionalized in Masonic lodges or philanthropic societies resembling the *Amis des noirs*.[48] Brissot de Warville, the founder and main publicist of the *Amis des noirs,* later emerged as the leader of the Girondins, who drew their name from the Gironde, the province surrounding Bordeaux, and who represented both the liberal and commercial spirit of the port cities. On most of the issues of the early Revolution, Brissot's natural allies were Bordelais leaders like Gaudet, Gensonné, and Vergniaud. Like Brissot, such men favored reforms that promised to strengthen ties between the colonies and the mother country; in Bordeaux humanitarian fervor could even extend to the hope for an eventual emancipation of West Indian

[47] Gabriel Debien, *Les Colons de Saint-Domingue et la Révolution: Essai sur le club Massiac, Août 1789—Août 1792* (Paris, 1953), pp. 235–61; Debien, *Esprit colon et esprit d'autonomie, à Saint-Domingue au XVIIIᵉ siècle* (2nd ed., Paris, 1954), pp. 44–49; Philip D. Curtin, "The Declaration of the Rights of Man in Saint-Domingue, 1788–1791," *Hispanic American Historical Review,* XXX (May, 1950), 162–66; Mitchell B. Garrett, *The French Colonial Question, 1789–1791* (Ann Arbor, 1916), passim; C. L. R. James, *The Black Jacobins: Toussaint L'Ouverture and the San Domingo Revolution* (2nd rev. ed., New York, 1963), pp. 66–67; J. Saintoyant, *La Colonisation française pendant la révolution, 1789–1799* (2 vols., Paris, 1930), I, 94–99; II, 33.

[48] On the ideology of the Bordelais leaders, I am much indebted to Elizabeth Fox Genovese, who kindly let me read her unpublished study, "Social Origins of the Girondist Bourgeoisie."

slaves.[49] But on immediate colonial issues the artisans, workers, merchants, and professional men of the port cities formed a united front. Early in 1790 a delegation from Bordeaux's *armée patriotique*, giving expression to the popular will, informed the Paris Assembly and Jacobin Club that five million men depended on colonial commerce for their livelihood, and that both the slave trade and West Indian slavery were vital supports to national prosperity. Accordingly, until 1793 the slave trade continued to receive an official subsidy.[50]

As we have seen, the Constituent Assembly delegated West Indian affairs to a Committee on Colonies, charging it, like the Constitutional Convention's Committee of Detail, to submit a report defining constitutional powers and jurisdiction. Like the American Committee of Detail, the French Committee on Colonies represented both planter and commercial interests, and struck a compromise intended to mollify all parties except the abolitionists.[51]

The Committee, chaired by Antoine Pierre Barnave, took the risk of alienating the colonists when it endorsed the mercantilist system as "an essential condition of the union of metropolis and colonies." The colonial deputies had told the Assembly that their constituents were starving because France could not supply them with sufficient quantities of grain. Barnave conceded that justice might require further modifications in the prohibitive regime. But bowing to the demands from French merchants, his Committee insisted that requests for reform be submitted to the National Assembly for final decision.[52]

As compensation, however, the Committee would allow the colonists the right to draft constitutions for their own internal government, to be approved by the king and National Assembly. In the resolution that

[49] In February, the Assembly received an address from some two hundred electors in Bordeaux asking that the various nations with American colonies "s'acheminer vers l'affranchisement des Noirs." But a deputy from Bordeaux demanded that the address be withdrawn (*Patriote français*, No. CLXXXIV [Feb. 8, 1790], 3).

[50] *Ibid.*, No. CCIII (Feb. 27, 1790), 1; No. CCIV (Feb. 28, 1790), 2; *Journal des Etats Généraux*, VI, 276–77.

[51] For an analysis of the Committee's composition and competing interests, see Valerie Quinney, "Decisions on Slavery, the Slave-Trade and Civil Rights for Negroes in the Early French Revolution," *Journal of Negro History*, LV (1970), 118–27. Clearly Brissot had expected that Barnave would produce a much more liberal report (J. P. Brissot, *Lettre de J. P. Brissot à M. Barnave, sur ses rapports concernant les colonies . . .* [Paris, 1790], pp. 17–18, 28–29).

[52] Quinney, "Decisions on Slavery," p. 120.

so pleased Sir William Young, speaking to the British Parliament, the Committee disavowed any future interference with the slave trade. And finally, in a decree which all slaveholders would have liked to incorporate in their respective constitutions, the Committee branded as treasonous any attempt to incite uprisings against the colonists or their property. When Mirabeau and Pétion de Villeneuve tried to speak against this measure, which they saw aimed at the *Amis des noirs,* the Assembly shouted them down.[53]

The Assembly adopted the proposals of Barnave's Committee on March 8, 1790; on March 28 the *Amis* had their first opportunity to challenge constitutional concessions that would give colonists a free hand with race relations. Although the West Indians had already begun drafting constitutions, the National Assembly presumed that it could still issue instructions governing the initial elections. The Committee on Colonies had considered granting suffrage to "every citizen" —and in one draft, "without exception of color"—who owned sufficient property or paid taxes in his parish. But Article 4 of the instructions submitted to the Assembly said nothing of citizenship or color, referring simply to "toutes les personnes." In the floor debate, the Abbé Grégoire demanded that the ambiguity be resolved, adding that Arthur Dillon had assured him the phrase included free mulattoes who could meet the property qualifications. Chevalier de Cocherel, a deputy for St. Domingue, replied that Dillon might speak as he wished for Martinique, but certainly not for St. Domingue. Some of the West Indians favored dropping the clause altogether; others conveyed the impression that well-to-do mulattoes already enjoyed political rights. The Assembly voted to shut off discussion, but in the confusion many deputies interpreted the response to Grégoire's question to mean that qualified mulattoes would have the right to vote. Like the phrases

[53] *Archives parlementaires,* XII (March 8, 1790), 72–73; *Patriote français,* No. CCXIII (March 9, 1790), 3; Brissot, *Lettre . . . à M. Barnave,* p. 28. The planters later tried to persuade Barnave to institute legal proceedings against Grégoire, under the provision of the March 8 law, but Barnave refused (Ruth F. Necheles, *The Abbé Grégoire, 1788–1831: The Odyssey of an Egalitarian* [Westport, Conn., 1971], p. 82). Julien Raimond, the mulatto leader, later claimed that after the March 8 decree, "Grégoire, Pétion de Villeneuve, Brissot et Clavière sont les seuls qui ont continué à défendre notre cause avec un zèle incomparable" (A. Brette, "Le Gens de couleur libres et leurs députés en 1789," *La Révolution française,* XXIV [1895], 403).

"importation or migration" and "such persons," "toutes les personnes" was ambigious enough to satisfy the Assembly.[54]

In the West Indies, however, the white colonists had no intention either of giving the vote to mulattoes or of allowing France to set suffrage requirements. The St. Domingue planters would change their minds about mulattoes' rights after the slaves had burned most of the estates and cane fields on the rich north plain. But in 1790, when all the forces seemed to be working in their favor, the colonists would stand for no ambiguity about "toutes les personnes." In St. Domingue the *petits-blancs* rioted against property qualifications for voting, and demanded secession if any attempt were made to enfranchise the non-whites. In August, royal troops dispersed the assembly at St. Marc, after it had opened the island's ports to free trade without the governor's approval.[55] In October, Vincent Ogé, a mulatto associate of the *Amis des noirs,* arrived in Le Cap and appealed to the authorities to enforce Article 4 of the Assembly's instructions. Professing his support for the slave system, Ogé also claimed that the Assembly had intended "toutes les personnes" to eliminate racial disabilities. Ogé did not count on the force of principle; he had secured arms and munitions in the United States. Soon after attacking Le Cap, he and his followers were crushed, tortured, and executed. Ogé's martyrdom would make him a hero in Revolutionary France, as well as among the mulattoes of St. Domingue. But meanwhile the news of violence and insubordination had caused the Constituent Assembly to order the dissolution of the general assemblies of St. Domingue and Martinique. As an olive branch, the punitive decree of October 12 also promised that France would not interfere with the status of persons in the colonies.[56]

[54] *Archives parlementaires,* XII (March 28, 1790), 317, 383; *Patriote français,* No. CCXXXII (March 28, 1790), 2; Quinney, "Decisions on Slavery," pp. 125–27.

[55] Curtin, "Declaration of the Rights of Man," pp. 163–68; Garrett, *French Colonial Question,* pp. 59–63, 68, 74–76; James, *Black Jacobins,* pp. 72–73.

[56] J. P. Brissot, *Mémoires, publiés avec étude critique et notes par Cl. Perroud* (Paris, 1910), II, 96–97; Hippolyte Carnot, ed., *Mémories de Grégoire, ancien évêque de Blois* . . . (2 vols., Paris, 1840), I, 396; Brissot, *Lettre* . . . *à M. Barnave,* p. 13; Eloise Ellery, *Brissot de Warville: A Study in the History of the French Revolution* (Boston, 1915), pp. 202–3; Grégoire, *Lettre aux philanthropes, sur les malheurs, les droits et les réclamations des gens de couleur de Saint-Domingue* . . . (Paris, 1790), pp. 2–7.

By the spring of 1791 there was growing support for the mulatto petitioners in France and increasing turmoil in the colonies. As royal authority disintegrated in the West Indies, it fell upon the Constituent Assembly to enforce its own authority by dispatching troops and civil commissioners. Few deputies could question the need for such action, but disputes over the commissioners' instructions brought dangerous delay and finally an agreement on open debate. It was the issue of mulatto rights that finally moved colonial affairs outside committee control.[57]

The mulatto petitioners charged the white colonists with openly violating Article 4 of the Assembly's earlier instructions. Moreau de Saint-Méry, the distinguished jurist from Martinique who had briefly governed Paris after the fall of the Bastille, bitterly attacked the *Amis des noirs* and warned that France must either renounce its commerce and wealth, or frankly declare that the Declaration of the Rights of Man did not apply to the colonies. Defending a proposed constitution for the colonies submitted by four associated committees on imperial affairs, Moreau emphasized that West Indian conventions must have an unequivocal guarantee that the French National Assembly would never pass a law on the status of persons unless formally requested to do so by the colonists.[58] This provision, embodied in the proposed constitution, provoked heated debate on May 13, 1791. Amendments were offered to change "no law on the status of persons" to "no law on the status of persons not free," or "no law on the status of slaves." Jean François Rewbell, a radical Jacobin, proposed instead, "persons not free, other than those born of free mothers and fathers." Moreau

[57] *Patriote français,* No. DXCIV, supplément (March 25, 1791), 319–21; *Adresse de la Société des Amis des Noirs, à l'assemblée nationale, à toutes les villes de commerce, à toutes les manufactures, aux colonies, à toutes les Sociétés des Amis de la Constitution* (March, 1791), *passim;* (2nd ed., July, 1791), *passim.* Armand Gensonné, Brissot's Girondin colleague, claimed that even "l'opinion des Bordelais est fortement prononcée: ils regardent comme une dérogation improposable à la déclaration des droits, de priver les citoyens de couleur libres des droits imprescriptibles que leur assure leur qualité de citoyens; l'initiative que réclament les colons leur paroît également contraire aux droits et à l'interêt de la métropole" (*Lettres importantes, relatives à la question des citoyens de couleur,* [May (?) 1791], reprinted in *La Révolution française et l'abolition de l'esclavage* [12 vols., Paris, n.d.], IV).

[58] *Archives parlementaires,* XXV (May 7, 1791), 639–40; (May 11, 1791), 737–41; *Journal des Etats Généraux,* XXV, 389–436; *Patriote français,* No. DXCIV, supplément (March 25, 1791), p. 319.

now reminded the Assembly of the fatal effects produced by the ambiguity of "toutes personnes"; it would do to speak vaguely of "persons not free." The moment had arrived when it was essential to reassure the colonists with precise words which could leave no room for doubt. He then demanded that the Assembly decree, as a new constitutional article, that the national legislature could adopt no law "on the status of slaves" except upon the formal and spontaneous request of the colonial assemblies. This was exactly the guarantee South Carolina had wanted in the United States Constitution.[59]

But Moreau's proposal played into the hands of the more extreme radicals. Like many members of the Philadelphia Convention, Robespierre objected to the dishonor of using the word "slaves" in a constitution. In a flaming speech, he also hinted that secret enemies of the constitution were opposing the rights of Negroes as a means of subverting the Revolution. Echoing the rhetoric of the Abbé Raynal, he declared: "Eh! périssent, vos colonies si vous les conservez à ce prix (murmures . . . *oui, oui;* applaudi). Ou, s'il falloit ou perdre vos colonies, ou perdre votre bonheur, votre gloire, votre liberté, je répétcrois. périssent vos colonies (applaudi) !" After hearing Robespierre's speech, Moreau announced he would not quibble over words, so long as the meaning were understood, and withdrew his amendment to include "slaves."[60]

On May 14 the Assembly heard testimony from mulattoes on the evils of racial discrimination. Julien Raimond, the chief mulatto pamphleteer and activist, argued that granting rights to his people would help keep the slaves in their place. Like Brissot and Grégoire, the mulattoes disavowed any intention of weakening the slave system. But Viefville des Essars then offered a detailed plan for the total emancipation of all slaves over a period of sixteen years. And on May 15, despite warnings of insurrection and slaughter of the whites, the Assembly adopted by acclamation Rewbell's amendment that no law would be passed on the status of "persons not free, other than those born of free mothers and fathers." Few mulattoes could meet this requirement, but it represented a break in the color wall. The West

---

[59] *Journal des Etats Généraux,* XXVI, 14; *Archives parlementaires,* XXVI (May 13, 1791), 60; (May 15, 1791), 96–97.

[60] *Journal des Etats Généraux,* XXV, 484; *Archives parlementaires,* XXVI (May 13, 1791), 42–48, 60–61; Necheles, *Abbé Grégoire,* pp. 83–84.

Indian deputies stalked out of the Assembly and for a time considered returning to the colonies to promote secession and resistance.[61]

In the explanatory instructions sent to St. Domingue, the Assembly condemned slavery in principle but acknowledged that the Declaration of the Rights of Man could not be extended to bondsmen without producing the gravest evils; however, the children of free parents, regardless of color, should enjoy the full rights of citizenship. As might be expected, the white colonists saw the proceedings of May 15 as a betrayal of the Assembly's promise of October 12, 1790. There was talk of secession and alliance with England. But the slaves themselves had not been blind to the struggles between royalists and patriots, between mulattoes and *petits-blancs*. On the night of August 22, 1791, a pivotal date in the history of New World slavery, they began to burn and kill.[62]

The well-planned insurrection in the North Province might have settled the issue of mulattoes' rights and led to the restoration of French authority in the Caribbean. The mulattoes of St. Domingue's West Province made a show of force that soon won official approval of their demands, since the whites knew they needed mulatto support to suppress the slaves. In France, Brissot was as eager as were his Girondin friends in the new Legislative Assembly to send enough troops to crush the slaves, protect private property, and restore normal commercial relations with France. By late November, 1791, the leaders of the rebellious slaves, including Toussaint L'Ouverture, offered to surrender to the newly arrived French commissioners if freedom were promised to a few hundred of their friends. It was only the intran-

---

[61] Debien, *Les Colons de Saint-Domingue*, pp. 262–90; James, *Black Jacobins*, pp. 76–77; *Journal des Etats Généraux*, XXVI, 11–12, 14; *Archives parlementaires*, XXVI (May 14, 1791), 66–70; (May 15, 1791), 96–97; Garrett, *French Colonial Question*, p. 105; Saintoyant, *La Colonisation française*, I, 115–29, 316–20. Grégoire portrayed the May 15 decree as a triumphant turning point, and while he expressed the hope that free mulattoes and blacks of the West Indies would be loyal and peaceful patriots, he also told them not to forget that the slaves, "comme vous, ils naissent et demeurent libres et égaux," and predicted that: "un jour le soleil n'éclairera parmi vous que des hommes libres; les rayons de l'astre . . . ne tomberont plus sur des fers et des esclaves" (*Lettre aux citoyens de couleur et nègres libres de Saint-Domingue, et des autres îles françaises de l'Amérique* [Paris, 1791], pp. 11–12). Such rhetoric would have pleased the mulattoes no more than the white planters.

[62] Curtin, "The Declaration of the Rights of Man," p. 170; Theodore Lothrop Stoddard, *The French Revolution in San Domingo* (Boston, 1914), pp. 124–28; James, *Black Jacobins*, pp. 85–96.

sigence of the assembly at Le Cap that convinced Toussaint that his own freedom was inseparable from that of his brothers. Yet even by the following summer, when Toussaint had organized a more disciplined black army, the cause of the slaves seemed hopeless. No one could have dreamed that this aging ex-steward of livestock would soon be virtual master of the island.[63]

Meanwhile, the quickening of the French Revolution in the summer of 1791 had distracted attention from colonial affairs, further delaying the dispatch of troops. On September 23, a few days after the king had been forced to accept the constitution, Barnave told the retiring Constituent Assembly that relations with the colonies had been good until the May 15 decree had undermined confidence and led to disaster. On September 24 the Constituent Assembly responded to Barnave's plea and tried to backtrack again, renouncing jurisdiction over the status of persons in the colonies. The Assembly was unaware that the mulattoes of St. Domingue had already made an alliance with the wealthier whites and would soon sign a concordat guaranteeing their rights. The news of the Assembly's action aggravated the conflict between the mulattoes and *petits-blancs*. In the West Province, where the mulattoes felt betrayed and launched a war of racial vengeance, they themselves aroused the slaves to insurrection. In the South Province the outnumbered whites armed their slaves against the mulattoes.[64]

Barnave had blamed the insurrections on the May 15 decree and on the agitation of the *Amis des noirs*. The *Amis* replied that many colonists were guilty of treason and had precipitated violence as a pretext for English intervention. Even French merchants had second thoughts when they learned that St. Domingue planters had appealed for aid from the governor of Jamaica. By December 1, 1791, the new Legislative Assembly could no longer ignore the colonial crisis. Brissot, an influential member, had threatened to make his own report if none

---

[63] James, *Black Jacobins,* pp. 95–117; Ellery, *Brissot,* pp. 210–11. In 1791 the mulattoes' cause was considerably strengthened by the withdrawal of Barnave and the Feuillants from the Jacobin Club, by Brissot's election as president of the club, and by the spread of pro-mulatto sentiment among the provincial clubs, partly through the efforts of the Jacobins of Angers (*Adresse de la Société des Amis des Noirs, à l'assemblée nationale* [2nd ed., July, 1791], pp. 210–32).

[64] Debien, *Les Colons de Saint-Domingue,* pp. 326–31, 352–65; Garrett, *French Colonial Question,* pp. 127–33; James, *Black Jacobins,* pp. 96–103; Saintoyant, *La Colonisation française,* II, 55–74.

were forthcoming from the Colonial Committee. Now he delivered an eloquent speech, demanding repeal of the September 24 law and warning that slaves could be kept at work only if their natural guardians, the mulattoes, were kept content. The strengthened political voice of the *Amis des noirs* provoked proslavery speeches that rivaled those in the First United States Congress. But the collapse of the conservative Feuillants and the rise to power of the Girondins made it easier to repudiate earlier constitutional guarantees. In the spring of 1792 the Legislative Assembly nullified the previous nullification of September 24, and, overriding the precedents of the Constituent Assembly, proclaimed equal rights to all free Negroes and mulattoes, whose support now appeared essential for the colonies' pacification and defense.[65]

By September, 1792, events in France had moved at such a rapid pace that any colonial response could only be hopelessly out of phase. Having first been assured a degree of constitutional autonomy, the white colonists faced in September a French army of six thousand troops, many of them imbued with Jacobin principles, led by three Girondin-appointed commissioners carrying dictatorial powers. The most influential commissioner, Léger-Félicité Sonthonax, was in effect an agent of Brissot's. The latter's ascendancy in the Legislative Assembly appeared to ensure military enforcement of the racial policies of the *Amis des noirs*. These policies now drew increasing support from merchants ready to seek mulatto allies in order to subdue the slaves and prevent white planters from delivering the colony to England. But the *Amis,* in this moment of triumph, had ceased to exist. Brissot had become preoccupied with a European war of "liberation" and with preventing the French Revolution from becoming more radical. He had denounced Lafayette and the more conservative *Amis des noirs* as enemies of the state; he and the Girondins were increasingly regarded as counterrevolutionary traitors by Robespierre, the Mountain, and the *sans-culottes.* The Mountain included radical but proslavery planters who joined Robespierre in accusing Brissot of plotting to destroy the colonies or ready them for English seizure. The so-called

[65] *Patriote français,* No. DCCCXLIV (Dec. 2, 1791), 637; (Dec. 4, 1791), 645–46; Ellery, *Brissot,* pp. 209–14. On December 10, Mathieu Blancgilly offered a plan to free slaves who had worked at least four years under a present master, and to emancipate the remaining bondsmen after eight more years (*Archives parlementaires,* XXXV, 713–16).

second Revolution, beginning with the storming of the Tuileries and the calling of the National Convention, undermined the power of the Girondins. In November, 1792, the Jacobin Club expelled Brissot and the Girondin commissioners. The Convention demanded that the latter return to France, but the order went unheeded.[66]

In response to these events, the St. Domingue planters began fighting the commissioners, in the name of the deposed French king and with the support of mulatto troops. The planters collaborated with invading Spanish and then English armies. The French army, sent to suppress the slaves, thus became engaged in suppressing royalist whites and fighting foreign enemies. When Sonthonax faced annihilation after being driven by royalists out of Le Cap, he promised pardon and freedom to the slaves surrounding the city, who then took the opportunity to destroy the city and send the terrorized inhabitants fleeing to the United States. For a time, however, Toussaint and other black leaders wisely sided with the invading Spanish and claimed to fight for the crown of France. It was essential for the slaves to exploit the division of their enemies, since the Revolutionary government of France promised no more than political rights for mulattoes, and a planter-English alliance pointed to a restoration of the old regime. Then on August 29, 1793, shortly before the planters welcomed a British expeditionary force from Jamaica, Sonthonax played his last card and decreed the emancipation of the slaves.[67]

Britain and the United States, after 1792, offer no parallels to the French experience with slavery. One can hardly imagine a scene in Parliament or Congress like the one in the French Convention on June 4, 1793, when the president warmly greeted a manumitted Negro woman who was reputedly one-hundred-and-fourteen years old. Martial music celebrated the arrival of colored delegates from St. Domingue; and the Abbé Grégoire, who had risen to power in the new Convention, expressed an ardent hope for the total abolition of slavery. But though Grégoire succeeded in abolishing the bounty to

[66] Debien, *Les Colons de Saint-Domingue,* pp. 381–82; Ellery, *Brissot, passim; Patriote français,* No. DCCLXXVI (Sept. 25, 1791), 370; Necheles, *Grégoire,* pp. 113–16. The Massiac club had also dissolved by the summer of 1792, after the planters had lost most of their merchant allies.

[67] Saintoyant, *La Colonisation française,* II, 115–36; Stoddard, *French Revolution,* pp. 156–205, 227–35; James, *Black Jacobins,* pp. 118–44; Charles Oscar Hardy, *The Negro Question in the French Revolution* (Menasha, Wisc., 1919), pp. 71–72, 76, 79.

slave traders, the government still refused to end the trade itself. When the Convention finally enacted universal emancipation, on February 4, 1794, it was not because of antislavery agitation. In St. Domingue the blacks had gone far toward freeing themselves and had proved that they alone could save the colonies from English conquest—indeed, the emancipation decree arrived too late to save Martinique from capture. By February, 1794, the leading abolitionists had either fled France or been guillotined, like Brissot, along with Arthur Dillon and most of the defenders of colonial slavery. The Convention was so out of touch with West Indian affairs that René Levasseur expressed astonishment when three delegates from St. Domingue, including one black and one mulatto, reported that there were still slaves in the French Caribbean. Levasseur's demand for immediate emancipation won enthusiastic acclaim. Danton, soon to be executed himself, predicted that future generations would find their glory in this decree of universal liberty. On 30 *Pluviôse,* year II of the Republic, the French celebrated the event in Notre Dame, now the Temple of Reason. Anaxagoras Chaumette, the attorney general of Paris, embraced colored citizens; someone raised a Negro child high in the air as the drums rolled and the soldiers marched. With tears in their eyes the people lifted the arms of the colored citizens and shouted "Vive la République! Vive la France!" Eight years later Napoleon Bonaparte would resolve to reenslave colonial Negroes and would send an army to crush Toussaint L'Ouverture.[68]

Expansion and Constraint

As we have seen, slavery proved to be a dangerously divisive issue in the assemblies of Britain, France, and the United States. The premises of antislavery philosophy were much the same in the three countries, but acquired quite different implications when adapted to the interests of a Wilberforce, a Brissot, or a Gouverneur Morris. Slave-

---

[68] *Archives parlementaires,* LXVI, 56–57; LXIX, 580; LXXXIV, pp. 283–84; [Pierre Gaspard] Chaumette, *Discours sur l'abolition de l'esclavage, prononcé par Anaxagoras Chaumette, au nom de la commune de Paris* (Paris, 1794), pp. 40–42; *Décret de la Convention Nationale . . . qui abolit l'esclavage des nègres dans les colonies,* reprinted in *La Révolution françaises et l'abolition de l'esclavage,* XII. Grégoire, who in 1794 was virtually the only member of the *Amis* still in power, later termed the emancipation decree "une mesure désastreuse: elle était en politique ce qu'est en physique un volcan" (*Mémoires,* I, 391).

holders shared a common determination to resist the slightest infringements on their property rights, even if this required renouncing allegiance to a national government. Yet the secessionist impulse was credible only in the United States, where southern delegates represented a substantial white population capable of fending for itself. In Britain and France the planter class drew temporary support from alliances with commercial interests, particularly those connected with the African trade. By 1787, New England's commercial interests were not significantly tied to the slave trade, but they gave the Deep South sufficient reinforcement to postpone prohibition and to gain an implicit Constitutional sanction for slavery. The various alliances between planters and merchants involved more than advantageous trade-offs: they rested on a common respect for the rights of property and a common fear of genuine revolution, especially after the slaves of St. Domingue had dramatized the meaning of revolution. In the 1790s the assemblies of all three countries styled themselves as temples of liberty, but tried to reassure planters by issuing formal statements denying or relinquishing any power to alter the status of slaves.

Yet controversy continued over the precise limits of governmental jurisdiction. If the United States Constitution gave slaveholders important protections, it could also be interpreted as granting Congress powers that were broad and flexible enough to ensure eventual emancipation throughout the nation. The significant point is that the South's social structure provided the political strength to block undesirable legislation. In contrast, British planters had to rely on the inertia and conservatism of the metropolitan social order, whose preservation might for a time be linked to the well-being of the Old Colonial System, but might ultimately depend on the social order's own adaptability to middle-class reforms. The looser British constitution provided slaveholders little protection from future encroachments as their economic power waned. French planters, like their British counterparts, relied less on the populousness of the colonies than on their economic importance to the mother country. But like the North American slaveholders, the French colonists sought to exploit a revolutionary situation in order to gain a degree of autonomy and fixed guarantees protecting their property. The National Assembly's vacillation in defining its jurisdiction over the status of mulattoes brought a loss of confidence which aggravated separatist impulses and fostered internal conflicts within the colonies. The relative stability and continuity of the British and American governments enabled British and American slavery to survive the Age of Revolution. But the institution itself proved too unstable to survive the extreme discontinuities of the French Revolution. It would appear, then, that while the political response to slavery followed roughly similar patterns in Britain, France, and the United States, the crucial differences arose from the opportunities available to the slaveholding classes, and from the constitutional structures that defined their rights and ultimate power.

These conclusions may gain added meaning if we glance briefly at subsequent efforts to promote or contain the expansion of Negro slavery. After 1800, French policy made it clear that the emancipation proclamation of 1794 had been an aberration signifying neither the growth of powerful antislavery opinion nor the emergence of a capitalist class bent on univeralizing the benefits of free labor. By the Peace of Amiens, in 1802, the principal question for France was whether something could be salvaged from the wreckage of her West Indian colonies. Inspired by grandiose visions of a new American tropical empire, Napoleon had already pressured Spain into secretly ceding Louisiana to France; as soon as preliminary peace arrangements had been signed, he sent a great armada and more than twenty thousand men to restore French authority in the Caribbean. For Napoleon there was to be no further nonsense about colonial constitutions extending the universal principles of the French Revolution. In 1801, Toussaint L'Ouverture had published a constitution for St. Domingue which not only prohibited slavery forever and made himself governor for life, but combined an allegiance to France with a denial of French authority to govern the island.[69] Napoleon's plan called for a period of seeming conciliation, during which black and mulatto leaders would be arrested and deported to France. After the unruly masses had been subdued, they would be re-enslaved, and the African trade would be restored.

French troops overwhelmed the rebels of Guadeloupe, where Victor Hugues, after defeating the English with a racially mixed army, had carried out the earlier emancipation decree under a dictatorial regime.

---

[69] *Constitution de la colonie française de Saint-Domingue, du 17 Août (29 Thermidor an 9)*, reprinted in *La Révolution française et l'abolition de l'esclavage*, XI. Article II begins: "Il ne peut exister d'esclave sur ce territoire; la servitude y est à jamais abolie. Tous les hommes y naissent, vivent et meurent libres et français." This turned out to be a rather empty guarantee.

Martinique presented few problems, since the island had been held in trust, as it were, by the British. During the later Napoleonic wars the British would again seize Martinique and Guadeloupe, ensuring the further stability of their slave systems until such time as the colonies would finally be restored to Bourbon France. The British had failed, however, to wrest St. Domingue from the mulattoes and the emancipated blacks who had fought alongside the French republican armies. By 1800, Toussaint had slowly eliminated white power in St. Domingue. He had also tried to reassure white settlers of his own good will and of his dependence on France, assuming that France made no attempt to reinstitute the old colonial regime. Toussaint's faith in compromise, unfortunately for him, helped to divide his followers and ultimately led to his capture. Only a few black leaders like Jean Jacques Dessalines recognized that French promises were as temporary as the Convention's decree of universal emancipation, although the truth became clear when news arrived from Guadeloupe that both slavery and the color line had been re-established. As for St. Domingue, as a result of the heroic resistance of black and mulatto troops, aided in the end by yellow fever, Napoleon's generals were not able to subdue the island before the resumption of war with England cut off both supplies and retreat.[70]

The triumph of Dessalines, the ex-slave founder of Haiti, makes it impossible to know what questions of jurisdiction might have been raised by the expansion of French slavery in the New World. The French Revolution had opened the way for the destruction of the world's richest slave colony and for the first large-scale emancipation. The ensuing reaction stifled all further attempts at reform. At the end of the Napoleonic period there was little French protest against the reopening of the African slave trade. With no opportunity for expansion, slavery would nevertheless persist in the remaining French colonies until the Revolution of 1848.

The United States had been closely involved with the fate of St.

[70] James, *Black Jacobins, passim.* On the assumption that blacks could never have won their own independence, white historians have commonly attributed the French defeat to yellow fever. No doubt Haitian independence, like that of the United States and the Latin American republics, depended on a variety of circumstances. But if the black population had been easily subdued, the yellow-fever epidemic would have made little difference. Both sides knew that the fever would come, like the tropical rain, but only the blacks used the knowledge to their own advantage.

Domingue. The American Revolution had not only opened the way for a brisk trade that supported the sugar boom of the 1780s, but had given military experience to St. Domingue mulattoes fighting with the French armies. In the late 1790s, during the undeclared naval war with France, American ships supplied and openly aided Toussaint. It is doubtful whether Haitian independence could have been achieved without American arms and provisions, although in 1803 American opportunism also helped supply Napoleon's troops. Under growing pressure from France, the United States finally placed an embargo, in 1806, on commerce with the rebellious black republic, whose continuing survival threatened the security of all slaveholding regimes. By then, however, there was no danger that France would colonize Louisiana as a supplier of provisions for her tropical empire.[71]

France's abandonment of Louisiana forced the United States to confront questions of governmental sanction and jurisdiction in their clearest terms. The central issue, as William L. Yancey later told the Democratic Party at its stormy convention in April, 1860, was whether the Constitution, framed to protect minorities, could prevent the government from discriminating against slaveholders in the competitive settlement of the West. Yancey's position, which drew support from the Dred Scott decision, was that slaves should be accorded the same status as other kinds of property; to bar them from any part of the public domain was invidious injustice and a violation of fundamental law.[72]

There is no need to review the complex history of this problem, except to identify the major contrasts between French, American, and British experience.[73] By the 1780s the populations of the North and South were roughly equal, and there was a general expectation that migration would move on latitudinal lines, extending westward the customs and institutions of the seaboard states. Seven of the original

---

[71] For relations between Haiti and the United States, see James G. Leyburn, *The Haitian People* (New Haven, 1941), *passim;* Ludwell Lee Montague, *Haiti and the United States, 1714–1938* (Durham, N.C., 1940), *passim;* Robinson, *Slavery in the Structure of American Politics,* pp. 361–77; Linda K. Kerber, *Federalists in Dissent; Imagery and Ideology in Jeffersonian America* (Ithaca, N.Y., 1970), pp. 43–49.

[72] *Speech of the Hon. William L. Yancey of Alabama, Delivered to the National Democratic Convention, Charleston, April 28, 1860.*

[73] For more detailed treatment, see Robinson, *Slavery in the Structure of American Politics,* pp. 378–423; and Robert R. Russel, "Constitutional Doctrine with Regard to Slavery in Territories," *Journal of Southern History,* XXXII (Nov., 1966), 466–86.

states had legal claims on much of the trans-Appalachian territory. To many Northerners it seemed only natural that Kentucky, which had long been an extension of Virginia, should be admitted as a new slave state in 1792. At that time neither New York nor New Jersey had taken steps to abolish slavery, and even Pennsylvania's emancipation act had not yet freed a single Negro. When North Carolina and Georgia finally ceded their western lands to the federal government, it was with the stipulation that slavery be permitted in the relinquished territories. In 1790, Congress omitted any mention of slavery when it enacted provisions for the territorial government of the Southwest.

We do not know precisely why southern representatives in the Continental Congress accepted the clause in the Ordinance of 1787 prohibiting slavery from the territory north of the Ohio River. Earlier proposals to exclude slavery from all the territories had had no chance of success and do not indicate, as has sometimes been alleged, any realistic expectation that the institution could be confined to the original states.[74] Perhaps Staughton Lynd is right in suspecting a

[74] The political maneuvering behind the Ordinance of 1784, which has been termed "the foundation stone of American territorial policy," is still shrouded in mystery. Robert F. Berkhofer, Jr., has recently argued that Jefferson was less responsible for the central provisions, embodied in Congressional committee reports of March, 1784, than scholars have commonly assumed ("Jefferson, the Ordinance of 1784, and the Origins of the American Territorial System," *William and Mary Quarterly*, 3rd ser., XXIX [April, 1972], 231–62). As chairman of the Congressional committee that drafted preliminary and revised plans for temporary government of the western territories, Jefferson endorsed and ultimately voted (on April 19) for a provision prohibiting slavery in any of the new states after 1800. The idea had earlier been proposed by Timothy Pickering, of Massachusetts, and "was a reform," in Berkhofer's words, "as dear to [David] Howell as to Jefferson."

Howell, a lawyer from Rhode Island, was a member of the three-man committee and played a leading role in drafting the Ordinance. Howell was also a close associate of Moses Brown, the Rhode Island philanthropist and antislavery leader, who loaned Howell money when Congress ran short of funds and suspended salaries. Howell kept Brown posted on the affairs of Congress, and solicited advice, especially regarding territorial policy and the interests of his Rhode Island constituents. But curiously, Howell made no mention of slavery, although on November 6, 1782, he referred to the probable cession of state claims to western territories and reported a "good prospect of carrying the most important points I have been labouring after" (Howell to Brown, Nov. 6, 1782, Moses Brown papers, IV, 945, 1005, Rhode Island Historical Society [hereafter RIHS]). On May 3, 1784, Brown apologized for not answering Howell's letter of August 24, 1783, and then hastened to add that "I was glad to find you were so thoughtful of Liberty as to prevent Slavery in the new States 16 years hence, I wish the old ones might be engaged no longer to abridge its black Inhabitants of those rights which they have so long been contending for, I mean liberty. Couldn't thou be Instrumental of prohibiting any further Importation from Africa, it would I believe be an acceptable service and cause of harmony with thy own better feelings notwithstanding some may be opposed to such a measure who ought to shew forth a better example." After referring to recent laws passed by Rhode Island and Connecticut, Brown added: "Could Virginia be induced to free their best Interest & give a Specimen of this touchstone of real Liberty it would I believe be happy for their Posterity & to their great Honour. Has Gen.¹ Washington free'd his Negroes or has he not? Can slave holders be Members of the Cincinnati & transmit testimonies of their being guardians to Liberty & expect the Hereditary Honours from their Country? This will indeed be a Paradox to Posterity" (Brown to Howell, May 3, 1784, Brown papers, RIHS).

Although Brown attributed this outburst to "nervous Fatigue," his letter reveals how isolated he was from national politics, though he was one of the wealthiest men in New England and a key coordinator of antislavery activity. On questions of territorial policy, the abolitionists could not begin to rival the lobbyists of the various land companies. And in Congress, it is clear that many other issues took precedence over slavery, particularly the need to reduce friction between the states that had claims to western land and the states that had none; the desire of the "landed" states to prevent private speculators from challenging the titles of previous land grants; and above all, the urgency of establishing a plan for the temporary government of the West before settlers could have a chance to secede. It is possible that the proposal to exclude slavery was part of a larger political strategy, or that it was intended to put pressure on the states south of Virginia which had not yet outlawed the importation of slaves from Africa.

In any event, Congress voted to delete the antislavery measure on April 19, 1784, two weeks before Brown congratulated Howell. The committee's proposal to outlaw slavery after the year 1800 lost by a single vote. Passage required the assent of seven of the ten states whose delegates were present. Six of the northern states approved the measure, and New Jersey would have added the critical seventh vote if one of its delegates, John Beatty, had not been ill. Jefferson and Hugh Williamson, of North Carolina, were the only southern delegates who voted in favor of the prohibition (see Julian P. Boyd, ed., *The Papers of Thomas Jefferson* [Princeton, 1950—], VI, 603–12; VII, 118).

Superficially, it appeared that Congress had come within a single vote of permanently confining slavery to the southern seaboard states. But though Virginia had just ceded her land claims north of the Ohio, none of the states had yet ceded territory south of the Ohio. The South thus retained considerable bargaining power on the question of slavery in the territories. Jefferson expressed disappointment over the outcome of the Congressional vote, but his correspondence is remarkably silent on the subject of barring slavery from the West.

In 1785, Rufus King ran into stiffer opposition when he offered a plan providing for the return of fugitives from the territories in exchange for an immediate exclusion of slaves (*Journals of the Continental Congress,* XXVI, 119, 247; XXVIII, 164). Nathan Dane, who proposed the exclusion clause in the Northwest Ordinance, had not expected it to be accepted and was evidently surprised by the sudden shift in southern policy (E. C. Burnett, ed., *Letters of Members of the Continental Congress* [Washington, 1921–1938], VIII, 622).

secret bargain in which the North won exclusion of slavery from the Northwest as the price for the three-fifths clause in the Constitution which the Convention adopted the day before Congress agreed to the antislavery ordinance. The South would have had still other motives for such an agreement. The Northwest Ordinance tacitly implied that there would be no opposition to the extension of slavery south of the Ohio. In general, Southerners had good reason for believing they would benefit from rapid settlement of the West, even if legislative encouragement required a moral concession to those who feared an agricultural alliance against northeastern commerce. If the federal government succeeded in protecting American commercial rights in Spanish New Orleans, planters could count on the Mississippi river system to knit the trans-Appalachian area into a cohesive economic unit. On the other hand, the Northwest Ordinance, which the new Congress re-enacted, set a precedent for barring slavery from prescribed areas.[75]

Some qualifications should be added to the current view of the South as initially committed to the westward expansion of slavery and the aggrandizement of political power. In 1787 no one could foresee the importance of cotton cultivation or anticipate that the American slave population would increase by more than one million in the first three decades of the nineteenth century. In both England and America abolitionists contended that ending the slave trade would reduce the density of slave populations and permit various ameliorative reforms. In 1798, when Congress debated a motion to extend the Northwest exclusion clause to Mississippi Territory, William Giles expressed a common variant on this thesis: "If the slaves of the Southern States were permitted to go into this Western country, by lessening the number in those States, and spreading them over a large surface of country, there would be a greater probability of ameliorating their condition, which could never be done whilst they were crowded together as they now are in the Southern States."[76] However credible

[75] Staughton Lynd, "The Compromise of 1787," *Political Science Quarterly,* LXXXI (June, 1966), 225–50; Duncan MacLeod, "Racial Attitudes in Revolutionary and Early National America," D.Phil. thesis, Cambridge, 1969, pp. 70–72. Congress was in session in New York City and the Convention in Philadelphia. There were close contacts between the two bodies, but I am inclined to doubt the notion of a definite bargain, since it is likely that later controversies would have brought it into the open.

[76] *Annals of Congress,* 5th Cong., 2nd Sess., 1309. In 1798 it was possible to

in 1798, this notion was far less convincing by 1804, when various Senators voiced alarm over the increase in slaves shown by the censuses of 1790 and 1800. In 1798, however, there were no official statistics to contradict the widespread assumption that Georgia's prohibition of further slave importations would result in a relatively stable Negro population.

Nevertheless, even in 1798, some southern Congressmen made it clear that on the question of slavery in the territories, two philosophies were at war. They could not tolerate any provision that would restrict the Southwest to settlers who brought no slaves. Even Albert Gallatin, who argued that Congress had a perfect right to prohibit a practice that would be detrimental in the long run to the happiness of the people, acknowledged that present settlers who had arrived under the laws of England, Spain, or Georgia, could not with justice be deprived of their property. And if Congress could not interfere with the slave property already brought into a given territory, how could it prevent future settlers from moving in with their bondsmen?[77]

This question would confound American politics for two generations to come, but the first crisis arose in 1804, as a result of the collapse of French power in the Caribbean. As we shall see in a moment, the same circumstance presented England with a similar problem and a similar turning point, but with consequences vastly different. Unlike the territories east of the Mississippi, Louisiana was free from the land claims of seaboard states and was beyond the reach of the ordinances that had made the Ohio river a dividing line between supposedly free and slave soil. President Jefferson's purchase of the immense and uncharted territory claimed by France, which doubled the area of the United States, raised Constitutional issues never contemplated by the Convention of 1787. Theoretically, since the Constitution granted Congress the power "to dispose of and make all needful Rules and Regulations respecting the Territory or other Property belonging to the United States," Louisiana might have been

---

consider such a motion because Georgia did not cede the territory until 1802, and the claims of the United States rested on treaties with England and Spain. The inhabitants of Natchez had appealed for territorial status.

[77] *Ibid.*, pp. 1306–10. Duncan MacLeod points out that Congress took no steps to free the slaves already living in the northwestern territory, but rather assured white settlers that the Northwest Ordinance applied only to the future introduction of new slaves ("Racial Attitudes," pp. 72–73).

governed for a time as a kind of crown colony, where experiments with labor reform could have served as a yardstick for the existing states. The Senate in fact insisted that the territorial legislature be appointed by the President and not elected by the inhabitants, in the belief that the inhabitants had had no training in self-government. On the other hand, the treaty of purchase guaranteed the white inhabitants equal citizenship, recognized their titles to slave property under French and Spanish law, and promised early admission to the Union. Louisiana contained, in 1803, more than sixteen thousand slaves. The number had been considerably augmented by refugees from the French Caribbean who had greatly stimulated Louisiana's production of sugar.[78]

No one seriously challenged the government's right to exclude new slaves from Louisiana, although northeastern Federalists did challenge the wisdom and Constitutionality of the purchase. No one seriously questioned the right of present inhabitants to retain their slaves. But the fear of black rebels from the French Caribbean brought overwhelming support for Senator James Hillhouse's motion to prohibit foreign slaves from being imported into Louisiana. In response to South Carolina's reopening of the African trade, the Senate also agreed to Hillhouse's proposal to exclude all Negroes who had been brought into the United States since 1798, at which time Georgia had stopped legal importation.[79] It is remarkable, in view of the South's adamant stand in 1807, that the Senate decided that slaves illicitly taken to Louisiana should be freed. This measure may also have been a slap at South Carolina, whose Senators were not present for the vote.[80] Even many Northerners thought that Hillhouse went too far,

[78] Ulrich Bonnell Phillips, *American Negro Slavery* (Gloucester, Mass., reprint ed., 1959), pp. 164–65; Robinson, *Slavery in the Structure of American Politics*, pp. 392–97.

[79] Everett S. Brown, ed., "The Senate Debate on the Breckinridge Bill for the Government of Louisiana, 1804," *American Historical Review*, XXII (1917), 340–64; Brown, *The Constitutional History of the Louisiana Purchase, 1803–1812* (Berkeley, 1920), *passim*.

[80] Robinson, *Slavery in the Structure of American Politics*, p. 398. On the other hand, Robert Goodloe Harper, of South Carolina, had proposed an amendment in 1798 to emancipate any slaves illegally smuggled into Mississippi territory. Robinson suggests that Southerners may have thought that this provision, a "peace-offering" to philanthropists, would also make the law unenforceable (*ibid.*, p. 313). But one must then explain why the South failed to adopt similar tactics in 1807. One should bear in mind that some South Carolinians had an interest

however, when he then moved that no slave brought into Louisiana in the future could be sold or held in servitude for more than one year. Congress had received strong memorials against the expansion of slavery into Louisiana; leaders from all sections were aware of the issue's broad significance. But Hillhouse, as a Connecticut Federalist, was subject to the suspicion of trying to impede the growth of the West. Other northern Federalists thought it unwise to risk an explosive debate on slavery. Stephen Bradley, the Vermont Republican who would sponsor the 1807 law prohibiting the slave trade, said he had done everything in his power to keep the question from being raised. Bradley assured the Senate he considered slavery "as a moral evil—as a violation of the laws of God—of nature—of Vermont," and even quoted Exodus on manstealers deserving to die. But he voted, along with both Senators from Massachusetts, with the South.[81]

In the end, the Senate accepted Hillhouse's compromise proposal to restrict the importation of slaves to the bona-fide property of actual settlers. Though opposed by Virginia, this measure drew support from South Carolina and Georgia, both of which had enacted similar regulations to avoid becoming a dumping ground for Virginia's unruly blacks. If we are to see the law in perspective, we should remember that most of the slaves who moved westward did so with their masters. In any event, the law was unenforceable and was soon interpreted to mean that South Carolinians could bring in slaves who had recently arrived from Africa.[82]

In effect, then, slavery could expand into Louisiana as freely as into Mississippi. This decision was the logical outcome of two premises the government had long accepted: that slaves were legitimate property; and that territories, being an extension of the nation, should be equally open to all citizens. If the Northwest Ordinance contradicted the last premise, there would soon be strong pressure for the Ordi-

---

in retaining control over southwestern slave markets, and that their fear of insurrection led to drastic measures against smuggling slaves into their own state (Brady, "Slave Trade and Sectionalism," p. 611).

[81] Brown, "Senate Debate on the Breckinridge Bill," pp. 340–64. Many northern Federalists still counted on a continuing alliance with the Deep South against the West, and even hoped to provoke the West into secession (James M. Banner, Jr., *To the Hartford Convention: The Federalists and the Origins of Party Politics in Massachusetts, 1789–1815* [New York, 1970], p. 112).

[82] Phillips, *American Negro Slavery*, p. 165. On slaves migrating with their masters, see Fogel and Engerman, *Time on the Cross*, I, 44–52.

nance's suspension in Indiana, where in 1807 the territorial legislature concocted a legal subterfuge to attract the settlement of slaveholders. Although proslavery movements ultimately failed in Indiana and Illinois, it was evident well before the Missouri crisis that slavery would not only be permitted to expand westward, enjoying the same protections it had in the original southern states, but that it would become the key to the sectional balance of power.[83]

As we have suggesed, French defeats in the Caribbean presented Britain with very similar problems. It was imperative to prevent black revolution from spreading to Jamaica and the other established colonies; military conquest opened enormous areas of virgin land, especially in Trinidad and the former Dutch colonies on the Guiana Coast. Having acquired considerable experience in imperial management, Britain denied the newly won colonies any right to legislative self-government. In the interest of security and centralized control, the crown colonies of Trinidad, St. Lucia, Essequibo, Demerara, and Berbice were to be governed directly by Orders-in-Council, administered by royal governors and nominated councils which the governors could overrule. With the exception of Tobago, which had a precedent of English representative government, the new territories joined the empire on a completely different footing from that of the older sugar colonies.

In 1805, William Pitt, the prime minister, took action somewhat similar to that of the United States regarding Louisiana. An Order-in-Council prohibited the importation of foreign slaves into the captured or ceded colonies, and restricted the annual introduction of any slaves to 3 per cent of the existing slave populations. At first the older colonies stood to gain by this discrimination. The prohibition of the African slave trade to the captured colonies gave a competitive advantage to land-hungry planters in the older islands who wished to migrate with their blacks to the frontier lands. Accordingly, the internal Caribbean slave trade could bring rich profits, although the older colonies soon began to fear overproduction of tropical staples and a fatal reduction in the price of sugar. Moreover, Britain, unlike the United States, successfully restricted the intercolonial traffic, so that only in Trinidad, and there for a brief period, did the inflow check the general decline in slave population after 1817. In Trinidad the labor

[83] MacLeod, "Racial Attitudes," pp. 74–87.

shortage grew so acute that some planters turned to Chinese immigrants or even to free blacks who had served in the imperial armies or been taken from America in the War of 1812. An equally serious threat appeared when antislavery leaders persuaded Spencer Perceval's Ministry to use the crown colonies as models for social experimentation.[84]

The West Indian legislatures had always conceded Parliament's right to regulate imperial trade, but had insisted on their own constitutional jurisdiction over internal affairs. The crown colonies, however, could not appeal to such arguments. In 1812, the planters of Trinidad expressed outrage when they received an Order-in-Council requiring the registration of all slaves and stipulating that, in the future, any unregistered Negro would be presumed to be free. The justification for the order fell within the realm of regulating commerce. To prevent the illegal importation of Negroes, it was argued, there had to be accurate records of all existing slaves. Yet as the West Indian planters clearly saw, a centrally administered registration would publicize statistics on slave mortality and provide the mechanism for government intervention and a wide variety of reforms. In 1815, when Wilberforce introduced a bill in the Commons for the registration of all slaves in the legislative colonies, the West Indian assemblies desperately appealed to the crown, warning that their constitutional liberties were in jeopardy. Reminding Parliament of its resolution of 1778 renouncing any future attempt to levy direct taxes on the colonies, they pointed to the fees that would be required by the Registration Bill, and hinted that the United States had rebelled against similar acts of despotism. But given the lesson of St. Domingue and the declining white population of the West Indies, British officials knew that secession was an empty threat.[85]

[84] Murray, *The West Indies and the Development of Colonial Government,* pp. 47–66; Lowell Joseph Ragatz, *The Fall of the Planter Class in the British Caribbean, 1763–1833* (New York, 1928), pp. 279, 292, 326–83; [Stephen], *Crisis of the Sugar Colonies, passim;* Henry Brougham, *An Inquiry into the Colonial Policy of the European Powers* (2 vols., Edinburgh, 1803), *passim;* Robert Isaac Wilberforce and Samuel Wilberforce, *The Life of William Wilberforce* (5 vols., London, 1838), II, 259–63; D. Eltis, "The Traffic in Slaves between the British West Indian Colonies, 1807–1833," *Economic History Review,* XXV (Feb. 1972), 55–64.

[85] *Seventh Report of the Directors of the African Institution, Read at the Annual General Meeting on the 24th of March, 1813* (London, 1813), pp. 45–83; Murray, *The West Indies and the Development of Colonial Government,* pp.

The abolitionists, who had won the ear of the government, argued that it was impossible to separate the power of regulating trade, as expressed in the slave-trade abolition law of 1807, from the internal regulations required for the law's enforcement. In 1824, Chief Justice John Marshall would point to a similar conclusion when he defined the power of Congress to regulate commerce *among* the several states as a power "not to be confined by state lines, but [which] acts upon its subject matter wherever it is to be found." As we have seen, the Senate had presumed in 1804 that the federal government could free slaves who had been illicitly imported into Louisiana. But given the strength of the South in the federal government, slaveholders had little reason to fear administrative encroachments at the hands of a hostile power. Indeed, in 1820 a Congressman from Georgia even proposed a national registry of slaves as a means of preventing illegal importation. Although John Randolph thought that the plan would dangerously enhance the powers of the central government, the Georgian apparently assumed that a national registry would be no more dangerous than a registry controlled by Georgia.[86]

Britain's Parliament had no intention of abandoning the imperial supremacy it had announced in the Declaratory Act of 1766. But the stormy debates over the Registration Bill of 1815 may have encouraged the slaves of Barbados to take matters into their own hands, since early the next year they burned many plantations and laid the cane fields as bare and black as those of St. Domingue's north plain. In response, Lord Bathurst, the colonial secretary, persuaded Wilberforce to withdraw his bill in order to give the West Indian legislatures an opportunity to save face by enacting registration laws of their own.

The history of British slavery from 1816 to 1833 proved Bathurst's hopes to be wrong. The West Indian legislatures drafted ineffective registration laws which were, of course, administered by slaveholding colonists. By 1823, antislavery leaders saw the necessity for Parliament's direct reform of the colonial slave codes in order to prepare the way for gradual emancipation. Bathurst followed the previous strategy of recommending to the colonies specific ameliorative measures which had been endorsed in principle by the House of Commons. In 1824

67–108; R. L. Schuyler, "The Constitutional Claims of the British West Indies," *Political Science Quarterly,* XL (March, 1925), 17–29.

[86] *Annals of Congress,* 16th Cong., 1st Sess., 925–26.

the government reinforced attempts at persuasion by an Order-in-Council designed to make Trinidad's slave code a model for the other colonies to follow. Again, West Indian assemblies talked of Parliamentary despotism, constitutional liberties, and the possibility of rebellion. But even with the leverage of the crown colony system and the doctrine of reserved transcendent power, the British government failed to pressure the slaveholding colonists into adopting meaningful reforms. When emancipation came, it was an act of coercive power, of sheer Parliamentary supremacy, softened, to be sure, by the award of monetary compensation. By 1833, the West Indians had been virtually stripped of indirect representation in Parliament, and their defeat signaled the eventual end of their own representative institutions.[87]

If any broad conclusion can be drawn from the British experience, it is that plantation slavery, even when declining economically, could not be ameliorated or gradually abolished by indirect means. Yet two striking achievements may in part be credited to the British policy of recommendation, warning, and example. First, in contrast to the United States, Britain successfully limited the growth of slavery in the "frontier" lands of Trinidad and Guiana, though at the expense of the colonies' economic development. The crown colony system encouraged both planters and statesmen to look to Asia and Africa for cheap sources of nominally free labor, but it also reduced the relative political power of the West Indian colonies. Hence the growth of the plantation labor force could not have the divisive consequences, even on a minor scale, that it had in the United States. Second, because of the gradual weakening of the white power structure in the West Indies, the British government could support the demands of the free colored population, using the crown colonies as models for removing legal barriers of discrimination. This achievement meant that before the slaves had been emancipated, Britain had moved far toward resolving the problem that had destroyed French authority in St. Domingue.[88]

---

[87] See especially Schuyler, *Parliament and the British Empire*, pp. 117–93; Mary Reckord, "The Colonial Office and the Abolition of Slavery," *Historical Journal*, XIV (Dec., 1971), 723–34; Murray, *The West Indies and the Development of Colonial Government*, pp. 146–204; David Brion Davis, "James Cropper and the British Anti-Slavery Movement, 1823–1833," *Journal of Negro History*, XLVI (July, 1961), 154–73.

[88] Charles H. Wesley, "The Emancipation of the Free Colored Population in the British Empire," *Journal of Negro History*, XIX (April, 1934), 137–70.

In retrospect, it appears that a few radical abolitionists had more insight into the nature and tendencies of slavery than did the Pitts and Jeffersons who expressed confidence that gradual progress would obviate the need for decisive national action. From any realistic viewpoint, to be sure, it was clear that in the period from 1770 to 1820 abolitionists had little chance of persuading any of the three national governments to take the direct and forceful action necessary to remedy the injustices of Negro slavery. Yet abolitionist doctrine had helped to fuse conflicts in value with specific conflicts of interest, making slavery a testing ground for disputes over representation, jurisdiction, and the limitation of power. If there had been no abolitionists, the injustices of slavery, which mankind had tolerated for several millennia, would hardly have seemed a serious problem.

Four

The Boundaries of Idealism

Introduction

By the eve of the American Revolution there was a remarkable convergence of cultural and intellectual developments which at once undercut traditional rationalizations for slavery and offered new modes of sensibility for identifying with its victims. Negro slavery had been morally condemned by figures as diverse as John Woolman, Denis Diderot, and John Wesley; its legality had been publicly debated in Jamaica as well as in Cambridge, Massachusetts.

"Antislavery" is a vague and flexible concept. It has been used to describe an organized social force; political activity aimed at eradicating the slave trade or slavery itself; a set of moral and philosophic convictions that might be held with varying intensities; or simply the theoretical belief that Negro slavery is a wasteful, expensive, and dangerous system of labor which tends to corrupt the morals of white Christians. The risk of homogenizing these meanings accompanies, at the other extreme, the risk of becoming distracted by an elaborate and artificial taxonomy. Any evaluation of antislavery thought or action must take account of specific social and historical contexts.

The Founding Fathers and the Debunkers

Among the slave societies of the New World the American South was a shining anomaly. No other plantation society exhibited such diversities in climate and topography; in demography and social structure; in religion and social norms. During the eighteenth century

no other plantation regime was so open to the antislavery doctrines of
the Quakers, the Methodists, and the *philosophes*. Nor did the West
Indies or Brazil produce national leaders of the stature of Washington,
Jefferson, and Madison.

Historians have never expressed surprise over the virtual absence of
antislavery activity in the West Indies, or over its belated and derivative development in Brazil. The South, however, has long raised per-
plexing problems—in part because of the belief that, prior to the
cotton boom, slavery was a dying institution; in part because of the
belief that as late as 1827 the number of antislavery organizations in
the slave states outnumbered those in the free states by at least four
to one; but largely because of the antislavery professions of eminent
Southerners like Washington, Jefferson, Madison, Patrick Henry, St.
George Tucker, Arthur Lee, and John Laurens.

Early in the Civil War, when northern writers were identifying the
Confederacy with historical forms of despotism and were making the
cause of emancipation synonymous with that of democracy, Andrew
Dickson White portrayed Thomas Jefferson as the patron saint of
antislavery. It would have been impossible, according to White, for
the great champion of man's inalienable rights to have been anything
less than a determined and consistent foe of slavery. What gave antislavery its driving force, in this idealistic view, was the Enlightenment
of Montesquieu, Voltaire, and Rousseau: "There was not one chance
in a thousand that any man who had once made any considerable
number of these ideas his own could ever support slavery." Anyone
who read Montesquieu "earnestly" was certain to be a fighter against
slavery.[1] White did not explain why Montesquieu's home city of
Bordeaux, which was a center of enlightened culture, should have
remained so united in support of the African slave trade. But White's
exaggerated emphasis on the power of democratic ideals has been
echoed and amplified in countless textbook histories. Even the most
careful Jefferson scholars have often shared White's conclusion that
beneath the Virginian's flexible tactics lay an unswerving commitment
to emancipation.

History must have its heroes, and it is extremely difficult to believe
that the causes we cheer were sometimes supported by scoundrels or

[1] Andrew Dickson White, "Jefferson and Slavery," *Atlantic Monthly,* IX
(Jan., 1862), 31.

feared by the men we most admire. In the decades preceding the Civil War, many defenders of slavery quoted Jefferson's arguments on Negro inferiority, cited his opposition to the Missouri Compromise and his failure to free his own slaves, and finally took refuge behind the Jeffersonian doctrine of states' rights. Robert Toombs, the proslavery Senator from Georgia, happily observed that Jefferson's most telling actions had always been in support of Negro slavery. William Lloyd Garrison exclaimed that if Jefferson had only put his theories into practice, "what an all-conquering influence must have attended his illustrious example!" Yet abolitionists enshrined his ringing tributes to human liberty and made the Declaration of Independence the touchstone of their crusade. Proponents of Negro colonization claimed that their plan was "Jefferson's solution" to America's racial problem. As the supposed originator of the Northwest Ordinance, he was also identified with the cause of free soil in the territories. And his name gave sanction to Stephen Douglas's demand for popular sovereignty. In a very real sense, our political motto has been "every man his own Jeffersonian."[2]

During the past decade, however, the debate has taken new directions and the "Jefferson image"—indeed the wider Founding Father image—has taken on a villainous hue. To the thousands of spectators who saw Martin B. Duberman's play, "In White America," the actor cast as Jefferson had only to recite selected passages from *Notes on Virginia,* often in a supercilious tone, to transform the father of democracy into the father of American racism. In a brilliant dissection of Jefferson's attitudes toward race, Winthrop D. Jordan has argued, somewhat more charitably, that Jefferson "never realized how deep-seated his anti-Negro feelings were." Jordan also stresses Jefferson's "heartfelt hatred of slavery," and the personal guilt he felt over violating the key commandments of his natural rights philosophy. And by focusing attention on Jefferson's racism, as a microcosm of conflicts permeating American culture, Jordan suggests that the Virginian had an authentic commitment to antislavery but was intellectually paralyzed by racial prejudice.[3]

[2] Merrill D. Peterson, *The Jefferson Image in the American Mind* (New York, 1960), *passim.* By the 1850s, however, most defenders of slavery had come to repudiate the Jeffersonian legacy, or at least that part of it that could easily be converted into abolitionist currency.

[3] Winthrop D. Jordan, *White over Black: American Attitudes toward the Negro, 1550–1812* (Chapel Hill, 1968), pp. 430–36.

William Cohen has more recently agreed that "the contradiction in Jefferson's intellectual position stemmed in large part from his equivocal stance on the question of racial equality." But Cohen also points out that Jefferson often owned more than two hundred slaves; that over one-seventh of his blacks chose to desert him, many fleeing to the British during the Revolution; that his holdings in land and Negroes made him "the second wealthiest man in Albemarle County and one of the richest men in Virginia"; that between 1783 and 1794, because of his debts, "he reluctantly sold about fifty slaves"; and that Jefferson's "wealth, his status, and his political position were tied to the system of slavery" and to "a societal environment which took for granted the enslavement of one race by another."[4]

Any explanation of the contradiction between Jefferson's principles and practice must also take account of Robert McColley's revisionist portrait of Virginia's plantation society, and of the "cliometric" calculations of Robert William Fogel and Stanley L. Engerman. If racism alone prevented the Jeffersonians from implementing their antislavery principles, how can one explain their anger and distress over the evacuation of thousands of slaves by the British? Or the continuing increase in the number of Virginia slaveholders? Or the high price of slaves and the rising aggregate demand? Or the westward movement of slaves with their Virginia masters?[5]

Moreover, although historians have generally believed that no Virginians openly defended slavery in the Revolutionary period, Fredrika Teute Schmidt and Barbara Ripel Wilhelm have recently discovered proslavery petitions containing 1,244 signatures, addressed in 1784 and 1785 to the Virginia General Assembly. These documents evidence considerable public hostility to the law of 1782 allowing private manumissions. They make repeated use of Scriptural sanctions for slavery—in response to the antislavery agitation of Quakers, Methodists, and other "Enemies of our Country, Tools of the British Ad-

---

[4] William Cohen, "Thomas Jefferson and the Problem of Slavery," *Journal of American History*, LVI (Dec., 1969), 503–26. See also, Donald L. Robinson, *Slavery in the Structure of American Politics, 1765–1820* (New York, 1971), pp. 88–97, and *passim*.

[5] Professor McColley's thesis that "the years of slavery's supposed decline were in fact the years of its greatest expansion" (*Slavery and Jeffersonian Virginia* [Urbana, Ill., 1964], p. 3) receives considerable support and elaboration from Robert William Fogel and Stanley L. Engerman, *Time on the Cross: The Economics of American Negro Slavery* (2 vols., Boston, 1974).

ministration." As the editors point out, the petitioners employ the rhetoric of the Revolution and the Lockean theme of property rights: "The tone of the petitions is not one of guilt and defensiveness. They contain a fierce assertion of property rights and liberty at the same time they deny the slaves' humanity and their right to enjoy freedom to participate in society."[6]

It is possible, of course, to acknowledge that slavery was a profitable and growing institution in Jeffersonian Virginia and that "Jefferson's world," in William Cohen's phrase, "depended upon forced labor for its very existence"—and still to credit Jefferson with effective anti-slavery leadership. Indeed, the greater the obstacles, the more enhanced the achievement. In response to the debunkers—or more properly, the disillusionists—William W. Freehling has pictured Jefferson as "the pragmatic statesman, practicing government as the art of the possible." Professor Freehling faults the revisionists for taking a short rather than a long-run view of the question:

What could be done—what Jefferson and his contemporaries did—was to attack slavery where it was weakest, thereby driving the institution south and vitiating its capacity to survive. In a variety of ways the Founding Fathers took positive steps that demonstrated their antislavery instincts and that, taken together, drastically reduced the slavocracy's potential area, population, and capacity to endure.[7]

Yet Professor Freehling tends to conflate Jefferson not only with all the Founding Fathers but with all the "men of the Revolution," and thus proceeds to tie a Jeffersonian banner to every measure or development that weakened American Negro slavery. But Jefferson himself did nothing to encourage gradual emancipation in the northeastern states; he was in France when Congress adopted the Northwest Ordinance, and he later issued no public statements to defend or extend its free soil principles; as President, he expressed no regret over the extension of slavery into Louisiana; he made no comment when fellow Virginians sought to legalize slavery in Indiana and even pressed Congress to repeal the Northwest Ordinance. The final exclu-

[6] Fredrika Teute Schmidt and Barbara Ripel Wilhelm, "Early Proslavery Petitions in Virginia," *William and Mary Quarterly*, 3rd ser., XXX (Jan., 1973), 133–46.

[7] William W. Freehling, "The Founding Fathers and Slavery," *American Historical Review*, LXXVII (Feb., 1972), 81–93.

sion of slavery from Illinois was no more or no less "Jeffersonian" than was the admission of Missouri as a slave state.

In any event, it is questionable to speak of an "abolitionist process" proceeding "slowly but inexorably from 1776 to 1860." No doubt Professor Freehling is right when he argues that if slavery had continued in the North and had expanded into the Northwest, if the African slave trade had not been abolished, "if, in short, Jefferson and his contemporaries had lifted nary a finger—everything would have been different." But one cannot really extract a few variables and then predict the course of history. The erosion of slavery in the North and later in the border states was the result of complex and continuing forces; more important, it was intimately related to the expansion of slavery in the Deep South. It may well be that "the long-run impact of the Founding Fathers' reforms . . . not only helped lead lower South Slavocrats to risk everything in war but also helped doom their desperate gamble to failure."[8] The idea is at least reassuring. But to understand the more immediate functions and fate of antislavery thought in the South, one's vision must be confined to the short-run.

Jefferson's Uncertain Commitment

There can be no question that by the 1760s many sensitive Virginians, even among the planter elite, regarded Negro slavery with the deepest moral repugnance. Writing privately in 1761, Robert Beverley confided " 'tis something so very contradictory to Humanity, that I am really ashamed of my Country whenever I consider of it; & if ever I bid adieu to Virginia, it will be from that cause alone." Governor Francis Fauquier, who was intimate with the Williamsburg intellectual circle that included George Wythe, Dr. William Small, and the young Thomas Jefferson, expressed the hope, in his will, that none of his slaves would condemn him on the Day of Judgment: "For with what face can I expect mercy from an offended God, if I have not myself shewn mercy to these dependant on me." George Washington spoke for the more enlightened sector of his class

[8] *Ibid.* It should be stressed that I am not offering a rebuttal to the theses of either Jordan or Freehling; I am pursuing a rather different set of questions, which have nevertheless been given new meaning and depth by the works cited above.

when he expressed the wish, in private correspondence, for legislative emancipation by "slow, sure, and imperceptible degrees." Can such sentiments be termed "antislavery" without diluting the concept of any meaning?[9]

Instead of ennobling the antislavery cause with a touch of his enormous prestige, President Washington privately discountenanced even a cautiously worded Quaker memorial against the slave trade, terming it "very mal-apropos," and an "illjudged piece of business [that] occasioned a great waste of time." One may note that Benjamin Franklin, as president of the Pennsylvania Abolition Society, signed a somewhat bolder companion petition; and in a published response to Congressional speeches vilifying the Quakers, Franklin satirized the southern defenses of slavery by putting them in the mouth of an Algerian pirate. In 1789, Beverley Randolph, then governor of Virginia, sent copies of Virginia slave laws to the Pennsylvania Abolition Society, adding that "it will always give me pleasure to give any aid in my Power to forward the humane & benevolent Designs of the Philadelphia Society." James Wood, also while presiding as governor of Virginia, served as vice-president of the Virginia Abolition Society.[10]

In contrast, Washington became indignant when the Pennsylvania Society sought to bring the slaves of government officials resident in Philadelphia under the protection of Pennsylvania law. Afraid that some of his own servants might find "the idea of freedom" "too great a temptation for them to resist," he instructed Tobias Lear to send back to Virginia any slaves who, being unregistered in accordance

[9] Thad W. Tate, Jr., *The Negro in Eighteenth-Century Williamsburg* (Williamsburg, Va., 1965), pp. 210–11; George Washington to John Francis Mercer, Sept. 9, 1786, *Writings,* ed. by John C. Fitzpatrick (Washington, 1931–1941), XXIX, 5 (see also, XXVIII, 408, XXXIII, 358; XXIV, 47–48; XXXVI, 2).

[10] Washington to David Stuart, March 28 and June 15, 1790, *Writings,* XXXI, 30, 52; Beverley Randolph to Pennsylvania Abolition Society, July, 1789, Pennsylvania Abolition Society MSS, II, 5; membership list of Virginia Abolition Society, V, 3, Historical Society of Pennsylvania (hereafter HSP). Similarly, Edmund Randolph wrote to Franklin in 1788, "merely as a private man: and in that character I am free to declare, that whensoever an opportunity shall present itself, which shall warrant me, as a *citizen,* to emancipate the slaves, possessed by me, I shall certainly indulge my feelings, as a man, impressed with a sense of the rights of this unfortunate people, and regardless of the loss of property" (Pennsylvania Abolition Society MSS, I, 36, HSP). James Wood rose to prominence as an officer in the Revolutionary army. In 1801 he became president of the Virginia Abolition Society. Even for a Virginia Federalist, such organizational activity was unusual among the military and political elite,

with Pennsylvania law, might seek liberation after six months' residence: "I wish to have it accomplished under pretext that may deceive both them and the Public; and none I think would so effectively do this, as Mrs. Washington coming to Virginia next month."[11] Washington's sincerity is not the issue. He often wished he could free himself, as well as his state, from this "very troublesome species of property." When he drew up his last will, in 1799, he provided for the emancipation of his own slaves, after "the decease of my wife." But antislavery is a questionable classification for a master who threatened to have a misbehaving youth shipped off to the West Indies, and who feared, two years before his death, that he would have to break his resolution against buying more slaves because his cook had run away.[12]

As I have already suggested, Jefferson's position is considerably more ambiguous. One must emphasize that he gave occasional and extremely quiet encouragement to Negro education and to antislavery opinion among the planter class. By 1835 this would have been unthinkable for any major political leader in the South. Nor were there many planters in any country who could write that

the whole commerce between master and slave is a perpetual exercise of the most boisterous passions, the most unremitting despotism on the one part, and degrading submissions on the other. Our children see this, and learn to imitate it.[13]

Such rhetoric soon acquired a life of its own, transmuting the "Jefferson image" into an antislavery force. No one can deny that Jefferson's democratic ideals were of monumental importance for the later antislavery cause. But the question of Jefferson's relation to the antislavery

[11] Washington to Robert Morris, April 12, 1786, *Writings,* XXVIII, 407–8; to Tobias Lear, April 12, 1791, XXXVII, 573.

[12] *Ibid.,* XXXII, 336; XXVI, 70 (for other evidence of Washington's dilemmas, see XXIX, 56, 81, 107, 116–18, 154; XXXII, 277, 463); James Thomas Flexner, *George Washington: Anguish and Farewell, 1793–1799* (Boston, 1972), pp. 445–46. Washington did not want to burden Martha with the disruptions and difficulties of emancipating his own slaves, many of whom were married or related to her dower slaves. But as Flexner notes, Washington "chose to ignore the situation Martha would find herself in when some hundred and fifty individuals eagerly awaited her death to set them free."

[13] Thomas Jefferson, *Notes on the State of Virginia,* ed. by William Peden (Chapel Hill, 1955), pp. 162–63.

of his time requires an examination of his various roles and specific audiences.

According to Professor Jordan, it was "neither timidity nor concern for reputation" which restrained Jefferson from public criticism of slavery or from endorsement of the antislavery cause. Rather, the statesman's caution arose from an acute consciousness of the depth of American racial prejudice and from a fear "that premature endorsement by a figure of his prominence might easily damage the antislavery cause."[14] This was essentially Jefferson's own explanation. But Benjamin Franklin, Alexander Hamilton, and John Jay were figures of prominence who either owned or had owned Negro slaves; they were by no means free from racial prejudice or unaware of the difficulties of emancipation. Yet none of these circumstances deterred them from joining and lending their prestige to the earliest abolition societies.

I am not concerned with assigning moral credit or with ranking political leaders according to their abolitionist "contributions." Neither Hamilton nor Jay boldly championed the cause; and it is likely that Jay's inaction, as governor of New York, delayed the enactment of New York's gradual emancipation law. The point to be stressed is that early antislavery organization posed no threat to the vital interests of the northeastern states. In the North, abolitionist societies could win sanction and support from national political leaders as well as from the reigning mercantile elites. In the South, however, the abolitionist societies carried far more subversive implications. It was not accidental that they were virtually ignored by Jefferson and the other major political leaders who professed an abhorrence of slavery.

From the time of Jefferson's election to the Virginia House of Burgesses to his departure for France as American Minister, his political experience with slavery amounted to a series of rebuffs from the class which first accorded him recognition and prestige. Late in life he recalled that soon after his election to the House of Burgesses, at the age of twenty-six, he succeeded in persuading Richard Bland to move "for certain moderate extensions of the protection of the laws" to slaves. Although Bland was "one of the oldest, ablest, and most respected members," he was "denounced as an enemy of his country, and was treated with the grossest indecorum." Jefferson, because of

14 Jordan, *White over Black,* p. 435.

his youth, "was more spared in the debate." He clearly thought this story contained a lesson for twenty-seven-year-old Edward Coles, who had written the aged and respected former President, hopeful that "in the calm of this retirement you might, most beneficially to society, and with much addition to your own fame, avail yourself of that love and confidence to put into complete practice those hallowed principles contained in that renowned Declaration, of which you were the immortal author." Jefferson urged Coles to work "softly but steadily" for emancipation, promising to give the cause "all my prayers, & these are the only weapons of an old man."[15]

As a young man, he had dared a good bit more. In his *Summary View* of 1774 he had attacked the British crown for refusing to allow colonies to restrict or prohibit the further importation of slaves. This was a safe stand in Virginia, but Jefferson also asserted that "the abolition of domestic slavery is the great object of desire in those colonies where it was unhappily introduced in their infant state." He surely knew this was an exaggeration, in the light of his experience with Richard Bland, but it strengthened the case against England and no doubt expressed his own true desire as well as that of mentors like Bland and George Wythe. In the Declaration of Independence, however, he made no mention of emancipation but condemned King George for enslaving innocent Africans, for encouraging the "execrable commerce" in men, and for inciting American Negroes to rise in arms against their masters. Congress struck out the entire section. Thus in writing the document that gave him international fame, Jefferson learned that on the question of slavery one yielded to older and more cautious men, and especially to outspoken objections from any segment of the planter class. In 1776 he also met defeat when, in his drafts of a constitution for Virginia, he introduced an unacceptable clause prohibiting any future importation of slaves.[16] At the end of

---

[15] Thomas Jefferson (hereafter TJ) to Edward Coles, Aug. 14, 1814, in Paul Leicester Ford, ed., *The Federal Edition of the Works of Jefferson* (10 vols., New York, 1892–1899), IX, 477–78; Edward Coles to TJ, July 31, 1814, "Letters of Governor Coles," *Journal of Negro History*, III (1918), 159.

[16] Julian P. Boyd, ed., *The Papers of Thomas Jefferson* (Princeton, 1950—), I, 130, 353, 414. In 1778 the Virginia legislature prohibited the further importation of slaves, but this provision was never made part of the state constitution, as Jefferson had wished. For evidence that Virginia's anti-slave-trade legislation had little to do with antislavery or with expectations of gradual emancipation, see McColley, *Slavery and Jeffersonian Virginia*.

the Revolution he was apparently emboldened by the national spirit of thanksgiving and the expectation of a new republican era. In his 1783 draft of a new constitution for Virginia he provided for the freedom of all children born of slaves after the year 1800. This is the only definite record of a formal proposal by Jefferson for gradual emancipation; along with the measure his committee submitted to Congress in 1784 for excluding slaves from the western territories, again after the year 1800, it represents the high-water mark of his reform zeal. But both propositions were defeated.

One cannot question the genuineness of Jefferson's liberal dreams. If he had died in 1784, at the age of forty-one, it could be said without further qualification that he was one of the first statesmen in any part of the world to advocate concrete measures for restricting and eradicating Negro slavery. One may add, parenthetically, that in 1780 Edmund Burke drafted a bill for ameliorating the treatment of West Indian slaves, in preparation for their ultimate emancipation; but since he feared splitting the Whig party, he kept the plan secret for twelve years, and termed the abolition of the slave trade a "very chimerical object." In Britain, however, there were far weaker forces limiting the assimilation of antislavery philosophy. It is significant that Jefferson's individual efforts had virtually ceased by the time the first abolition societies appeared.

Jefferson played a central role in revising the laws of Virginia. Since this prodigious undertaking aimed at bringing the entire structure of law into conformity with republican principles, it offered unprecedented opportunities for the reform of slave codes, for the amelioration of slavery, or even for experiments at gradual emancipation. Surprisingly enough, Jefferson's proposed bills retained most of the inhumane features of the colonial slave law, and his innovations were largely too conservative for the legislature to adopt. For example, he was particularly harsh in depriving free Negroes of legal protection and in insisting on their expulsion from the commonwealth. Jefferson later claimed that the revisers had planned on introducing on the floor of the legislature an amendment for gradual emancipation and colonization. No draft of the amendment has survived, and it seems clear that its supporters were not prepared to defend the measure against legislative opponents and the angry petitioners already mentioned. As Merrill D. Peterson has recently written, Jefferson continued to favor the plan of gradual emancipation proposed in the *Notes on Virginia* in 1785; yet "neither he nor any other prominent Virginian was ever willing to risk friends, position, and influence to fight for it."[17]

In 1786, when Jefferson was in France and was contributing detailed information for an article on the United States in the *Encyclopédie méthodique,* he wrote a strained reply to the editor's question: Why had Virginia adopted a new slave law without some provision for emancipation? Jefferson told of his planned amendment, hastening to add that his own presence in the Virginia legislature would not have reversed the decision to suppress the untimely clause. He seemed anxious to avoid raising any suspicion of political conflict over slavery. The disposition of the legislature was simply not "ripe" for emancipation. And here Jefferson began experimenting with the locutions which for the rest of his life would characterize his response to such questions. Since his replies became so standardized, it is not unfair to conflate a number of examples: there was "not a man on earth" who more "ardently desired" emancipation, or who was more prepared to make "any sacrifice" to "relieve us from this heavy reproach, in any practicable way"; but—and Jefferson's buts deserve underscoring —the public mind needed "ripening" and would not yet "bear the proposition." To a French audience conditioned by the Abbé Raynal's bombastic rhetoric he exclaimed over the inconsistency of a slaveholding nation that fought for natural rights: "What a stupendous, what an incomprehensible machine is man!" In the style of Raynal, Jefferson talked, with uncharacteristic awkwardness, of "exterminating thunder" and "cosmic justice": when the slaves' groans "shall have

---

[17] Boyd, ed., *Papers,* II, 470–78; Merrill D. Peterson, *Thomas Jefferson and the New Nation* (New York, 1970), p. 153. The discovery of the 1,244 signatures on proslavery petitions gives added meaning to Madison's report to Washington on Nov. 11, 1785: "The House have engaged with some alacrity in the consideration of the Revised Code prepared by Mr. Jefferson, Mr. Pendleton & Mr. Wythe. The present temper promises an adoption of it in substance. . . . The pulse of the H. of D. was felt on thursday with regard to a general manumission, by a petition presented on that subject. It was rejected without dissent, but not without an avowed patronage of its principle by sundry respectable members. A motion was made to throw it under the table, which was treated with as much indignation on one side as the petition itself was on the other. There are several petitions before the House against any step towards freeing the Slaves, and even praying for a repeal of the law which licenses particular manumissions" (*Writings,* ed. by Gaillard Hunt [New York, 1900–1901], II, 192–93).

involved heaven itself in darkness, doubtless a god of justice will awaken to their distress."[18]

It is curious that the author of the Declaration of Independence should now justify inaction on the ground that an unsuccessful struggle against injustice would "rivet still closer the chains of bondage, and retard the moment of delivery to this oppressed description of men." We do not ordinarily associate Jeffersonian democracy with a quietistic surrender to fate; yet he advised his French editor that we must "await with patience the workings of an overruling providence, and hope that that is preparing deliverance of these our suffering brethren." At the age of forty-three Jefferson placed all his hope in the younger generation. In Virginia, he said, the emancipation cause was winning the support of "nearly the whole of the young men as fast as they come into public life."[19] But what would these young men think when they heard their intellectual mentor recommending faith in providence as a substitute for social action? Jefferson gave no public sanction or moral encouragement to this alleged army of young emancipators; there is no record of his approving or even acknowledging the existence of the Virginia Abolition Society. Instead, his icy caution provided a precedent and model for the younger generation of politicians from both North and South who would attack every effort to discuss the slavery question as a reckless tampering with the "seals" which Jefferson and the other Founders had "wisely placed" on the nation's most incendiary issue. If the great father of democracy had refrained from giving public voice to his convictions, how could lesser men presume superior wisdom?

[18] Boyd, ed., *Papers*, X, 18, 61–63. Although Jefferson attacked Raynal's theory of American degeneracy, his rhetoric on slavery, especially on slave revolts, bears the strong imprint of Raynal's influence. For the views on slavery of Raynal and his collaborators, see Davis, *The Problem of Slavery in Western Culture* (Ithaca, N.Y., 1966), pp. 12–17, 417–21. In his *Notes on Virginia,* Jefferson replied to Raynal's suspicion of American inferiority by arguing that it was unfair to disparage American culture for not producing a poet until "we shall have existed as a people" as long as the Greeks and Romans had before producing a Homer or Virgil. Yet later on, in the same work, he reasoned that since there had been poets and scholars among the Roman slaves, and since no comparable men of genius had arisen among the American Negro slaves, "it is not their condition, then, but nature, which has produced the distinction" (see Ford, ed., *Works*, III, 168, 247–48).

[19] Boyd, ed., *Papers,* X, 18, 63.

It is true that Jefferson's celebrated *Notes on Virginia* combined the antislavery ideals of the Enlightenment with a clinical diagnosis of Negro inferiority. But one must not forget that this work originated in 1781 as a body of information on Virginia for a small audience of French statesmen and intellectuals; that Jefferson opposed publishing the enlarged manuscript, in part because of his strictures on slavery; and that he intended the small and anonymous edition published in France in 1785 for strictly private circulation. He seems to have had two purposes for digressing on the general subject of Negro slavery: he wished to show that American planters shared the prevailing spirit of *bienfaisance* and *éclaircissement;* he also sought to explain why the abolition of slavery would require the deportation and colonization of Negroes.[20] When it appeared that the book might be published without his consent, Jefferson became alarmed at the thought of American planters reading his antislavery rhetoric. In 1785 he wrote the Marquis de Chastellux that the passages on slavery, if made public, might "produce an irritation" that would damage the cause of emancipation. In the next year Chastellux would damage the cause of emancipation by making derogatory comments on American Quakers, Negroes, and abolitionists, in his *Voyages dans l'Amérique septentrionale,* a book which drew heavily on Jefferson's *Notes* and which provoked an angry rebuttal from the abolitionist Brissot de Warville. Jefferson did not indicate how he expected to encourage the cause of emancipation without producing irritation. He told Chastellux that if he received sufficient reassurance from American friends, he would present a copy of the *Notes* to each student at William and Mary College: "It is to them I look, to the rising generations, and not to the one now in power

[20] Jefferson began writing *Notes on Virginia* in response to queries from François de Marbois, secretary of the French legation in Philadelphia. The original intended readers were thus America's wartime allies who were familiar with the antislavery declamations of Montesquieu and Raynal, and who had been subjected to highly romanticized pictures of America, many of which Jefferson sought to counteract. After later being challenged by the Abbé Grégoire on the subject of Negro equality, Jefferson told Joel Barlow that he had written a "very soft answer," adding that "it was impossible for doubt to have been more tenderly or hesitatingly expressed" than it was in the *Notes on Virginia* (Ford, ed., *Works,* IX, 261–64). After reading his notorious passages on Negro inferiority (for example, the statement that Negroes prefer whites "as uniformly as is the preference of the Oran-ootan for the black women over those of his own species"), one can only wonder what his uninhibited doubts would have been.

for these great reformations." And yet John Adams, who belonged to the generation in power, wrote Jefferson that the passages on slavery were "worth Diamonds." James Monroe thought the *Notes* could be safely circulated, but promised to keep the book private until Jefferson consented to general publication. Jefferson agreed to have copies distributed among members of Congress, but was adamant that his authorship remain unknown. He would not take the risk of placing his own prestige squarely behind his antislavery views. Some thirty years later he could still affirm his willingness to make any sacrifice for the cause of emancipation and then add, with tragic opacity, "But I have not perceived the growth of this disposition in the rising generation, of which I once had sanguine hopes."[21]

The truth was that Jefferson had only a theoretical interest in promoting the cause of abolition. When still in France, and incidentally while helping one J. D. Derieux buy land and slaves in America, he received inquiries from both the French and British abolition societies. Brissot reported the formation of the *Amis des noirs,* whose immediate object, like that of the parent London society, was limited to combating the slave trade. Brissot and Etienne Clavière requested that Jefferson attend a general meeting. No doubt it would have been imprudent if not improper for the American Minister to have joined a French reform society (John Jay, for example, resigned from the New York Manumission Society when he was appointed Chief Justice of the Supreme Court). Jefferson knew that he represented South Carolina as well as Virginia; his efforts to find new markets for American produce, including rice, had increased his awareness of the importance of slave labor in the national economy. He might informally have provided the *Amis* with valuable information, but he clearly wanted nothing to do with antislavery organizations. One fears, in any event, there was something disingenuous about his insistence to Brissot that while he was "willing to encounter every sacrifice" for the abolition of slavery as well as of the slave trade, any association with the *Amis* might render him less able to serve the cause in America.[22] The purity he preserved in France did not equip him to speak out later against

[21] Boyd, ed., *Papers,* VIII, 159–60, 184, 295; IX, 38; Ford, ed., *Works,* X, 77. Jefferson also feared that his strictures on the Virginia constitution might give offense.

[22] Brissot de Warville to TJ, Feb. 10, 1788, and TJ to Brissot, Feb. 11, 1788, Boyd, ed., *Papers,* XII, 577–78.

the spread of slavery into Kentucky, Tennessee, Mississippi Territory, or Louisiana.

The communication from London was less demanding. Edward Bancroft, an American inventor and double agent in the Revolution, had been talking with some friends who were members of the London Abolition Society.[23] He had retailed a story he had heard Jefferson tell at a dinner in France, concerning a benevolent Virginia planter who had tried to free his Negroes and pay them wages for labor. The point of the story, as Bancroft recalled, was that the Negroes had proved incapable of self-government, the "most sensible" desiring to return to slavery. Since the British abolitionists wanted more than hearsay evidence, Bancroft appealed to Jefferson for exact particulars. After a four-month delay, Jefferson replied that he could not remember telling such a story. He refused to go on record with any conclusions about the effects of emancipation. But so far as he knew from the experiments in Virginia, to free Negroes was "like abandoning children." Slavery had rendered them utterly incapable of self-control. Even the Quakers had been obliged to give daily supervision and even to whip the Negroes they had emancipated. This was essentially the message British abolitionists would continue to receive from West Indian planters. But Jefferson was unwilling to abandon his role as scientist and philanthropist. He abruptly announced to Bancroft that he personally intended to import German workers equal in number to the adult slaves he owned, intermingling them on farms of fifty acres. Presumably the Germans, with their "habits of property and foresight," would set an example for the slaves. But since Jefferson was at this time in critical financial straits and was faced with the need of selling land or slaves to pay his debts, he could not have taken the plan very seriously.[24]

After his return to America the most remarkable thing about Jefferson's stand on slavery is his immense silence. The revolution in St. Domingue, followed by the Gabriel plot in Virginia, prompted him to occasional apocalyptic warnings about being "the murderers of our

[23] Edward Bancroft to TJ, Sept. 16, 1788, Boyd, ed., *Papers*, XIII, 606–8. Bancroft erroneously said that the London society had been formed to abolish slavery. He may have received this impression by talking with Granville Sharp, who was interested in plans for gradual emancipation.

[24] TJ to Edward Bancroft, Jan. 26, 1789 [misdated 1788], Boyd, ed., *Papers*, XIV, 492.

own children," or being forced, "after dreadful scenes and sufferings to release them in their own way, which, without such suffering we might now model after our own convenience." But such insights into the nature of power were balanced by Jefferson's self-comforting assurance that "interest is really going over to the side of morality. The value of the slave is every day lessening."[25] If this seemed true in 1805 (and it was not true), how would Jefferson define morality when the value of slaves was every day increasing?

Political responsibilities help to justify Jefferson's policy of having "carefully avoided every public act or manifestation" on the subject of slavery. As President he felt he could not even reply to a warm appeal for his subscription to an antislavery poem, although he subscribed to other literary works and apparently had no hesitation over the public act of signing a law which opened Louisiana to settlement by slaveholders. He wrote to his friend Dr. George Logan, who was the only Quaker in the United States Senate, asking him to explain to the antislavery poet why the President could not openly support the "holy" cause: "Should an occasion ever occur in which I can interpose with decisive effect, I shall certainly know & do my duty with promptitude & zeal. But in the meantime it would only be disarming myself of influence to be taking small means."[26] Again we find Jefferson conserving his influence and power for some decisive and well-timed blow against Negro bondage. But during his long retirement, when he was unencumbered by the responsibilities of office and was being deified as the apostle of liberty and the sage of Monticello, he kept his peace.

He was challenged, then, "in the calm of this retirement" by Edward Coles, one of the members of the rising generation in whom he had invested such hope. Coles had attended William and Mary and was thus part of the select audience Jefferson had hoped would read

[25] TJ to St. George Tucker, Aug. 28, 1797, Ford, ed., *Works,* VII, 167–69; TJ to William A. Burwell, Jan. 28, 1805, MS in the Henry E. Huntington Library (hereafter, HEH).

[26] TJ to Dr. George Logan, May 11, 1805, Ford, ed., *Works,* VIII, 351–53. The poem, dramatizing the injustice of enslavement in Africa and the evils of the Middle Passage, was written by Thomas Branagan, a former slave trader and overseer on a West Indian plantation. In the letter asking Logan to soothe Branagan's feelings, the President showed particular concern over political schism in Pennsylvania.

Notes on Virginia. By 1814, Coles had determined to emancipate the slaves he had inherited from his father, even if this required moving to a free state or territory. After apologizing for seeming so presumptuous, Coles confronted Jefferson with the truths he had tried so hard to evade. Obviously it would be easier for "the revered fathers of all our political and social blessings" to begin the work of gradual emancipation than it would be for any succeeding statesmen. "And it is a duty," Coles went on, "as I conceive, that devolves particularly on you, from your known philosophical and enlarged view of subjects, and from the principles you have professed and practiced through a long and useful life." Coles, who had been President Madison's private secretary, was familiar with Jefferson's rationalizations: "I hope the fear of failing, at this time, will have no influence in preventing you from employing your pen to eradicate this degrading feature of British Colonial policy, which is still permitted to exist, notwithstanding its repugnance as well to the principles of our revolution as to our free institutions." Coles tried to persuade Jefferson that temporary failure could not damage his future reputation. After the former President had been "taken from us by the course of nature," his memory would be "consecrated"; his opinions and writings would have an "irresistible influence . . . in all questions connected with the rights of man."[27]

Since Coles put Jefferson's antislavery commitment to the test, it is well to examine the statesman's reply with some care. Although he had postponed speaking out against slavery until the time was ripe, he now insisted that his views had "long since been in possession of the public." Nevertheless, the younger generation had not been aroused to action: "Your solitary but welcome voice is the first which has brought this sound to my ear; and I have considered the general silence which prevails on this subject as indicating an apathy unfavorable to every hope." To this excuse Coles made the obvious reply: it required men of influence and reputation "to arouse and enlighten the public sentiment, which in matters of this kind ought not to be expected to lead, but to be led; nor ought it to be wondered at that there should prevail a degree of apathy with the general mass of mankind, where a mere

[27] Edward Coles to TJ, July 31, 1814, "Letters of Governor Coles," pp. 158–60. Of course Jefferson replied to other letters concerning slavery, but was mainly content to repeat his old apprehensions and to recommend the emancipation plan outlined in *Notes on Virginia.*

passive principle of right has to contend against the weighty influence of habit and interest."

Jefferson tried to reassure Coles that moral progress was inevitable: "It is an encouraging observation that no good measure was ever proposed, which, if duly pursued, failed to prevail in the end. We have proof of this in the history of the endeavors in the English parliament to suppress that very trade which brought this evil on us." But surely Jefferson knew that both Pitt and Fox had given their immense prestige to the British abolition cause; nor had British reformers talked about awaiting with patience the workings of an overruling providence. In response to Jefferson's familiar plea that "this enterprise is for the young," Coles reiterated the importance of experience, influence, and reputation, and pointed out that Jefferson was not as old as Franklin had been when leading the antislavery movement in Pennsylvania. But what must have disheartened Coles the most was Jefferson's strong advice that he should remain in Virginia and take good care of his slaves: "I hope then, my dear sir, you will reconcile yourself to your country and its unfortunate condition." Although Coles would remain a loyal disciple of Jefferson's, he realized there was no hope of working for gradual emancipation in Virginia. The only alternative to reconciling himself to slavery was emigration to Illinois.[28]

The exchange with Edward Coles dramatized Jefferson's fundamental commitment to his "country" as well as his extraordinary capacity to sound like an enlightened reformer while upholding the interests of the planter class. By "class" I mean something far more complex than a group united or governed by purely economic interest. Jefferson lived and moved within a cultural milieu dominated by the master-slave relationship, a relationship that included considerably more than "the most unremitting despotism on the one part, and degrading submissions on the other." The first childhood memory of the author of the Declaration of Independence was of being carried on a pillow by a mounted Negro slave. Jefferson was attuned to the values, loyalties, sanctions, taboos, and expectations of Virginia's wealthiest families, most of whom owned more than one hundred slaves. To a large extent he shared their collective sense of propriety, their moral imperatives, their definitions of available options. When

---

[28] TJ to Coles, Aug. 25, 1814, Ford, ed., *Works*, IX, 478–79; Coles to TJ, Sept. 26, 1814, "Letters of Governor Coles," p. 161.

Jefferson feared that he might harm the cause of liberty by over-stepping prudent bounds, he gave expression to the genuine conviction that his power to do good depended on maintaining his reputation, or in other words, his social identity.

In some respects, of course, Jefferson transcended both his society and his age; in other respects he shared the more generalized opinions and prejudices of his time. For example, he felt that the only "practicable plan" of emancipation would be to liberate and eventually deport some future generation of Negroes; the children would be put to "industrious occupations," as wards of the state, as soon as their labor equalled the cost of their maintenance. This would mean permanently separating the children from their mothers, but the program would reduce both the public expense of emancipation and the compensation due to the mothers' owners. It must be stressed that there was nothing peculiarly "southern" about such reasoning. Neither racism nor a calculated concern for the rights of property was a monopoly of the slaveholding class.

On the other hand, if Jefferon could blame England for the "trade which brought this evil on us," he could also blame northeastern Federalists for trying to divide the nation by excluding slaves from Missouri. Ironically, in defending the extension of slavery into Missouri, Jefferson used precisely the same arguments which British slave traders had used long before. It was not a moral question, he insisted, since the removal of slaves from one state or country to another did not make new slaves; their status remained unchanged. Moreover, if slaves were spread over a larger surface, "their happiness would be increased."[29]

Jefferson's record on slavery can only be judged by the values of his contemporaries and by the consistency between his own professed beliefs and actions. One needs to remember that he was a man burdened by many conflicting fears, roles, and responsibilities. One can understand and sympathize with his occasional feelings of despair, as when he wrote in 1820 that "we have a wolf by the ears, and we can neither hold him, nor safely let him go. Justice is in one scale, and self-preservation in the other." But for Jefferson the scale tipped heavily toward self-preservation, which meant the preservation of a social order based on slavery. Despite his glimpses of a more humane and

[29] TJ to Albert Gallatin, Dec. 26, 1820, Ford, ed., *Works,* X, 177–78.

just world, he could not doubt the basic legitimacy of his social universe. He knew that any serious threat to slavery was also a threat to this universe, however he might wish to dissociate the two. He was, to be sure, equivocal and indecisive; because of his immense prestige, he thereby sanctioned equivocation and indecision. But when the chips were down, as in the Missouri crisis, he threw his weight behind slavery's expansion, and bequeathed to the South the image of antislavery as a Federalist mask for political and economic exploitation. If early antislavery became identified with political partisanship and with conservatives like Hamilton, Jay, and Rufus King, it was partly by default.

Philosophes of the Caribbean

I do not mean to suggest that anyone who owned slaves or who shared Jefferson's social background was incapable of a deeper commitment to antislavery. Neither economic interest nor involvement in the slave system predestined men's attitudes toward human bondage. Edward Coles, a birthright member of the Virginia planter elite, helped to lead the struggle to prevent Illinois from becoming a slave state. So, too, an impressive number of abolitionist leaders emigrated from Virginia to the North or West.[30] As young men, the British abolitionists James Stephen and Zachary Macaulay worked for several years in the West Indies, the latter supervising the labor of plantation slaves. But all of these men moved away from the plantation, severing ties with any class or occupation that rested directly on Negro labor; none of them depended for recognition and approval on even an enlightened portion of the planter class. Although there was genuine antislavery sentiment in such states as Virginia, North Carolina, and Tennessee, it was largely limited to marginal groups like the Quakers, or to nonslaveholders who did not yet identify with the planter interest.

Ironically, the same point can be made in reverse, since it was possible for a number of political radicals and revolutionaries from other societies to find refuge by accommodating to southern norms.

[30] Dwight Lowell Dumond, *Antislavery Origins of the Civil War in the United States* (Ann Arbor, 1939), pp. 6–8; Merton L. Dillon, "Sources of Antislavery Thought in Illinois," *Journal of the Illinois State Historical Society*, L (Spring, 1957), 37–40; W. H. G. Armytage, "The Editorial Experience of Joseph Gales, 1786–1794," *North Carolina Historical Review*, XXVIII (July, 1951), 332–61.

Thus Joseph Gales, the Sheffield journalist, represented the radical wing of British abolitionism, which was finally decimated—along with other democratic causes—by the reactionary suppression of the 1790s. Gales fled to North Carolina, where he became editor of the *Raleigh Register*. Similarly Thomas Cooper, of Manchester, a radical democrat and outspoken opponent of Negro slavery, escaped Pitt's reign of terror and finally found haven in South Carolina, where he became a slaveowner, an antidemocrat, and an extreme racist. The only element in Cooper's world view that remained unchanged was his hostility to organized religion.[31]

One can put Jefferson's views on slavery in a clearer (and more flattering) perspective by comparing him with two foreign contemporaries who shared many of his interests, prejudices, and opportunities. Both Bryan Edwards and Moreau de Saint-Méry were men of the Enlightenment who looked to plantation slavery as the basis of their livelihood. Both combined legal and political interests with literary ambitions. They wrote works, in the genre of *Notes on Virginia*, which were highly acclaimed by critics. Like Jefferson, they moved from membership in provincial governing bodies to positions of power in the metropolitan government. Inevitably, they played important roles in the slavery controversies of the Age of Revolution. Since they are not nearly so well known as Jefferson, it will be helpful to sketch their biographies.

Bryan Edwards was born in Wiltshire in 1743 and at the age of sixteen went out to Jamaica to work for a wealthy uncle. He eventually took over his uncle's business, inherited considerable property, and rose to a prominent position in the colonial assembly. As a Jamaican legislator Edwards sympathized with the grievances of the North American colonists, and in 1784 published a work attacking British restrictions on trade with the United States. "The war with America on the part of Great Britain," he wrote, "was conceived in wickedness, and continued through insanity."[32] He was a man of liberal views and

---

[31] Dumas Malone, *The Public Life of Thomas Cooper, 1783–1839* (New Haven, 1926), pp. 19–22, 281–90, 387; Thomas Cooper, *Letters on the Slave Trade* (Manchester, 1787); E. P. Thompson, *The Making of the English Working Class* (New York, 1963), pp. 132, 151–52, 180.

[32] Bryan Edwards, *Thoughts on the Late Proceedings of Government, Respecting the Trade of the West India Islands with the United States of North America* (London, 1784), p. 4.

benvolent instincts; after acquiring a great fortune and settling permanently in England, he was said to have relieved the sufferings of many poor. He was even much disturbed by what slaves had told him concerning the fraud, oppression, and bloodshed occasioned in Africa by the slave trade. In a speech in 1789 before a free conference of the Jamaican Council and Assembly, called in response to Wilberforce's Parliamentary attack on the slave trade, Edwards agreed with the abolitionist's description of how Negroes were made captive, and admitted it was a mockery and insult to claim that most African slaves were criminals deserving of punishment. A bit later he wrote, in very Jeffersonian terms, that large numbers of Africans "have been torn from their native country and dearest connections, by means which no good mind can reflect but with sentiments of disgust, commiseration, and sorrow. . . . Nothing is more certain than that the Slave Trade may be very wicked, and the planters in general very innocent."[33] Stephen Fuller, Jamaica's agent in England, complained to Edwards that there were passages in his 1789 speech which "cut up by the root" all the evidence the Liverpool merchants had been trying to establish at a cost of £4,000 and three years of labor. Fuller, who feared that the abolitionist zealots would make "very bad use of your compassionate sentiments," wished that Edwards could come to England, where he would surely change his mind on the slave trade and where he could put his obvious abilities to work fighting for Jamaica's survival as a sugar colony.[34]

In the 1790s, after viewing the ravages in St. Domingue with a British "relief" expedition which was welcomed by Moreau's terrorized planter friends, Edwards returned to England for good. He prospered as a West India merchant and banker. In 1796 he was elected to the House of Commons, and having been convinced that Jamaica's survival as a sugar colony depended on the successful defense of the slave trade, he joined the powerful faction which had beaten down Wilberforce's repeated motions. By this time Edwards's two-volume *History*,

[33] Bryan Edwards, *A Speech Delivered at a Free Conference Between the Honourable the Council and Assembly of Jamaica . . . on the Subject of Mr. Wilberforce's Propositions in the House of Commons, Concerning the Slave Trade* (Kingston, Jamaica, 1789), pp. 13–14; Edwards, *The History Civil and Commercial, of the British Colonies in the West Indies* (4 vols., Philadelphia, 1806), II, 236.

[34] Stephen Fuller to Bryan Edwards, March 3, 1790, Stephen Fuller Letterpress book, Fuller papers, Duke University Library.

Civil and Commercial, of the British Colonies in the West Indies had given him a deserved reputation as an expert on the economy and society of the British Caribbean. His literary productions ranged from a volume of poems to admirably lucid and detailed accounts of Caribbean topography, agriculture, trade, and social customs. After publishing in 1797 *An Historical Survey of the French Colony in the Island of Santo Domingo,* which included an account of the revolution, he succeeded Sir Joseph Banks as secretary of the Association for Promoting the Discovery of the Interior Parts of Africa. Edwards made an abridgment of Mungo Park's account of African travels; he became a Fellow of the Royal Society. But his Jeffersonian interest in scientific exploration was cut short by death in the year Jefferson was elected President.

Moreau de Saint-Méry was born in Martinique in 1750, and at the age of nineteen he traveled to France, where he had wealthy relatives, in order to study classics and Roman law. Moreau's family had long held the leading judicial posts in Martinique. His mother, it is said, imbued him with a humanitarian spirit, and while still in his teens he became a legal counselor and defender of Negro slaves accused of infractions of the *Code noir.* Despite his lack of preparatory study, Moreau achieved a brilliant record in France, rapidly earning a law degree and becoming an *avocat du parlement.* He was, it should be emphasized, steeped in the philosophy of Diderot and Rousseau. But unlike Alexander Hamilton, who was born and reared in the Leeward Islands, Moreau did not sever ties with the Caribbean slave society when he traveled to the metropolis for education. After returning briefly to Martinique, he moved on to St. Domingue to practice law and to become a member of the colonial *conseil supérieur.*

As a result of his interest in scholarship and colonial administration, Moreau was not in St. Domingue when the great slave uprising sent shock waves from Edwards's Jamaica to Jefferson's Virginia. After returning to Paris, Moreau had published a massive six-volume compilation of the laws and constitutions of the French Windward Islands. He had also helped found the somewhat subversive Museum of Paris, of which he became president in 1787. This activity led to Moreau's political elevation in 1789 as president of the Electors of Paris and as one of the city's revolutionary leaders. It was Moreau who received the keys of the fallen Bastille, who was responsible for placing Lafayette in command of the National Guard, and who presided for a time over the Paris Commune. He then represented Martinique as a deputy in the Constituent Assembly. Though a strong advocate of domestic reform in France, Moreau sided with the colonial planter interest in opposing any interference with the slave trade or with the status of persons in the colonies. He violently denounced the Abbé Grégoire, the *Amis des noirs,* and the French mulattoes who agitated for equality of rights in the colonies. As the Revolution swung sharply to the left, Moreau's position became as insecure as that of his abolitionist opponents. In the fall of 1793 he would have died on the guillotine, along with his enemy Brissot, if he had not been lucky enough to escape from France. Although he had planned on returning to St. Domingue, he abandoned this hope after traveling to the United States and encountering refugees from the war-torn island. Between 1794 and 1798 he ran a bookstore and printing press in Philadelphia, where he became a member of the American Philosophical Society and where he also published his monumental *Description topographique, physique, civile, politique et historique de la partie française de l'isle Saint-Domingue.* Napoleon's rise to power brought Moreau back to Europe, where he served as administrator of the states of Parma, Piacenza, and Guastalla before suffering a second and more permanent fall from political grace.

Although Moreau and Edwards were obviously lesser figures than Jefferson, they can be thought of as the pre-eminent statesmen-intellectuals of their respective slaveholding societies. These societies were profoundly different in many respects, but the three men had much in common.

Their formative experiences occurred in regions dominated by the plantation system, from which their wealth was directly or indirectly derived. While they lived many years in capital cities where they interacted with men of diverse backgrounds and interests, their main orientation was toward a slaveholding planter class. It was a plantation society with which they identified, and which their political efforts were designed to protect.

Yet all three were widely read men who absorbed the liberal and humanitarian ideas of their age. Moreau knew English; Edwards and Jefferson knew French, and were familiar with the works of the *philosophes.* Like Jefferson's *Notes on Virginia,* Moreau's *Description* and Edwards's *History* display a passion for measurement and for specific information on geography, meteorology, ethnology, and political economy. All were acute observers, intensely inquisitive about their environments. With a mixture of pride and unflagging curiosity they presented the world with detailed descriptions of Virginia, Jamaica, and St. Domingue.

The three men acquired legislative experience at an early age. And as enlightened lawmakers they shared an interest in ameliorating Negro slavery. Moreau, for example, was much encouraged by his discoveries at Dubuisson, in St. Domingue, where the natural increase of slaves exceeded the rate of mortality. This fact proved, he insisted, that slavery and happiness could be combined.[35] Bryan Edwards emphasized that he was no friend of slavery in any form. He knew, like Jefferson, that the institution could corrupt both master and slave: "So degrading is the nature of slavery," he wrote, "that fortitude of mind is lost as free agency is restrained." In Jamaica he worked for humane regulations that would reduce mortality and perhaps eliminate the necessity of importing Africans. His most radical proposal was to bind slaves to the soil, in the manner of serfs, to prevent their sale apart from an estate. He bitterly opposed an English law allowing creditors to sell slaves, even in foreign markets, for the recovery of a master's debt. Although this "execrable statute" had brought excruciating misery to hundreds of slaves, Edwards observed that abolitionists had remained silent on the subject: "They are men of the world, and with all their philanthropy, probably consider no rights so sacred as those of creditors." It was Edwards himself who finally secured the law's repeal.[36]

Neither Edwards nor Moreau proposed a plan for gradual eman-

---

[35] Moreau de Saint-Méry, *Description topographique, physique, civile, politique et historique de la partie française de l'isle Saint-Domingue* (2 vols., Philadelphia, 1797–1798), I, 174. Moreau later said that the misfortunes of St. Domingue had led many Frenchmen to praise North Americans for the humane way they treated their slaves. He found, however, that Negro servants were cruelly treated in New York as well as in the South. He also acquired the bizarre notion that George Washington had said in the Constitution that all slaves would be freed in the year 1800, but that Congress had ignored the promise in order to avoid a civil was (see Moreau de Saint-Méry, *Voyage aux Etats-Unis de l'Amérique, 1793–1798,* ed. with introduction by Stewart L. Mims [New Haven, 1913], pp. 67, 170–71, 324–34).

[36] Edwards, *History Civil and Commercial* (3 vols., ed., London, 1793–1801), I, vii; (4 vols., 1806 ed.), II, 284, 357, 363–68; Lowell J. Ragatz, *The Fall of the Planter Class in the British Caribbean, 1763–1833* (New York, 1928), p. 272. Edwards proposed that slaves be given wages for extra labor, that they be given legal rights to property, or a *peculium,* and that they be permitted to have their own juries to judge one another for minor offenses.

cipation and colonization. Far more than Jefferson, they were reconciled to the "unfortunate condition" of their countries, largely because
they could willingly abandon their countries for a more exciting
metropolis without severing ties of economic interest and social
identity. They talked more of the inevitability of human imperfection
and could argue that slavery, like sickness and poverty, had always
been a part of human existence. Despite this difference, the three men
shared the conviction that any sudden emancipation would result in
economic ruin and racial warfare.[37]

In an era of revolutionary challenge to central authorities, they
agreed that any reforms in the plantation system must be the work of
local governments, which would of course be dominated by slaveholding planters. They shared a common hostility to any interference with
slavery or race relations on the part of a central government. Moreau
expressed the underlying fear and threat: if French slaves should ever
suspect that their fate could be governed by an authority independent
of the will of their masters; if they should see free mulattoes acquiring
full equality with whites, without the consent of the whites—then
France would have no hope of preserving her colonies. Both Moreau
and Edwards hinted that the political machinations of abolitionists
might drive the colonies to independence, if they were not first destroyed by racial warfare. At the time of the Missouri crisis Jefferson,
in the same vein, warned that the Federalist antislavery conspiracy
might force the South to secede.[38]

From a West Indian point of view the North American colonies had
enjoyed a great tactical advantage as a result of their diminishing need
for African labor. But like the North Americans, Moreau and Edwards
blamed Europe for beginning the slave trade. The colonists, who were
ignorant of how slaves were procured, simply bought laborers who had
been made legitimate objects of sale by the laws of metropolitan governments. Of course, once the imperial governments had guaranteed a
regular and continuing supply of labor, any reversal in policy would
bring disaster to planters, merchants, investors, and the holders of

[37] Edwards, *History Civil and Commerical* (1806 ed.), II, 338–39, 347, 363–
64; IV, xiv; Moreau de Saint-Méry, *Considérations présentées aux vrais amis de
repos et du bonheur de la France, à l'occasion des nouveaux mouvemens de
quelques soi-disant Amis-des-Noirs* (Paris, 1791), pp. 30, 56–57, 68.

[38] Edwards, *History Civil and Commercial* (1806 ed.), II, 347–49, 362–66;
Moreau, *Considérations*, pp. 47–57, 70; TJ to Albert Gallatin, Dec. 26, 1820,
Ford, ed., *Works*, X, 177.

annuities and mortgages. In Edwards's words, "every thing that is dear and important to us all" was staked on the outcome of the slave-trade debates.[39]

Edwards admitted that he had once hoped England would abolish the slave trade, setting a humane example for other nations. His investigations had convinced him, however, that such a step would produce unspeakable suffering. Foreign traders would swoop in to buy the prime Negroes abandoned by the British; the rest would be slaughtered by their captors, to avoid the expense of maintenance. In the Caribbean, where the number of Negro women was insufficient to keep the population from declining, each slave would have to assume a heavier burden of work. To avoid these misfortunes, the slave trade should obviously be reformed instead of abolished. The worst abuses of the past had arisen from overcrowding (as has been said of today's ghettos), and much had already been done to provide wholesome food and sanitary, fumigated "apartments." In any event, as Edwards and Moreau repeatedly emphasized, the Negroes were much happier in America than in Africa. If a few unscrupulous Europeans exploited the Africans' native bent for violence, the victims were at least redeemed from barbarism by the West Indian colonists. According to Moreau, the African-born slaves in St. Domingue generally remained indolent, garrulous, and quarrelsome; they were liars and thieves incapable of grasping a religious idea. The fact that the creole blacks were in every way superior disproved the malicious charge that masters debased and mistreated their slaves.[40]

Jefferson took as little note as possible of organized abolitionism; when forced to respond, he made his negatives so delicate that they sounded positive. He clearly considered most antislavery efforts chimerical and irresponsible and resented, as much as any planter, the moral aspersions directed against his class. After shuddering over the nightmare of St. Domingue he was doubtless thankful that he had not compromised himself with the *Amis des noirs*.[41] When the southern

---

[39] Moreau, *Considérations*, p. 30; Edwards, *History Civil and Commercial* (1806 ed.), II, 321–22, 334, 336; Edwards, *Speech*, pp. 4, 6–7.

[40] Edwards, *Speech*, p. 14; Edwards, *History Civil and Commercial* (1806 ed.), II, 315–25, 327–32; Moreau, *Description*, I, 35–40.

[41] As early as Dec. 25, 1789, William Short wrote Jefferson that the *Amis* were accused of being a "set of illuminés" in the pay of Pitt's government (Boyd, ed., *Papers*, XVI, 46).

slaveholders met their first serious challenge, in the Missouri contest, Jefferson was quick to see attacks on slavery as part of a diabolical conspiracy to weaken or destroy the southern states.

The Caribbean planters had heard their "firebell in the night"—to use Jefferson's phrase—a good bit earlier. Edwards and Moreau tried to maintain a sharp distinction between the well-intentioned proponents of "rational reform" and the antislavery fanatics who, as Edwards said, disgraced both humanity and letters. The difficulty was that "some of the best friends of freedom and virtue," including leaders like Pitt, had been taken in by abolitionist propaganda. Edwards was even willing to concede that Wilberforce had become the victim of misinformation, whereas for Clarkson's "monstrous calumnies" against West Indian slaveholders he had nothing but indignant rage: "I declare to God, I do not believe that a series of more abominable falsehoods ever blotted a page in the wide history of human depravity!" In order to vindicate the planter class from abolitionist accusations, Edwards painted an idyllic picture of the liberality, warm hospitality, and proud, independent spirit of white creole society. The portrait was remarkably similar to the southern "plantation myth" of the next generation.[42]

Moreau's response was virtually the same. He was frank in saying he admired and honored some of the men who had joined the *Amis des noirs*. They clearly had no idea of what they were doing, or of how they were being used by fanatical agitators like Brissot and Clarkson. In order to awaken these benevolent dupes, Moreau explained how the British had exploited the French Revolution, entering into a treasonous conspiracy with the *Amis des noirs* for the destruction of the French colonies.[43] He claimed that Brissot, while traveling in North America, had seized upon the Quakers' antislavery doctrines as a means of winning fame in France. After Brissot had returned to France, Moreau continued, he had collaborated with Clarkson, who had come over from England, "ivre de joie," intent on further inflaming the French abolitionists. Moreau charged that Brissot and Clarkson had prepared the way for the mulatto Ogé to purchase arms and munitions in the United States. As an agent of the abolitionists, Ogé had then sailed for St. Domingue, where early in 1791 he had led an

[42] Moreau, *Considérations,* pp. 68–69; Edwards, *Speech,* pp. 7–11, 31, 59–63; Edwards, *History Civil and Commercial* (1806 ed.), II, 201–4, 210–15.
[43] Moreau, *Considérations,* p. 4; Moreau, *Voyage aux Etats-Unis,* pp. 324–34.

abortive insurrection and had become a celebrated martyr. Moreau's hostility toward the *Amis des noirs* was hardly lessened when he learned that a report had reached Martinique to the effect that he himself had proposed the abolition of slavery! As a result, a mob had nearly lynched his cousin and brother-in-law, and his relatives had gone into hiding for six weeks.[44]

Moreau and Edwards agreed that the *Amis des noirs* and the London Abolition Society were directly responsible for all the calamitous events in the French Caribbean. Although both organizations had supposedly misled the public by claiming they favored only the abolition of the slave trade or equal rights for free mulattoes, their actions could not have been more perfectly designed to incite slaves to insurrection. The wonder was, Edwards wrote, that the explosion had not begun in the British islands, which had first been showered with the abolitionists' sparks. Domestic servants traveling from England to the West Indies had carried news of the Parliamentary debates; at great expense the abolitionists had deluged the colonies with tracts and pamphlets maligning the planters, preaching equality and natural rights, and asserting that the act of men illegally held in bondage could not be considered crimes. For the instruction of slaves who could not read such incendiary pamphlets, the philanthropists had struck a medal picturing a naked Negro, loaded down with chains, kneeling and begging for mercy.[45]

In describing the consequences of such reckless provocations, Edwards gave explicit content to what North Americans had uneasily referred to as a *bellum servile*. As a West Indian Virgil who had seen the outer fringes of hell, he takes us down into the pit, past the hideous tableaux: the white infant impaled on a stake; the white women being repeatedly raped on the dead bodies of the husbands and fathers; the fair eyes being scooped out of their sockets by black

---

[44] Moreau, *Considérations*, pp. 5–19, 25, 29, 47; Edwards, *History Civil and Commercial* (1806 ed.), IV, xiv–xvi, 19–67, 87–93. Edwards claimed that Ogé first learned of the "miseries of his condition" from the *Amis des noirs*. There is no evidence I have seen to support C. L. R. James's contention that Clarkson "aided and abetted" Ogé's plans for the mulatto revolt (see James, *The Black Jacobins* [2nd ed., New York, 1963], p. 73 and footnote). Such activities would have been wholly out of keeping with Clarkson's character. Before leaving France, Ogé had publicly accused Moreau of selling a mulatto woman to the Chevalier de Redouin, a charge which Moreau angrily denied (see *Patriote français*, No. 253 [April, 18, 1790], 4; Moreau, *Considérations*, p. 73).

[45] Edwards, *History Civil and Commercial* (1806 ed.), IV, 68–98.

men's knives; and Madame Séjourné having a babe cut from her
womb and fed to the pigs in her own sight, and then her husband's
head sewed up in the bloody cavity. This, Edwards tells us, is the
final triumph of philanthropy. It is the fruit of the doctrine that
resistance is always justifiable where force is substituted for right.
Edwards makes no mention of the atrocities which the white Frenchmen (and Englishmen) committed on the blacks.[46]

From a modern point of view both Bryan Edwards and Moreau de
Saint-Méry were white supremacists. Yet in very significant ways their
racism differed from that of Thomas Jefferson. Like Jefferson, they
said that Negro slaves were prone to theft and dissimulation, that they
were carefree and submissive, that they never thought of the future
and were promiscuous in their sexual attachments, having no capacity
for delicate or refined love. Both writers described the Negroes' un-
pleasant odor, and Edwards even denied them musical ability. But
neither Edwards nor Moreau had even a "suspicion," as Jefferson did,
that Negroes were an inferior race. Africans were simply "savages"
who came from a "barbarous" continent.[47]

Indeed, Edwards and Moreau were far less inclined than Jefferson
was to make sweeping generalizations about "Negroes." Accustomed
to large populations of newly imported slaves, they were acutely aware
of tribal and cultural differences. They were fascinated by various
"Africanisms," and presented detailed and often sympathetic accounts
of African dances, speech, behavior, and cultural characteristics. And
since they were eager to prove that Caribbean slaves would be the
"objects of envy to half the peasantry of Europe," their attitude toward
creole slaves, who had enjoyed the benefits of plantation life since
birth, was far more positive than that of Jefferson. One gets the
distinct impression that both Moreau and Edwards actually *liked*
Negroes. It strains the imagination to think of Jefferson interrupting
the flow of *Notes on Virginia* to include an ode to "The Sable Venus."
Yet Bryan Edwards sings to us of a "sable queen of love" whose "skin
excell'd the raven plume, / Her breath the fragrant orange bloom, /
Her eye the tropick beam."

Edwards's ode accompanied his admission that Jamaican planters

---

[46] *Ibid.*, (1793 ed.), II, 89; (1806 ed.), II, 266, 284–88, 292; Moreau, *Description,* I, 25–26, 40ff, 62. Both writers explicitly rejected the theory of racial
inferiority.
[47] Edwards, *History Civil and Commercial* (1793 ed.), II, 32–38.

generally kept colored mistresses, and his insistence that the colored females were not to blame. Although he granted that the offspring of such unions were a "burden and reproach" to society, degraded both in their own eyes and in the eyes of the community, he thought them capable of freedom, and advocated legal reforms. Moreau, who was said to have a trace of African blood in his veins, cited the number of free blacks and mulattoes in St. Domingue as evidence of the colonists' humanity. To be sure, he opposed racial equality or assimilation, and pointed to the plight of Jews in France as proof of the strength of prejudice. But both he and Edwards accepted an interracial society in a way that Jefferson never could.[48]

No West Indian could entertain fantasies about his island being a "white man's country." He could not dream of deporting the Negroes to some out-of-the-way spot; they were there to stay. He knew, as few North Americans would admit, that much of his country's wealth depended on slave labor, and that Negroes would irrevocably play a central role in his country's destiny.

The significant point, however, is that while Edwards and Moreau were relatively free from Jefferson's aloof distaste for Negroes, they were far more unequivocally opposed to antislavery. And yet they were cosmopolitan men of the Enlightenment, exposed to the writings of Diderot and Rousseau, as well as of Montesquieu. If we take Moreau and Edwards as representative of the enlightened "planter mentality," then Jefferson is atypical both in his early radicalism and in the depth and morbidity of his racial prejudice, which, as Winthrop Jordan has shown, had developed from conditions peculiar to North America. But the three men responded much the same way when the slaveholding system appeared to be threatened by an outside force, which they invariably perceived as a conspiracy. When we compare their underlying attitudes toward Negro slavery it thus seems plausible that neither racial prejudice nor the absorption of enlightened ideas was so important a variable as a continuing identification with the interests and culture of a planter class.

[48] *Ibid.,* (1806 ed.), II, 218–21; Moreau, *Considérations,* p. 30; Moreau, *Description,* I, 68ff; *Avertissement,* April 4, 1791, for the *Amis des noirs'* March *Adresse à l'assemblée nationale.* For a thoughtful discussion of the differences between Caribbean and North American societies in the acceptance of mulattoes, see Jordan, *White over Black,* pp. 175ff. I tend to agree with Jordan that "the question of Jefferson's miscegenation . . . is of limited interest and usefulness even if it could be satisfactorily answered" (*ibid.,* p. 467).

The Neutralization of Antislavery in the South

Obviously antislavery activity carried far more subversive implications in the southern states than in Philadelphia, New York, or London. It was all very well for men like St. George Tucker and Ferdinando Fairfax to speculate on plans that would gradually free slaves at no cost to their owners and that would then remove the unwanted "separate interest," as Fairfax delicately put it, to some remote country.[49] But any direct move to undermine the institution challenged the economic and political foundations of the social order. It was difficult, therefore, to define such moves as purely "moral" acts, devoid of political significance.

It is true that the example of a wealthy Quaker planter like Robert Pleasants could be embarrassing to political leaders who professed to see Negro slavery as Virginia's tragic curse. Pleasants, whose father had been restrained by colonial law from freeing all his slaves outright, made personal antislavery appeals to such enlightened Virginians as Washington, Madison, Tucker, and Patrick Henry. Henry, to whom Pleasants sent a copy of Benezet's *Some Historical Account of Guinea,* replied with a revealing mixture of bombast and candor. He lavished praise upon the Quakers, a people "whose system imitates the Example of him whose Life was perfect.—And believe me I shall honour the Quakers in their noble Effort to abolish Slavery." He exhorted Pleasants "to persevere in so worthy a resolution," adding, however, that "some of Your people disagree or at least are lukewarm in the abolition of Slavery." As for Henry himself and his views of the future:

Would any one believe that I am Master of Slaves of my own purchase! I am drawn along by ye general Inconvenience of living without them; I will not, I cannot justify it. However culpable my conduct, I will so far pay my devoir to Virtue, as to own the excellence & rectitude of her Precepts & to lament my want of conformity to them. . . . If we cannot reduce this wished for Reformation to practice, let us treat the unhappy Victims with lenity, it is the furthest advance we can make towards Justice. It is a debt we owe to the purity of our Religion to shew that it is at variance with that law which warrants Slavery.[50]

[49] "Plan for liberating the negroes within the United States, by Mr. Ferdinando Fairfax," *American Museum,* VIII (Dec., 1790), 285–87; St. George Tucker, *A Dissertation on Slavery, with a Proposal for the Gradual Abolition of It in the State of Virginia* (Philadelphia, 1796).

[50] Patrick Henry, Jr., to Robert Pleasants, Jan. 18, 1773, in George S. Brookes,

The homage to virtue served to disarm criticism of Henry's "want of conformity" to virtue's precepts. Thus Quakers like Pleasants could at least rejoice in the knowledge that the hearts of the nation's leaders were in the right place. Henry's rhetoric also tended to soften his central point: namely, that antislavery principles could be transmuted into a program for ameliorating the plight of slavery's "unhappy Victims." This transmutation would in fact become the fate of antislavery in the southern states.

Quaker lobbyists were apparently responsible for the temporary and unpopular Virginia law of 1782 allowing private manumissions.[51] It was Pleasants, encouraged by the Philadelphia Quakers, who in 1790 founded the Abolition Society in Richmond; who addressed memorials to the state and federal governments; and who, as the leading abolitionist in Virginia, tested the boundaries of permissible dissent. In 1791, Madison frankly advised him not to submit a general emancipation measure to the Virginia assembly, and also admitted that "those from whom I derive my public station are known by me to be greatly interested in that species of property, and to view the matter in that light." Even Pleasants's cautious experiments with private manumissions soon brought him into sharp conflict with the laws of Virginia as well as with hostile neighbors. When he began treating his slaves as free workers, giving them tenancy on his own extensive lands, he was ordered to pay a heavy fine for allowing his Negroes to "go at large"; the Negroes were beaten and robbed by white terrorists. This reaction occurred, incidentally, well before the impact of the cotton gin, and when slavery was supposedly a dying and unpopular institution in Virginia. Between 1788 and 1796 the Virginia Yearly Meeting of the Society of Friends adopted the radical tactic of employing an agent, Christopher Johnson, to travel through Georgia and South Carolina recovering Negroes who had been seized and sold into bondage after being manumitted. But by 1798 Virginia laws had barred any member of an emancipation society from serving as a juror in a freedom suit and had virtually prevented humanitarians from advising or aiding blacks in any legal action for freedom.[52]

Friend Anthony Benezet (Philadelphia, 1937), pp. 443–44; Henry to Benezet, Jan. 18, 1773, MS in Friends House, London.

[51] William Dillwyn to Robert Valentine, Jan. 19, 1783, RV43, HEH. According to Dillwyn, his brother George, Warner Mifflin, and John Parrish had spent fifteen days lobbying with members of the Virginia assembly.

[52] James Pemberton to Robert Pleasants, Feb. 28, 1790; May 9, 1790; Aug. 25,

In North Carolina, where substantial numbers of Quakers had settled in the Piedmont region, there were few political leaders like Madison and Patrick Henry who would at least pay lip service to the Quakers' idealism. The conflict between Quaker policy and the law was thus sharper and more immediate. Like their Moravian neighbors, the North Carolina Quakers were a group apart, looked upon as religious fanatics and isolated from the dominant structures of political and economic power. In his recent study of the antislavery movement in North Carolina, John Michael Shay has argued that much of the abolitionist impulse among North Carolina Quakers came from pressures outside the state. If there had been no strain to conform to the evolving policy of Friends in Philadelphia and London, the North Carolina Quakers might conceivably have followed the path of the Moravians, who tried to adapt Negro slavery to the paternalistic patterns of their *Gemeinschaft* communities, who made cautious efforts to discourage slaveholding, but who finally absorbed much of the racism and commercial spirit of their secular neighbors.[53] In any event, the North Carolina Friends were attuned to the norms of the international Quaker community, and from the 1750s they continued to receive visits from antislavery missionaries like John Woolman and Warner Mifflin. By 1781 their Yearly Meeting gave sanction to the disownment of masters who could not be persuaded to free their slaves. Unfortunately, in 1777 the new state had re-enacted a colonial law forbidding manumission except for some act of meritorious service that would satisfy a county court. The legislature could not be swayed by the lobbying efforts of Joshua Evans and others, nor could the Quakers at first prevent the re-enslavement and sale of Negroes whom they had freed. Finally, between 1808 and 1810 the Yearly

---

1790; Oct. 5, 1790, Box 12, Brock Coll., HEH; Christopher Johnson's expense account, Box 13, Brock Coll., HEH; Robert Pleasants, memorial to the governor and council of Virginia, Box 12, Brock Coll., HEH; McColley, *Slavery and Jeffersonian Virginia*, pp. 156, 161, 187. Pleasants was in close touch with antislavery activities in Philadelphia and London. His papers include many manumission documents, but also show that he continued to own slaves to his death. A complex legal case, Pleasants *v.* Pleasants, arose over the family's efforts to free their slaves.

[53] John Michael Shay, "The Antislavery Movement in North Carolina," ch. 4, Ph.D. thesis, Princeton, 1971; Philip Africa, "Slaveholding in the Salem, N.C., Community of Moravians, 1771–1847," unpublished paper (I am much indebted to Professor Africa for allowing me to read his study).

Meeting created a special agency which could nominally "own" manumitted slaves and employ them for wages until they could safely be sent out of the state. It has been estimated that the North Carolina Quakers removed some fifteen hundred manumitted blacks from the peril of re-enslavement. Yet the conflict also contributed to a mounting Quaker emigration from the state. As early as 1804, Philadelphia Meeting for Sufferings reported the exodus to London, adding that it was "probable that few if any friends will remain long in Georgia, South Carolina or the eastern part of North Carolina." In the same year the American Convention of Abolition Societies confessed that nothing could be done to change the proslavery public opinion in North Carolina: "At present, the inhabitants of that state, consider the preservation of their lives, and all they hold dear on earth, as depending on the continuance of slavery; and are even riveting more firmly the fetters of oppression."[54]

Two questions haunted the minds of the South's more genuine opponents of slavery. Where could freedmen be sent, in order to prevent their re-enslavement and to satisfy the popular objection that the two races could never coexist as free men? Barring a satisfactory answer to this question, where could an antislavery Southerner go without being followed by the slave plantation? By 1817 the American Colonization Society offered a specious answer to the first question, and evoked particular enthusiasm in states like Maryland which had a large and growing population of free Negroes. There is no need here to discuss the history of the Colonization Society and its many state and local auxiliaries. The point to be stressed is that the movement mixed with and diluted earlier southern attempts at antislavery organization. Some colonizationists were sincere and even militant aboli-

[54] Stephen B. Weeks, *Southern Quakers and Slavery: A Study in Institutional History* (Baltimore, 1896), pp. 209–10, 217–22; Patrick Sowle, "The North Carolina Manumission Society, 1816–1834," *North Carolina Historical Review,* XLII (Winter, 1965), 47–49; H. Shelton Smith, *In His Image, But . . . : Racism in Southern Religion, 1780–1910* (Durham, N.C., 1972), pp. 33–34; "Notices of David Cooper," *Friends' Review,* XVI (Sept. 6, 1862), 3, 20; Shay, "Antislavery Movement in North Carolina," pp. 165, 213, 299, 506, and *passim;* John S. Bassett, *Anti-Slavery Leaders in North Carolina* (Baltimore, 1898), pp. 53–54; Philadelphia Meeting for Sufferings to London Meeting for Sufferings, Dec. 28, 1804, "Letters Which Passed Betwixt the Meeting for Sufferings in London, and the Meeting for Sufferings in Philadelphia . . ." Friends House, London; Gordon E. Finnie, "The Antislavery Movement in the Upper South before 1840," *Journal of Southern History,* XXXV (Aug., 1969), 327–28.

tionists; others responded to the missionary appeal of Christianizing Africa. But there can be no doubt that in the Upper South, as well as in North Carolina and Tennessee, the colonization movement provided a safe distraction for people whose misgivings over slavery were too strong to be kept entirely private. It also fostered the tacit understanding that slavery itself should not be openly denounced, since the movement's success required the support of slaveholders who were interested only in getting rid of free Negroes, but whose hearts were supposed to soften once there were no racial deterrents to emancipation. The tendency for antislavery to merge with colonization suggested that there could be no moderate and yet effective opposition to a system of labor which was not only expanding geographically but which had come to dominate the market and power relationships of the South.[55]

The increasing attractiveness of colonization as a surrogate for antislavery coincided with the exodus of potential abolitionist leaders. A brief glance at a representative roster tells much.

George Bourne, an English emigrant, began preaching against slaveholding as an independent Presbyterian minister in the mountainous regions of western Virginia. The central issue Bourne raised was whether a genuine Christian, and especially a Presbyterian churchman, could also be a slaveowner. In 1815 the Lexington Presbytery tried Bourne on charges of un-Christian conduct toward fellow Presbyterians who happened also to be slaveholders. The General Assembly reversed the Presbytery's decision to unfrock Bourne and ordered a new trial. Meanwhile, in 1816, Bourne published *The Book and Slavery Irreconcilable,* the most radical abolitionist tract yet to appear in the United States—a work which attacked the complicity of the churches in the sin of slavery, which rejected the palliative of colonization, and which demanded nothing less than total and immediate emancipation. In 1817, Bourne wrote the Lexington Presbytery from Pennsylvania, humbly apologizing for his offending acts, and begging to be dismissed to some other presbytery "which chuses to receive me into their communion." He feared, however, that his life might be in danger if he returned to Virginia for the second trial. In 1818, the

[55] P. J. Staudenraus, *The African Colonization Movement, 1816–1865* (New York, 1961), *passim;* Shay, "Antislavery Movement in North Carolina," pp. 329–30; Finnie, "Antislavery Movement in the Upper South," *passim.*

General Assembly upheld Lexington's second decision to expel Bourne from the ministry.[56]

James Gilliland, also a Presbyterian clergyman, appealed in 1796 to the Synod of the Carolinas after his local presbytery, in South Carolina, refused to ordain him unless he promised not to preach against slavery. The Synod sustained the rule, and in 1804 Gilliland emigrated to southern Ohio, where he eventually joined other southern antislavery refugees, including John Rankin, James H. Dickey, and Samuel Crothers.[57]

David Rice, the son of a poor farmer in Hanover County, Virginia, the center of the Presbyterian Great Awakening, was converted by the revival, entered the ministry, and moved on to Kentucky, where in 1792 he delivered an eloquent speech against slavery at the state's first constitutional convention. After losing the struggle to outlaw slavery in Kentucky, Rice pressed the Transylvania Presbytery to follow the Quakers' example of requiring masters to manumit their slaves as a condition for continuing communion.[58]

David Barrow, also the son of a small Virginia farmer, entered the Baptist ministry and in 1784 freed his few personal slaves. In 1790 he issued a circular letter to the Baptists of Southampton County, explaining his reasons for emigrating to Kentucky. Barrow said that in eastern Virginia he could not support his family without owning slaves, a practice he had forsworn as a violation of the laws of God and nature. After moving to Kentucky, Barrow encountered bitter hostility and disciplinary action from various Baptist associations. He finally helped to found a new association of antislavery Baptists, the Baptized Licking-Locust Association, Friends of Humanity. James Lemen, also a Virginia Baptist and a friend of Jefferson, followed Barrow's example after he had moved to Illinois and had been excommunicated from a church for his antislavery views.[59]

---

[56] Smith, *In His Image*, pp. 61–64; George Bourne, *The Book and Slavery Irreconcilable; With Animadversions Upon Dr. Smith's Philosophy* (Philadelphia, 1816).

[57] Smith, *In His Image*, p. 60; Dumond, *Antislavery Origins*, p. 7.

[58] Smith, *In His Image*, pp. 56–58; Asa Earl Martin, *The Anti-Slavery Movement in Kentucky prior to 1850* (n.p., 1918), pp. 14–18, 22–24; David Rice, *Slavery Inconsistent with Justice and Good Policy; Proved by a Speech Delivered in the Convention Held at Danville, Kentucky* (Philadelphia, 1792).

[59] Miles M. Fisher, "Friends of Humanity: A Quaker Anti-Slavery Influence,"

The Quakers not only took the leadership in forming antislavery societies in the South, but achieved remarkable success, even in the face of obstructive laws, in manumitting their own slaves. This achievement was particularly striking in regions like Delaware and Maryland's Eastern Shore, where John Woolman had persuaded the schismatic followers of Joseph Nichols to free their slaves; where the Quakers themselves manumitted hundreds of blacks; and where the Methodist Francis Asbury found in 1778 that "the more pious part of the people called Quakers, are exerting themselves for the liberation of the slaves. This is a very laudable design; and what the Methodists must come to, or, I fear the Lord will depart from them."[60] The key question for southern antislavery was whether the Quaker example would be taken up by the churches of the evangelical revival—and thus by the mass of "plain folk," including yeomen farmers, artisans, tradesmen, and small slaveholders.

There is evidence of a strong Quaker influence on the Protestant revivalists who struggled to keep slavery from spreading into Kentucky, Tennessee, and Illinois. David Barrow and Carter Tarrant called their Kentucky Baptist association, "Friends of Humanity"; and like the Quakers, they barred slaveholders from fellowship. James Lemen adopted the same name and exclusionary principle for his Illinois church. For small farmers and artisans who sought to escape the encroaching domination of the plantation system, the Quaker testimony showed the way to self-purification and independent identity. The Quakers proved that in some sections of the South, at least, one could achieve dignity and economic independence without purchasing slaves. Thus Elihu Embree, who edited *The Emancipator* at Jonesboro, in eastern Tennessee, owned a nail factory valued at $150,000. But economic success did not bring independence from slaveholder sanctions. Many of Embree's sympathetic, non-Quaker correspondents were afraid to give him their names.[61]

Church History, IV (Sept., 1935), 189–95; Smith, *In His Image,* pp. 49–53, 130–31; Carlos R. Allen, "David Barrow's 'Circular Letter' of 1798," *William and Mary Quarterly,* 3rd ser., XX (1963), 440–51; Dillon, "Sources of Early Antislavery Thought in Illinois," p. 37.

[60] Kenneth L. Carroll, "Religious Influences on the Manumission of Slaves in Carolina, Dorchester, and Talbot Counties," *Maryland History Magazine,* LVI (June, 1961), 176–97; Finnie, "Antislavery Movement in the Upper South," pp. 321–22; Smith, *In His Image,* p. 37.

[61] Fisher, "Friends of Humanity," 187–202; Smith, *In His Image,* pp. 48–52; Embree papers, HSP.

Evangelical religion, whether in England or America, combined a reformist impulse with a sometimes countervailing need for social conformity. Even in England, as Leland J. Bellot has recently argued, there was no necessary connection between religious evangelicalism and hostility to colonial slavery. English missionaries to the West Indies were interested in religious conversion, not revolution, although some West Indian planters were too blind or bigoted to see the difference—a fact which incalculably strengthened the hand of British abolitionists.[62] But in England itself the Methodist and Anglican revivalists who preached on the themes of humility, subordination, and acceptance of worldly privation had little need to accommodate the pious slaveholder. On the contrary, the godless character of West Indian society made it easy to perceive slavery as a product of irreligion and infidelity, closely linked to the sins of intemperance, profanity, and shameless sexuality. Similarly, many representatives of the established order in New England—who were the heirs of a different revivalistic tradition—could think of antislavery as an expression of "disinterested benevolence" precisely because slavery was not a powerful "interest" in New England.

In contrast to New England, however, the southern antislavery leaders were not wealthy lawyers, merchants, jurists, or Yale-educated ministers. Nor were they spokesmen for the established order. The southern revival, which spread from Virginia to the west and south, was essentially a populist movement. As Donald G. Mathews has suggested, it was an immense organizing process, providing common people with a diversified range of decision-making and participatory experience. It also assimilated republicanism and the belief in natural rights to a simple, Bible-centered faith.[63] For preachers like David Barrow, slavery was not only an obstacle to a Christian life and a God-fearing society. Every man, black or white, he insisted, had a right to "a good character."

For a time it appeared that the evangelical churches were only a step behind the Quakers in purging themselves of slaveholding. The Methodists worked from the unequivocal precedents established by

[62] Leland J. Bellot, "Evangelicals and the Defense of Slavery in Britain's Old Colonial Empire," *Journal of Southern History*, XXXVII (1971), 19–40; John Vickers, *Thomas Coke, Apostle of Methodism* (London, 1969), pp. 169–72.

[63] Donald G. Mathews, "The Second Great Awakening as an Organizing Process, 1780–1830: An Hypothesis," *American Quarterly*, XXI (Spring, 1969), 23–43.

Wesley, who had called slavery the "execrable sum of all villainies," and who had written into the rules of Methodist societies a prohibition against buying or selling men with the intention of enslaving them. After some earlier and more cautious preparatory steps, the constituent 1784 Christmas Conference at Baltimore, which organized the Methodist Episcopal Church, determined "to take immediately some effectual method to extirpate this abomination from among us," and proceded to adopt a detailed plan requiring members to begin manumitting their slaves, in accordance with state laws, or to face excommunication.[64]

In 1785 the General Committee of Virginia Baptists, which was only an advisory body, condemned slavery as "contrary to the word of God." Five years later the same body adopted a resolution proclaiming that slavery "is a violent deprivation of the rights of nature, and inconsistent with a republican government." They called upon all Baptists to "make use of every legal measure, to extirpate the horrid evil from the land," and looked forward to the day when the legislature could "proclaim the general Jubilee, consistent with the principles of good policy." In 1787 the Ketocton Association took a similar stand and approved a plan for gradual emancipation.[65] In the same year, the Presbyterian Synod of New York and Philadelphia, acting as the supreme tribunal of the church, debated an "overture" that all members and churches be exhorted "to promote the abolition of slavery, and the instruction of negroes, whether bond or free." As a compromise measure, the Synod endorsed the general principle of emancipation, recommending that Presbyterians prepare their slaves for freedom, and that they use "the most prudent measures, consistent with the interest and the state of society . . . to procure eventually the final abolition of slavery in America." In Kentucky, the Transylvania Presbytery not only urged members to prepare their slaves for freedom, but to manumit those who could assume the responsibilities of liberty.[66]

[64] Donald G. Mathews, *Slavery and Methodism: A Chapter in American Morality, 1780–1845* (Princeton, 1965), pp. 3–11; Wade Crawford Barclay, *History of Methodist Missions* (2 vols., New York, 1949–1950), II, 63–64, 71–72; William B. Gravely, "Early Methodism and Slavery: The Roots of a Tradition," *Wesleyan Quarterly Review*, II (May, 1965), 84–87.

[65] Joseph Michael Shea, "The Baptists and Slavery, 1840–1845," p. 10, M.A. thesis, Clark University, 1933; Smith, *In His Image*, pp. 47–53.

[66] Smith, *In His Image*, pp. 47–53; Martin, *Anti-Slavery Movement in Kentucky*, pp. 22–24.

Even these cautiously worded pronouncements bear a striking similarity to the earlier evolving policies of the Society of Friends. But the Quakers were not a proselytizing church whose desire for converts required accommodation to economic interest and popular prejudice. The very openness and self-direction of the southern revival made it a weak vehicle for antislavery discipline. If the revival helped to encourage private manumissions, especially in Kentucky, it also led to schisms and bitter conflicts over slavery within church congregations. And since the strength of American Protestantism lay in its dynamic balance between local autonomy and national consensus, the general governing or advisory bodies were soon forced to exert moderating pressures in the interest of denominational unity.

Thus in Virginia the Roanoke Association of Baptists questioned the right of the General Committee to issue resolutions on an issue so complex as slavery, and added, with respect to the 1790 statement, that "we are not unanimously clear in our minds whether the God of Nature ever intended that one human should ever hold another in slavery." The Strawberry District Association advised the General Committee "not to interfere" with slavery. In 1793, according to W. Harrison Daniel, "the subject of hereditary slavery was officially mentioned for the last time by the General Committee," which prudently decided that emancipation was a political issue which "belongs to the legislative body." Two years later the Presbyterian General Assembly sidestepped the issue of excluding slaveholders from membership, thus beginning a sustained retreat from earlier idealistic pronouncements.[67]

The declension was more dramatic, prolonged, and anxiety-ridden in the Methodist Episcopal Church, which had come closest to the Quakers in its antislavery commitments. The Methodist governing structure was more authoritarian than that of either the Baptists or Presbyterians; but in the 1780s some eighty per cent of the church's membership lived south of Maryland. Only a few months after the Christmas Conference of 1784, Thomas Coke began to discover the significance of this fact. While touring Virginia, Coke visited "leading members" who told him that the rule against slaveholding would prove disastrous for the church. Far more alarming, Coke encountered

---

[67] W. Harrison Daniel, "Virginia Baptists and the Negro in the Early Republic," *Virginia Magazine*, LXXX (Jan., 1972), 65–67; Smith, *In His Image*, pp. 47–48, 58, 66–68; Irving S. Kull, "Presbyterian Attitudes toward Slavery," *Church History*, VII (1938), 102–3.

angry, club-wielding mobs and narrowly escaped being flogged, if not lynched. Along with his clerical associate, Bishop Francis Asbury, Coke sought the personal aid of George Washington in support of a petition to the Virginia assembly for gradual emancipation. But during his southern tours Coke also began to address Negroes on the duties of slaves to their masters. At the Baltimore Conference of 1785 the Methodist leadership decided to suspend the controversial rule on slavery, since as Coke said, the religious work was "in too infantile a state to push things to extremity." At that time Coke, like the Quakers who had preceded him, was still trying to persuade his Virginia hosts that being kind to slaves was not sufficient. Eight years later, when the Methodist mission had expanded to the West Indies, Coke could applaud a Grenada slave law as an "honour to the whole island." By 1798, Bishop Asbury had concluded that slavery would "perhaps exist in Virginia for ages."[68]

Meanwhile, after years of "postponement," the Methodist General Conference tried in 1796 to follow the Quaker path of decentralized gradualism. The church hierarchy still condemned slavery as an unmitigated evil, even as a "crying sin," but passed the initiative for self-purification to local meetings and officials. The system, in the words of Donald G. Mathews, was one of "formalized frustration." The church made some provision for excommunicating members who sold slaves or who spurned the recommendations of a quarterly meeting. In 1800 the General Conference even directed the annual conferences to prepare petitions for gradual emancipation in states which had not yet enacted such measures. At the same time, however, the Conference rejected a motion to require Methodist masters to free upon maturity all slaves born after July 4, 1800.[69]

The Methodists faced obstacles even greater than those the Quakers had overcome. They were not an exclusive, self-contained sect with intricate ties of communication and endogamous marriage. Their disciplinary machinery was neither as subtle nor as effective as that of the Quakers. Whereas the Quakers relied on the quiet persuasion

[68] Mathews, *Slavery and Methodism*, pp. 11–61; Vickers, *Thomas Coke*, pp. 95–98, 169–71; Smith, *In His Image*, pp. 39–46, 69; Albert Matthews, "Notes on the Proposed Abolition of Slavery in Virginia in 1785," *Publications of the Colonial Society of Massachusetts*, VI (Boston, 1904), 371–77.

[69] Mathews, *Slavery and Methodism*, pp. 19–24; Barclay, *History of Methodist Missions*, II, 74–82.

of visiting committees, Methodists like James O'Kelly were given to violent denuncaition, which in O'Kelly's case contributed to a bitter schism. Between 1784 and 1816, Methodist membership soared from 15,000 to 172,000, much of the growth centering in the South. Finally, the Methodists began their antislavery activities at a time of national expansion, when an evangelical church could either spread westward with slavery or not advance at all. Consequently, in the early nineteenth century, Methodist conferences learned the arts of equivocation and softened language, and began to devise numerous exceptions and exemptions—as in 1808, when the General Conference decided to delete the offensive rule on slavery from copies of the *Discipline* to be used in Georgia and the Carolinas. In the end, the church concentrated its efforts on the religious instruction of slaves. As George Whitefield had perceived, during his stay in Georgia many decades before, the best way to save slaves' souls was not by offering worldly liberty but by teaching Negroes to be grateful that they were spared the temptations of the free. Bishop Asbury, who had once vowed that Methodists should emulate the Quakers, asked in 1809, "What is the personal liberty of the African which he may abuse, to the salvation of his soul, how may it be compared?"[70]

H. Shelton Smith has noted a seeming paradox concerning the Quakers: "In view of this unparalleled ministry to the Negro race, one would have expected the Society of Friends to reap a bountiful harvest of black members. Yet extremely few joined the Society."[71] The question obscures and yet points to a profound social truth. There were no greater illusions than the belief that emancipators would embrace ex-slaves in religious communion; or above all, the belief that religious instruction was a step toward the slaves' emancipation. The Quakers were a highly exclusive sect, intent on purifying their own lives in accordance with in-group norms. Insofar as they were a "people among peoples," to use Sydney V. James's phrase, they sought to diffuse a spirit of benevolence and to create a social environment congenial to their own discipline. They could achieve this objective more readily in Philadelphia than in the southern Appalachians. In the major plantation districts of the South, the Quakers could only become apostate accommodationists, genuine subversives, or emi-

[70] Mathews, *Slavery and Methodism, passim;* Smith, *In His Image,* pp. 41–47; Gravely, "Early Methodism and Slavery," pp. 88–92.
[71] Smith, *In His Image,* pp. 34–35.

grants. Almost by self-definition, they were morally insulated from the mass of Negro slaves. In the South as a whole, the ultimate effect of the Quakers' achievement was a tightening of the bars to private manumission. The contest between the internal discipline of the sect and the external discipline of the slave regime could have but one outcome: the Quakers alerted the South to the danger of a gradual erosion of slavery through private emancipation.

On the other hand, the great lesson of the eighteenth-century Presbyterian and Baptist revivals was that Christianity could safely be extended to Negro slaves without endangering the slave regime. The only way a church could affect the lives of the mass of slaves—and the Baptists took the lead in proving the point—was to show that even Negro preachers, if they understood the true precepts of Christianity, would never think seriously of emancipation, let alone insurrection.[72] By 1822 the South had become ideologically committed to the notion that authentic Christianity made Negroes better slaves. In sentencing ten of the "criminals" linked with the Denmark Vesey conspiracy, the South Carolina court not only charged them with "the vilest ingratitude," since:

Servitude has existed under various forms, from the deluge to the present time, and in no age or country has the condition of slaves been milder or more humane than your own. You are, with few exceptions, treated with kindness, and enjoy every comfort compatible with your situation. You are exempt from many of the miseries, to which *the poor* are subject throughout the world. In many countries the life of the slave is at the disposal of his master; here you have always been under the protection of the law.

But even worse, in the eyes of the court, the slaves were guilty of "the grossest impiety":

You have perverted the sacred words of God, and attempted to torture them into sanction for crimes. . . . Are you incapable of the Heavenly influence of that Gospel, all whose "paths are peace?" It was to reconcile us to our destiny on earth, and to enable us to discharge with fidelity all

[72] Daniel, "Virginia Baptists and the Negro," pp. 60–69. In his new work *Roll, Jordan, Roll* (New York, 1974), Eugene D. Genovese not only demonstrates the success of the Baptists in bringing Christianity to the slaves, but shows what different uses the whites and blacks made of their supposedly common faith. The black preacher, whether slave or free, played a far more complex role than the whites ever suspected.

our duties, whether as master or servant, that those inspired precepts were imparted by Heaven to fallen men. . . . Had you listened with sincerity to such doctrines, you would not have been arrested by an ignominious death.[73]

The Reverend Richard Furman, president of the South Carolina Baptist State Convention, felt an imperative need to distinguish authentic Christianity from the perverted doctrines of Charleston's African Methodist Episcopal Church, to which some of the conspirators had belonged, and which had been "intimately connected with a similar Body in Philadelphia . . . whose Principles are formed on the Scheme of General Emancipation." Furman assured Governor Thomas Bennett that the blacks "composing the great Body, of well-known, regular, & esteemed Members of Churches, have not been impeached. It would indeed seem that the Conspirators were afraid to trust them." Hence the evidence furnished at the trials served to vindicate one of the fundamental lessons of the past revivals:

that one of the best Securities we have to the domestic Peace & Safety of the State, is found in the Sentiments & correspondent Dispositions of the religious Negroes; which they derive from the Bible.—If this Sentiment is just, it would seem, that instead of taking away the Bible from them, & abridging the truly religious Privileges they have been used to enjoy, to avoid Danger; the better Way would be, to take Measures for bringing them to a more full & just acquaintance with the former; & to secure to them the latter, under Regulations the least liable to abuse.[74]

Since Furman simply extended the doctrines that Whitefield had advanced in the mid-eighteenth century and that Asbury had come to accept by 1809, it might appear that the antislavery pronouncements from the Protestant associations of the 1780s were a relatively meaningless aberration. The retreat of evangelical Protestantism left scattered pockets of antislavery sentiment across the Upper South, but precluded the possibility of an organized southern movement. One can easily be misled by the large number of reported antislavery societies in North Carolina, Tennessee, and Kentucky during the second and third decades of the nineteenth century. The records of few societies survive, and most of our information comes from Quaker abolitionists

[73] Robert S. Starobin, ed., *Denmark Vesey: The Slave Conspiracy of 1822* (Englewood Cliffs, N.J., 1970), pp. 55–56.
[74] *Ibid.*, p. 122.

like Benajmin Lundy, who were victims of wishful thinking and who were eager to record unconfirmed reports of meetings and expanded membership.[75]

Virtually all of these southern societies were concentrated in the Piedmont counties of North Carolina and across the mountains in eastern Tennessee. Of the leadership of the North Carolina Manumission Society, seventy-eight per cent were Quakers. There was evidently a similar Quaker predominance in the Tennessee societies, though not in Kentucky. And in Kentucky the early Methodist and Baptist leaders failed to sustain a continuing movement. It seems likely that most of the reported southern organizations were auxiliaries which died almost as soon as they were born. Moreover, the typical manumission society was exceedingly cautious and conservative, its survival depending largely on its unobtrusiveness. Several scholars have recently concluded that the "southern antislavery movement" was more apparent than real; and that much that passed for antislavery was in essence "deportationist, proslavery, and anti-Negro."[76] The most significant point, perhaps, was the growing isolation of these Quaker-dominated groups. One occasionally encounters mention of "friends" in the Deep South, but their names are seldom mentioned. By 1804 the societies in Richmond, Alexandria, and Delaware were clearly being overwhelmed by expensive legal suits, by a shortage of funds, and by the "lukewarmness" or disaffection of many members. The critical event that helped to paralyze antislavery zeal in the South was the disclosure in 1800 of a well-organized slave conspiracy, led by Gabriel Prosser, to destroy Richmond and to ignite a general insurrection. The subsequent mass execution of accused slaves dramatized both the seriousness of the plot and the peril facing anyone who dared to question the precarious establishment. By 1806, few ties remained between the southern antislavery societies and the larger "parent" groups in Philadelphia and New York.[77]

[75] Finnie, "Antislavery Movement in the Upper South," pp. 319–42; Shay, "Antislavery Movement in North Carolina," *passim.*

[76] Finnie, "Antislavery Movement in the Upper South," *passim;* Sowle, "North Carolina Manumission Society," *passim;* H. M. Wagstaff, ed., *Minutes of the North Carolina Manumission Society* (Chapel Hill, 1934), *passim;* Ruth Nuermberger, *Charles Osborn in the Anti-Slavery Movement* (Columbus, Ohio, 1937), *passim;* James W. Patton, "The Progress of Emancipation in Tennessee," *Journal of Negro History,* XVII (Jan., 1932), 67–102; Smith, *In His Image,* pp. 69–73.

[77] John S. Tyson, *Life of Elisha Tyson, the Philanthropist* (Baltimore, 1825),

Though recent scholarship has correctly emphasized the weakness of antislavery in the South, the persistence of any antislavery activity is a remarkable social fact. The very diversity of southern society for a time made slavery a more vulnerable institution than in any other plantation regime. If Virginia could produce an enlightened planter-statesmen culture, it could also produce a religious revivalist culture, some of whose spokesmen condemned slavery as a sin. Far more than the West Indies, the South also absorbed elements of the Protestant work ethic. Even the great Virginia planters could express occasional anxiety over the idleness of some of their neighbors, over the waste and economic stagnation that slavery supposedly entailed, and over the stigma that slavery attached to "honest labor." And if many of the later romanticized "plain folk" actually aspired to become slaveholding planters, they could also resent the wealth and ostentation of the elite, and fear the competition of slave labor.

Yet this potentiality for internal dissent ultimately became the South's major source of strength. For among plantation societies, the South alone was forced to test the limits of dissent and to resolve a moral challenge by assimilating and transmuting it. Compared to the West Indians, the southern slaveholders were acutely sensitive to their reputation and "right to a good character." They could not retire to an English or French estate, leaving an original and less savory identity behind. The various expressions of southern antislavery senti-ment raised genuine moral doubts that had to be resolved by a redefi-

---

pp. 21–22; *Minutes and Proceedings of the Fifth Convention of Delegates from the Abolition Societies* . . . (Philadelphia, 1798), p. 12; MS Minutes of the American Convention, I (1800), 186; II (1805), 19–21; II (1806), 60–61, HSP; Pennsylvania Abolition Society MSS, IV, 23–25; VI, 6, HSP; P. E. Thomas to John Parrish, Aug. 31, 1806, Cox. Parrish, Wharton papers, V, HSP; *Minutes and Proceedings of the Seventh Convention of Delegates* . . . (Philadelphia, 1801), pp. 30–32. By 1817, Charles Osborn's *The Philanthropist* claimed that even in Delaware, Maryland, and Virginia, no member of the legislature would dare to make a motion on the subject of slavery; and that in the District of Columbia, as well as in the southern states, printers would publish nothing intimating that slavery was an evil—at best, they would touch the subject lightly and then hurry away (*The Philanthropist* [Dec. 5, 1817], 99). On the other hand, as late as 1823 the American Convention received an encouraging report from Tennessee, which said that there were twenty branches of the state manumission society, comprising six hundred members, and that the legislature had appointed a committee to consider a petition for ameliorating the condition of slaves (*Minutes of the Eighteenth Session of the American Convention* . . . [Philadelphia, 1823], pp. 16–18).

nition of collective norms. And the redefinition did not begin with the Reverend Furman or the later proslavery apologists. Jefferson himself pointed to the solution: the ownership of slaves was a heavy burden, carrying the strictest moral obligations; to emancipate one's Negroes would be a betrayal of duty, since only a few exceptional slaves could fend for themselves. If the burden brought the satisfactions of any paternalistic guidance, it was also considered expensive. In the 1790s Washington repeatedly complained of his slaves' laziness, inefficiency, and wastefulness; they knew he would support them regardless of their behavior. Between 1786 and 1799 their numbers grew from 216 to 317, and all looked upon the father of the country as their provider.[78] Although Washington resolved to emancipate his slaves by will, most planters already believed that such a step was misguided idealism, as well as a breach of solemn trust. The Negro's supposed incapacity for freedom, coupled with his supposedly ineffective labor, disguised the profitability of the system.

In the South, therefore, an indigenous questioning of slavery did not lead to a parallel development of antislavery and proslavery traditions. It led rather to a resolution which channeled idealism toward the goals of Christian trusteeship, and which committed the entire society to a moral defense of the slaveholder, a defense demanded by the major Protestant churches and by the political and military power of an immense and diversified white population.

[78] Flexner, *George Washington: Anguish and Farewell*, p. 444.

Five ∽

The Quaker Ethic and the
Antislavery International

The Quaker Initiative

The Quakers, more than any other religious group, had long expressed misgivings over the possible sinfulness of buying and selling men. During the first half of the eighteenth century, however, they had been content to issue cautionary warnings about the African slave trade; to exhort Quaker masters to treat their black servants with Christian charity; and to ignore or disown the few deviants, like Benjamin Lay, who shrilly proclaimed that "all slave-keepers" were "apostates." The Quaker commitment to bear collective testimony against slavery came surprisingly late and coincided with the publication of secular antislavery arguments from jurists, philosophers, moralists, and men of letters.[1] Quaker writers did not play a con-

[1] See Davis, *The Problem of Slavery in Western Culture* (Ithaca, N.Y., 1966), ch. 10 and Epilogue. My discussion of Quakerism in general draws on William C. Braithwaite, *The Beginnings of Quakerism* (London, 1912); Braithwaite, *The Second Period of Quakerism* (London, 1919); Rufus M. Jones, *The Later Periods of Quakerism* (London, 1921); Thomas Drake, *Quakers and Slavery in America* (New Haven, 1950); Sydney V. James, *A People among Peoples: Quaker Benevolence in Eighteenth-Century America* (Cambridge, Mass., 1963); Richard Bauman, *For the Reputation of Truth: Politics, Religion, and Conflict among the Pennsylvania Quakers, 1750–1800* (Baltimore, 1971); Anne T. Gary, "The Political and Economic Relations of English and American Quakers," D.Phil. thesis, Oxford, 1935. Most of these and other secondary accounts give the impression of an immanent unfolding of Quaker antislavery testimony, as if there were an unbroken continuity from George Fox to Anthony Benezet, and as if

213

spicuous part in creating this international body of antislavery literature, although Anthony Benezet helped to anthologize and disseminate
it. Indeed, it was the emergence of an enlightened climate of opinion,
defining liberty as a natural and fundamental right, that brought outside sanction to Quaker reformers like Benezet and John Woolman.[2]

Quaker leaders simply waited until the time was ripe. There are a number of
arguments that cast strong doubt on this view: (1) The Quakers in the West
Indies did no more than attempt to Christianize their slaves, and even this
aroused fierce resistance and persecution (Richard S. Dunn, *Sugar and Slaves:
The Rise of the Planter Class in the English West Indies, 1624–1713* [Chapel
Hill, 1972], pp. 104–6, 184, 249, 339). (2) The Quaker-dominated government
of colonial Pennsylvania enacted a harsh slave code, and as late as 1730 Quaker
merchants in Philadelphia were actively importing and selling West Indian
Negroes; as late as the 1760s the Rhode Island slave trade involved leading Quaker
families; some of the most powerful English Friends were members of the Royal
African Company (Darold D. Wax, "Quaker Merchants and the Slave Trade in
Colonial Pennsylvania," *Pennsylvania Magazine of History and Biography,*
LXXXVI [April, 1962], 144–59; Gary, "Political and Economic Relations," pp.
194–97). (3) During the Seven Years' War, when the Quaker leaders of Philadelphia agreed to take active measures to discourage slaveholding among their
brethren, the city faced a growing shortage of white indentured servants, a
shortage which increased the demand for slaves. Gary B. Nash has estimated that
by 1767 Quakers "were somewhat overrepresented among Philadelphia slaveholders in proportion to their numbers," and has concluded that "when faced
with a direct choice between forgoing the human labor they needed or ignoring
the principles enunciated by their leaders and officially sanctioned by the
Society through its Quarterly and Yearly Meetings, the rank and file of Philadelphia Friends chose the latter course." Quaker ideology did not become effective until the supply of white indentured servants increased and the supply of
slaves decreased in the years immediately prior to the Revolution (Nash,
"Slaves and Slaveholders in Colonial Philadelphia," *William and Mary Quarterly,*
3rd ser., XXX [April, 1973], 252–54). (4) The early Quaker doubts over the
African trade were not so clear-cut as the earlier doubts of the seventeenth-
century Dutch clergy, who advised the Dutch West India Company to keep clear
of the slave trade; and in neither case did the doubts prevent involvement
(Johannes Postma, "Slaving Techniques and Treatment of Slaves: The Dutch
Activities on the Guinea Coast," paper presented at the M.S.S.B. Conference on
Systems of Slavery, March, 1972, University of Rochester). (5) The Moravians'
ethical and religious views were similar to those of the Quakers, and the
Moravians expressed a similar sensitivity to the possible corruptions of slaveholding; but though the Moravians of North Carolina made attempts at communal supervision of slaveholders, they continued into the nineteenth century to
buy and hire slave labor. My point, then, is that the Quakers' decision to disengage themselves from slavery was not an inevitable outgrowth of George Fox's
cautious advice in 1657 to treat slaves with Christian mercy and if possible limit
their terms of bondage to thirty years.

[2] For example, in 1783 and 1784, *Gentleman's Magazine* reported Lord North's
compliments to Quaker humanitarianism; published the epistle of the Yearly

But then climates of opinion do not give virgin birth to social movements. By the 1780s the British and American Quakers could provide
what no other group seemed capable of: decision, commitment, and
most important, organization.

It would be difficult to exaggerate the central role Quakers played
in initiating and sustaining the first antislavery movements. During
the Seven Years' War, Philadelphia Yearly Meeting moved from the
ideal of Christianizing the master-slave relationship to the ideal of
preparing slaves for freedom. By 1758 official committees were visiting
and prodding individual slave owners, although a shortage of white
servants, occasioned by the war, put a premium on the value of slaves.
In 1760, New England Yearly Meeting ruled that the importers of
slaves would be subject to discipline. The following year London
Yearly Meeting, under some pressure from Philadelphia, took the
decisive move of authorizing disownment for Quakers still engaged in
the slave trade. In 1774, Philadelphia Yearly Meeting finally adopted
rules that threatened disownment for any buying or transfer of slave
property, that barred Quakers from serving as executors of estates
involving slaves, and that required masters to treat Negroes like other
servants and to manumit them at the earliest opportunity.[3]

These efforts at self-reform, especially in Pennsylvania and Delaware, soon involved the Quakers in legal battles to protect slaves who

---

Meeting, in angry response to an anti-Quaker parody; and printed the American
Quaker petition to the Continental Congress (LIII [June, 1783], 524; [Nov.,
1783], 919; LIV [Feb., 1784], 121. Even from Liverpool, John Pemberton reported to his wife, on July 16, 1783, that the Quaker petition was generally
well-spoken of, and he thus felt encouraged over the prospects of further efforts
to enlighten the English public (Pemberton papers, XXXIX, Historical Society
of Pennsylvania [hereafter HSP]). As early as the 1730s Voltaire had idealized
the "Good Quaker" as a symbol of religious tolerance, and the legend continued
to grow in France, receiving nourishment from some of the physiocrats and
especially from Crèvecoeur.

[3] In 1757, London Meeting for Sufferings appointed a committee to investigate
the problem of Quaker engagement in the slave trade. On February 1, 1759,
Philadelphia Meeting for Sufferings took comfort and satisfaction in the warnings
from London against dealing in Negroes and other slaves. By August 22, 1766,
however, London Meeting for Sufferings had grown more cautious about
political involvement in general: "If above all things we make the great work of
Religion our chief Concern, every other Circumstance will be so directed, or
permitted, as to conduce the most effectually to our real Happiness and
Security. . . . If we honestly labour to mind our proper Business and truly
study to be quiet, we shall be found in a State both safe and acceptable (MS
Letterbook, Friends House, London).

claimed to be free. For example, Israel Pemberton and Thomas Harrison tried to defend an Indian woman and her children who had been brought from Virginia to Philadelphia; because Harrison had given the family shelter, the court forced him to pay heavy damages, for which he was later reimbursed £25 in Anthony Benezet's will. It was this contest that led in 1775 to the formation of the Society for the Relief of Free Negroes Unlawfully Held in Bondage.[4] The Revolutionary War soon disrupted the organization, but early in 1784 the reported suicides of two blacks who had been illegally enslaved prompted the restoration of what was to become the Pennsylvania Society, for Promoting the Abolition of Slavery, for the Relief of Free Negroes Unlawfully Held in Bondage, and for Improving the Condition of the African Race. The phrase "abolition of slavery" reflected the new state law of 1780 providing for mandatory gradual emancipation. In New York, where no such law had yet been passed, the organization formed in January, 1785, bore the title, Society for Promoting the Manumission of Slaves in New York City.[5]

The Pennsylvania Abolition Society served as the model and inspiration for the various state societies which began in 1794 to send representatives to Philadelphia for the annual Convention of Delegates from the Abolition Societies. Prominent non-Quakers, like Benjamin Franklin and Benjamin Rush, served at one time or another as presidents of the Pennsylvania Society. But from the outset it was a predominantly Quaker organization. After selecting sixty-eight of the Society's most active members during its first twenty-five years of existence, I have identified more than three-quarters as Friends. I have also identified as Quakers about one-half of the most active mem-

---

[4] W. J. Buck, MS History of the Pennsylvania Abolition Society, Pennsylvania Abolition Society MSS, HSP (this section of the history was based on an earlier MS account by Thomas Harrison).

[5] The New Jersey Society for Promoting the Abolition of Slavery was formed at Burlington in 1793, at the instigation of the Pennsylvania Society, well before New Jersey had passed a gradual emancipation act (Pennsylvania Abolition Society MSS, III, 15, HSP; *The Constitution of the New-Jersey Society, for Promoting the Abolition of Slavery* . . . [Burlington, 1793]). On the other hand, the Rhode Island organization was simply the Providence Society for Abolishing the Slave-Trade, and in Connecticut the title was Society for the Promotion of Freedom and the Relief of Persons Unlawfully Holden in Bondage.

Anthony Benezet referred to the Negroes' suicides in a letter of August 10, 1783, to James Pemberton (George S. Brookes, *Friend Anthony Benezet* [Philadelphia, 1937], p. 397).

bers of the New York Manumission Society. In 1805 seven of the ten officers of the same Society were Friends. Except in Connecticut and Kentucky, Quakers were the chief organizers and most active supporters of the early American antislavery societies. In the North Carolina movement the proportion of Quakers ran as high as eighty per cent.[6]

[6] Thomas Drake notes that twelve of the original eighteen members attending the New York Manumission Society were Friends (*Quakers and Slavery*, p. 98). I have checked the MS membership lists against a large number of directories and genealogical guides. The problem is complicated by the number of Quakers who were disowned or who left the Society as a result of outside marriage or active participation in the war against England. John Michael Shay estimates that 80 per cent of the participants in the North Carolina antislavery organizations were from Quaker families ("The Anti-slavery Movement in North Carolina," Ph.D. thesis, Princeton, 1971). The initiative in Kentucky came from Baptist and Methodist ministers.

In Rhode Island and Connecticut, Quakers were the moving spirit behind antislavery organization. As early as 1784 Moses Brown issued a circular letter, trying to win support from the New England Congregationalist clergy, but was deterred by anti-Quaker feeling from organizing a society in Providence. In the same year Samuel Hopkins, a Congregationalist minister and leading opponent of the slave trade in Newport, said he was pleased by Brown's zeal and perseverance, but confessed that he was "apt to sink under discouragements which you seem easily to surmount." Hopkins anticipated a strong movement to repeal Rhode Island's recent emancipation act, since the towns resented the prospect of maintaining the freeborn children of slaves. Although he hastened to add that his own church had condemned slavery, he feared that present circumstances would prevent Congregationalists from taking effective political action (Friends' Moses Brown pamphlets, MRV Austin, 5, Rhode Island Historical Society [hereafter RIHS]; Samuel Hopkins to Moses Brown, April 29, 1784, Moses Brown papers, IV, 1130, RIHS; *The Works of Samuel Hopkins*, ed. by E. A. Park [Boston, 1853], I, 119–20; *The Literary Diary of Ezra Stiles*, ed. by Franklin B. Dexter [New York, 1901], I, 174; David S. Lovejoy, "Samuel Hopkins: Religion, Slavery, and the Revolution," *New England Quarterly* [June, 1967], 227–43; Mack Thompson, *Moses Brown, Reluctant Reformer* [Chapel Hill, 1962], *passim;* James F. Reilly, "The Providence Abolition Society," *Rhode Island History*, XXI [April, 1962], 33–48). Hopkins's fears were not unfounded. Peter Ecles, a Newport printer, wrote Moses Brown that while he personally hated slavery, he could not print Hopkins's "Crito" essay without ruining his business and bringing disaster upon himself and his family (Hopkins papers, VI, 1537, RIHS).

Quaker antislavery leaders outside New England, such as James Pemberton of Philadelphia and John Murray, Jr., of New York, encouraged Brown to organize an antislavery society. Brown, in turn, sent Hopkins pamphlets he had received from British Quakers, observing that the English Dissenting clergy were "uniting their Endeavours for the removal of slavery from the British Domineouns [*sic*] & for the suppression of the African Trade for Slaves." After expressing his wish that the American clergy could unite in a similar effort, he offered to donate $20

For reasons I shall soon discuss, the American Revolution not only stimulated the antislavery zeal of American Quakers but encouraged them to exert pressure on the British and American governments for the abolition of the slave trade. Even before the war had ended, Philadelphia Meeting for Sufferings, an executive committee concerned with political and legal defense, urged its counterpart body in London to organize efforts against the African trade. As a result of this correspondence, Philadelphia and London Quakers succeeded in coordinating petitions in 1783 both to Parliament and to the Continental Congress. Partly in response to pressure from visiting American Quakers, London Meeting for Sufferings appointed in 1783 a special committee on the slave trade. Some of the members of this committee had already formed an unofficial committee of six to consider steps "for the Relief & Liberation of the Negro Slaves in the West Indies, & for the Discouragement of the Slave Trade on the Coast of Africa." This small public-relations committee soon began collecting and reprinting a wide range of antislavery literature, making arrangements especially to submit regular contributions to the London and provincial press.[7]

---

toward a prize essay on the evils of slavery, in imitation of . the Cambridge University prize won by Thomas Clarkson, to be offered to the students at Yale, Princeton, or Harvard. Brown feared that the officers of the Providence college (Brown) were too involved in the slave trade to consider such a prize (Brown papers, V, 1300, 1344, RIHS).

By 1788, Brown and Hopkins had succeeded in arousing the Connecticut Congregationalists, whose General Assembly petitioned the state legislature to outlaw the slave trade. Early in 1789 Brown could assure the Philadelphia Quakers that lobbyists were at work in Connecticut and Massachusetts, and that he had helped to organize an abolitionist society in Providence (Friends' Moses Brown pamphlets, MBV Austin 5, RIHS; Moses Brown papers, VI, 1614, 1635, RIHS). In Chapter Seven I shall give fuller consideration to antislavery sentiment in New England, and for now simply observe that in New Haven the organizational activity was weak and short-lived, and that in Providence it depended on continuing Quaker initiative. Elsewhere in New England, the zeal inspired by the Revolution died very early.

Although John Murray of the New York Society proposed the idea of an annual convention of delegates, he also recognized the Philadelphia Society as the unofficial leader of the movement (Pennsylvania Abolition Society MSS, III, 17–18). The Pennsylvania Society not only corresponded actively with the societies in London and Paris, but sent letters to the governors of such states as Connecticut and Delaware.

[7] MS Minutes, Committee on the Slave Trade, Meeting for Sufferings, 1783–1792, Box F, Friends House, London; MS Minutes of informal slave-trade com-

Between 1783 and 1787 there were thus two overlapping Quaker abolition committees in London. By 1785 the slave-trade committee of the Meeting for Sufferings had expanded its goals to include gradual emancipation and had pressed its parent body to request detailed information from Philadelphia on the good effects of slave manumission.[8] It was the same committee which decided on February 26, 1787, that the time had arrived for a renewed application to Parliament for the abolition of the slave trade. Since the sequence of related events highlights the importance of Quaker initiative, I shall briefly summarize the chronology.

In 1774, during his first trip from America to England, William Dillwyn had made the acquaintance of Granville Sharp and other non-Quakers with whom Anthony Benezet had corresponded on the subject of slavery. On April 25, 1783, after Dillwyn had returned to England and several months before he helped organize the two Quaker committees, Sharp answered his request for arguments and new evi-

----

mittee, Thompson-Clarkson scrapbook, II, 9, Friends House. The latter committee consisted of Thomas Knowles, Joseph Woods, Samuel Hoare, Jr., William Dillwyn, John Lloyd, and George Harrison, all of whom became active members of the famous 1787 Abolition Committee. Dillwyn was an American, and the movement within London Meeting for Sufferings was clearly inspired by visiting American ministers, including John Pemberton; by epistles from Philadelphia Meeting for Sufferings; and perhaps most important, by renewed prodding from the aged Anthony Benezet, who prior to the Revolution had urged the leading English Quakers to take decisive action to end the slave trade. Through John Lloyd, the publicity committee submitted weekly antislavery extracts to *Lloyds' Evening Post;* they soon secured access to papers in Liverpool, Cork, Dublin, Bristol, Bath, Norwich, York, Newcastle-upon-Tyne, and numerous other cities and towns.

[8] The minute for Sept. 30, 1785, contains the crossed-out words "to promote the overthrow" of slavery and also "to abolish slavery"; but the committee recorded that steps had already been taken "to discourage the practice of keeping slaves" (MS Minutes, Box F, Friends House). London Meeting for Sufferings did request the information from Philadelphia Meeting for Sufferings, but the Philadelphians feared that any evidence they could send on the condition of free blacks might be used against the cause of emancipation (London Meeting for Sufferings to Philadelphia Meeting for Sufferings, Dec. 2, 1785; Philadelphia Meeting for Sufferings to London Meeting for Sufferings, May 18, 1786, MS Letterbook, Friends House). London's request could not have been unrelated to the worsening plight of the London black population, much of it made up of refugees from the American war. In 1786 a non-Quaker Committee for the Relief of the Black Poor succeeded in sending three shiploads of blacks to Sierra Leone (James Walvin, *Black and White: The Negro and English Society, 1555–1945* [London, 1973], ch. 9).

dence against the slave trade. The two men soon engaged in long conferences and continued to meet during the next few years.[9] In 1784, James Phillips, the Quakers' official printer and a member of the slave-trade committee of the Meeting for Sufferings, published James Ramsay's *An Essay on the Treatment and Conversion of African Slaves in the British West Indies*. Ramsay, an Anglican clergyman who had spent many years in the West Indies, sent Phillips instructions on how to get copies of his book to the king and queen, and continued to suggest names of others who should receive antislavery literature. Meanwhile, Thomas Clarkson, who was eager to publish the essay on the slave trade which had won him a prize at Cambridge in 1785, found his way to Phillips's shop, where he soon met Dillwyn and the other Quaker activists.[10] It was well before 1787, therefore, that the Quaker abolitionists had established cooperative ties with outsiders like Sharp, Ramsay, and Clarkson. On May 14, 1787, after frequent previous meetings, the committee of the Meeting for Sufferings concluded that it was too late in the term to petition Parliament. But in determining to mount a campaign directed at the next session of Parliament, they had apparently decided to broaden the membership of the informal publicity group. For on May 19, Dillwyn recorded a meeting at James Phillips's shop of a committee on the slave trade "now instituted." Two nights later Clarkson met William Wilberforce and other dignitaries at the famous anti-slave-trade dinner at the home of Bennet Langton, a host who moved in London's highest social circles. The next day, May 22, twelve men met at Phillips's shop and officially organized the Society Instituted in 1787 for Effecting the Abolition of the Slave Trade. Except for Sharp, Clarkson, and Philip Sansom, all were Quakers and all were veterans of the earlier Quaker

[9] William Dillwyn, MS Diaries, July 23 and 27, 1774; Jan. 27, 1781; May 23, 1783; May 21, 1784, National Library of Wales, Aberystwyth (hereafter NLW); Sharp to Dillwyn, April 25, 1783, British and Foreign Bible Society. In the latter communication Sharp enclosed material on the shocking *Zong* incident, in which 133 slaves had been thrown overboard after the *Zong*'s rations had run low. Dillwyn had been especially interested in having information on Spanish slave regulations and on West Indian laws.

[10] James Ramsay to James Phillips, July 12, 1784; Nov. 26, 1785, Misc. MSS R, New-York Historical Society (hereafter NYHS); Dillwyn, MS Diaries, Dec. 12, 1786; March 30, 1787; April 3, 1787, NLW. In 1808, Clarkson said he had conversed with Dillwyn as early as March 13, 1786 (*The History of the Rise, Progress and Accomplishment of the Abolition of the African Slave-Trade by the British Parliament* [2 vols., London, 1808], I, 218).

abolitionist efforts. Five were members of the informal publicity group, and at least four were on the Meeting for Suffering's slave-trade committee.[11]

Quakers always predominated as the most regular attenders and active workers of the nominally non-Quaker Abolition Committee, even after Evangelicals had begun to take over political leadership of the movement. Moreover, Quakers played a leading role in organizing anti-slave-trade societies in most of the provincial cities and towns. It was through Quaker example and Quaker encouragement that figures like Sharp and Clarkson became involved in abolitionist organization; it was the Society of Friends that the Parisian *Amis des noirs* sought to imitate.

Although Quakers in general shared a similar heritage and subculture, they lived in very different environments that inevitably affected the outcome of their antislavery views. In the southern states there were severe obstacles that delayed implementation of the sect's emerging policy of self-purification. In the South, even more than in England or in the North, the Quaker governing bodies were anxious to dissociate themselves from any official link with manumission societies or with the antislavery movement as a whole.[12] In the Middle Atlantic states, however, some of the "weightiest" religious leaders were among the minority of reformers who wished to go beyond the Society's official stand.

Pennsylvania Friends were of course the heirs of William Penn's Holy Experiment; they could draw on traditions of leadership and

[11] MS Minutes, Box F, Friends House; Dillwyn, MS Diaries, May 19, 1787, NLW; MS Proceedings of the Committee for the Abolition of the Slave Trade, 1787–1819, I, 2, British Museum Add. MSS 21254–21256 (hereafter Abolition Committee Minutes). Dr. Thomas Knowles, the only member of the original publicity group who was not at the May 22 meeting, soon joined and became an active member of the Abolition Committee. In 1788 the men who really seem to have run the Committee and to have directed Clarkson's evidence-gathering activities were: Dillwyn, John Lloyd, James Phillips, Richard Phillips (James's cousin and a soliciter at Lincoln's Inn), Dr. Thomas Knowles, Samuel Hoare, Jr., Joseph Woods, and George Harrison. Late in 1786 George Dillwyn candidly informed Moses Brown that the British clergy were not sufficiently united against the slave trade, and observed that the Quakers had superior advantages over the Dissenting clergy with respect to unpopular movements (George Dillwyn to Moses Brown, Nov. 29, 1786, Friends' Moses Brown pamphlets, MBV Austin 5 and MBV Austin 12, RIHS).

[12] Shay, "Antislavery Movement in North Carolina," pp. 431–32; Stephen B. Weeks, *Southern Quakers and Slavery* (Baltimore, 1896), *passim.*

power. It is true that the immigration of non-Quakers had slowly undermined their political dominance, and that the Seven Years' War had forced many conscientious Quakers to withdraw from the colonial legislature. The American Revolution, coming so soon after the war with France, reinforced popular suspicion that the pacifist Quakers were loyalist sympathizers if not outright traitors. Yet as Sydney V. James has perceptively shown, the Pennsylvania Quakers did not abandon their traditions of social leadership as a result of persecution and lessening political power. On the contrary, they took the lead in a variety of benevolent causes, including antislavery, partly as a means of reasserting their influence, of vindicating their reputation, and of restoring cooperative ties with Revolutionary patriots like Franklin and Rush. Social reform helped to give Quakers the sense of being "a people among peoples," and thus a part of the sovereign people. Even when fearing and disapproving violence, American Quakers could appeal to the principles of natural rights or to the Declaration of Independence. When Quaker merchants called for an end to the slave trade, they were in effect supporting colonial grievances against British imperial policy.[13] For their English brethren, the same move not only implied a challenge to an institution sanctioned by church and state, but had to be addressed to a traditional order that denied them political rights.

There is evidence that antislavery activity brought American Quakers into sharp conflict with rival ethnic groups, such as the Germans in Pennsylvania and the Dutch in New York.[14] Yet it also served to rehabilitate former leaders like James Pemberton. Pemberton was a Quaker merchant who belonged to one of Philadelphia's wealthiest and most powerful families. He was also one of the Quakers who had

[13] James, *A People among Peoples,* pp. 193–213, 240–58, 282–83, and *passim;* Benezet to Robert Pleasants, April 8, 1773; Benjamin Franklin to Benezet, Aug. 22, 1772, in Brookes, *Friend Anthony Benezet,* pp. 298–302, 422; Philadelphia Meeting for Sufferings to London Meeting for Sufferings, April 22, 1773, MS Letterbook, Friends House; Richard K. MacMaster, "Arthur Lee's 'Address on Slavery'; An Aspect of Virginia's Struggle to End the Slave Trade, 1765–1774," *The Virginia Magazine,* LXXX (April, 1972), 141–53.

[14] Owen S. Ireland, "Germans against Abolition: A Minority's View of Slavery in Revolutionary Pennsylvania," *Journal of Interdisciplinary History,* III (Spring, 1973), 685–706. The Germans were not, for the most part, slaveholders. Professor Ireland suggests that their political opposition to emancipation sprang from ethnic rivalry, from uncertain identity, and from a deep and possibly unconscious fear of further radical social change.

resigned from the Assembly during the Seven Years' War. After returning to the legislature during the brief interim of peace, Pemberton was arrested during the Revolution as a security risk and sent, along with nineteen other Friends, to Virginia for detention. After the war, however, Pemberton regained prestige as an antislavery leader. He was one of the principal founders of the Pennsylvania Abolition Society, over which he presided in place of the nominal chairman, Benjamin Franklin. He then succeeded Franklin as the Society's president, and was succeeded himself by the illustrious Rush.[15]

Unlike their brethren in Pennsylvania, English Quakers had always been outsiders. As Dissenters they were excluded from public office and from the universities. The professions were virtually closed to them, and they were barred by religious scruples from many other employments that could have been sources of influence and power. On the other hand, they had achieved a pragmatic accommodation with the British political order and were acutely sensitive to any public actions which might rekindle prejudice or jeopardize their informal mechanisms of influence. Thus David Barclay, whose wealthy and eminent family had entertained the king, sent an angry letter to James Pemberton in 1783, complaining of the impetuosity of the American *"Reformers"* who had recently arrived in England and who had agitated the slave-trade question at London Yearly Meeting. The Americans had presumed to tell Barclay that he should not quote William Penn because Penn "had dealt or approved the dealing in slaves!" Even worse, they had pressed the English Quakers to address the king "to *use his influence* with his Parliament to discountenance that trade," a move not only highly improper but self-defeating. Barclay, who said he spoke for "some of our most weighty valuable Friends," told the American leader that he hoped "Friends will be wise enough to submit with propriety to the powers placed over them or that such as do not approve thereof will leave the country!"[16]

Barclay had actually deflected the move to petition the king and had persuaded London Yearly Meeting of the propriety of sending a

[15] Janet Whitney, *John Woolman: American Quaker* (Boston, 1942), p. 36; John Woolman, *The Journal and Essays of John Woolman,* ed. by Amelia Mott Gummere (New York, 1922), p. 513.

[16] MS Minutes, London Yearly Meeting, XVII (June 16, 1783), 298–307, Friends House; David Barclay to James Pemberton, July 2, 1783, Pemberton papers, XXXIX, HSP.

delegation to Parliament, which was about to consider a measure prohibiting servants of the African Company from engaging in the slave trade "to the detriment of their masters." As a result of Barclay's strategy, Lord North and Lord John Cavendish courteously received the Quaker delegation; Sir Cecil Wray praised Quaker benevolence when he introduced in the Commons their petition to end the slave trade; and though Parliament tabled the proposal, since it went so far beyond the measure before them, the Quakers received favorable publicity in the public press. It was this occasion that prompted both London Yearly Meeting and Meeting for Sufferings to give official approval to a pamphlet drafted by William Dillwyn and John Lloyd, *The Case of Our Fellow Creatures, the Oppressed Africans, Respectfully Recommended to the Serious Consideration of the Legislature of Great-Britain, by the People Called Quakers.* The slave-trade committee of the Meeting for Sufferings succeeded in getting copies to the king, the queen, the secretaries of state, and then to M.P.'s. Following this achievement, the slave-trade committee printed more than ten thousand copies and devised an elaborate plan for personal distribution to virtually every institution, office holder, and influential man in the realm. By 1786 it was not accidental that the Quaker testimony was commonplace knowledge in Great Britain, or that a pamphlet by Benezet should be readily accessible to anyone who cared to read it.[17]

The availability of such channels and media of persuasion was only one of the circumstances that differentiated British and American

[17] Barclay to Pemberton, July 2, 1783, Pemberton papers, XXXIX, HSP; MS Minutes, Sept. 26, 1783; May 14, 1784; July 23, 1784, Box F, Friends House; London Meeting for Sufferings, MS Minutes, XXXVII (June 18, 1784), 65; Clarkson, *History,* I, 121; *Gentleman's Magazine,* LIII (Nov., 1783), 919; Russell S. Mortimer, "Quaker Printers, 1750–1850," *Journal of the Friends' Historical Society,* L (1963), 103–6. According to Patrick Cleburne Lipscomb, the London Quakers not only retained a standing committee to review Parliamentary legislation, but regularly paid doorkeepers at both Houses of Parliament to distribute Quaker propaganda ("William Pitt and the Abolition of the Slave Trade," pp. 74–76, Ph.D. thesis, University of Texas, 1960). Dillwyn indicated that the Quakers had qualms over printing certain antislavery material that contained ideas to which they could not subscribe (Dillwyn to John Pemberton, Dec. 6, 1783, Pemberton papers, XL, HSP). Yet there can be no question that the Quakers' dissemination of antislavery literature had tremendous impact; by 1787 the slave trade had become a lively issue for a considerable segment of the English reading public, and an audience had been prepared for the 51,432 copies of books and pamphlets and the 26,526 briefer reports that the Abolition Committee would print by mid-July, 1788 (Clarkson, *History,* I, 571).

Quakers. English Quakers had been mainly concerned with freeing their expanding commercial enterprises from any direct involvement with the slave trade, especially since so much Quaker capital had been invested in colonial commerce. London Yearly Meeting exhorted the various colonial meetings to "clean" themselves from the unrighteous practice of keeping bondsmen, but few English Friends had had any direct experience with slaveholding. Thus when David Barclay discovered that he and his brother had acquired thirty-two Jamaican slaves as payment for a debt, he was ultimately forced to rely on the assistance of James Pemberton and the Philadelphia Quakers. His own Jamaican agent refused to emancipate the blacks in Jamaica, because the example would be "unpopular in the island." Barclay finally had to send another agent to Jamaica, who with some difficulty persuaded the blacks to embark with him to Philadelphia, where they were apprenticed under the supervision of the Abolition Society, after a committee had decided "what they are fit for."[18]

If the British Quakers were attuned to publicity campaigns and to the subtle means of reaching men of power, they were unfamiliar with the problems of committees appointed to "free Negroes unlawfully held in bondage," or for "improving the condition of free blacks." In the North, at least, American Quakers acquired their main knowledge of slavery through experience with domestic servitude and through their commercial activities in port cities like Philadelphia, New York, and Newport. Understandably, their main antislavery interests focused on stopping the further importation of Negroes, on removing legal obstacles to private manumission, on preventing the re-enslavement of free blacks, and on providing education, apprenticeship, and old age assistance for the objects of their benevolence. Far more than their English brethren, the Americans understood the extent and depth of racial prejudice, as well as the painful complexities of converting domestic servants into free men. They tended to assume, however, that their English correspondents, being free of such obstacles

[18] London Yearly Meeting, Epistles Sent, I (1774–1790), 1, 9, 95, 321–22, Friends House; David Barclay, *An Account of the Emancipation of the Slaves of Unity Valley Pen, in Jamaica* (2nd ed., London, 1801). In the latter work a chart (pp. 13–14) shows that children from four to seven were bound to masters who took no black adults. Caesar, age six, was bound for fifteen years but immediately died and was buried in the potter's field. Several of the blacks were said to be very grateful to the Quakers, although they complained of the cold.

and being closer to the centers of imperial power, could take the leadership in eradicating the Atlantic slave system.[19]

Despite the diversity of Quaker experience and the lack of a central ecclesiastical authority, the Society of Friends maintained unity by a communications network unparalleled in the eighteenth century. This achievement was partly the cause and partly the result of the incredible commercial success of enterprising Quakers. The network's growth had also been encouraged by persecution, which had led not only to transatlantic migration, but to institutions for communal discipline and mutual aid. Above all, the communications network drew strength from the Quaker ethic, which gave its adherents the confident sense of being members of an extended family whose business and personal affairs were united in a seamless sphere. The decisions of London Yearly Meeting radiated outward through an intricate structure of regional Yearly, Quarterly, Monthly, and local meetings, affecting the personal and economic lives of Friends from North Carolina to Ireland.

A word about the nature and scope of the Quaker communication system reveals some of the social implications of the Quaker antislavery initiative. Although Friends relied heavily on informal correspondence and on official epistles between the various meetings, it was the traveling ministry that brought distant congregations into living fellowship. By gently rebuking the families they visited for retaining Negro slaves or for displaying worldly vanities, the itinerants also helped to define as well as to apply the consensual values of the Society.

---

[19] Philadelphia Meeting for Sufferings to London Meeting for Sufferings, May 18, 1786, MS Letterbook, Friends House; Benezet to William Dillwyn, Aug. 20, 1783, Misc. MSS, B, NYHS. Of course, many Philadelphia Quakers had seen plantation slavery in the Deep South (John F. Watson, *Annals of Philadelphia and Pennsylvania, in the Olden Time* [2 vols., Philadelphia, 1845], I, 595–96). We have already noted that Quakers who remained in the West Indies had difficulty even in giving their slaves religious instruction. Dr. John Coakley Lettsom, a native of Tortola, rendered medical service to hundreds of slaves, but finally emigrated to England. In 1791 and 1792, Richard Nisbet wrote rather plaintive letters to James Pemberton from St. Kitts and Nevis, expressing a wish to join the Quakers, since of all religions they most closely approximated the primitive Christian church. Yet Nisbet insisted that Christianity did not forbid slaveholding. He professed an abhorrence for the African trade, but thought that the relatively mild servitude in the West Indies was the only "means of improvement & happiness." He assured Pemberton that he was trying to give religious instruction to his own slaves (Nisbet to Pemberton, Aug. 1, 1791; May 30, 1792, Misc. MSS, N, NYHS).

Theoretically, any Friend of either sex might feel called to a traveling mission and receive the assent of the appropriate meetings. In practice, however, traveling ministers won recognition only if they could serve as models of authentic religious purity, proving themselves "acceptable" to the various congregations they visited. Though far lesser known than the Wesleys and Whitefields, they were a powerful arm of the international Great Awakening.

The eighteenth-century Quaker revival had two overlapping phases. Many of the early traveling ministers were imbued with a quietistic yearning for self-effacement. Often inclined toward mysticism, they developed spiritual exercises to cleanse themselves of every taint of worldliness. Both in England and America, the quietists' appeal for absolute purity and selflessness struck the consciences of Friends who were dismayed by bloody Indian wars on the American frontier or by their own indirect complicity in the wars with France. John Churchman, for example, saw the Indian raids on the Pennsylvania frontier as a sign of divine disapproval for slaveholding. Churchman, a saintly American quietist, was the mentor and friend of John Woolman. At times Churchman joined Woolman in visiting and expostulating with Quaker slaveholders. And in a sense, Woolman's continuing and lonely crusade against slavery was an objectification of the older minister's spiritual quest for purity.[20]

The second phase of Quaker revivalism came closer to the evangelicalism of the major Protestant denominations, and coincided with Quaker efforts to enlist outsiders in various benevolent causes. Like Anglican and Methodist evangelicals, the younger Quakers stressed the sinfulness of natural man and the mercies of Christ the Redeemer. Among the leading Quaker preachers of this Christ-centered faith was Rebecca Jones, a convert from Philadelphia's Anglican church. A close friend of Benezet, the Pembertons, and the Dillwyns, Rebecca Jones achieved various triumphs on a mission to England, not the least of which was the conversion of young William Allen to a life of "serious" religion. Later on, in the early nineteenth century, Allen's serious interest in religion led him to work cloesly with British diplomats on the international suppression of the slave trade, and to confer personally on that subject with Emperor Alexander I of Russia.[21]

[20] For expressions of Benezet's quietistic yearnings, see Brookes, *Friend Anthony Benezet*, pp. 210, 222–23.
[21] *Memorials of Rebecca Jones*, comp. by William J. Allinson (London, n.d.);

Rebecca Jones's most noted co-worker was her fellow Philadelphian, William Savery, who converted both Isaac Hopper and Elizabeth Gurney (later Fry) to serious religion, thereby channeling the former toward a life of abolitionism and the latter toward worldwide fame as a prison reformer. Savery even tried to bring off the *coup* of the century by laboring in France to persuade Thomas Paine, the Great Infidel himself, to return to his parental faith.[22]

The distinction between quietistic and evangelical ministers, however, is less important than the role both played as catalysts of antislavery commitment. It is true that the journals of the great itinerants are almost wholly preoccupied with religion. Yet there can be no question that virtually all the early Quaker antislavery leaders were profoundly influenced by the same traveling ministers. Woolman and Churchman, for example, were intimate with the Pemberton brothers, Israel, James, and John, whose family not only owned slaves but had amassed a fortune from the West India trade and from the sale in Europe of slave-produced sugar, rum, tobacco, and rice. Notwithstanding their worldly interests, the Pembertons became deeply moved by the spirit of the revival. Partly at the instigation of Samuel Fothergill, a visiting English minister, they threw their powerful support behind the Quaker withdrawal, in 1756, from the Pennsylvania Assembly. They helped to create and manage Philadelphia Meeting for Sufferings. And while the Pembertons continued to draw wealth from the produce of West Indian slaves, they freed their own Negroes and became leaders in a variety of philanthropic activities. It was on a Pemberton ship that Woolman planned to sail to the West Indies in 1769 to preach against slavery.[23]

Jones, *Later Periods, passim.* I have mentioned only a few of the influential traveling ministers; Thomas Shillitoe, Stephen Grellet, Mary Dudley, and several others were part of the same movement.

[22] Jones, *Later Periods,* I, 280. Benjamin Rush, who cooperated with Benezet and other Quaker abolitionists in Philadelphia, met Paine in 1775 and was much pleased that Paine's first published work was an attack on slavery. Antislavery, coupled with a defense of the colonists' rights, served to unite the two men; but Rush was later much put off by Paine's *Age of Reason* (*Letters of Benjamin Rush,* ed. by L. H. Butterfield [Princeton, 1951], II, 1007, 1009; *The Autobiography of Benjamin Rush . . . ,* ed. by George W. Corner [Princeton, 1948], pp. 113–14).

[23] Gummere, introduction to *Journal and Essays of John Woolman,* p. 110; Theodore Thayer, *Israel Pemberton, King of the Quakers* (Philadelphia, 1943), *passim;* Pemberton papers, *passim,* HSP.

Meanwhile, in the early 1750s John Churchman had persuaded young John Pemberton to give up business for a religious life. For three years the two men traveled together through Britain and the Continent, struggling against Quaker declensions in faith. John Pemberton's strictures against card playing and violations of the Sabbath anticipated the mood of evangelical "puritanism." He was so shocked by the visibility of English drunkards, whores, and "profane swearers" that he thought divine punishment must be at hand. For ministers like Pemberton, involvement with slavery was simply one of many worldly sins; and "queries" about slavery could be taken as a prime test of how "clear" Quakers were of contamination. When Woolman himself finally arrived in England twenty years later, he expressed astonishment that many Friends were still indirectly connected with the African trade, a fact he interpreted as the prime symbol of their worldliness and degeneracy.[24]

The mainspring of the Quaker revival lay in such transatlantic lines of influence and personal acquaintance. As the highest official in Philadelphia Meeting for Sufferings, John Pemberton could put considerable weight behind the coordination of antislavery activity. Through commercial as well as religious correspondence, he and his brother James were close to Quaker planters like Robert Pleasants and to Quaker merchants like Moses Brown, the leader of the antislavery cause in Rhode Island. Beginning in 1770 the Pembertons aided and spread news about Benezet's school for Negro children. Even before the American Revolution ended, John Pemberton sailed again for England, where he joined his cousin William Dillwyn in urging London Meeting for Sufferings to take action against the slave trade. When Rebecca Jones arrived in London in 1784, she was delighted to encounter six American Quaker ministers, in addition to Pemberton, most of whom were actively engaged in the antislavery cause.[25]

---

[24] John Pemberton, MS Journal, June 1, 1752–Nov. 27, 1752, Pemberton papers, HSP; *Journal and Essays of John Woolman*, pp. 307–8.

[25] James Pemberton to Robert Pleasants, Aug. 14, 1788; Nov. 16, 1789; April 20, 1790, Brock collection, Henry E. Huntington, Library (hereafter, HEH); Moses Brown to James Pemberton, Sept. 14, 1781; March 20, 1784, Pemberton papers, XXXVI, XL, HSP; James, *A People among Peoples*, pp. 235–37; *Memorials of Rebecca Jones*, p. 65. On August 20, 1783, Benezet wrote Dillwyn about the plight of Philadelphia's blacks and the need for funds to give them legal protection against being unlawfully enslaved. He reminded Dillwyn of the

The revival moved both ways across the Atlantic. In 1755, two years before Woolman's most famous mission through the South, Israel Pemberton and Samuel Fothergill had traveled the same route, quietly preaching against slavery. A leader of the revival in England, Fothergill also quickened the move for self-purification among Philadelphia Friends. Upon returning to England, he helped to indoctrinate future English abolitionists like George Harrison and the Gurneys of Norwich. It was Samuel's brother John, an internationally renowned physician, who welcomed John Woolman to England. A member of London Meeting for Sufferings, Dr. Fothergill moved in the highest circles of enlightened culture. He was a close friend of Benjamin Franklin and a Licentiate of the Royal College of Physicians (though excluded, as a Quaker, from being a Fellow). Dr. Fothergill's interests ranged from projects for prison reform to a plan for colonizing emancipated Negroes in Africa, a plan for which he said he would contribute £10,000. A correspondent of Benezet's, he also had a link through Joseph Priestley, whom he aided with money and apparatus, with the Nonconformist radicals of the Birmingham Lunar Society. It is tempting, therefore, to see a stream of antislavery influence running from the Quaker revival through Fothergill to men like Priestley, Richard Price, Thomas Day, and Josiah Wedgwood, who laid the foundations for a more secular and radical abolitionism in Birmingham and Manchester. One can speak with more confidence about Fothergill's influence on younger Quaker physicians like Thomas Knowles, Joseph Hooper, John Coakley Lettsom, and George Vaux, all of whom became involved in the British antislavery movement. Although Quaker physicians were few in number, since they could seek degrees only in Scotland or on the Continent, they gave representation, in the ranks of British abolitionists, to a profession that seems generally to have been indifferent or hostile to reform.[26]

---

large unappropriated fund that Quakers had raised in England and Ireland for the relief of their American brethren during the war (Brookes, *Friend Anthony Benezet,* pp. 382–83). Dillwyn wrote John Pemberton on June 7, 1784, that the London Quakers had agreed to send some of the money to Philadelphia (he wished that the amount had been doubled), but had not yet decided whether it should be for Benezet's plan or for the Negro school (Pemberton papers, XLI, HSP). In 1787, David Barclay sent the sum of £500 for the school.

[26] James, *A People among Peoples,* p. 137; Arthur Raistrick, *Quakers in Science and Industry: Being an Account of the Quaker Contributions to Science and Industry During the 17th and 18th Centuries* (London, 1950), pp. 264, 278,

The traveling ministers prepared the way by exhorting influential Friends to cast off worldly contaminations, which included ties with slavery. The transatlantic connections provided a framework for co-ordinated action. The deepening imperial crisis, however, precipitated the first Quaker efforts to shift from internal reform to a program for changing the course of history. In the years immediately following the Stamp Act crisis, American Quakers sought to use the leverage of their English connections as a means of modifying British imperial policy. There were mixed motives behind the colonial attempts to tax or pro-hibit the importation of slaves. But for American Quakers like Benezet and Robert Pleasants, the actions of the Virginia General Assembly—coupled with Arthur Lee's much-quoted "Address on Slavery"—could be used to show that the colonial cause was not only sincere but em-bodied the noblest principles of an enlightened age. The Americans exhorted the more influential British Friends to use the slave-trade issue as an instrument of reconciliation. In 1773, after considerable prodding from the Americans, David Barclay led a delegation to visit the Lord of Trade, in futile support of Virginia's attempts to levy a prohibitive tax on imported Africans. By then, British Friends recog-nized that a political breach with the colonies would pose grave threats to business as well as to religion.[27]

Between English and American Quakers there was a subtle competi-tion in registering antislavery influence. Writing soon after the Somer-set decision had removed any legal basis for slavery in England,

---

292, 295–99. On October 13, 1788, Granville Sharp gave John Coakley Lettsom a report on the new settlement at Sierra Leone, saying that he shared the opinion which Dr. William Thornton had adopted from the late Dr. Fothergill; namely, that establishing a free settlement on the coast of Africa would be the most effectual way to destroy the slave trade. Thornton, a Quaker physician and associate of Fothergill and Lettsom, had emigrated to Philadelphia, where he had begun to promote the cause of Negro colonization (Sharp to Lettsom, N147, HEH).

[27] Philadelphia Meeting for Sufferings to London Meeting for Sufferings, Nov. 21, 1777, MS Letterbook, Friends House; Gary, "Political and Economic Rela-tions," pp. 221–22; MacMaster, "Arthur Lee's 'Address on Slavery,'" pp. 143–53. Lee's "Address," which appeared in the *Virginia Gazette* in 1767, was later widely publicized by Robert Pleasants and Benezet; but when Benezet reprinted it, he removed the strongest passages, which warned that the slaves might with justice rise in mass insurrection. One should add that Benezet's letters to Gran-ville Sharp, from 1772 to 1774, gave a candid and realistic assessment of the self-interested motives behind Maryland and Virginia's opposition to the slave trade (see Chapter Nine, n. 17).

London Yearly Meeting rejoiced in the growing testimony against slavery in America but expressed a rather paternalistic hope that the colonies would work harder at enacting laws that discouraged the institution. In 1782, Philadelphia Meeting for Sufferings proudly cited Virginia's law allowing private manumissions as a sign that "through the favour of divine Providence the Light of Truth hath evidently broken forth in many places amongst those whom temporal Considerations, and long accustomed prejudices have held in obdurate blindness." Yet British authority still supported the "Crying Enormity" of the slave trade (as well as the war against America). The Philadelphians hoped that "divine Wisdom will be afforded to qualify you as Instruments in the hand of the Lord . . . to the gradual Extirpation" of the slave trade. In reply, London Meeting for Sufferings promised to put Philadelphia's request before the Yearly Meeting, but warned of the great opposition that could be expected from "interested parties" in the government. Philadelphia then responded, perhaps with intentional irony, that if the "temper of humanity" was gradually prevailing among British statesmen—as the London Quakers had claimed in a letter of 1773—then there should be grounds for hope, notwithstanding the power of interested parties. With the end of hostilities, the Philadelphia Quakers actually shifted their major hopes to the personal influence of Americans like William Dillwyn and John Pemberton, who had arrived in England. As James Pemberton pointed out to his brother, John, the Americans were more familiar with slavery than were their English brethren; they could obviate the objections which timidity or "ill-founded fears" might suggest. Some of the English leaders were annoyed by the Americans' rashness and disregard for political proprieties, but through the 1780s the British and American Quakers continued to spur each other on, proudly reporting their antislavery gains on both sides of the Atlantic.[28]

[28] London Meeting for Sufferings to Philadelphia Meeting for Sufferings, Oct. 2, 1772; April 4, 1783; Dec. 5, 1783; Jan. 28, 1785; Nov. 3, 1787; Feb. 28, 1788; Philadelphia to London, Nov. 21, 1777; Aug. 15, 1782; July 17, 1783; Aug. 19, 1784; Dec. 2, 1785; Oct. 18, 1787, MS Letterbook, Friends House; London Yearly Meeting, Epistles Sent, V (1774–1790), 1, 9, 95, 321–22; London Yearly Meeting, Epistles Received, V (1788–1801), 234, 272–73, 317–18, Friends House; James Pemberton to John Pemberton, July 19, 1783; to Daniel Mildred, July, 1783, Pemberton papers, XXXIX, HSP. The Philadelphia Quakers were extremely reluctant to send London detailed information on the condition of emancipated blacks, arguing that the cause of emancipation must be defended

The Solvent of Wealth

Few accounts of early Quaker abolitionists give any indication of their most conspicuous characteristic, which was, quite simply, their incredible economic success. Although it is generally acknowledged that Quakers epitomized the "Protestant ethic," the central role they played in eighteenth-century commerce, banking, and industry is seldom appreciated. Cut off from traditional sources of wealth and power, the English Friends searched for new opportunities in "innocent" trades. To a variety of small-scale enterprises, ranging from pottery and china to iron production, they brought a seriousness of purpose, a discipline of mind, and a compelling commitment to "useful" work. They were natural innovators, fascinated by the possibility of "useful improvements." Their sectarian exclusiveness, resulting in an intricate web of intermarriages, linked one successful enterprise with many others. By the second half of the eighteenth century the English Quakers had established themselves as the founders and managers of great firms manufacturing porcelain, clocks, instruments, drugs, and china; they were leaders in mining, particularly of lead, and in the production of brass, zinc, copper, and other metals. According to Paul Mantoux, the history of three generations of the great Quaker Darby dynasty "sums up that of the whole English metalworking industry." Nor was it accidental that the names of two great Quaker families, the Lloyds and the Barclays, should ultimately come to designate two of the world's greatest banks. The very embodiment of the capitalist mentality, the English Quakers were in the vanguard of the industrial revolution.[29]

One gets some sense of the linkage of Quaker interests from the diaries of William Dillwyn, whom Thomas Clarkson praised as the

---

on its own grounds, not on a possibly misleading study of the consequences. When London Meeting for Sufferings finally received the information they sought, early in 1788, they rejoiced over the progress made by certain free blacks, and indicated that the heart-warming stories sent from Philadelphia had resolved various doubts.

[29] Raistrick, *Quakers in Science and Industry, passim;* Paul H. Emden, *Quakers in Commerce: A Record of Business Accomplishment* (London, n.d.), *passim;* Isabel Grubb, *Quakerism in Industry before 1800* (London, 1930), *passim;* Frederick B. Tolles, *Meeting House and Counting House: The Quaker Merchants of Colonial Philadelphia, 1682–1763* (Chapel Hill, 1948), *passim;* Paul Mantoux, *The Industrial Revolution in the Eighteenth Century,* rev. ed., tr. by Marjorie Vernon (New York, 1929), p. 307.

chief organizer of the British antislavery movement. Born in Philadelphia in 1738, Dillwyn was a pupil of Anthony Benezet and then a merchant associated with the Pembertons. In 1773 he wrote his cousin James Pemberton from Charleston, reporting his success in exchanging West Indian rum for Carolina rice; in the same year he published a cautious and anonymous pamphlet suggesting the "expediency" of gradual emancipation, and also joined a Quaker delegation petitioning the New Jersey Assembly for a more liberal law regulating slave manumisions. In 1774, Dillwyn sailed for England, carrying with him letters from Benezet to a variety of people, including Granville Sharp and John Wesley. Soon after arriving, Dillwyn called upon Sharp, Benjamin Franklin, the Fothergills, and Samuel Hoare. The latter, a wealthy Quaker merchant, had recently formed a banking firm that would eventually merge, as a result of intermarriages, with the Gurney and Barclay banking houses, forming the nucleus of Barclays Bank. Dillwyn went with John Gurney and George Harrison to drink tea at David Barclay's, where he also met Joseph Bevan and John and Ambrose Lloyd. John Gurney was the co-founder of the famous Gurney bank at Norwich; Harrison was a barrister-at-law; Bevan was a leading drug manufacturer; and the Lloyds, who had family connections with the Pembertons, had already expanded from their Birmingham iron and metal trades into banking and industry. Samuel Darby, of the great iron family, took Dillwyn on a tour of the Liverpool docks. In the same city he visited William Rathbone, a rich timber merchant and later a Quaker abolitionist.[30]

It was Manchester, however, that seems to have excited Dillwyn the most. In that "thriving populous Town" he inspected the warehouses filled with domestic manufactures, and spent hours marveling at the linens, cottons, velvets, fustians, hats, and threads. In Birmingham, he dined with Sampson Lloyd, who has been called the true father of Lloyds Bank, and then toured "Taylor's famous Beltt Manufacturies where abundance of Women are employed." He described the pump machinery used to draw water from Quaker-owned lead mines, and in Dorset he viewed

[30] Dillwyn to James Pemberton, Jan. 27, 1773; July 10, 1774, Pemberton papers, XXIV, XXVI, HSP; Sharp to Dillwyn, July 25, 1774, British and Foreign Bible Society; Dillwyn, MS Diaries, NLW. Here and elsewhere I have drawn on the invaluable MS Dictionary of Quaker Biography at Friends House, and on the Emlen-Dillwyn papers, Library Company of Philadelphia (hereafter, LCP).

the curious Silk Mill for winding raw silk in and about which [I] was informed near 300 Persons were constantly employed but many of them are young Children who watch the winding of the silk of the Reels and twisting it. The Machinery is admirable and consists of many thousand wheels of different sizes.[31]

As Dillwyn continued to make notes on British industry and on his business meetings with leading entrepreneurs, he also grew increasingly gloomy over the news that "a bad Ministry is resolving to enslave my Country." He attended meetings of merchants who were angered by British policy and by Parliament's refusal to heed their petitions. After a seventeen-month stay in England, Dillwyn received a certificate from London, addressed to his own Monthly Meeting in West Jersey, attesting to his good conduct while abroad. When he departed for America in 1775 he was on intimate terms with the men who would launch the British antislavery movement: Joseph Woods, Thomas Knowles, John Lloyd, George Harrison, Samuel Hoare, Jr., Joseph Gurney Bevan, Philip Sansom, and Granville Sharp. He had also met the families that would found some of England's greatest industries, banks, railroads, and insurance companies. When Dillwyn returned to England for good, in 1781, he called on Sharp to discuss the slave trade; having married Sarah Weston, a wealthy heiress, he also joined the firm of Weston, James & Dillwyn. He later bought the Cambrian pottery works at Swansea, which produced china of international fame.[32]

The family connections between Quaker business and reform were extraordinarily complex. One of the centers of early British antislavery activity was the home of Joseph Gurney Bevan, at Plough Court, London. As apothecaries and chemists, the Bevans had built up a prosperous pharmaceutical concern at Plough Court (through Dr. John Fothergill, they won the contract to supply Pennsylvania Hospital). By the 1780s the firm had grown sufficiently to allow Joseph Gurney Bevan the leisure to dabble at poetry, to write a refutation of "the misrepresentations of the Quakers," and to devote considerable time to the Quaker slave-trade committee and then to the London Abolition Society. When Rebecca Jones visited the Bevan home, she

[31] Dillwyn, MS Diaries, Oct. and Nov., 1774, NLW.
[32] In 1785, Dillwyn purchased a summer house and forty acres of land, some of which he began to farm (Dillwyn to Susannah Dillwyn, June 16, 1785; July 16, 1786, Emlen-Dillwyn papers, LCP).

was welcomed by Bevan's close friend, William Dillwyn, whom she found living "elegantly." Bevan was also an intimate friend of the Quaker's official publisher and bookseller, James Phillips. On Lombard Street, close to David Barclay's house and to such Quaker banking firms as Hanbury, Taylor, Lloyd and Bowman, Phillips printed the thousands of antislavery pamphlets authorized by the Quaker committee and the later Abolition Society.[33]

The Bevans were related by marriage both to the Barclays and the Gurneys. Joseph Gurney Bevan was a cousin of Elizabeth Gurney Fry; his half-brother was a banking partner of the Barclays. His own production of drugs and chemicals soon led into the chemistry of brewing. In 1781 a Bevan and a Barclay bought the Anchor Brewery for £30,000 and, with help from members of the Gurney clan, converted it into a highly profitable enterprise. The brewery soon passed into the hands of Robert Barclay of Clapham, whose mother was a Gurney and who was himself an active member of the Abolition Committee, along with his good friends John Lloyd and William Dillwyn.[34]

Thomas Fowell Buxton, of the next generation, led the Parliamentary struggle against slavery in the 1820s. Although Buxton was not a Friend himself, his mother belonged to the Quaker Hanbury family, which had founded a tobacco empire prior to the American Revolution and had then turned to banking, brewing, and iron before eventually launching the age of chocolate. Buxton's wife was the daughter of the banker John Gurney, and was thus the sister of both Elizabeth Fry and of the abolitionist Joseph John Gurney. When in 1808 Buxton joined the brewing firm of Truman, Hanbury & Co., he helped to consolidate, according to Arthur Raistrick, the Hanbury iron interests with both the iron and banking interests of the Lloyd dynasty and the banking and brewing interests of the Barclay group. Buxton later became associated with a great insurance firm founded by Samuel Gurney, Alexander Baring, and Sir Moses Montefiore. Buxton's wife,

[33] Raistrick, *Quakers in Science and Industry*, pp. 283–85; R. S. Sayers, *Lloyds Bank in the History of English Banking* (Oxford, 1957), *passim; Memorials of Rebecca Jones*, p. 63. Lombard Street became London's great banking street. Phillips's shop was a short walk from the Old Jewry, where Granville Sharp lived until 1786 and where the Abolition Committee found a permanent office.

[34] MS Dictionary of Quaker Biography, Friends House; Raistrick, *Quakers in Science and Industry*, pp. 286–88; William Dillwyn to Thomas Parke, Sept. 13, 1781, Cox, Parrish, Wharton papers, HSP.

I may add, was the niece of Samuel Hoare, Jr., one of the most diligent members of the Abolition Committee. Hoare, whose father was a wealthy banker, had worked at Henry Gurney's bank in Norwich before entering the London firm that eventually became the core of Barclays Bank. To round matters off, Hoare was related by marriage to the merchant and woolen draper Joseph Woods, who was also in the nucleus of the Abolition Committee.[35]

I need not labor the point that Quaker antislavery activity was closely associated with complex ties of intermarriage and with fortunes made from shipping, banking, mining, insurance, and industry. And despite the Quakers' valiant efforts to stay clear of the African slave trade, their quest for profit sometimes compromised their quest for innocence. William Rathbone, one of the few abolitionists in Liverpool, was also one of the city's wealthiest merchants. Although he dealt in timber instead of slaves, his firm was the first in England to receive a consignment of cotton grown in the United States. Such historical ironies were common wherever Quakers took the leadership in the economic revolution. Thus Moses Brown, the organizer of the Providence Society for Abolishing the Slave Trade and a leader of the antislavery movement in New England, supported various philanthropic causes with a fortune made from the West India trade and from the distillation of rum. In 1773, just before his formal conversion to Quakerism, Brown freed his own slaves and began active work against the African trade, hoping to atone for his sin of eight years before when he had fitted out a slave ship as a quick way to secure profits for investment in an iron furnace. Yet for all of Brown's attempts to dissociate himself from slavery and to make up for a guilty past, he was the great promoter of early New England cotton manufacturing and the patron of Samuel Slater, whose reconstructed spinning frame prepared the way for the American cotton textile industry.[36]

Like their English brethren, the American Quaker abolitionists were distinguished by their mercantile wealth and above all by their entre-

---

[35] MS Dictionary of Quaker Biography, Friends House; Emden, *Quakers in Commerce, passim;* Raistrick, *Quakers in Science and Industry,* p. 147.

[36] Friends' Moses Brown pamphlets, MBV Austin 5, RIHS; Moses Brown papers, II, 328, 331, RIHS. Rathbone, it should be added, was disowned in 1805, four years before his death, but not for importing cotton. Moses Brown had been much influenced by reading the religious testimony of Samuel Fothergill.

preneurial leadership. The Pemberton fortune arose from international trade that depended on slave-produced sugar, molasses, rice, and tobacco, as well as on Caribbean markets for North American commodities. But even by the 1750s the elder Israel Pemberton was discovering that speculation in land, mortgages, and bonds was safer and less time-consuming than investment in commercial shipping. Robert Waln, an active abolitionist and a great Philadelphia merchant of the next generation, moved from the China and East India trade to insurance, cotton manufacturing, and iron. Both in his worldly success and in the diversity of his economic and philanthropic interests Waln was typical of the Quaker leaders of the Philadelphia and New York abolition societies.

There were a number of such influential personages. Among them was Samuel Coates, considered an old-style Philadelphia merchant, a man who was a business correspondent of Moses Brown, a manager of Pennsylvania Hospital, and a director of the First Bank of the United States. Thomas Pym Cope, a promoter of the Chesapeake-Delaware canal, had drawn his wealth from a Philadelphia-to-Liverpool packet line. Isaac Hicks, a prominent New York banker, was close to the merchant interests represented politically by John Jay. John Murray, Sr. was a great New York shipowner and importer, whose insurance, banking, and real estate interests (Murray Hill) helped him to accumulate a fortune of one-half million dollars. John Murray, Jr., a nephew of the latter and an affluent brewer, gave $10,000 in relief to the yellow-fever victims of 1798. Thomas Eddy, who moved from Philadelphia to New York after making a fortune in insurance and speculation in the public debt, turned to various public services, becoming a governor of New York Hospital, the chief founder of Newgate prison, and a promoter of the Bible Society, the Historical Society, the New York Savings Bank, and the Erie Canal. The younger generation of urban Quakers included Jeremiah Thompson, who by 1827 was said to be the largest shipowner in the United States and one of the leading cotton dealers in the world.[37]

The Quakers constituted the largest identifiable group in the Philadelphia and New York abolition societies, but it is important to ask what kinds of outsiders they attracted to their pioneering efforts. It

[37] In sketching profiles of both Quaker and non-Quaker abolition society members in New York and Philadelphia I have drawn on many city directories and biographical guides, far too many to be listed here.

would be useful to have a comprehensive and quantitative analysis of the active membership of all the abolition societies. Here I can only venture a few general and preliminary observations.

Except in Philadelphia, the major abolition societies represented an extremely narrow and affluent cross section of any given population. The English provincial societies often included artisans, tradesmen, and shopkeepers, many of whom were Quakers or Dissenters, along with a striking number of clergymen, a group conspicuously underrepresented in the American societies, except in Connecticut, Rhode Island, and Kentucky.[38] Among the more active members of the Pennsylvania Abolition Society, during its first twenty years of existence, I have identified a saddler, a hatter, a tanner-currier, a tailor, a ladies' shoemaker, a cooper, three carpenters (probably), two clock and watchmakers, and a number of teachers, booksellers, and printer-stationers. Although most of these skilled workers were probably Quakers and may have been relatively well-to-do, they represent a class that was unseen among the Parisian *Amis des noirs,* the London Abolition Society, or, with two or three exceptions, among the New York Manumission Society. In any event, the committees of the Pennsylvania Society were clearly dominated by merchants, lawyers, doctors, and the holders of high public office. Because the Society was oriented toward enforcement of the emancipation law, in a city close to neighboring slaveholding states, it retained a large legal counsel and counted among its members an unusually high proportion of attorneys. A study of forty-nine of the more active New York abolitionists shows that at least twenty-three were merchants and shipowners; eight were bankers, including several bank presidents and directors; eight were lawyers and judges; the remaining number included a few ministers, doctors, and college professors, along with a scattered assortment of canal promoters, land speculators, and the owners of drug firms, drygoods stores, sawmills, and boardinghouses.[39]

[38] For the English provincial societies, the best guide is E. M. Hunt, "The North of England Agitation for the Abolition of the Slave Trade, 1780–1800," M.A. thesis, University of Manchester, 1959. Except in Scotland, the clergymen were mostly Dissenters. West of the Pennines, the abolition societies contained more wealthy manufacturers and were also, especially in Manchester and Birmingham, more independent of the London Abolition Society.

[39] The New York Manumission Society initially required dues of 8 shillings upon joining and 4 shillings every quarter. In 1789 the average skilled carpenter or mason in New York earned about 4 shillings a day, which was twice the wages

Although the overwhelming majority of Americans were farmers, the abolition societies contained virtually no members with agricultural "interests," unless one counts those involved in speculation in confiscated Tory estates and western lands. German, Dutch, and French names are conspicuously scarce in the membership rosters. The New York Society included, at least nominally, the high command of the Federalist party: Hamilton, Jay, Colonel Robert Troup, General Matthew Clarkson, John B. Murray, and many others. But neither the New York nor Pennsylvania societies was a Federalist club. They contained prominent anti-Federalists, Clintonian and Jeffersonian Democrats, former Liberty Boys, and the sons of Tory families. The striking point is not party affiliation but the number of active abolitionists who held important offices. Among the members of both societies were United States Senators, Congressmen, Federal judges and diplomats, Federal and state attorneys general, members of state legislatures, of constitutional conventions, and of city councils. The abolition societies were, in short, one of the municipal meeting grounds for men of wealth, influence, and political power.

During the post-Revolutionary decades American municipal life was invigorated by a movement for cooperative organization in the public interest. This spirit partly reflected the commercial and philanthropic ideals of the European Enlightenment, which had led to similar planning and civic organization in cities like Edinburgh. In America, however, there were special circumstances that quickened the sense of local responsibility. Political independence forced merchants to find new markets and routes of trade, while simultaneously opening new opportunities in business, banking, and manufacturing. Interurban rivalry spurred local leaders to improve transportation facilities and to found, by various charters and acts of incorporation, institutions for public service (the Pennsylvania Abolition Society was officially incorporated in 1789). In both Philadelphia and New York, the abolition societies were thus parts of an interlocking network of public and private

---

of an unskilled laborer. I have identified one hatter and one tanner-currier among the New York members. There was at least one Jewish member, Moses Judah, a merchant, Revolutionary War veteran, and active Freemason. Unlike the Pennsylvania Society, the New York Society did admit slaveholders, a fact which resulted in tense debate and which may have strained relationships between Quaker and non-Quaker members (see especially the minutes for Nov. 10, 1785; Feb. 8, 1786; Nov. 9, 1786; Feb. 15, 1787, New York Manumission Society MS Minutes, NYHS).

organizations designed to give order and direction to municipal life. In both cities the leading abolitionists could also be found in the chambers of commerce and in companies promoting canals and improved inland navigation; on the boards of savings banks, libraries, hospitals, Bible societies, and Sunday School societies; as the commissioners and directors of almshouses, poorhouses, and prisons. The London abolitionists exhibited a similar profile, except for the affiliation of many non-Quakers with the Evangelical movement.[40]

In one sense these interlocking directorates can be taken as evidence of the civic pride and philanthropic spirit of successful men who met in the same social clubs and in the same banks and exchanges, and who shared a common interest in the collective health and welfare of their fellow townsmen. Their concern for the Negro cannot be dismissed as a substitute for broader social concerns: the members of the abolition societies worked to extend and improve the education of the poor, to help imprisoned debtors, to provide free smallpox vaccination for the indigent, and to give information and assistance to newly arrived immigrants. And unlike the London and Parisian abolitionists, the reformers of New York and Philadelphia were an unrivaled elite, free from the restraints of an established aristocracy and from the fear of what Jefferson termed the *canaille*.

On the other hand, by the 1790s America's two largest cities were hardly immune from labor conflict. Immigration from Europe was on the rise, the old apprenticeship system continued to decay, and skilled artisans and mechanics complained of cheapened standards and of unfair competition from poorly trained and underpaid workers. In the face of unemployment and a growing pool of cheap labor, some skilled workers saw the manumission of slaves as a further threat to their former dignity and independence.[41] There is no reason to suspect that the entrepreneurial abolitionists were conspiring to lower wages by increasing the free labor force or by preventing the southward drain of Negroes. They were concerned, however, with the broader question

[40] Sidney I. Pomerantz, *New York, an American City, 1783–1803* (New York, 1938), *passim;* Louis Hartz, *Economic Policy and American Democratic Thought in Pennsylvania, 1776–1860* (Cambridge, Mass., 1948), p. 9 and *passim.* In order to avoid losing some members, the New York Manumission Society changed the night of its quarterly meeting so there would be no conflict with the Hand-in-Hand Fire Company (MS Minutes, VI, 57).

[41] Pomerantz, *New York*, pp. 209–10, 223 and *passim;* Jackson Turner Main, *The Social Structure of Revolutionary America* (Princeton, 1965), pp. 35–37, 73.

of labor discipline and with devising efficient institutions to replace older methods of social control. For example, in both Philadelphia and New York they helped to create the modern prison system, dedicated to the rehabilitation of deviants by means of steady work, habit-shaping regimen, and strict control over all aspects of life. Instead of being whipped or branded and then set free with an unchanged heart, the offender would now be placed behind walls, ostensibly for his own good as well as that of society, and transformed into a dependable and willing worker. Most of the philanthropies linked with the abolition cause had two broad aims: to protect an urban population from disease and disorder, thereby ensuring the smooth functioning of the social and economic system; and to inculcate the lower classes with various moral and economic virtues, so that workers would want to do what the emerging economy required. Slavery seemed entirely antithetical to this public-spirited ideology. Like sanguinary punishments, it seemed to be a relic of the barbarous past. And if slaves could be converted into sober, self-disciplined workers, the same could presumably be done with vagabonds, whores, felons, and deviants of every kind.

The point to be stressed is that the Quaker example included considerably more than a decision to manumit their slaves. Both in England and in the northern states the Quakers worked tirelessly for improved credit and insurance facilities; for canal systems and better roads; for transatlantic mail packets; for chambers of commerce and, ultimately, for railroads. And they linked such "useful improvements" with a variety of civic and philanthropic projects. For in the Quaker world view there were no disparities between business enterprise and devoting one's leisure time to the dissemination of Bibles, to the promotion of science, to the building of hospitals and prisons, and to the eradication of slavery. God's plan for human progress, revealed through reason and natural law, was all of a piece. The canals, banks, and technological improvements would be of little use unless workers understood the dynamic core of the Quaker ethic: responsibility. It was not by chance that Franklin issued his famed homilies from the Quaker City.

William Allen and the Limitations of Quaker Philanthropy

William Allen, a key figure in the British antislavery movement, epitomizes the meaning of Quaker science and philanthropy in the face of revolutionary change. I have already mentioned that Rebecca Jones, the missionary from Philadelphia, imbued young Allen with the spirit of the evangelical revival. Much earlier Allen had developed a keen interest in chemistry and astronomy, and at fourteen had built his own telescope. At eighteen, however, Allen's mind became absorbed with religious introspection and with a daily struggle, recorded in his spiritual diary, against self-indulgence. At that time, in 1788, his models of Quaker piety included Rebecca Jones, George Dillwyn, and John Pemberton. He was deeply moved by Pemberton's account of Quaker committees visiting and helping Negroes in Philadelphia. As a symbol of his own quest for purity, Allen resolved to abstain from sugar until its West Indian cultivators had been emancipated—a vow he kept for forty-three years.[42]

It happened that Allen was born and grew up in one of the first parts of London to feel the more devastating effects of the economic revolution. His father had moved from Scrooby, the home of the Plymouth Pilgrims, to become a silk manufacturer in Spitalfields, which had a long tradition, in E. P. Thompson's words, of "anti-authoritarian turbulence." According to Thompson, the Spitalfields silk weavers were the first "large group of domestic workers . . . whose conditions anticipate those of the semi-employed proletarian outworkers of the 19th century." As a result of exploitive innovations in management and of increasing competition from Lancashire cottons, the Spitalfields silk weavers were degraded to a ghastly level of poverty and overcrowding.[43] In short, young Allen lived in the midst of a noxious ghetto which threatened at any moment to explode into violence. Much to his father's disappointment, he left the family silk mill at the age of twenty-two and began working at Plough Court for Joseph Gurney Bevan. By 1786 he was on the slave-trade committee of the London Meeting for Sufferings. He married a Hanbury of the tinplate industry and soon became proprietor of Bevan's pharmaceutical concern, which ultimately became Allen & Hanburys.[44]

[42] My account of Allen draws mainly on *Life of William Allen, with Selections from His Correspondence* (3 vols., London, 1846), and from his papers at Allen & Hanburys, Ltd., London.

[43] E. P. Thompson, *The Making of the English Working Class* (New York, 1963), pp. 21, 69, 143, 261, 266.

[44] MS Minutes, Aug. 14, 1786, Box F, Friends House. Allen's third wife was a Birkbeck, and was related to Morris Birkbeck, who in 1788 was a correspondent

It might be tempting to conclude that Allen's antislavery activities were a hypocritical effort to divert attention from the sufferings of English workingmen. Thompson, for example, quotes a remarkable address to the public from an anonymous Manchester journeyman cotton spinner who seemed to suspect that humanitarians had contrived a double standard for judging the condition of English workers and West Indians slaves. English workers supposedly enjoyed the equal protection of law and were free to leave their places of employment. Yet:

The negro slave in the West Indies, if he works under a scorching sun, has probably a little breeze of air sometimes to fan him: he has a space of ground, and a time allowed to cultivate it. The English spinner slave has no enjoyment of the open atmosphere and breezes of heaven. Locked up in factories eight stories high, he has no relaxation till the ponderous engine stops, and then he goes home to get refreshed for the next day; no time for sweet association with his family; they are all alike fatigued and exhausted.[45]

The difficulty is that William Allen was fully aware of the human misery in Spitalfields and of the later degradation of English mill workers. As a rich entrepreneur who had close ties with Evangelicals like William Wilberforce and Henry Thornton, he would probably have endorsed the first part of Burke's famous message of 1795 to the starving poor: "Patience, labour, sobriety, frugality, and religion, should be recommended to them; all the rest is downright fraud." But Allen was also heir to the Quaker variant of Dissent, which, for all its inward-turning spirituality and its dilution by wealth, still contained both a latent dissatisfaction with the social order and the vision of a more harmonious and equalitarian world. Beginning in 1797, he helped to organize a committee to distribute soup to the ragged masses of Spitalfields. By 1812 his reorganized "Soup Society" was conducting street-by-street surveys of the area, recording data on population, age, literacy, religion, and families without Bibles. Allen may have considered the possession of a Bible as important as the possession of a job and the doles of soup as an antidote to revolution. The fact remains that Allen's journal, *The Philanthropist*, designed to stimu-

---

of the Abolition Committee and who in 1817 emigrated to the United States, where he promoted English settlement as well as antislavery doctrine in Illinois.

[45] Thompson, *Making of the English Working Class*, p. 201.

late "virtue and active benevolence," combined information on West Indian and American slavery with detailed reports on the plight of the English poor.[46]

Except for limitations of time and energy, there is no inherent reason that a concern for one species of injustice should blind a man to other species of injustice. Indeed, Allen probably weakened his effectiveness by engaging in such an incredible number of benevolent activities. And his passion for philanthropy was partly a way of justifying his active hobby of science. As a student of science Allen faced a growing conflict between his faith in God's intelligible design and his fear of French and German natural philosophy (late in life, while writing a paper for the Royal Society on the respiration of pigeons, he threatened Henry Brougham that he would withdraw his sponsorship from the Library of Useful Knowledge unless Kant's works were suppressed!). A friend of Sir Humphrey Davy, Allen gave popular lectures at the Royal Institution, helped write a notable paper on carbonic acid, and was elected Fellow of the Linnaean and Royal Societies. He was confident that "the pursuits of science, properly conducted, tend to enlarge our views, to banish narrow prejudices, to increase our love of truth and order, and give tone and vigour to the mind." Nevertheless, throughout his life Allen kept reminding himself, "beware, lest chemistry and natural philosophy usurp the highest seat in thy heart." Discovery of truth in natural science only "'exalted the creature," whereas spiritual truth always "lays him low." In 1812, Allen comforted himself by the thought that his main object had been the good of others, "for if, instead of these things, my time were devoted to philosophical pursuits and experiments, to which I am so naturally prone, the path to honour and distinction stands far above me. May the sacrifice be accepted above!"[47]

These inner conflicts provide insight into the goals Allen sought in philanthropy. Social reform, though secular by traditional standards, was a "spiritual" outlet that balanced worldly success in business and science. It also furnished an inner test of moral worthiness. Allen hoped that his efforts to do good did not spring merely from "benevolent intentions," but also from the humble sense that he was an instru-

---

[46] *Life of William Allen*, I, 33–34; *The Philanthropist: or Repository for Hints and Suggestions Calculated to Promote the Comfort and Happiness of Man*, II (1812), 173–96, 395–404, and *passim*.

[47] *Life of William Allen*, I, 143, and *passim*.

ment in the hand of the Lord.[48] Above all, reform led to acceptable external ties with the non-Quaker world. An analysis of the nature and limitations of such external ties will help illuminate the subtle connections between class ideology and the Quaker evangelical faith.

The early Quaker revivalists foreshadowed the moralistic concerns of the great evangelical awakening of the late eighteenth and early nineteenth centuries—the Evangelical crusade within the Church of England, the triumphs of Methodism on both sides of the Atlantic, and parallel movements within the Baptist and Presbyterian churches. Apart from important theological differences, the Quaker itinerants called for the moral uplift of the common people, inveighing against drunkenness, sexual immorality, ignorance of religion, and desecration of the Sabbath. If the Quaker ethic could lead to more radical and secular critiques of the social order—and one may cite Thomas Paine as a witness—the Quaker evangelicals were as horrified by Paine and by the French Revolution as were Wilberforce and Hannah More.[49] Like the Evangelicals within the Church of England, their program for reforming the nation's morals had two goals: to produce a sober, self-disciplined, and industrious working population; and to persuade the upper classes to devote their time and wealth to ennobling causes rather than to gay parties, gambling, and other conspicuous forms of waste and self-indulgence. The result of such reforms, even if not uppermost in the reformers' minds, would be a society free from the threat of class conflict and revolution.

This ideology had considerable appeal for the young Quakers of Allen's generation, born into an affluent environment but surrounded by the boredom and erosion of wealth. Allen's friend, Elizabeth Gurney, frankly confessed that she had been leading a frivolous and un-Quaker social life before her conversion to serious religion. To families like the Gurneys, Barclays, and Hoares, wealth had brought a slackening of Quaker discipline, exogamous marriage, and a drift away from religious identity. But paradoxically, the same communications network that helped to create the toxin of wealth also accelerated the movement for self-purification. A further pardox was that the Quaker revival, while restoring a sense of religious identity and purpose, also brought Quakers into cooperative alliance with outsiders, most notably with

[48] *Ibid.*, I, 180.
[49] Jones, *Later Periods*, I, 243, 265–75, 280.

the Wilberforce-Thornton syndicate of reformers. In a sense, it was this latter group that appropriated Quaker programs and Quaker modes of organization as a means of reforming and "saving" the nation. But for Quakers, both in Britain and America, membership in nondenominational societies provided a means of confirming economic success with social acceptability. When a man like Allen collaborated with the British ruling elite in the African Institution, the British and Foreign Bible Society, and the British and Foreign School Society, he became at least a half-way member of the moral establishment, and he assimilated many of its values. The great benevolent societies helped to shape a consciousness of class identity and purpose, and, when leading merchants, bankers, and manufacturers met together in reform societies, they were not unmindful of useful contacts for business purposes.

On the other hand, such alliances could not altogether surmount religious prejudice. Granville Sharp once remarked that Anthony Benezet, his antislavery correspondent, was "unhappily involved in the errors of Quakerism." Wilberforce bluntly wrote Allen that he wished "for your own sake, and that of the world [that] . . . your religious principles and my own were more entirely accordant." Allen's Quaker friend, Richard Reynolds, commented bitterly on such condescension: after all that Quakers had done for the Bible Society and to secure Wilberforce's election in Yorkshire, Reynolds would hope "that class to which he, Thornton, and Stephen belong, should be convinced that we are, as we are willing to admit they may be, real genuine Christians." Yet for Wilberforce and his associates, the interests of "true" Christianity took precedence over any benevolent cause, and Nonconformists like Allen could only be looked upon pathetically as "poor creatures."[50]

If Allen's ties with liberal reformers were limited, they also qualify

[50] Prince Hoare, *Memoirs of Granville Sharp, Esq., Composed from His Own Manuscripts* . . . (London, 1820), p. 97; *Life of William Allen,* I, 178–79. Similarly, Granville Sharp could praise Benezet in a letter to Benjamin Rush, but also say that he could speak more frankly and candidly to Rush because of religion (Sharp to Rush, July 2, 1774, Rush papers, HSP). Samuel Hopkins admitted that even though Quakers did not celebrate the Lord's Supper, they had led other Christians in freeing their slaves; who could say, he asked, whether the Quakers' neglect of church institutions was worse than keeping slaves? (*Works,* II, 594).

any conclusion that he was solely interested in preserving the social order through moral regeneration.[51] Whereas Hannah More's Sunday Schools were intended to produce a dutiful and tractable working population, whose "education" would stop with religious indoctrination, Allen was genuinely dedicated to the cause of educating the public. Despite their close cooperation in the antislavery cause, Wilberforce declined Allen's invitation to join the committee of subscribers to the Lancasterian Society, an organization that included such Utilitarian associates of Allen's as James Mill and David Ricardo. Allen was undisturbed by the democratic implications of the Lancasterian system, which was intended to multiply the effectiveness of knowledge by converting pupils into participating teachers. Unlike the Evangelical leader, Charles Simeon, Allen did not think that the movement to reform the penal code was unsuitable for "religious people" so long as a rationalist like Samuel Romilly led the cause. Allen also campaigned against capital punishment, exchanging information with American Quaker philanthropists like John Murray, Jr., as well as with European monarchs.[52] But Allen's most revealing involvement with secular reform came with his encouragement of Robert Owen's paternalistic experiments at New Lanark. In Allen's eyes, Owen's experiments promised to solve the otherwise catastrophic problems of industrialism. He therefore furnished substantial funds that helped Owen take over the mill town and carry out his reforms. As one of the proprietors of

[51] As early as 1811 *The Philanthropist* printed a remarkable essay on "the most rational means of promoting civilization in barbarous states" (in the British Museum copy someone has attributed it to Clarkson), which argued that missionaries should not denounce customs like infanticide and abandonment of the aged if conformity to Christian ethics would simply lead to starvation; the first step toward Christianizing a barbarous people should be "to furnish them with a permanent supply of food"; "You must first improve the worldly condition of those, whom you mean thus morally to serve. You must produce, with this view, a change in their character and habits." In other words, Christian values depended on Western civilization, and the plow and "mechanic" should precede the Bible and priest (*Philanthropist*, I, 16–21).

[52] Although Wilberforce displayed a more liberal or at least a more pragmatic spirit on such subjects than did most of the Evangelicals, he wrote Buxton on Feb. 12, 1819, that he did not think the principles regarding capital punishment had as yet been "clearly ascertained," and that he had long disdained the idea of himself bringing forward any proposition on the subject. He thought that Sir James Mackintosh was ideally suited for the cause, but regretted that Mackintosh was so infected by party spirit (Gurney papers, Friends House).

New Lanark, Allen was delighted by the unmistakable improvements in working and social conditions.

The rupture came when it began to dawn on the devout Quaker that Owen was a "determined enemy" of all revealed religion. Indeed, at New Lanark, Owen seemed bent on proving that human happiness required emancipation from the belief in the divinity of the Bible. "We came into the concern," Allen wrote Owen in 1815, "not to form a manufactory of infidels, but to support a benevolent character in plans of a very different nature, in which the happiness of millions, and the cause of morality and virtue, are deeply concerned." Together with Joseph Fox, Allen forced Owen to introduce the Bible in New Lanark schools; he himself lectured the workers on the importance of revealed religion. Allen perfectly trusted the Russian Emperor's professions of humanitarianism and his promises to promote public education—presumably in line with Quaker principles—while, in contrast, Allen threatened to withdraw from New Lanark unless Owen surrendered all control over educating the children, who had proved to be deficient in Scriptural knowledge. It was precisely because the eyes of the enlightened world were fastened upon New Lanark that Allen resolved to do anything in his power, even if it meant removing Owen as manager, to prevent the model town from becoming "an infidel establishment."[53] The more contact Allen had with secular radicalism, the more importance he attached to religious orthodoxy. Among the "sound" causes that increasingly absorbed his energies were the dissemination of Bibles and of antislavery doctrine.

A Preliminary Assessment: The Symbolism of Slave and Free Labor

Quaker testimony against slavery was an extension of the sect's traditional stand against war and violence. Such testimony also served, in time of crisis and persecution, both as a test of purity and as an emblem of distinctive identity. But the early Quaker revival, which spawned collective efforts to rid the Society of Friends of slaveholding, issued a broader challenge to the ethical basis of capital accumulation. Unlike their antislavery disciples and successors, Woolman and Benezet were content to live in the most humble circumstances. Benezet, whom

[53] *Life of William Allen,* I, 96–97, 130–32, 180–81, 209, 244–45, 324–25, 344–46, 349–53; II, 226, 236–37, 362–63.

wealthy friends described as extremely unprepossessing in appearance, expressed skepticism over the "cant" he heard about the stewardship of wealth. Writing to Samuel Fothergill in 1755, he questioned the rationalizations by which Quaker capitalists justified their success:

And there are some who, though they have already a large affluence of wealth, yet are toiling hard to add thereto, without knowing wherefore they thus toil, and whether a wise man or a fool shall possess it after them. . . . Why do so many suffer the God of this world so to blind their eyes, and vitiate their reasonable as well as religious senses, as to suffer them to toil after gain, and think it is a mighty thing, and themselves notably employed, if they can add £1,000 to £1,000, or £10,000 to £10,000, and that often by a trade far from being pure from defilement, as such gain often arises chiefly from the purchase and sale of things at least needless and vain, if not of a defiling nature; an instance of which I have often painfully observed amongst us, where it is frequent to see even Friends, toiling year after year, enriching themselves, and thus gathering fuel for their own and their children's vanity and corruption, by the importation and sale of large quantities of rum, &c. . . . Now, that such a person shall esteem himself, and be esteemed, a religious man, and perhaps be the more regarded, even by religious people, because he is rich and great, is a mere paradox; yet is it too often the case. . . . Shall we desire to be great and rich, when our Saviour has so plainly declared it a situation so very dangerous; and that his predominant choice is of the poor of this world?[54]

Such words, warning against the allure of security and accommodation, echo the spirit of seventeenth-century religious radicalism. Insofar as Benezet's critique represented the spirit of the Quaker revival, the revival itself struck at the heart of the business ethic that was enriching families like the Pembertons, Hoares, Gurneys, and Barclays, on whose consciences the revival had a profound impact. From the Benezets, Fothergills, and Churchmans the wealthy Friends acquired their zeal for education, temperance, and antislavery. They showed little inclination, however, of abandoning their ideology of progress which justified toiling hard "to add £10,000 to £10,000."

No one should expect the Quaker capitalists to have renounced their wealth; and the possession of wealth does not cast doubt on the moral sincerity of Quaker abolitionists. They were, after all, a pioneering minority who were among the first modern capitalists to recognize both

[54] *Memoirs of the Life and Gospel Labours of Samuel Fothergill, with Selections from his Correspondence. . .*, ed. by George Crossfield (New York, 1844), 363–65.

the social responsibilities of wealth and the social consequences of economic action. Yet it is essential to distinguish individual motive from the larger ideological functions of a movement like antislavery.

The Society of Friends interpreted each step toward a total disengagement from slaveholding as a tangible sign of growing religious purity. For men disturbed by the revival's strictures against wealth, antislavery suggested the compromise of limited sacrifice, though obviously a sacrifice of keener anguish for a few Quaker planters in the South.[55] Abolitionist activity allowed many of Benezet's "rich and great" Quakers to "be esteemed" religious men, and in accordance with moral criteria which Benezet himself had helped establish. It also brought them into contact with the rich and great of other denominations, enabling them to escape some of the exclusiveness and inwardness of their sect. To moralists and reformers of other faiths, the Quakers demonstrated that testimony against slavery could be a social correlative of inner purity which seemed to pose no threat to the social order—at least to that capitalist order in which the Quakers had won so enviable a "stake." As a social force, antislavery was a highly selective response to labor exploitation. It provided an outlet for demonstrating a Christian concern for human suffering and injustice, and yet thereby gave a certain moral insulation to economic activities less visibly dependent on human suffering and injustice. Viewed from one perspective, the Quakers were at the headwaters of a widening stream of philanthropy and social reform. From another viewpoint they created the liberal tradition of being "kind" to Negroes as proof of one's humanitarianism.

The simplistic thesis that Quaker abolitionists were governed by "economic interest" in the sense that they stood to profit from the destruction of the slave trade or a weakening of the plantation system cannot bear examination.[56] But Negro slavery was a system of labor

---

[55] Some prominent Quakers refused to make even a limited sacrifice, and either left the Society of Friends or were disowned, like Stephen Hopkins, former governor of Rhode Island. Even in Pennsylvania some Quaker families had to free as many as ten or fifteen slaves, and often helped to compensate the blacks for past services. In Virginia, Warner Mifflin's father manumitted nearly one hundred slaves (Drake, *Quakers and Slavery,* pp. 75–77). Yet as Stephen B. Weeks shows, there was soon a conservative reaction among Virginia Quakers, many of whom opposed the policy of emancipation and many of whom left the Society of Friends (*Southern Quakers and Slavery,* p. 216).

[56] Although there were a few exceptions, like James Cropper, the Liverpool

which raised fundamental questions about the meanings of freedom, dependability, and discipline; the Quaker reformers represented an entrepreneurial class which confronted, at least in Great Britain, an unruly labor force, much of it recently uprooted from village or rural life—a labor force which even in the early nineteenth century had not yet been disciplined to the factory system, and which expressed its frustrations in riots, crime, sabotage, and other acts of uninhibited violence.

The Quakers engaged in the antislavery cause were also deeply concerned over domestic problems of labor discipline. William Dillwyn, for example, praised Quaker manufacturers for being more attentive to the welfare of the children in their mills, and for being careful "to preserve good order among them, and employ a man to instruct them in reading, &c., during certain hours, for which no deduction is made from their wages." The wider adoption of such practices, Dillwyn thought, would reduce the public complaints that factories were nurseries of vice. David Barclay circulated large broadsides giving "advice to servants," some of which echoed the sermons of American slaveholders: "Be not what is called an eye-servant, appearing diligent in sight, but neglectful when out of it." "Avoid pert answers; for civil language is cheap, and impertinence provoking." "Never stay when sent on a message; waiting long is painful to a Master, and a quick return shows diligence." Barclay's central message, however, was that "a good character" should be the supreme goal of servants, "for it is their bread." Therefore, servants should watch the company they keep and never provoke their superiors. As for their freedom to change employers, "the Servant that often changes his place works only to be poor."[57]

Consider also the following specimen. On July 15, 1787, Dr. John Coakley Lettsom wrote Dr. Benjamin Rush on the subjects of prisons and slavery. Rush, who read Lettsom's letter to the Philadelphia Prison Society, had become convinced that "a prison sometimes supplies the place of a church and out-preaches the preacher in conveying useful instruction to the heart." Lettsom reported that "villainy" was accum-

---

importer of East India sugar, it would appear that many eighteenth-century Quaker merchants actually stood to lose by any weakening of the Atlantic slave-trade system.

[57] *Memoir of the Life and Religious Labors of Henry Hull* (Philadelphia, 1873), p. 203; David Barclay, "Advice to Servants," broadside, Friends House.

ulating so fast in England that "necessity" would soon cure the prejudice against prisons. He had himself favored condemning convicts to public labor out of doors, assuming that the beneficial example to spectators would be more permanent than that of the gallows. Lettsom was struck, however, by Rush's argument that the example might serve to render any physical labor "ignominious." On the other hand, he cited an instance of convicts who were chained at night on a ship and who worked on the land in day. Although voluntary laborers performed the same drudgery within sight of the convicts, the proximity enhanced their appreciation of their own liberty, "for however the body may be occupied alike, the mind is impressed very differently, as differently as voluntary labour, and condemned slavery can impress the mind." Hence "the example of the latter may be beneficial to the morality of the community, without entailing disgrace upon any species of voluntary industry." Without pause, Lettsom then proceeded to express his joy over the joint British and American efforts to abolish the slave trade.[58]

What distinguished the Quakers from earlier mercantilist writers, who had also pondered schemes for suppressing "villainy" and for putting the unruly poor to work, was the Quakers' gift for assimilating utility and national interest to a humanitarian ethic. The Quakers, unlike the mercantilists, deplored visible or overt forms of social cruelty, such as the slave trade. But they also helped to create a moral climate in which a highly ethical purpose could disguise the effects of power. Although eighteenth-century Quakers were not responsible for the consequences of a nineteenth-century free labor market—or for the consequences of British efforts to stamp out the slave trade in the heart of Africa—they unwittingly drew distinctions and boundaries which opened the way, under a guise of moral rectitude, for unprecedented forms of oppression.

Clearly, for Rush and Lettsom there was no comparability between "condemned slavery" and Negro slavery, except for the possibility that both might render voluntary labor ignominious. For Barclay, it was inconceivable that English servants were in any sense unfree. For Dillwyn, the children in the English mines and factories were the beneficiaries of wholesome discipline, except where the factories had become nurseries of vice; the children of American slaves, who seldom

---

[58] Lettsom to Rush, July 15, 1787, Rush MSS, XXXII, LCP.

endured such regular work or supervision, were the victims of unquestioned oppression. Despite what we have said concerning William Allen's Soup Society and educational reforms, antislavery ideology served to isolate specific forms of human misery, allowing issues of freedom and discipline to be faced in a relatively simplified model. And by defining slavery as a unique *moral* aberration, the ideology tended to give sanction to the prevailing economic order. If we look on antislavery as a game certain people played—which as a conceptual device implies no lack of seriousness on the players' parts, but simply points to the definition and acceptance of arbitrary rules—then we can appreciate how the movement helped to reshape attitudes toward work, liberty, exploitation, and proper discipline.

What made the Negro slave ideally suited as a counter in such a game was his lack of responsibility for his own status. By definition, he was innocent of the burdens and coercions of the Protestant work ethic, almost as if his forced labor had freed him from the unhappy legacy of Adam's curse. Accordingly, Quakers and others could commiserate with his sufferings and attack his exploiters while reaffirming both the validity of economic law and God's wisdom in assigning men unequal stations in life.

Yet there can be no greater disparity of power than that between a man convinced of his own disinterested service and another man who is defined as a helpless object. As representatives of the emerging capitalist order, extending charity to the lowliest segment of laborers, Quaker reformers could not view Negroes as even potentially autonomous beings. Most of the Negroes freed by Quaker masters were quietly dissuaded from trying to join the Society of Friends. Liberation from slavery did not mean freedom to live as one chose, but rather freedom to become a diligent, sober, dependable worker who gratefully accepted his position in society. Freedom required the internalization of moral precepts in the place of less subtle forms of external coercion. No doubt it was a sign of progessive enlightenment when Moses Brown showed concern over providing secure savings deposits for his freed slaves; William Allen promoted the same idea for the workers of New Lanark. Yet neither man doubted that he knew the best interests of the laboring class, or that saving from wages was an act of freedom.

Six

The Emancipation
of America, I

The Limits of Revolutionary Ideology

The doctrines of the American Revolution, we have often read, presented a direct challenge to Negro slavery. By the end of the war, according to Winthrop D. Jordan, "it was perfectly clear that the principles for which Americans had fought required the complete abolition of slavery; the question was not *if*, but *when* and *how*." Although Jordan acknowledges that the majority of Americans failed to face the question of "when and how," he tends to confuse liberal principles with antislavery commitment. He thus concludes, along with many other historians, that the last quarter of the eighteenth century was a time of missed opportunity. Perhaps, he suggests, the bitter legacy of Garrisonian abolitionism, Civil War, and Reconstruction could have been avoided. In an optimistic passage that seems to ignore his own emphasis on racial exploitation as a source of national identity, Jordan writes:

In retrospect, the pity of antislavery's failure was that in the decade after the Revolution, success against slavery seemed almost within reach. If the Negro had been freed in the late eighteenth century rather than in 1863, if only in Virginia, he would have suffered far less degradation. The implications of the natural rights philosophy and religious equalitarianism would have operated directly upon his nature unimpeded by the glaring fact of his inferior status as a slave, and he would then have been in a far

255

stronger position to meet the challenge of Darwinism. . . . The protracted battle for abolition in the nineteenth century generated by reaction defenses of slavery which deliberately subverted his equality; just as important, that battle forced reformist energies to concentrate more exclusively upon the single goal of abolition. . . . A general emancipation after the Revolution would have been more than an improvised weapon in a fratricidal war. It would have come as a glorious triumph, the capstone of the Revolution; guilt could easily have been foisted onto the British and the whole nation stirred with pride.[1]

Such speculation would be harmless if it did not distort our understanding of the forces that maintained slavery and of the kind of struggle that abolition required. Although Jordan carefully takes note of other factors, his thesis shifts attention to the internal weaknesses of early antislavery principles. Yet such weaknesses cannot be gauged by what legislators did or left undone. The Revolution could not have opened avenues toward general emancipation unless the slaves themselves had become involved as a significant military force. Historians have too often underestimated the economic strength of slavery during the Revolutionary period, exaggerated the force of antislavery sentiment in the Upper South, and minimized the obstacles that abolitionists faced even in the northern states. The American colonists were fighting, after all, for self-determination. And it is now clear that slavery was of central importance to both the southern and national economies, and thus to the viability of the "American system."[2]

The significance of early antislavery does not lie in its marginal successes or major failures. We can hardly expect that reformers should have persuaded southern planters to give up their slaves. Even in times of crisis, no other group of planters accepted emancipation except when coerced by a central government or by the slaves themselves. In America, Revolutionary patriotism was seldom a sufficient inducement even for raising taxes or recruiting troops. Nor should we expect

---

[1] Winthrop D. Jordan, *White over Black: American Attitudes toward the Negro, 1550–1812* (Chapel Hill, 1968), pp. 342, 374. Jordan is careful to say success against slavery *seemed* almost within reach; four recent works that present a contrary view are: Donald L. Robinson, *Slavery in the Structure of American Politics, 1765–1820* (New York, 1971); Robert McColley, *Slavery and Jeffersonian Virginia* (Urbana, 1964); Gerald W. Mullin, *Flight and Rebellion: Slave Resistance in Eighteenth-Century Virginia* (New York, 1972); Robert William Fogel and Stanley L. Engerman, *Time on the Cross: The Economics of American Negro Slavery* (2 vols., Boston, 1974).

[2] See Chapters One, Two, and Three, above.

eighteenth-century legislators to have embraced a vast program of social engineering, equivalent or superior to that of Reconstruction. A general emancipation, even if gradually administered, would have required an unprecedented bureaucracy; new mechanisms for raising and dispensing revenue; and an army of agents to register the age and value of slaves, to supervise labor contracts, to protect freedmen from *de facto* re-enslavement, to institute judicial proceedings, to provide temporary sustenance, and to implement a program for education and economic self-sufficiency. To recall the fears and suspicions aroused by the Federal Constitution, or the vehement opposition to Hamilton's modest experiments with centralized planning, is to begin to appreciate the distance between the ideal of emancipation and its effective implementation.

But what, then, is the significance of an ineffective movement? The easiest answer, of course, is that the movement was not ineffective in the long run. It is a fact of great importance that William Lloyd Garrison, Wendell Phillips, and Abraham Lincoln could all appeal to the antislavery principles and pronouncements of the Revolutionary generation. But there are hazards in imagining antislavery as a telic force, flowing irresistibly toward its moment of destiny. It is more promising to analyze the meaning of antislavery within its own historical context. The way in which reformers define and respond to a national problem may tell much about the needs and internal strains of a social system. For example, the patriots of the Revolution were self-professed enemies of every form of tyranny; yet their liberal ideology may have raised obstacles to "unearned" emancipation. Since the Revolution tended to define liberty as the reward for righteous struggle, it was difficult to think of freedom as something that could be granted to supposedly passive slaves. As a reform movement, antislavery probed and helped to define the boundaries of an emerging republican ideology. It embodied some of the central tensions of eighteenth-century thought, and also revealed the limits of change which a given society could envision or assimilate.

A pragmatic regard for limits, coupled with uncompromising moral judgment, characterized the entire Enlightenment's approach to slavery. The later achievement of men like Garrison and Phillips lay, to a large extent, in freeing abstract principles and judgments from a heavy ballast of qualifications. I have discussed elsewhere the two sides of rationalism, as applied to slavery by eighteenth-century *phi-*

losophes, and have suggested that both reformers and defenders of slavery could make effective use of the ideas of utility, social equilibrium, and the moral economy of nature.[3] One example will be sufficient to show how, in a single work, a fear of abrupt change could compromise the rhetoric of militant abolitionism. In 1789, Benjamin Frossard, a French Protestant, summarized several decades of philosophic writing against slavery. The institution was a criminal violation of the rights of man and the citizen; it stood opposed to peace, Christian morality, public order, sound policy, and economic law; it contradicted a century of growing benevolence and enlightenment, arousing the indignation of apostles of liberty, such as the American Quakers, and of the best and most generous minds in England and France. And yet no pen could be eloquent enough to convince planters to give up their slaves or governments to impose such an obligation. "Il faut un siècle de bonnes actions pour corriger trois siècles de tyrannie." If justice required the eventual emancipation of slaves, it would also require compensation to any planters who, having acquired property under the protection of law, were forced to relinquish it. Moreover, Negroes were as yet too uncivilized to perceive the connection between individual and general interests; if liberated, they would fall into idleness and crime. Frossard favored the British plan of ending the slave trade. This, he thought, would force planters to improve the condition of their slaves and would also give hope and incentive to Negroes, who could be taught that freedom and responsibility are the rewards of industry.[4]

Of course, Frossard was right in predicting that it would take a century to eradicate slavery from the New World. No doubt it would have taken longer if everyone had kept saying the same thing. Yet gradualism was the hallmark of the liberal mind, in England and

[3] *The Problem of Slavery in Western Culture* (Ithaca, N.Y., 1966), chs. 13 and 14.

[4] Benjamin Frossard, *La Cause des esclaves nègres et des habitans de la Guinée, portée au tribunal de la justice, de la religion, de la politique . . .* (2 vols., Lyon, 1789), I, 20–24, and *passim.* Frossard was one of the few antislavery writers who analyzed the psychology of sympathy and commitment. Since Negro slaves lived so far away, he argued, their sufferings could not arouse an immediate and authentic compassion. When Europeans read accounts of the slave trade, their emotions were as fleeting as those evoked by a sentimental romance. It was therefore necessary for writers to make direct appeals to reason and conscience.

America no less than in France. And the gradualist mentality reflected something more than a willingness to subordinate human rights to property rights. The two were inseparable, at least according to the Harringtonian or "classical republican" tradition which served as a foundation for liberal political thought of the eighteenth century. J. G. A. Pocock summarizes the Harringtonian political outlook as follows:

Society is made up of court and country; government, of court and Parliament. . . . The court is the administration. The country consists of men of independent property; all others are servants. The business of Parliament is to preserve the independence of property, on which is founded all human liberty and all human excellence. The business of administration is to govern, and this is a legitimate activity; but to govern is to wield power, and power has a natural tendency to encroach.[5]

A free society, in other words, was by no means incompatible with dependent classes of workers. Its central prerequisite was a large class of freeholders, unencumbered by feudal, military, or political obligations. Liberty required independence, and independence required freehold property. As Pocock shows, these axioms were not confined to the "Commonwealthman" tradition of religious and political dissent; they permeated eighteenth-century political thought and left an imprint on conservative as well as democratic theory. The assumptions of "Country ideology" had a decided influence on antislavery writers on both sides of the Atlantic, enabling them to maintain, for example, that slavery was repugnant to the "ancient constitution" and that the slave-trading interests were allied with a mercantilist and power-hungry court. Yet so far as this ideology held sway, any scheme of emancipation ran the risk of undermining property, of increasing the powers of government, and thus of endangering the very foundations of liberty.

If demands for freedom weakened the traditional justifications for slavery, demands for self-determination raised new obstacles to emancipation. During the Age of Revolution, insistent appeals to constitutional rights and liberties were often a reaction against the administrative reforms of a centralizing power. Philosophical speculation drew nourishment from a succession of widespread conflicts between

[5] J. G. A. Pocock, "Machiavelli, Harrington, and English Political Ideologies in the Eighteenth Century," *William and Mary Quarterly,* 3rd ser., XXII (Oct., 1965), 565, and *passim.*

kings and nobles, between elites in central and local constituted bodies, and between landed aristocrats and the bourgeoisie. Thus in 1789 and 1790 some of the Hungarian nobility formed revolutionary committees of correspondence to defend their liberties from the encroaching reforms of the Austrian Empire. Traditionally, their rights had included autonomous dominion over serfs who had not been considered subjects of the emperor but who now looked to the central government for protection. Faced with a genuine danger of peasant insurrection, the local diets echoed the favorite arguments of North American slaveholders: peasant unrest had been stirred up by outside agitators; agricultural workers would soon starve if they were allowed to leave the estates; peasants were fully accustomed to hard work and physical punishment; they were far too lazy, childish, and stupid to respond to monetary incentives; the Bible justified involuntary servitude, and Providence had assigned men to their proper ranks.[6]

It was within this larger framework of contested rights and powers that the British and French metropolitan governments first moved to reform the slave systems of the New World. In most respects the West Indian assemblies were more vulnerable than the constituted bodies of central Europe. Caribbean slaveholders could hardly make claim to noble lineage and ancient tradition. For protection they were wholly dependent on the imperial armies and navies. They did not resist the innovations of an enlightened despot but rather the authority of a Parliament or National Assembly which represented powerful segments of bourgeois opinion. On the other hand, within the metropolitan governments they could count on allies who would exploit every domestic fear of social and political disorder. The defense of slavery, or even of slave trading, could easily be conflated with a defense of liberty and public order.

In North America an additional factor defined the boundaries of revolutionary ideology. Edmund S. Morgan has recently drawn attention to a central paradox of American colonial life: the rise of liberty and equality coincided with the rise of slavery; in effect, Americans "bought their independence with slave labor."[7] In Morgan's view,

[6] Robert R. Palmer, *The Age of the Democratic Revolution: A Political History of Europe and America, 1760–1800* (Princeton, 1959), pp. 387–96.

[7] Edmund S. Morgan, "Slavery and Freedom: The American Paradox," *The Journal of American History*, LIX (June, 1972), 6. I am much indebted to

this was not a fortuitous "inconsistency." The paradox involved more than racial prejudice or even the subtle psychological exploitation documented by Winthrop Jordan.

Clearly there was nothing novel about the freedom and independence of some men depending on the coerced labor of others. What distinguished American colonists was their magnificent effrontery. They rejoiced to find their ideals of freedom and equality reflected in the actual social order, but resolutely denied that the social order rested on a "mudsill" of slavery, as Southerners would later acknowledge. Yet like their English contemporaries, the American colonists equated social responsibility with independence, and independence with land ownership. They feared and mistrusted men, regardless of race, who lacked any tangible stake in society. During the seventeenth century, when England hatched various schemes for colonizing the idle poor, Virginia's governing elite feared that the colony was becoming "a sinke to drayen England of her filth and scum." With numerous British theorists, including John Locke, James Burgh, and Francis Hutcheson, the Americans shared the view that idle rogues and vagabonds were a menace to society unless impressed into involuntary servitude. Morgan thus contends that large-scale importations of Africans enabled the South to avoid the problem of an unruly and undisciplined white lower class: "The increase in the importation of slaves was matched by a decrease in the importation of indentured servants and consequently a decrease in the dangerous number of new freedmen who annually emerged seeking a place in society that they would be unable to achieve." It follows that eighteenth-century southern leaders could promote the ideal of a free white yeomanry and profess allegiance to the rights of all Englishmen precisely because black slaves had taken the place of a lower caste of whites. The fears and prejudices that had long been directed against the landless poor could now conveniently be confined to a restricted and highly visible group. Indeed, Morgan implies that the idea of deporting emancipated blacks, as a troublesome and dangerous population, originated in the English schemes for colonizing lower-class whites. Hence it was slavery

that transformed the Virginia of Governor Berkeley to the Virginia of Jefferson, slavery that made the Virginians dare to speak a political

Professor Morgan for allowing me to see an early version of this presidential address to the Organization of American Historians.

language that magnified the rights of freemen, and slavery, therefore, that brought Virginians into the same commonwealth political tradition with New Englanders.[8]

One should add that New England's own prosperity and equalitarian society had been nourished by the carrying trade with the slave isles of the Caribbean. On the eve of the American Revolution, Massachusetts alone could boast sixty distilleries producing rum, the export of which provided the region with its chief supply of specie. And if Massachusetts contained no more than five thousand Negro slaves, its West Indian trade employed some ten thousand seamen, to say nothing of the workers who built, outfitted, and supplied the ships.[9]

The American colonists were not trapped in an accidental contradiction between slavery and freedom. Their unique social order had arisen from many choices. They had resolved some of mankind's deepest social dilemmas, but at a heavy price. Their rhetoric of freedom was functionally related to the existence—and in many areas to the continuation—of Negro slavery. In a sense, then, demands for consistency between principles and practice, no matter how sincere, were rather beside the point. Practice was what made the principles possible.

Slavery as an Obstacle to Man's True Destiny

There was, then, no automatic connection between a defense of natural rights and the imperative that slavery be abolished, although slavery, at least in the abstract, was repugnant to the whole spirit of the Enlightenment.[10] Slavery always represents a moral contradiction, for it carries to extreme form the tendency to define and treat other men as physical objects—a tendency which moralists have deplored since ancient times. Moralists and social theorists have found ways of accommodating the contradiction to various ethical systems, though not without strain. Since the concept of slavery carried a penumbra of

[8] *Ibid.*, pp. 25, 29.

[9] "Statement of Trade and Fisheries of Massachusetts," Fitch Papers, Connecticut Historical Society, *Collections* (Hartford, 1920), XVIII, 266; Arthur Meier Schlesinger, *The Colonial Merchants and the American Revolution, 1763–1776* (New York, 1957), pp. 25–26.

[10] For elaboration of this theme, see *The Problem of Slavery in Western Culture,* chs. 11–14.

associations involving sin, punishment, obedience, self-surrender, and deliverance, the strains were related to central antinomies in the structure of Western thought. And for that reason, fundamental changes in attitude toward the nature and destiny of man could not help but give new resonance to the idea of human bondage.

For eighteenth-century thinkers who contemplated the subject, slavery stood as the central metaphor for all the forces that debased the human spirit. The treatment of man as property dramatized the moral dilemmas of the age. At the risk of gross oversimplification, it can be said that the Enlightenment was torn between the ideal of the autonomous individual and the ideal of a rational and efficient social order. These terms refer, of course, to complex tendencies of thought, not to static or uniform positions. The ideal of the autonomous individual involved a repudiation of both original sin and subservience to worldly authority, and thus required the reordering of social relations on some moral and voluntaristic basis. The ideal of the rational society involved the elimination of social and economic waste, the exaltation of utility, and the introduction of predictable system in place of arbitrary choice. Both major and minor thinkers of the Enlightenment strove to reconcile some notion of individual liberty with some notion of a rationally functional state. Negro slavery dramatized the difficulties of any synthesis; antislavery provided an illusory means of resolution.

There is no inherent reason that slavery should be incompatible with the ideal of a functional or utilitarian state. Indeed, for later champions of individual liberty, like William Lloyd Garrison and Mikhail Bakunin, all states were founded on the principle of slavery. For Thomas Hobbes, slavery was an inevitable part of the logic of power; the bondsman had no cause for complaint when he was provided with sustenance and security in exchange for being governed. Samuel Pufendorf agreed with Hobbes that the majority of men were governed by selfish impulse, and that slavery was therefore a highly useful instrument of social discipline which might solve the problem of Europe's idlers, thieves, and vagabonds. John Locke recommended compulsory labor for England's landless poor, and especially for their small children who needed to be "inured to work." Francis Hutcheson, one of the prime sources of antislavery thought, also argued that nothing was so "effectual" as perpetual bondage in promoting industry and restraining sloth, especially in the "lower conditions" of society.

He therefore argued that slavery should be the "ordinary punishment of such idle vagrants as, after proper admonitions and tryals of temporary servitude, cannot be engaged to support themselves and their families by any useful labours."[11]

A similar emphasis on public order and useful labor appears in the writings of mercantilists and later defenders of colonial slavery. But by the 1760s, even the most ardent proponents of social utility refrained from recommending *slavery* as the most suitable condition for England's poor. If I may offer a corollary to Profesor Morgan's thesis: the Virginians could defend man's inalienable rights because Negro slavery had precluded the need to discipline a white proletariat; Englishmen could later condemn the principle of slavery, as a demonstration of their own liberality, because they were beginning to find new uses for the idle poor, who, after "proper admonitions and tryals," could be molded into a compliant working class.[12] The dominant ideology— to which Hobbes, Harrington, Locke, and Hutcheson had all contributed—required that the utilitarian state be at least nominally "free." In other words, the ideal of rational order, if it were to win acceptance, needed to be limited by some compromise version of the ideal of individual autonomy. And what could be a more convenient symbol for exceeding limits than total and perpetual bondage?

Slavery is the perfect antithesis of individual autonomy or self-sovereignty, an ideal which derived in part from the humanist image of man as microcosm and in part from the sectarian and pietistic emphasis on the inner light and on man's capacity to partake of divine perfection. At the end of the eighteenth century the ideal reached its fullest development in Germany, especially in the works of Kant and Wilhelm von Humboldt. Whereas most antislavery writers assumed that freedom was a release from external restraint, to be granted only after sufficient preparation, Kant held (with respect to the French Revolution) that freedom is the "precondition of acquiring the maturity for freedom." Humboldt's *The Limits of State Action* (completed in 1792) drew on Kant's dictum that "each individual must be treated as an end and never simply as a means," and developed the thesis that man's true end is

[11] *Ibid.*, pp. 116–21, 374–78.
[12] See Sidney Pollard, "The Adaptation of the Labor Force," in *The Genesis of Modern Management* (Cambridge, Mass., 1965), pp. 160–206.

the highest and most harmonious development of his powers to a complete and consistent whole. Freedom is the first and indispensable condition which the possibility of such a development presupposes; but there is besides another essential—intimately connected with freedom, it is true— a variety of situations. Even the most free and self-reliant of men is hindered in his development, when set in a monotonous situation.[13]

Though Humboldt's ideal of self-development had no influence on antislavery thought, it dramatizes the contingency and limitations of the conventional definitions of freedom. Humboldt's faith in individuality, spontaneity, and diversity rested on an organic view of human nature and on the central concept of *Bildung*, by which he meant, in J. W. Burrow's words, "the fullest, richest and most harmonious development of the potentialities of the individual, the community or the human race." Though he wished to free individuals from social coercion, Humboldt by no means depreciated the importance of social ties. Indeed, it can be argued that his brand of liberalism was less antisocial than the liberalism which located individual freedom in the proprietorship of person and property. Humboldt wanted to limit "state action" not because he valued the rights of property, but because he saw that the state tends to "make man an instrument to serve its arbitrary ends, overlooking his individual purposes."[14] He was alert to the varieties of oppression that require no physical restriction, and to the ways by which the state can convert nominally free men into mindless mechanisms, ostensibly for their own true welfare.

In contrast to Humboldt, even the more radical Anglo-American social theorists tended to identify freedom with the individual's legal status, his ownership of property, including his own person, and his external rights within the social compact. In effect, this represented a middle position between Hobbes, who would have the state treat all citizens as slaves, and Humboldt, who argued that the only meaningful freedom lay in the removal of all impediments to self-development. Within the framework of British liberalism, Negro slavery could stand as the antithesis not of autonomy but of a "freedom" which in practice included various kinds of coercion and manipulation. Negro slavery could thus be of considerable symbolic importance for the British

---

[13] J. W. Burrow, introd. to Wilhelm von Humboldt, *The Limits of State Action* (Cambridge, England, 1969), pp. vi–xliii; Humboldt, p. 16.

[14] *Ibid.*, Burrow, pp. xviii–xxi, Humboldt, *passim;* Noam Chomsky, "Notes on Anarchism," *The New York Review of Books* (May 21, 1970), pp. 31–35.

liberal, since it focused attention on physical restraint and legal rights as the test of authentic freedom. Society's repudiation of the most extreme form of treating man as an instrument could have the effect, at least temporarily, of vindicating less flagrant varieties of coercion. The nonslave was, by definition, a free man.[15] Individual liberty—in the form, for example, of Adam Smith's economic man—could thus be made compatible with utility and social order.

There were, however, two major obstacles to the use of antislavery as an ideological instrument. Defenders of slavery did their best to assimilate the institution to other forms of dominion and to accuse antislavery writers of undermining the foundations of all authority. It was therefore necessary to show that the kind of liberty which was opposed to slavery, in the words of John Allen, "is a power of acting agreeable to the laws which are made and enacted by the consent of the PEOPLE." Even absolute freedom, according to Anthony Benezet,

can only consist in *restraining Evil Doers* by just and equitable *Laws,* that the *Weak & Poor,* may be as *free* as the *Rich & Strong,* for all men ought to be *absolutely free to do good* according to their ability; & if they are *not free to do evil,* it is not to be accounted a restraint upon *liberty;* but a restraint *only upon Tyranny.*

This was essentially the distinction John Winthrop had drawn in 1645 between man's natural liberty "to do what he lists; it is a liberty to evil as well as to good . . . [and] is incompatible and inconsistent with authority," and a civil or moral liberty which "is the proper end and object of authority, and cannot subsist without it; and it is a liberty to that only which is good, just, and honest." Like Winthrop, eighteenth-century antislavery writers saw consent—or at least the fiction of consent—as the necessary seal for lawful subordination.[16]

---

[15] It should be emphasized that this vindicating effect later gave way to a tendency to move from antislavery to a critique of all forms of social coercion. The dialectic between these two positions is one of the principal themes of the present study, and will be developed in subsequent chapters. On the other hand, even the more radical abolitionists of the nineteenth century never quite escaped the consequences of focusing on physical restraint and legal rights as the crucial tests of freedom.

[16] [John Allen], *The Watchman's Alarm to Lord N---h; or, the British Parliamentary Boston Port-Bill Unwraped* [sic] (Salem, Mass., 1774), p. 5; Anthony Benezet, MS marginal comments in Thomas Thompson, *The African Trade for Negro Slaves, Shewn to be Consistent with Principles of Humanity, and with the Laws of Revealed Religion* (Canterbury, n.d.), pp. 22–23, Rutgers University

It was difficult to hold this position with perfect consistency, for defenders of slavery could point to examples of unquestioned subordination—such as that of man to God or children to parents—which involved no voluntary contract. Yet these relationships were justified by a supposed righteousness or altruism which seemed incompatible with slaveholding. John Woolman, who was uncommonly sensitive to the moral complexities of individual cases, refrained from accusing all masters of injustice. It was right, he thought, that some men should be servants and that others should be punished for their crimes. No blame could be attached to a pious man who maintained slaves for no other motive than a sense of duty and charity. But Woolman felt that whatever a master's good intentions, he could not long escape the corruptions of absolute power. Involuntary servitude deprived both master and servant of the special liberty, as defined by Winthrop, "to that only which is good, just, and honest."[17]

The second obstacle to isolating slavery as a unique infringement on liberty was the unfortunate fact that slaves were defined by law as property, and property was supposedly the foundation of liberty. Liberal theorists needed a strategy that would remove slaves from the protective category of private property without doing injury to the category itself.

The traditional approach to this problem rested on a distinction between legitimate and illegitimate enslavement, which was itself part of a precapitalist ideal of Christian business ethics. It was not a modern discovery that slavery might involve the sins of manstealing and acceptance of stolen property. Such moral discriminations were perhaps more easily made when men never dreamed of condemning *all*

Library; John Winthrop, speech to the General Court of Massachusetts, July 3, 1645, in Perry Miller and Thomas H. Johnson, eds., *The Puritans* (New York, 1938), pp. 206–7. One should note that Winthrop defined civil liberty as a means of upholding the authority of magistrates, whereas John Allen, a radical Baptist who emigrated in 1769 from England to America, spoke of civil liberty as an inherent right, "the power of the people which *binds kings in fetters and nobles in irons.*" Yet Allen, like Benezet, thought of "the liberty which is opposed to slavery" as a freedom to obey just laws.

[17] [Theodore Parsons and Eliphalet Pearson], *A Forensic Dispute on the Legality of Enslaving the Africans, Held at the Public Commencement in Cambridge, New England . . .* (Boston, 1773), pp. 10–11; John Woolman, *Considerations on Keeping Negroes; Recommended to the Professors of Christianity, of Every Denomination* (Philadelphia, 1762), pp. 21–24, 48–50.

slavery or of defending an unqualified right to legitimate private property. In the eyes of a few Catholics like Tomás de Mercado and Bartolomé de Albornoz, and of a few English Protestants like Richard Baxter and Morgan Godwyn, the purchase of Negro slaves entailed grave moral risks, since the majority of Africans had been illegally seized, and the purchaser could seldom be certain of lawful title. American slavery thus fell within a larger realm of economic practice in which greed had overcome equity. As phrased in more absolutist terms by Samuel Sewall, the New England Puritan: "There is no proportion between Twenty Pieces of Silver, and Liberty. The Commodity it self is the claimer."[18]

The idea of the commodity as claimer lent itself easily to what C. B. Macpherson has termed "the political theory of possessive individualism," which is well illustrated by the following argument of Thomas Paine: "But none can lawfully buy without evidence that they are not concurring with Men-Stealers; and as the true owner has a right to reclaim his goods that were stolen, and sold; so the slave, who is proper owner of his freedom, has a right to reclaim it, however often sold."[19] Although Paine begins on the conventional note of "evidence that they are not concurring with Men-Stealers," he abruptly shifts to the notion that freedom is a possession, "owned" by all men, and always reclaimable when stolen. This argument carried both conservative and radical implications.

The conservative implications derived from the equation of liberty with ownership. This formula reinforced the absolute character of proprietorship and obscured the conflict between human rights and property rights, a conflict which men like Albornoz and Baxter had found epitomized in slavery. For Paine, as for far more conservative antislavery writers, Negro slavery was not simply one of many abuses resulting from the unrestrained pursuit of economic self-interest. The pursuit of authentic self-interest led to wealth, industry, and happiness. But Negro slavery was founded on usurpation, according to Adam Ferguson, and on "RAPINE THEFT OR NOTORIOUS INJUSTICE," according to Granville Sharp. By categorizing slave trading with piracy and

[18] For documentation, see *The Problem of Slavery in Western Culture,* pp. 187, 190, 338, 340, 345.

[19] C. B. Macpherson, *The Political Theory of Possessive Individualism* (Oxford, 1962); Thomas Paine, "African Slavery in America," in *The Writings of Thomas Paine,* ed. by Moncure D. Conway (New York, 1894), p. 5.

highway robbery, such writers helped to eliminate any gradations between "crime" and lawful economic activity. The latter, by implication, could not be characterized by greed, luxury, brutality, or exploitation.

The equation of slaves with stolen property also had radical implications. Paine, who published his essay in 1775, did not specify how the slave was to reclaim his stolen freedom. In 1760 George Wallace, a young Scottish jurist, was more explicit. In a passage later reprinted by Anthony Benezet and plagiarized by Louis de Jaucourt in an influential essay in Diderot's *Encyclopédie,* Wallace contended that human beings cannot be the objects of trade and cannot be bought or sold at any price:

For these reasons, every one of those unfortunate men, who are pretended to be slaves, has a right to be declared to be free, for he never lost his liberty; he could not lose it; his prince had no power to dispose of him. Of course, the sale was *ipso jure* void. This right he carries about with him, and is entitled every where to get it declared. As soon, therefore, as he comes into a country, in which the judges are not forgetful of their own humanity, it is their duty to remember that he is a man, and to declare him to be free.[20]

Although Wallace addressed himself to Scottish judges, urging them to free any Negro brought to his native land, he also denounced American slave laws as contrary to the law of nature. Significantly, he explicitly rejected the theory of possessive individualism: "A man is not the *proprietor* of himself; can he, therefore, be the proprietor of another?"[21] Accordingly, any supposed owner "has nobody but himself to blame, in case he shall find himself deprived of a man, whom he thought he had, by buying for a price, made his own; for he dealt in a trade, which was illicit, and was prohibited by the most obvious dictates of humanity."

[20] George Wallace, *A System of the Principles of the Law of Scotland,* I (Edinburgh, 1760), 95–96. For Wallace, Benezet, and the *Encyclopédie,* see my article, "New Sidelights on Early Antislavery Radicalism," *William and Mary Quarterly,* 3rd ser., XXVIII (Oct., 1971), 585–94.

[21] Wallace, *System of the Principles,* p. 95. It should be noted, however, that Wallace's position was based on the superior right of the state: " 'Tis agreed among all philosophers, that no man has a right to do an unnecessary injury to himself; for the public has a superior interest in all the individuals, of whom it consists. It is interested in their welfare; for its prosperity depends upon theirs" (pp. 93–94).

Wallace's principles presented a direct challenge to established authorities. In another passage disseminated by Benezet, he held:

If this trade admits of a moral or a rational justification, every crime, even the most atrocious, may be justified. Government was instituted for the good of mankind: Kings, princes, governors are not proprietors of those, who are subject to their authority; they have not a right to make them miserable. On the contrary, their authority is vested in them, that they may, by the just exercise of it, promote the happiness of their people.[22]

Governmental sanction, then, served only to show the illegitimacy of government. In 1772, Granville Sharp concluded that any magistrate who neglected to relieve an oppressed slave, as Wallace had demanded, would be certain to partake in the guilt of the original theft. Moreover, if the British legislature should ever

become so miserably degenerate as to repeal, or annul, the Habeas Corpus Act, and adopt, instead of it, the most horrid and diabolical of the West Indian Laws; yet, even in this case, the natural *unlawfulness* and wickedness of such principles as those laws contain, would *still remain;* for [and here Sharp quoted from a pamphlet by Anthony Benezet] "No Legislature on Earth, which is the supreme power in every Civil Society, can alter the Nature of things, or make that to be lawful, which is contrary to the Law of God. . . ."[23]

This statement of "higher law" doctrine, often attributed to Benezet, came originally from an anonymous pamphlet, *Two Dialogues on the Man-Trade,* published in London in 1760.[24] The author carried his radical premises much farther than either Sharp or Benezet was prepared to go. In a passage not reprinted in later collections of antislavery argument, he held:

And so all the black men now in our plantations, who are by unjust force deprived of their liberty, and held in slavery, as they have none upon earth to appeal to, may lawfully repel that force with force, and to recover their liberty, destroy their oppressors; and not only so, but it is the

[22] *Ibid.,* p. 95.

[23] Granville Sharp, *An Appendix to the "Representation"* . . . (London, 1771), pp. 19, 25. The quotation was taken from Benezet's *A Short Account of that Part of Africa, Inhabited by the Negroes* . . . (Philadelphia, 1762).

[24] J. Philmore [*pseud.*], *Two Dialogues on the Man-Trade* (London, 1760), p. 44. Although Benezet attributed the statement to "Philmore" in *A Short Account,* he failed to do so in *Some Historical Account of Guinea* . . . (Philadelphia, 1771), p. 131. For a discussion of "Philmore's" very rare pamphlet, see Davis, "New Sidelights on Early Antislavery Radicalism."

duty of others, white as well as blacks, to assist those miserable creatures, if they can, in their attempts to deliver themselves out of slavery, and to rescue them out of the hands of their cruel tyrants.

Since England, in prosecuting the slave trade, had been for more than a century "at war and enmity with mankind in general," any nation would be justified in declaring war to liberate the colonial slaves by force.[25]

If no other writer pushed the "higher law" doctrine to such a logical extreme, the author of *Two Dialogues* nevertheless illustrated the revolutionary possibilities of early antislavery thought. And by quoting the main premises of such works, Anthony Benezet, a devout and peace-loving Quaker, became a vehicle for some of the more subversive ideas of the secular Enlightenment.

The arguments he disseminated cut two ways. If governments were allowed to justify slavery, they could justify any crime. But if reformers could nullify the legal sanctions for slavery, they could also limit a government's powers and impeach the sanctions for any form of injustice. How could a government that fostered slavery have any claim to legitimacy? Benezet could offer only one excuse for the men who ruled the British empire: no doubt they were ignorant of the facts. This charitable conviction led him to address epistles to various institutional authorities, including the queen, the Archbishop of Canterbury, and the Society for the Propagation of the Gospel. But as American patriots were soon to learn, appeals which presumed governmental ignorance also presumed unprecedented power on the part of the governed. Benezet defined and therefore narrowed the options open to the authorities: once they had been informed of their violations of divine and natural law, they would have to rectify their mistakes or presumably forfeit their claims to legitimate power.[26]

---

[25] Philmore, *Two Dialogues,* pp. 54, 57. This inflammatory statement appeared, of course, during the Seven Years' War.

[26] Thomas Clarkson later claimed that Benezet's *Some Historical Account* was "instrumental, beyond any other book ever before published, in disseminating a proper knowledge and detestation of this trade" (*The History of the Rise, Progress and Accomplishment of the African Slave-Trade by the British Parliament* [2 vols., London, 1808], I, 169). Along with the "higher law" doctrines of Philmore and Wallace, Benezet reprinted the antislavery arguments of earlier moralists like Francis Hutcheson and James Foster. For his assumption that "worthy men in power, both of the laity and clergy, have been unacquainted with the horrible wickedness with which the trade is carried on," see his letters

By the late 1760s and early 1770s these arguments obviously had a bearing on the colonial protests against British tyranny. Yet paradoxically, the same years witnessed a growing Anglo-American consensus, except in the South and the West Indies, that Negro slavery was a flagrant violation of the natural rights of man. Thus William Warburton, the Bishop of Gloucester, could ridicule the arrogant notion that Negroes were happiest as slaves. "Nature," he proclaimed, "created man free, and grace invites him to assert his freedom." And John Wesley, despite his Tory politics and his obsession with original sin, could announce that "liberty is the right of every human creature, as soon as he breathes the vital air." Adam Ferguson, James Beattie, and William Blackstone, all enormously influential figures, popularized Montesquieu's arguments on the incompatibility of slavery with free institutions.[27] Clearly, liberty did not mean the same thing to Methodists, to Latitudinarian clergy, and to American rebels complaining of unjust taxation. But despite their diverse aims, an increasing number of writers did agree that liberty was an original and fundamental right.

Georg Simmel has suggested that the various political, economic, and religious conflicts of the eighteenth century were sublimated into an "abstract need" for human freedom: "This is the general category that came to cover what was common in the various complaints and self-assertions of the individual against society."[28] Simmel's insight helps to explain how the Negro slave could become an abstract symbol for the deprivation of freedom, so long as his status was dissociated from property rights and from accepted forms of subordination.

But this dissociation involved an implicit defiance of law. It also encouraged a shift in perspective from individual to collective liberty. George Wallace and the author of *Two Dialogues* were primarily concerned with the preservation of British institutions, which they saw

---

to Queen Charlotte and the Archbishop of Canterbury, reprinted in George S. Brookes, *Friend Anthony Benezet* (Philadelphia, 1937), pp. 273–74, 402. Benezet was also confident that Queen Elizabeth and Louis XIII had been misled concerning the true nature of the slave trade (*Some Historical Account,* pp. 57–58).

[27] William Warburton, *A Sermon Preached Before the Incorporated Society for the Propagation of the Gospel in Foreign Parts* . . . , Feb. 21, 1766, Stephen Fuller, Letterpress Book, I, 177, Duke University Library; John Wesley, *Thoughts Upon Slavery* (Philadelphia, 1774), p. 56.

[28] Georg Simmel, *The Sociology of Georg Simmel,* ed. and tr. by Kurt H. Wolff (Glencoe, Ill., 1950), pp. 63–68.

threatened by "those arbitrary and inhuman usages, which prevail in a distant land." The laws of America deserved no respect; nor were American sugar and tobacco worth the price of collective guilt and a collective loss of freedom. For American colonists, on the other hand, Negro slavery was one of the unhappy legacies of British oppression. Thomas Jefferson, in the famous suppressed clause of the Declaration of Independence, charged that King George

has waged cruel war against human nature itself, violating the most sacred rights of life and liberty in the persons of a distant people who never offended him, captivating and carrying them into slavery in another hemisphere, or to incur miserable death in their transportation thither. . . . Determined to keep open a market where MEN should be bought and sold, he has prostituted his negative for suppressing every legislative attempt to prohibit or to restrain this execrable commerce; and that this assemblage of horrors might want no fact of distinguished die, he is now exciting these very people to rise in arms among us, and to purchase that liberty of which *he* deprived them, by murdering the people upon whom *he* also intruded them; thus paying off former crimes committed against the *liberties* of one people, with crimes which he urges them to commit against the *lives* of another.[29]

The Penalty for Being Inconsistent

The American colonists had long been absorbing and energizing the English "Commonwealthman" tradition of religious and political dissent. At the core of this tradition, as Bernard Bailyn suggests, was the belief that political liberty requires constant vigilance and struggle. Freedom was not so much an achieved state as a guarded relationship. Even the "mixed" constitution that emerged from Britain's Glorious Revolution of 1688 could easily be undermined by the plots of corrupt politicians. Whenever men were unprepared to defend their natural rights, there was no check on the multiplier effects of superior power. And behind each successful encroachment on liberty hovered the specter of slavery. Bailyn argues that Americans genuinely believed that men who were taxed without their consent were literally slaves, since they had lost the power to resist oppression, and since defenselessness inevitably led to tyranny. Given such assumptions, American Negro slavery offered an ideal example of masses of men subordinated

[29] Julian P. Boyd, ed., *The Papers of Thomas Jefferson* (Princeton, 1950—), I, 426.

to a self-appointed elite that dominated all sectors of local society and government. No image could have been more diametrically opposed to the ideal of a rational nation state whose citizens distribute power according to social function.[30]

The fear of a British conspiracy to "enslave" America had an obvious but complex bearing on Negro bondage.[31] In the late 1760s Benjamin Rush wrote to a French correspondent that "it would be useless for us to denounce the servitude to which the *Parliament of Great Britain* wishes to reduce us, while we continue to keep our fellow creatures in slavery just because their color is different from ours." Rush did not explain why inconsistent protest would be useless. Few men, or nations, are consistent. The "strain for consistency" did not prevent Rush from being both a crusader for freedom and a personal tyrant who imprisoned his son for life in his own mental hospital and who tortured alcoholics and mental deviants for the supposed good of society.[32] It has commonly been said that antislavery sentiment spread through the rebellious colonies as people recognized the "monstrous inconsistency" of tolerating Negro slavery while defending the natural rights of man. Yet in times of crisis, men have been known to accept glaring inconsistencies. Nor does the fear of losing freedom necessarily lead men to sympathize with slaves. In 1774, for example, the Jamaican assembly addressed a petition and memorial

[30] Bernard Bailyn, *The Ideological Origins of the American Revolution* (Cambridge, Mass., 1967), pp. 55–143, 232–46. See also Edmund S. Morgan, "The Puritan Ethic and the American Revolution," *William and Mary Quarterly,* 3rd ser., XXIV (Oct., 1967), 3–43.

[31] According to Winthrop Jordan, the natural rights theory "led inescapably to realization that Americans were indulging in a monstrous inconsistency" (*White Over Black,* p. 289). Bailyn takes a more complex view, but both historians tend to exaggerate the autonomous power of ideas.

[32] Rush to Jacques Barbeu Dubourg, printed in *Ephémérides du citoyen,* IX (1769), 172–74; Thomas S. Szasz, *The Manufacture of Madness: A Comparative Study of the Inquisition and the Mental Health Movement* (New York, 1970), pp. 139–59. Taking his cue from John Stuart Mill ("Was there ever any domination which did not appear natural to those who possessed it?"), Szasz writes of Rush: "His eyes thus beheld the world in terms of sickness and health. He categoried opposition to the Revolution as illness; support of it, as therapy. Americans loyal to the British Crown tended to suffer from a disease which Rush christened 'revolutiona.' " In Rush's own words, the absence of right reason "annuls a man's social compact, disfranchises him." After his son John had run away to sea and had then returned in a sullen mood, with a long beard and uncombed hair, Rush became, as Szasz puts it, "his doctor, psychiatrist, and jailer."

to the king, protesting against the tyrannical usurpation of power by Parliament, and expressing amazement over the execution of a plan for "enslaving" the colonies. The locutions were the same as those of the mainland assemblies. But with unconscious irony, the Jamaican legislators attributed their own lack of resistance to the vulnerability of the island and to the "encumbrance" of a population of over 200,000 slaves.[33]

To cite another example, the spokesmen for northern workingmen, in the Jacksonian era, outdid even the pamphleteers of the Revolution in invoking images of impending bondage: the factory system was a "species of slavery," worse in most respects than the plantation slavery of the South; workers were being treated as mere machines, as the property of aggrandizing merchant capitalists; if workers continued to lose control over the price of labor and the hours of work, they would sink deeper and deeper into helpless bondage. But these same protesters were notoriously unsympathetic to the abolitionist cause, which they tended to view as a distractive maneuver of the capitalists. Like southern proslavery apologists, they often maintained that factory workers enjoyed less leisure and genuine liberty than did Negro bondsmen.[34] One could multiply examples to show that men could speak rhetorically of enslavement, in order to dramatize the danger of a progressive loss of independence, without feeling compelled by consistency to demand a universal emancipation.

Since British and Tory writers taunted the rebels with charges of hypocrisy—as in Samuel Johnson's memorable quip: "How is it that we hear the loudest *yelps* for liberty among the drivers of negroes?"—the colonists might well have devised a defensive strategy that would dissociate Negro slavery from political oppression. To the modern ear, at least, the alarm over "enslavement" by taxation sounds rather more hyperbolic than the later fears that factory workers were becoming "enslaved" by the owners of capital. Even in 1776 Samuel Hopkins observed that the slavery of which the colonists complained was

[33] *Journals of the Assembly of Jamaica,* VI (Jamaica, 1800), 569–70.
[34] Lorman Ratner, *Powder Keg: Northern Opposition to the Antislavery Movement, 1831–1840* (New York, 1968), pp. 63–64; Leon F. Litwack, *North of Slavery: The Negro in the Free States, 1790–1860* (Chicago, 1961), pp. 159–62; Joseph L. Blau, ed., *Social Theories of Jacksonian Democracy* (New York, 1954), pp. 306–9, 321–22; Bernard Mandel, *Labor, Free and Slave: Workingmen and the Anti-Slavery Movement in the United States* (New York, 1955), pp. 65–95.

"lighter than a feather" compared with the heavy doom suffered by the blacks. One might conclude, therefore, that to link the two forms of oppression, as Hopkins in fact tried to do, would diminish the forcefulness of the colonists' complaints. Perhaps the Virginia Convention of 1776 had this point in mind when the delegates amended George Mason's original definition of natural rights in a way that excluded Negro slaves.[35] Yet there can be no doubt that in the 1770s a growing number of American writers and political leaders were becoming sensitive to the inconsistency of holding Negro slaves while resisting a British plot to enslave the colonies. How can this be explained?

At the outset, one should not underestimate the "restiveness," as it was termed, of the black population. Philosophical inconsistency pinched harder when slaves began to speak the language of natural rights. The blacks, as Hopkins pointed out, did not have to be told how miserable they were; yet every day they heard the whites expressing indignation over British threats to civil liberties. Even by the early 1770s petitions from northern slaves appealed to the same principles the colonists were using against Great Britain: "We have in common with all other men," said a typical plea, "a naturel right to our freedoms without Being depriv'd of them by our fellow men as we are a freeborn Pepel and have never forfeited this Blessing by aney compact or agreement whatever."[36] Such language raised the specter of a rebellion within a rebellion, both of them justified on the same grounds. The obvious discontent of the blacks, coupled with the uncertainties of war, made it difficult for writers to ignore certain parallels and relationships between political oppression and Negro slavery.

An interesting illustration of this point can be found in John Allen's *An Oration Upon the Beauties of Liberty, or the Essential Rights of the Americans,* an immensely popular pamphlet that appeared in 1773, after the burning of the *Gaspée,* to defend Rhode Islanders against retaliation. One of Allen's examples of English tyranny was

[35] [Samuel Hopkins], *A Dialogue Concerning the Slavery of the Africans, Showing it to be the Duty and Interest of the American States to Emancipate All Their African Slaves* (2nd ed. [originally published 1776] New York, 1785), pp. 37–38; Jordan, *White over Black,* p. 295.

[36] *Collections* of the Massachusetts Historical Society, 5th ser., III (Boston, 1877), 432–36.

that a white colonist could "be confined, and tried for his life, by the accusation of a negro." Like various protesters in the future, Allen apparently saw Negro rights as a weapon for destroying the liberties of white Americans. But in the fourth edition, also printed in 1773, Allen substituted the following passage for his example of tyranny against whites: "Such cruelty and tyranny ought ever to be held in the most hateful contempt, the same as you would *a banditti of slave-makers on the* coast of Africa." And in a new section, "Remarks on the Rights and Liberties of the Africans," he observed that no one would deny the Africans' right to freedom if they were kept as slaves by Indians, Moslems, or Turks. Yet Christians, who professed to believe in the brotherhood of man and who struggled to preserve their own liberties, continued to oppress the Negroes. Significantly, Allen printed a letter that had been rejected by the "free" press, presumably because it referred ominously to the Negroes' bloody revolts against tyranny in the West Indies. He then appended another letter written by four slaves, on April 20, 1773, addressed to the Massachusetts assembly. The slaves promised to wait patiently for their award of freedom, after which they would return to Africa, making no claims for compensation for past wrongs. Their humility stood out in sharp contrast to Allen's own radical stance against England; yet the mention of West Indian revolts gave hint that Americans could not always count on such patience and forgiveness.[37]

During the Great Awakening ministers of various denominations had promoted the religious conversion of slaves as a means of ensuring meekness, docility, and obedience. But resistance to British authority tended to blur traditional distinctions between spiritual liberty and external status. "It was no longer possible," writes Winthrop Jordan,

[37] [John Allen], *An Oration, Upon the Beauties of Liberty, Or the Essential Rights of the Americans* (Boston, 1773), p. 27; 3rd ed., "corrected" (New London, 1773), p. 21; 4th ed., "carefully corrected" (Boston, 1773), pp. 61, 73–80. The pamphlet was formerly attributed to Isaac Skillman. For Allen's authorship and life, see John M. Bumsted and Charles E. Clark, "New England's Tom Paine: John Allen and the Spirit of Liberty," *William and Mary Quarterly*, 3rd ser., XXI (1964), 561–70. The oration was originally delivered on Dec. 3, 1772, at the Second Baptist Church of Boston. The title page of the 4th ed. states that the new remarks on the rights and liberties of the Africans were "inserted by particular desire." With respect to slavery, the immigrant Allen was clearly far in advance of his American co-religionists (see William G. McLoughlin, *New England Dissent, 1630—1833; the Baptists and the Separation of Church and State* [2 vols., Cambridge, Mass., 1971], I, 584; II, 766–69).

"for American ministers to urge Negro slaves to remain content as Christians in their bondage when they were urging white members of their congregations to resist oppression."[38] Slaveholders had long interpreted contentment as a form of consent. But the redefinition of consent lay at the heart of America's controversy with Great Britain.

Again, interest stiffened the force of logic. A Virginia planter like Robert Carter, thinking of himself as a benevolent patriarch, found it necessary to appeal to his "people" at Coles Point quarter, imploring them not to run off and join the British army. George Washington reluctantly approved the re-enlistment of Negroes who had served in his army around Boston in 1775, because he feared that they might join the enemy. Even southern blacks were familiar with the rumor that any slave who set foot on English soil would be free. Lord Dunmore, the loyalist governor of Virginia, reinforced this message by promising freedom to any fugitives who took up arms for the king. Neither England nor America was prepared to risk a full-scale social revolution by issuing emancipation proclamations or mobilizing large armies of black troops. Assuming that the South could easily be pacified, the British were especially reluctant to antagonize loyalist planters. Nevertheless, some eight hundred Virginia slaves had time to respond to Dunmore's short-lived offer. Many more later flocked to Count Rochambeau's French army or met Sir Henry Clinton's offer of freedom to slaves who served the crown against their masters' cause. Rhode Island, when largely occupied by British troops, resorted to the ultimate weapon of promising freedom to slaves who enlisted in a "black battalion." And perhaps more important than the actual number of blacks serving in both armies was the knowledge that war could lead to widespread emancipation. According to Gerald W. Mullin, Virginians had been surprisingly complacent about fugitives— even communities of fugitives—in the decades prior to Dunmore's proclamation. For white Southerners the Revolution brought new fears and new needs for self-justification. For blacks it opened possibilities for new postures of militancy and defiance.[39]

[38] Jordan, *White over Black,* p. 296.

[39] Peter Force, comp., *American Archives* (9 vols., Washington, 1837–1853), 4th ser., III, 1385–87; Robinson, *Slavery in the Structure of American Politics,* pp. 98–130; Mullin, *Flight and Rebellion, passim;* Benjamin Quarles, *The Negro in the American Revolution* (Chapel Hill, 1961), *passim;* Quarles "The Colonial Militia and Negro Manpower," *Mississippi Valley Historical Review,* XLV

There were, of course, other reasons for the rebellious colonists' sensitivity to the issue of inconsistency. From the mid-1760s the Americans had confidently and self-righteously resisted imperial authority. Yet they seemed to be unprepared, psychologically, for the Boston Massacre, for the Coercive Acts of 1774, and for armed invasion and military defeats. Rebels and protesters are often curiously shocked by the punitive action of once-respected authorities. Even when the authorities are defined as tyrants, it is difficult to understand why one's virtue and courage should be punished. And for Americans the defense of freedom was entirely consistent with Britain's noblest heritage; it was the mother country that had become a lawless rebel.

Prior to the Revolution, few colonists were capable of the imaginative leap of placing themselves in their slaves' position. They were, to paraphrase Peter Berger, the sociologist, "fully encased" in their identity as free white men. The Revolution may not have been disruptive enough to destroy the existing social order, but it did result in a period of uncertainty, self-doubt, and unpredictable identity. To cite the most obvious example: the distinction between patriot and traitor depended, pragmatically, on the outcome of war. Situations of extreme disorder and unpredictability often make it easier to imagine a reversal of roles. Thomas Paine expressed the thought that occurred to many minds: "If they could carry off and enslave some thousands of us, would we think it just? One would almost wish they could for once; it might convince more than Reason, or the Bible." The theme of reversing roles with slaves had long been used as a literary device, and had been a commonplace in English and French journals such as the *London Magazine* and *Ephémérides du citoyen*. But for the Revolutionary generation there was a new immediacy to the question: suppose that *we* were *their* slaves! According to Jefferson himself, this was an event that "may become probable by supernatural interference!"[40]

(March, 1959), 643–52. Rhode Island was not the only state that enlisted slaves with the promise of freedom. Despite the excellent coverage by Quarles, Robinson, and Mullin, there is much more to be learned about the fear of slave conspiracy and the role of slaves in the struggles between patriots and Tories. An even more elusive but highly significant question pertains to the "ill-disposed" whites, briefly treated by Mullin, who "entertained" blacks. These independent and irreverent fraternizers appear in the record from the 1741 New York slave "conspiracy" to the Denmark Vesey trials in Charleston in 1822, but their history is as yet unwritten.

[40] Paine, "African Slavery in America," p. 6; *London Magazine*, VII (March,

The colonists may have sincerely believed, as Bernard Bailyn maintains, that taxation without consent would literally make them slaves of the British, if not of the blacks. But understandably, a note of strident defensiveness runs through the sermons and tracts that led finally to the Declaration of Independence. Moderate appeals had been rejected by the world's reputedly freest government. Suppose that posterity or "the opinion of mankind" finally dismissed the American cause as self-interested opportunism? How could men who believed themselves to be sincere prove their sincerity to the world? As far south as Darien, Georgia, there were groups of colonists who found the answer in a public testimonial: "To show the world that we are not influenced by any contracted or interested motives," said the people of Darien, "but a general philanthropy for all mankind, of whatever climate, language, or complexion, we hereby declare our disapprobation and abhorrence of the unnatural practice of Slavery in *America.*"[41]

In 1776, a year after the Darien Resolutions, Samuel Hopkins

1738), 129; *Ephémérides du citoyen,* VI (1766), 189–90; Adrienne Koch and William Peden, eds., *The Life and Selected Writings of Thomas Jefferson* (New York, 1944), p. 279. Anthony Benezet suggested that the Irish had been conquered and judged by God as a penalty for enslaving Englishmen! (*A Caution and Warning to Great Britain and Her Colonies* [Philadelphia, 1766], p. 33). American colonists had, of course, long been vulnerable to the threat of being captured by Indians, especially by Indians serving the cause of the French. Richard Slotkin has brilliantly analyzed the immensely popular captivity narratives, in which "the Indians become the instruments of God for the chastisement of his guilty people—a reversal of the missionary and war narratives' insistence that the whites are God's means for the salvation or destruction of the Indians" (*Regeneration through Violence: The Mythology of the American Frontier, 1600–1860* [Middletown, Conn., 1973], p. 99). He also suggests that "the success of the captivity as an archetype of the American experience lies in its aptness as an expression of the Puritans' anxieties" arising both from guilt over abandoning "ancestral England" for a strange wilderness, and from fear that captives would lapse into savagery or become converted to French Catholicism (pp. 98–99). A sensitivity to the psychological hazards of captivity may have prepared some Americans for an imaginative reversal of roles with their slaves. I am more struck, however, by the failure of antislavery writers to make greater use of a rich literary and religious tradition. No doubt the subject deserves further study, but I would tentatively conclude that most Americans failed to see any connection between their own Negro captives and the whites held captive by Indians. There must be some limits, after all, to what a culture can allow one to perceive.

[41] Force, comp., *American Archives,* I, 1136. C. Vann Woodward has drawn my attention to the irony that Darien was one of the few towns deliberately burned to the ground by Union troops during the Civil War.

contended that if the Continental Congress' resolutions against the slave trade had been made in good faith, and not for "political reasons" only, the country's leaders would use their influence to effect a total abolition of slavery in the colonies. In the same year William Gordon quoted the Virginia Declaration of Rights and the Declaration of Independence, and concluded: "The Continent has rang [*sic*] with affirmations of the like import. If these, Gentlemen, are our genuine sentiments, and we are not provoking the Deity by acting hypocritically to serve a turn, let us apply earnestly and heartily to the extirpation of slavery from among ourselves." And at the end of the war David Cooper repeated the now plaintive argument:

Now is the time to demonstrate to Europe, to the whole world, that America was in earnest, and meant what she said, when . . . she pled the cause of human nature. . . . Let not the world have an opportunity to charge her conduct with a contradiction to her solemn and often repeated declarations; or to say that her sons . . . have been actuated in this awful contest by no higher motive than selfishness and interest. . . . Ye rulers of America beware![42]

There was more to such appeals than national pride. The ideology of the American Revolution involved a repudiation of established sovereignty, and thus touched the most fundamental religious and political principles. Few resistance movements have been so psychologically dependent on a consistent defense of abstract principles. The conflict also stimulated self-conscious reflection on the "American identity," heightening an awareness of the differences that distinguished the colonial societies from Europe. In Gordon Wood's words, the revolutionary ideology entailed "a fundamental shift in values" and was "used to mobilize the society into revolution." At the heart of this ideology, according to Wood, was a concept of "republicanism" that contained, supposedly, the distilled wisdom of the science of political economy. In theory, a republic was the most desirable of all

[42] Hopkins, *Dialogue*, pp. 8–9; George H. Moore, *Notes on the History of Slavery in Massachusetts* (New York, 1866), pp. 176–77; [David Cooper], *A Serious Address to the Rulers of America on the Inconsistency of Their Conduct Respecting Slavery* . . . (London, 1783), pp. 6–9, 14; Benezet, *Caution and Warning*, pp. 3–4, 35; Benezet, *Serious Considerations on Several Important Subjects* . . . (Philadelphia, 1778), pp. 28–29; Nathaniel Appleton, *Considerations on Slavery* (Boston, 1767), pp. 19–20; [Allen], *Watchman's Alarm*, pp. 27–29; John Cooper, letter in *New Jersey Gazette*, Sept. 20, 1780; "Anti-Slavetrader," in *Pennsylvania Chronicle*, Nov. 21–28, 1768.

forms of government, since the proper end of a republic could only be the welfare of the people. On the other hand, history had shown that republics were exceptionally fragile, particularly when a people fell short of the highest standards of public virtue.[43]

The American colonists felt that they were uniquely qualified for republican life. They had been idealized by various European writers as an industrious, equalitarian people, content with the simple joys of life. The blessings of Providence were clearly evidenced by prosperity, expanded settlement, and population growth. Yet as Wood shrewdly observes, this candidacy for republicanism involved new strains and pressures. If Americans could think of themselves as being in some sense emancipated from the coercions of history, they were obviously not immune from the kind of greed, factionalism, and self-indulgence that had undermined freedom in England. Like a repentant sinner who feels the first inward stirrings of grace, the colonists were both heartened and perplexed by unpredictability: republican virtue was a tangible goal, but not guaranteed. The success of the American cause would depend on a reformation of public manners, morals, and institutions. True liberty was not, as Kant would maintain, a precondition of acquiring the maturity for liberty, but rather the reward for struggle and self-purification. Moreover, there was considerable urgency to collective regeneration, since the unhappy events beginning with the Stamp Act crisis showed that Americans were increasingly vulnerable to corruption and to the punishment that inevitably follows corruption. Precisely at this point religion and the "sociology" of the Enlightenment converged.

The Darien Resolutions illustrate some of the connections between slavery and the republican ideal. Negro slavery, according to the inhabitants of Darien, was "highly dangerous to our liberties (as well as lives), debasing part of our fellow-creatures below men, and corrupting the virtue and morals of the rest; and is laying the basis of that liberty we contend for (and which we pray the Almighty to continue to the latest posterity) upon a very wrong foundation." One should note the easy merger of religious and secular concerns. The revolutionary generation could lay either the right or wrong foundations for a free

[43] Gordon S. Wood, "Republicanism as a Revolutionary Ideology," in John R. Howe, Jr., ed., *The Role of Ideology in the American Revolution* (New York, 1970). pp. 83–91; Wood, *The Creation of the American Republic, 1776–1787* (Chapel Hill, 1969), pp. 3–124; Bailyn, *Ideological Origins, passim.*

society, a society which, with God's blessing, would flourish to the end of time. Throughout the literature, slavery appears, with metaphorical regularity, as the architectural flaw, the noxious weed in a garden, the hidden disease in an otherwise sound and growing body. Precisely because America was a place of unlimited space and of time without bounds, a deformed birth might lead to a monstrous and unchecked growth. As Anthony Benezet warned, the persistence of Negro slavery could well reverse the gradually liberating effects of a thousand years of Christianity, leading America back to the ignorance and barbarity of the darkest ages, then slowly reducing Europe to a similar fate.[44]

The Revolution was the central moment of decision that would govern the meaning of past and future history. The colonists must realize, pleaded Benjamin Rush, that "the plant of liberty is of so tender a Nature, that it cannot thrive long in the neighborhood of slavery." The eyes of all Europe, he added, "are fixed upon you, to preserve an asylum for freedom in this country, after the last pillars of it are fallen in every other quarter of the Globe." At this momentous time, slaveholders should remember that in God's Providence, "national crimes require national punishments." And Rush now added a significant historical dimension to the issue:

If domestic Slavery is agreeable to the Will and Laws of God, political Slavery is much more so. —Then it follows, that our British Constitution was obtained unjustly—King Charles the First did no wrong—Passive Obedience was due to Oliver Cromwell—King James the Second was the Lord's Anointed—the Revolution was a Rebellion—King William was a Tyrant—The illustrious House of Hanover are Usurpers—and the Right of the British Parliament to tax the American Colonies, is unlimited and indisputable.[45]

For Rush, writing before the move for independence, resistance to British taxes was a continuation of the epic struggle for Protestantism and a free constitution. Obviously, God had not been on the side of

[44] Force, comp., *American Archives,* I, 1136; Benezet, *Some Historical Account,* pp. 67–68; [Cooper], *Serious Address,* pp. 5–6; Robert C. Smith, " A Philadelphia Allegory," *Art Bulletin,* XXXI (1949), 323–26; Smith, "Liberty Displaying the Arts and Sciences: A Philadelphia Allegory by Samuel Jennings," *Winterthur Portfolio,* II (1965), 85–105.

[45] [Benjamin Rush], *An Address to the Inhabitants of the British Settlements in America, upon Slave-Keeping* (Philadelphia, 1773), pp. 28, 30; [Rush], *A Vindication of the Address* . . . (Philadelphia, 1773), pp. 48–49.

despotism and popery: His will had been clearly revealed by history. But if Americans were to be the legitimate heirs of the Children of Light, they could not continue violating the law of liberty.

This mode of thought was not confined to supposedly "religious" minds any more than natural rights arguments were confined to secular rationalists. John Jay, an Epicopalian and hardly a religious enthusiast, could write from Spain in 1780 that America's "prayers to Heaven for liberty will be impious," until measures were adopted for the gradual abolition of slavery. Thomas Paine, a Deist, agreed that the threat of tyranny as punishment was "perfectly suited" to the nature of America's crime against the Negro. Paine also held, like the New England clergy who would soon regard him as the devil incarnate, that Christians had a special obligation to spread the true spirit of their religion among the heathen of Africa, in order to change the bad "impression" left by slave traders. During the Revolutionary years the notion of collective guilt and judgment seemed no less real to disciples of the Enlightenment than to sons of the Puritans. It was in the midst of war that Jefferson wrote the following well-known words, addressed to an audience of French rationalists:

And can the liberties of a nation be thought secure when we have removed their only firm basis, a conviction in the minds of the people that these liberties are the gift of God? That they are not to be violated but with His wrath? Indeed I tremble for my country when I reflect that God is just; that his justice cannot sleep forever.[46]

[46] Henry P. Johnston, ed., *John Jay, Correspondence and Public Papers* (New York, 1890–1893), I, 406–407; Paine, "African Slavery in America," pp. 7–9; Koch and Peden, eds., *Life and Selected Writings of Thomas Jefferson*, pp. 278–79.

Seven ∽

The Emancipation
of America, II

How Negroes Could Help Emancipate White Americans

If Edmund S. Morgan is right in maintaining that Americans "bought their independence with slave labor," then the pronouncements we have quoted from Jay, Paine, and Jefferson were freighted with some of the cruelest irony in human history. American leaders could "dare to speak a political language that magnified the rights of freemen" precisely because they had no need to fear a dependent and exploited class of whites. Yet that very political language contributed to their abhorrence of Negro slavery—and made them dare to speculate aloud about God's justice! Perhaps the speculation itself helped to confirm what Jefferson called "a conviction in the minds of the people that these liberties are the gifts of God." Perhaps a just God would make allowance for the Americans' good intentions, as well as for their inability to do anything about the unfortunate "source" of their freedom.

But there was more to this conflict than irony. If the American Revolution could not solve the problem of slavery, it at least led to a *perception* of the problem. Nor was the desire for consistency a matter of empty rhetoric. It appeared in the antislavery resolutions of New England town meetings, in the Vermont constitution of 1777, in individual wills that manumitted slaves, in Rhode Island's law of 1774 that prohibited future importations of slaves, and in Pennsylvania's gradual emancipation act of 1780, adopted, according to a preamble written by Thomas Paine, "in grateful commemoration of our own happy deliverance" from British occupation.[1]

One may doubt whether inconsistency was of pressing concern to the majority of Americans, even in New England. Of the vast number of speeches, sermons, and resolutions warning of a British plot to enslave America, only a handful made the unsettling leap to the Americans' enslavement of Negroes. During the early years of imperial conflict, the Quakers led the way in exploiting the theme of inconsistency. Having blamed slaveholding, among other sins, for their own sufferings during the French and Indian War, the Quakers helped to popularize the ideal of voluntary manumission as a means of self-purification and avoidance of divine retribution. But the Quakers' pacifism, coupled with their suspected Tory bias, soon deprived the sect of an effective voice. The patriots' cause won more substantial support from the liberal Protestant clergy, who had been open both to the ideals of the Enlightenment and to the Latitudinarian spirit of English theology. As a group, the theological liberals may well have agreed that Negro slavery had no place in a free society. But their domestic views, like those of the majority of patriot lawyers and political leaders, were moderated by a concern for public order, for property rights, and for southern sensibilities. For a brief period, the most profound and uncompromising exposures of America's dilemma came from the Calvinist heirs of the Great Awakening.

Alan Heimert has recently given us a controversial portrait of Calvinist radicals and Lockean liberals battling for America's soul.[2] One need not accept Heimert's thesis—or his idealization of the "progressive" post-millennialist followers of Jonathan Edwards—in order

[1] For Paine's authorship and the text of the preamble, see Philip S. Foner, ed., *The Complete Writings of Thomas Paine* (2 vols., New York, 1945), II, 21–22.

[2] Alan Heimert, *Religion and the American Mind: From the Great Awakening to the Revolution* (Cambridge, Mass., 1966). Heimert's thesis has received, along with much praise, a number of devastating critiques (see, for example, Edmund S. Morgan's review, *William and Mary Quarterly*, 3rd ser., XXIV [July, 1967], 454–59; and James W. Davidson, "Searching for the Millennium: Problems for the 1790s and the 1970s," *New England Quarterly*, XLV [June, 1972], 241–61). I am much indebted, however, to some of Heimert's searching insights, as well as to the more traditional interpretation of Alice M. Baldwin's *The New England Clergy and the American Revolution* (New York, 1958; first published, 1928).

to apply some of his arguments to the origins of New England abolitionism, a subject he oddly ignores. As Heimert convincingly shows,
the imperial conflict brought out a militant, apocalyptic strain of New
England Calvinism that probed the ultimate boundaries of permissible
dissent. The ideas of collective accountability and collective judgment
were by no means confined to the "New Divinity" followers of Jonathan Edwards; it is highly debatable whether such "New Lights" were
any more predisposed toward social justice than their clerical opponents. Yet it was only among New England Calvinists that traditional
eschatology gave form to an antislavery rhetoric which challenged the
Neo-Harringtonian conception of liberty, which pointed to a more
radical definition of freedom, and which anticipated the "immediatism" of the later Garrisonians. The doctrines of the New England
Awakening did not lead directly or necessarily to militant abolitionism,
but by the 1770s Edwards's leading disciples had come to see Negro
slavery as the providential means for bringing freedom and redemption
to white America. Unlike the theological liberals, the Calvinists had
always insisted that God, in His infinite wisdom, had permitted sin
and had designed a world in which evil may be the occasion for good.
As phrased much later by Wendell Phillips, an heir of the Puritans
and a convert of Lyman Beecher's revivalism, "slavery, by the necessity of its abolition, has saved the freedom of the white race from
being melted in luxury or buried beneath the gold of its own success."[3]

Evangelical Calvinism may not have been, as Heimert contends,
"profoundly hostile to the emerging capitalist ethic of eighteenth-
century America," or a "counterthrust to the seeming tendency of
American history."[4] Attempts to extrapolate political outlook from
theological doctrine have met with little success. Yet it cannot be
denied that the heirs of the New England Awakening approached
the Revolution with a set of values and expectations very different
from those of Hamilton, Jefferson, and Washington. If one is to

[3] Quoted by Irving H. Bartlett, "The Persistence of Wendell Phillips," in
Martin Duberman, ed., *The Antislavery Vanguard: New Essays on the Abolitionists*
(Princeton, 1965), p. 119. James W. Davidson points out that while the Calvinists
and liberals agreed that God uses human agencies as well as natural disasters to
accomplish His purposes, they violently disagreed on the question of God's
allowance of sin as a means of promoting virtue ("Eschatology in New England,
1700–1763," Ph.D. thesis, Yale University, 1973).

[4] Heimert, *Religion and the American Mind,* pp. 55, 481.

understand their response to Negro slavery, it is first necessary to look
at their changing assumptions regarding historical time, individual and
collective guilt, and above all, liberty.

Millennial thought has been linked both with militant rebellion
and with quietistic withdrawal from the world. Sometimes post-mil-
lennialism—or the belief that a thousand years of peace and brotherhood will precede Christ's second coming—has encouraged active
effort to redeem the world; sometimes pre-millennialism has had the
same effect. As James W. Davidson has pointed out, eighteenth-century millennialists were anything but consistent. They were less
troubled by "the ambiguities of the prophesies" than by "the ambiguities of the world."[5] It is therefore possible to read millennial prophecies as projective fantasies, mirroring individual or collective fears,
anxieties, and aspirations. Visions of an impending millennium could
bridge the gap between the known world and the unknown future.
They could give sanction to disruptive change, help explain misfortune, and furnish a reassuring sense of historical continuity. Yet in
eighteenth-century New England—and to some extent in all the
colonies touched by the Great Awakening—millennialism also supplied
a shared set of symbols and preconceptions which defined the wider
meaning of historical experience. Thus a national crisis took on the
overtones of an individual's spiritual crisis wherein the morphology
of individual redemption, including the discovery of one's own sinfulness and the subsequent trials of humiliation and repentance, served
as a model for "saving" the nation. If millennialism cannot quite be
thought of as an autonomous force or "influence," it can be interpreted

---

[5] Davidson, "Searching for the Millennium," p. 261; Davidson, "Eschatology
in New England," *passim.* I have profited greatly from correspondence with
Davidson, who, along with a number of other young historians, has pointed out
the ambiguities and inconsistencies of the pre- and post-millennialist distinction
in the eighteenth century. We need not consider the complexities of the subject
here, except to observe that among millennialists of the eighteenth century there
were no clear-cut schools or traditions that account for optimistic activism or
pessimistic withdrawal. The Great Awakening did not alter the traditional
eschatological framework or affect the general assumption that Biblical prophecies
were meant to be obscure until fulfilled. Biblical prophecies were ambiguous
enough to be read in countless ways, and the critical questions do not concern
taxonomy but the social functions of prophecy at a given moment of time. For
the New Lights, prophecy served to justify mass conversions, to explain the
continuing opposition of the antirevivalists, and to vindicate the belief in God's
absolute sovereignty.

as a language that merged individual and collective needs, providing a vehicle for the transference of personal aspirations to a larger social sphere.

The Great Awakening had not only condemned the depravity of the existing social order, but had aroused new faith that Americans stood within reach of Christ's millennial kingdom. It is perhaps impossible for the modern secular mind to grasp the revolutionary implications of an imminent millennium, especially when it is to occur in history as the result of natural causes. Throughout the colonies, the revivals induced a heightened sense of expectancy, an almost obsessive need to "look for the beginnings" of the great drama of redemption. Joseph Bellamy, one of Edwards' more militant disciples, pictured the world as a participatory theater: God, who would exhibit His own perfections as the "scenes" came to a climax, also wanted His creatures to "give a true specimen of themselves, that it might be known what was in their hearts." For expectant Calvinists, the unfolding scenes included economic distress, wars with the French antichrist, and finally, collision with British imperial authority. Already suspicious of worldly power and fashion, their imaginations superheated by struggles against Popish despotism, the New England clergy were well prepared to interpret political independence as the first stage of collective redemption.[6]

A holy cause imposes uncompromising obligations. Edwards himself had said that "a great degree of holiness" would render "a man unable to take complacence in wicked persons or things." Therefore, if the struggle for American liberty was part of the great "Work of Redemption," there was no room for moderation or lukewarm emotion. For militant Calvinists the question of sincerity took on cosmic dimensions. The sincere in heart were partners of God, the troops of

---

[6] Heimert, *Religion and the American Mind,* pp. 66–67, 343–44; Baldwin, *New England Clergy,* pp. 66, 85–104. Antislavery was by no means a monopoly of the New Light clergy. But as might be expected, the opponents of religious revivalism were more likely to adopt a judicious and restrained tone when discussing any manifestation of collective sin. While one may debate the gradations between "New Light," "Old Light," and "Arminian" factions, the source of New England's militant abolitionism can unmistakably be traced to the Calvinist followers of Jonathan Edwards, who were united by friendship and marriage as well as by a common religious cause. At the center of this group stood Nathaniel Emmons, Joseph Bellamy, Samuel Hopkins, Levi Hart, and Jonathan Edwards, Jr.

his millennial army. To the rough militia and Minute Men the New England clergy preached the duty to fight, as soldiers for the Lord.[7]

It is easy to miss two radical implications of this evangelized resistance. First, the American armies were fighting not for individual liberty but for collective liberty, not for private interest but for the public good. Nathaniel Niles and other followers of Edwards explicitly repudiated the notion of a social compact for the protection of property and other private interests—in Niles's view this was "the maxim on which pirates and gangs of robbers live in a kind of unity." Revolutionary unity was not to be based on bribes, on the mutual protection of booty, or on any formula that apportioned power between the rich and the "undeserving." All had an equal stake in the public good, which would be most safely defined by the "voice of a majority." Fulfillment of the moral law would depend on persons of "a disinterested benevolent spirit," and Niles believed "that by far the greater part of these are to be found among the lower classes of mankind, and that a very small proportion of them are among the great."[8]

The second point, which Heimert ably develops, is that resistance to Britain became a "surrogate" for the kind of religious revival which was supposed to purify society, overcome theological confusion, and create an organic community. It followed that the revolutionary state must be an instrument of the divine will, enforcing the moral law and preparing the way for collective redemption. The state itself was morally accountable, and legislators could not be allowed to tolerate any form of oppression or unrighteousness.[9]

Political commitment involved changing and seemingly inconsistent images of liberty and slavery. Calvinists still talked of liberty as God's reward for obedience and of slavery as God's punishment for dis-

[7] Heimert, *Religion and the American Mind*, pp. 343–50, 466, 482–86, 516; Baldwin, *New England Clergy*, pp. 122–33.

[8] Heimert, *Religion and the American Mind*, pp. 515, 517, 522; Nathaniel Niles, *Two Discourses on Liberty, Delivered at the North Church, in Newbury-Port* (Newburyport, Mass., 1774), pp. 11–14, 44–45. Niles was a member of the Connecticut legislature during the Revolution and later became Speaker of the Vermont House of Representatives, a member of Congress, and a judge of the Vermont Supreme Court.

[9] Heimert, *Religion and the American Mind*, pp. 299, 300, 398–400; Perry Miller, "From the Covenant to the Revival," in James Ward Smith and A. Leland Jamison, eds., *The Shaping of American Religion* (Princeton, 1961), 322–68.

obedience, even when they defined liberty as the necessary precondition for obedience. They tried to preserve the conventional distinctions
between spiritual and civil liberty, between the perfect liberty of
heaven and the imperfect liberty of a sinful world. Yet Edwards's
arguments had helped to blur conventional dualisms.

Assuming man was free from external compulsion, Edwards had
posited a necessary connection between "choice" and inner disposition.
We perceive what we want to perceive; we are free only to follow our
own strongest motives. Spiritual liberty therefore meant a freedom
from being disposed to choose sin. Once transformed by grace, a man
would spontaneously relish and choose the greatest good. If, however,
a man were to act according to his "moral ability" and hence exercise
his spiritual freedom, he could not be bound by any physical or legal
restraints. A threat to physical liberty was therefore a threat to spiritual
liberty. Since Edwards himself had tended to take physical liberty for
granted, his theology had focused attention on the absolute disparity
between true and spurious virtue. But the imperial conflict enabled his
followers to reverse priorities. If the struggle against England were at
one with the Work of Redemption, it would be self-defeating to raise
doubts over the moral ability of Americans. The colonists individually
would have no opportunity of proving their regeneration if they
allowed themselves to become "enslaved" by external coercion; their
collective resistance might be the providential means of offering that
very proof.[10]

Some of the Revolutionary Calvinists took the momentous step of
identifying liberty with grace. Liberty was "divine," "the finished work
of Heaven," the very "image of JEHOVAH." Like grace, it was the
precondition for virtue. According to Niles, who was a student of
Bellamy's:

The first effects of liberty, on the human mind, are calmness, serenity and
pleasing hope; and all the various fruits of liberty produce the same happy
effects. Thus liberty, first divides itself, as it were, into various streams;
which, at length, all meet together again in soothing sensations and sweet

---

[10] Niles, *Two Discourses*, pp. 8–9; Heimert, *Religion and the American Mind*,
pp. 456–60; Paul Ramsey, introd. to Jonathan Edwards, *Freedom of the Will*
(Vol. I, *The Works of Jonathan Edwards*) (New Haven, 1957), pp. 11–47;
Edwards, *Freedom of the Will, passim;* Perry Miller, *Jonathan Edwards* (n.p.,
1949), pp. 235–63.

emotion of soul. . . . How great then must be the collective happiness that a community derives from a state of perfect freedom.[11]

As Heimert points out, Niles's millenarian society of "perfect liberty" depended less on God's arbitrary will than on the colonists' determination to throw off British enslavement. Among the rewards, or "fruits" of liberty, would be economic prosperity and a thriving growth of the arts, sciences, and purified religion.[12] Niles and his contemporary Edwardseans did not link freedom with the independence of property. Their ideal of liberty was closer to that of Humboldt than to that of the Neo-Harringtonian tradition. In a society of perfect liberty, each individual would be autonomous in his own sphere, but would move in harmony with all other individuals, spontaneously uniting for the highest good of the whole. And since the crimes of an influential man were particularly damaging to social harmony, "the offenses of the great should be punished with greater indignity and severity, than the crimes of persons in low life."[13]

Niles warned the people of Newburyport that "a free spirit is no more inclined to enslave others than ourselves. If then it should be found upon examination that we have been of a tyrannical spirit in a free country, how base must our character appear! And how many thousands of thousands have been plunged into death and slavery by our means?" Niles's central admonition sounds much like those of Benezet or Rush: "For shame, let us either cease to enslave our fellow-men, or else let us cease to complain of those that would enslave us."[14] But the question of "inconsistency" has now taken on far subtler dimensions. Americans had not been compelled to enslave Negroes (or to buy their independence with slave labor); but neither were they free, from the Edwardsean viewpoint, to change their minds and respond to rational appeals to justice. The central question involved the state of America's soul. A free soul, as Niles emphasized, "is no more *inclined* to enslave others than ourselves" (my ital.). "Perfect

[11] Niles, *Two Discourses,* pp. 22–23; Levi Hart, *Liberty Described and Recommended* (Hartford, 1775), p. 9; Heimert, *Religion and the American Mind,* pp. 401, 455–56, 459–60.

[12] Perry Miller perceptively develops the theme of prosperity as reward and peril in "From the Covenant to the Revival," *passim.*

[13] Niles, *Two Discourses,* pp. 27–31; Heimert, *Religion and the American Mind,* pp. 456–57.

[14] Niles, *Two Discourses,* pp. 37–38.

liberty" was the absolute antithesis of slavery. By definition, the two could not coexist in the same society.

Calvinists thought of slavery as God's punishment for disobedience even when they defined liberty as the necessary precondition for obedience. The key to this riddle lay in the contingency of Revolutionary time. When Niles spoke of "a tyrannical spirit in a free country," he meant that it was not yet certain whether America would "choose"—in the Edwardsean sense—the blessings of freedom or the curse of slavery. Liberty, he pointed out, could give no pleasure to a tyrannical or licentious people. Moreover, in a state of slavery men exhibited a "dumb, sullen, morose melancholy" spirit. This was the fate Americans might bring upon themselves. And since they held innocent Negroes in bondage, they could not expect the divine protections enjoyed by a just society. According to Levi Hart, another of Bellamy's students, the colonists were already enslaved to sin and were thus particularly vulnerable to various forms of secular tyranny. If, however, they abolished Negro slavery and were "consistent" with the law of liberty, "the hard bondage of sin and satan" would be thrown off and they could enjoy "the most perfect liberty." Emancipation of the blacks would allow Americans to fight, as Hart put it, under the banner of the Lord's host. This would ensure even more than victory, since "liberty shall be your lasting reward, for whom the Son maketh *free* shall be *free indeed.*"[15]

Hart's millennial vision shows how far the New England clergy had gone in adapting the hopes of the Great Awakening to the uncertainties of the Revolution. Edwards's followers had long agonized over man's illusions of freedom, his infinite capacity for self-deception, and his blindness to counterfeit virtue. But now Americans had the opportunity to demonstrate their own moral accountability, suspending, as it were, any anxious doubts over the inner state of their souls. Accordingly, when England sent mercenary troops to kill, rape, and enslave Americans, this was outrageous tyranny which demanded armed resistance; yet the colonists' sufferings were also a sign of divine judgment that called for immediate repentance and reform.

Thus in 1776 Samuel Hopkins observed that if slaveholding was "a

[15] *Ibid.*, pp. 26, 36; Hart, *Liberty Described*, pp. 16–22; Bernard Bailyn, *The Ideological Origins of the American Revolution* (Cambridge, Mass., 1967), pp. 242–43.

sin of a crimson dye, which is most particularly pointed out by the public calamities which have come upon us, from which we have no reason to expect deliverance till we put away the evil of our doings, this reformation cannot be urged with too much zeal, nor attempted too soon, whatever difficulties are in the way." Benjamin Colman agreed that the nature of America's woes pointed to slaveholding as the "capital sin of these States." No doubt the colonists were guilty of many transgressions, "yet this crime is more particularly pointed at than any other. WAS BOSTON THE FIRST PORT ON THIS CONTINENT THAT BEGAN THE SLAVE-TRADE, and are they not the first shut up by an oppressive act, and brought almost to desolation. . . ?"[16]

Viewed from one perspective, men like Colman and Hopkins were infusing the slavery issue with highly charged religious symbolism; from another viewpoint, they were secularizing the religious vocabulary of their Puritan forebears. However the process is described, it amounted to more than a mechanical pouring of old wine into new bottles. The transference had momentous consequences both for religion and for the future of American radicalism.

First of all, there was an imaginative conflation of freedom from sin with freedom from secular bondage—both the bondage of Negroes and the bondage with which the colonists were threatened. Again, Hopkins's language is especially revealing since he theoretically held that no man had the capacity to act righteously without the aid of

[16] [Samuel Hopkins], *A Dialogue Concerning the Slavery of the Africans, Showing It to be the Duty and Interest of the American States to Emancipate All Their African Slaves* (2nd ed., New York, 1785; originally published 1776), p. 39; George H. Moore, *Notes on the History of Slavery in Massachusetts* (New York, 1866), pp. 146–47; Joshua Coffin, *A Sketch of the History of Newbury, Newburyport, and West Newbury, from 1635–1845* (Boston, 1845), p. 339; Ebenezer Baldwin, *An Appendix, Stating the Heavy Grievances the Colonies Labour Under from Several Late Acts of the British Parliament* (New Haven, 1774), p. 78; Jacob Green, *A Sermon Delivered at Hanover, April 22nd, 1778* (Chatham, N.J., 1779), pp. 4, 12–15; John Cooper, letter to *New Jersey Gazette,* Sept. 20, 1780. Again, it should be emphasized that the providential mentality was not confined to New England Congregationalists or even to Calvinists. I am using the latter term as a label for a general set of mind, not a rigid set of doctrine. The important point is that the antislavery vocabulary of men like Hopkins was less congenial to liberal rationalists than to the Quakers and New Light Presbyterians of the Middle Colonies; it had resonance with the world of John Wesley and Granville Sharp, but not that of Adam Smith. One must, of course, keep obvious distinctions in mind. Thus the Quakers might interpret the war as a divine punishment for the sin of slaveholding, but unlike the Calvinists they did not see armed resistance as a holy obligation.

divine grace. As Hopkins approached the question of divine judgment, he placed purely secular concerns, such as public safety, within a vague framework of Providence. His words take us back to the "restiveness" of the black population:

God is so ordering it in his Providence, that it seems absolutely necessary something should speedily be done with respect to the slaves among us, in order to our safety, and to prevent their turning against us in our present struggle, in order to get their liberty. Our oppressors have planned to gain the blacks, and induce them to take up arms against us, by promising them liberty, on this condition.

Hopkins then reveals, however, that Jehovah is in more direct command of events, and will doubtless punish Americans with enslavement unless they expiate their guilt: "God has raised up men to attempt to deprive us of liberty; and the evil we are threatened with is slavery. This, with our vigorous attempts to avoid it, is the ground of all our distresses." Clearly nothing could be more foolish than to postpone emancipation to a more "convenient" time. Americans must arise, Hopkins warned, "all as one man, and do it with all our might, without delay, since delaying in this case is awfully dangerous, as well as unspeakably criminal." There is no "insurmountable difficulty," Hopkins affirmed, "but that which lies in your own heart."[17]

By making emancipation a religious issue, Hopkins came close to secularizing religious commitment. Obviously this meant something very different from advocating emancipation as an act of Christian charity. Though Hopkins never said that men could be freed from *individual* sin by working for Negro emancipation, he did see individual conversion—a change of "heart"—as the key to collective redemption. He also pictured Negro slavery as the epitome of national sin and the cause of national suffering. Faced with the imminent threat of God's vengeance, it mattered little whether an individual American was a saint or sinner. Individual salvation would have to be of subordinate concern until the people had collectively appeased God's wrath.

This frame of mind gave an almost chiliastic urgency to emancipation, reinforcing the legalistic argument that Negroes had an "equal right to freedom." The result, even outside New England, was often a sharpened sense of moral realism which anticipated the later Gar-

[17] Hopkins, *Dialogue*, pp. 38–39, 55–57.

risonians. John Cooper, for example, in commenting on Pennsylvania's gradual emancipation act of 1780, warned that the Lord would not be satisfied with halfway measures: "And if we keep our present slaves in bondage, and only enact laws that their posterity shall be free, we save that part of our tyranny and gain of oppression, which to us, the present generation, is of the most value." Such measures, Cooper continued, really meant telling the slaves "we will not do justice unto you, but our posterity shall do justice unto your posterity." Until Americans abandoned such hypocrisy, they could never expect to achieve liberty and peace.[18]

One source of antislavery immediatism can be found in the writings of secular thinkers, such as George Wallace, who sought to dissociate slavery from the protective category of private property. A more vital source, in America, at least, was the largely Calvinist impulse to find social correlatives for sin, repentance, and redemption. As an alternative to the prudent and "rational" approach of the gradualists, a more impatient morality survived the Revolution. Occasionally it found expression among frontier Calvinists; it was later nourished by Yale and Andover Seminaries, which became Edwardsean seedbeds for radical reform. It is therefore legitimate to see Bellamy, Hopkins, Hart, Niles and Jonathan Edwards, Jr., as the precursors of Garrison, Phelps, Pillsbury, Wright, and Phillips.[19]

[18] John Cooper, letter to *New Jersey Gazette,* Sept. 20, 1780. On the other hand, David Cooper, a prominent Quaker leader, approved the Pennsylvania law because it provided for a total emancipation (see [David Cooper], *A Serious Address to the Rulers of America on the Inconsistency of Their Conduct Respecting Slavery* . . . [London, 1783], p. 22n.).

[19] Sometimes the Wallace "higher law" tradition merged with the concepts of New England theology, as in Theodore Dwight's *An Oration, Spoken Before "The Connecticut Society, for the Promotion of Freedom and the Relief of Persons Unlawfully Holden in Bondage"* (Hartford, 1794), pp. 9–13. It is worth noting that the Edwardseans, like Wallace, saw slaveholding as a form of rampant individualism that violated the common good. The Edwardsean influence on nineteenth-century reform has not yet been adequately explored. As I have tried to suggest, Edwards's immediate followers anticipated the language and concepts of militant abolitionism; they would have had no difficulty in comprehending Amos A. Phelps's later explanation of immediatism as "a yielding up of the PRINCIPLE of slavery as a practical principle. . . . All that follows is the carrying out of the new principle of action, and is to emancipation just what sanctification is to conversion" (*Lectures on Slavery and its Remedy* [Boston, 1834], p. 179). If the very success of the American Revolution helped to dissipate millennial expectations, the republic's growth and good fortune also en-

But there were grave weaknesses in the providential approach to slavery and American independence. Perhaps Calvinism advanced moral consciousness by insisting that liberty cannot be earned by good works. The doctrine appears to be a refreshing antidote to the more common rationalistic view that some slaves could be freed without harm, since they were better behaved than many whites.[20] But insight had its price, even for a democratic Calvinist like Nathaniel Niles. If a freed Negro seemed to lack moral capacity, as defined by the revivals, he was not really suited for freedom. One could not demand industry, frugality, and temperance as conditions for freedom. But these virtues, in addition to "decent conversation and courteous behavior," were the necessary fruits of freedom. Slaves were not sinners, but sinners could not expect to benefit from liberty. By making liberty equivalent to grace, Niles could conclude that it would be better to be born a slave than to be guilty of abusing liberty.[21]

By making the urgency of Negro emancipation depend on the fears evoked by war, abolitionists of various kinds invited an obvious reply: the times could not be more "inopportune," since it was difficult enough to mobilize the people without increasing further discord, threatening additional property, and turning loose a savage, vengeful, and propertyless swarm of marauders. Fear, in short, could be countered by fear. To be effective, the abolitionist jeremiads required a proper timing of victories and defeats. Hopkins advanced the rather strained argument that the Americans' early military successes were a reward for the Congressional resolutions ending the slave trade. He warned, of course, that the patriot armies could expect nothing but defeat if this

---

couraged more optimistic estimates of human "ability" among theologians who associated salvation with forms of self-effacement. It would be difficult to overemphasize the influence of the Andover and New Haven theologies on such radical reformers as Phelps, Parker Pillsbury, Henry Clarke Wright, John Humphrey Noyes—and indirectly, on Garrison himself. On the other hand, a very similar brand of abolitionism could emerge from the Calvinism of an English immigrant, George Bourne; from the pulpit of a popular Scottish evangelical, Andrew Thomson; and from a militant English Quaker, Elizabeth Heyrick. It was this parallel development of religious radicalism which eventually enabled the American Garrisonians to find sympathetic supporters among the Nonconformists of Glasgow, Dublin, and Edinburgh.

[20] [Anon. American editor], "Appendix No. 1" to Granville Sharp, *An Essay on Slavery, Proving from Scripture its Inconsistency with Humanity and Religion* (Burlington, West Jersey, 1773; reprinted London, 1776), p. 13.

[21] Niles, *Two Discourses,* pp. 23, 26, 57–58.

preparatory step were not followed by emancipation. But to anyone who took this logic seriously, the final American victory could only prove that Negro emancipation was not one of God's supreme concerns.[22]

Above all, the retributive approach focused on the guilt, fears, and aspirations of white Americans. Shocked by the harshness of British coercion, threatened with defeat and paternal vengeance, the Calvinist clergy searched for the hidden guilt that could account for God's displeasure. Some of them fastened on slaveholding, but usually in a spasmodic or intermittent way. Significantly, Hopkins thought it necessary to say that by emphasizing the national sin of slaveholding he did not mean to exclude other sins "such as impiety and profaneness—formality and indifference in the service of Christ and his religion." These, of course, were among the sins that had been the traditional province of the clergy, and their partial displacement by slavery was the result of an unprecedented crisis. After independence had been achieved, it would have been unthinkable for a minister like Levi Hart to assure Americans that they could throw off "the hard bondage to sin and satan" and enjoy "the most perfect liberty" simply by abolishing Negro slavery. One may also note that impiety, profaneness, and religious indifference are predictably enduring problems, at least until the millennium. By linking the sin of slaveholding with these perennial human failings, the abolitionist clergy implied that the condemnation was what really mattered.[23]

[22] [Hopkins], *Dialogue,* p. 59; Green, *Sermon Delivered at Hanover,* p. 17; "A Whig," in *New Jersey Gazette,* Oct. 4, 1780; "A Friend of Justice," in *New Jersey Gazette,* Nov. 8, 1780; "Impartial," in *New Jersey Gazette,* Jan. 10, 1781; *Pennsylvania Packet,* March 25, 1780. For the hostility Hopkins encountered from the slave-trade interests, see his letter to Moses Brown, April, 29, 1784, in Elizabeth Donnan, ed., *Documents Illustrative of the History of the Slave Trade to America* (Washington, 1930–1935) III, 335–336.

[23] [Hopkins], *Dialogue,* p. 58; Baldwin, *Appendix,* p. 78. Hopkins was later distressed when Hart expressed doubts on the propriety and effectiveness of a state law prohibiting the importation of slaves (see Hopkins to Hart, Sept. 8, 1788, Simon Gratz collection, Historical Society of Pennsylvania [hereafter HSP]). But Hopkins himself evidenced a philosophical passivity, possibly the outgrowth of his theology of self-effacement, when he expressed faith that God had allowed the horrors of the slave trade in order to promote the Christianization of Africa by Black American missionaries (see E. A. Park, ed., *The Works of Samuel Hopkins* [Boston, 1852], I, pp. 136ff); Samuel Hopkins to Moses Brown, Apr. 29, 1784, Moses Brown papers, IV, 1130, Rhode Island Historical Society.

If the revival's logic had been taken with literal seriousness, America might have experienced a genuine social revolution, culminating in a theocratic state. There were grim dangers, as the clergy seemed to sense, in substituting military victories for mass conversions or in portraying the state as an instrument of the Lord. By the end of the war, the clergy had already begun to compromise their millennial goals and to reaffirm the separation between religion and worldly politics. Victory, which in one sense marked the fulfillment of the revival's most daring hopes, also promoted a spirit of accommodation. In January, 1788, for example, Hopkins could express dismay to Levi Hart over the news that *"these States, which have been fighting for liberty, and consider themselves as the highest and most noble example of zeal for it,"* could not come together "in any political constitution, unless it indulge and authorize them to inslave their fellowmen!" Yet he favored adoption of the Constitution, thinking that the alternative would be "a state of anarchy, and probably of civil war."[24] Instead of being the instrument for American emancipation, the slave, it appeared, had become the greatest peril to union.

Race and Reality

The ideology of the American Revolution cannot be divorced from the momentous question of race. But then racial attitudes cannot be taken as an irreducible and self-explanatory "fact." If racial differences came to symbolize a kind of irreducible reality, one must ask what functions the symbol served. How, precisely, were racial attitudes related to more general questions concerning labor, subordination, social discipline, and moral progress? Winthrop D. Jordan has mapped much of this terrain in his account of American attitudes toward the Negro's physical characteristics, the self-conscious "discovery" of prejudice, and the environmentalists' attempts to "explain" the Negro's various deficiencies. There is something to be added, however, to his insight that Americans had reason "to emphasize the physical differences between themselves and Negroes in order to confirm the validity of their social order."[25]

The antislavery arguments of the Revolutionary period were notably

[24] Hopkins to Hart, Jan. 29, 1788, Misc. MSS, H, New-York Historical Society (hereafter NYHS); Donnan, ed., *Documents*, III, 342–44.
[25] Winthrop D. Jordan, *White over Black: American Attitudes toward the Negro, 1550–1812* (Chapel Hill, 1968), p. 255.

abstract and seldom touched on the actual condition, interests, or future of Negro Americans. Some of the younger generation of patriots, having a literary bent, sought to enliven the debate by writing parodies of the proslavery argument. This device added comic dress to lofty theory, and presumably indicated which principles a writer could assume his audience would *not* take seriously. Thus John Trumbull, writing in the *Connecticut Journal and New Haven Post-Boy,* was clearly confident that his Swiftian irony would not be misunderstood: "It is strange," he remarked, "that any persons should be so infatuated, as to deny the right of enslaving the black inhabitants of Africa." Trumbull could not look on silently "and see this inestimable privilege, which has been handed down inviolable from our ancestors, wrenched out of our hands, by a few men of squeamish consciences."[26] He knew, of course, that the idea of prescriptive authority commanded little popular respect, though it is doubtful whether a contemporary English writer could have made the same assumption.

It was perhaps more hazardous to do a caricature of amoral utilitarianism, although in 1773 an anonymous pamphleteer must have known that angry colonists were not in a mood to agree with his initial quotations from Pope: *"Whatever is, is right";* and from "Machiavelus Americanus": "However amiable Justice and Virtue may be in our abstract ideas of them: the policy of Kingdoms and Commercial States, ought ever to be regulated by the more important considerations of necessity and convenience."[27] Judged by the latter criteria, even

---

[26] John Trumbull, "The Correspondent, No. 8," in "Documents," *Journal of Negro History,* XIV (Oct., 1929), 493.

[27] [Anon.], *Personal Slavery Established, by the Suffrages of Custom and Right Reason: Being a Full Answer to the Gloomy & Visionary Reveries, of All the Fanatical & Enthusiastical Writers on that Subject* (Philadelphia, 1773), title page. Although Winthrop Jordan has discovered one "antislavery proslavery" hoax, which also appeared in Philadelphia in 1773 (see Jordan, "An Antislavery Proslavery Document?" *Journal of Negro History,* XLVII [1962], 54–56), he oddly accepts the above pamphlet as a genuine defense of the slave trade (*White over Black,* pp. 305–8, 484–85). But in 1773 no American, or Englishman for that matter, would have dedicated a work to the committeemen of the bankrupt Royal African Company, for their "generous disinterested exertion of benevolence and philanthropy, which has been the principal means of heaping wealth and honours on Europeans and Americans, and rescuing many millions of wretched Africans, *as brands from the fire*" (p. 3). The pamphlet is clearly a parody, written as a spoof on Richard Nisbet's *Slavery Not Forbidden by Scripture* (Philadelphia, 1773), and as a defense of Benjamin Rush's *An Address to the Inhabitants of the British Settlements in America, upon Slave-Keeping*

West Indian slavery emerged as one of the most efficient and beneficent institutions ever devised by man. The blacks had "fewer cares, and less anxiety about to-morrow, than any people in the whole world." If the people of Britain and Ireland should ever become aware of the bliss and security of colonial slavery, Parliament would have to pass stringent legislation to prevent the entire population from fleeing to "this terrestrial elysium." Unhappily, the agitation over slavery might force West Indians to break off the provision trade with the northern colonies. Even then, however, utility could provide a sensible solution: the West Indians could find a perfect substitute for pork and ham if they pickled or smoked the bodies of the 20,000 slaves who perished every year on their trip from Africa![28]

The Revolutionary generation felt equally confident in ridiculing the notion of natural subordination. Thus in Hugh Henry Brackenridge's *Modern Chivalry*, Captain Farrago scoffs at natural rights, claiming that slaveholding is justified by "the economy of nature" which everywhere illustrates "the subserviency of one thing to another." Farrago then reveals the Hobbesian basis for his position, when he admits that since "it is difficult to determine, *a priori,* who are intended for slavery or freedom, so as to make a judicious distribution, things must take their course; and the rule be, catch, catch can; and every man have a servant when he can get one. It is vain to be squeamish, and stick at colour. It is true, I would rather have a white person, if such could be got."[29]

This is the antislavery principle of "consistency" turned upside down. It also illustrates a common tendency to subordinate questions of race to questions of dominion, utility, and social order. Since Farrago rested his case on expediency and superior power, his only inconsistency was an added assurance that Negroes were not of the same species as whites.

(Philadelphia, 1773). It also gave publicity to current antislavery literature. Long after writing the above conclusions, I am pleased to find them confirmed by Lester B. Scherer, "A New Look at 'Personal Slavery Established,' " *William and Mary Quarterly,* 3rd ser., XXX (Oct., 1973), 645–52.

[28] [Anon.], *Personal Slavery Established,* pp. 3, 5–9, 15, 24–26.

[29] Hugh Henry Brackenridge, *Modern Chivalry: Containing the Adventures of Captain John Farrago, and Teague Oregan* [sic], *his servant* (2 vols. in one, Philadelphia, 1792), II, 108–14. In view of my previous discussion, it is noteworthy that Brackenridge, the Jeffersonian rationalist, had graduated from Princeton and was an ordained Presbyterian minister.

Montesquieu had provided the classic model for satirizing this latter position: "It is impossible for us to suppose that these beings should be men; because if we supposed them to be men, one would begin to believe that we ourselves were not Christians." Brackenridge, among others, took up the theme:

That it is justifiable I have no doubt. Is there any religious denomination, except the fanatical people called Quakers, that have made it a term of communion not to hold a slave. In admitting to church privileges, I have never heard of the question asked, Have you any negroes, and do you keep slaves: If it was a matter of conscience, would not conscientious persons themselves make it.[30]

But this line of argument was clearly dangerous, even apart from its anticlericalism. It was one thing to parody abstract arguments that could be turned against any assertion of natural rights, and quite another to satirize racial antipathies which served the important function of qualifying natural rights. In a "forensic dispute" on the legality of slavery, held at Harvard's commencement ceremony in 1773, the student taking the abolitionist side realized that the argument was driving his opponent back to the defensive wall of Negro inferiority. At this point he asked, "I suppose you will hardly imagine the darkness of a man's skin incapacitates him for the direction of his conduct," and added some quips, borrowed from Montesquieu, on slavery being justified by kinky hair or a flat nose. The reply exposed the hazard of such light attempts to dismiss the racial question: "My friend, I am no enemy to humour, but I think it rarely serves to illustrate a logical conclusion." The real issue, according to Harvard's defender of slavery, was neither physical difference nor abstract right, but the Negro's present capacity for self-determination.[31]

Since the Revolutionary debates over slavery moved irresistibly to the question of race, abolitionist writers tried to focus attention on the superficiality of physical differences. "A black, tawny or reddish skin," said William Gordon, "is not so unfavorable an hue to the genuine son of liberty, as a tory complection." Benjamin Rush felt it necessary to

[30] Charles Louis de Secondat de Montesquieu, *Oeuvres complètes de Montesquieu* (publiées sous la direction de M André Masson, Paris, 1950), I, 330–31; Brackenridge, *Modern Chivalry*, II, 117–18.

[31] [Theodore Parsons and Eliphalet Pearson], *A Forensic Dispute on the Legality of Enslaving the Africans, Held at the Public Commencement in Cambridge, New England* . . . (Boston, 1773), pp. 6–7, 21–25, 28, 38–40; "Impartial," *New Jersey Gazette,* Jan. 10, 1781.

begin his 1773 *Address to the Inhabitants of the British Settlements in America, upon Slave-Keeping* by denying the necessity of saying anything in favor of the Negroes' intellect or capacity for virtue and happiness (after which, of course, he said a good deal). And in his *Vindication* of the same *Address,* he added that even if Negro inferiority had been proved, "Would it avail a man to plead in a Court of Justice that he defrauded his Neighbour, because he was inferior to him in Genius or Knowledge?"[32]

Such arguments were blunted by strategic and ideological barriers. The strategy of the Revolutionary debate left little ground for an abstract or generalized defense of slavery. Given the widespread enthusiasm for liberty and equal rights, it was difficult for an apologist to show that the freedom of some Americans depended on the exploitation of others. He could not plead in favor of honest tyranny or unadulterated self-interest. The abolitionists, by resting their case on the highest moral principles, helped to isolate the Negro's supposed incapacity for freedom—whether inherent or the result of long oppression—as the only obstacle to emancipation. When the argument acquired this structure, it obscured the national interests served by slavery. The terms of the debate also gave a subtle tactical advantage to the opponents of abolition. As the principles of the Revolution became more hallowed and abstract, racial fears and prejudices could acquire all the symbolic connotations of "reality." The "realist" could agree with the "visionary" that the principles for which Americans had fought, to use Jordan's phrase, "required the complete abolition of slavery." Yet reality required that the Negroes' "equal right to freedom" be consigned to that pantheon of ideals which evoked rhetorical respect but did not impinge on the immediate world of affairs.

Both parties in the Revolutionary debate helped to make race the central excuse for slavery. They thus diverted attention from a pattern of exploitation, and of prejudice toward the exploited, which America had supposedly never shared with the Old World. Obviously the blacks differed from other *under*castes in being racially distinct and sharply segregated from the poorer classes of whites. Nor can one overlook the racial fears, tensions, and stereotypes which, as Jordan has shown, were not necessarily a product of slavery. But the "reality" that weak-

[32] Moore, *Notes on History of Slavery,* p. 186; [Rush], *Address, passim;* [Rush], *Vindication,* pp. 32–33.

ened antislavery ideology had less to do with race *per se* than with the discipline of a potentially disruptive lowest class.

The question of discipline must be understood within the context of religious perfectionism and Revolutionary aspirations. The newborn Christian could demonstrate his own spiritual liberty by championing the cause of the downtrodden; the nation could live up to its Messianic motto, *Novus Ordo Seclorum,* by repudiating the principle of slavery. The blacks themselves, however, were deprived of this opportunity to act on their inner volition and thus to fulfill their inherent destiny. They did not, as a group, emancipate themselves. As a result, white Americans retained the prerogative of telling blacks what their inner volitions should be. Levi Hart, for example, could assure the freemen of Farmington, Connecticut, that his antislavery remarks would not make the blacks unruly since they were bound both by duty and their own interest to remain obedient. The formula allowed emancipators to define their own external behavior as an expression of internal freedom and purity; unhappily, the objects of emancipation could be externally freed only as they gave evidence of an internal enslavement to the benefactor race.[33]

A few examples of the reformers' programs for uplift and rehabilitation will suggest that racial distinctions were not the central concern. The reformers feared, above all else, the kind of uncontrolled behavior they already associated with unruly whites—the very class of "idle vagrants" that liberals like Burgh and Hutcheson had wanted to have enslaved. In colonial America, the availability of Negro slaves limited the need to exploit a large mass of unskilled white labor. Consequently, for the emancipated slave, the only nearby reference groups were the remaining slaves and a marginal group of "depraved" whites who had refused or failed to internalize the norms of the dominant class. The really serious question, which had nothing to do with racial characteristics, was whether emancipated slaves would greatly augment this intractable population? Would the freed black fail to show up for work? Would he carouse in taverns with Jack Tar? Would Crispus Attucks, resurrected, lead mobs that defied American troops?[34]

[33] Hart, *Liberty Described,* pp. 2–6. I am indebted to Daniel Kelly, a Yale undergraduate, for bringing out this point in a brilliant paper on Anthony Benezet.

[34] Obviously, the goals of social discipline continued to change, and immigration from Europe continued to complicate problems of acculturation. For a

The slave codes, in the North as well as South, provide suggestive images of the kind of disorder that affluent Americans most feared: Negroes, slave or free, who had time to dance, gamble, or drink; who fraternized with white beggars, vagrants, sailors, and prostitutes; who hung out at low taverns or other spots notorious for intrigue and trading in stolen goods; who defied all curfews, or engaged in brawls, or simply laughed at dignified authority. There were no masters who could be held responsible for the offenses of the lower order of whites, but a slave's owner could be harshly fined for lapses in discipline. European lawmakers might well have envied such a system of delegated authority over a highly visible lower class. In cities like New York and Philadelphia, on the other hand, slave owners must have wondered whether profit outweighed legal liability. As private manumissions increased in the North, even antislavery spokesmen looked for substitute controls that could serve the functions of slavery, especially in keeping blacks at work and insulated from the corruptions of the lower white "counterculture."

For example, William Dillwyn, the American Quaker who helped catalyze the British antislavery movement, opposed in 1774 the idea of any general emancipation. By encouraging private manumissions, he argued, reformers could teach slaves to avoid idleness and to acquire habits of conduct that would fit them for liberty. When Moses Brown freed his own slaves in 1773, he admonished them against such "profaneness and wickedness, as stealing, lying, swearing, drinking, lusting after women, frolicking and the like sinful courses." The depravity of "frolicking" appears often in the eighteenth-century literature. Pennsylvania's proposed law for gradual emancipation provided that any Negro or mulatto found loitering or "mispending his time" could be sold as a servant for one year upon the order of two justices. A New Jersey "Lover of True Justice" suggested in 1781 that factories be built in which slaves would be prepared for freedom; while aiding the economy, such factories would presumably "manufacture" a moral and industrious labor force. Similarly, the pious Benezet proposed that emancipated slaves be made to work under the supervision of overseers

---

penetrating discussion of the persistence of nonindustrial cultures and of nineteenth-century resistance to the Protestant work ethic, see Herbert G. Gutman, "Work, Culture, and Society in Industrializing America, 1815–1919," *American Historical Review*, LXXVIII (June, 1973), 531–88.

of the poor, who would oblige them "to act more circumspectly, and make proper use of their liberty." The blacks would then be "profitable members of society"; and they and their children "might gradually become useful members of the community." Benezet also recommended that Negroes be forced to settle and improve western lands ("when not hired out to work for the white people"): "Hence both planters and tradesmen would be plentifully supplied with chearful [*sic*] and willing minded laborers, much vacant land would be cultivated; the produce of the country be justly encreased."[35]

Here, one suspects, is the true "reality" of race: cheerful and willing-minded laborers. The success of emancipation would not depend on the Negro's capacity for liberty, but on finding a substitute for the labor discipline of slavery. In preindustrial America no one could envision the social controls of nineteenth-century industry or the staggering task of transforming an immense population of immigrants into an efficient and orderly working class. In the 1770s the black's performance as a freedman could not be measured against a large existing class of white peasants and laborers; thus for a century or more to come, it would be measured against his previous performance as a slave.

The Perishability of Revolutionary Time

As later antislavery writers searched for a vocabulary that would resonate with the largest possible audience, they turned repeatedly to the examples and principles of the War of Independence. A petition of 1786 to the Virginia legislature, from Frederick and Hampshire counties, restated the central argument of inconsistency:

That the Glorious and ever memorable Revolution can be Justified on no other Principles but what doth plead with greater Force for the emancipa-

[35] William Dillwyn to John Mehelm, Feb. 16, 1774, Simon Gratz collection, HSP; William D. Johnston, "Slavery in Rhode Island, 1755–1776," *Publications of Rhode Island Historical Society*, new ser., II (July, 1894), 162; Raymond A. Mohl, *Poverty in New York, 1783–1825* (New York, 1971), *passim;* American Convention of Abolition Societies, "To the Free Africans and Other People of Color in the United States," in *Minutes of the Proceedings of the Third Convention of Delegates* . . . (Philadelphia, 1796), pp. 12–13; *Pennsylvania Packet,* March 4, 1779; "A Lover of True Justice," in *New Jersey Gazette,* Feb. 14, 1781; Anthony Benezet, *Some Historical Account of Guinea, its Situation, Produce and the General Disposition of its Inhabitants* . . . (Philadelphia, 1771), pp. 139–41.

tion of our Slaves in proportion as the oppression exercised over them exceeds the oppression formerly exercised by Great Britain over these States.[36]

To illustrate the same point, David Cooper reminded his readers of the colonists' outrage over General Howe's atrocities in Boston, especially the separation of men from their families. Yet the American people had authorized similar and far worse crimes against the Africans. "In vain has the tyranny of kings been rejected," said the delegates of the 1794 Convention of Abolition Societies, "while we permit in our country a domestic despotism, which involves, in its nature, most of the vices and miseries that we have endeavoured to avoid." In the less temperate words of a writer in the *American Museum,* the inconsistency was "the most abandoned apostasy that ever took place, since the Almighty fiat spoke into existence this habitable world."[37]

These arguments acquired new implications as they were repeated through the postwar decades. The "Glorious and ever memorable Revolution" kept receding into the past, secure now from any need for justification. There was, inevitably, a widening chasm of time between the transcendent moment of rebirth—when the "Word of Liberty" created a nation—and the recurring rediscoveries of America's unredeemed sin. What was the meaning of this elongating interval? Did the persistence of slavery—and thus the growing permanence of America's inconsistency—mean that the Revolution had been lost,

[36] "Anti-Slavery Petitions Presented to the Virginia Legislature by Citizens of Various Counties," *Journal of Negro History,* XII (Oct., 1927), 670. A perceptive analysis of the significance of the Revolutionary heritage is in Duncan MacLeod, "Racial Attitudes in Revolutionary and Early National America," D.Phil. thesis, Cambridge, 1969.

[37] [Cooper], *Serious Address,* pp. 9–10; American Convention of Abolition Societies, *Address of a Convention of Delegates from the Abolition Society* [sic], *to the Citizens of the United States* (Philadelphia, 1794), p. 5; *American Museum,* IV (Nov., 1788), 415; XII (Oct., 1792), 195; New York Manumission Society, MS Minutes, VI, 42–43, NYHS; [Samuel Hopkins] "Crito," "The Slave Trade and Slavery," originally published in the *Providence Gazette and Country Journal* (Oct. 13, 1787), in E. A. Park, ed., *The Works of Samuel Hopkins* (Boston, 1852), II, 616–21, 624; Zephaniah Swift, *An Oration upon Domestic Slavery; Delivered at the North Meeting-House in Hartford* . . . (Hartford, 1791), pp. 3–4; George Bourne, *The Book and Slavery Irreconcilable; With Animadversions upon Dr. Smith's Philosophy* (Philadelphia, 1816), pp. 65–67; Fourth of July oration at meeting of Manumission Society of North Carolina, in *The Emancipator,* Oct. 31, 1820; *The Genius of Universal Emancipation,* I (July 4, 1821), 4; (Dec., 1821), 89.

in both senses of that word? Would post-Revolutionary America be simply an extension of pre-Revolutionary America, at least with respect to national sin and guilt? Or did institutionalized inconsistency mean that America would soon acquire all the infections and diseases of the Old World? The power of Revolutionary ideals depended on the sense of a continuing Revolutionary time—a time not simply of completion and rounding out, but a time of creation, marked by the same contingency, fears, and openness of the Revolution itself.

Such considerations make understandable the attempts by anti-slavery writers to find "signs of the times" that would reanimate the sense of collective peril generated by the Revolution. If God had rewarded the American people with military victory, He could be expected all the more to punish them for violating His covenant. In the 1780s His displeasure over slavery became manifest in the nation's prolonged economic distress, in the dissension between states, and in Shays's Rebellion. In the following decade slaveholding provoked even more ominous signs of divine wrath: yellow-fever epidemics; warfare with Barbary pirates and western Indians; the slave revolt in St. Domingue; the danger of being engulfed in a European war. The Barbary states, by their continuing raids on American shipping, showed that whites were not immune from enslavement and thus encouraged the antislavery literary device of role reversal. Yet when compared with the armed might of Great Britain, Indians and corsairs were weak instruments of vengeance. Unlike the redcoats, they could hardly be portrayed as threatening to "enslave" the entire American people.[38]

[38] Royall Tyler, *The Algerine Captive; or, the Life and Adventures of Doctor Updike Underhill, Six Years a Prisoner Among the Algerines* (Hartford, 1816; originally published 1797), pp. 99–101; Hilda Justice, *Life and Ancestry of Warner Mifflin* (Philadelphia, 1905), pp. 95–96, 101; American Convention of Abolition Societies, *Minutes of the Proceedings of a Convention of Delegates from the Abolition Societies . . .* (Philadelphia, 1794), pp. 25–26; American Convention, *Address* (1794), pp. 6–7; American Convention, "Documents," *Journal of Negro History,* VI (July, 1922), 359; [Hopkins] "Crito," "Slave Trade and Slavery," 621–22; Curtis Dahl, "The American School of Catastrophe," *American Quarterly* (Fall, 1959), 380–83; Joel Barlow, *The Columbiad, a Poem* (London, 1809; originally published 1794), *passim;* Benjamin Franklin, *The Complete Works of Benjamin Franklin,* ed. by John Bigelow (New York, 1888), X, 196–200; George Buchanan, *An Oration upon the Moral and Political Evil of Slavery, Delivered at a Public Meeting of the Maryland Society for Promoting the Abolition of Slavery, July 4, 1791* (Baltimore, 1793), p. 9; Thomas Branagan, *Political and Theological Disquisitions on the Signs of the Times, Relative to*

By 1806, John Parrish was forced to rely on a more tenuous example of divine retribution for America's declension:

The worm and the wevil [*sic*], like an army, have entered the stacks and barns, and rendered the grain in some places of little value. Our fruit-trees of latter years have been remarkably smitten. . . . The rain has been withheld, at seasons, in a remarkable manner, so that a shower has not been witnessed to moisten the earth for upwards of ninety days in some places.

Thomas Branagan detected signs of God's anger in the moral dissipation of his countrymen:

And who, that is not judicially blind, can not discover the finger of an avenging God, in the greatest curse that ever befel this country—ARDENT SPIRITS, the very produce of slavery, which is our greatest scourge.[39]

---

the Present Conquests of France . . . (Trenton, N.J., 1807), pp. 3, 83–84, and *passim; Genius of Universal Emancipation,* I (Jan., 1822), 112. Although anti-slavery writers trotted out the Indian warfare of the 1790s as one of many signs divine displeasure, they did not emphasize the theme of white captivity which had played such a major role in the colonial literature on Indian warfare (for the latter, see Richard Slotkin, *Regeneration through Violence: The Mythology of the American Frontier, 1600–1860* [Middletown, Conn., 1973], *passim*). Slotkin finds intriguing continuities between the themes of colonial experience and the archetypes of nineteenth-century antislavery literature, particularly as seen in *Uncle Tom's Cabin.* Without debating his argument, I think it is significant that Slotkin has so little to say about Negro slavery in the pre-Garrisonian era, and that the abolitionists' first important references to Indian warfare, as a sign of divine judgment, came long after the fighting had moved to the western territories. For most Americans, especially for slaveholders, the danger of being captured by Indians in the 1790s was a remote worry. Abolitionist writers gave considerably more attention to the Barbary pirates.

[39] John Parrish, *Remarks on the Slavery of Black People; Addressed to the Citizens of the United States* . . . (Philadelphia, 1806), pp. 2, 4; Thomas Branagan, *The Penitential Tyrant; or Slave Trader Reformed* . . . (Philadelphia, 1807; originally published 1805), p. vi. Parrish concluded, in words that would become better known in the future: "A house divided against itself cannot stand; neither can a government or constitution" (p. 9). Branagan exploited the danger of slave insurrection as a sign of divine retribution. Other writers and orators invoked Jefferson's well-known warnings to support the same argument, especially at the time of the Missouri crisis (see, for example, Asa Cummings, *A Discourse Delivered at Brunswick, April 6, 1820, the Day of The Annual Fast in Maine and Massachusetts* [Brunswick, Maine, 1820], pp. 23–24). But by the early 1820s it was already clear that providence could have other meanings. In 1823, Dr. Richard Furman, of South Carolina, expressed thanksgiving for the divine goodness that had led to the timely exposure of Denmark Vesey's insurrection. And since God had expressed His will, it was essential to convince the

When Parrish and Branagan looked across the Atlantic, they had no trouble finding a more terrifying example of the national punishment that slavery would inevitably provoke. For there could be no doubt that God had raised up Napoleon, as an avenging spirit, to punish the nation that had long led the world in the slave trade. England's calamities, Parrish wrote, were the direct result of her failure to comply with the British abolitionists' petitions.[40]

This was, in fact, precisely the judgment of the British abolitionists. In 1807, for example, James Stephen suggested that God had "winked" at British failings during an age of ignorance. But by the late eighteenth century, statesmen had become aware of the national crimes against Africa, and their refusal to abolish the slave trade had been followed by war, treason, famine, mutiny, debt, loss of specie, oppressive taxes, and now, the threat of invasion: "Can it be denied then, that we have in this great national offence, an adequate cause of the displeasure of Heaven, and of the calamities which have fallen upon the country? or can it be alleged, that there is any contemporary provocation that bears any proportion to the slave trade." Ironically, Stephen went on to ask, "Has not the hand of Providence distinguished some portion of the earth with blessings equally unusual?" He meant, of course, "the rising western empire," whose leaders had

done much to redeem themselves from those sins to which I chiefly ascribe the calamities of Europe. Indeed, their government and legislature, with whom the corporate responsibility in every country chiefly rests, have done all that was in their immediate power; while every state in the union but one, has long since finally delivered itself from the guilt of the African slave trade.[41]

---

slaves that an insurrection could never succeed and that slavery was perfectly harmonious with true religion (*Exposition of the Views of the Baptists Relative to the Colored Population of the United States* . . . [Charleston, 1823], pp. 4–7).

[40] Parrish, *Remarks*, pp. 34–35; Branagan, *Political and Theological Disquisitions*, pp. 7–8, 149–60. But Branagan added that Americans should blush when they heard how many Englishmen were protesting against the slave trade.

[41] [James Stephen], *The Dangers of the Country* (Philadelphia, 1807), pp. 132–140. Stephen wrote soon after hearing of Jefferson's annual message of December, 1806, urging Congress to abolish the slave trade at the end of the period of Constitutional limitation. His praise of America is remarkable in view of his highly influential pamphlet, *War in Disguise* (1805), which attacked America for supplying Napoleon's Europe with West India produce, under the cover of neutrality, and which persuaded the British Ministry to adopt the Orders-in-Council that led to the War of 1812. As Leslie Stephen later

Stephen's words indicate that American and British abolitionists lived in a common intellectual world, but were also separated by important situational differences. They agreed that God punishes or rewards nations through the "secondary causes" of history; that the American and French Revolutions had ushered in an era of unprecedented hope and peril; that the African slave trade entailed monstrous burdens of national guilt which would either lead to horrifying retribution or afford an opportunity for moral regeneration. By 1803, however, it was England that feared "enslavement" by a foreign enemy.[42] Psychologically, the Napoleonic Wars could provide a counterpart for the millennial hopes and fears of the American Revolution. And it was during this crisis, when the tide of victory had begun to turn in their favor, that the British abolished the slave trade. This triumph consummated twenty years of often discouraging struggle and helped vindicate as the true champion of liberty the most powerful of France's foes.

The differences between British and American antislavery provide a perspective on the meaning of America's Revolutionary heritage. In England it was possible to think of antislavery as a continuously unfolding force, hampered perhaps by temporary setbacks, but moving irresistibly toward the distant goal of universal emancipation.[43] In 1808, when Thomas Clarkson presented this view in the first full-scale history of the movement, it could still be assumed that the African slave trade was the root evil, and that its abolition would set in motion a chain of forces that would improve the West Indian slave's condition, prepare him for freedom, and eventually emancipate him. Public policy made clear that the nation was committed, as the world's strongest sea power, to an international suppression of the slave trade.

---

wrote, "I fear that my grandfather was thus partly responsible for the unfortunate war with the United States; but he clearly meant well" (*The Life of Sir James Fitzjames Stephen, a Judge of the High Court of Justice, by his Brother* [New York, 1895], p. 19). Further, James Stephen blamed West Indian slavery, as well as the slave trade, for the calamities England suffered. He also resented American criticism of England for initiating the slave trade, but hoped that mutual abolition would provide new ground for Anglo-American unity.

[42] Stephen's *Dangers of the Country* was entirely devoted to this theme. See also [George Harrison], *Notices on the Slave-Trade: in Reference to the Present State of the British Isles* (London, 1804), p. 5.

[43] One should add that part of the difference can be attributed to the continuity of British antislavery leadership from the 1790s to the 1820s for which there was no American counterpart.

Abolitionists could hold the government accountable for fulfilling the national pledge of 1807.

The American commitment, stemming from the Revolution, was considerably more ambiguous. Reformers might read the Congressional resolution of 1774 against importing slaves as a pledge to begin the slow work of redeeming America. But in contrast to England, American political history showed that opposition to the slave trade could be combined with a defense of domestic slavery. Given the natural increase in the slave population, abolitionists could not count on undermining the institution, at least after census statistics were known, simply by cutting off the supply of Africans. From the beginning, they had also been more impatient than their British counterparts and had made emancipation their unequivocal goal. As we have seen, no lower purpose would have fit the millennial expectations of the Revolution. A people who, with divine favor, could win their own freedom from the most powerful kingdom on earth should meet no insuperable obstacle in emancipating their own slaves—so long as they had the will to do so. As later antislavery writers looked back upon the Revolution, they discovered a time of selfless commitment, when the people had entered into a "solemn league and covenant to vindicate the rights of man, and promote national righteousness."[44] Such dedication could be followed only by apostasy or social regeneration.

The rewards for America's victory were union and prosperity; yet union required sectional compromise, and prosperity was not unrelated to the labor of 700,000 slaves. By 1785, Samuel Hopkins acknowledged that since America had been so generously rewarded (despite many ominous warnings), some of his readers might conclude that

[44] The quotation is from Warner Mifflin, referring to the 1774 resolution (Justice, *Warner Mifflin*, p. 189). See also *American Museum*, IV (Aug., 1788), 173; (Nov., 1788), 414; New Jersey Society for Promoting the Abolition of Slavery, *The Constitution of the New Jersey Society* . . . (Burlington, N.J., 1793), pp. 3–4; American Convention of Abolition Societies, *Address* (1794), pp. 3–7. Unlike their British counterparts, American reformers emphasized the hypocrisy of condemning the brutal way slaves were obtained in Africa without recognizing that the present owners were as guilty as the original captors (see David Rice, *Slavery Inconsistent with Justice and Good Policy* . . . [Philadelphia, 1792], pp. 3–4, 9; David Barrow, *Involuntary, Unmerited, Perpetual, Absolute, Hereditary Slavery, Examined; on the Principles of Nature, Reason, Justice, Policy and Scripture* [Lexington, Ky., 1808], pp. 43–49; *Annals of Congress*, 9th Cong., 2nd sess., 200–3; Jesse Torrey, Jr., *A Portraiture of Domestic Slavery, in the United States* [Philadelphia, 1817], p. 39).

slavery was not quite the "Heaven-provoking sin" he had earlier made it out to be. There were reasons, however, why a long-suffering God might have allowed the United States a reprieve. Slavery had been outlawed in the proposed state of Vermont and had disappeared in Massachusetts and New Hampshire. Pennsylvania, Rhode Island, and Connecticut had all adopted acts for gradual emancipation. Even Virginia had removed legal obstructions to private manumission. Only five states had yet shown no "disposition" to promote the cause of freedom.[45]

During the 1780s these signs were highly encouraging to the reformers, who worked from Delaware to Rhode Island to secure laws prohibiting slave importations and providing for gradual emancipation. Interstate communication gave them a sense of united effort in overcoming powerful interests, in implementing the principles of the Revolution, and thus in preventing any historical validation of America's inconsistency. Early in 1784 Moses Brown passed on the news that Congress had proposed the year 1800 as the terminal date for slavery in the new states and perhaps even in the existing states. In 1785, it appeared that even political squabbles could not prevent New York from joining the three other northern states that had adopted laws for gradual emancipation. In 1791, Jonathan Edwards, Jr., predicted that, at the present rate of progress, within fifty years it would "be as shameful for a man to hold a Negro slave, as to be guilty of common robbery or theft." Many Northerners were heartened by reports, especially from Virginia and Maryland, that Southerners were beginning to doubt the profitability of slave labor. The Upper South's hostility to the slave trade could easily be interpreted as the first step toward general emancipation. Benjamin Rush hoped that even South Carolina would respond to the idealism of the Revolution and refuse to import further slaves.[46]

---

[45] [Hopkins], *Dialogue,* appendix to 2nd ed., pp. 69–70.

[46] Moses Brown to James Pemberton, March 20, 1784, Pemberton papers, HSP; Jonathan Edwards, Jr., *The Injustice and Impolicy of the Slave-Trade, and of Slavery of the Africans* . . . (Providence, 1792), p. 30; David Cooper, diary entries, Nov. 1, 1785, Aug. 25, 1786, in *Friends' Review,* XVI, No. 1 (Philadelphia, 1862), pp. 21, 37; John Parrish to William Dillwyn, Oct. 4, 1787, "Slavery Miscellaneous," MSS, Box 2, NYHS; Philadelphia Meeting for Sufferings to London Meeting for Sufferings, Dec. 18, 1788, MS Letterbook, Friends House, London; Benjamin Rush to Nathaniel Greene, Sept. 16, 1782, Lyman H. Butterfield, ed., *Letters of Benjamin Rush* (2 vols., Princeton, 1951), I, 286. For

Above all, the years immediately following the Revolution brought a mood of self-congratulation. For the first time, numerous writers began to review the history not only of slavery, but of antislavery sentiment. To their astonishment, they found that except for a few isolated voices Negro slavery had been virtually unopposed prior to the imperial crisis. Such research gave a new self-consciousness to antislavery leaders. It also led to two conclusions that would have contradictory consequences: first, it appeared that the exertions of a few dedicated individuals could transform the public consciousness; second, since so much had been accomplished in so brief a time, it seemed that post-Revolutionary Americans should marvel less at their own remnants of inconsistency than at the incredible progress of antislavery sentiment.[47]

These themes provided a formula for evasion, or for what the American Convention in 1794 termed "our consolation and encouragement." Recent history showed that one could count on "the irresistible, though silent progress of the principles of true philosophy." "Let us remember," the Convention urged its constituent abolition societies, "although interest and prejudice may oppose, yet the fundamental principles of our government, as well as the progressive and rapid influence of reason and religion, are in our favour."[48] The more

---

some reason Moses Brown thought that the antislavery provision in the Ordinance of 1784 might apply to existing states. The proposal to exclude slavery after 1800 from the new western states had been incorporated in the March 1 report of Jefferson's committee, and was unchanged in the revised report submitted to Congress on March 22. Brown wrote his optimistic letter to John Pemberton on March 20. On April 19, Congress voted to delete the antislavery clause. It is possible that Brown received his earlier mistaken impression from David Howell (see Chapter Three, n. 74).

[47] Swift, *Oration*, pp. 17–21; Noah Webster, *Effects of Slavery, on Morals and Industry* (Hartford, 1793), pp. 33n., 34; Jeremy Belknap and St. George Tucker, "Queries Respecting the Slavery and Emancipation of Negroes in Massachusetts . . . ," *Collections* of the Massachusetts Historical Society, for the Year 1795, IV (Boston, 1795), pp. 193–203, 391–94; James Dana, *The African Slave Trade: A Discourse Delivered in the City of New-Haven, September 9, 1790, before the Connecticut Society for the Promotion of Freedom* (New Haven, 1791), pp. 13ff; [Anon.], *A Poetical Epistle to the Enslaved Africans, in the Character of an Ancient Negro, Born a Slave in Pennsylvania . . .* (Philadelphia, 1790), pp. 3–8, 12–19; Thomas Clarkson, *An Essay on the Slavery and Commerce of the Human Species . . . with Additions* (Georgetown, 1816; originally published 1786), pref.

[48] American Convention, "Appeal of the American Convention of Abolition Societies," *Journal of Negro History*, VI (April, 1921), 200–1; Pennsylvania

that reformers praised American institutions and congratulated themselves on living in an enlightened age, the more prepared they were to postpone the Revolution's goal to future centuries. Thus William Griffith, addressing the New Jersey Abolition Society in 1804, expressed "wonder and gratification" over the immense progress America had made in eradicating slavery and assimilating Negroes to the standards of their superiors. Much was still to be done, especially before "riches increase, and corruption (as it will) gains on the public morals." It was imperative to act while "individual and national feelings are alive to sentiments of charity and justice." Yet Griffith cautioned: "Nor is it to be wished, much less expected, that sudden and general emancipation should take place. A century may and probably will elapse, though every fair exertion shall be made, before it can be eradicated from our country."[49]

In 1793, Noah Webster was not quite so optimistic, although he had no rival in celebrating the glories and promise of American life. His predictions about slavery must be comprehended in juxtaposition with his introductory paean to the new republic:

Here the equalizing genius of the laws distributes property to every citizen. . . . here no tithes, no rack rents, no lordly exactions of gratuities and fines for alienation, no arbitrary impositions of taxes, harass the cultivator of the soil and repress his exertions. Here no beggarly monks and fryars, no princely ecclesiastics with their annual income of millions, no idle

---

Abolition Society to London Committee for the Abolition of the Slave Trade, May 6, 1794, Pennsylvania Abolition Society MSS, IV, HSP; New York Manumission Society, MS Minutes, VI, 95, NYHS; Benjamin Franklin, *The Works of Benjamin Franklin*, ed. by Jared Sparks (Chicago, 1882), II, 515–16. Even in 1820, Elihu Embree, the Quaker editor of the Jonesborough, Tennessee, *Emancipator*, could exclaim over the remarkable progress of antislavery sentiment during the past twenty years. If the trend toward enlightenment continued another twenty years, he wrote, the prediction that slavery would be as universally unpopular as piracy was "almost deducible from mathematical calculation" (*Emancipator*, June 30, 1820). However, a few months later Embree was much distressed by a letter from Governor George Poindexter of Mississippi, which turned the providential argument against even gradual abolition: "The same providence which has permitted African slavery in the new world, will point to the period of its happy termination" (*ibid.*, Sept. 30, 1820). In response, Embree warned that if slavery should continue a few generations longer, it "will produce such scenes of misery and destruction for our posterity to wade through, as have not been exceeded in the history of man."

[49] [William Griffith], *Address of the President of the New-Jersey Society, for Promoting the Abolition of Slavery, to the General Meeting at Trenton* . . . (Trenton, N.J., 1804), pp. 5–8.

court-pensioners and titled mendicants, no spies to watch and betray the unsuspecting citizen, no tyrant with his train of hounds, bastards and mistresses. . . . Here no commercial or corporation monopolies give exclusive advantages to favored individuals . . . no sacramental test bars the conscientious sectary from places of trust and emolument . . . here no monasteries, convents and nunneries, the retreats of idleness and the nurseries of superstition and debauchery. . . . Here every man finds employment, and the road is open for the poorest citizen to amass wealth by labor and economy, and by his talents and virtue to raise himself to the highest offices of State.

And so on and so on, to the vista of wealth, manufacturing, and commerce: "and in the short period of 170 years, since our ancestors landed on these shores, a trackless wilderness, inhabited only by savages and wild beasts, is converted into fruitful fields and meadows, more highly cultivated than one half of Europe."

During his travels Webster had seen how the fields were cultivated in South Carolina, and he reminded his readers that the proportion of slaves in the American population was "a circumstance which cannot fail to allay the joy, that the prosperous state of the country would otherwise inspire in every patriotic bosom." In Webster's view this circumstance was an unfortunate accident, the product of the misguided policy of an unenlightened age. Oddly enough, however, his model for emancipation had nothing to do with the brave new world where "the mind of man, as free as the air he breathes, may exert all its energy, and by expanding its powers to distant and various objects, its faculties may be enlarged to a degree hitherto unknown." Rather, when Webster thought of emancipation his mind turned to the gradual elevation of serfs, which had presumably taken place in the depraved environment that Americans had escaped: "Indeed if we judge from the fate of villanage [*sic*] in many parts of Europe, it is no illfounded prediction, that slavery in this country will be utterly extirpated in the course of two centuries, perhaps in a much shorter period, without any extraordinary efforts to abolish it."[50]

Webster recognized that such progress would be too slow to satisfy "the friends of humanity, in this enlightened period of the world," and he called for efforts, both public and private, "to accelerate the progress of freedom, with all convenient speed." Nevertheless, the whole point of his argument was the peril of any sudden abolition.

[50] Webster, *Effects of Slavery*, pp. 32–34, 37.

Negro emancipation would come inevitably, without extraordinary effort, although the task might take as long as had America's slow emancipation from Europe. Webster was not alone in seeing the post-Revolutionary years as a midpoint between the origins of North American slavery (and colonization), and a terminal date of about 1960. Nor was he alone in screening out any perceptions that might cast doubt on his belief in irresistible progress. Like various other anti-slavery writers of the time, Webster found himself in the anomalous position of exclaiming over the "improved" condition of southern slaves. Masters had been touched by the benevolent spirit of the age, and had also come to appreciate that kindness was good policy. American slaves already enjoyed many of the privileges of English villeins, and could never again be forced, for example, to dig more than a quarter of an acre of land in a day or to work on the days they called their own! Indicating a similar frame of mind, the American Convention urged in 1798 that slaves should be quietly submissive to their masters, since this would lead to better treatment and might also help persuade masters of the injustice of human bondage.[51]

But however sanguine Americans might be about the distant future, they could not escape the idea of declension, since virtually any statute on slavery was bound to compromise the "higher law" principle of natural rights. It was clear that union required the postponement of emancipation, not only in the South, but in most of the northern states as well. Yet the Revolution had been rooted in the "higher law" doctrine, as quoted by Benezet, that "No Legislature on Earth . . . can alter the Nature of things, or make that to be lawful, which is contrary to the Law of God." The success of the Revolution presumably showed the danger as well as the illegitimacy of laws based on expediency, of laws like those of Parliament which had sanctioned the Guinea trade, and which, as Benezet put it, had brought "under hard Bondage a people over whom the Parliament had not the least shadow of Rights." In 1783, Benezet exhorted British Quakers to begin pressing the king and Parliament to abolish the iniquitous traffic. At the same time, however, he wrote to Benjamin Franklin, then in Paris, observing that it was "sorrowfully astonishing that after the declaration so strongly and clearly made of the value & right of liberty on this

[51] *Ibid.,* p. 37; Swift, *Oration,* p. 17; Justice, *Warner Mifflin,* pp. 99–100; American Convention of Abolition Societies, *Minutes and Proceedings of the Fifth Convention of Delegates* . . . (Philadelphia, 1798), p. 18.

continent, no state but that of Pennsylvania & that imperfectly, have yet taken a step towards the total abolition of slavery."[52]

Hugh Henry Brackenridge mockingly praised Pennsylvania's act on the grounds of expediency which, he said, should be extended still further:

On this principle, I have always thought a defect in the criminal codes of most nations, not giving license to the perpetrators of offences, to proceed, for a limited time, in larcenies, burglaries, &c. until they get their hands out of use to these pursuits, and in use to others. For it must be greatly inconvenient to thieves and cut-throats, who have engaged in this way of life, and run great risks in acquiring skill in their employment, to be obliged all at once to withdraw their hands, and lay aside picking locks, and apply themselves to industry in other ways, for a livelihood.

Legislators, he warned, should never confuse the slavery issue with moral doubts regarding the original right of capturing or subjugating Africans, since that would raise difficulties over the *"natural right to hold a slave for a moment, even whether the law sanctioned it or not;* in which case we should find it necessary to go as far as the fanatics in religion, and set our slaves *free altogether."*[53]

This was the "higher law" doctrine advanced by George Wallace, by the French Encyclopedists, and by a scattering of American Quakers and Calvinists. In America the state constitutions supposedly embodied the "higher law" of natural rights. Yet David Cooper expressed dismay over the constitutions which showed such extraordinary care in guarding the rights and privileges of white citizens, but which gave "no gleam of notice" to the oppressed Africans.[54] The Vermont constitution of 1777 specifically outlawed slavery. Several Massachusetts towns objected to the lack of such a clause in the Massachusetts constitution of 1778. But the framers of the new 1780 constitution contented themselves with a general declaration that "all men are born free and equal, and have certain natural, essential, and unalienable rights."

[52] [Anthony Benezet], *A Short Account of that Part of Africa, Inhabited by the Negroes* . . . (2nd ed., Philadelphia, 1762), p. 52; Benezet, *Some Historical Account of Guinea* . . . (Philadelphia, 1771), p. 131; Benezet to John Gough, May 29, 1783; to Benjamin Franklin, March 5, 1783; to John Pemberton, Aug. 10, 1783, in George S. Brookes, *Friend Anthony Benezet* (Philadelphia, 1937), pp. 375–76, 387, 396.

[53] Brackenridge, *Modern Chivalry*, II, 138–40.

[54] [Cooper], *Serious Address*, p. 21.

Jeremy Belknap later wrote that this bill of rights, which roughly followed the wording of the Virginia Convention of 1776, had been inserted "with a particular view to establishing the liberty of the negroes on a general principle, and so it was understood by the people at large; but some doubted whether this was sufficient." Moses Brown, for one, was convinced by 1784 that the Massachuetts constitution had put an end to slavery, and that Negroes had been adjudged to be free. Various historians have tried to penetrate the obscurity surrounding the now famous "Quock Walker cases," but have reached little agreement on the actual process of emancipation in Massachusetts. Here it is sufficient to say that by the early 1780s Massachusetts slaveholders had little confidence in their legal claims to proprietorship, in part because of the actions of town governments; that an attorney like Levi Lincoln was prepared to write an eloquent brief condemning slavery on religious and "higher law" principles, but with little reference to the constitution; and that while individual slaves were freed by jury decisions—or by their boldness in simply leaving their masters—no court specifically and clearly ruled that slavery was unconstitutional, although Chief Justice William Cushing instructed a jury in 1783 that slavery was inconsistent with the constitution. Regardless of popular opinion in Massachusetts, there was no publicized case that encouraged constitutional emancipation in other states with similar bills of rights. In 1794, for example, the counsel of the Pennsylvania Abolition Society was evenly divided on whether the 1790 state declaration of rights had outlawed slavery. Though the Society pursued the question in court, the High Court of Errors and Appeals judged that slavery had existed legally in the state prior to the 1790 constitution, and was unaffected by the declaration of rights.[55]

[55] Arthur Zilversmit, "Quok Walker, Mumbet, and the Abolition of Slavery in Massachusetts," *William and Mary Quarterly,* 3rd ser., XXV (Oct., 1968), 614–24; Horace Gray, "The Commonwealth *v.* Nathaniel Jennison," Massachusetts Historical Society *Proceedings,* 1st ser., XIII (Boston, 1875), 293–99; William O'Brien, "Did the Jennison Case Outlaw Slavery in Massachusetts?" *William and Mary Quarterly,* 3rd ser., XVII (April, 1960), 219–41; John D. Cushing, "The Cushing Court and the Abolition of Slavery in Massachusetts: More Notes on the 'Quock Walker Case,'" *American Journal of Legal History,* V (1961), 118–44; Elaine MacEacheren, "Emancipation of Slavery in Massachusetts: A Re-examination, 1770–1790," *Journal of Negro History,* LV (Oct., 1970), 289–306; Robert M. Spector, "The Quock Walker Cases (1781–1783)—

Encouraged by signs of unmistakable progress, abolitionists also fell within the yawning gap between Revolutionary expectations and political realities. In 1776, Samuel Hopkins could assure the honorable members of the Continental Congress that their resolution against the slave trade "leaves in our minds no doubt of your being sensible of the equal unrighteousness and oppression, as well as inconsistence with ourselves, in holding so many hundreds of thousands of blacks in slavery, who have equal right to freedom with ourselves." He could express confidence that they would apply their wisdom "to bring about the total abolition of slavery." By 1787 he was reporting to Moses Brown that various Rhode Island clergymen objected to petitioning the state assembly on the subject of the slave trade, since "the present ruling part in the Assembly, have appeared to be so destitute of all principles of justice, or regard to it . . . that there is an impropriety in applying to them for justice." No doubt Hopkins was surprised when the assembly, in that very year, voted to prohibit the slave trade![56]

But in 1787 Hopkins was well aware of the debates in a larger

---

Slavery, Its Abolition, and Negro Citizenship in Early Massachusetts," *Journal of Negro History*, LIII (Jan., 1968), 12–32; "Letters and Documents Relating to Slavery in Massachusetts" (the Jeremy Belknap papers), *Collections* of the Massachusetts Historical Society, 5th ser., III (Boston, 1877), 197–203, 390–91, 438–42; Moore, *Notes on History of Slavery*, pp. 187, 202–21; Moses Brown to James Pemberton, March 20, 1784, Pemberton papers, XL, HSP; Pennsylvania Abolition Society, MSS, III, 5 (April 29, 1794), HSP; Edward R. Turner, *The Negro in Pennsylvania* (Washington, 1911), pp. 82–83; Jabez D. Hammond, *The History of Political Parties in the State of New-York* (Syracuse, 1852), I, 580–81. O'Brien and Zilversmit discuss the correspondence on the constitutional issue between Massachusetts officials and Jared Ingersoll, an attorney for the Pennsylvania Abolition Society. Although the Pennsylvania courts refused to declare slavery unconstitutional, a legislative committee, appointed to consider petitions that French West Indian refugees be exempted from the provisions of the abolition act, reported in 1792 that slavery was contrary to the laws of nature, to the dictates of justice, and to the constitution of the state. Since the institution was "unlawful in itself," it was beyond the authority of the legislature "to authorize it under any modification whatsoever." One may also note that according to Charles Cotesworth Pinckney, some of the framers of the federal Constitution had opposed a bill of rights because such bills usually began by declaring "all men are by nature born free," when in fact "a large part of our property consists in men who are actually born slaves" (Max Farrand, ed., *The Records of the Federal Convention of 1787* [4 vols., New Haven, 1937], III, 256). Of course there was no such statement in the bill of rights finally adopted.

[56] [Hopkins], *Dialogue*, pp. 8–9; Hopkins to Moses Brown, Oct. 22, 1787, Donnan, ed., *Documents*, III, 343.

political arena. Along with other antislavery leaders, he felt that the Constitutional Convention should be bound by the precedents of the Revolution, particularly the 1774 slave-trade resolution and the Declaration of Independence. There is fragmentary evidence of organized attempts on the part of abolitionists to influence the Philadelphia delegates. Since 1783 the Quakers, especially, had gained experience from their lobbying campaigns with state assemblies, with the Continental Congress, and, via their British connections, with Parliament. In petitioning the Constitutional Convention, the Pennsylvania Abolition Society appealed to the Revolutionary resolutions against the slave trade, to Europe as a judge of hypocrisy, and to the certainty of divine judgment. Tench Coxe, a member of the Society and one of the earliest champions of the Constitution, later confided to James Madison that it had required tremendous efforts to suppress the pleas of overzealous but honest men. "A very strong paper was drawn & put into my hands," he wrote, "to procure the signature of Dr. Franklin to be presented to the federal convention—I enclosed to the Dr. with my opinion that it would be a very improper season & place to hazard the Application."[57]

At this time Coxe was in correspondence with prominent British abolitionists who were eager for information on the achievements of emancipated Negroes.[58] Coxe, an ardent Federalist and proponent of industrial progress, shared with the more progressive British reformers a common set of values. What separated them—and what proved to be a liability to American antislavery—was the different meaning of rising "establishments." In 1787, even in 1792, England could hardly match America in the number of prominent citizens who theoretically embraced the antislavery cause: statesmen of international rank, legislators, lawyers, clergymen, merchants, bankers, manufacturers,

[57] Pennsylvania Abolition Society MSS, I, 17, HSP; Tench Coxe to James Madison, March 31, 1790, Farrand, ed., *Records*, III, 361. On August 17, 1787, the New York Manumission Society was informed that the Convention would probably not consider the question of slavery. The Society resolved not to send a memorial to the Convention on the subject of "manumission of slaves." This latter phrase is crossed out in the existing manuscript, and at least one page has clearly been destroyed, a fact which probably indicates the sensitivity of the question (New York Manumission Society, MS Minutes, VI, 72–74, NYHS). The Convention's explosive debate on the slave trade came five days later, on August 22.

[58] See James Phillips to Tench Coxe, Dec. 5, 1787, Pennsylvania Abolition Society MSS, I, 19, HSP.

and prophets of the new age. But the leading English spokesmen for abolition were not faced with a constitutional convention, the success of which depended on the compliance of West Indian delegates.

One may object that accommodation is the fulcrum of politics, that British antislavery leaders could bend when the occasion demanded, and that the weaknesses of antislavery principles cannot be gauged by what legislators did or left undone. In America, however, it was the Revolutionary expectations that made the difference. Nor could Europe offer examples of virgin states, such as Kentucky, where colonizers were re-enacting the drama of separation and self-determination. As David Rice exhorted the Danville convention (which did not heed his words): "Holding men in slavery is the national vice of Virginia; and, while a part of that state, we were partakers of the guilt. As a separate state, we are just now come to the birth; and it depends upon our free choice whether we shall be born in this sin, or innocent of it."[59]

The logic of the Revolution suggested that such principles might have prevailed at the Constitutional Convention. For a time it was by no means clear exactly which principles had prevailed. The text, like that of the King James Bible, scrupulously avoided the word "slave."[60] On November 8, 1787, an anonymous Pennsylvanian complained that "the words, dark and ambiguous, such as no plain man of common sense would have used, are evidently chosen to conceal from Europe, that in this enlightened century, the practice of slavery has its advocates among men in the highest stations."[61]

Luther Martin, who as a disgruntled delegate had walked out of the Convention and had refused to sign the Constitution, explained what

[59] David Rice, *A Kentucky Protest Against Slavery: Slavery Inconsistent with Justice and Good Policy, Proved by a Speech, Delivered in the Convention, Held at Danville, Kentucky* (New York, 1812; originally published 1792), p. 13.

[60] Luther Martin pointed out that the Convention had disingenuously avoided a number of "offensive" words, such as "national," "stamps," and "slaves" (Jonathan Elliot, ed., *The Debates in the Several State Conventions* . . . [Philadelphia, 1876], I, 372). For the reasons behind the avoidance of the word "slaves," see *ibid.*, III, 98. The translators of the King James Bible used the word once once (Rev. 18:13), as the equivalent of *mancipium* in the Vulgate; ordinarily, they chose "bondsman," "bondmaid," or "servant" for such terms as *doulos, servus, mancipium,* and *ancilla,* all of which denoted varieties of slavery (P. R. Coleman-Norton, ed., *Studies in Roman Economic and Social History* [Princeton, 1951], pp. 155–56n.).

[61] Quoted in W. E. B. DuBois, *The Suppression of the African Slave-Trade to the United States of America, 1638–1870* (New York, 1896), p. 63.

lay behind the dark and ambiguous words. Leading a campaign in Maryland to oppose ratification, he exposed the deal within the committee, of which he was a member, whereby the New England states had agreed to give the slave trade a twenty-year immunity from federal restriction in exchange for southern votes to eliminate any restrictions on navigation acts. To the rest of the world, Martin wrote, it must appear "absurd and disgraceful to the last degree, that we should *except* from the exercise of that power [to regulate commerce], the *only branch* of *commerce* which is *unjustifiable in its nature,* and *contrary* to the rights of *mankind.*" Moreover, the authors had been so anxious to avoid a word "which might be odious in the ears of Americans" that they had inadvertently authorized Congress to impose a duty of ten dollars on any free immigrant who entered the United States.[62]

Martin, who had graduated from the Presbyterian College of New Jersey in the afterglow of the Great Awakening, expanded eloquently on the themes and inconsistency, apostasy, and divine judgment. The slave-trade and three-fifths compromises "ought to be considered as a *solemn mockery of,* and *insult to that God* whose protection we had then implored, and could not fail to hold us up in *detestation,* and render us *contemptible* to every *true friend* of liberty in the world." It ought to be considered, Martin warned,

that national *crimes* can only be, and *frequently are punished* in this world, by national punishments; and that the *continuance* of the slave-trade, and thus giving it a *national sanction* and *encouragement,* ought to be considered as *justly exposing* us to the *displeasure* and *vengeance* of *Him,* who is equally Lord of all, and who views with equal eye the poor *African slave* and his *American master.*[63]

At the Convention, a number of delegates made such arguments, but were seldom free from the suspicion of ulterior motives. George Mason, for example, who also refused to sign the Constitution, had much to say about the evils of slavery and the dangers of divine judgment. Like Martin, he was outraged by the coalition between the states of New England and the Deep South, a coalition which had shattered the expected alignment of agrarian interests. Yet in opposing ratifica-

[62] Elliot, ed., *Debates,* I, 372–73; Farrand, ed., *Records,* III, 210–12.
[63] Farrand, ed., *Records,* III, 211. Martin advocated gradual emancipation carried out by the federal government.

tion in Virginia, Mason qualified his antislavery principles by arguing that "though this infamous traffic be continued, we have no security for the property of that kind which we have already. There is no clause in this Constitution to secure it; . . . So that 'they have done what they ought not to have done, and have left undone what they ought to have done.' "[64]

During the Convention debates Charles Cotesworth Pinckney, of South Carolina, explained that Virginians could afford a specious humanitarianism: "S. Carolina & Georgia cannot do without slaves. As to Virginia she will gain by stopping the importations. Her slaves will rise in value, & she has more than she wants." Oliver Ellsworth, of Connecticut, pointed out that if slavery were to be considered in a moral light, "we ought to go farther and free those already in the Country." This was a gibe at Mason. In justice to Georgia and South Carolina, Ellsworth argued, the delegates should remember that slaves "multiply so fast in Virginia & Maryland that it is cheaper to raise than import them, whilest in the sickly rice swamps foreign supplies are necessary." He was confident, in any event, that poor laborers would soon become so plentiful "as to render slaves useless. Slavery in time will not be a speck in our Country. Provision is already made in Connecticut for abolishing it." Pinckney, on the other hand, held "that the importation of slaves would be for the interest of the whole Union. The more slaves, the more produce to employ in carrying trade; the more consumption also, and the more of this, the more of revenue for the common treasury."[65]

It is not surprising that the Constitution was subject to a variety of interpretations or that its defenders helped to popularize conflicting expectations. General William Heath assured the Massachusetts ratifying convention that "the federal convention went as far as they could; the migration or importation, &c. is confined to the states, now *existing only,* new states cannot claim it." Congress, he promised, had already prohibited slavery in the new states. William Dawes added "that although slavery is not smitten by an apoplexy, yet it has received a mortal wound and will die of a consumption." With these judgments James Wilson entirely agreed. Speaking to the Pennsylvania convention, as one of the framers of the Constitution, he interpreted the slave-trade clause "as laying the foundation for banishing slavery out

[64] *Ibid.,* II, 221–22, 370; Elliot, ed., *Debates,* III, 452–53.
[65] Farrand, ed., *Records,* II, 370–71.

of this country; and though the period is more distant than I could wish, yet it will produce the same kind of gradual change which was pursued in Pennsylvania." Wilson also expressed confidence that Congress would never allow the introduction of slaves in the new states.[66]

In Virginia, however, Governor Edmund Randolph, also one of the framers, hinted at undisclosed understandings which convinced even South Carolina that slavery would be secure: "I believe, whatever we may think here, that there was not a member of the Virginia delegation who had the smallest suspicion of the abolition of slavery." Farther to the south, Charles Cotesworth Pinckney had to meet objections that South Carolina had conceded too much. Unfortunately, he explained, "your delegates had to contend with the religious and political prejudices of the Eastern and Middle States, and with the interested and inconsistent opinion of Virginia, who was warmly opposed to our importing more slaves." Yet the Constitution in no way ruled that the slave trade must cease in 1808; it provided security that the general government could never emancipate slaves in the states; it guaranteed the right "to recover our slaves in whatever part of America they may take refuge, which is a right we had not before." All things considered, Pinckney said, "we have made the best terms for the security of this species of property it was in our power to make. We would have made better if we could; but, on the whole, I do not think them bad." Robert Barnwell was even more sanguine. By 1808, he predicted, the New England states would be the main carriers of slaves cargoes, and it would thus be in their interest to encourage the trade as long as possible. "I am of opinion," he concluded, "that, without we ourselves put a stop to them, the traffic in negroes will continue forever."[67]

A few of the antislavery leaders appreciated that a fundamental law which satisfied so many interests could only be interpreted as the ultimate and fatal betrayal of the Revolution. In a letter to Moses Brown, William Rotch anticipated the view of Garrison: the Constitution was "founded on *Slavery* and that is on *Blood*." But the sharpest public attacks on the Constitution came from men like Luther Martin

[66] Elliot, ed., *Debates,* I, 60, 123–24n.; II (Philadelphia, 1891 ed.), 451–52. For problems in the reporting of Wilson's speech, see Farrand, ed., *Records,* III, 437n.

[67] Farrand, ed., *Records,* III, 253–54; Elliot, ed., *Debates,* IV, 272–73, 286, 296–97.

and George Mason, who opposed ratification on a variety of grounds. And as Benjamin Rush informed Jeremy Belknap, the vast majority of Quakers were "highly Federal": "The appeals, therefore, that have been made to the humane & laudable prejudices of our Quakers by our Antifederal writers upon the subject of negro slavery, have been greeted by that prudent society with silence and contempt."[68]

By 1789 the Pennsylvania Abolition Society could assure the British abolitionists that no apostasy had occurred. The large number of Negroes in some states simply prevented "making a general arrangement *at this moment,* that should carry the American principles on this subject to their full length." Nevertheless, the Constitution should be considered as a testimonial against the slave trade, which would doubtless be abolished by the individual states in the near future. Then, in a classic use of projection, the Pennsylvanians added: "We are very sensible of the difficulties, that must arise to you in Great Britain from the prejudices & arts of interested men. But similar prejudices have been *removed,* & similar arts have been *defeated* in this country."[69]

Declension and Justification

The American people, according to the First American Convention of Abolition Societies, could take pride in having originated the international movement against the slave trade. Yet by allowing slavery itself to continue, Americans were impeding the cause of political liberty in Europe. A slaveholding nation could not serve the world as a model of freedom.[70]

[68] Thomas Drake, *Quakers and Slavery in America* (New Haven, 1950), p. 102; Donnan, ed., *Documents,* III, 342, n. 4, 343; Jeremy Belknap papers, *Collections* of the Massachusetts Historical Society, 6th ser., IV (Boston, 1891), 397. In 1790, Rhode Island proposed a Constitutional amendment condemning the slave trade and calling on Congress "as soon as may be" to promote and establish laws and regulations to prevent the importation of slaves (Pennsylvania Abolition Society MSS, II, 38, HSP).

[69] Pennsylvania Abolition Society MSS, II, 14, HSP. For an explanation of the sudden apotheosis of the Constitution, see Lance Banning, "Republican Ideology and the Triumph of the Constitution, 1789 to 1793," *William and Mary Quarterly,* 3rd ser., XXXI (April, 1974), 167–188.

[70] American Convention, *Minutes* (1794), p. 22; American Convention, *Address* (1794), p. 5; Dana, *African Slave Trade,* p. 30; Buchanan, *Oration,* pp. 13–14; H. M. Wagstaff, ed., *Minutes of the North Carolina Manumission Society* (Chapel Hill, 1934), p. 39; [Joseph Blunt], *An Examination of the Expedience*

This argument had far-reaching implications. If the entire world was on the eve of revolution, as Zephaniah Swift told the Connecticut Abolition Society in 1791, did this mean Americans would cheer for black slaves who fought for their own inalienable rights? In 1786 a correspondent wrote *The New York Journal* that recent murders in the West Indies indicated what punishment the buyers of human flesh could expect. Tyrannical countries everywhere would soon face the deluge, and "the greatest philanthropist will not afford even a pitying sigh for those who have been, or may be plundered, tormented, and even massacred by the avenging hands of their purchased slaves."[71]

Five years later the blacks of St. Domingue put the American ideology to its most critical test: if slaves could demonstrate their capacity for freedom by fighting for it, then how could white Americans sustain their double standard and still remain loyal to their Revolutionary ideals? Abraham Bishop, a Connecticut radical and Yale classmate of Noah Webster, Joel Barlow, and Zephaniah Swift, put the issue in clear-cut terms: "If freedom depends upon colour, and if the blacks were born for slaves, those in the West India islands may be called insurgents and murderers." But surely, Bishop hoped, Americans were too open-minded to believe that color changes the natural rights of men. The cause of the blacks was as just as that of the white American patriots. The latter had drawn blood in order to rid themselves of illegitimate taxes. The West Indian slaves had been subjected to the most barbarous cruelty: "Then shall we preach lessons of coolness and moderation to the blacks?" If the slaves had been treated with mildness, they might have used milder measures for achieving their natural rights. Until this moment, Bishop noted, Americans had seen the hand of Providence in every struggle against despotic rule. "Shall we now sacrifice principle to a paltry partiality for colour?"[72]

---

and Constitutionality of Prohibiting Slavery in the State of Missouri (New York, 1819), p. 13.

[71] Swift, *Oration*, pp. 22–23; Dwight, *Oration*, pp. 6, 16–18, 23; Buchanan, *Oration*, pp. 15–16; *New-York Journal, or the New-York Journal Weekly Register*, June 22, 1786. The latter newspaper also carried advertisements for slave sales and runaways.

[72] J. P. Martin [Abraham Bishop], *American Museum*, XII (Nov., 1792), 299–300; *National Gazette*, ed. by Philip Freneau, II (No. 79, July 31, 1793), 314–15; *Columbian Centinel*, XVI (Sept. 21, 1791), 10; Dwight, *Oration*, pp. 16–17; Franklin B. Dexter, "Abraham Bishop, of Connecticut, and his Writings,"

But as the Marquis de Condorcet had said, in 1776, "ils sont noirs et cela change toutes nos idées." Some months before Abraham Bishop celebrated the cause of the blacks, the *Amis des noirs* had issued a public manifesto that echoed the "higher law" doctrine of George Wallace and the *Encyclopédie:*

Nous croyons bien que tous les hommes naissent libres et égaux en droits, quelle que soit la couleur de leur peau, quel que soit le pays où le sort les fasse naître.

Nous croyons bien que nul homme ne peut aliéner sa liberté, que nul homme ne peut . . . ravir la liberté de son semblable, que nulle société ne peut consacrer ou légitimer un pareil brigandage.

Nous croyons bien, que malgré les loix, les habitudes, les usages contraires, l'esclave reste libre, parce qu'on ne peut proscrire contre la nature; qu'en conséquence, la restitution de la liberté n'est pas un bienfait, une faveur; mais un devoir rigoureux, mais une acte de la justice, qui déclare ce qui est, plutôt qu'il ne décrète ce qui doit être.

Nothing could be clearer or more uncompromising. None of the early American antislavery societies issued a declaration that so directly challenged the lawfulness of human bondage. Yet the French reformers seemed far less sensitive to the question of "inconsistency" when it came to reconciling "les intérêts de l'humanité avec les intérêts des propriétaires":

Mais nous croyons aussi . . . qu'affranchir subitement les esclaves noirs, seroit une opération, non-seulement fatale pour les colonies, mais que, dans l'état d'abjection et de nullité où la cupidité a réduit les noirs . . . ce seroit abandonner à eux-mêmes, et sans secours, des enfans au berceau, ou des êtres mutilés et impuissans.[73]

Proceedings of the Massachusetts Historical Society, 2nd ser., XIX (1905), 190–99. Bishop toured France in 1787, opposed ratification of the Constitution, and ultimately became an ardent Jeffersonian in Federalist Connecticut.

[73] Marie Jean Condorcet, *Remarques sur les pensées de Pascal,* in *Oeuvres* (Paris, 1847–1850), III, 647; *Adresse de la Société des Amis des Noirs, à l'assemblée nationale, à toutes les villes de commerce, à toutes les manufactures, aux colonies, à toutes les sociétés des amis de la constitution* (1st ed., Paris, 1791), p. 76; (2nd ed., Paris, 1791), pp. 107–08. The quotation can be freely translated as follows:

"We hold that all men are born free and with equal rights, regardless of their color, their nationality, or their condition of birth.

"We hold that no man can give up his freedom, that no man can seize the freedom of his fellow man, and that no society can legitimate such crime.

"We hold that, regardless of contrary laws, customs, and practices, the slave

In France, as in America, this was the formula for dulling the edge of revolutionary doctrine: the evil of slavery justified its perpetuation, since avarice and oppression had rendered the blacks incapable of freedom; they were objects for compassion, candidates for uplift and reform; on a conceptual level, they had never lost their liberty or human rights; existentially, they were defined as being incapable of free choice.

In 1793, French refugees, many accompanied by their personal slaves, began streaming into American port cities. In 1804 the triumphant blacks proclaimed the republic of Haiti. In the interim, which witnessed Gabriel Prosser's slave conspiracy in Virginia, Americans became terrified by what Winthrop Jordan has termed "the cancer of revolution." As Jordan observes, there was more than a concern for security behind the shrill warnings, the laws excluding West Indian blacks, and the attempts to suppress all discussion of slavery: "The ostentatiousness of all this caution is suggestive: beyond a reasoned fear of domestic insurrection seems to have lain a desire to banish the reality of St. Domingo."[74] For that reality demolished the myth that slaves were "les enfans au berceau . . . êtres mutilés et impuissans." It also exposed the hollowness of American pretensions. If St. Domingue strengthened the clamor to end the slave trade, it also dealt a crushing blow to the abolition movement.

The unwelcome spread of revolutionary violence—in France as well as in the West Indies—made it all the easier for abolitionists to rationalize the succession of grim events which undercut earlier ex-

---

is always free, since the law of nature cannot be annulled. Accordingly, the restoration of a slave's freedom is not a gift or an act of charity. It is rather a compelling duty, an act of justice, which simply affirms an existing truth—not an ideal which ought to be.

"But we also hold that the immediate emancipation of Negro slaves would be a measure not only fatal for our colonies, but a measure which, since our greed has reduced the blacks to a degraded and impotent state, would be equivalent to abandoning and refusing aid to infants in their cradles or to helpless cripples."

[74] Jordan, *White over Black,* pp. 380, 384. The "Gabriel plot," according to the American Convention, showed the urgency of the amelioration and gradual abolition of slavery (*Minutes of the Proceedings of the Seventh Convention of Delegates* . . . [Philadelphia, 1801], pp. 37–39). Thomas Branagan warned that unless the slaves were freed and colonized in the West, the blacks would reenact another St. Domingue, avenging themselves against whites softened by luxury (*Serious Remonstrances, Addressed to the Citizens of the Northern States* . . . [Philadelphia, 1805], pp. 15–17, 46–47, 78–79).

pectations. The defeats began even before the fear of revolutionary contagion: in the First Congress, the explosive reaction of Southerners to moderate antislavery petitions defined the terms of the federal "compact," intimidated future protest, and virtually precluded the British strategy of working through "friends" in the central government. This critical setback was followed by the Fugitive Slave Act of 1793 and by the clear indication that American lawmakers put the supposed property rights of slaveholders above the "inalienable rights" of northern free Negroes who were being kidnapped and sold into the South in ever-increasing numbers. The abolition societies then had to reconcile themselves to the admission of Kentucky and Tennessee as slave states; to North Carolina's re-enslavement of manumitted blacks; to Virginia's and Maryland's legal retaliation against abolitionists who sponsored freedom suits (in 1797, Virginia reformers complained that a new law was "calculated to destroy almost every suggestion of hope, that any person . . . can obtain liberty by due process of law, however valid their claim, or however indiputable their claim, or however indisputable their title"); to the infiltration and subversion of the Alexandria (Virginia) Abolition Society; to Congress' acceptance of slavery in Louisiana; to South Carolina's reopening of the slave trade; and finally, to the shock of the Missouri crisis and the attempts to legalize slavery in Indiana and Illinois.[75]

During the first two decades of this declension, the abolition societies called for renewed dedication, warned against discouragement, emphasized the need for caution, and complained that their aims and

[75] Pennsylvania Abolition Society MSS, II (1790) 28–31; IV (1797), 23–24, HSP; Warner Mifflin, *A Serious Expostulation with the Members of the House of Representatives* (Philadelphia, 1793), pp. 3–15; Justice, *Warner Mifflin*, p. 134; American Convention, *Minutes and Proceedings* (1798), p. 11; *Minutes and Proceedings* (1801), pp. 30–33; *Minutes and Proceedings of the Eighth Convention of Delegates* . . . (Philadelphia, 1803), p. 26; *Minutes and Proceedings of the Ninth American Convention* . . . (Philadelphia, 1804), pp. 40–42, 47; *Minutes and Proceedings of the Tenth American Convention* . . . (Philadelphia, 1805), pp. 19, 21; *Minutes of the Eighteenth Session of the American Convention* . . . (Philadelphia, 1823), p. 11; American Convention, MS Minutes of the Acting Committee of the American Convention, pp. 5–7 (July 12, 1804); p. 17 (June 3, 1805), HSP; MacLeod, "Racial Attitudes," pp. 200–10; Edwards, *Injustice and Impolicy*, pp. 23–24; Philadelphia Meeting for Sufferings to London Meeting for Sufferings, Dec. 28, 1804, MS Letterbook, Friends House, London; [Blunt], *Examination*, pp. 3–15; *Philanthropist*, Dec. 5, 1817; Jeremiah Evarts, "The Missouri Question," *Panoplist and Missionary Herald*, XVI (Jan.–Feb. 1820), 15–24, 59–72.

methods had been badly misrepresented. It was essential, by 1804, to select officers who

have their zeal tempered with prudence and knowledge; for we are Sensible, that for want of Sound discretion on the part of some well meaning, but over zealous individuals, the views and conduct of the Body at large have been grossly misunderstood: the Cause has suffered undeserv'd reproach in the minds of some of our fellow Citizens.[76]

In 1808 the Pennsylvania Society concluded that it would be too risky to authorize formal agencies in the southern states, as their Acting Committee had recommended. More attention should be given to the "moral and intellectual improvement" of the blacks in Philadelphia, since the abolitionists' very success had encouraged an influx of black paupers and criminals who had damaged the cause. The Philadelphians noted that both public sentiment and the attitude of the courts were much less liberal than they used to be. The Ninth American Convention urged the New York Society to impress free blacks with the thought that future emancipations might well depend on their own good conduct. In 1809 the Wilmington (Delaware) Society assured the Convention: "We feel with you, that Liberty may become an *evil*, without a previous qualification for it's [*sic*] enjoyment, and a preparation on the part of the subject, of becoming useful to himself, to his family, and his country."[77]

Despite such pressures of fear and accommodation, there were con-

[76] New York Manumission Society, MS Minutes, VI, 161, 164–66, VII, 115–16, NYHS; Pennsylvania Abolition Society MSS, III, 16, HSP; Philadelphia Meeting for Sufferings to London Meeting for Sufferings, March 15, 1792, MS Letterbook, Friends House, London; Jeremy Belknap to Ebenezer Hazard, May 7, 1790, *Collections* of the Massachusetts Historical Society, 5th ser., III (Boston, 1877), 220–22; American Convention, *Minutes and Proceedings* (1798), p. 19; *Minutes and Proceedings* (1804), pp. 38–39; MS Minutes of Acting Committee (1809), pp. 94–95, HSP.

[77] Pennsylvania Abolition Society to Twelfth American Convention, Jan. 2, 1808, Pennsylvania Abolition Society MSS, VI, HSP; P. E. Thomas to John Parrish, Aug. 31, 1806, Cox, Parrish, Wharton papers, HSP; American Convention, *Minutes and Proceedings* (1796), pp. 12–13; *Minutes and Proceedings* (1798), p. 18; *Minutes and Proceedings of the Fifteenth American Convention . . .* (Philadelphia, 1817), p. 43; MS Minutes of Acting Committee, Address of Wilmington Society, Jan. 4, 1809, HSP. In 1806 a committee of the New York Manumission Society approved the recommendation to establish agencies in the South, but cautioned that the names of agents should not be divulged without their consent (MS Minutes, IX, 160, 162, NYHS). In 1808, however, the New Jersey Society decided against appointing such agents.

tinuing restatements of "higher law" absolutism. "No terrestrial legislators," wrote George Bourne, "without the most diabolical impiety,
can legalize this claim upon the human family." During the Missouri
controversy, Rufus King brought the antislavery doctrines of George
Wallace and Granville Sharp to the United States Senate:

> I have yet to learn that one man can make a slave of another. If one man
> cannot do so, no number of individuals can have any better right to do it.
> And I hold that all laws or compacts imposing any such a condition upon
> any human being, are absolutely void, because contrary to the law of
> nature, which is the law of God, by which he makes his ways known to
> man, and is paramount to all human control.[78]

King's speech predictably outraged Senator William Smith, of
South Carolina, who was also infuriated by a militant antislavery
pamphlet entitled *Horrors of Slavery*. Yet the author, John Kenrick,
posed in 1817 some fundamental questions that had become obscured
by wishful thinking. Surely the obstacles to emancipation were not
lessened by a prudent "delay" that brought a substantial increase in
the number of slaves:

> Is it resolved by the nation that negro slavery shall be perpetual in this
> land of liberty? Shall those who have their eyes open, with respect to the
> magnitude of the evil, hold their peace, and do nothing to purge them-
> selves and their country from this dreadful guilt, until a righteous God
> shall repeat in our land the horrors of St. Domingo?[79]

For Kenrick and a few other writers, the imperatives of justice
required a flexible approach to Constitutional theory. The entire Constitution should not be considered a flawless and unchangeable expression of "higher law." The temporary acceptance of slavery in the
states existing in 1787 could not be allowed to subvert the principles
of the Declaration of Independence, of the declarations of rights in
the state constitutions, or of the preamble to the federal Constitution.
According to John Parrish, the Declaration of Independence was a
solemn "covenant," the obligations of which had been validated, along

---

[78] Bourne, *The Book and Slavery Irreconcilable*, pp. 58–59, 65, 114–18; Rufus
King papers, Box 18A, 217, NYHS; Joseph L. Arbena, "Politics or Principle?
Rufus King and the Opposition to Slavery, 1785–1825," *Essex Institute His-
torical Collections*, CI (Jan., 1965), 56; Webster, *Effects of Slavery*, p. 33;
Barrow, *Involuntary . . . Slavery*, pp. 9–13; Dwight, *Oration*, pp. 9–12; Rice,
Slavery Inconsistent with Justice, pp. 4–6; John Kenrick, *Horrors of Slavery*
(Cambridge, Mass., 1817), pp. 38–39; *Emancipator*, May 31, 1820.

[79] Kenrick, *Horrors of Slavery*, p. 40.

with other prior debts, by Article VI of the Constitution. By any fair construction, Parrish argued, all slaves had been declared free in 1776, and the Constitution imposed the obligation of carrying out that promise. Other writers stressed Article IV, Section 4, which guaranteed to every state a republican form of government, a form which was said to be incompatible with slavery. The Constitution's overriding purposes included promoting the general welfare and securing the blessings of liberty. Therefore, Kenrick pointed out, if the powers of the general government were too restricted to deal with slavery, it was up to the people to enlarge those powers.[80]

These views, which anticipated important Constitutional arguments of the 1840s and 1850s, were clearly unacceptable to the great majority of early abolitionists. There seemed to be no way, prior to the great struggles over slavery in the territories, to reconcile the "higher law" heritage of the Revolution with an acceptance of the established order. There appeared to be no realistic choice between compromise and total inaction. "If we dare not strain legislative authority so as to root up the evil at once," William Pinkney said in 1789, "let us do all we dare, and lop the exuberance of its branches. I would sooner temporize than do nothing." Pinkney was then attacking the report of a Maryland legislative committee that endorsed laws prohibiting the voluntary manumission of slaves. Abolitionists reprinted the speech to embarrass

[80] *Ibid.*, pp. 58–59; Parrish, *Remarks*, pp. 2–3, 30–32, 47; Barrow, *Involuntary . . . Slavery*, p. 47; Bourne, *The Book and Slavery Irreconcilable*, p. 25; [Blunt], *Examination*, pp. 16–19; [Robert Walsh], *Free Remarks on the Spirit of the Federal Constitution, the Practice of the Federal Government, and the Obligations of the Union, Respecting the Exclusion of Slavery from the Territories and New States* (Philadelphia, 1819), pp. 5–15, 23, 30–31, 44, 54–56. Philip F. Detweiler has traced the slow evolution of the Declaration of Independence as a hallowed statement of "higher law" principles ("The Changing Reputation of the Declaration of Independence: The First Fifty Years," *William and Mary Quarterly*, 3rd ser., IXX [Oct., 1962], 557–74; "Congressional Debates on Slavery and the Declaration of Independence, 1819–1821," *American Historical Review*, LXIII [April, 1958], 598–616). My own reading would indicate that the Declaration was used more frequently by antislavery writers than Detweiler suggests. If the Declaration was not yet regarded as the supreme statement of "higher law," it formed an integral part of the argument on "inconsistency," from the end of the Revolution to the Missouri crisis.

Kenrick's doctrine that the people had the right and duty to enlarge the powers of government, in order to eradicate slavery, was expressed even earlier in Kentucky, where the state constitution prohibited the legislature from manumitting slaves (Concord Abolition Society, *A Circular Letter, from Concord Abolition Society, to the Inhabitants of Kentucky . . .* [n.p., 1814], pp. 4–8).

Pinkney at the time of the Missouri crisis, when his "temporizing" had led him to champion the proslavery cause in the United States Senate.[81]

Even for more persevering antislavery spokesmen, accommodation had its costs. While proclaiming that human beings could never be legitimately enslaved, abolitionists also pledged themselves to respect the laws of states and the supreme rights of property. They congratulated themselves on gradual emancipation acts which ensured that slaveholders would suffer little if any pecuniary loss and which guaranteed that freedmen would be deprived of equal civil rights. When the abolition societies found that Congress would not "step to the very verge of the power vested in you" for discouraging the slave trade, they tried, without success, to implore the legislators to impose the ten-dollar head tax authorized by the Constitution. In 1795 the American Convention congratulated Georgia for passing a self-protective law that prohibited slave imports from any country *other* than Africa. By 1818, ten years after the slave trade had been outlawed, the Convention was forced to protest the sale of contraband slaves in Georgia for the benefit of the United States Treasury! In spite of such accommodation—or because of it—the moderate abolitionists kept insisting on the need for prudence, and pointed happily to the improved condition of southern slaves. After 1816 the colonization movement gave new hope to this gradualist mentality, since deportation promised to fulfill God's purposes without altering the structure of American politics. The temporizing approach also suited the northeastern mercantile elites, such as the Boston Unitarians, who managed to reconcile both "higher law" platitudes and a theoretical abhorrence of slavery with a genteel distaste for controversy.[82]

---

[81] William Pinkney, *Speech of William Pinkney, Esq. in the House of Delegates of Maryland* (Philadelphia, 1790), p. 4. In January, 1790, Pinkney reported to the Pennsylvania Abolition Society that advocates for freedom could not dare too much in Maryland for fear of losing everything (Pennsylvania Abolition Society MSS, II, 15, HSP). Benjamin Lundy later made much of Pinkney's desertion to the proslavery camp (*Genius of Universal Emancipation,* I [Dec., 1821], 89).

[82] American Convention, *Minutes and Proceedings of the Second Convention of Delegates* . . . (Philadelphia, 1795), p. 24; *Minutes of a Special Meeting of the Fifteenth American Convention* . . . (Philadelphia, 1818), pp. 8–9, 47–50, 65; *Minutes of the Eighteenth Session* (1823), pp. 5–6, 16; *Address of the American Convention* . . . (Philadelphia, 1804), pp. 6–7; Evarts, "Missouri Question," pp. 63–68; Daniel Walker Howe, *The Unitarian Conscience: Harvard*

It is true that a number of religious radicals veered toward the opposite extreme. The revivals of the early nineteenth century re-kindled the millennial visions of the Great Awakening, illuminating the contrast between the corruptions of a secular society and the ideal of a New Jerusalem. The persistence of slavery, along with other vices, showed that the nation was not "under God," that it had not chosen freedom—in the Edwardsean sense—and that it respected no prin-ciples higher than self-interest. This renewed respect for moral law could easily breed an indifference toward the affairs of a sordid world. A deep aversion to partisan politics would underlie the evangelical quest for a holy community. On the other hand, as early as 1816 the "come-outer" spirit could result in militant abolitionism:

Every water for a public officer, who will not destroy the system, is as culpable as if he participated in the evil, and is responsible for the pro-traction of the crime. . . . No human law must be obeyed when it con-travenes the divine command; but slavery is the combination of all iniquity, and therefore every man is obligated not to participate in its corruption.[83]

This was, of course, the uncompromising position that Garrison would later popularize. Prior to 1831 it constituted no more than a minor aberration in American thought, overshadowed by the domi-nant faith in conciliation and gradual moral progress. Between these two poles there seemed to be no alternative response.

Yet even by the 1790s a few writers began experimenting with other ways of dealing with the Revolution's heritage of inconsistency. In his *Dissertation on Slavery*, St. George Tucker correctly described

Moral Philosophy, 1805–1861 (Cambridge, Mass., 1970), pp. 270–305. The founders of the American Colonization Society outdid the earlier abolitionists in claiming the blessings of divine Providence. As Samuel Finley put it: "I know the scheme is from God" (Henry N. Sherwood, "The Formation of the American Colonization Society," *Journal of Negro History*, II [July, 1917], 219–21). A report of the Fifteenth American Convention warned that the Colonization Society was not friendly to abolition, and asserted that blacks were as much Americans as whites. But the constituent abolition societies were by no means unanimous in rejecting the Colonization Society.

[83] Bourne, *The Book and Slavery Irreconcilable*, pp. 114–18, 133; Elias Hicks, *Observations on the Slavery of the Africans and their Descendents, and on the Use of the Produce of their Labour* (Philadelphia, 1839; originally published 1811), pp. iv–vii, 9, 18–21. For the revival's political implications, see John R. Bodo, *The Protestant Clergy and Public Issues, 1812–1848* (Princeton, 1954), *passim;* and Charles C. Cole, Jr., *The Social Ideas of the Northern Evangelists, 1826–1860* (New York, 1954), esp. pp. 144–53.

the condition of free Negroes in the North as a form of civil slavery. Though Tucker was a liberal Virginian who deplored the moral and social consequences of Negro slavery, he pointed to a line of argument that would increasing appeal to many Northerners as well as Southerners: if emancipated Negroes were to be no better off than those in the North, manumission itself was of questionable wisdom. It was thus hypocritical for Northerners to interpret their gradual emancipation laws as proof of moral superiority. The fact of oppression could serve as an excuse for continued oppression. And by 1806, as has been seen, a southern Congressman could feel free to be more candid: "I will tell the truth. A large majority of the people in the Southern States do not consider slavery as even an evil."[84]

Such frankness invited Northerners, and especially Northern Federalists, to express sentiments they had only partially suppressed before. Even during the Revolutionary crisis Samuel Hopkins, among other New Englanders, charged that slaveholders were petty tyrants who would gladly suppress freedom of speech and inquiry. It had to be admitted, Noah Webster wrote, that the southern states were still tinged with European aristocratic tendencies; one could only look forward to the day when the large plantations would be broken up and replaced by small farms and industrious free workers. In the 1790s national political conflict gave a sharper edge to sectional contrasts. "Pelham," writing in the *Connecticut Courant*, was unusually blunt:

The existence of Slavery may be viewed as one forcible cause of a final separation of the United States. . . . The extreme wickedness of holding our fellow men in chains, merely to serve our own interested plans, is very generally acknowledged in the northern states, and the sentiment is steadily gaining ground. We are shocked to hear reverential ideas of liberty and equality, uttered by mouths, worn smooth with curses against their fellowmen. . . . How can the hands of men, accustomed to do to others, as they would that others should do to them, clasp in the fraternal

[84] St. George Tucker, *A Dissertation on Slavery, with a Proposal for the Gradual Abolition of It, in the State of Virginia* (Philadelphia, 1796), pp. 8–9; *Annals of Congress,* 9th Cong., 2nd sess., 238. For examples of the incipient proslavery arguments of James Jackson, William L. Smith, and Thomas Tucker, see *Annals of Congress,* 1st Cong., 2nd sess. 1240–44. Timothy Ford of Charleston was claiming by 1794 that slavery was a positive support to free institutions (MacLeod, "Racial Attitudes," p. 155). Even earlier, "Marcus Aurelius" cited the examples of Greece and Rome to prove that slave labor could strengthen national freedom (*New Jersey Journal,* Jan. 17, 1781).

embrace, those who brood over misery and blood, who smile at murder, and ridicule despair?[85]

"Amynto," reflecting on "the inconsistency of man," charged that a "furious jacobin democracy" was emerging in the South alongside Negro slavery: "He that is accustomed to rule as a tyrant, cannot even bear to be ruled under the mildest system of freedom." There was thus an inner logic to the South's seeming inconsistency: "Consistant mortals! Opposing, as tyrannical, not only the free monarchy of Great Britain, but also the much freer republican government of America, while they themselves reign, not only as absolute monarchs, but as the worst of tyrants over the much injured Africans." Thomas Boylston Adams agreed that "there is a spirit of domination engrafted on the character of the southern people. Of all the inhabitants of this continent, they are the most imperious in their manners."[86]

During the Revolution, Tory and English writers had delighted in casting similar barbs, which would later prove serviceable against the West Indian "nabobs." In the United States, however, such words sizzled with danger. New England had been, in effect, an accomplice in freeing southern slaveholders from any fear of future Parliamentary interference with slavery; New England had also helped protect Georgia and South Carolina from any immediate prohibition of the slave trade. The compact of 1787 showed what was essential for national political solidarity: the family secret could not be mentioned in public, except perhaps as an unfortunate heritage from the past. Southern Federalists, after all, would hardly relish northern Federalist speeches portraying all plantation owners as bloodthirsty tyrants. Presumably for this reason one Connecticut Federalist wrote privately, during a trip in the South, that "if I was an enthusiast, I shou'd launch out into the most extravigant [*sic*] denunciation against slavery." He quickly added, however, that he was "no enthusiast."[87]

[85] [Hopkins], *Dialogue*, p. 37; Noah Webster, "An Essay on the Political Advantages of America," *American Museum*, VI (Nov., 1789), 390; "Pelham," "The Existance of Slavery," *Connecticut Courant*, Dec. 12, 1796.

[86] "Amynto," *Reflections on the Inconsistency of Man, Particularly Exemplified in the Practice of Slavery in the United States* (New York, 1796), pp. 12–15; Linda K. Kerber, *Federalists in Dissent: Imagery and Ideology in Jeffersonian America* (Ithaca, N.Y., 1970), pp. 25–26; [Hopkins], *Dialogue*, p. 37; Rice, *Slavery Inconsistent with Justice*, pp. 10–11; Thaddeus M. Harris, *Discourse Delivered Before the African Society in Boston . . .* (Boston, 1822), pp. 13–15.

[87] Kerber, *Federalists*, pp. 24–25. It should be noted that there was a continuing

When northern Federalists did allow their enthusiasm to burst occasionally into public, the enthusiasm was not fueled by unadulterated humanitarianism. There were a variety of reasons that explain why some of the shriller Federalist voices should attack the hypocrisy of Virginia *democrats* ("A democrat in the southern states is a planter, or other person, who owns a large number of slaves; who is above labor himself"); why they should oppose the westward expansion of slavery; should favor the independence of Haiti from France; and should suggest that a dissolution of the union would be no loss to the northeastern states.[88]

On the other hand, some of the antisouthern outbursts displayed more than partisan interest. "Amynto," for example, exposed one meaning of the slave-trade clause in the Constitution. It meant that the American people, despite their idealistic professions, really believed

that the Negroes of Africa, because they are black, and we are white—because it is necessary for us to live in genteel refinement, at the expense of the misery of the stupid negroes—because liberty and property are our rights, and necessarily extinguish theirs: we therefore maintain it to be perfectly right, and just, to keep them and their children to languish in hopeless bondage.[89]

Few Americans had so clearly perceived the connection between white liberty and black slavery. For "Amynto," an antislavery challenge to the South was a necessary step toward the genuine emancipation of America. In the words of "Gustavus," writing in 1797, the question

---

literature that repeated the Revolutionary theme that England was responsible for America's seeming inconsistency. For example, in 1819 Robert Walsh, Jr., charged that England had been responsible for the slave trade; that slaves in Virginia were as well off as English peasants; that the British abolition of the slave trade was ineffective and hypocritical; that England would be a slave nation if the West Indians had been allowed representation in Parliament (*An Appeal from the Judgments of Great Britain Respecting the United States of America* [Philadelphia, 1819], pp. 306–87). For a detailed discussion of American replies to British antislavery attacks, see MacLeod, "Racial Attitudes," pp. 37–40. This was another aspect to the geographic sectionalizing of moral inconsistency.

[88] Kerber, *Federalists,* pp. 23–66; James M. Banner, Jr., *To the Hartford Convention: The Federalists and the Origins of Party Politics in Massachusetts, 1789–1815* (New York, 1970), *passim.*

[89] "Amynto," *Reflections,* pp. 9–10. Though "Amynto" condemned Jacobinism, I cannot be sure he was a Federalist. In 1796 he hoped that the French and American Revolutions "are but introductory movements towards a general emancipation of human nature" (p. 27).

of union or disunion was perhaps "the most important problem which had ever become a subject of public investigation":

On it may be suspended the decision, whether the civilized part of mankind, after improvement of three thousand years, shall revert to a state of savage barbarity, or whether the present heathen world shall emerge from their native darkness, to the knowledge of arts and sciences—of christianity, and of future glory.[90]

Such words foreshadow William Seward's view, in 1858, of "an irrepressible conflict between opposing and enduring forces." There was, indeed, a striking similarity between the antisouthern imagery of New England Federalists, as recently analyzed by Linda K. Kerber, and the later "Republican critique of the South," as delineated by Eric Foner.[91] The Federalists, unlike the Republicans of the 1850s, did not glorify westward expansion or exalt the upward mobility of labor. They did picture the South, however, as a land of tyranny and decay, where power made men brutal, insolent, and irresponsible; where indolence extinguished ambition; where slavery degraded the worth of labor; where self-indulgence drained the springs of progress.

Whatever the actual role of slavery in the nation's economic development, the South symbolized, even by 1800, a set of styles and values directly antithetical to the emerging capitalist ideology. The early recitals of evidence were virtually the same as those of the 1850s: exhausted or uncultivated soil, bad roads, dilapidated buildings, and unpainted fences. The unpainted fences seem to have been especially grating to New England travelers. Nor should modern suburbanites wonder at such a compelling concern over outward appearance, without regard for utility. Southern whites, whether slaveholders or not, had evidently failed to internalize those values that were to provide a basis not only for northern economic enterprise but for northern class and social discipline. A farmer who painted his fences would also presumably pay his debts and feel a sense of common interest with various improvers and developers. A populace that saw dignity in labor would know that "even Betas are useful." Slavery could easily be

[90] *Connecticut Courant*, Aug. 14, 1797. In 1820 even the Pennsylvania Abolition Society considered the possibility of a separation of the North from the slaveholding states (Pennsylvania Abolition Society MSS, VII, 6, HSP).

[91] Kerber, *Federalists*, pp. 23–66; Eric Foner, *Free Soil, Free Labor, Free Men: The Ideology of the Republican Party Before the Civil War* (New York, 1970), pp. 11–72.

identified as the source of a divergent and threatening system of values; above all, it threatened the indispensable myth that American society was founded on a harmony of interests.[92]

There were powerful forces, however, that inhibited the temptation to sectionalize America's inconsistency. James M. Banner, Jr. has suggested a number of reasons for antislavery's peripheral character in New England's early sectional consciousness. The chief function of government, according to Federalist ideology, following the Harringtonian tradition, was to protect the security of property. New England Federalists esteemed the Constitution as a product of the highest statesmanship, by which the art of compromise had defined the common good. Although they increasingly identified the South as the bastion of their Republican enemies, they viewed the West with even greater alarm, and at times indulged in hopeful fantasies of a western secession that would bring a renewed sense of unity and common interest to the original thirteen states. The threat of the South as a divergent culture ran counter to lingering hopes for an alliance of conservative elites. In addition, the hysteria provoked by the French Revolution intensified the Federalists' mistrust of aliens or of any population—including emancipated blacks—who had no stake in local society and traditions. Professor Banner also points to the split between Federalist politicians and the Federalist clergy, the latter being faced with waning power, schism, and denominational competition. As New Englanders felt increasingly isolated from the sources of national growth and power, they could well be expected to turn inward and to avoid any backlash that might result from intermeddling with the domestic institutions of others.[93]

The themes of antislavery literature were part of a wider American ideology that defined the hopes and perils of independence. Although I have necessarily focused attention on the slavery issue, it was by no means the only symbol of a gap between the millennial expectations of the Revolution and the political realities of union. By the time of the Constitutional Convention, both Federalists and anti-Federalists were obsessed with an apparent decline in public virtue. Both feared the emergence of contending political interests (other than their own) that endangered the supposedly selfless standards of the Revolution.

[92] See, for example, [Samuel Blodget], *Economica: A Statistical Manual for the United States of America* (Washington, 1806), pp. 80–82, 197.

[93] Banner, *Hartford Convention*, pp. 24–52, 58–69, 89–109, 112–21, 153–67.

For New Englanders, who later looked back on the administrations of Washington and Adams as an age of golden virtue, the expansion of slavery was only one of many ominous signs of declension. Some of the more terrifying examples of divine retribution—such as Jefferson's election, the Louisiana Purchase, the Embargo, and the War of 1812—were not necessarily identified with slavery.[94]

We still have much to learn, however, about the continuities of antislavery and sectionalism. Why, for example, did New England Federalists show less restraint in attacking slavery in the 1790s, when they still had powerful political allies in the South, than in the early nineteenth century, when southern Federalism had all but disappeared? Why were pro-English Federalists so little influenced by the 1807 triumph of British abolitionists? Perhaps Professor Banner is right in maintaining that the growing weakness of the Federalist Party "further dampened the Federalists' interest in the antislavery cause." Yet political strength, as later history testifies, could have the same effect. Federalist leaders showed no caution in demanding a Constitutional amendment to repeal the three-fifth clause on slave representation, though such a measure would actually have increased the representation of their political opponents. If Federalists could mistakenly perceive the three-fifths clause as the source of Republican power, why did they hesitate at the next step, taken a generation later, to challenge directly the "Slave Power"?[95]

This is not the place to pursue such political questions, though they may involve, in addition to the changing style and character of political leadership, a desire to suppress the more radical social implications of the Edwardsean tradition, which had already given shape to a militant, uncompromising abolitionism that anticipated the immediatist spirit of the 1830s. In a few brief and tantalizing passages, Professor Banner refers to the sons of Federalist fathers who assumed leading roles in the later abolition crusade, and to a "larger Federalist ideology" which somehow taught "a third generation of political leaders to understand that slavery lay at the root of New England's

[94] Jonathan C. Clark, "The Hopes and Fears of a Yesteryear," Ph.D. thesis, Yale University, 1972, *passim;* Banner, *Hartford Convention, passim.*

[95] Banner, *Hartford Convention,* pp. 100–5. Although I have drawn heavily on Banner's discussion, it seems to me that he skirts these questions and never really explains why by 1815 "the antislavery cause in Massachusetts was dead, a victim of political needs and moral indifference" (p. 104).

powerlessness."[96] The antislavery cause doubtless suffered, during a period of exuberant nationalism, from the sour taint of Federalist partisanship and conspiracy. Yet it is also true that by 1820 the main ingredients of the sectionalist Slave Power thesis had appeared as an explanation for the nation's moral declension and as a program for militant restoration. The Missouri crisis pointed to a sectional reformulation of the Revolution's great dilemma.

Ironically, the Revolutionary generation had seen Virginia as the originator of the nation's first antislavery commitments: the disavowal of the slave trade and the formal proclamation of man's inherent rights. Yet Virginia's early leadership made it all the easier to sectionalize the national burden of inconsistency. For Virginia, as critics discovered at the time of the Missouri debates, had never been sincere. She had eagerly welcomed the importation of slaves, so the argument ran, until further numbers posed the threat of declining slave prices and possible insurrection. This moment had fortuitously coincided with the rise of Revolutionary idealism in the North, and northern patriots had thus been deceived by the appearance of a united humanitarian will. The Missouri debates revealed Virginia's true colors.[97] Henceforth, the contradiction between Revolutionary and secular time, which had seemed to lead to irreversible declension, could be conceived as a contradiction between two cultures—or as a contradiction in American space.

[96] *Ibid.*, pp. 108–9. See also Kerber, *Federalists*, pp. 62, 66.

[97] [Joseph Dennie], *The Port Folio, by Oliver Oldschool*, III (July 30, 1803), 245–46; John Wright, *A Refutation of the Sophisms, Gross Misrepresentations, and Erroneous Quotations Contained in "An American's" "Letter to the Edinburgh Reviewers"* . . . (Washington, 1820), pp. 43–44. For northern discouragement over reports of the unpopularity of antislavery in the Upper South, see Pennsylvania Abolition Society MSS, IV (1797), 23–24, HSP; New York Manumission Society, MS Minutes, IX (1804), 118, NYHS; American Convention, MS Minutes of the Eleventh American Convention, II (1806), 60–61, HSP.

Eight ∾

The Preservation of
English Liberty, I

The English Context Compared with That of America and France

The ideology of the American Revolution was largely British in origin, and the arguments that American reformers used against Negro slavery had long been commonplace in British political and moral philosophy. Yet by the 1770s antislavery thought had considerably different implications in the two countries.

In England there was no "fundamental shift in values" that mobilized the society into revolution. There was no counterpart to the American need for self-justification. No new hopes or obligations arose from an attempt to build a virtuous republic. Such phrases as "created equal," "inalienable rights," and "the pursuit of happiness"—all of which had appeared in classic liberal texts—were qualified by a reverent constitutionalism that looked to Saxon precedent to legitimize ideals of freedom. The notion of man's inherent rights, when assimilated to the historical concept of British "liberty," implied little challenge to traditional laws and authorities. And by the 1790s the very idea of inherent rights was giving way to radical and conservative forms of Utilitarianism. Like the Americans of a later generation, most Englishmen looked back to a long sanctified revolution—the Glorious Revolution of 1688—which had supposedly restored the foundations of a free society. Reformers and critics often expressed alarm over the corruption of that "revolutionary" heritage. But even when they called for an extension of political liberties, it was usually in the name of purifying or restoring balance to the existing political order.

The stability of English institutions made antislavery appear less dangerous than in revolutionary America or France. In the latter two countries, where leaders at least thought of themselves as creating new social orders, there was the possibility of judging any institution against the abstract ideals of liberty and equal rights. Since slavery epitomized hereditary power, it could be denounced as one of the vestiges of a barbarous past, along with royalty, primogeniture, feudal dues (in France), or an established church. The creation of new political authorities opened the way for sweeping change that could easily overleap national or continental boundaries.

In the words of the Abbé Grégoire: "Le volcan de la liberté allumé en France amènera bientôt une explosion générale et changera le sort de l'espèce humaine dans les deux hémisphères."[1] Yet even enthusiasts like Grégoire knew that revolutions require priorities and that "higher law" ideals must be selectively applied. What Grégoire had in mind, in the passage just quoted, was a revolutionary alliance of colonial mulattoes and nonslaveholding whites. In order to win full civil rights for free blacks and mulattoes, he was quite willing to postpone the question of slavery. I have already noted the wide discrepancy between the *Amis des noirs'* declaration of principles and their belief that any "sudden" emancipation would be disastrous for the colonies. In both France and America there was a notable gap between antislavery rhetoric and the realities of revolutionary politics. The slavery issue could not be allowed to divide revolutionary alliances or to take precedence over such critical questions as military defense and political reconstruction. And in both countries, there was a need for qualifying the immediate implications of manifestoes concerned with man's natural equality. Within the context of revolution, the postponement of Negro emancipation could be one of various checks against an uncontrolled assault upon private property.

In France, unlike America, few men had ever seen a Negro slave, except perhaps in Paris and the port cities, and fewer still had grown

[1] Quoted in Paul Grunebaum-Ballin, *Henri Grégoire, l'ami des hommes de toutes les couleurs, la lutte pour la suppression de la traite et l'abolition de l'esclavage, 1789–1831* (Paris, 1948), p. 27. Grégoire's words can be translated as follows: "The volcanic eruption of freedom in France will soon bring on a general explosion which will transform the destiny of mankind in both hemispheres."

accustomed to slavery as part of their immediate universe. The anti-slavery cause could easily be applauded by any enlightened man who had no personal or economic ties with the colonial system. Yet precisely because the French colonies were so remote, the plight of slaves could remain low on the agenda of reform. As the Revolution widened, the agitation of the *Amis des noirs* seemed at best a pious irrelevancy, at worst a dangerous distraction, inspired no doubt by the British in order to divide the colonies from France. In addition, the bewildering pace of revolutionary events left little time for antislavery organization, and it was soon too late for white reformers to decide the destiny of the St. Domingue blacks.

In England, however, the remoteness of the colonies had profoundly different implications. As in France, only a few men who had lived in the West Indies had become habituated to slavery as one of the necessary realities of life. They and their proslave trade allies did their best to evoke fears that any humanitarian tampering with the slave system would open Pandora's box, as the Earl of Abingdon put it, and let loose democratic forces that would ultimately destroy both monarchy and rank: "The Order, and Subordination, the Happiness of the whole habitable Globe is threatened," Abingdon warned. "What anarchy, confusion, and bloodshed," Gilbert Francklyn asked, "may follow too nice and critical an enquiry into the exact portion of each man's particular liberty, the society of which he is a member may have a right to deprive him of?" He added:

What would the people of England think of men, who, under a similar pretext of zeal for the rights of humanity, should erect themselves into a society, and endeavour, by preaching, writing, and publishing, to stir up the soldier, the artisan, and the peasant, to assert their rights to an equal portion of liberty with those who now lord it over them? Could any religious man amongst the present petitioners [against the slave trade] object to, or decline promoting an agrarian law, in favour of the distressed poor of Great Britain?[2]

But equality had never been a goal of the earlier petition campaigns for "Wilkes and Liberty," for annual Parliaments, for enlarging the

---

[2] *Speech of the Earl of Abingdon on His Lordship's Motion for Postponing the Further Consideration of the Question for the Abolition of the Slave Trade* . . . (London, 1793), pp. 5–6; Gilbert Francklyn, *Observations, Occasioned by the Attempts Made in England to Effect the Abolition of the Slave Trade* . . . (Kingston, Jamaica, 1788; reprinted London, 1789), pp. xvii-xviii.

membership of the House of Commons, or for reducing the court's influence in the legislature. English reformers, with the exception of a few isolated radicals, had shown no enthusiasm for the American doctrines of direct representation and continuous public "consent." And since most Englishmen looked upon existing institutions as effective safeguards of liberty, it seemed improbable, except perhaps in 1792 and 1793, that antislavery arguments could be extended to domestic forms of oppression and inequality. On the contrary, for men who sincerely believed that the English workers were a free and contented people, there could be little hazard in cautiously extending to the colonies Whiggish notions of liberty. Antislavery, far from being an innovation justified by a Declaration of Independence or a Declaration of the Rights of Man, could be embraced as a reinforcement of tradition.

Some Political and Ideological Implications

In 1838 an English critic pondered the remarkable discrepancy between the public's apathy toward the most critical political and economic issues of the day, and the public "convulsions upon the question, whether the Black Apprentices [in the West Indies] shall have their indentures cancelled in August next, or be compelled to serve out their time!" Matters of politics and finance, he noted, appeared as lifeless abtractions; local evils became blurred by familiarity. "But slavery *proves* itself; its evils are embodied, and animated by a living spirit. It has action, actors, and horrors. . . . Ordinary home questions, in short, are as dull as lectures or sermons—slavery has the excitement of a tragedy." Moreover,

except with planters, activity on this subject is followed by no injury or ill-will. A Tory or a Whig aristocrat may call a tenant or a tradesman, who agitates for "instant abolition" . . . an enthusiast, but he does not withdraw his custom or turn a man out of his farm. Individuals, who are disgusted with the state of home politics, but dare not move in them lest they should "bring in the Tories," find here a safe opportunity to "take an interest in public affairs."[3]

When applied retroactively, these remarks suggest that British leaders had much to gain, in ensuring stability, if reform energies

[3] "Sources of English Zeal for the Blacks," *The Spectator*, No. 509 (March 31, 1838), 301.

could be channeled outward toward a symbol of unparalleled oppression. The critic of 1838 implied nothing about conscious motive. There is no evidence that politicians like William Pitt cannily supported abolition of the slave trade as a means of evading domestic reform or dampening radical discontent. Nor can one ignore the political risks that inhibited Edmund Burke, for example, from taking an early leadership in the antislavery cause. It would be naïve, however, to overlook the political and ideological context within which British antislavery emerged as an organized force.

Adam Smith, who was much esteemed by Pitt and the abolitionists, provides us with a classical precedent for asking what "interests" antislavery might have served. Here is Smith's evaluation of the first achievement of antislavery in America:

The late resolution of the Quakers in Pennsylvania to set at liberty all their negro slaves, may satisfy us that their number cannot be very great. Had they made any considerable part of their property, such a resolution could never have been agreed to. In our sugar colonies, on the contrary, the whole work is done by slaves, and in our tobacco colonies a very great part of it. The profits of a sugar-plantation in any of our West Indian colonies are generally much greater than those of any other cultivation that is known either in Europe or America: And the profits of a tobacco plantation, though inferior to those of sugar, are superior to those of corn, as has already been observed.[4]

Since Smith considered self-interest to be the governing principle of life, it was inconceivable that Quakers or any other group would emancipate their slaves if slaves constituted "any considerable part of their property." Of course, Smith heartily favored the reform of a colonial system of labor that was artificially subsidized and that drained capital from more productive investment at home. There could be no "natural identity of interests" between English consumers and American planters unless the latter were subjected to free market forces.

Today even the authority of Adam Smith is likely to raise the bugaboo of "economic interpretation" and the specter of Eric Williams's controversial book, *Capitalism and Slavery*. The shortcomings of Williams's thesis, which argues that British self-interest led to the abolition of the slave trade and to West Indian emancipation, have been exposed

[4] Adam Smith, *An Inquiry into the Nature and Causes of the Wealth of Nations* (New York, 1937), p. 366.

by a host of historians. In one of the most convincing rebuttals, Roger Anstey has pointed to the absence of any organized or self-conscious group in Parliament that represented the "developing economic forces"; to the fact that a bill for immediate abolition of the slave trade nearly passed in the House of Commons in 1796, at the very peak of the sugar boom; and to the lack of evidence that English reformers or politicians thought of the overproduction of sugar as a reason for slave-trade abolition. Anstey's most intriguing argument concerns the abolitionists' first major breakthrough, in 1806, when as a tactical maneuver they deliberately suppressed humanitarian arguments and concentrated their fire on the neutral (mainly American) slave trade to enemy colonies, and on the British slave trade to foreign and temporarily conquered territories. Anstey appears to turn Williams upside down. Appeals to the national interest cloaked hidden humanitarian motives, and succeeded "by a side wind," as Colonel Banastre Tarleton put it, in annihilating more than half of the total British slave trade. And the precedent of 1806 meant that a total abolition, even if demanded for true humanitarian motives, would not be regarded as a dangerous innovation.[5]

Williams's critics have shown us the inadequacy of a naïve determinism and of too literal a conception of "self-interest." On the other hand, if the majority in Parliament feared the consequences of "any innovation upon a long-established practice," and shifted ground only when aroused to the danger and short-sightedness of supplying slaves to foreign colonies, it is of little importance that few M.P.'s had direct personal ties with the West Indies. And if the most powerful political leaders later championed abolition as the cause of national interest as well as of moral righteousness, it is hardly crucial that they represented the large English landholders—for whom Adam Smith was also a spokesman—more than the rising manufacturers.

The key questions concern the relationship between antislavery and the social system as a whole. Why did a seemingly liberal movement emerge and continue to win support from major government leaders in the period from 1790 to 1832, a period characterized by both poli-

---

[5] Roger Anstey, "A Re-interpretation of the Abolition of the British Slave Trade, 1806–1807," *The English Historical Review,* LXXXVII (April, 1972), 304–32; Anstey, "Capitalism and Slavery: A Critique," *The Economic History Review,* 2nd ser., XXI (1968), 307–20. I am also indebted to Professor Anstey for allowing me to read chapters of his forthcoming study of British abolition.

tical reaction and industrial revolution? How could such a movement be embraced by aristocratic statesmen and yet serve eventually as a vehicle for the triumphant middle class, who regarded West Indian emancipation as the confirmation of the Reform Bill of 1832, and who used antislavery rhetoric and strategy as models for their assault upon the Corn Laws? How could antislavery help to ensure stability while also accommodating society to political and economic change? Antonio Gramsci defined "hegemony," in the words of his biographer, as "the predominance, obtained by consent rather than force, of one class or group over other classes"; or more precisely, as "the 'spontaneous' loyalty that any dominant social group obtains from the masses by virtue of its social and intellectual prestige and its supposedly superior function in the world of production."[6] The paramount question, which subsumes the others, is how antislavery reinforced or legitimized such hegemony.

Ideological hegemony is not the product of conscious choice and seldom involves insincerity or deliberate deception. As Peter Berger has written, "deliberate deception requires a degree of psychological self-control that few people are capable of. . . . It is much easier to deceive oneself. It is, therefore, important to keep the concept of ideology distinct from notions of lying, deception, propaganda or legerdemain." Ideology is a mode of consciousness, rooted in but not reducible to the needs of a social group; indeed, it helps to define those very needs and interests, as well as to frame the boundaries of conscious tactics and objectives. As phrased by Berger, ideology "both

---

[6] John M. Cammett, *Antonio Gramsci and the Origins of Italian Communism* (Stanford, 1967), pp. 204–5. Gramsci distinguishes "the apparatus of state coercive power which 'legally' enforces discipline on those groups who do not 'consent' either actively or passively . . . ," from "the 'spontaneous' consent given by the great masses of the population to the general direction imposed on social life by the dominant fundamental group" (*Selections from the Prison Notebooks of Antonio Gramsci,* ed. and tr. by Quentin Hoare and Geoffrey Nowell Smith [London, 1971], p. 12). In his illuminating essay, "On Antonio Gramsci," Eugene D. Genovese stresses that "the success of a ruling class in establishing its hegemony depends entirely on its ability to convince the lower classes that its interests are those of society at large—that it defends the common sensibility and stands for a natural and proper social order" (Genovese, *In Red and Black: Marxian Explorations in Southern and Afro-American History* [New York, 1971], p. 407). In other words, hegemony rests on a credible and adaptable *Weltanschauung.* For a brilliant application of Gramsci's theory of hegemony to American history, see Aileen S. Kraditor, "American Radical Historians on Their Heritage," *Past and Present* (Aug., 1972), 136–53.

justifies what is done by the group whose vested interest is served and interprets social reality in such a way that the justification is made plausible."[7] At issue, then, are not conscious intentions but the social functions of ideology; not individual motives but shifting patterns of thought and value which focused attention on new problems, which camouflaged others, and which defined new conceptions of social reality.

The antislavery movement, like Smith's political economy, reflected the needs and values of the emerging capitalist order. Smith provided theoretical justification for the belief that all classes and segments of society share a natural identity of interest. The antislavery movement, while absorbing the ambivalent emotions of the age, was essentially dedicated to a practical demonstration of the same reassuring message. It appealed, of course, to the highest ideals of man. Yet the very effectiveness of ideals requires a certain blindness to their social power and social consequences. They must be taken as pure and transcendent, free of ambiguous implication. Thus for abolitionists it was unthinkable that an attack on a specific system of labor and domination might also validate other forms of oppression and test the boundaries of legitimate reform. But from the perspective of our different world view —which no doubt equally restricts our vision in ways we cannot suspect—we can see that abolitionism helped to define the permissible character of a "popular" or "spontaneous" social movement. Antislavery not only reflected the needs and tensions of a transitional social system, but provided a new conceptual and categorical framework that imposed its own "logic" on events. As abolitionists sought support from men in power and from middle-class opinion, they discovered, though not without travail, the common denominators that gave both zeal and limits to an emerging consensus. In a more positive sense, they succeeded in making a sincere humanitarianism an integral part of class ideology, and thus of British culture.

These themes can be approached initially on three levels of analysis: the relationship between antislavery and economic theory; the significance of antislavery as a channel for political action; and the use of antislavery literature as a medium for resolving conflicts inherent

[7] Peter Berger, *Invitation to Sociology: A Humanistic Perspective* (Garden City, N.Y., 1963), pp. 109, 112. In framing these general propositions, I am heavily indebted to the generous and perceptive criticism of Aileen S. Kraditor.

in the emerging system of liberal values. Let me try to spell out the implications of each "level."

By 1776 England was well-prepared for a marshaling of argument and evidence against the mercantilist system, and *The Wealth of Nations* acquired immediate popularity. Adam Smith's great mentors, Hutcheson and Hume, had both questioned the economic utility of Negro slavery. The Physiocrats had linked antislavery with the ideal of laissez faire. In a negative way, the defenders of the slave trade confirmed this association of ideas by invoking mercantilist dogma: the slave trade was a source of naval power and a great "nursery" for seamen; as a form of state-regulated exploitation, the slave colonies were essential to a favorable balance of trade and were the main source of the nation's economic surplus. No statesman had doubted the value of the slave system during those decades of war and competition with Spain and France which had resulted in England's unquestioned supremacy. Yet these backward-looking arguments missed the significance of Smith's challenge: after supremacy has been achieved, the means of achieving it may become obsolete.[8]

Smith's views on slavery present a paradox. He complains that

We see frequently societies of merchants in London and other trading towns, purchase waste lands in our sugar colonies, which they expect to improve and cultivate with profit by means of factors and agents; notwithstanding the great distance and the uncertain returns, from the defective administration of justice in those countries. Nobody will attempt to improve and cultivate in the same manner the most fertile lands of Scotland, Ireland, or the corn provinces of North America, though from the more exact administration of justice in these countries, more regular returns might be expected.

[8] Joseph A. Schumpeter, *History of Economic Analysis,* ed. by Elizabeth Boody Schumpeter (New York, 1954), pp. 185–86, 210–20, 267–68; E. A. J. Johnson, *Predecessors of Adam Smith: The Growth of British Economic Thought* (New York, 1937), *passim;* Ronald Hamowy, "Adam Smith, Adam Ferguson, and the Division of Labour," *Economica,* new ser., XXXV (Aug., 1968), 249–59; Jacob Viner, "Adam Smith and Laissez Faire," *Journal of Political Economy,* XXXV (April, 1927), 198–232; Edward Mead Earle, "Adam Smith, Alexander Hamilton, Friedrich List: The Economic Foundations of Military Power," in *Makers of Modern Strategy,* ed. by Edward Mead Earle (Princeton, 1941), pp. 117–28. As Earle notes, Smith favored state intervention whenever essential for military security, and defended navigation acts for preserving the strength of the British navy and merchant marine. Similar arguments would be used in defense of the slave trade. However, Smith considered overseas colonies a liability, in part because of the costs of military defense.

Slave-grown sugar is not only more profitable than other crops, but "it is commonly said, that a sugar planter expects that the rum and the molasses should defray the whole expence of his cultivation, and that his sugar should be all clear profit." On the other hand, "the experience of all ages and nations" demonstrates that the labor of slaves, "though it appears to cost only their maintenance, is in the end the dearest of any. A person who can acquire no property, can have no other interest but to eat as much, and to labour as little as possible."[9]

The question of incentive brings us to Smith's central concern, which is the price and productivity of labor as the source of national wealth. For Smith a commodity's price is not the real measure of its value (and he thought the price of sugar artificially inflated); rather, a commodity's value lies in the amount of labor it enables a purchaser to command, in a kind of balancing of pains and pleasures. English consumers of sugar were not getting their money's worth of labor, and the surplus from cheap English labor was paying for the extravagance of slavery: "The prosperity of the English sugar colonies has been, in great measure, owing to the great riches of England, of which a part has overflowed . . . upon those colonies." Even worse, the duties on sugar fell chiefly on people of "middling or more than middling fortune."[10]

The slave system, then, epitomized those artificial market conditions which multiplied conflicts of interest. The heavy losses of English seamen engaged in the slave trade, together with the depopulation of the slave-labor force (at a time when the demand for labor in England was increasing), were sufficient proof of the impediments to authentic self-interest.[11] For Smith and his disciples, the abolition of the slave trade

[9] Smith, *Wealth of Nations,* pp. 157, 364–67.
[10] *Ibid.,* 547–56, 625–26, 837; Elie Halévy, *The Growth of Philosophic Radicalism,* tr. by Mary Morris (London, 1949), pp. 88–120; Schumpeter, *History of Economic Analysis,* pp. 267–69; Ronald L. Meek, "Physiocracy and Classicism in Britain," *The Economic Journal,* LXI (March, 1951), 26–47. In 1788, Arthur Young argued that Britain would enjoy far greater prosperity if one-half of the capital invested in the West Indies were reinvested in domestic industry ("On the Abolition of Slavery in the West Indies," *Annals of Agriculture,* IX [1788], 96).
[11] On May 24, 1787, Thomas Clarkson presented the newly-formed Committee for the Abolition of the Slave Trade with evidence and arguments on the unprofitability of the slave trade (the papers included an outline of his own forthcoming and highly influential *Essay on the Impolicy of the African Slave*

and gradual emancipation could be justified on the same grounds as the removal of other artificial restrictions on enterprise, such as the Poor Laws and Laws of Settlement, or regulations governing wages, apprenticeship, food prices, and usury rates (Jeremy Bentham's early cause).

This philosophy left no room for opposing a hypothetical slave trade resulting from free market conditions. And if one could show that the enslavement of a minority group increased the sum of total happiness, it is difficult to see how Smith—or Bentham and Burke, Smith's followers on economic questions—could raise any objections. Although the three thinkers stood together as emancipationists, they also denounced all forms of "false charity" that limited the free exercise of individual self-interest. For unless the egoistic principle were given free play, there could be no natural identity of interests. Moreover, in adopting Hume's defense of private property, Bentham echoed the most powerful argument of slave traders: government, by sanctioning private property, creates the expectation that such property will bring future pleasure; to negate such expectation not only inflicts great pain—greater, that is, than the denial of immediate gratifications— but destroys the psychological basis for all security. Burke pushed the argument from utility still further when he insisted that time validates laws and property of illegitimate origin.[12]

Logically, the rapid growth of Utilitarianism should have been a boon to the defenders of colonial slavery, who had long needed weap-

---

Trade). From this point on, abolitionists emphasized the following arguments: an end to the slave trade would greatly benefit the national economy by preventing the annual loss of thousands of seamen; by encouraging the development of the cheapest market for the raw materials needed by industry; by opening new markets for British manufactured goods; by eliminating a wasteful drain of capital and a cumbersome system of credit (Clarkson pointed out that trade in produce would bring returns two or three times a year to merchants and manufacturers, whereas the slave trade required as much as three years' credit); and by creating in the colonies a self-sustaining labor force that would in time consume more British produce (MS Proceedings of the Committee for the Abolition of the Slave Trade, 1787–1819 [hereafter Abolition Committee Minutes], I, 4; III, 4–6, British Museum Add. MSS 21254–21256).

[12] Halévy, *Growth of Philosophic Radicalism*, pp. 17–18, 46–47, 88–120, 174–76. Bentham saw both the American Declaration of Independence and the French Declaration of Rights as revivals of metaphysical "scholasticism"; every law, he pointed out, is a restriction on human liberty; every fine or tax is an attack on property; all human interaction involves a balancing of pains and pleasures.

ons that could demolish the champions of sentiment and natural rights.[13] But given the intellectual climate of the late eighteenth century, any serious attempt to accommodate slavery to the doctrine of natural identity of interests could only have succeeded in exposing the self-serving character of the doctrine. Or put the other way, an invalidation of slavery would help prove the beneficence of the doctrine of self-interest.

One of the striking features of British intellectual history, in the decades following *The Wealth of Nations,* is the sharp divergence of the standards of utility and moral sentiment. Hutcheson, among others, had assumed that the Creator had perfectly synchronized utility with man's moral sentiment; but Smith, his pupil, could never reconcile *The Theory of Moral Sentiments* (1759) with *The Wealth of Nations* (1776). Indeed, the latter work makes it perfectly clear that man's benevolent feelings can be disastrous, if allowed to interfere with public policy. As Elie Halévy and other historians have shown, a dominant theme that connects the writings of Smith, Burke, Joseph Townsend, Bentham, Godwin, and Malthus, is the need to free social philosophy from sentimental notions of charity and human rights. John Millar, a pupil and later colleague of Smith, and an influential opponent of slavery, actually undercut the governing premises of the antislavery movement. Progress, Millar insisted, was always the "natural" consequence of impersonal economic forces. It was never the result of benevolent intent, individual good will, or a changed disposition of the people.[14]

[13] Utilitarian arguments appeared, of course, in various antiabolition pamphlets. An especially interesting specimen is "A West India Planter," *Considerations on the Emancipation of Negroes and on the Abolition of the Slave Trade* (London, 1788). It was not accidental, however, that the main stream of Utilitarian thought, beginning with Bentham and William Paley, was profoundly antithetical to West Indian slavery. Henry Brougham thought that it was "a gross and intolerable perversion of the most liberal and enlightened in modern policy," when slaveholders appealed to the principles of laissez faire. One might as well, he argued, extend the principles of liberty to the destruction of criminal jurisprudence (*An Inquiry into the Colonial Policy of the European Powers* [4 vols., Edinburgh, 1803], II, 472).

[14] Halévy, *Growth of Philosophic Radicalism*, pp. 153–54, and *passim;* J. R. Poynter, *Society and Pauperism: English Ideas on Poor Relief, 1795–1834* (London, 1969), pp. 23–27, 53, 138; Duncan Forbes, " 'Scientific' Whiggism: Adam Smith and John Millar," *The Cambridge Journal*, VII (Aug., 1954), 643–70. Viner, in "Adam Smith and Laissez Faire," notes the discrepancy between

Yet paradoxically, the age of early Utilitarianism was also dominated by the cult of sensibility and by Evangelical benevolence. Nor did a divergence of the two mentalities lead to ideological warfare. Bentham once confided that he would have been a Methodist "had I not been what I am." He added, significantly, "if to be an anti-slavist is to be a saint, saintship for me. I am a saint!" Halévy has helped to explain why Christian philanthropy could for a time be compatible with antireligious Utilitarianism. Both schools of thought looked upon life as a perpetual struggle; both stressed the need to sacrifice present pleasure for the hope of future happiness; both valued efficiency and practical technique, and preached a form of socially oriented individualism.[15] One may add that both Utilitarian intellectuals and Christian missionaries were experimenting with new methods that would have the effect of ensuring the hegemony of an emerging ruling class.

Eventually, Utilitarianism would become a "radical" instrument in the hands of middle-class reformers, and the landed aristocracy would come to symbolize the retrogressive forces of monopoly. But during the early stages of the antislavery movement, no one could envision the meaning of an industrial society or predict the full implications of utility and laissez faire. The wars of the French Revolution helped to delay any sense of sharp division between industrialists and

---

Smith's *Theory of Moral Sentiments* and *The Wealth of Nations*. One of Smith's anonymous converts published some advice to the abolitionists which embodied the hard realism of the Utilitarians: "Instead of employing the money of your subscribers in paying people for collecting instances of cruelty and oppression, which, if true, only prove what no one denies, that *slaves* are *slaves*," the abolitionists should gather evidence to show "that the West Indian islands, so far from being of the importance commonly ascribed to them, have . . . long been, and while the present system remains, must continue to be, a dead weight about the neck of this country, to stifle its efforts and distract its strength." Humanitarian zeal, the author predicted, would only lead "the man of reflection to distrust a cause undertaken by such missionaries." Any legislative attempts to prohibit the slave trade would be as unenforceable as were the early Spanish efforts to prohibit the export of gold and silver. But if the West Indies were deprived of monopolistic privileges and subjected to the forces of free competition, the artificial demand for slaves would cease, and the islands would be inhabited and cultivated by "a much more useful body of men" (*A Letter to Granville Sharp, Esq., on the Proposed Abolition of the Slave Trade* [London, 1788], pp. 32–43).

[15] Elie Halévy, *England in 1815* (*A History of the English People in the Nineteenth Century*, I), tr. by E. I. Watkin, and D. A. Barker (London, 1949), pp. 586–87.

landlords, between free traders and protectionists, or between Utilitarian reformers and Evangelicals. William Wilberforce, for example, who represented the Christian paternalism of the landed aristocracy, could good-naturedly act as Bentham's intermediary with Cabinet ministers, and conclude, after the government had finally abandoned Bentham's plan for a "Panopticon" prison, that "never was any one worse used than Bentham."

Such philanthropic causes as prison reform and antislavery provided a meeting ground for Utilitarians and Christian "Saints." And if few of the early abolitionists were advocates of unqualified laissez faire, their popular movement served as a vehicle for the economic doctrines of Smith's disciples. It was perhaps accidental that Smith's influence on public policy, beginning with Lord North's tax reforms and Lord Shelburne's short ministry of 1782, coincided with the emergence of antislavery activism. Less coincidentally, Pitt, who personally consulted Smith in 1787 on an unknown economic matter, supported Smith's doctrines along with antislavery. Charles James Fox, Burke, and Wilberforce, all eloquent opponents of the slave trade, enhanced Smith's reputation in the House of Commons. By 1797, W. N. Pultney could assure the House that Smith would persuade the living generation and govern the next.[16]

More striking, however, are the parallels between the rise of antislavery and a profound transformation in attitudes toward the English poor, a transformation that reflected the growing contradiction between paternalistic traditions of local charity and the demands of a free-market economy. The first two decades of antislavery agitation were times of confusing contrasts: manufacturing towns grew in the midst of an agricultural and aristocratic society; famine and unemployment coexisted with a rising demand for industrial labor; for a time, cotton manufacturers profited from the Old Poor Law which supplied them with parish apprentices and which threw most of the

---

[16] For the difficulties in assessing Smith's influence, see E. G. West, *Adam Smith* (New Rochelle, N.Y., 1969), pp. 165–73; Jacob H. Hollander, "The Founder of a School," in *Adam Smith, 1776–1926: Lectures to Commemorate the Sesquicentennial of the Publication of "Wealth of Nations"* (New York, 1966 reprint), pp. 22–52; Halévy, *Growth of Philosophic Radicalism*, p. 107; Wesley C. Mitchell, *Types of Economic Theory: From Mercantilism to Institutionalism*, ed. by Joseph Dorfman (New York, 1967), pp. 152–62; C. R. Fay, "Adam Smith: A Bicentenary Appreciation," *The Dalhousie Review*, III (Jan., 1924), 403–22.

burden of supporting paupers on the country squires; a staggering increase in welfare costs (the poor rates) was offset by lingering paternalism and by the fear of hungry Jacobin mobs. Karl Polanyi has documented the slow and painful emergence of the ideal of a self-regulating labor market, in which the avoidance of starvation and the pursuit of self-gain would be the only incentives for work. The English squirearchy, in particular, resisted any measures that would erode their authority, disrupt the paternalistic order of the countryside, or destroy a sense of reciprocity and personal obligation as economic incentives. It was not until 1795 that Parliament loosened the restrictions of the 1662 Act of Settlement, which had virtually bound certain categories of workers to a parish. But this move toward a national labor market was counterbalanced by the famous Speenhamland Law, also of 1795, which established an allowance system designed to assure the poor of a minimum income, irrespective of earnings, and to prevent a further drain of rural labor. The allowance system had the effect of depressing wages, of guaranteeing a public subsidy to employers, and of exacerbating the problem of pauperism. As late as the 1820s British statesmen feared any sudden removal of the allowance system—much as they feared an immediate emancipation of West Indian slaves. By then, however, the English middle class had become increasingly dissatisfied with piecemeal reforms. In 1834, the same year that witnessed the nominal emancipation of West Indian slaves, the Poor Law Amendment liberated the English workers from public welfare and offered the unemployed a choice between starvation and the humiliating workhouse. Both "emancipations" had been made possible by the political triumph, in 1832, of the middle class.[17]

[17] Karl Polanyi, *The Great Transformation* (New York, 1944), pp. 68–102. John Clive has pointed to the first post-Reform Bill election in Leeds "as a microcosm of the social and economic forces in conflict during the 1830s." On the Tory side was Michael Thomas Sadler, a champion of maximum-hours legislation for working children. The Whig opposition consisted of a prominent mill owner and Thomas Babington Macaulay, the son of the abolitionist and a rising spokesman for laissez-faire and middle-class ideology. William Cobbett and working-class radicals supported Sadler. Macaulay, who had savagely reviewed a book by Sadler attacking Malthusian economics, maintained that "the lower orders" (he discreetly redefined the group as "the labouring class") would benefit far more from free trade than from a ten-hour-day law for persons under eighteen. As Clive perceptively observes, "the views of Sadler and Macaulay illustrate the differing directions in which tributaries from the stream of Evangelical social teaching could flow in the course of the nineteenth century." Sadler

There was no consistent or inevitable connection between antislavery doctrine and the laissez-faire ideal of a competitive labor market. The early abolitionists reflected the ambivalent attitudes of a transitional age and economy. Wilberforce and the Evangelicals tried to preserve traditional notions of deference and paternalism. The Quakers, on the other hand, had long taken the leadership in proposing labor reforms that would provide relief for the unemployed while making pauperism profitable for enlightened entrepreneurs. Yet the tension between forward- and backward-looking desires should not obscure a significant fact: the first decades of antislavery agitation also witnessed an out-pouring of tracts on the problem of labor discipline. And the chief figures who helped to revise the traditional paternalism toward the "laboring poor" were all outspoken opponents of Negro slavery: Pitt, Burke, Samuel Romilly, Bentham, William Paley, Hannah More, and Thomas Malthus.

In 1786, the year of Thomas Clarkson's famous *Essay on the Slavery and Commerce of the Human Species,* the Reverend Joseph Townsend suggested the relationship between antislavery and the ideal of a free and self-regulating market for labor. In his influential attack on the Poor Laws, Townsend wrote:

The poor know little of the motives which stimulate the higher ranks to action—pride, honour, and ambition. In general it is only hunger which can spur and goad them on to labour; yet our laws have said, they shall never hunger. The laws, it must be confessed, have likewise said that they shall be compelled to work. But then legal constraint is attended with too much trouble, violence, and noise; creates ill will, and never can be productive of good and acceptable service: whereas hunger is not only a peaceable, silent, unremitted pressure, but, as the most natural motive to industry and labour, it calls forth the most powerful exertions. . . . The slave must be compelled to work; but the freeman should be left to his own judgment and discretion; should be protected in the full enjoyment of his own, be it much or little; and punished when he invades his neighbor's

_____

had retained both his Evangelical faith (he had been a friend of Wilberforce) and a paternalistic sense of social responsibility "that could eventually lead to a dutiful acceptance of the need for state intervention." Macaulay, who had moved away from his Evangelical upbringing, had adapted "the doctrine of a providentially ordered class system . . . to the iron decrees of the classical economists. The laws of supply and demand were no less ineluctable than the divine edicts, and both seemed to be dependent for their working on a reserve army of labor" (John Clive, *Macaulay: The Shaping of the Historian* [New York, 1973], pp. 221–25).

property. By recurring to those base motives which influence the slave, and trusting only to compulsion, all the benefits of free service, both to the servant and to the master, must be lost.[18]

Sir Frederick Morton Eden, one of Adam Smith's many disciples, followed the precedents of the slave-trade investigations when he gathered empirical data on "the state of the poor." Paley, in his *Reasons for Contentment* (1795), echoed the West Indian planters by contending that poor workers were much happier than their rich employers, since they were spared from so many cares. The abolitionist Burke, in his *Thoughts and Details on Scarcity, Originally Presented to the Right Honourable William Pitt* (1795), pointed out that "the labouring people are only poor, because they are numerous. Numbers in their nature imply poverty. . . . Patience, labour, sobriety, frugality, and religion, should be recommended to them; all the rest is downright *fraud*. It is horrible to call them 'The *once happy* labourer.' " Malthus asserted that no public relief should be given to illegitimate or deserted children; only the threat of starvation would teach the poor to depend on themselves. Yet Malthus became highly indignant when William Cobbett's *Political Register* used his "profound work" to defend both the slave trade and West Indian slavery![19] The central point for Townsend, Burke, Paley, and Malthus was that the problem of English labor should be seen as entirely distinct from West Indian slavery, except in so far as "false charity" had kept the English poor in bondage.

The *Edinburgh Review*, a leading organ for antislavery propaganda, also disseminated Malthusian economics (the rival Tory journal, the *Quarterly Review*, attacked Malthus and defended the West Indian planters). Henry Brougham, one of the founders of the *Edinburgh Review*, first won national attention by attacking the slave trade and by demanding a total reformation of the colonial system.

---

[18] [Joseph Townsend], "A Dissertation on the Poor Laws," in [J. R. McCulloch], *A Select Collection of Scarce and Valuable Economical Tracts* (London, 1859), p. 404.

[19] Edmund Burke, *The Works of the Right Honourable Edmund Burke,* (London, 1889), V, p. 84; Poynter, *Society and Pauperism,* pp. 20–24, 53, 157, 166; *Cobbett's Political Register,* VII (Feb. 16, 1805), 229–32; IX (Jan. 18, 1806), 72–76. Unlike later reformers, Burke thought that alcohol would be of some help to the poor: "It is not nutritive in *any great* degree. But, if not food, it greatly alleviates the want of it. It invigorates the stomach for the digestion of poor meagre diet, not easily alliable to the human constitution. Wine the poor cannot touch. Beer . . . will by no means do the business" (*Works,* V, 106).

Although his abolitionism gave Brougham entrée to the Wilberforce circle, he remained independent of their Tory sympathies and helped to revitalize a Whig Opposition based on the values and aspirations of the new middle class. In 1812 he borrowed and perfected abolitionist methods when he mobilized a vast petition campaign against the Orders-in-Council that had attempted to control the trade of neutral nations (mainly the United States). Brougham's victory was hailed as a triumph for free-trade principles, as a triumph for the new industrialists, and above all, as a triumph for public opinion. According to Asa Briggs, the campaign of 1812 was as instrumental in organizing middle-class self-consciousness as was the Luddite movement in organizing working-class resistance to the bourgeoisie. Briggs has also shown how Brougham's success in shaping middle-class opinion culminated in the anti-Corn Law movement, which was heavily indebted to the precedents of antislavery agitation. The 1826 *Catechism on the Corn Laws*, for example, not only followed the familiar question-and-answer format of abolitionist literature, but included this exchange: *Q.* asserts that the relation between landlords and others, arising out of the Corn Laws, is a "source of kindly feelings and mutual virtues." *A.* replies, "exactly the same was said of slavery." No more needed to be said.[20]

[20] Halévy, *England in 1815*, p. 574; Asa Briggs, "The Language of 'Class' in Early Nineteenth-Century England," in *Essays in Labour History: In Memory of G. D. H. Cole*, ed. by Asa Briggs and John Saville (London, 1960), pp. 55–60; Chester W. New, *The Life of Henry Brougham, to 1830* (Oxford, 1961), pp. 36–44, 59, 67–70. Brougham was anything but doctrinaire; he easily bridged the worlds of James Mill, the Utilitarian reformer, and of Zachary Macaulay, the Evangelical reformer. His personal loyalty to abolitionists transcended partisan politics, as he evidenced when appointed Lord Chancellor, in dispensing patronage. He was perfectly attuned to the causes—antislavery, Catholic Emancipation, Parliamentary reform, education, and free trade—which defined the emerging self-consciousness of the middle class. It was Brougham's antislavery alliance with Zachary Macaulay that helped to pave the way for the latter's son, Thomas Babington, to rise to prominence as a writer and public speaker. As John Clive suggests, Tom Macaulay's abolitionism kept him in favor with his father at a time when Tom was drifting away from Evangelical orthodoxy. In the 1820s antislavery served a similar legitimizing function in British politics, as the banner passed from the Tories to Brougham and even to the great Catholic leader, Daniel O'Connell. Clive's analysis of Tom Macaulay's emerging social philosophy illuminates the meaning of class hegemony in the 1820s: "The important thing was that those who were going forward should feel that they were doing so as part of a general movement that embraced all classes. Since it was plainly impossible to unteach the poor, it was essential to teach those who could by comparison, be called the rich, that is, the middle class." For Macaulay, who wished

Such continuities do not imply that antislavery was a cloak for selfish interests. No doubt the movement unconsciously reflected the interests and aspirations of the English middle class. More important, however, it helped to crystallize an awareness of those interests and to identify them with those of the nation. An end to economic protectionism could thus be styled as the ultimate "emancipation." This conclusion is not weakened by the fact that the free-trade issue divided both the abolitionists and the middle class. Most abolitionists were far less concerned with extending the potential impact of their ideology than with the need to prevent a direct challenge to property rights in human beings from undermining the sanctions for property rights in general. The question of middle-class ideology does not involve individual motives but rather the ways in which antislavery precedents were actually used. Antislavery was a transitional social movement that served to mediate values and to prepare the way for the largely unforeseen things to come.

In some respects, the movement also fits Oliver MacDonagh's abstract "model" for later British reforms, although MacDonagh has specifically excluded antislavery as an appropriate example. The model can be summarized, wtih some oversimplification, as follows: a sudden and sensational exposé of a social evil is followed by a popular outcry, by a reaction from endangered interests, and by legislation that falls short of original reform objectives; soon it is discovered that the original evils still exist, and the precedent of the first law opens the way for further legislation and stricter rules of enforcement; a need for supervision and regulation replaces the earlier demands for abolition, and investigative commissions give way to more permanent bureaucratic agencies.[21] For our purposes the mechanisms of a "revolution in government" are less significant than a point which MacDonagh does not develop. The interaction between middle-class reformers and

---

above all to avoid democracy or revolution and to link the general progress of society with social stability, the middle class was " 'not likely to carry its zeal for reform to lengths inconsistent with the security of property and the maintenance of social order' " (Clive, *Macaulay,* pp. 58–60, 70, 103, 112).

[21] Oliver MacDonagh, "The Nineteenth-Century Revolution in Government: A Reappraisal," *The Historical Journal,* I (1958), 52–67; MacDonagh, *A Pattern of Government Growth, 1800–1860* (London, 1961). Brian Harrison has shown that the British temperance movement fails to fit MacDonagh's model (*Drink and the Victorians: The Temperance Question in England, 1815–1827* [Pittsburgh, 1971], pp. 28–29).

government provides an outlet for noisy and indignant agitation and gives a sanctioned recognition of limited conflict. Yet it also ensures some kind of compromise and the illusion of an ultimate harmony of interests. England was not governed by a slaveholding class, though the ruling elites had included and tolerated a few slaveholders. An attack on the slave system could thus become a permissible means of responding to change without a weakening or discrediting of class hegemony.

On another level, antislavery provided a new channel for political action. The year 1787 marked the transformation of the Quaker anti-slave-trade committee into a secular pressure group that soon began collecting evidence and petitions for Wilberforce's great Parliamentary campaign, a campaign initially proposed by Pitt and later endorsed enthusiastically by such rival leaders as Fox and Burke. Seven years earlier the so-called Gordon Riots, which had convulsed London in a week of pillage climaxing in an attack on the Bank of England, had shown how popular agitation could unleash diverse grievances. By 1780, mainly as a result of the American war, it was also clear that large segments of the middle class would continue to demand some form of extraparliamentary political activity, and that such activity could prove exceedingly useful to strong factions, like the Rockingham Whigs, when they were out of power. From 1779 to 1785 the York-shire-based movement for Parliamentary reform provided a safe channel for controlled agitation. The "Association" movement served a multitude of purposes: it allowed the "out" factions to embarrass the "in" factions, so long as the latter did not appropriate the reform cause; it enhanced the popular reputation of aspiring leaders like Fox and Pitt; it enabled a practical-minded organizer, the Reverend Christopher Wyvill, to neutralize the more radical demands of metropolitan supporters; above all, it tested the amount of popular participation the system was willing to allow. But in 1783, with the achievement of peace, the reform movement suffered serious division and disillusionment when Fox sacrificed his principles and entered the "infamous coalition" with Lord North in the Portland Ministry. By 1786, after Pitt as prime minister had been defeated in his third and last attempt at moderate Parliamentary reform, there appeared to be no further hope. As Ian Christie has pointed out, the American crisis had raised the specter of a court conspiracy undermining the liberties of the ancient constitution; but the period of fear and agitation barely survived the war.[22]

Meanwhile, Wyvill had swung his Yorkshire Association behind Pitt, who had acquired the popular image as a champion of liberal causes. Wyvill's political protegé, William Wilberforce, was also an intimate friend of Pitt. By 1788, Wilberforce was writing Wyvill that "our little kingdom" of Yorkshire should not be backward in organizing district meetings to petition Parliament against the slave trade (adding, *"entre nous,"* that Wyvill would be delighted to hear Pitt talk on the slave question). Veteran organizers of Wyvill's Yorkshire Association were soon at work collecting petition signatures. Eugene Charlton Black is perhaps too harsh when he writes that "Wilberforce learned his techniques for antislavery agitation in the Yorkshire Association school, and, intriguingly enough, Pitt used Wilberforce much the same way that he had previously used Wyvill."[23] On the other hand, if we suspend questions of personal motive and deliberate strategy (and there can be no doubt that both Pitt and Wilberforce found the slave trade morally repugnant), confining our view to the history of extraparliamentary association, it seems apparent that antislavery petitioning revived enthusiasm among a constituency that had become bored or disillusioned over the futile struggle to "purify" Parliament. Indeed, the slave-trade issue gave Parliament a chance to vindicate its own moral purity and to prove its responsiveness to "respectable" petitioning. And the new movement provided the public with a safe distraction—or to put it more charitably, with a mode of political participation which did not directly threaten the sources or structure of political power.

As Pitt was quick to perceive, extraparliamentary groups could be

[22] George Rudé, *Wilkes and Liberty: A Social Study of 1763–1774* (Oxford, 1962), pp. 135–48; Ian R. Christie, *Wilkes, Wyvill and Reform: The Parliamentary Reform Movement in British Politics, 1760–1785* (London, 1962), pp. 70–81, 110–32, 146–66, 202–23; Eugene Charlton Black, *The Association: British Extraparliamentary Political Organization, 1769–1793* (Cambridge, Mass., 1963), pp. 14, 31–33, 60–66, 87, 99–105, 111–21, 132, 201–4.

[23] Wilberforce to Wyvill, Jan. 25, 1788, Wilberforce papers, in possession of C. E. Wrangham, Esq. (hereafter CEW) (I am much indebted to Mr. Wrangham for allowing me to consult this collection); E. M. Hunt, "The North of England Agitation for the Abolition of the Slave Trade, 1780–1800," M.A. thesis, University of Manchester, 1959, pp. 252–53; Black, *The Association*, p. 124.

as useful to the government as to factions aspiring to power, although he personally detested the word, "association." During the early years of the French Revolution, his own administration gave support and encouragement to vigilante societies, such as the Association for the Preservation of Liberty and Property, which helped to terrorize the advocates of liberal reform. Abolitionist agitation was still on the rise when loyalist mobs were attacking the premises of men like Joseph Priestley and Thomas Walker, and when other dissidents were being tried for treason and sedition. The key question, then, is whether antislavery would be perceived as potentially subversive, or as a force that helped to preserve "liberty and property."

The second part of this question will require extensive development in Chapter Nine, but I shall touch on the first part now. Until 1792 there were still ideological ties between the antislavery movement and the Constitutional societies that were beginning to distribute Painite literature to the working class. It was to be expected that English radicals like Thomas Paine and Thomas Hardy, who embraced the ideals of the American and French Revolutions, should include antislavery among the political causes they espoused. When Thomas Cooper combined anti-slave-trade agitation with more radical activities in the north of England, a hysterical pamphlet accused Cooper, Paine, Clarkson, and Wilberforce of being "the JACOBINS OF ENGLAND." Wilberforce himself, who saw that it was only "natural" that Jacobins should be friendly to abolitionism, sent word to Clarkson that any further talk of the French Revolution "will be ruin to our cause." In some of the provincial centers, middle-class abolitionists complained that no one except "Republicans" would sign petitions against the slave trade.[24]

Consequently, the more frightened and conservative members of the antislavery committees tended to withdraw from the cause at the very time when radicals were becoming wholly absorbed with the struggle against domestic suppression. By the summer of 1792 Thomas Hardy,

[24] Austin Mitchell, "The Association Movement of 1792–1793," *The Historical Journal,* IV (1961), 56–77; Maurice J. Quinlan, *Victorian Prelude: A History of English Manners, 1700–1830* (London, 1965), pp. 73–86; James Walvin, "How Popular Was Abolition? Popular Dissent and the Negro Question, 1787–1833," unpublished paper; Black, *The Association,* pp. 223–67; *A Very New Pamphlet Indeed! Being the Truth* . . . (London, 1792), pp. 3–5; Robert Isaac Wilberforce and Samuel Wilberforce, *The Life of William Wilberforce* (5 vols., London, 1838), I, 343.

of the London Corresponding Society, was not alone in fearing that abolitionism might divert attention from more pressing and critical issues. The Manchester Abolition Committee, which contained a growing preponderance of radicals, held its last meeting on April 17, 1792; eleven days later the radical *Manchester Herald* delivered what E. M. Hunt has termed "the last blast of the campaign in Manchester," announcing "with grief" that the House of Commons had decided to sanction the slave trade for seven more years: "she weeps, indignant, whilst she announces to the world the tardiness of the REPRESENTATIVES of the people of BRITAIN to do JUSTICE." Yet the movement as a whole survived both the suppression of radical dissent and the growing disillusion of radical reformers. It also survived middle-class defections from more dangerous causes. The London Abolition Committee continued to meet, though with growing infrequency, until 1797. And if the tides of reaction finally made it prudent to suspend further public agitation, antislavery remained popular in the House of Commons, which as late as 1796 rejected Wilberforce's immediate abolition bill by the narrow margin of seventy-four to seventy votes. British antislavery suffered for a while from the taint of Jacobinism, but it largely purged itself of the embarrassing association.[25]

I have already noted the apparent discrepancy between the political economists' sympathy for the slave and their hostility toward the "false charity" that had kept the English poor in a state of moral bondage. The contemporary interpretations of that discrepancy require a third level of analysis: the use of antislavery literature as a means of resolving conflicts in value.

Much as white Americans had learned to deny or rationalize the worst evils of Negro slavery, so had middle-class Englishmen learned to screen out most of the oppression and suffering in their midst. If the cult of sensibility encouraged sympathy for individual misfortune, the cult of utility gave grounds for believing that such misfortune was a

[25] Hunt, "North of England Agitation," pp. 57–58, 105–13; Walvin, "How Popular Was Abolition?" The Abolition Committee met three times in 1796, once in 1797, and then suspended meetings until May 23, 1804. It is significant that when Clarkson was contemplating retirement, for personal reasons, in August, 1793, he gave a candid prediction to Wilberforce, William Smith, Josiah Wedgwood, and Matthew Montagu that it would be "two or three years" before the cause succeeded (Clarkson to Matthew Montagu, Aug. 28, 1793, Clarkson papers, Henry E. Huntington Library [hereafter HEH]).

necessary part of the general good. It is true that the mechanisms of denial were becoming increasingly sensitive, especially after the French Revolution evoked a consciousness of peril. Yet a half-century later, as E. P. Thompson observes, "when the girls were brought half-naked out of the pits, the local luminaries seem to have been genuinely astonished." Thompson adds: "We forget how long abuses can continue 'unknown' until they are articulated: how people can look at misery and not notice it, until misery itself rebels."[26] Although the various religious and benevolent societies helped to foster an awareness of domestic suffering, it was blunted by the fear of revolution and by the reigning attitudes toward property and responsibility. Yet the misgivings of men of good will, arising from the "inconsistency" between liberal profession and daily practice, could be psychologically displaced in a concern for "the unfortunate slave."

This is a difficult thesis to substantiate. At best it can illuminate no more than one aspect of an enormously complex movement. The central questions do not concern conscious intent but rather selectivity, context, and emphasis.

For our first illustration, let us return to James Stephen's musings, early in 1807, on the reasons for God's vengeance against England. It should be noted in passing that Stephen was perhaps the most powerful intellect of the British abolition movement, and that for some thirty years he had a decisive influence on the movement's policy. His indictment of the inconsistency of English practice is also a panegyric of English society:

Who are the people that have provoked God thus heinously, but the same who are among all the nations of the earth, the most eminently indebted to his bounty. He has given to us an unexampled portion of civil liberty; and we in return drag his rational creatures into a most severe and perpetual bondage. Social happiness has been showered upon us with singular profusion; and we tear from oppressed millions every social, nay, almost every human comfort. . . . For our plenty we give them want; for our ease, intolerable toil; for our wealth, privation of the right of property; for our equal laws, unbridled violence and wrong. Science shines upon us, with her meridian beams; yet we keep these degraded fellow-creatures in the deepest shades of ignorance and barbarity. Morals and manners, have happily distinguished us from the other nations of Europe; yet we create

[26] E. P. Thompson, *The Making of the English Working Class* (New York, 1963), p. 342.

and cherish in two other quarters of the globe [Africa and the West Indies], an unexampled depravity of both.[27]

This was hardly the England perceived by the London Corresponding Society, by Francis Place or William Cobbett, by John Thelwall, Henry Hunt, or "General Ludd." Yet for Stephen an attack on the slave system provided the occasion for an explicit vindication of the English social order. What could account, he asked, for the divine vengeance that had heaped so many calamities upon England? According to Scripture, the causes most frequently assigned for the chastisement of sinful nations were "the sins of oppression, injustice, and violence towards the poor and helpless; and the shedding of innocent blood." To English radicals these words might have recalled the domestic oppression of the 1790s, the Irish blood bath of 1798, or Cobbett's charge, made in 1806, that England was "daily advancing to the state in which there are but two classes of men, *masters,* and abject *dependents.*"[28] Stephen's own view is important enough to quote at some length:

If we cast our eyes around us in this happy island, there is still less matter of charge against the national conscience on the score of violence and oppression. In no other part of the globe, are the poor and helpless so well protected by the laws, or so humanely used by their superiors. Nor are the laws chargeable with injustice towards the less fortunate peasantry of our sister island; though here perhaps, there is much that ought to be reformed. If the legislature be now culpable in regard to Ireland, it is for omission and neglect, rather than for positive wrong; nor does the fault arise from any of those unrighteous principles, or from that oppressive use of power, which are so peculiarly offensive to heaven. If therefore we are suffering for such offences as have usually provoked the scourge of the Most High, if it be as the protector of the poor and destitute, that God has entered into judgment with us, we must, I repeat, look to Africa, and to the West Indies, for the causes of his wrath.[29]

It should be stressed that Stephen, a deeply religious man, was obsessed by fears of collective guilt and retribution. Unlike his brother-in-law, Wilberforce, he personally knew the meaning of oppression and poverty. His father, a tempestuous Scot who had admired the

---

[27] James Stephen, *The Dangers of the Country* (Philadelphia, 1807; originally printed London, 1807), p. 121.

[28] *Ibid.,* p. 112; Raymond Williams, *Culture and Society* (New York, 1958), pp. 14–15.

[29] Stephen, *Dangers of the Country,* pp. 115–16.

French *philosophes* and who had sent young James to the school of Peter Annet, the notorious Deist, had not been "well protected by the laws" or "humanely used" by his superiors. As a result of bankruptcy he had, in fact, been thrown into King's Bench Prison and then transferred to a more secure jail after leading an attempted breakout to protest the illegality of imprisonment for debt. Along with his destitute mother, James had lived for a time in the squalid jail, surrounded by spectacles of drunkenness and despair.[30] England had been for him anything but a "happy island" until he returned, as a young lawyer, from the West Indies and won acceptance in the Clapham Sect. Apart from his own experience with poverty, he was clearly aware of England's conduct in India (which he goes on to defend), as well as of the torture, arbitrary imprisonment, and massacre that had marked the suppression of Irish dissent (Henry Grattan had proclaimed that "the Irish Protestant can never be free until the Irish Catholic has ceased to be a slave"). And yet the meaning of Stephen's language is quite explicit. Interpreting God's justice to his countrymen, he made an attack on Negro slavery serve as an all-redeeming atonement.[31]

But the ideological functions of antislavery literature were still more complex. The wider connotations of Negro slavery appear in a portion of William Cowper's "Charity," a long sermon in verse which had immense and continuing appeal to abolitionists and which is virtually a paradigm of early British antislavery thought.[32] Writing five years after

[30] James Stephen, MS Memoirs "written by himself for the use of his children," British Museum Add. MSS 46443–46444. Stephen was the father of Sir James Stephen and the grandfather of Leslie and Sir James Fitzjames Stephen.

[31] Henry Grattan is quoted in J. Steven Watson, *The Reign of George III, 1760–1815* (Oxford, 1960), p. 392. Stephen's theme also appeared in Parliamentary speeches and, more significantly, in handbills like *The Contrast; or, the African Slave, and the English Labourer* (c.1805?), which announced that the English worker was blessed with a twelve-hour day, that he had wages with which to buy food, that "he is as independent as his employer," and that he "would be ready to strike his master to the ground if he saw him degrade a woman" by flogging her on the naked breasts. James Walvin has pointed out that English radicals like John Thelwall employed antislavery rhetoric to dramatize the similar plight of English workers and West Indian bondsmen. Although more research is needed on the subject, I suspect that Walvin exaggerates the continuing appeal of antislavery to working-class leaders (for later proslavery feeling among English radical leaders, see Mary Ellison, *Support for Secession; Lancashire and the American Civil War* [Chicago, 1972]).

[32] William Cowper, "Charity," in *The Poems of William Cowper,* ed. by J. C. Bailey (London, 1905), pp. 165–78. In the spring of 1788 Lady Hesketh

the publication of *The Wealth of Nations,* Cowper sings the praises of Captain Cook and of international trade, which is providentially designed "To give the pole the produce of the sun, / And Knit the unsocial climates into one." Commerce is the great engine of human progress; it "Spreads foreign wonders in his country's sight, / Imports what others have invented well / And stirs his own to match them or excel."

But this happy lesson in political economy brings us to the slave merchant, who grows "rich in cargoes of despair." Clearly the expansion of Europe has not been a universal blessing to mankind. The name Cortez is "odious for a world enslaved!" Catholic Iberia has suffered divine vengeance for centuries of greed and plunder. The lesson should not be lost on traders who "buy the muscles and the bones of man." Cowper pictures the conventional sable warrior, "frantic with regret / Of her he loves, and never can forget." Slavery is the "most degrading of all ills": "Yes, to deep sadness sullenly resigned, / He feels his body's bondage in his mind; / Puts off his generous nature; and, to suit / His manners with his fate, puts on the brute." Cowper boldly advises the slave to "Wait for the dawning of a brighter day, / And snap the chain the moment when you may." This leads the poet to a lyrical passage on natural liberty, which moves from an external command to exuberant release, subsiding into pastoral contentment:

> Nature imprints upon whate'er we see
> That has a heart and life in it, "Be free!"
> The beasts are chartered neither age nor force
> Can quell the love of freedom in a horse:
> He breaks the cord that held him at the rack;

---

suggested that Cowper write some songs on the slave trade "as the surest way of reaching the public ear." Cowper was at first reluctant; he had "already borne my testimony in favour of my black brethren [in "Charity"] and . . . was one of the earliest, if not the first, of those who have in the present day expressed their detestation of the diabolical traffic." After writing five ballads, including "The Negro's Complaint" and "Pity for Poor Africans," he wrote Lady Hesketh: "I shall now probably cease to sing of tortured negroes—a theme which never pleased me, but which, in the hope of doing them some little service, I was not unwilling to handle." These poems were immensely popular on both sides of the Atlantic, and were read by many who would never have opened an antislavery pamphlet. See Thomas Wright, *The Life of William Cowper* (London, 1892), pp. 471–72; Gilbert Thomas, *William Cowper and the Eighteenth Century* (2nd ed., London, 1948), pp. 28–29; Lodwick Hartley, *William Cowper: The Continuing Revaluation* (Chapel Hill, 1960), pp. 8–9.

> And, conscious of an unencumbered back,
> Snuffs up the morning air, forgets the rein;
> Loose fly his forelock and his ample mane;
> Responsive to the distant neigh, he neighs;
> Nor stops till, overleaping all delays
> He finds the pasture where his fellows graze.

This is an artful blend of British primitivism and natural rights philosophy, appealing to our impulsive yearnings to throw off the restraints and encumbrances of society, to be as free as a prancing horse. Yet there are striking ambiguities even in Cowper's image of spontaneous natural liberty. As an active force, nature "imprints" upon passive life its command of freedom. The beasts are "chartered" with an irrepressible desire to break all cords of bondage, to forget the rein. But charters restrict and prescribe, as well as protect. In effect, Cowper defines our love of freedom in words that suggest passivity and bondage. Liberation ends, finally, in a complacent grazing with "fellows."

After this pastoral excursion, Cowper returns to human slavery:

> Canst thou, and honoured with a Christian name,
> Buy what is woman-born, and feel no shame?
> Trade in the blood of innocence, and plead
> Expedience as a warrant for the deed?

Expediency, he reminds us, is the excuse for all crime and aggression:

> So may the wolf, whom famine has made bold
> To quit the forest and invade the fold;
> So may the ruffian, who with ghostly glide,
> Dagger in hand, steals close to your bedside;
> Not he, but his emergence forced the door,
> He found it inconvenient to be poor.

Thus far Cowper has used the slavery issue as a medium for expressing fairly radical but ambiguous attitudes toward liberty and authority. He equates liberty with the unrestrained release of natural instincts, which are nevertheless externally prescribed and which lead the horse to a peaceful and uncoerced sociability with his "fellows." Significantly, the idyll of pasture and sheepfold is threatened by the wolf, whose boldness has apparently been "chartered" by the famine and brutality of the wilderness; and, analogously, by the criminal, who voluntarily places self-interest and expediency above natural justice. Later in the poem Cowper insists that "the foe of virtue" has no claim on charity: "Let just restraint, for public peace designed, / Chain up the wolves and tigers of mankind." In line with conventional imagery, the native African is associated with pastoral innocence and natural liberty. His European abductor is linked with the wolf who invades the fold and with the ruffian who finds it "inconvenient to be poor." Neither famine nor poverty justifies violent resistance. But presumably the slave has a perfect right to break the cord that holds him at the rack, and we should feel the same empathy toward the fugitive slave that we feel toward the escaped horse "overleaping all delays."

But Cowper was an Evangelical and a devoted admirer of John Newton and Henry Thornton. It was one thing to experiment with imagery of natural freedom and quite another to suggest that all men should snuff up the morning air and forget the reins of society.[33] Cowper's nostalgic yearning for rustic innocence is always balanced by his conviction that man, the "progeny and heir of sin," can never learn his duty from reason and nature alone. It is precisely the tension between these values which gives force to Cowper's concept of charity and which gives him a solution to the moral problem of European expansion.

Cowper cannot believe that New World slavery is part of God's design for human progress. Surely God has not "Built a brave world, which cannot yet subsist, / Unless His right to rule it be dismissed?" And even if one grants the plea of economic necessity, there is still room for charity. Souls have no "discriminating hue." Christ's love paid one price for all men. And on this proselytizing note, Cowper shifts key and begins discussing spiritual slavery, by which he means ignorance of Christ's saving truth. Any nominal Christian who scorns the "godlike privilege" of saving others is "himself a slave." This brings us to the consummate image of "charity"—a Negro slave kneeling before his evangelical liberator:

[33] Though Cowper was much distressed by the plight of the Olney poor, he was even more distressed by the failure of the poor to embrace serious Christianity. In 1782 he expressed typical doubts about the value of "charity": "The profane are so profane, so drunken, dissolute, and in every respect worthless, that to make them partakers of his bounty would be to abuse it" (Wright, *Life of Cowper*, p. 319). For Cowper's alarm over the Gordon Riots and the state of English society, see Maurice J. Quinlan, *William Cowper: A Critical Life* (Minneapolis, 1953), pp. 108–9.

And slaves, by truth enlarged, are doubly freed.
Then would he say, submissive at thy feet,
While gratitude and love made service sweet,
"My dear deliverer out of a hopeless night,
Whose bounty bought me but to give me light,
I was a bondman on my native plain,
Sin forged, and ignorance made fast, the chain;
Thy lips have shed instruction as the dew,
Taught me what path to shun, and what pursue;
Farewell my former joys! I sigh no more
For Africa's once loved, benighted shore;
Serving a benefactor I am free;
At my best home, if not exiled from thee."

Our picture of freedom has swung abruptly away from the polarity of natural innocence. Note that the slave was a bondman on his "native plain," which is now a "benighted shore." He was not enslaved by a rapacious European but by sin and ignorance. Unlike the liberated horse, the black learns to "sigh no more / For Africa's once loved, benighted shore" (the horse, we should recall, neighs in response to the distant neigh, "nor stops till, overleaping all delays, / He finds the pasture where his fellows graze"). The black's liberator has taught him "what path to shun, and what pursue." His freedom lies in a conversion from unwilling to willing servitude. "Gratitude and love" enable him to internalize his new master's commands. His submission is legitimized by his sense of obligation.

For Cowper, as for many of his contemporaries, the image of Negro slavery evoked a contrary image of release, liberation, and natural freedom. Since slavery required physical coercion, its implied antithesis was a perfect freedom of will, instinct, and physical movement, or in other words, a state of self-sovereignty. This concept of freedom had considerable appeal, on levels of theory and emotion, to men of the late eighteenth century. It can be found in primitivistic fantasies, in portraits of the American as a New Adam, and in highly qualified form, in the Wesleyan ideal of the sanctified Christian.

But natural self-sovereignty threatened traditional Christian values as well as secular ideologies that justified social rank and social control. Had nature imprinted the mandate, "Be free!" upon the hearts of common laborers as well as upon horses? (And of course no one who took vicarious delight in a horse's freedom advocated the burning of saddles.) Was every man who wielded power in the name of expediency to be likened to a thief who finds it "inconvenient to be poor"? Cowper did not have to fret over such questions. The subjects of slavery and emancipation provided him with a medium for bridging two worlds of contradictory value. The remote institution of Negro slavery represented an idealized model of physical oppression which allowed both a paean to natural liberty and the rejection of expediency as an excuse for injustice. The fantasy of emancipation and conversion, with the grateful servant submissive at his benefactor's feet, gave sanction to dependence and authority by redefining the relationship— in contrast to physical slavery—as one of natural freedom. Charity redeemed the fruits of trade as well as the existing social order. "Some men," Cowper assures us, "make gain a fountain, whence proceeds / A stream of liberal and heroic deeds." In a leap of psychological imperialism, Cowper exorcized the guilt of commercial exploitation— first, by associating slavery with the loss of primitive liberty; then, by picturing emancipation as a conversion to voluntary servitude. In so doing, he helped define the identity of the evangelical deliverer.

Antislavery as Reinforcement of Legitimate Authority

For a time it was at least conceivable that British antislavery might become part of a wider challenge to traditional authorities. During the mid-eighteenth century the most outspoken protests against Negro slavery had come from anonymous revolutionaries like "Philmore" or from egalitarian theorists like George Wallace.[34] By 1780 opposition to the American war, coupled with alarm over Ministerial corruption, brought Granville Sharp, Thomas Day, and Richard Price, all noted opponents of slavery, together with metropolitan reformers like John Jebb, Capel Lofft, and Major John Cartwright. The methods and goals of their Society for Promoting Constitutional Information (S.C.I.) were far more radical than those of Wyvill's Yorkshire Association. And in 1783 the Society endorsed the Quaker petition to Parliament against the slave trade, a remonstrance which at least raised

---

[34] In 1787, Major Cartwright sent Granville Sharp a subscription "towards the Emancipation of the Negroes" from the Reverend John Charlesworth, who had also loaned Cartwright Philmore's radical pamphlet, *Two Dialogues on the Man-Trade,* which Cartwright thought had been published forty or fifty years before (John Cartwright to Granville Sharp, Oct. 15, 1787, Clarkson papers, HEH). Though Benezet had quoted from the pamphlet in 1762, two years after its actual publication, I have encountered no other references to it. See Chapter Six.

the question whether the "benevolent purposes" of government had been perverted, "that its terrors have fallen on the innocent, while evil doers, and oppressors, have been openly encouraged?" There is some truth to Eugene Black's argument that antislavery served as one of the distractions that diluted the effectiveness of the S.C.I. Yet in the provincial cities like Manchester antislavery retained a radical flavor into the 1790s, and was frequently associated with bolder programs for political and economic reform. E. M. Hunt has pointed to the ties between antislavery and the Dissenters' campaign to repeal the Test and Corporation Acts. And according to Hunt, the anti-slave-trade cause gave Manchester radicals like Thomas Walker and Thomas Cooper their first experience in national agitation. In 1790, Walker linked antislavery with the "general principles of universal Liberty (unconfined to Colour or to Clime) . . . so recently and so widely adopted on the European continent." A few years later Walker stood trial for high treason after defending his premises against a drunken loyalist mob.[35]

The resistant power of traditionalism can be seen in Dr. Daniel Burton's serene reply, in 1768, to a letter from Anthony Benezet. Burton, who had been Chancellor of the Diocese of Oxford, was then secretary of the Society for the Propagation of the Gospel (S.P.G.), which

[35] London Yearly Meeting and London Meeting for Sufferings, *The Case of our Fellow-Creatures, the Oppressed Africans, Respectfully Recommended to the Serious Consideration of the Legislature of Great Britain, by the People Called Quakers* (London, 1783), pp. 3–4; Black, *The Association,* pp. 84, 177–78, 200–4; Hunt, "North of England Agitation," pp. 12–14, 22–23, 33, 58–69, 99–115; Thomas Walker, printed sheet, 1790, William Smith papers, Duke University Library (hereafter DUL); Thomas Cooper, *Letters on the Slave Trade: First Published in "Wheeler's Manchester Chronicle"* (Manchester, 1787), *passim;* "Junius," "An Expostulatory Address to the *People* of *England* on the Late Memorable Decision Against the Abolition of the Slave Trade," *Gentleman's Magazine,* LXI (June, 1791), 537–38; Thompson, *Making of the English Working Class,* pp. 11–12, 120. Walker affirmed that since Britons had been "the *foremost* to propagate" such principles of liberty, they should not be the last to practice them. The principle of universalism, which Thompson finds in the London Corresponding Society, was also endorsed by the Manchester radicals, who called for the total abolition of *slavery* throughout the world (Hunt, p. 113). Walker, a wealthy textile manufacturer, frequently attended meetings of the London Abolition Committee, and continued to send the Committee money and petitions as late as March, 1792 (Abolition Committee Minutes, III, 42). That summer he was close to Thomas Paine, and in December defended his premises against the loyalist mob.

Benezet had attacked for oppressing slaves on the Society's Barbadian plantations. Burton expressed a patronizing "esteem" for the Quaker's feelings of tenderness and humanity toward Negroes. He assured Benezet (quite without foundation) that members of the S.P.G. paid strict attention to the welfare and Christian instruction of their slaves: "But they *cannot condemn* the *Practice* of *keeping Slaves* as unlawful, finding the contrary very plainly implied in the precepts given by the Apostles, both to Masters & Servants, which last were for the most part Slaves." In other words, the doctrine that slave-keeping was unlawful might undermine the authority of Scripture. Furthermore, the dissemination of such a doctrine would tempt slaves to rebel and would make masters "more suspicious & cruel, & much more unwilling to let their Slaves learn Christianity." The S.P.G. advised the deluded but well-intentioned Quaker "not to go further in publishing your Notions, but rather to retract them, if you shall see cause, which they hope you may on further consideration."[36]

It was Granville Sharp, the grandson of an Anglican archbishop and a complex figure, in many ways atypical of English antislavery leaders, who countered this strategy by converting antislavery into a defense of traditional authority.[37] By 1767, Sharp had developed the following line of argument: no one could claim a Negro as private property, in the manner of a horse or dog, unless he could prove that Negroes were not human beings and thus *subjects* of the king; all men, women, and children including aliens and strangers, were in a relative sense the "property" of the king; as subjects, they were bound by the king's laws and were entitled to the king's protection; the latter included the Habeas Corpus Act of 1679, which protected subjects from

[36] Quoted in George S. Brookes, *Friend Anthony Benezet* (Philadelphia, 1937), pp. 417–18.

[37] Sharp was in fact much upset by Burton's letter, and sent a private complaint to the Bishop of Llandaff (July 25, 1774, Sharp papers, British and Foreign Bible Society). He declined, however, Benezet's request for public support. "I had too much veneration for the Society," he later wrote the Archbishop of Canterbury, "to permit their opinion to be called publickly in question." Sharp did answer the S.P.G.'s "missionary," the Reverend Thomas Thompson, who had gone further than Burton by trying to vindicate the slave trade; and Burton's position led Sharp into Scriptural studies designed to remove the "stigma" Burton had thrown on "our Holy Religion" (Sharp to the Archbishop of Canterbury, Aug. 1, 1786, John A. Woods's transcripts of Sharp papers [hereafter JAW]; also printed in Prince Hoare, *Memoirs of Granville Sharp, Esq. Composed From His Own Manuscripts* . . . [London, 1820], p. 262).

arbitrary imprisonment or from being involuntarily shipped out of the realm; the importation or exportation of slaves was thus an innovation, unjustified by either law or precedent; a master's rights could derive only from contract, and any contract would be nullified if it permanently deprived a servant of his corporal liberty. Indeed, Sharp assumed the position of a discoverer and vindicator of the true law of England. In 1769, he could write the Lord High Chancellor, protesting that a public advertisement for the sale of a black girl was a breach not only of the laws of nature, humanity, and equity, but of "the established law, custom, and constitution of England." Three years later he won international fame when, in the case of James Somerset, the Court of King's Bench appeared to say that he was right.[38]

In Chapter Ten the facts and implications of the Somerset case will be discussed at some length. The point to be stressed here is that Sharp drove a wedge between the defense of slavery and the defense of traditional privilege. His more knowledgeable opponents, like Samuel Estwick, the assistant colonial agent for Barbados, conceded that Negro slavery was an innovation, unknown to common law and "totally different" from ancient villeinage. In his commentary on the Somerset case, Estwick fell back upon the argument that where there was no law, there could be no remedy. If slavery was incompatible with the maxims of common law, so were other practices, such as the impressment of seamen, which were justified by special circumstances. And though Parliament had not specifically enacted a slave code, it had authorized the slave trade and had thus recognized legal claims to property in men. Estwick tried to avoid discussing servitude and dominion, claiming that the question must be confined to the ownership of legitimate articles of commerce. He admitted, however, that Parliament had the right to remedy any defects in the law. And by focusing on the bare "facts" of property rights and Parliamentary sanction, he helped to sever the authority of slaveholders from more traditional forms of dominion.[39]

---

[38] Granville Sharp, *A Representation of the Injustice and Dangerous Tendency of Tolerating Slavery; or of Admitting the Least Claim of Private Property in the Persons of Men, in England* (London, 1769), pp. 10–41; Hoare, *Memoirs of Granville Sharp,* pp. 44–45, 49.

[39] Samuel Estwick, *Considerations on the Negro Cause Commonly So Called, Addressed to the Right Honourable Lord Mansfield, Lord Chief Justice of the*

Antislavery ideology is usually considered as part of a wider egalitarian and liberalizing movement. Most of the arguments used against human bondage could have been turned against the forms of religious and hereditary privilege which dominated eighteenth-century England. Yet on the eve of the American Revolution, Granville Sharp's legal triumph helped to frame the boundaries of future controversy. The Somerset decision—which would be looked upon as the opening act of the antislavery drama—was interpreted as a vindication of law and tradition. It defined slavery as essentially "un-British," as an alien intrusion which could be tolerated, at best, as an unfortunate part of the commercial and colonial "other-world." A denunciation of colonial slavery therefore implied no taste for a freer or more equal society.

On the contrary, much of the early British antislavery writing reveals an almost obsessive concern with idealizing hierarchical order. The Reverend James Ramsay begins his highly praised *Essay on the Treatment and Conversion of African Slaves* (1784) by stating that "there is a natural inequality, or diversity, which prevails among men that fits them for society." When founded upon nature or revelation, such inequalities serve the best interests of both superiors and inferiors: "Each man takes that station for which nature intended him; and his rights are fenced around, and his claims restrained, by laws prescribed by the Author of nature."[40]

Ramsay praises the "voluntary" relationships between servant and master, blending a traditional ideal of organic interdependence with a Whiggish emphasis on implicit contract. Thus he finds that the entrepreneur's "superiority," derived from the ownership of material, is balanced by the workman's "liberty" to accept or refuse employment. Yet law and mutual interest must be reinforced by religion—meaning the established church—which inculcates obedience to legitimate authority. Such arguments seem closer to those of Daniel Burton than to the equalitarian rhetoric of the more radical American and French abolitionists. Indeed, Ramsay makes no attempt to disguise his admiration for the discipline of the sugar plantation. Drawing on his own

---

Court of King's Bench . . . (2nd ed., London, 1773), pp. xiii, 21, 25–26, 31, 38–39.

[40] James Ramsay, *An Essay on the Treatment and Conversion of African Slaves in the British Sugar Colonies* (London, 1784), pp. 1–2. A naval surgeon before he took holy orders, Ramsay had spent some twenty years in the West Indies.

experience in St. Kitts, he speaks glowingly of a system which ensures that every hour will have its employment and every piece of work its overseer: "Nor are any families among us so well regulated as those connected with plantations, where method in correction and work makes some amends for the want of principle in our manner of managing slaves."[41]

Nevertheless, this "want of principle" means that slavery is the very "negation of law":

Opposed to this law of nature, and of God, that gives and secures to every man the rights adapted to his particular station in society, stands the artificial, or unnatural relation of master and slave; where power constitutes right; where, according to the degree of his capacity of coercion, every man becomes his own legislator, and erects his interest, or his caprice, into a law for regulating his conduct to his neighbor.[42]

Slavery, then, is an evil not because of its inherent injustice, its inequality, or its permanent subordination of one class of men. It is an "artificial" and "unnatural" relation which lacks the legitimacy of tradition and which removes both master and slave from the restraints that should control all men. The institution presupposes that superior and inferior "are natural enemies to each other," that there should be "tyranny on one side, treachery and cunning on the other." And what clearly disturbs Ramsay the most is the lack of sufficient control over the moral conduct of the slaves. His solution, as one might expect, is to replace physical terror with internalized controls. He offers us images of young Negro children repeating moral precepts as they pick grass for the cattle; of "religious examinations" of families marshalled for review; of "merrymaking" under the strict direction of slaves noted for sobriety; and of rare corporal punishments "inflicted with solemnity, in presence of the gang, accompanied with some short explanation of the crime, and an exhortation from the chaplain, to abstain from it." Such were the mechanisms for creating a society of free and willing laborers.[43]

If Ramsay's respect for discipline was a bit excessive, he was by no means unusual in his respect for traditional order. The year 1788, marking the centennial of the Glorious Revolution, gave a brief impetus to domestic reform, but also provided opportunities for convert-

[41] *Ibid.*, pp. 9–11, 172–73.
[42] *Ibid.*, pp. 3, 18.
[43] *Ibid.*, pp. 107–8, 173–75, 184–88.

ing antislavery into a vehicle for social control. In the preface to a sermon preached at Cambridge University, Peter Peckard, the Vice-Chancellor and master of Magdalen College, supported the abolition of both slavery and the slave trade as part of a wider reformation of manners. He noted that a century had passed since Providence had blessed England with a free constitution. Let this year be a Jubilee of Commemoration, he pleaded, a time not for riot and drunkenness, but for the extension of the blessings of all Englishmen to the suffering Negro slaves. It was a time for "breaking every yoke, and setting the poor Captive free." Peckard hoped that by infusing into students a loyalty to the king, an obedience to magistrates, and a reverence for the constitution, a firm foundation could be built for the abolition cause. Thus, he coupled the emancipation of slaves with a call for domestic obedience and loyalty, and with an affirmation that the Glorious Revolution had defined the boundaries of legitimate freedom.[44]

In 1788, Edward White went even further in equating antislavery with a respect for governmental power. Though he disclaimed any intent of praising absolutist government, White suggested that a free people might find something worthy of imitation in the despotic regime of France. "That arbitrary power should ever be a friend to liberty," he wrote, "or to the alleviation of slavery, may appear a thing too opposite to its very nature to be admitted. But so it is." White had hit upon a profound point, one which Adam Smith had already underscored in *The Wealth of Nations*. He went on to argue that the French slaveholder could never dare be tyrannical: "He is kept in awe by a higher and stronger hand, that would instantly crush him, should avaricious views of private emolument tempt him to dishonour or endammage the community." The worst abuses of the British slave system were thus the product of too much freedom.[45]

---

[44] Peter Peckard, *Justice and Mercy Recommended, Particularly with Reference to the Slave Trade* . . . (Cambridge, 1788), pp. viii–x. In his sermon, however, Peckard expressed a warm belief in moral progress. In 1788 the *Annual Register* hailed the slave-trade debates as proof that "liberty, humanity and science are daily extending, and bid fair to render despotism, cruelty and ignorance subjects of historical memory, not of actual observation" (quoted in Anstey, "A Re-interpretation of the Abolition of the British Slave Trade," p. 311).

[45] [Edward White], *Hints for a Specific Plan for an Abolition of the Slave Trade, and for Relief of the Negroes in the British West Indies* (London, 1788), pp. 18–19.

Even after the St. Domingue insurrection had cast doubts on one part of White's thesis, English writers continued to link slaveholding with an immunity from authority, and emancipation with an extension of governmental power. By 1792, British abolitionists were alarmed and divided by the revolutionary events in France and St. Domingue. At the outset, in 1789, they had generally rejoiced at the news of "a most extraordinary & wonderful Revolution," as Granville Sharp put it, which they interpreted as a restoration of government by law. Even skeptics, like James Beattie, who feared that the French and North Americans understood liberty to mean the privilege of being subject to no laws but those of one's own making, expressed hope that the Revolution would benefit the "poor Negroes."[46] After the conservative reaction had begun to grow, abolitionists were increasingly embarrassed by accusations of Jacobinism, by Thomas Clarkson's continuing support for the Revolution, and by Anglican suspicions that the anti-slave-trade cause was linked to the radical plots of Dissenters. In time, the fear of Jacobinism would become the official rationalization for Parliament's refusal to end the slave trade: it was not that the crown and House of Lords were deficient in a sense of justice; they were simply swayed by an understandable if irrelevant dread of Jacobin principles. There was one point, however, on which all antislavery men could agree, whatever their differences in timing in disavowing the French Revolution: the St. Domingue insurrection was not the result of protests against the slave trade or of the activities of the *Amis des noirs*. Rather, the savage violence of the blacks was a direct response to the brutal tyranny of their masters. The revolt should demonstrate to England, wrote William Roscoe, "that the preservation of our own islands from similar disasters, depends on the early adoption of measures which, whilst they are vigorous and decisive, are just, conciliatory, and humane."[47]

[46] Granville Sharp to John Sharp, July 6, 1789, JAW; William Forbes, *An Account of the Life and Writings of James Beattie* (3 vols., Edinburgh, 1807), III, 66–67.

[47] Samuel Hoare, Jr., to William Wilberforce, Feb. 20, 1792, Robert Isaac Wilberforce and Samuel Wilberforce, eds., *The Correspondence of William Wilberforce* (2 vols., London, 1840), I, 89–90; Thomas Clarkson, *The History of the Rise, Progress and Accomplishment of the Abolition of the African Slave-Trade by the British Parliament* (2 vols., London, 1808), II, 208–12; *Parliamentary History of England*, XXXI, 467–70; [William Roscoe], *An Inquiry into the Causes of the Insurrection of the Negroes in the Island of St. Domingo* . . .

In 1794, William Fox, an unusually radical abolitionist, used similar arguments to defend the French decree of emancipation. It was altogether wrong, he argued, to interpret this measure as a step toward anarchy. For the first time, French Negroes had been brought under the *subjection* as well as the protection of the law. Slaveholders had never cared whether their slaves practiced personal vices unacceptable to any genuine society. Paradoxically, slaves had been "free" to commit the worst sins. As a result of emancipation, however, French blacks would presumably be subject to the full powers of civil government. Even infants and idiots, Fox pointed out, were never given over to the arbitrary will of an individual. If Negroes were deficient in any human capacities—and Fox suspected they were superior in character to the English lower classes—this was all the more reason for bringing them under the protection and control of government. By 1802, James Stephen could find merit even in the brutal military regime that Victor Hugues had established in Guadaloupe. For the private authority of masters, Hugues had substituted the public authority of municipal law and military policy. If English governors had issued similar proclamations for ensuring industry by means other than "a mere physical effect to be excited by the application of the lash," every English planter would have considered it an impertinent interference with the "interior discipline of his plantation."[48]

These arguments carry implications that I have touched upon before but may now develop somewhat further. British antislavery writers expressed particular indignation over the arbitrary authority of West Indian slave masters, whom they portrayed, essentially, as the modern and anachronistic counterparts of feudal lords and barons. The abolitionists demanded that bonds of personal dependence give way, however gradually, to uniform and impersonal standards. And in their preference for objective, bureaucratic authority, they appeared to look forward to a future when all workers would be citizens, sub-

---

(London, 1792), pp. 1–3, 10, 18–26; Henry Roscoe, ed., *The Life of William Roscoe* (2 vols., Boston, 1833), I, 67–71; Samuel Romilly to Mme. G., Dec. 6, 1791, *Memoirs of the Life of Sir Samuel Romilly,* ed. by his sons (2 vols., London, 1840), I, 455.

[48] William Fox, *A Defence of the Decree of the National Convention of France for Emancipating the Slaves* (London, 1794), pp. 12–16; [James Stephen], *The Crisis of the Sugar Colonies; or, an Enquiry into the Objects and Probable Effects of the French Expedition to the West Indies . . .* (London, 1802), pp. 17–25.

ject to the same laws and to the same forces of the market. From our point of view, one could justify exploitation only by making it impersonal. According to Thomas Clarkson, there was nothing inequitable about slavery when considered merely as a form of labor. Any state, for example, might legitimately use convicts to clear rivers, repair roads, or work in mines. Granville Sharp suggested that "Negroes that are not capable of managing and shifting for themselves, nor are fit to be trusted, all at once, with liberty, might be delivered over to the care and protection of a *County Committee* (in order to avoid the baneful effects of *private property in Men*)." The committee could then hire out such servants, "the *Hire* to be paid (*also in produce*) towards the discharge of the *Registered Debt* for each Man's original price." Nor did Sharp object to the purchase of slaves by a corporate entity, such as an African colonizing company, so long as the purchase price was considered a "mere pecuniary debt" that the slave could redeem by working for the company.[49] What Sharp and Clarkson did object to were claims of personal proprietorship which gave a master exclusive control over the body and produce of a dependent, and which deprived the dependent of selling his labor in a reasonably free market. And it followed, in accordance with this outlook, that the master-slave relationship epitomized those artificial restraints, including monopoly and guaranteed subsistence, that prevented self-interest from being harnessed to the general good. Gilbert Francklyn, a Tobago planter and propagandist for the West India Committee, reported a credible story about Sharp which would hardly have shocked the new disciples of laissez faire. As a promoter of Sierra Leone colonization, Sharp was distressed to find many of London's Negroes unwilling to embark for Africa, despite their current misery and destitution. According to Francklyn, Sharp then distributed handbills around the city, requesting gentlemen not to relieve blacks in distress, since charity would blind them to their own best interest.[50]

[49] Thomas Clarkson, *An Essay on the Slavery and Commerce of the Human Species, Particularly the African* . . . (Philadelphia, 1786; originally printed London, 1786), pp. 75–76; Granville Sharp to Benjamin Rush, July 18, 1775; Aug. 1, 1783, Rush papers, Historical Society of Pennsylvania (hereafter HSP); Sharp to the Archbishop of Canterbury, Oct. 9, 1788, JAW.

[50] Francklyn, *Observations*, pp. xii-xiii. Christopher Fyfe, in his masterly *A History of Sierra Leone* (Oxford, 1962), touches on the difficulty of persuading London blacks to embark for Sierra Leone (pp. 14–19). James Walvin's *Black and White: The Negro and English Society, 1555–1945* (London, 1973), pro-

On the other hand, Wilberforce and other antislavery writers clung to the paternalistic ideals of the past and expressed considerable ambivalence toward Adam Smith's exaltation of self-interest and market relations. Even the classical economists, it should be stressed, approved acts of private benevolence which did not stifle individual initiative. Wilberforce (like Sharp) devoted much of his personal income to private charity; in 1800, when he was alarmed by the plight of starving workers in the West Riding, he attacked the callousness of those who "servilely" accepted Smith's principles without allowance for the thousand circumstances which might qualify a general principle. Later, when the same region was threatened with rebellion, he associated the insubordination of the lower orders with

the modern system of making expediency the basis of morals and the spring of action, instead of the domestic and social affections and the relations of life and the duties arising out of them. Not that the lower orders understand this generalizing abstract way of thinking and feeling; but the opinions and emotions which are taught and imbibed in this school, receiving their stamp in the mint of the higher orders . . . obtain a currency throughout the inferior classes of society.[51]

The early industrial revolution coincided with defensive attempts to rehabilitate the values of the old social order. The 1780s and 1790s

---

vides a more detailed account of the plight of London's blacks, many of whom had joined the king's armed forces during the American Revolution. Although Sharp helped to organize relief for this destitute population, he was convinced that African colonization afforded the only permanent solution. In 1786 the Committee for the Black Poor acknowledged that, "considering the disposition of the Blacks and their want of discipline," it would be difficult to fill the three Royal Navy ships scheduled to embark for Sierra Leone. The government tried to increase incentive by stopping daily welfare payments of 6d per person. Early in 1788, when Sharp heard the news of the disastrous mortality of the first expedition, he assured his brother that "I cannot find that the Climate has been at all to blame; nothing but the intemperance of the people, and their enervating indolence in consequence of it" (quoted in *Black and White*, p. 147). In a letter of Oct. 13, 1788, to Dr. John Coakley Lettsom (Huntington Library), Sharp admitted that over fifty blacks had died soon after the ships had left the Thames, and that by September, 1787, only 276 were still alive in Sierra Leone, out of the 439 to 441 who had embarked. Again, he blamed intemperance.

[51] Wilberforce, *Life of William Wilberforce*, II, 163–64, 387–88; IV, 28–29. Of course abolitionists also delighted in quoting Adam Smith to the effect that a slave's only "interests" could be to eat much and labor little. See, for example [Thomas Burgess], *Considerations on the Abolition of Slavery and the Slave Trade, Upon Grounds of Natural, Religious, and Political Duty* (Oxford, 1789), pp. 154, 158.

produced a considerable literature that outlined the duties of the higher ranks and that eulogized the deference and loyalty of the poor. The two classes were united, in the idealized view, by an invisible "chain" or "bond."[52] Abolitionists never tired of contrasting the impersonality of slavery to the benevolent paternalism that most English workers supposedly still enjoyed. As we have seen, Cowper's emancipated slave is not abandoned to the cold winds of the marketplace. Submissive at his liberator's feet, he vows: "Serving a benefactor I am free; / At my best home, if not exiled from thee." The reformers' alternative to slavery was not the modern factory but a master-servant relationship based on mutual respect, obligation, and above all, belief in the legitimacy of each man's station. Moreover, it was absenteeism, in the eyes of abolitionists, that accounted for many of the worst evils of the plantation system. The Negro slave, from the time of his sale on the West African coast, could appeal to no responsible authority. Neither the slave-ship captain nor the agent who managed a plantation had any interest beyond "private emolument." Obviously this "artificial" way of delegating authority and manipulating a labor force was not a vestige from the archaic past. It was a mark of the emerging capitalist order.

There were, to be sure, contradictory tendencies within colonial slavery itself. In some respects, plantation slavery prefigured the salient features of the factory system; yet it also retained the characteristics of preindustrial labor discipline.[53] The institution's mixed character helps to explain why the British abolitionists' critique could be significantly selective. It was neither a traditionalist attack on a capitalistic innovation, nor a capitalist attack on an archaic form of authority. In some ways it was a combination of both.

British antislavery helped to ensure stability while accommodating society to political and economic change; it merged Utilitarianism with an ethic of benevolence, reinforcing faith that a progressive policy of laissez faire would reveal men's natural identity of interests. It opened

[52] Briggs, "Language of 'Class,' " pp. 43–54.

[53] Eugene D. Genovese has given this point theoretical elaboration in *The Political Economy of Slavery: Studies in the Economy and Society of the Slave South* (New York, 1965) and in *The World the Slaveholders Made: Two Essays in Interpretation* (New York, 1969), pp. 3–113. I have particularly profited, however, from reading chapters of Professor Genovese's *Roll, Jordan, Roll* (New York, 1974), a profound study of the accommodations and contradictions of New World slavery.

new sources of moral prestige for the dominant social class, helped to define a participatory role for middle-class activism, and looked forward to the universal goal of compliant, loyal, and self-disciplined workers. The abolitionists' ideal of the plantation's future was thus a strange hybrid: a kindly, paternalistic master ministering to his grateful Negro "yeomen," both subject to the administrative agents of the king and both dedicated to the commercial prosperity of the empire! And the realization of this dream was supposed to have profound reverberating effects. The abolition of the slave trade would not only reform the motives and character of planters, but would lead to the more important goal of Christianizing and civilizing Africa. In Ramsay's vision, "this measure promises to realize the fabulous golden age, when mutual wants and mutual good, will & shall bind all mankind in one common interest."[54]

[54] James Ramsay, MS volume, fols. 71, 95, Phillipps MS 17780, Rhodes House, Oxford. For the influence of the anti-slave-trade movement on later imperialist ideology, see Ralph A. Austen and Woodruff D. Smith, "Images of Africa and British Slave-Trade Abolition: The Transition to an Imperialist Ideology, 1787–1807," *African Historical Studies,* II (1969), 69–83. It is perhaps symbolic that in 1834, the year of West Indian emancipation, Thomas Babington Macaulay sailed to India for precisely the same motive that had earlier led would-be planters to the Caribbean: he was almost penniless and aspired to become financially independent. He returned to England in three-and-a-half years, wealthy enough to avoid any future financial worries. But whereas the Caribbean planters had been unconcerned with transforming Caribbean culture, Macaulay, as a member of the lawmaking Council of India, had helped to lay the groundwork for momentous change. He had seen India as a testing ground for his ideology of progress—for the formation, as phrased in his influential "Minute on Indian Education," of "a class who may be interpreters between us and the millions whom we govern; a class of persons, Indian in blood and colour, but English in taste, in morals, and in intellect." Macaulay's struggles for a free press, for a humane penal code, and for the teaching of English language and literature were essentially struggles for cultural hegemony, as distinct from dominion by physical force. Significantly, he argued that a free press could not endanger British rule, since India lacked any class "analogous to that vast body of English labourers and artisans whose minds are rendered irritable by frequent distress and privation, and on whom, therefore, the sophistry and rhetoric of bad men often produce a tremendous effect" (Clive, *Macaulay,* pp. 330–31, and *passim; Macaulay; Prose and Poetry,* selected by G. M. Young [London, 1952], pp. 722, 729).

Nine ∿

The Preservation of
English Liberty, II

Slavery as the Prime Symbol of Corruption

In the United States, northern writers increasingly claimed that southern slaveholders, accustomed to rule as tyrants, could not bear to be ruled under the mildest laws of freedom. Americans have seldom recognized that this temptation to sectionalize a national burden of "inconsistency" first arose in England—or that in English eyes all the Caribbean and North American colonies constituted "slave soil."

In 1769, Granville Sharp quoted an advertisement from the *New York Journal,* offering the separate sale of a mother and three-year-old daughter, as if they were cow and calf. The presence of slaves in the North, he argued, proved how the institution could spread into climates where there could be no plea of economic "necessity" (Sharp was of course well aware that the contagion had spread to London, where newspapers also advertised the sale of Negroes). In colonies like New York the existence of slavery clearly infringed upon civil and domestic liberty, "notwithstanding that the political controversies of the inhabitants are stuffed with theatrical bombast and ranting expressions in praise of liberty." Every petty planter in America was in truth an arbitrary monarch; his *"boasted liberty"* masked a new form of tyranny that subverted the British constitution.[1]

[1] Granville Sharp, *A Representation of the Injustice and Dangerous Tendency of Tolerating Slavery; or of Admitting the Least Claim of Private Property in the Persons of Men, in England* (London, 1769), pp. 81–82, 84.

How could one account for the contrast between the just and equal laws of England, which *Gentleman's Magazine* termed "the garden of Europe," and the despotism of the American slave colonies? Benjamin Franklin, the colonial agent, complained in 1772 of "the hypocrisy of this country, which encourages such a detestable commerce by laws for promoting the Guinea trade; while it piqued itself on its virtue, love of liberty, and the equity of its courts, in setting free a single negro."[2] But according to James Ramsay, "slavery takes place among Europeans, on in the Western world, where their proper religion and laws are not deemed to be in full force; and where individuals too often think themselves loosened from ties, which are binding in the mother country." Negro slavery was thus a symptom of institutional disintegration; it was one of the many unhappy products of too much liberty. Whereas Americans blamed the evil on British mercantile policy, Englishmen pointed to the corrosive forces of the New World environment. Ramsay held out hope that Europe would ultimately redeem America, that the time would come

when the perfect law of liberty shall extend her protection to and bring within her pale every oppressed suffering son of sorrow. The abolition of slavery equally with that of arbitrary divorces and plurality of wives may be concluded to be a necessary step in the improvement of human nature, which enters into the views of providence respecting man, and will in proper time be fully accomplished.[3]

Sharp, though no less concerned with redeeming America, found his first mission in protecting English law from being subverted by a New World innovation. Sharp's views on America, as well as on corruption and redemption, were most complex. And since he did much to formulate some of the initial assumptions of British antislavery—especially

[2] *Gentleman's Magazine* (Oct. 1780), 458; Benjamin Franklin to Anthony Benezet, Aug. 22, 1772, in George S. Brookes, *Friend Anthony Benezet* (Philadelphia, 1937), p. 422. Franklin wished success to Benezet and the antislavery cause, and soon cooperated with Sharp in urging acceptance of colonial restrictions on slave importation. Yet he had also written an anonymous letter to the London *Public Advertiser*, exposing the hypocrisy of English critics, and offering arguments and apologies that would soon become clichés in the literature defending American slavery (Verner Crane, "Benjamin Franklin on Slavery and American Liberties," *The Pennsylvania Magazine of History and Biography*, LXII [Jan., 1938], 1–11).

[3] Ramsay, MS volume, fols. 69–70, Phillipps MS 17780, Rhodes House, Oxford.

with respect to law and authority—it will be helpful to provide a more extended analysis of his thought.[4]

Sharp's moral absolutism led to ambivalent attitudes toward English institutions and American innovations. In a letter to Sharp of 1774, Benjamin Rush argued that physical causes could pervert or even suspend man's innate moral faculty. For Rush, a hopeful environmentalist, this meant that man was malleable and that human nature might be improved by "physical" means. The thesis furnished a secular basis for any number of reforms, including antislavery. Yet it also permitted the conclusion that slave traders could not be held accountable for their acts if their moral faculties had been corrupted by physical environment. Sharp detected the dangers of such possible relativism. It was man's capacity for self-condemnation, he replied, that testified to his knowledge of good and evil and thus to his assent to the justice of God's laws. Rush's examples no doubt showed that a few men were exempt from this responsibility, if insanity or some other physical cause had suspended their moral faculties. But Sharp feared that such "suspension" was also caused by "invisible spiritual Enemies." In these "latter days of Infidelity & Deism," the devil would use subtle stratagems, "lest the more refined modern Sadducees should discover their errors, and be enabled to resist his secret & invisible influence by those beneficial means which the Almighty has mercifully revealed to us." Sharp asked how men who disbelieved even in the existence of spiritual enemies could be sufficiently on guard? (One wonders whether he had Rush in mind?) Of one thing he was certain: "Those unhappy persons who sink into *spiritual bondage* by neglecting the necesary *resistance* are certainly guilty of a *willful Offence*." Resistance could thus be man's highest duty. And while Sharp implied that America might be especially vulnerable to "refined modern Sadducees," he expressed warm approval for the "moderation" and "true loyalty" shown by the people's instructions to their deputies in the Continental Congress.[5]

---

[4] In many ways, however, Sharp's constitutional theories were highly atypical of British antislavery thought.

[5] Benjamin Rush to Granville Sharp, July 9, 1774, "The Correspondence of Benjamin Rush and Granville Sharp, 1773–1809," ed. by John A. Woods, *Journal of American Studies,* I (1967), 6–8 (hereafter "Rush-Sharp Correspondence"); Sharp to Rush, Oct. 31, 1774, Rush papers, Historical Society of Pennsylvania (hereafter HSP; I sometimes refer to the latter for the full text).

Sharp's fascination with the devil's stratagems seems closer to the world of Cotton Mather than to the world of Blackstone and Adam Smith. There is also a seventeenth-century flavor to his notions of representation and consent. Though unquestioningly loyal to church and king, he accepted the legitimacy of an *ad hoc* congress, and thus challenged the prevailing Whig belief in the absolute and indivisible sovereignty of king, Lords, and Commons. In a sense, Sharp endorsed the American Puritans' view of their original mission: migration to the New World did not represent a rebellious separation from England, but rather an extension and purification of English law. Yet ironically, and as a mark of his own divided loyalties, Sharp insisted that the experiment in purification could be made secure only by establishing an American Episcopacy![6]

Sharp was something of an anomaly in eighteenth-century England; he still embodied the polarized traits of a Puritan reformer. The double nature of his mission fits Kai T. Erikson's aphorism: "Humility is the badge of his sanctity; but sanctity, in turn, is his warrant for converting the whole world to his way of thinking."[7] Like the Puritan, Sharp never doubted his ability, or duty, to distinguish truth from error. Doubt and skepticism were the weapons of the devil. He shared the Puritan belief in the Bible as a guide to everyday life and as an unambiguous source of law and prophecy. Above all, Sharp saw himself as the vindicator of a primal and eternal law which had been obscured by centuries of encrustation. A quotation from his *The Law of Liberty*,

[6] Granville Sharp, *The Law of Retribution; or a Serious Warning to Great Britain and her Colonies, Founded on Unquestionable Examples of God's Temporal Vengeance Against Tyrants, Slave-holders, and Oppressors* (London, 1776), pp. 331–32, n. 194; Prince Hoare, *Memoirs of Granville Sharp, Esq. Composed From His Own Manuscripts* . . . (London, 1820), pp. 207–8. The prospect of an American Episcopacy had long been the *bête noir* of the Dissenting colonial clergy, especially in New England. On the other hand, Sharp favored the free election of bishops. The lack of such election, he said, was the "only" defect of the Church of England—a defect of some magnitude in Dissenter eyes.

[7] Kai T. Erikson, *Wayward Puritans: A Study in the Sociology of Deviance* (New York, 1966), p. 51. Sharp campaigned against the indecency of the theater, especially the performance by males of female roles, or by females of male roles. He sent a remonstrance to the Archbishop of York, after learning that the latter's son had acted the part of *Thaïs* in Terence's "Eunuch," at a Westminster School performance. Sharp's favorite text of Scripture was thoroughly Puritan: "The tree which beareth not good fruit shall be cut down, and cast into the fire" (Hoare, *Memoirs of Granville Sharp*, pp. 206, 476).

or, Royal Law, by Which All Mankind Will Certainly Be Judged!
(1776) will serve to underscore the Puritan—and Reformation—
parallel:

Now a continued multiplication of Statutes (as in England, where the
number exceeds the capacity of the human Memory) affords matter only
for *Equivocation, Doubt,* and *Evasion,* whereby SOUND LAW is vitiated
and corrupted; and the loathsome *Prostitute,* still retaining *the Name of
Law, arises* (like the Harlot POPERY from pure CHRISTIANITY) *in another
Dress!* She is clothed with the many-coloured garment of misconstruction,
and sets herself at the right hand of the unjust judge, prompting him with
wily Subterfuges, and *bad Precedents* instead of LAW.[8]

Sharp devoted his first layman's researches to Holy Scripture. When
apprenticed to a London linen draper, he encountered a Jewish boarder
who accused him of misrepresenting Biblical prophecies. In order to
find the true Word of God and thus vindicate Christianity, Sharp
began learning Hebrew. Some years later, at the age of thirty, he confidently challenged the accuracy of a Hebrew Bible published by a
learned Dr. Kennicott. Sharp's quest for the purified text soon carried
over to a dedicated study of the law, which commenced in 1767, when
he had never before opened a law book. The circumstances of this
delayed search for identity, which would soon lead Sharp to international fame, can be illuminated by Erik H. Erikson's description of
Gandhi: "There is every reason to believe that the central identity
which here found its historical time and place was the conviction that
among the Indians in South Africa, he was *the only person equipped
by fate* to reform a situation which under no conditions could be
tolerated."[9]

Of course, Sharp differed from Gandhi—and from other great reformers—in many important ways. Although he helped redefine the
boundaries of what his society could tolerate, and was in that sense a
"deviant" from accepted norms, he retained a secure niche in English
society. The traditions and cohesiveness of his family gave Granville's

[8] Granville Sharp, *The Law of Liberty* . . . (London, 1776), p. 21. For
Sharp's place in the English "higher law" tradition, see J. W. Gough, *Funda-
mental Law in English Constitutional History* (Oxford, 1955), pp. 185–200.
Gough holds that Sharp himself was guilty of bad history and bad law.

[9] Hoare, *Memoirs of Granville Sharp,* pp. 23, 29, 31, 38–39; Granville Sharp,
MS diary, John A. Woods's transcripts of Sharp papers (hereafter JAW); Erik
H. Erikson, *Gandhi's Truth: On the Origins of Militant Nonviolence* (New
York, 1969), p. 166.

oddities a kind of protective coloration. As the grandson of the Archbishop of York, and son of the Archdeacon of Northumberland, who
had himself wielded extensive powers of patronage, Granville had easy
access to the bishops and peers of the realm. His wealthy older brothers
were leading philanthropists, and the family, including Granville, won
special esteem for their musical concerts, given from a summer barge,
which delighted London's elite as well as the royal family itself.

On the other hand, Granville had been taken from school and
and apprenticed to an undistinguished trade. At an impressionable
age, while living in the metropolis three hundred miles from home, he
had been exposed to the religious arguments of a Quaker, a Presbyterian, a Catholic, a Socinian, and a Jew. Granville continued to defend the faith of his heritage, especially that of the illustrious grandfather whom he idolized. Yet it was apparently the death of his parents
that gave him freedom to abandon his trade as linen draper and seek
a minor post in the government's Ordnance office. Whatever the ego
needs of this least-successful son, his self-assertion was circumscribed
by unusual bonds of family loyalty and love. Sharp's obsession with
the corruption of justice may have reflected some deep-seated grievance
over the three-generational decline from archbishop to linen draper's
apprentice. In any event, he harbored what Sir James Stephen described as a settled conviction of the wickedness of the human race,
"tempered by an infantile credulity in the virtue of each separate member of it . . . a burning indignation against injustice and wrong,
reconciled with pity and long-suffering towards the individual oppres-
sor." Sharp's associates respected his saintlike naïveté, but recognized
him as an eccentric. And the role of eccentric allowed him to expose
the moral compromises of his society without being branded as a
rebel.[10]

[10] Sharp, MS diary, JAW; Hoare, *Memoirs of Granville Sharp,* pp. 12–20,
27–30, 253–60, 450–55, 480–82; Sharp, *Law of Retribution,* pp. 253–55; Sharp,
The Just Limitation of Slavery in the Eyes of God . . . (London, 1776), p.
44n.; Sir James Stephen, *Essays in Ecclesiastical Biography* (4th ed., London,
1860), pp. 538–43. Granville's eldest brother, John, succeeded their father as
Archdeacon of Northumberland; Thomas became a parish priest; James was a
wealthy ironmonger, inventor, and canal promoter; William an eminent London
surgeon. We are told that young Granville was withdrawn from grammar school
and put to a trade because his father's fortune had mostly been spent on educating the older sons. One suspects there may have been other reasons. In 1767,
however, he declined his uncle's offer of a ministerial living, arguing that as a

Like Gandhi, Sharp moved from a humiliating personal conflict to unswerving mission. In 1765, while working at his monotonous job in Ordnance, he gave help to a Negro youth, Jonathan Strong, who had been savagely beaten and then abandoned by his master, a lawyer from Barbados. Two years later the master tried to seize Strong, intending to sell him for shipment to Jamaica. Sharp's successful interference resulted in a challenge to a duel, which he declined, and to a law suit. When Sharp then sought the aid of eminent attorneys, he was shocked to learn of the prevailing opinion, supported by the Lord Chief Justice, Baron Mansfield, that no slave could claim freedom merely as the result of being in England. Therefore, Sharp determined to undertake his own defense, and for two years immersed himself in the study of law.[11]

He soon hit upon a discovery that his first biographer likened to Newton's reflections on the fallen apple. Slavery was totally illegal in England. The 1729 rulings of the Attorney-General and Solicitor-General had been "mere opinion," unjustified by any law. Much as the Catholic church had buried religious truth under encrustations of error and deception, so had English lawyers obscured the law of liberty with deposits of false precedent. Even "sensible and learned persons" could be heard referring to the ancient practices of villeinage as a legal sanction for Negro slavery. Yet villeinage, Sharp maintained, had always been contrary to both natural and common law and had finally been abolished by the force of the latter. Nothing could be more dangerous than to revive obsolete forms of oppression which could easily subvert the traditional liberties of Englishmen.[12]

For Sharp, the only true law transcended both custom and human authority. Its two foundations, which often merged in his mind, were the maxims of common law and the law of God. The essence of all

---

layman he could better serve the cause of religion. In 1775, when Granville quit his job at the Ordnance office, in protest against the American war, he went to live with his brothers, James and William, who offered him support. He later lived with his sister-in-law, whose business he managed; and in 1787 he inherited an estate from Mrs. James Oglethorpe. By that same year, he had personally donated over £1,700 to the cause of Sierra Leone colonization. He never married.

[11] Granville Sharp, "An Account of the Occasion which compelled Granville Sharp to study Law, and undertake the Defence of Negro slaves in England," MS, JAW; Hoare, *Memoirs of Granville Sharp,* pp. 32–37; Sharp to Benezet, July 7, 1773, in Brookes, *Friend Anthony Benezet,* p. 424.

[12] Hoare, *Memoirs of Granville Sharp,* pp. 38–40; Sharp, *Representation,* pp. 107–8, 135, 158.

law lay in the first two Commandments to Moses, which could be compressed into the single word "love." It followed that any custom or practice should be abolished if it violated the maxims of common law or their ultimate and divine source. Nor could any legislative authority enact a valid statute repugnant to such "higher law."

After a series of legal battles and inconclusive decisions, Sharp had mixed feelings over his seeming triumph in the Somerset case. Lord Mansfield reluctantly ruled that no positive law entitled a slaveholder to detain a slave forcibly in England or transport him out of the country. What alarmed Sharp the most was Mansfield's advice that West Indian merchants appeal to Parliament for a legislative remedy. "It is on this account," Sharp wrote to Benezet, "that I have now undertaken to write once more upon the subject, in order to apprise disinterested people of the dangerous tendency of such a measure; and I shall endeavour to prepare what few friends I have in Parliament, for an opposition to such a destructive proposal." Sharp had assumed, when writing his first classic tract, that a clarification of English law would be sufficient. But by August, 1772, he faced the same threat that was disturbing North American colonists· Parliament's claim to legislative supremacy. For this reason, he told Benezet, "my former tracts were built chiefly on the laws of England; but my present work is for the most part *founded on Scripture,* to obviate the doctrines of some late writers and disputers, who have ventured to assert that slavery is not inconsistent with the Word of God."[13]

By the eve of the American Revolution, Sharp's outlook had become remarkably similar to that of the New England pamphleteers who demanded an abolition of slavery, as a means of self-purification, to appease God's wrath. One of his tracts of 1776 bears a title that would have suited Nathaniel Niles or Levi Hart: *The Law of Retribution; or a Serious Warning to Great Britain and her Colonies, Founded on Unquestionable Examples of God's Temporal Vengeance Against Tyrants, Slaveholders, and Oppressors.* Like many Americans of his generation, Sharp had first found his identity as a defender of tradition—both an English tradition of political liberty stemming from an idealized Saxon constitution, and a natural-law tradition descending from Cicero to Bracton, Grotius, and Pufendorf. Historically, both

[13] Sharp to Dr. Findlay, July 21, 1772, JAW; Sharp to Benezet, Aug. 21, 1772, in Hoare, *Memoirs of Granville Sharp,* pp. 100–1.

streams of liberty had clarified God's will.[14] Sharp did not make
the theoretical leap, as did many Americans, from these historical
precedents to an assertion of abtract natural rights. But the "chance"
encounter with Jonathan Strong, followed by the legal research for his
own defense, brought Sharp to an "unhesitating commitment—when
the time is ripe," to borrow another of Erik Erikson's descriptions of
new-found identity. The unhesitating commitment led him to oppose
England's war against America and to question the legitimacy and
stability of much of his social environment.

If lawyers could long justify the detention of slaves in England, any
deception seemed possible. Sharp vaguely associated colonial slavery
with the domestic corruptions that had long alarmed political reformers: the national debt, the abuse of privilege, political faction, the
pensioners and placemen who increased the powers of the Court and
upset the balance of the ancient constitution. His expanding range of
protests and prescriptions involved a curious mixture of "liberal" and
"conservative" causes. Yet no critic could claim that Sharp's war on
Negro slavery distracted his attention from domestic ills. He fought for
Parliamentary reform and Irish home rule. He denounced the impressment of seamen as a form of slavery. He wrote a tract against the
sin of dueling. He complained that a proposed bill on divorce would
allow the guilty party to remarry, contrary to the law of God. He
labored for the conversion of Jews to Christianity. He continued to
rescue Negroes from being shipped into slavery. Nor did his concern
over the destitution of London's blacks blind him to the suffering of
enslaved Scottish miners or to the starvation of England's poor. He
worked tirelessly to redeem America through the establishment of an
apostolic Episcopacy. He advocated, especially for the salvation of
Sierra Leone, the restoration of King Alfred's "frank pledge"—an
ideal form of government, supposedly derived from Moses, based on
group self-discipline and the election of officers from organized sub-
divisions of population. And he excoriated the English upper class for
its lewdness, adulteries, and other immoralities, all of which he saw,
along with slave trading, as sufficient cause for divine vengeance.[15]

---

[14] Granville Sharp, *An Appendix to the Representation* . . . (London, 1772),
pp. 2–8, 55, 193–202, 383–92; Sharp, *Serious Reflections on the Slave Trade and
Slavery; Wrote in March, 1797* (London, 1805), pp. 34–39. In 1789, Samuel
Hopkins initiated a correspondence with Sharp, mainly concerning Sierra Leone.
[15] Sharp's reform causes are described by Hoare, but his correspondence pro-

Sharp's central foe, of course, was the "Demon of Demons," the author of all injustice and tyranny. And from a providential perspective Sharp's various causes were indivisible. For example, he became convinced that his own legal researches had helped make Americans aware of their constitutional rights. This conviction gave him a kind of proprietary interest in redressing colonial grievances as well as in eradicating colonial slavery. And the two issues, in Sharp's mind, were inseparable. As he wrote Benjamin Rush, on July 27, 1774:

> I must observe that the impending Evils which threaten the Colonies abroad, and the general misunderstanding of the British Constitution which at present prevails at home (circumstances which presage the mutual destruction of both) may, with great probability of Truth, be looked upon as a just punishment from God, for the enormous Wickednesses which are openly avowed and practised throughout the British Empire, amongst which the public Encouragement given to the Slave Trade by the Legislature at home, and the open Toleration of Slavery and Oppression in the Colonies abroad, are far from being the least![16]

Earlier that year, Sharp had had a private conference with Lord Dartmouth, the Secretary of State, on the subject of colonial petitions to prohibit further slave importations. He had assured Dartmouth that the petitions from Virginia and Pennsylvania expressed a spirit of pub-

---

vides a richer sense of the man's zeal and incredible range of interests. Hoare also tends to soften the radical edges of Sharp's thought, which were more pronounced during the American Revolution (for example, *A Declaration of the People's Natural Right to a Share in the Legislature* [1775], *The Claims of the People of England* [1782]; Sharp to John Wilkes, Jan. 12, 1780, British Museum Add. MS 30872, f. 168). But Sharp's demands for reform always centered on the restoration of ancient law. He associated the "frank-pledge," for example, with the ideal theocratic commonwealth of ancient Israel, which he wished to see revived in England as well as in America and Sierra Leone. It should be further emphasized that his first and primary loyalty lay with the Church of England. The underlying motive for much of his antislavery activity was to vindicate the honor of the only true church. And after earnestly conversing with most of the archbishops and bishops in England, he could credulously assume that he had converted the Church of England to antislavery. It is perhaps not unfair to see a waning of radical spirit after Sharp has acquired financial independence and had become involved in Sierra Leone colonization, a role which intensified his obsession with social discipline.

[16] Granville Sharp to Col. Dalton, Feb. 7, 1812, JAW; Hoare, *Memoirs of Granville Sharp*, pp. 116–17; Sharp, *Law of Retribution*, pp. 3, 34–35, 68, 250–52; Sharp, *The Case of Saul, Shewing That his Disorder was a Real Spiritual Possession* (London, 1807; originally published 1777), *passim;* Sharp to Rush, July 27, 1774, "Rush-Sharp Correspondence," p. 10.

lic virtue, that the people of New York and Boston were favorably inclined toward emancipation, and that the whole kingdom could expect dreadful judgments if such liberal tendencies were blocked by political or mercenary policies. To his American correspondents Sharp sent a continuing flow of advice, along with tracts on their Biblical and constitutional rights: they should address petitions to the king and not to Parliament, since the latter's authority should not be acknowledged except with regard to the slave trade in general; they should not allow Congress to create a standing army, or they would find themselves "enslaved" by an American Cromwell; above all, they should realize that if Congress had acted "nobly" in forbidding further importations of slaves, "the business is but half done, 'till they have agreed upon some equitable & safe means of gradually enfranchising those which remain."[17]

Sharp's divided attitudes toward law and authority involved him in a number of contradictory positions. He regarded the colonial slave codes as "null and void." As the American editor of one of his tracts pointed out, the colonists claimed the rights and privileges of the British constitution, while upholding an institution that had been ruled unconstitutional. Yet Sharp believed that since the invalid laws had long been in force and had won the assent of kings, they had to be formally repealed by the colonial assemblies, in order to preserve "in each branch of the legislature, that reciprocal faith, which is due to all solemn compacts." He did not explain why unlawful compacts should be solemn or deserving of faith. This point aside, Sharp felt certain

[17] Granville Sharp to Lord North, Feb. 18, 1772, in Hoare, *Memoirs of Granville Sharp*, p. 79 (also pp. 101–2); Sharp to Benezet, Aug. 21, 1772, in Brookes, *Friend Anthony Benezet*, pp. 420–21; Benezet to Sharp, Nov. 8, 1772, Sharp papers, New-York Historical Society (hereafter NYHS); Sharp to Benezet, Jan. 7, 1774, JAW; Sharp to Rush, Feb. 21, 1774; July 18, 1775; August 4, 1783, "Rush-Sharp Correspondence," pp. 4–19; Benezet to Sharp, Nov. 18, 1774, JAW. Sharp distinguished between petitions against the slave trade in general and petitions against the further importation of slaves into a given colony. He was clearly disappointed when Benezet explained that most of the sentiment against the slave trade, especially in Maryland and Virginia, arose from self-interested motives. Sharp insisted that the colonial legislatures had the right to stop further importations, and was confident he could obtain the king's concurrence by appealing to the good will of Lord Dartmouth. It was up to the colonies, he suggested, to prove their own disinterestedness by petitioning against slaveholding itself. Benezet, on the other hand, warned that English reformers should not expect too much from the nonimportation agreements, and argued that the slave trade could only be stopped by England and other European nations.

that the imperial conflict would be advantageous to the abolition cause. Parliament's infringements on the civil rights of Americans should awaken even slaveholders to "the horrid Effects and unlawfulness of Arbitrary Power." But this meant that neither the king nor Parliament, in waging an unjust war, had the right to interfere with colonial slavery. Sharp agreed essentially with the American—and later West Indian—position that Parliament could not legislate for territories it did not represent.[18]

The Revolution might have been avoided, in Sharp's eyes, if the king's Ministers had heeded his prophetic warnings of divine vengeance. For American slaveholders, however, political independence could hardly be interpreted as a form of divine punishment. And the war further complicated Sharp's problems with "higher law" authorities. Instead of appealing to the Somerset precedent, he turned increasingly to Deuteronomy, 23:15: "Thou shalt not deliver unto his master the servant which is escaped from his master unto thee." This meant, he wrote to Rush, that "no Man can *lawfully* be prosecuted for protecting a Negro, OR ANY OTHER Slave whatever, that has '*escaped from his Master*,' because that would be punishing a Man for doing his *indispensable* Duty, according to the *Laws of God*." Further, it was a maxim of common law that "the inferior law must give place to the Superior"; and this maxim must prevail, Sharp added, not knowing how far America might go in rejecting English precedents, in "every Christian Nation." This doctrine was clearly an outgrowth of Sharp's own experience in sheltering and defending London Negroes. But it was also a religious version of George Wallace's radical position that every slave had an immediate right to be declared free. If put to practice, it would soon undermine any slave system. When Sharp talked of emancipation, however, he pictured slaves gradually working off their "debt" under regulations that would reciprocally improve the morals of masters and servants, leading to a free and happy peasantry, content to "improve" the estates of "landed gentlemen." He did not wish to see "domestick Slavery" abolished at

[18] Sharp to Lord North, Feb. 18, 1772, in Hoare, *Memoirs of Granville Sharp*, pp. 78–79; Sharp, *An Essay on Slavery, Proving from Scripture its Inconsistency with Humanity and Religion* (Burlington, West Jersey, 1773; reprinted London, 1776), pp. 7–8; Sharp to Rush, July 27, 1774, "Rush-Sharp Correspondence," p. 10.

the expense of "publick Liberty," and assured Rush that he trembled at the probable consequences of a slave insurrection.[19]

Samuel Johnson, who felt a lofty scorn for both West Indians and North Americans, and who reportedly toasted at Oxford "to the next insurrection of the negroes in the West Indies," took up the black man's cause with a seriousness that distresed Boswell, with whom he engaged in heated argument—Boswell supporting both the cause of Negro slavery and the legitimacy of North American resistence to taxation. For Johnson, who observed that colonial laws provided no redress for even a black prince or scholar, the Americans' "inconsistency" was no more than one could expect from hypocrites and scoundrels.[20] Similarly, for James Ramsay the loss of the colonies was good riddance; no treaty could be lasting with a society "where a designing demagogue, working on an ignorant town committee, can prescribe to the legislature."[21]

Even liberals sympathetic to the American cause could adopt a tone of biting sarcasm. Thus in 1776 Thomas Day wrote a scathing letter to an American slaveholding acquaintance, but refrained from publishing it until the end of the war. America, he charged, was dominated by avarice:

Is money of so much more importance than life? Or have the Americans shared the dispensing power of St. Peter's successors, to excuse their own observance of those rules which they impose on others? If there be an object truly ridiculous in nature, it is an American patriot, signing resolutions of independency with the one hand, and with the other brandishing a whip over his affrighted slaves. . . . You do not go to Africa to buy or steal your negroes; perhaps, because you are too lazy and luxurious; but you encourage an infamous, pitiless race of men to do it for you, and conscientiously receive the fruits of their crimes. You do not, merciful men, reduce your fellow creatures to servitude! No, men of your independent spirits, that have taken up arms against the government that had protected and established them, rather than pay a tax of three pence . . . would never make flagitious attempts upon the liberties and happiness of their brethren! . . . Did you not carry the rights of men into the un-

---

[19] Sharp to Rush, July 27, 1774; Jan. 31, 1775; July 18, 1775; Oct. 10, 1785, Rush papers, HSP.

[20] James Boswell, *The Life of Samuel Johnson, LL.D.* (New York, n.d.), pp. 747–49.

[21] [James Ramsay], *An Inquiry into the Effects of Putting a Stop to the African Slave Trade, and of Granting Liberty to the Slaves in the British Sugar Colonies* . . . (London, 1784), pp. 12–13, 26–27.

cultivated desart and the howling wilderness? Not of Frenchmen, nor of Germans, nor of Englishmen, but of men? . . . Yes, gentlemen, as you are no longer Englishmen, I hope you will please to be men; and, as such, admit the whole human species to a participation of your unalienable rights.

Although Day implied that America might represent a new beginning for mankind, he insisted that the continuance of slavery contradicted the fundamental rule of "universal morality": "the greatest possible degree of happiness" for the whole human species. Anyone who presumed the authority to deprive other men of their rights and happiness was a tyrant "whom it is permitted to destroy by every possible method." But Day, a zealous Utilitarian, had seen no tyranny in his own attempt to "buy" and train a future wife! His plan was to select two little girls—a blond and a brunette—from an orphan asylum. He would then perfect their mental and physical powers by a rigorous system of education, suggested by Rousseau's *Emile.* He assumed, erroneously as it turned out, that the better-trained girl would marry him.[22]

Though less extreme, the liberal Scottish philosopher John Millar agreed, with respect to slaveholding republicans, that "fortune perhaps never produced a situation more calculated to ridicule a liberal hypothesis, or to show how little the conduct of men is at the bottom directed by any philosophical principles." Dr. Richard Price not only upheld the cause of the rebellious colonists, but in England supported such measures as universal manhood suffrage and the separation of church and state. Regarding Negro slavery, however, he could rejoice that "on this occasion I can recommend to them the example of my own country—in *Britain,* a *Negro* becomes a *freeman* the moment he sets his foot on British ground." Notwithstanding their glorious experiment in human government, the outcome of which might determine the fate of man's progress, the American people would never deserve their liberty until they had renounced both slavery and the slave trade: "For it is self-evident," Price wrote, "that if there are any men

---

[22] [Thomas Day], *A Letter From ********, in London, to his Friend in America, on the Subject of the Slave-Trade* . . . (New York, 1784), pp. 5–9, 14–17 (other editions, printed in London and Philadelphia in 1784, carry the title, *Fragment of an Original Letter on the Slavery of the Negroes: Written in the Year 1776*); George Warren Gignilliat, *The Author of Sandford and Merton; A Life of Thomas Day, Esq.* (New York, 1932), *passim;* Leslie Stephen, "Thomas Day," in *Dictionary of National Biography,* XIV).

whom they have a right to enslave, there may be others who have had a right to hold them in slavery."[23]

British reformers would later offer similar strictures to their French correspondents. Thomas Clarkson warned Bouvet de Cressé in December, 1789, that "the French Revolution can never be kept from the Negroes. The Efforts of good Men, who are hourly increasing in their Favour throughout all Europe, must unavoidably reach their Ears." And how could any Frenchman, believing the Revolution to be a virtuous and noble cause, "prevent the Negroes from accomplishing their Design?" National honor, as well as self-interest, required France to end the slave trade and ameliorate the condition of her slaves:

If she continues it, the Principles, on which She has brought about the Revolution, will be justly considered to have flowed from a polluted source, her Declaration of the Bill of Rights will be considered as the Declaration of Hypocrites, her Word will not be attended to for the future, and She will become the Derision of Europe.

Three years later the London Revolution Society exhorted the Society of Friends of the Constitution at Cognac to measure the French slave trade against the Declaration of Rights: "To defend your own liberties is noble, but to befriend the friendless is Godlike; complete then your Revolution by demanding Commerce to be just, that Africa may bless you as well as Europe."[24]

[23] John Millar, *The Origin of the Distinction of Rank* . . . (3rd ed., London, 1781), pp. 359–60; Richard Price, *Observations on the Importance of the American Revolution, and the Means of Making it a Benefit to the World* (London and New Haven, 1785), pp. 4–5, 7–8, 68–70; Edward Rushton, *Expostulatory Letter to George Washington of Mount Vernon, in Virginia, on his continuing to be a Proprietor of Slaves* (Liverpool, 1797), pp. 9, 12–13, 16–17, 21 (MS note on p. 24 of the Bibliothèque Nationale copy [Pb 2317] reads: "The Negroes are as free and as equal to Kings as the Americans are themselves and nothing can look more ridiculous than to see an assertor of American liberties with his Constitution in one hand and his negro lash in the other").

[24] Clarkson to Auguste Jean Baptiste Bouvet de Cressé, Dec. 1, 1789, Clarkson papers, Henry E. Huntington Library (hereafter HEH); George R. Mellor, *British Imperial Trusteeship, 1783–1850* (London, 1951), p. 22. See also Ghita Stanhope and G. P. Gooch, *The Life of the Third Earl Stanhope* (London, 1914), pp. 107–8; *Memoirs of the Life of Sir Samuel Romilly*, ed. by his sons (2 vols., London, 1840), I, 388; Granville Sharp to a member of the National Convention of France, Oct. 23, 1792, JAW. Clarkson, whom Wilberforce had sent to France as an abolitionist agent, expressed contradictory attitudes toward Negro violence. He assured Bouvet de Cressé that France could "avert the impending Blow," and that ameliorative measures would calm the minds of the

Such admonitions, coming even from outspoken critics of the British political system, suggested that if reformers had failed to purge the "corruptions" from their own constitution, England at least offered a moral vantage point for gauging the shortcomings of other people's revolutions. In the popular view, Sharp's judicial victory proved that slavery violated the fundamental law of England. And even for Price, this was one occasion for looking on England as the true model of liberty. In some respects Sharp himself regarded the new American Constitution as a purified version of the original British model. But this made him "the more sincerely grieved," as he wrote Benjamin Franklin, "to see the new Federal Constitution stained by the insertion of two most exceptionable clauses." The provision allowing the slave trade to continue for twenty years dishonored the solemn commitment made by the First Continental Congress. Sharp was even more indignant over the fugitive-slave clause, which defied the "higher law" of Deuteronomy. The Constitution purported to be the supreme law of the land. Sharp found these two clauses "so clearly null and void by their iniquity, that it would be even a *crime* to regard them as law."[25]

This statement virtually put Sharp in Garrison's later position of branding the Constitution as "a covenant with death and an agreement with hell." And in his response to the Fugitive Slave Law of 1793, Sharp gave support to the radical strain of American abolitionism that would culminate in in the civil disobedience of the 1850s. In 1793 the Maryland Abolition Society published and circulated a long letter from Sharp explaining why the forcible recovery of fugitives violated the laws of reason, nature, and Holy Scripture. If southern lawyers and legislators could offer any argument against his "high legal authorities," Sharp wrote, "they must have more subtile heads, and worse hearts, than I am willing to attribute to any one, who is not obviously actuated by the grand spiritual enemy of man!" Sharp went on to identify slavery with the apocalyptic "Beast." He warned that if Maryland and the Carolinas had escaped the restraints of mon-

---

blacks, who "will be flattered greatly by the attention." Yet to Mirabeau he exclaimed over the "Scenes of the brightest Heroism," when Negroes had temporarily seized control of slave ships. The leaders of such revolts, he wrote, "often eclipse by the Splendour of their Actions the celebrated Characters both of Greece and Rome" (Clarkson to Mirabeau, Dec. 9, 1789, HEH).

[25] Sharp to Franklin, Jan. 10, 1788, in Hoare, *Memoirs of Granville Sharp*, pp. 252–53.

archy, they were not beyond the reach of divine vengeance. Most important, he advocated a "higher" loyalty to the betrayed and only true constitution: "for no man can be truly *loyal* to God and his country, who is so totally devoid of *first principles* as to favour *slavery!*"[26]

This was revolutionary language in America, where Sharp's antislavery doctrines directly collided with the supreme law of the land. But in England, as abolitionists increasingly emphasized, the institution could claim no legal or constitutional sanction. And though Sharp was sometimes a bold critic of the evils in his own society, his arguments also strengthened the reassuring image of England as a land of freedom—notwithstanding the repeated failures at Parliamentary reform or the fact that during the first decades of antislavery effort, increasing numbers of English women and children were being pushed into mines, mills, and workhouses, where dehumanizing labor, physical punishment, sexual exploitation, and division of families approximated the "un-English" evils that abolitionists selected as their prime targets for attack.[27]

[26] Granville Sharp, *Letter from Granville Sharp, Esq. of London, to the Maryland Society for Promoting the Abolition of Slavery, and the Relief of Free Negroes and Others, Unlawfully Held in Bondage* (Baltimore, 1793), pp. 3–11 (the 1793 London edition is entitled, *Extract of a Letter to a Gentleman in Maryland; Wherein is Demonstrated the Extreme Wickedness of Tolerating the Slave Trade . . .*). The themes developed by Sharp, Price, Day, and Rushton were repeated endlessly, though sometimes with qualification, in later British travel accounts of America. For example, Richard Flower, *Letters from Lexington and the Illinois . . .* (London, 1819), pp. 96–98, 106; Morris Birkbeck, *Letters from Illinois* (Philadelphia, 1818), p. 102; John M. Duncan, *Travels Through Part of the United States and Canada in 1818 and 1819* (2 vols., Glasgow, 1823), II, 58–60, 256; William Newnham Blane, *An Excursion Through the United States and Canada During the Years 1822–1823* (London, 1824), pp. 73, 171–72, 201, 214, 221; James Flint, *Letters from America* (London, 1824), pp. 197–200. On the other hand, British opponents of the slave trade also made much of American census returns which proved that in an "enlightened" nation the slave population would increase naturally, without benefit of new importations (Samuel and Susannah Emlen to William Dillwyn, May 14, 1807, Emlen-Dillwyn papers, Library Company of Philadelphia [hereafter LCP]; Thomas Clarkson, *Three Letters . . . to the Planters and Slave-Merchants Principally on the Subject of Compensation* [London, 1807], p. 14).

[27] Elie Halévy, *England in 1815,* tr. by E. I. Watkin and D. A. Barker (London, 1949), pp. 262–63, 279–81. I am aware that a modern school of historians has presented a far happier view of the early stages of industrialization, which supposedly increased the real income of British workers and reduced their want and suffering. Similar arguments can be made regarding Negro slavery. But as Karl

Benevolence as the Redemption of Politics

If antislavery was a highly selective response to the exploitation of labor, it also represented an implicit challenge to English traditions of constituted authority. It is true that British abolitionists, unlike their American co-workers, could rejoice in the absence of conflict between the "higher law" of liberty and the fundamental law of the land. Yet it was one thing for Granville Sharp to plead with patient bishops and Cabinet secretaries, and quite another to bring organized public pressure upon an unreformed Parliament. Sharp expressed confidence that the English government had not intentionally allowed the introduction of slavery in the colonies; the evil had simply arisen from "want of a fixt attention *to the first principles of law* and religion." But this meant that ignorance could no longer serve as an excuse.[28] And by 1789 a few abolitionist converts had arrived at the antinomian conclusion that a government which lent its authority to crimes punishable by death had become "as much the common pest and scourge of mankind as any of the piratical states of Barbary."[29]

The conflict with the North American colonies had already shown how popular political discussion could overleap boundaries and spread the contagion of discontent. If the antislavery cause were to serve a hegemonic function, its leaders would have to find means of blocking this tendency and of striking a precise balance between respect for governmental authority and responsiveness to the voice of the "respectable" public. The success of the movement's leaders is admirably described by Sir Reginald Coupland, in words that say more than he probably intended: "Never before had the politically passive, quiescent, oligarchic Britain of the eighteenth century witnessed such a lively and widespread movement. It had shown how much could be done to mobilize public opinion outside the walls of Parliament, yet

---

Polanyi has observed, the critical questions have nothing to do with income or material standards of life. They rather involve the disintegration of preindustrial culture, psychological insecurity, and the dehumanizing effects of divorcing the "economic sphere" from life itself (Polanyi, *Primitive, Archaic, and Modern Economies. Essays of Karl Polanyi,* ed. by George Dalton [New York, 1968], p. 18 and *passim*).

[28] Sharp, *Extract of a Letter to a Gentleman in Maryland,* p. 12.

[29] "Atticus," to the printer of the *Diary,* April 16, 1789, Misc. Slavery, Box 1, A46, NYHS. Later letters from "Atticus" were more moderate (to Lewes *Journal,* Jan. 22 and March 24, 1796, A44–45).

strictly within the liberties of the constitution." The abolitionists' methods, Coupland adds, quoting another historian, " 'became the model for the conduct of hundreds or even thousands of other movements . . . which have been and still are the chief arteries of the life-blood of modern Britain.' "[30] In other words, in both conscious and unconscious ways, the movement showed the governing elites how to channel moral idealism and satisfy public opinion without risk to vital interests.

But it took a subtle political process to define—or redefine—the boundaries of vital interest. Petitions against the slave trade offered no direct threat to rotten boroughs, to the Test and Corporation Acts, or to other unpopular elements of the existing political structure. When such groups as the Commissioners of Supply and Heritors of the County of Stirling addressed Parliament, they expressed confidence that a "virtuous" Commons would always listen to the "sense" of the nation, and would do so with no greater glory than by abolishing the slave trade. Even Dissenters warned one another that the African cause would be severely damaged by any association with political reform. As early as July, 1788, the London Abolition Committee created a subcommittee to supervise Clarkson's establishment of provincial abolition committees, "paying regard to the advise [sic] contained in Mr. Wilberforce's Letter to the Treasurer . . . to avoid giving any possible occasion of offence to the Legislature by forced or unnecessary Associations." In the same month, when plans were under way for a public meeting, the Committee unanimously voted to suspend the idea after receiving "forcible" arguments from Wilberforce.[31] This was a full year before the French Revolution. Antislavery leaders

---

[30] Reginald Coupland, *Wilberforce: A Narrative* (Oxford, 1923), p. 160.

[31] Resolution of the Commissioners of Supply and Heritors of the County of Stirling, March 16, 1792, clipping, William Smith papers, Duke University Library (hereafter DUL); Robert Benson to James Phillips, March 26, 1792, Misc. MSS, B, NYHS; MS Proceedings of the Committee for the Abolition of the Slave Trade, 1787–1819 (hereafter Abolition Committee Minutes), II, 40–41, 44, British Museum Add. MSS 21254–21256. It is no doubt true that many of the M.P.s who voted for abolition in 1792 or 1796 were also inclined to vote for moderate Parliamentary reform and for repeal of the Test and Corporation Acts. Wilberforce, as we have seen, thought that it was "natural" that even Jacobins should flock to the abolition banner. The significant point, however, is that the abolitionist leaders perceived their movement as far less controversial and divisive than other reforms, and took considerable pains to keep the slave-trade issue from becoming associated with a broader reform program.

were always in need of convincing symbols of disinterestedness and "respectability." But Parliament, in turn, acquired from the cause a new image of moral purity. For surely no legislature dominated by selfish interests and party spirit could evoke the antislavery eloquence of a Pitt, a Wilberforce, a Fox, or a Burke. Between the antislavery movement and Parliament there was thus a kind of reciprocating process of legitimation: the cause served to vindicate the tarnished reputation of national politics, and demonstrated that the House of Commons, at least, was "responsive" to public opinion; it also proved that public opinion, even when mobilized by a network of corresponding committees, could be safe and respectable. But the resulting equilibrium would collapse without constant adjustment and compromise. The moral credibility of Parliament would ultimately require more than eloquent speeches and investigations of evidence. And if the antislavery movement were to preserve a convincing image of loyalty, after the outbreak of war with France, it would have to mute the voices of liberal reformers, of Dissenters, and even of organized pressure groups.

The dynamics of political interaction can best be approached by examining the abolitionists' first and most important tactical decision: the choice of the slave trade as an exclusive target. At first sight the decision appears to have been a simple and clear-cut matter, the logical result of a chain of preceding circumstances. The Quakers had established the precedent of disengaging from the slave trade as a prelude to gradual and peaceful manumission. When Anthony Benezet addressed an influential London Quaker in 1773, he recommended that political action be confined to ending the African trade: "If this could be obtained, I trust the sufferings of those already amongst us by the interposition of the government, and even from selfish ends in their master, would be mitigated; and, in time, Providence would fit them for freedom." Although Granville Sharp had first focused attention on the unlawfulness of chattel slavery, he became increasingly preoccupied with rescuing Negroes from ships outbound from English ports. In 1783, when Quakers like William Dillwyn were planning a concerted campaign against the slave trade and were writing Sharp for fresh information, the latter disclosed the shocking details of the *"Zong* case." As Sharp wrote Dillwyn, the Court of King's Bench had been asked to judge an insurance claim for the loss of one hundred and thirty-three slaves who had been thrown overboard at sea to preserve the *Zong's* dwindling rations. Sharp's unsuccessful effort "to prosecute the *Murderers*" helped dramatize the criminality of the slave traffic and fixed an unforgettable image in the mind of the reading public. Clarkson, in his celebrated *Essay* of 1786, presented the Zong atrocity as a usual occurrence. Wilberforce, who had dreamed in 1781 of becoming "the instrument of breaking, or at least easing, the yoke" of West Indian slaves, concluded by 1787 that Africa and the Atlantic slave trade should be the key objectives for reform. It was to be expected, then, that the 1787 Abolition Committee would decide to limit its goal, over Sharp's objections, to an outlawing of the slave trade. The only surprise, if we may believe Clarkson's later testimony, is that the Committee considered alternatives and concluded that it did not really matter where they began, since an ending of either slavery or the slave trade would bring an end to the other evil.[32]

The Committee's choice had obvious tactical merits. No one questioned the right of Parliament to regulate commerce, but the American Revolution had cast doubts on the wisdom, to say the least, of interfering with the domestic affairs of the colonies. Since British "antislavery" writing usually combined salutes to abstract liberty with an insistence on duty and discipline, proposals for anything bolder than

[32] Benezet to John Fothergill, April 28, 1773, in Brookes, *Friend Anthony Benezet*, p. 303; Sharp to Dillwyn, April 25, 1783, Sharp papers, British and Foreign Bible Society; Thomas Clarkson, *An Essay on the Slavery and Commerce of the Human Species, Particularly the African* (Philadelphia, 1786), p. 88; Robert Isaac Wilberforce and Samuel Wilberforce, *The Life of William Wilberforce* (5 vols., London, 1838), I, 149; IV, 306; Clarkson, *The History of the Rise, Progress and Accomplishment of the Abolition of the African Slave-Trade by the British Parliament* (2 vols., London, 1808), I, 283–89. In a letter to Benjamin Rush, written over a month after the decision on objectives, the Committee defined its "immediate aim" as "diffusing a knowledge of the subject, and particularly of the Modes of procuring and treating Slaves, to interest men of every description in the abolition of the Traffic." The inclusion of slave treatment suggests a broad-gauged program of dispensing information on the slave system; and though Rush's Pennsylvania Society explicitly worked for emancipation, the London group talked of "our respective Designs, so nearly allied in their Nature & Tendency." On the other hand, opposition attacks soon made the Committee more circumspect in defining its objectives, as when John Vickris Taylor reported that a manuscript by Edward White went "beyond the Views of this Society but not withstanding it contained some valuable information on the subject of Slavery" (Abolition Committee Minutes, I, 8; II, 6; *Society Instituted in 1787 for Effecting the Abolition of the Slave Trade* [Report] [London, 1788], p. 1).

gradual amelioration would be certain to alienate many potential supporters.

Moreover, though West Indian profits depended on a predictable supply of African labor, there was anything but a harmony of interests between planters and slave merchants. West Indians resented their dependence on English merchants and longed for an opening of unrestricted trade with North America. Philip D. Curtin estimates that the volume of the British slave trade in the period 1701–1810 exceeded slave imports into British colonies by over 23 per cent; during the same period the French slave trade supplied only 62 per cent of the Africans imported into French colonies. British traders sold some 404,000 slaves to competitive territories.[33] Given the uncertainties of the market for sugar, the startling increase in French sugar production, the mounting debts of the British planters, and the declining demand for slaves in Barbados and the Leeward Islands, it was not unreasonable to expect that many planters would fail to rally to the merchants' cause. A disavowal of any intent to interfere with slavery itself might thus soothe both West Indian proprietors and the owners of other property who recoiled at the thought of "abolitions" and of "liberating" a wild and savage people.

A closer look at the sources, however, reveals a frequent blurring of the distinction between slavery and the slave trade. Indeed, the confusion is so widespread and persistent that it must have had some significance. Benjamin Rush, among other early writers, talked as if slavery and the slave trade were the same thing. It was a cardinal point of Quaker antislavery doctrine that the receiver was as guilty as the thief. Between 1785 and 1788 the London Meeting for Sufferings, which contained members of the Abolition Committee, kept asking the Philadelphia Meeting for Sufferings for detailed evidence on the good effects of emancipation, a subject much discussed in Quaker transatlantic communication. Joseph Woods, a charter member of the Abolition Committee, in an anonymous pamphlet of 1784, called for "the gradual indeed, but total abolition of slavery, in every part of the British dominions." Both Ramsay and Clarkson expanded on the horrors of the West Indian plantation.[34]

[33] Philip D. Curtin, *The Atlantic Slave Trade: A Census* (Madison, Wisc., 1969), p. 219.
[34] [Benjamin Rush], *An Address to the Inhabitants of the British Settlements*

On February 12, 1788, the Abolition Committee heard a report on a paper by the Bishop of Peterborough which contained "many valuable hints" on the future emancipation of West Indian slaves. As late as 1790, Sharp referred in his diary to the Committee for the abolition of "slavery" (he was titular chairman of the Committee). In 1807 he told David Barclay that he had earlier made a declaration to the group, stating that whenever he acted with them, his own opposition would be aimed not merely at the slave trade but at toleration of slavery itself. The manuscript minutes of the same Committee contain a recommendation by Clarkson to send agents into the counties to convince people of the evils of "slavery"—the word, however, was later crossed out and "slave trade" written above. A similar uncertainty runs through countless sermons and pamphlets.[35]

There can be no doubt that the people themselves were confused. In January, 1788, Stephen Fuller sent Lord Hawkesbury a list of those who had petitioned "for the abolishing of Slavery." A 1788 campaign poster for Edward Protheroe, entitled "The Negro Mother's Petition to the Ladies of Bristol," made no mention of the African trade. Rather, it implored the ladies of Bristol to tell their fathers, brothers, and husbands about the plight of the West Indian slave:

> "Missey, Missey, tink on we,
> Toder side de big blue sea—
> How we flogg'd, and how we cry—
> How we sometimes wish to die. . . .
> When de Buckra 'peaker sent
> To de House call Parliament,
> Send *such* Buckra 'peaker dere
> As regard poor Neger prayer.
> Massa PRODEROE—*he* good man!
> Send *him*, Missey—SURE YOU CAN!"[36]

Wilberforce appeared to face the issue squarely in Parliamentary debate: "I am not afraid of being told I design to emancipate the

in America, Upon Slave-Keeping (Philadelphia, 1773), p. 1; "Letters Which Passed Betwixt the Meeting for Sufferings in London, and the Meeting for Sufferings in Philadelphia," MSS, Friends House, London; [Joseph Woods], *Thoughts on the Slavery of the Negroes* (London, 1784), pp. 31–32.

[35] Abolition Committee Minutes, I, 38, II, 28; Sharp, MS diary, and letter to David Barclay, May 28, 1807, JAW.

[36] Stephen Fuller to the Jamaican Committee of Correspondence, Jan. 30, 1788, MS Letterpress Book, I, 152 (Protheroe poster, p. 179). Fuller papers, DUL.

slaves; I will not indeed deny that I wish to impart to them the blessings of freedom. . . . But the freedom I mean is that of which, alas!
[they] are not capable. . . . The soil must be prepared for its recep-
tion." Yet Wilberforce drafted long lists of questions, to be asked of
witnesses examined by Parliament, dealing solely with West Indian
slavery. In 1806 Thomas Clarke complained in a public letter to
Cobbett that it was unfair to accuse the abolitionists of aiming at
emancipation, when they had always drawn a "broad line" of distinction between slavery and the slave trade. In the same year, however,
Wilberforce confided to his co-worker William Smith why he could
not support a proposal for importing contract Chinese labor into the
West Indies: there was grave risk "in exposing the cause of Abolition
(to you I may add, & finally of Emancipation also) to the discredit it
would incur from the failure of a fair trial by ourselves, (so our
opponents would represent it) whether another system could not be
substituted in the place of working West Indian Estates by Slaves'
Labour."[37]

Earlier, the abolitionsts' boycott movement had been directed against
West Indian sugar, not against the British suppliers of exports for the
African trade. Granville Sharp kept insisting that a corrupt system of
colonial law was the ultimate source of the slave trade. And the
pamphlets and Parliamentary speeches calling for slave-trade abolition
were usually filled with graphic accounts of West Indian atrocities.
Understandably, there was considerable confusion among foreign observers. British abolitionists tried to explain to their French and American correspondents that the movement's objectives were confined to
the African trade.[38] But in America, Ezra Stiles, for example, thought

[37] *The Debate on the Motion for the Abolition of the Slave-Trade, in the
House of Commons, on Monday the Second of April, 1792. Reported in Detail*
(London, 1792), p. 12; William Wilberforce, *A Letter on the Abolition of the
Slave Trade; Addressed to the Freeholders and Other Inhabitants of Yorkshire*
(London, 1807), pp. 258–59; Wilberforce, MS questions for witnesses, CN 191,
HEH; Arthur Young. "On the Abolition of Slavery in the West Indies," *Annals
of Agriculture*, IX (1788), 88–96; Thomas Clarke, *A Letter to Mr. Cobbett on
His Opinions Respecting the Slave-Trade* (London, 1806), pp. 8–10; Wilber-
force to William Smith, Sept. 5, 1806, Smith papers, DUL; Stanhope to Henry
Dundas, April 4, 1792, in Stanhope and Gooch, *Life of Charles, Third Earl
Stanhope*, p. 108; "Review of Wilberforce on the Abolition of the Slave Trade,"
Christian Observer (May, 1807), 322, 326.

[38] [Zachary Macaulay], *The Horrors of the Negro Slavery Existing in Our
West Indian Islands, Irrefragably Demonstrated from Official Documents*

that Wilberforce had presented a bill for the "total abolition of Slavery," which had then been amended to a *"gradual* Abolition." Clavière wrote to the Pennsylvania Abolition Society in 1788, reporting that the French had founded a society modeled on those in England and America, aimed at securing the abolition of slavery and the slave trade. In the same year the *Analyse des papiers anglais* reported the activities of the London Committee under the heading, "Plan pour abolir entirement *l'esclavage* des *Nègres,* dans les possessions Britanniques." In 1789 La Rochefoucauld d'Enville asked the National Assembly to follow the example of Parliament and consider "la liberté des noirs."[39]

Such confusion no doubt served a useful purpose in attracting humanitarian support for a vague "Negro's cause" while also reassuring those who feared the results of emancipation. But the ambiguity of ultimate goals threw the West Indians instantly on guard. They knew that even the cautious law of 1788 regulating the ratio of slaves to ship tonnage was publicly defended as a righteous blow against slavery. In January, 1788, Stephen Fuller, the Jamaican agent and lobbyist, reported to the colony's Committee of Correspondence: "I believe the plan of proceeding is not yet agreed upon, but I understand the attack is to be made upon the Trade itself on the Coast of Africa." Two weeks later he became convinced that the abolitionists were "determined, if they can, to abolish the Slave Trade entirely, and in the end to set all the Slaves in the Sugar Colonies free." The abolitionists' tactics kept their opponents guessing, but also made them expect the worst. Fuller was especially alarmed by the steady flow of petitions, from all parts of the kingdom, "stating no grievance or injury of any

---

Recently Presented to the House of Commons (London, 1805), pp. 4–5, 36; Wilberforce to William Eden, Oct. 20, 1787, in *The Journal and Correspondence of William, Lord Auckland* (4 vols., London, 1861–1862), I, 240; New York Manumission Society, MS Minutes, VI, 111, NYHS; Clarkson to Bouvet de Cressé, Dec. 1, 1789, Clarkson papers, HEH. The draft of the latter letter contains numerous deletions, indicating uncertainty on several critical points; for example: "The Colonial Slavery, Sir, does not enter into our Plan. We are of Opinion that the immediate [crossed out] Emancipation of the Slaves would be of no Benefit to them at present." Clarkson also predicted that the planters should not oppose a plan that did not interfere with their property.

[39] Ezra Stiles, *Literary Diary of Ezra Stiles,* ed. by F. B. Dexter, III (New York, 1901), p. 456; Pennsylvania Abolition Society MSS, I (April 29, 1788), HSP; *Analyse des papiers anglais,* XIX (Jan. 31–Feb. 1, 1788); *Archives parlementaires,* VIII (June 27, 1789), 165.

kind or sort, affecting the Petitioners themselves." The West Indians would at least have known where they stood if the reformers had introduced a specific bill in Parliament and had then called for public support, instead of "blowing up the flame first, and then telling you for what purpose afterwards." Fuller spent a considerable amount of Jamaican money in an effort to defeat the Slave Trade Regulating Act. This move did not reflect a stubborn hostility to regulation, which the West Indians were prepared to agree to as an eventual bargaining "concession." Rather, like other West Indian representatives, his suspicions were aroused by the bill's sudden and unexpected introduction, and by the antislavery arguments it evoked. Above all, Fuller was concerned over the symbolic effect of an overwhelming vote. As he wrote the Duke of Richmond, "I have nothing to say as to the merits or demerits of the Bill . . . but the passing it will certainly be tantamount to a publick declaration to all the negroes in the Island of Jamaica, that their friends in the House of Commons are in the proportion of 58 to 7."[40]

Even if the planters had not been blinded by the allure of short-run profit and an exaggerated estimate of future labor needs, the abolitionists' tactics would have thrown them into the arms of the slave merchants. Unlike the North Americans, they could not divorce the slave-trade issue from their own domestic security. The fear that Parliamentary debates would spark a slave insurrection was both genuine and realistic. If the slaves should learn, as Fuller pointed out, that they had powerful "friends" in Parliament, that the people of England had rallied to the "Negro's cause," how could one expect them to make fine discriminations about tactical objectives or "wait with patience for a tardy event," when they might "by a sudden blow

[40] Fuller, Letterpress Books, I, 141, 149, 159, 167, 258, 335–36, DUL; MS Minutes of the Society of West India Planters and Merchants, III, June 30, 1788, West India Committee Archives, London; *Journals of the Assembly of Jamaica*, VIII (Jamaica, 1804), 406–10; letter from a "gentleman in Jamaica" to Lord Hawkesbury, April 12, 1788, Liverpool papers, Add. MS 38416, fols. 127–28, British Museum. In 1790, Robert Norris testified before the Select Committee of the Commons that when Clarkson was gathering evidence in Liverpool, he had specified emancipation as one of the abolitionists' objectives. The charge was denied and was no doubt malicious, but one must also take account of Clarkson's injudicious enthusiasms, as expressed, for example, to Mirabeau (*Minutes of the Evidence Taken Before a Committee of the House of Commons* . . . [2 vols., London, 1790], II, 57).

finish the business themselves . . . without giving their zealous friends here any further trouble?"[41]

Nor was it unrealistic for West Indians to fear that humanitarian zeal would justify the encroaching power of Parliament, that internal political stability would require external symbolic achievement, or that the demand for a Slave Trade Regulating Act would be followed successively by demands for immediate abolition, for the registration of slaves, for "amelioration," and for immediate emancipation. In the final debates on ending the slave trade, in 1807, Earl Percy unexpectedly proposed freeing every Negro child born in the colonies after January 1, 1810. As the planter George Hibbert bitterly predicted, "that young nobleman will be treated like a gallant soldier who outsteps the line, and anticipates the charge; but the line is advancing, and the charge will soon be made." By 1812, Wilberforce was writing Macaulay that "we've been too dilatory in our proceedings respecting slavery" in the West Indies, and should be "guarded against any measures which might ever totally obstruct our future reforms."[42]

From the very outset an astute lobbyist like Fuller knew that slavery itself was the central issue. For that reason, as early as 1788 he concentrated his energies on publicizing the supposedly humane provisions

----

[41] Elsa V. Goveia stresses the planters' short-sightedness, arising from unrealistic hopes for high profits from expanded production (*Slave Society in the British Leeward Islands at the End of the Eighteenth Century* [New Haven, 1965], pp. 21–23). Though her general argument is valid, the planters were not so blind to the future or so rigidly opposed to slave-trade regulation as she and others imply. A committee appointed by the Jamaican House of Assembly reported on Oct. 16, 1788, that the Slave Trade Regulating Act should ultimately prove highly beneficial to the sugar colonies, "inasmuch as it is notorious that vessels have been frequently crowded with a greater number of negroes than they ought in prudence to have contained." The committee called for further regulations, including steps to equalize the sex ratio and to prevent the purchase of slaves who had been kidnapped or deprived of liberty "contrary to the usage and custom of Africa"! (*Journals of the Assembly of Jamaica,* VIII, 409–10). Fuller's correspondence makes it clear that the West Indian agents opposed regulation because they feared that the character of the debates would convince slaves that the English people wanted to set them free, and because Parliament, after passing the 1788 bill, had nothing left "to give to the Petitioners that will not lead to the ruin and destruction of the colonies" (Letterpress Books, I, 285, 335–36, DUL).

[42] *Parliamentary Debates,* IX (March 16, 1807), 131; Wilberforce to Macaulay, Aug. 6, 1812, Wilberforce papers, in possession of C. E. Wrangham, Esq. (hereafter CEW); Clarkson to J. Wadkin, June 10, 1813, Bod. C107/166, Rhodes House, Oxford.

of the Jamaican Consolidated Slave Act, which he later credited with blunting the abolitionist attack. *"That act,"* he reported to Jamaica, *"has saved the West Indies."* By 1791, in response to Fox's blistering speech in Parliament, the West Indian agents were pleading to the colonial legislatures for sweeping reforms of the slave codes. They knew, looking to the future, that only gestures of humanitarianism would allow the colonies to retain a voice in British politics.[43]

Ironically, abolitionist leaders were prepared to deal with the West Indians if they accepted the abolitionists' rules. In 1794, Wilberforce told Clarkson that he was inclined to think the West Indians would cooperate in abolishing the slave trade "if they conceiv'd they could thereby preclude Emancipation. This is a compromise to which so far as I am concern'd I should not be indispos'd."[44]

The West Indians, however, were well aware that abolition would not preclude emancipation. They envisioned compromise as a succession of steps that would strengthen the slave system while eliminating its worst abuses. As early as 1791 Sir William Young pointed out, appropriating the mantle of benevolence, that a sudden ending of the slave trade would not only increase the work load of existing slaves but lead to the ruin of many planters and hence to the suffering and starvation of their dependents. On the other hand, a positive policy of improving the slaves' condition and encouraging their natural increase would ultimately make the African trade unnecessary. In 1797, Young and Charles Rose Ellis seized the offensive in Parliament and pushed through a motion requesting the king to recommend to the colonies ameliorative measures that would gradually "diminish the Necessity of the Slave Trade and ultimately . . . lead to its complete Termination." Much to Wilberforce's distress, the West Indians had not only learned to play the new game, but had succeeded temporarily in defining the terms of consensus.[45]

[43] Fuller, Letterpress Books, I, 198, 201, 287, 316, 329, 491–97; II, 66, 68–74, DUL. Even the Abolition Committee was much impressed by the Jamaican Consolidated Slave Act, and hoped that planters would soon begin to realize that the slave trade was not in their best interest (Abolition Committee Minutes, II, 117). Yet it is also clear that the West Indian legislatures lagged far behind their London agents in comprehending the requirements necessary for compromise.

[44] Wilberforce to Clarkson, Oct. 29, 1794, Thompson-Clarkson scrapbooks, I, 319, Friends House, London.

[45] Goveia, *Slave Society in the British Leeward Islands,* pp. 26–27, 33–35;

As events would prove, the abolitionists were right when they doubted both the ability and willingness of West Indians to smooth the way toward emancipation. Prompted in part by a memory of Ellis's resolutions of 1797, Wilberforce would warn Buxton in 1826 that it would be "nothing less than treachery to the cause . . . if all our chief friends were not with one concurrent voice to declaim against the utter hopelessness of any honest co-operation from the Colonial assemblies."[46] On the other hand, by insisting on the priority of the slave trade, even when they attacked the entire slave system, the abolitionists became trapped by their own untenable assumptions. Their early reliance on slave-trade abolition was wedded to laissez-faire ideology in a way that precluded *any* legislation to improve the condition of West Indian slaves.

Thus prior to 1818 Wilberforce repeatedly emphasized the unenforceability of laws regulating slaves' food and clothing, the hours of their labor, their punishments, their medical care, or their education. In a highly revealing passage he asked:

Put the case of a similar law, applicable to servants in this country; how impossible would it be found to enter into the interior of every family, and with more than inquisitorial power to ascertain the observance or the breach of the rules which should have been laid down for our domestic economy. . . . But supposing the means of enforcing the regulations to be found, how odious, how utterly intolerable would such a system be found in its execution![47]

This position ruled out plans like the one proposed to Parliament in 1796 by Philip Francis, who called on the government to ensure that slaves be guaranteed their own land, that conflicts with masters be settled by arbitration, and that slaves be allowed to develop their

Dale H. Porter, *The Abolition of the Slave Trade in England, 1784–1807* ([Hamden, Conn.] 1970), pp. 96–101.

[46] Wilberforce to Thomas Fowell Buxton, March 23 and April 28, 1826, Bod. C. 106/7,9, Rhodes House, Oxford; Wilberforce to Henry Brougham, March 28, 1826, *The Correspondence of William Wilberforce*, ed. by Robert Isaac Wilberforce and Samuel Wilberforce (2 vols., London, 1840), II, 495–97; Clarkson to William Stevens, Jan. 11, 1826, Clarkson papers, DUL.

[47] Wilberforce, *Letter on the Abolition of the Slave Trade*, pp. 222–23. Wilberforce had earlier argued in Parliament that all regulatory laws, such as the French *Code noir* and Spanish slave codes, were ineffective (*Parliamentary History*, XXIX [1791–1792], 272–74). Clarkson made the same point in *An Essay on the Comparative Efficiency of Regulation or Abolition, as Applied to the Slave Trade* (London, 1789), p. 40.

own legal and social institutions.[48] It also shut the door on tactics which Wilberforce and Clarkson came finally and reluctantly to accept.

As they looked into the future, the abolitionists distinguished two ethical dispensations. They expected nothing from the West Indians' self-interest prior to abolition, but everything from such self-interest after abolition. In Clarkson's words, the ending of slave importations would force the planters to "find that resource within themselves, which their avarice has taught them to reject, and they must immediately turn a system of calculated oppression, and murder, into that of lenity, tenderness, and preservation." Wilberforce took up the same theme:

All ideas of supply from without, being utterly cut off, it would immediately become the grand, constant, and incessant concern of every prudent man, both proprietor and manager, to attend, in the first instance, to the preservation and increase of his Negroes. Whatever may have been the case in the instance of men at once both liberal and opulent, the mass of owners have, practically at least, gone upon the system of working out their Slaves in a few years, and recruiting their gangs with imported Africans. The abolition would give the death-blow to this system. The opposite system, with all its charities, would force itself on the dullest intellects, on the most contracted or unfeeling heart. Ruin would stare a man in the face, if he did not conform to it.[49]

In other words, the sin of "avarice" was responsible for a brutal system of exploitation, but the desire for profit would force planters to breed and nourish their domestic labor force. And as they discovered "the waste incidental to the providing sustenance for large numbers," the planters would soon see advantage in leaving it "in the power of

[48] *Parliamentary History,* XXXII (1796), 959–80. Fox and William Smith came to Francis's defense, but Pitt, Dundas, and others were horrified by the idea of infringing on slaveholders' property rights. Francis was best known as the mortal enemy of Warren Hastings, with whom in India he had fought a duel. It was Francis who persuaded Fox and Burke to push for Hastings's impeachment, and who helped rally the anti-Hastings forces during the long impeachment trial of 1788–1795. Pitt's equivocation prevented the Whigs from appropriating all the credit as crusaders for justice in India. In 1796 he and Dundas were clearly determined to prevent Francis from exploiting another moral issue, whereas Francis and Fox were clearly bent on embarrassing the government.

[49] Clarkson, *An Essay on the Impolicy of the African Slave Trade* . . . (Philadelphia, 1788), p. 91; Wilberforce, *Letter on the Abolition of the Slave Trade,* pp. 243–44.

each individual to sustain himself more cheaply."[50] The blacks would thus gain their freedom as the planters grew richer; economic ruin would be the fitting penalty for any planter who disregarded the laws of benevolence and of Adam Smith.

This position necessitated a fairly sanguine view of slavery in the United States, despite all that had been said in 1776 about the whip-brandishing Sons of Liberty. Henry Brougham, for example, cited Jefferson's *Notes on Virginia* for evidence that a cutting off of slave imports would lead to better treatment and to a rapid natural increase in the Negro population. As a group, the British abolitionists found it virtually impossible not to interpret North America's growing Negro population as evidence that slavery itself was in the process of amelioration and rapid extinction. It was thus not altogether coincidental that British disillusionment over their own original tactics came with a belated recognition of the severity and geographic expansion of slavery in the United States.[51]

Wilberforce's expectations seem to have been related to his larger assumptions concerning the triumph of "practical" Christianity over original sin. By striking the evil at its "root," the reformers would allow the natural growth of a new "operative principle," somewhat comparable to grace, which would ensure to self-interest benevolent effect. Wilberforce hoped that the conversion of the English upper class to Evangelical religion would lead to the moral regeneration of domestic society. He placed similar reliance on the influence of absentee proprietors, whose motives the act of abolition would immediately transform. The key mechanism, in both instances, would be moral example reinforced by economic power. After abolition, the "credit and character" of each plantation manager would depend on increasing the stock of blacks, "not as hitherto on . . . the immediate and clear returns from the estate." And as absentee landlords took a closer interest in the well-being of their property, the cumulative effect would amount to a moral transformation of West Indian society: "the settlement of families, the discouragement of adultery; the coun-

---

[50] "Review of Wilberforce," *Christian Observer*, pp. 327–28; Abolition Committee Minutes, I, 5; Clarkson, *Essay on Impolicy*, pp. 90–94; Clarkson, *History of the Abolition of the African Slave-Trade*, I, 285–87.

[51] Henry Brougham, *A Concise Statement Regarding the Abolition of the Slave Trade* (London, 1804), pp. 60–61.

tenancing, by example as well as precept, among bookkeepers or over-seers, of morality and decency."[52]

It should now be clear that the tactical decision to attack the slave trade carried profound ideological meaning. Although Sharp and other writers continued to denounce the unlawfulness of slaveholding, the movement's leaders attributed the evils of slavery to the available supply of new labor, not to exploitation itself. As pointed out by the *Christian Observer,* the organ of the Evangelical party: "They who affirm that nothing may be tolerated which occasions robbery and murder, must not only emancipate our slaves in the West Indies, but raze our great cities, and fire our mines and manufactories. The abolitionists however are not chargeable with this paradox."[53]

The abolitionists embraced a different paradox. God had prohibited the commission of certain crimes, not institutions that might provide the occasion for crime. The slave trade was inseparable from the commission of crime and was therefore "the greatest practical evil which has ever afflicted the human race" (these were actually Pitt's words, from the debate of 1792).[54] This rather forced distinction allowed Wilberforce to declare that slaves were entitled to the blessings of liberty, but then to liken them to unfortunate prisoners who had been "driven into a state of utter madness," which required, out of charity, "salutary restraint" and even "the harsher expedient of wholesome discipline." The distinction allowed Brougham to say more frankly that Negro labor would long be essential for West Indian cultivation; that such labor would require coercion, though not mal-treatment; and that abolition would force the West Indian legislatures to pass ameliorative laws: "Of their superior ability to devise and execute such measures, we cannot entertain the smallest doubt."[55]

---

[52] Wilberforce, *Letter on the Abolition of the Slave Trade,* pp. 244–46.

[53] *Christian Observer* (April, 1807), pp. 254–55; (June, 1804), p. 368.

[54] *Ibid.*

[55] Wilberforce, *Letter on the Abolition of the Slave Trade,* p. 258; Henry Brougham, *An Inquiry into the Colonial Policy of the European Powers* (4 vols., Edinburgh, 1803), II, 449–505. Bishop Beilby Porteus was outraged over the "insidious effect" of Earl Percy's proposal in 1807 for gradual emancipation. The true friends of abolition, he noted, had always been careful to disavow any intent of interfering with slavery, which was not, after all, contrary to Christianity (Porteus MS 2104, 102 [I am most grateful to Roger Anstey, and indirectly to John A. Woods and Lambeth Palace Library, for supplying me with transcripts

But a few abolitionists did express doubt over the naïveté and inflexibility of official doctrine. James Stephen, Wilberforce's well-informed brother-in-law, knew that profits and amelioration would not mix.[56] "Would to God," he exclaimed, "that the interest of the master were really so involved in the well being of the slave, as has been asserted and admitted in Parliament!" Maltreatment, he insisted, was not confined to a few cruel or indigent masters; nor could one expect, even on the best-regulated estates, that the planter's self-interest would reduce excessive hours of labor or increase "the ordinary subsistence, which is far too small." In 1802, Stephen predicted that nothing less than direct Parliamentary intervention would be required: "When an efficient moving power shall be obtained, it will be time enough to consider how the parts of the machine may be best constructed and applied." During the next few years Stephen himself would work quietly and efficiently toward the creation of that "efficient moving power." A confirmed Tory, he had the good fortune to be close to Spencer Perceval and Lord Liverpool (the latter secured him a seat in the Commons in 1808); more important, in 1811 he was appointed

---

of the Porteus MSS]). Even more liberal abolitionists agreed that slavery had incapacitated the West Indian Negroes for freedom. William Smith, for example, used the common analogy of sickness and health, an analogy that allowed continuing confinement for the good of the patient (*A Letter to William Wilberforce, Esq., M.P. on the Proposed Abolition of the Slave Trade* . . . [London, 1807], pp. 27–28). Yet Clarkson expressed the similarly common view that regulatory laws would be ineffective since the ferocity of African-born blacks required harsh discipline. The worst evils of plantation discipline would thus disappear as increasing numbers of blacks were born into West Indian slavery! (*Essay on the Comparative Efficiency of Regulation or Abolition,* pp. 40–44).

[56] Initially there was a sharp divergence between Stephen's "statist philosophy" and the laissez-faire position of Brougham and the *Edinburgh Review.* In a review of *Crisis of the Sugar Colonies,* Brougham attacked Stephen's scheme for colonizing Trinidad with free blacks, under centralized controls; objected to any direct interference in the relations between slaves and masters; and urged that England cooperate with France in restoring order and white supremacy in the Caribbean (*Edinburgh Review,* I [Oct., 1802], 232–36). Late in 1804 both Brougham and Wilberforce feared that Stephen's writing would distract attention from Africa and the slave trade, and would unnecessarily alarm the West Indian planters (Brougham to Wilberforce, Dec. 27, 1804, CEW; Wilberforce, *Life of Wilberforce,* III, 198–200). Many years later, however, Wilberforce would secretly ask for Brougham's opinion on "what specific measures we ought to endeavor to prepare for the Universal Emancipation of the W. Indian slaves" (Wilberforce to Brougham, March 13, 1823, Brougham papers, University College, London).

Master in Chancery and in 1813 his son James became legal counselor to the Colonial Office. It was James, Jr., later to become permanent Undersecretary of the Colonial Office, who finally drafted the 1833 act of emancipation.[57]

As early as 1815 Clarkson had learned the "melancholy lesson, that, whereas the abolition of the Slave-trade ought in common Prudence, to have secured better Treatment to the Slave, yet such is the force of custom and prejudice . . . that *Legislative Authority is actually necessary* to *produce so desireable* an End." The colonial legislatures had *"forfeited their Charter"* and *"must be compelled to obey"* reason: *"They must be over awed by the public Voice."*[58] And in 1830 Clarkson would confess that abolitionists had been "deceived" in their first expectations:

We supposed that when by the abolition of the slave trade the planters could get no more slaves, they would not only treat better those whom they then had in their power, but that they would gradually find it to their advantage to emancipate them. . . . We did not sufficiently take into account the effect of unlimited power on the human mind. No man likes to part with power, and the more unbounded it is, the less he likes to part with it. Neither did we sufficiently take into account the ignominy attached to a black skin as the badge of slavery, and how difficult it would be to make men look with a favourable eye upon what they had looked [upon] formerly as a disgrace. Neither did we take sufficiently into account the belief which every planter has, that such an unnatural state as that of slavery can be kept up only by a system of rigour, and how difficult therefore it would be to procure a relaxation from the ordinary discipline of a slave estate.[59]

[57] [James Stephen], *The Crisis of the Sugar Colonies; or an Enquiry into the Objects and Probable Effects of the French Expedition to the West Indies . . .* (London, 1802), pp. 123–28, 140–51; D. J. Murray, *The West Indies and the Development of Colonial Government, 1801–1834* (Oxford, 1965), pp. 47–126. After the defeat of his scheme for a central registry for all slaves, Stephen resigned his seat in the Commons, writing Lord Liverpool that he could best serve the Negroes outside of Parliament (Stephen to Liverpool, March 2, 1815, Liverpool papers, Add. MS 38261, fols. 81–82, British Museum).

[58] Clarkson to Wilberforce (?), 1815, Clarkson papers, HEH. Clarkson significantly termed Stephen's Registry Bill, which had been proposed supposedly as a means of preventing illicit slave importations, as "the Foundation-stone of a constitution for their better treatment." The British people, he added, "have a right to consider the Negroes in our Islands as *British subjects*. If they are not subjects, then the government of the Islands is only an Excrescence on the *English Constitution* which the Mother-C should prune or cut away."

[59] Clarkson, unidentified letter in private possession, quoted in Ulrich Bonnell

Yet the original assumptions had served an important political purpose. The British attempt to control West Indian slavery by prohibiting further slave imports bore certain parallels with the later American
attempt to contain the peculiar institution by prohibiting its expansion
into the western territories. Thus the early British "abolitionists" were
content with a compromise that resembled the later "antislavery" position of American Freesoilers and Republicans. Like the Americans,
the British disavowed any intention of interfering with slavery where
it had long existed—though in both instances slaveholders had reason
to suspect the disavowals. Once contained, the institution would no
doubt wither and disappear (that is, if slaveholders knew their own
best interest). And if this faith really amounted to a containment of
moral protest, it allowed antislavery sentiment to be assimilated to the
political process. The differences, however, are more revealing than the
similarities. Unlike most of the American Free Soilers and Republicans, the British abolitionists genuinely wished to improve the life of
Negroes, and mistakenly thought that amelioration would rapidly
undermine the institution of slavery. Yet in England, during the first
phase of the antislavery movement, the governing classes accepted an
expedient—the abolition of the slave trade—that virtually required
further intervention if planters failed to conform to abolitionist expectations. In America, the compromise of containment emerged as
the final expedient, after a long official "conspiracy of silence." And
of course the "compromise" demand to exclude slavery from the territories provoked a crisis which succeeded in destroying the entire slave
regime.

In the 1790s, however, it was quite inconceivable that the English
government or the government of any imperial nation would adopt
an emancipationist program like the one proposed by Philip Francis.
Abolition of the slave trade was hardly more conceivable, unless jointly
agreed to by the principal maritime powers. Even the debates on slave-

---

Phillips, *American Negro Slavery* (reprint ed., Gloucester, Mass., 1959), pp.
148–49. There was also, however, a persistence of the original hopes of killing
slavery at the "root." Thus in 1838 Buxton solicited Clarkson's support for his
ambitious program of introducing Christian civilization into West Africa as the
only sure means of stopping the slave trade at its source. If the abolitionists were
to sit back and wait, he wrote, until "our" antislavery principles had ripened in
Cuba and Brazil, it would cost "us" a half-century and twenty-five million lives
(Buxton to Clarkson, Nov. 16 and Dec. 11, 1838, Howard University Library).

trade regulation, in 1788, raised explosive issues of national interest. In return for extremely moderate regulations, Pitt agreed to compensation for financial loss, as well as to government bounties for the preservation of lives. And for this token victory he faced abuse from members of his own Cabinet and party, and was finally forced to threaten a Cabinet crisis.[60]

On the other hand, the "spontaneous" loyalty that supports class hegemony is always the product of a subtle interaction between rulers and the ruled. During the American Revolution, the domestic turmoil in England had sharpened suspicions of Ministerial corruption, given an edge to the grievances of the disfranchised, and created a need for new symbols of legitimacy. Nor could any political faction safely ignore the growing sensitivity of the middle class, including, it should be stressed, middle-class women, to humanitarian issues. Thus in 1788 Pitt realized that the political value of an antislavery measure might justify certain short-run sacrifices. And in May of that year, when Wilberforce was incapacitated by serious illness and when Parliament received over one hundred petitions against the slave trade, Pitt's leadership was put to the test. Various factions in the House of Commons tried to seize the slave-trade issue from Pitt's grasp, or failing that, to strand him in an embarrassing position.[61]

The politics of abolition involved a collective definition of vital interests. But what, precisely, did this mean in practice? In the first place, it meant that both the opponents and defenders of the slave trade accepted the rules of Parliamentary procedure and assumed that Parliament was the scene where the issue would be decided. And though each side accused the other of procrastination, they both welcomed the formal hearing of evidence—which became a kind of choric ritual—as a means of delaying action and mobilizing votes.[62]

[60] *Parliamentary History*, XXVII (1788), 495–501; Elizabeth Donnan, ed., *Documents Illustrative of the History of the Slave Trade to America* (Washington, 1930–1935), II, 582–88; Richard Pares, *King George III and the Politicians* (Oxford, 1967), p. 42, n. 2. For admirals like Lord Rodney, the issue was one of national survival; the reformers, under a "masque of Religion," were in effect traitors giving aid to England's historic enemy (Rodney to Hawkesbury, March, 1788, Liverpool papers, Add. MS 38416, fols. 72–76).

[61] *Parliamentary History*, XXVII (1788), 495–501; Fuller, Letterpress Books, I, 249, DUL.

[62] Abolition Committee Minutes, II, 50; III, 6; Fuller, Letterpress Books, I, 209, 224, 418–20, DUL; MS Minutes of the Society of West India Planters and Merchants, III, April 24, 1789, Feb. 11, 1790. Of course, either side would have

Everyone understood the critical importance of timing. In January, 1788, Wilberforce expected a quick and easy victory, in part because of optimistic reports from France, in part because of his confidence in Pitt's support. By May, however, after Pitt's Privy Council Committee for Trade and Plantations had heard testimony from prestigious admirals, the slave-trade faction was equally confident. Like the Abolition Committee, the West Indian merchants and planters were unsure of Pitt's intentions. They hoped, however, that an early discussion and vote in the House of Commons would put an end to further agitation.[63] Thus began a long game of calculating the most favorable time to stop examining or cross-examining witnesses, a game that would be transferred to a select committee of the House and to the House of Commons itself. During 1790 and 1791 the West Indian faction generally opposed excessive delays and pressed for early votes; on occasion, however, they reached agreement with Wilberforce on postponing debate.[64]

The great slave-trade investigations embodied the spirit of the scientific Enlightenment. They gave expression to the desire to question traditional assumptions, to gather a multitude of facts, to weigh evidence, and to reject unprovable claims, including those arising from humanitarian zeal. The abolitionists were embarrassed by the moral character and social status of many of their witnesses; the West Indians were embarrased by the difficulty of finding "disinterested" witnesses. Yet each side was confident that testimony had unmasked the hypocrisy of their opponents and had revealed the nation's true best interest.[65] From a psychological perspective, the investigations can be

gladly dispensed with hearing evidence if they had been able to count on a quick and easy victory. When not appearing before a committee, witnesses gave testimony to the clerk of the House of Commons instead of to the assembled membership. The prolonged delays did not signify, therefore, that the entire House of Commons was eagerly studying and digesting the details of the Atlantic slave trade.

[63] Wilberforce to Wyvill, Jan. 25, 1788, CEW; Wilberforce, *Life of Wilberforce,* I, 160–61; Fuller, Letterpress Books, I, 41, 154, 209, 224, 235–41, 391, DUL; Abolition Committee Minutes, II, 14.

[64] Fuller, Letterpress Books, I, 418, 428–29, 491–97, 501–2, DUL; William Dillwyn to Susannah Dillwyn, March 13, 1791, Emlen-Dillwyn papers, LCP.

[65] *Minutes of the Evidence Taken Before a Committee of the House of Commons,* I, 29, 79–88, 467–77; II, 3–16, 22–23, 142–43, 181–93; *An Abstract of the Evidence Delivered Before a Select Committee of the House of Commons in the Years 1790 and 1791* . . . (2nd ed., London, 1791), *passim;* William Bell

seen as a ritual of expiation that temporarily exorcised the slave trade's worst evils. For surely it was morally preferable for M.P.'s to shudder at a recital of horrors than to pretend that the evils did not exist. Wilberforce's calling of witnesses, quite apart from the timing of votes, helped to prolong a public catharsis.

Wilberforce kept insisting that abolition itself would involve no greater sacrifice than did the public catharsis: "Here you can do good by wholesale, and at no expense; you may enrich others and be yourselves no poorer." In his memorable speech of May 12, 1789, he read from a document that echoed the West Indian merchants' predictions of economic ruin; then he informed the House that it had been written in 1774 and concerned the loss of the North American colonies, which occurrence, as it turned out, had hardly impoverished Great Britain.[66]

Yet apart from profits and losses, the investigations did raise a fundamental principle of economic enterprise. As pointed out by Robert Norris, who supplied Clarkson with information on Africa and who then became a leading witness and propagandist for the slave traders:

The principle which has raised the commerce and navigation of this country, and with them the landed interest and revenues of the kingdom, from inconsiderable beginnings to their present greatness, is the *right* which every man in it possesses, to carry on his own business, in the way most advantageous to himself and the society, without any sudden interruption in the pursuit of it; and the *consciousness* which he has, of the steady protection of the laws, in the prosecution of what has been shown to be legal.[67]

Crafton, *A Short Sketch of the Evidence* . . . (London, 1792), *passim;* [Anon.], *A Short Sketch of the Evidence for the Abolition of the Slave Trade* . . . (London, 1792) *passim.* The William Smith papers contain detailed lists and notes which show a conscientious attempt to evaluate the consistency and reliability of witnesses. Since the abolitionists took pains to distinguish their "true and faithful" accounts from the "pathetic poetry" of earlier antislavery writers like Thomas Day, they were particularly embarrassed by witnesses like Robert Norris, who double-crossed them, as well as by the admirals, whose character could not be impeached. The latter, it was argued, had simply had little opportunity to observe West Indian slavery.

[66] *Debate on a Motion for the Abolition of the Slave-Trade* (1792), p. 44; *Parliamentary History,* XXVIII (1789), 54.

[67] [Robert Norris], *A Short Account of the African Slave Trade, Collected from Local Knowledge, from Evidence at the Bar of Both Houses of Parliament; and, from Tracts Written Upon that Subject* (Liverpool, 1787), pp. 168–69.

This line of argument struck a far more vital nerve than did Fox's refutation of Aristotle or Clarkson's discussions of Pomponius and Cicero. It was one thing to dissociate the slave system from the rest of the economy, to make it a symbol of all oppression, and to provide Parliament with the chance to prove, as Pitt would have it, that nations are bound by the laws of morality. But no governmental action could be allowed to undermine the public's faith that there would be no "sudden interruption" in the pursuit of enterprises long sanctioned by Parliament. A considerable amount of capital had been invested in land, slaves, and shipping, on the assumption that the African trade would continue. And one senses that the issue of public trust carried greater weight than did conflicting evidence on the slave trade's value to the national economy.

Public trust had to be balanced, however, against the moral pretensions of government, against the desire to prove that government could be a vehicle for what Clarkson termed, in the rhetoric of the age, "that divine sympathy, which nature has implanted in our breasts, for the most useful and generous of purposes." Even opponents of abolition, such as London's Alderman Nathaniel Newnham, felt it necessary to defend their humanitarianism before the House of Commons. Stephen Fuller acknowledged the political potency of antislavery when he warned that Fox might take the cause from Pitt's hands, in order to regain support from Dissenters and disillusioned Whigs.[68]

Certainly Fox embarrassed both Pitt and Wilberforce by assimilating the public demand to his own theories of political reform and by defining the issue as a clear-cut struggle between expediency and justice. He claimed that Pitt's move to delegate investigation to the Privy

More specifically, it was argued that 100,000 acres of land in Dominica had been sold on the condition that it be cultivated; that one-half of the purchasers had borrowed capital for the purchase price; that if slave importations were stopped, the entire labor force would disappear in less than fifteen years. Abolition of the slave trade would not only represent a breach of contract, but would jeopardize British property estimated at £70,000,000 (*No Abolition; or an Attempt to Prove to the Conviction of Every Rational British Subject, That the Abolition of the British Trade with Africa for Negroes, Would be a Measure as Unjust as Impolitic* . . . [London, 1789], pp. 15–16, 25, 29; *Minutes of the Evidence Taken Before a Committee of the House of Commons,* I, 79–82; *Journals of the Assembly of Jamaica,* VIII, 425, 536; *Parliamentary History,* XXVIII, 89–95).

[68] Clarkson, *Essay on the Slavery and Commerce of the Human Species,* p. 22; *Parliamentary History,* XXVIII, 76; Fuller, Letterpress Books, I, 249, DUL.

Council Committee deprived the people's representatives of their constitutional right to hear petitions and examine evidence. The slave trade could never survive open debate; its abolition could be prevented only by stifling inquiry. Yet we must not, Fox warned, confuse the slave-trade question with more partisan issues, including even political freedom. Though he had always championed political liberty, this "great blessing sinks to nothing when compared with personal freedom." On a question of crime there could be no compromise. When Henry Addington recommended a bounty for transporting more female slaves, Fox thought it tantamount to asking the government to pay for kidnapping and murder. William Belsham, a prominent Unitarian Whig, had written that any "honest man," presented with the bare facts of the slave trade, would have to agree it was a crime. Surely public virtue had progressed beyond the point of requiring a formal train of argument to prove the traffic to be "the height of moral and political depravity." Fox agreed with this view that the issue transcended politics and foreclosed serious debate. Should his fellow M.P.'s reject abolition, he said in 1791, having been informed of the slave trade's true nature, this would be "more scandalous, and more defaming in the eyes of the country and the world, than any vote which any House of Commons had ever given."[69]

Fox's rhetorical strategy placed an uncomfortable burden upon Parliament. He more than implied that a responsible government must follow the lead of disinterested public opinion. And when he and other speakers tried to elevate the slave-trade question above the gamesmanship of politics, they in effect raised the stakes of the game and transformed defeat into a simple triumph of avarice that discredited the political order. In the debates of April, 1791, Pitt himself insisted that the issue transcended politics and even humanitarian feeling; it was a test of nothing less than whether the laws of morality were binding on nations. Lord Carysfort observed that any doubts he might have had were removed by the manner in which abolition had been opposed. Not one solid argument had been given in favor of the trade. When several members snickered at William Smith's tale of a slave-ship atrocity, Smith indignantly replied that he would have thought such

[69] *Parliamentary History,* XXVII (1788), 497–99; XXIX (1791), 344–46; *The Speeches of the Right Honourable Charles James Fox, in the House of Commons* (6 vols., London, 1815), IV, 180–83; [William Belsham], *Remarks on the African Slave Trade* (London, 1790), pp. 5–6.

unfeeling impossible, that he was almost ashamed of sitting in an assembly where such a disgrace could occur. Yet despite the eloquent speeches of 1791, despite the coalition of great names, the House gave a crushing defeat to Wilberforce's motion to introduce an abolition bill. Afterwards, Samuel Romilly brooded that "nothing can be more disgraceful to the nation than such a decision after so long an enquiry too."[70]

Even defeat, however, did not necessarily impair the ideological function of debate. The discouraging delay of 1789 was perhaps less memorable than the tides of eloquence—Burke, who received admiring praise himself, compared Wilberforce to Demosthenes. The expressions of humanitarian sentiment caused James Martin to remark that he was now prouder of being an Englishman than ever before. In spite of Parliament's failures, Wilberforce could express satisfaction in 1792 to see the effects of a great public movement, to see

so great and glorious a concurrence, to see this great cause triumphing over all lesser distinctions, and substituting cordiality and harmony in the place of distrust and opposition: nor have its effects amongst ourselves been in this respect less distinguished or less honourable; it has raised the character of Parliament.

So the moral cause, however unsuccessful in achieving its ostensible objective, had at least raised the character of Parliament. Even more important, it had taught the English people and other nations that

there is a point of elevation where we get above the jarring of the discordant elements that ruffle and agitate the vale below: in our ordinary atmosphere, clouds and vapours obscure the air, and we are the sport of a thousand conflicting winds and adverse currents; but here we move in a higher region, where all is peace and clear and serene, free from perturbation and discomposure.

And here, Wilberforce, pleaded, on "this august eminence, let us build the temple of benevolence."[71]

Even in a speech aimed at conciliation and compromise, it is re-

[70] *Parliamentary History*, XXIX, 330–43; C. G. Oakes, *Sir Samuel Romilly, 1757–1818* (London, 1935), p. 87; William Roberts, *Memoirs of the Life and Correspondence of Hannah More* (4 vols., London, 1834), II, 86. Bishop Porteus blamed the defeat on the abolitionists' uncompromising stand; he thought a bill for gradual abolition would have won (Diary entry, April 12, 1791, Porteus MS 2100, 33–36).

[71] *Debate on a Motion for the Abolition of the Slave-Trade*, pp. 44–45.

markable to find the movement for abolition described as "substituting cordiality and harmony in place of distrust and opposition." But one must understand that for Wilberforce the abolition movement was only one prong of a vast religious crusade to reform an unregenerate social order by first infusing government with the spirit of Christian morality. Thus Wilberforce often lamented that his friend Pitt had not felt the call of "serious" religion, which would have allowed Pitt, as prime minister, to exercise his enormous patronage in church and state, leading to a "descending series of official appointments" of truly pious men, until "religious and moral secretions" permeated the entire body politic as well as the private spheres of life. This was Wilberforce's great dream—a downward diffusion of Evangelical piety channeled through the structures of power. But Wilberforce could at least take comfort from Pitt's sincere commitment against the slave trade. This was the one issue that could unite men of good will, regardless of party or religious persuasion, and thus serve as a touchstone for measuring the moral regeneration of power.[72]

Historians have generally interpreted the Parliamentary struggle for abolition either as a contest between humanitarianism and selfish interests, or as a contest between opposing economic interests, one of which wore a humanitarian mask. The key questions, from either viewpoint, involve Pitt's moral integrity and the political feasibility of an abolition law, especially prior to Britain's declaration of war in 1793. For our purposes, however, the responsibility for defeat or delay is of less significance than the symbolic meaning of the compromise of April 3, 1792.

Before turning to the event itself, it is well to summarize some of Richard Pares's penetrating observations on the nature of British politics in the reign of George III. As Pares writes, "the Government existed, in those days, not in order to legislate but in order to govern: to maintain order, to wage war and, above all, to conduct foreign

---

[72] [Archibald P. Primrose], *Pitt and Wilberforce* (Edinburgh, 1897), pp. 21–25, and *passim*. The question of Pitt's role in the politics of abolition is both controversial and complex. Primrose's book is invaluable, but is unfortunately rare and relatively unknown. An excellent guide to the issues and literature is Patrick Lipscomb, "William Pitt and the Abolition of the Slave Trade," Ph.D. thesis, University of Texas, 1960 (condensed and updated as "William Pitt and the Abolition Question: A Review of an Historical Controversy," *Proceedings of the Leeds Philosophical and Literary Society; Literary and Historical Section,* XII [June, 1967], 87–128).

affairs." It was a government dominated by local oligarchies and local interests, by family alliances and personal connections. The House of Commons founded its claim to supremacy "on its historical function as a check on the Crown." The prestige and authority of the Commons arose from its supposed independence of judgment and from its "virtual" representation of an "undefined community of interests and sympathy in feelings and desires." In the slave-trade debates of 1792, for example, Pitt took exception to Fox's insistence that it was the House's *duty* to respond to public opinion. No doubt the petitions were sincere, Pitt said, and testified to the humanity and benevolence of the English people (he had already begun to suppress public meetings). Yet the prime minister assured the House that he would oppose the slave trade even if all the petitioners supported it; one could never barter justice for popular clamor.

The House of Lords, Pares points out, was considered as

an occasionally useful longstop [in the game of cricket, a kind of backstop], which could be perfectly relied upon to reject any measure which the Ministry could not, or durst not, resist in the Commons. This was particularly true of bills or motions which the members of the House of Commons were obliged to patronize because the electorate and the public, generally, were known to favour them.[73]

By April, 1792, it was clear that another crushing rejection of abolition would seriously discredit the House of Commons in the minds of thousands of the most "respectable" petitioners. The nation had been saturated with antislavery literature; the cause had won the support of local dignitaries and of the clergy, especially in Scotland and the north of England; a movement to boycott slave-produced rum and sugar was well under way. On March 16, King Christian VII of Denmark set England an example of benevolence by allowing his subjects only one more decade to transport slaves from Africa to the Danish colonies (he also encouraged foreigners to help stock the colonies with slaves).[74] Most important, the House of Commons had

[73] Pares, *King George III and the Politicians,* pp. 2–11, 34–43, 51–54; *Parliamentary History,* XXIX (1792), 1261.

[74] *Forording om Neger-Handelen,* March 16, 1792, copy in Kronberg castle. The Ordinance also prohibited the re-export of slaves. When American slave ships began flying the Danish flag, Secretary of State Timothy Pickering reported that President Adams did not feel able to interfere "in Danish affairs," notwithstanding the fact that the United States had prohibited its citizens from supply-

not only accumulated a vast body of evidence, but in effect had defined the issue as a test of its own moral legitimacy.

On the other hand, the passage of an actual abolition law might have shaken public confidence in the security of property, given encouragement to more radical reforms (across the Channel the Girondins, led by the abolitionist Brissot,[75] were preaching a war of liberation), and aroused the slaves in the British islands to follow the lead of their French brothers (an uprising had already occurred in British Dominica). Apart from the House of Lords' "spontaneous dislike of all change," to borrow Pares's happy phrase, the very idea of abolition was anathema to the Chancellor, Lord Thurlow, who had been asked by the king to exercise joint leadership with Pitt, his bitter enemy. It was equally repugnant to the young Duke of Clarence and to the king himself, who was apparently determined to keep Pitt from making abolition a Cabinet measure. Four years later, in 1796, the king wrote to Henry Dundas, Pitt's shrewd confidant and party manager, venturing the opinion that the prime minister's arguments against the slave trade were not of his own "sterling growth" but had been hatched by others.[76] Some of Pitt's powerful supporters seem to have regarded his abolitionism as an unfortunate foible, and considered it no disloyalty to rescue him from the awkward bind produced by his friendship with Wilberforce.

The compromise of April 3, 1792, can be quickly summarized. On April 2, Wilberforce asked the House to resolve that the slave trade

ing slaves to foreign markets (Pickering to the American Convention, June 1, 1798, Pennsylvania Abolition Society MSS, V, 9, HSP).

[75] Wilberforce succeeded in persuading James Phillips and the Abolition Committee to suppress the publication of a speech by Brissot (Wilberforce to William Phillips, Sept. 30, 1799, autograph letters, PHS).

[76] Mellor, *British Imperial Trusteeship*, pp. 70–71; Lipscomb, "William Pitt and the Abolition Question," pp. 93, 108–9, 115; Porter, *Abolition of the Slave Trade in England*, p. 104. In 1795, Stephen Fuller assured Jamaica that the king was a sincere friend of the colonies, and that they owed him more than was generally known "in regard to the defeat of the absurd attempt of abolishing the Slave Trade, which I think we shall hear no more of" (Letterpress Books, II, 501, DUL). For Pitt's relations with the king, see Donald Grove Barnes, *George III and William Pitt, 1783–1806* (Stanford, 1939), which argues that George III was able to exploit Pitt's great popularity while also preventing undesirable reforms. After the king's mental breakdown and the Regency crisis of 1788–1789, it became especially important for the prime minister to avoid any critical conflict which might require his own resignation or lead to a recurrence of the king's illness.

"ought to be abolished." According to Roger Anstey's calculations, the Commons contained in the 1790s approximately the same number of hard-core abolitionists as "West Indians" and others normally allied with the West Indian interests. The decisive swing vote hinged largely on definitions of national self-interest, particularly with respect to national power and the welfare of the larger British empire. No figure was more influential in crystallizing opinion on such issues than Henry Dundas, who presided over colonial affairs as Pitt's Home Secretary, who sat as president of the East India Company Board of Control, and who, in Dale H. Porter's words, "controlled much of the patronage in both ends of the Empire and influenced the votes of thirty-four Scots M.P.'s and eleven Scots peers."[77] Dundas replied to Wilberforce's proposal by arguing that the condition of West Indian slaves must be improved before imports from Africa could be stopped; he therefore moved to amend Wilberforce's motion by adding the word "gradually." On the morning of April 3, the House accepted Dundas's amendment by a majority of 193 to 125, and then passed the resolution favoring gradual abolition of the slave trade by a vote of 230 to 85.

Stephen Fuller, the Jamaican agent, was convinced that the West Indians would have had no difficulty maintaining a majority in the Commons if Henry Dundas had not moved the surprise amendment.[78] Dundas's motives aroused the suspicions of his contemporaries and of

[77] Porter, *Abolition of the Slave Trade in England,* pp. 80–82; G. P. Judd, *Members of Parliament, 1734–1832* (New Haven, 1955), pp. 89, 94. Roger Anstey has convincing evidence for increasing the "West-Indian interest," as of 1796, from twenty-four members, as listed by Judd, to thirty-four. Yet only twenty-six, or possibly thirty-six (if one allows for unknown West Indian connections) of these "West Indians" were among the seventy-four House members who voted against abolition in 1796 (Anstey, private communication to me). In fairness to Professor Anstey, I should like to dissociate him from my ideological interpretation of anti-slave-trade politics about which he has certain politely expressed reservations.

[78] Fuller to the Jamaican Committee of Correspondence, May 2, 1792, Fuller papers, DUL. Fuller seemed to be critical only of Dundas's tactics, since he emphasized that when the Commons had finally settled on the year 1796 as the terminal date for the slave trade, Dundas had resigned the bill to the abolitionists "to do what they please with it." In fact, Dundas consistently opposed later abolition bills. Wilberforce, in a MS autobiographical sketch, noted the close ties between the West Indies and Scotland, where Dundas exercised enormous patronage (CEW). Much to Wilberforce's distress, Dundas was Pitt's closest political ally.

later historians, but will probably never fully be known. Fuller had long been warning him that continuing debates on the slave trade would inevitably turn Jamaica into another St. Domingue. It was imperative, Fuller had earlier pleaded, for governmental leaders to put "an immediate and decisive stop" to the agitation by "taking the sense of Parliament upon it, by such means as they shall think proper, upon the first open day after the meeting [of the 1792 session]." On February 1, Fuller complained to Bryan Edwards that only Pitt could stop Wilberforce from introducing a new motion, but that Pitt would not do so because of his own "consistency." In fact, Pitt tried to persuade Wilberforce to postpone his motion, but without success. More significant, however, was Fuller's report to Jamaica that Dundas wanted to bring a "speedy end" to Parliamentary discussion of the slave trade, but was at a loss to know how to do so.[79]

Although Dundas's motion pleased neither the West Indians nor the abolitionists, it precisely answered the needs of Parliament, which could now become a "temple of benevolence" without sanctioning a "sudden interruption" in the pursuit of business. Dundas's plea for moderation allowed Fox to declaim to the crowded galleries, asking whether murder and theft were more justified when done with moderation. Pitt, in what was generally regarded as the most eloquent speech of his career, talked of the forgiveness of Heaven, of "the guilt and shame with which we are now covered," and of the sublime prospect of civilizing Africa as a means of national redemption. If Parliament had decided that the slave trade was unjust, he asked, "why ought it not to be abolished by the vote of this night?" But Pitt also applauded the fact that the dispute had been narrowed to "mere" differences over when the trade should end. By agreeing on the goal of ultimate abolition, the House had redeemed its moral character. The majority of members who voted for Dundas's amendment evinced a sensible fear of "hasty or precipitous" action, but there could be no question that their hearts were in the right place.[80]

[79] Fuller to Dundas, Nov. 16, 1791; April 5, 1792; to the Jamaican Committee of Correspondence, July 5, 1791; Dec. 8, 1791; to Bryan Edwards, Feb. 1, 1792 (Fuller papers, and Letterpress Books, II, 105, 140, 146, 152–53, 203, DUL).

[80] *Debate on a Motion for the Abolition of the Slave-Trade*, pp. 104–16, 124–35, 142–43, 164–67; *Speeches of the Right Honourable Charles James Fox*, IV, 378, 393–402; Philip Henry Stanhope, 5th Earl Stanhope, *Life of the Right Honourable William Pitt* (4 vols., London, 1861–1862), II, 143.

The *Morning Chronicle* hailed the vote as proof that the English constitution provided sufficient vitality for the reform of every abuse "without convulsion." Even abolitionist writers echoed this theme: the vote demonstrated the excellence of the constitution, showed the beneficent effects of the people's right to petition, and pointed to the legal and successful method of accomplishing every political improvement.[81]

Yet the House of Commons still faced the embarrassing question of what was being amended, since no bill had been proposed, and since Dundas had talked vaguely of ameliorative "regulations," the most important of which would depend on the West Indian legislatures, as a means of slowly eliminating the need for further importations of slaves. Dundas had no intention of introducing a bill for gradual abolition, and Wilberforce refused to do so on grounds of moral principle. It was Fox who finally forced Dundas to offer a bill, and Pitt who finally secured the bill's passage. But when the House agreed to 1796 as a terminal date for the slave trade, Dundas completely dissociated himself from the measure. From then on he not only actively opposed any renewal of abolitionist action, but in 1795 persuaded the House to postpone the desired terminal date until the end of the war with France.[82]

---

[81] Lipscomb, "William Pitt and the Abolition of the Slave Trade," p. 322; Thomas Somerville, *A Discourse on Our Obligation to Thanksgiving for the Prospect of the Abolition of the African Slave-Trade* (Kelso, 1792), pp. 21–22; Wilberforce to Wyvill, April 9, 1792, CEW.

[82] Wilberforce, *Life of Wilberforce,* I, 345–46, 348–49. Dundas told Bishop Porteus that the West Indian planters and merchants, with whom he was in close touch, would have acquiesced in a terminal date of 1800. Porteus believed that the compromise date of 1796 ensured the loss of the measure (Porteus MS 2100, 57–58). It is not clear why the difference of four years should have been so important. Possibly some planters thought that within eight years the islands could be sufficiently stocked with slaves; it is more likely that within an interval of eight years the colonial legislatures could be expected to adopt ameliorative laws that would undermine the abolitionists' most effective arguments and thus serve as an excuse for further delay. Dale H. Porter defends Dundas as a realistic stateman who, "in a way no abolitionist had dared to do . . . openly explored the long-range prospects of West Indian society" (*Abolition of the Slave Trade in England,* pp. 80–83). Yet the long history of British antislavery surely demonstrates the futility of relying on colonial legislatures to prepare the way for emancipation. Dundas's professed desire to bring a gradual end to both the slave trade and slavery is made suspect by his vehement opposition to all abolition measures proposed after 1792, including Francis's plan for gradual emancipation. On March 22, 1796, the Standing Committee of the society of West India

The Abolition Society voiced bitter disappointment over the supposed delay of four years, which ran counter to the will of the people as expressed in hundreds of petitions. They drew comfort, however, from the symbolic *precedent*. The House of Commons had officially declared itself in favor of abolition. In May, 1792, Sir Samuel Romilly was confident that the House would vote for immediate abolition at its next session. And though the House of Lords would probably reject the first bill,

> they will hardly venture to do so a second time, and they will certainly have a second Bill sent to them. However sincere the Lords are in their zeal for slavery, they will hardly carry their sincerity so far as to endanger their own authority; and the cause of the negro slaves is at present taken up with as much warmth in almost every part of the kingdom as could be found in any matter in which the people were personally and immediately interested.[83]

But the question of authority was precisely the point. Wilberforce understood the necessity of maintaining a delicate balance between public pressure and the authority of government. He acknowledged that all the "great men" in government hated public meetings, though in "this instance" abolitionists had sought the support of people "of a better sort than the generality of such cattle." He accepted the verdict of Lord Grenville, who told him any attempt to influence the House of Lords would be "an excess of zeal" that would seriously injure the cause. In 1793 the Commons refused to pressure the Upper House by renewing the previous year's resolution. The West Indian merchants and planters never doubted that the Lords' examination of evidence would ensure prolonged delay and an ultimate killing of the bill. Wilberforce later admitted that the gradual abolition measure had had no chance of passing the House of Lords. And as he looked back upon the vote of 1792, he became convinced that it had not had the slightest effect on the final outcome of abolition.[84]

Planters and Merchants officially voted to thank Dundas for his effective opposition to abolition (MS Minutes, IV). Wilberforce rightly stressed that "our most dangerous enemies" were those "who professed to concur with us in design, but to adopt a more moderate, and as they contended more effectual, method of accomplishing our common purpose" (Wilberforce, *Life of Wilberforce*, I, 351).

[83] Abolition Committee Minutes, III, 54, 64; Samuel Romilly to Mme. G., May 15, 1792, *Memoirs of Sir Samuel Romilly*, II, 2.

[84] Wilberforce, *Life of Wilberforce*, I, 333, 336–37, 351–52. It is clear that the bill never had a chance in the House of Lords. On March 10, 1794, the Bishop

Yet the commitment to gradual abolition provided the government, including the prime minister, with a fund of moral capital that would not deplete for some years. Pitt kept assuring Wilberforce that the slave trade had received its sentence of death; the execution would be carried out as soon as the time was ripe. The conflict with France required national unity and the leadership of a strong political coalition, but the coalition unfortunately included many enemies of abolition. It was only sensible, therefore, to be content with the symbolic resolution of 1792, which could be commemorated by the ritual of Wilberforce's annual motions. According to the logic of gradualism, there was really no necessity for further action. Since Pitt and Dundas had committed the government to the principle of abolition, the West Indians would be moved by self-interest to adopt reforms that would eventually render the slave trade obsolete. This was the assumption underlying the Ellis resolutions of 1797 and the resulting recommendations sent to West Indian governors.[85] The government's policy could thus be described, in modern jargon, as the "winding down" of a national mistake.

The compromise of 1792 did entail certain risks. The House of Lords' inaction evoked public criticism which threatened to merge with the more radical spirit of discontent brought on by war and domestic oppression. In 1795 the London Abolition Committee dared to say that the members of the legislature, by rejecting the petitions of the people, "have taken the whole weight of the trade on themselves." In the same year even Wilberforce privately concluded that the "infamous vote" of the Commons was an argument for Parliamentary reform.[86]

---

of Rochester moved that the examination of evidence be taken in committee, in order to prevent interminable delay. There were fourteen votes, half of them from bishops, for the measure; forty-two opposed (Porteus MS 2103, 78–79).

[85] Porter points out that the tactics of delay were ultimately self-defeating for the West Indians, since in 1804 Parliament was shown the correspondence with West Indian governors relating to the Ellis proposals. Parliament thus learned of the West Indians' evasions at a time when there was growing anger over the planters' illicit trade with the United States, a trade which meant "defaulting on consignments to England which guaranteed the security of merchants' advances and other West Indian investments" (*Abolition of the Slave Trade in England,* pp. 123–24).

[86] Abolition Committee Minutes, III, 95; Wilberforce to Wyvill, Feb. 28, 1795, CEW; J. Yule to William Smith, Aug. 13, 1792, Smith papers, DUL; William Fox, *A Defence of the National Convention of France, for Emancipating the*

For a brief time it appeared that the boycott movement might undercut the government's control over abolitionism. Since 1787 a number of abolitionists had proposed a popular boycott of West Indian sugar and rum, in the event that political action should fail. Though few middle-class Englishmen were prepared to forego sugar in their tea, East Indian sugar presented a possible substitute. And the prospect of public coercion through self-denial had particular appeal to the Nonconformist conscience. Instead of directly challenging Parliament by creating an "anti-Parliament" of public conventions or associations, individual Dissenters could abstain from sin-tainted produce and thus by transcending law and government bring the downfall of the slave system. It was the lowly consumer, wrote William Fox, who bore the guilt of the slave trade and who possessed the power to destroy it. For the consumer of slave-grown sugar was not only a participant in crime but an accessory to murder. "They may hold it to our lips," Fox wrote, "steeped in the blood of our fellow creatures, but they cannot compel us to accept the loathsome potion." Samuel Bradburn, a Methodist preacher, appealed in 1792 to the sense of disillusionment and powerlessness of the Dissenting public. The "same usurping power" that made men slaves, he warned, may "endeavour to enslave you and your posterity." Bradburn claimed that 400,000 consumers had joined in the popular protest (Clarkson and William Dillwyn estimated the number at 300,000); one-half of the abstainers were women, Bradburn noted, "who *(from might overcoming right)* have no voice at present in these matters."[87]

Slaves in the West Indies (London, 1794), *passim;* "Junius," "An Expostulatory Address to the *People* of *England* on the Late Memorable Decision Against the Abolition of the Slave Trade," *Gentleman's Magazine,* LXI (June, 1791), 537–38. The latter essay presented revolutionary arguments that would later appear in the letters of some of William Smith's abolitionist correspondents; namely: that the great men of England were corrupt; that effective reform could come only from the decent middle class, which was not represented in Parliament; and that England should look to France for a model of enlightenment.

[87] Thomas Cooper, *Letters on the Slave Trade: First Published in "Wheeler's Manchester Chronicle"* (Manchester, 1787), *passim;* [Anon.], *Remarkable Extracts and Observations on the Slave Trade, with Some Considerations on the Consumption of West India Produce* (London, 1791), pp. 8–10; [William Allen], *The Duty of Abstaining from the Use of West India Produce* (London, 1792), *passim;* [William Fox], *An Address to the People of Great Britain on the Consumption of West India Produce* [London, 1971], pp. 2–12 (another edition is entitled *An Address to the People of Great Britain, on the Propriety of Abstaining from West India Sugar and Rum* [reprinted London, 1830]); Samuel Brad-

The free-produce pamphlets, which reached an audience of at least 100,000 were filled with subversive implications. For abolitionist leaders they posed a critical problem of defining the boundaries of approved agitation. On June 20, 1793, a meeting of the Abolition Committee, including Wilberforce, Sharp, and Clarkson, resolved to recommend that the public abstain from West Indian sugar and rum, and appointed a subcommittee to draw up a plan of action. On August 13 the Committee decided to suspend the recommendation and to suppress the plan. Wilberforce had earlier expressed fears that the boycott scheme was associated with the "turbulent elements" of the abolition movement, and that the idea was certain to alienate moderates. He therefore favored holding the weapon in reserve, until it might be used with effect by "general concurrence." The weakness of the boycott movement, which like most popular enthusiasms was short-lived, lay in its dependence on individual action. Abstention was presented as a moral alternative to political organization, at a time when all organization raised the specter of Jacobinism, and when any interference with British commerce could be interpreted as treasonous aid to the enemy. The Abolition Committee, by continuing to defer to Parliamentary leadership, reinforced the image of British abolitionism as a force maintaining the existing political and constitutional structure.[88]

---

burn, *An Address, to the People Called Methodists; Concerning the Evil of Encouraging the Slave Trade* (Manchester, 1792), pp. 11–15; William Dillwyn to Susannah Dillwyn, Jan. 2, 1792; Feb. 2, 1792; April 4, 1792, Emlen-Dillwyn papers, LCP; Clarkson, *History of the Abolition of the African Slave-Trade,* II, 349–53; Romilly to Mme G., May 15, 1792, *Memoirs of Sir Samuel Romilly,* II, 3; Gwynne E. Owen, "Welsh Anti-Slavery Sentiments, 1790–1865: A Survey of Public Opinion," M.A. thesis, University College of Wales, Aberystwyth, pp. 7–9; E. M. Hunt, "The North of England Agitation for the Abolition of the Slave Trade, 1780–1800," M.A. thesis, University of Manchester, 1959, pp. 107–9. William Fox, in *A Second Address to the People of Great Britain: Containing a New and Most Powerful Argument to Abstain from the Use of West India Sugar* (London, 1792), contended that rum was permeated with the sweat and blood of slaves, that sugar was packed by "near-naked, sweaty slaves," and thus contained lice from their hair and "secretions" from yaws; the body of a roasted Negro, he claimed, had been found in a rum cask, apparently added for flavor (pp. 5–10). Presumably East Indian sugar, which the abolitionists recommended, was purer.

[88] Abolition Committee Minutes, III, 81, 84–87; Wilberforce, *Life of Wilberforce,* I, 338–39. Though William Dillwyn worked actively in the movement for East Indian sugar, he reported to Susannah that the Abolition Committee had taken no part (Jan. 2, 1792, and Feb. 2, 1792, Emlen-Dillwyn papers, LCP). On

It is true that opponents of abolition did their best to link the cause with Jacobin France, and this view won favor in the House of Lords and among the courtiers who surrounded the royal family. But no one could deny that a profoundly non-Jacobin Commons had voted to outlaw the African trade. Nor could one impeach Wilberforce's reputation as a stalwart loyalist who, if he opposed the war, nevertheless supported the harshest suppression of domestic disorder. In replying to the charge of Jacobinism in 1799, the Bishop of Rochester observed that abolitionists had never talked of the equality or the imprescriptible rights of man; they had strenuously upheld the existing gradations of society, objecting only to a power which no good king would claim.[89]

The British abolitionists, unlike the later American Garrisonians, were never pushed toward a position of independence and defiance which would have allowed them to assimilate radical thought and to appeal for a broad coalition of all enemies of slavery. From the outset, antislavery organization was dominated by the strategic goal of Parliamentary legislation. As result, the movement acquired a sense of deference, of patience, and of self-discipline. But the dependence on Parliament also required an often painful acceptance of the government's terms and definitions. Thus it became essential to believe that when the time was opportune Pitt would redeem the pledge of 1792. It was essential to draw hope from the debates of 1796, and to assume the cause was gaining when it nearly won sanction for a second time in the Lower House.

The exigencies of war placed Wilberforce in an increasingly awkward position. His ability to symbolize disinterested benevolence was an asset both to Pitt and to the abolition movement. His friendship

---

March 12, 1795, Dillwyn reported to James Pemberton that the Committee was so discouraged by their recent defeat in Parliament that they had decided to discontinue regular meetings, leaving it up to individuals to work for the cause as they saw fit. He seemed to have little hope in the effectiveness of consumer action, since he foresaw a slave revolt as a likely way for the slave trade to bring on its own end (Pennsylvania Abolition Society MSS, IV, 16). Yet in August, 1795, *Gentleman's Magazine* printed a cautious report from the Committee which urged the public to consume East Indian rather than West Indian produce (LXV [August, 1795], 635–36; also report of June 25, 1795, Abolition Committee Minutes, III, 95).

[89] *The Senator: or, Clarendon's Parliamentary Chronicle* . . . , X (1794), 1131; Clarkson, *History of the Abolition of the African Slave-Trade*, II, 481; Wilberforce, *Life of Wilberforce*, II, 114–15, 125–31, 134–35.

with the prime minister gave him supposed political leverage that enhanced his leadership among abolitionist followers. Yet Wilberforce's divided roles as politician and reformer were also a source of embarrassment for everyone concerned. Convinced that the political Opposition (such as it was) posed threats to church and state, he could not become an outspoken critic. But as an independent supporter of the administration, he felt it his duty to protest lapses from antislavery principle. He remained convinced, with some reason, that Pitt sincerely desired abolition. The prime minister had simply been distracted by the emergencies of war and then seduced by Dundas, now the Secretary of War, into a number of unfortunate policies, such as the attack on St. Domingue, with the hope of suppressing the black revolt; the conquest of the rich lands of Dutch Guiana and Trinidad; and the use of slaves from the older British colonies to clear and settle plantations in St. Vincent and Trinidad.[90]

To his abolitionist friends Wilberforce kept apologizing for Pitt. James Stephen, who was especially outraged over the plan for settling Trinidad, angrily wrote that Wilberforce had become "the Moses of the Israelites, though at the same time the courtier of Pharaoh." A man whose political friends were the "high priests of Moloch" could not escape responsibility. There could be no doubt that the government's war policies had given renewed sanction to Negro slavery, or that the destruction of St. Domingue had opened the way for a world

---

[90] Wilberforce, *Life of Wilberforce,* II, 266; Wilberforce to William Smith, Feb. 20, 1798, Smith papers, DUL; Wilberforce, MS autobiographical sketch, CEW; [Primrose], *Pitt and Wilberforce, passim;* Wilberforce to John Scandrette Harford, Oct. 22, 1814, Wilberforce papers, DUL. In the latter letter, Wilberforce wrote: "But *I solemnly declare* to *you* my firm conviction that Mr. Pitt was a sincere friend to the Abolition." He admitted, however, that if he were to express any criticism, it would not only be used to support the unjust censures of the *Edinburgh Review,* but would be interpreted as spite for never having received any personal rewards from his thirty-years' friendship with Pitt. He then confessed that some criticism of Pitt was both plausible and just: "In the phrase justly I allude to Mr. Pitt's suffering the Demerara & Berbice & the Slave Trade to go on year after year, tho' he promised me an Order in Council which at last was signed, but which Dilatoriness & Procrastination, his *great vices,* overcame him to delay again & again." Britain temporarily restored Guiana to Holland in 1802, but retained Trinidad, which had been captured from Spain in 1797 and which contained enormous expanses of uncleared land suitable for the cultivation of sugar. The British had earlier claims on St. Vincent, where a pro-French revolt of blacks and "Caribs" gave Pitt the excuse to deport dissident laborers and to encourage rapid settlement by British planters and British slaves.

sugar boom and for an increased demand for slaves, which was being met, even in the Spanish colonies, by British ships. These events brought Wilberforce the keenest anguish. But always there was the memory of Pitt's great speech of 1792, and the hope that Providence would ultimately permit the prime minister to act on his true principles.[91]

Providence did intervene in behalf of the abolitionists, but not early enough to redeem Pitt's reputation as a reformer. The complex details of the abolitionist triumph have been freshly analyzed in a number of recent studies.[92] It is sufficient to summarize a few salient points that help put the victory in wider perspective.

One must first give a nod to the "economic factors" which at least made abolition conceivable to practical statesmen. By 1799 the supply of sugar temporarily began to outrun European demand, and within a few years the price had sunk to an unprecedented low. Planters in the older British colonies might hope for better times, but they could not be blind to the effects of competitive cultivation in the captured colonies of Guiana and Trinidad, where land was plentiful and far more fertile. Moreover, speculative investment in land and slaves might simply aid the development of colonies that would ultimately be restored, on the precedent of the Treaty of Amiens, to rival nations. And clearly the easiest way to limit superfluous production was to cut off the flow of labor.[93]

By 1804 there had also been a decisive change in the goals and

[91] Wilberforce, *Life of Wilberforce,* II, 256–58, 262–65, 331–32, 369, Brougham to James Stephen, Sept. 7, 1804, CEW.

[92] See especially Anstey, "A Re-Interpretation of the Abolition of the British Slave Trade"; Lipscomb, "William Pitt and the Abolition Question"; Porter, *Abolition of the Slave Trade in England;* Alan Rees, "Pitt and the Achievement of Abolition," *Journal of Negro History,* XXXIX (July, 1954), 167–84.

[93] See especially Lowell Joseph Ragatz, *The Fall of the Planter Class in the British Caribbean, 1763–1833* (New York, 1928), pp. 209–14, and *passim.* Sugar production increased with the introduction of Bourbon and Tahitian canes; even before the sharp drop in price in 1799, the price on the English market had been influenced by increasing supplies of East Indian sugar, notwithstanding its higher import duty. The continuing Jamaican interest in the slave trade arose partly from hopes for rich profits in coffee. The small settlers or "pioneers" who were cultivating coffee wanted to be able to buy slaves at cheap prices (*Journals of the Assembly of Jamaica,* XI [Jamaica, 1805], 216; Edward Brathwaite, *The Development of Creole Society in Jamaica, 1770–1820* [Oxford, 1971], pp. 147–48).

strategy of imperial conflict. Neither Britain nor France was prepared to squander further resources in a struggle to capture colonies that had proved to be financial and military burdens. The new republic of Haiti symbolized the defeat of Napoleon's mercantilist dream of a French New World. The British, having achieved mastery in the Caribbean, could find neither adequate markets for their produce nor means of preventing their West Indian subjects from trading illicitly with the United States, which as a neutral reaped the rewards of carrying colonial staples to Napoleon's Europe. Even before Britain had won full naval supremacy (and it is worth remarking that the Battle of Trafalgar was not fought in the Caribbean, though both fleets had just dashed there and back), it was clear that the economic struggle would center not on the control of colonial production but on the control of colonial commerce to European markets. By 1804 Britain had no need to fear a rival slave trade augmenting the productive capacity of her competitors. The crucial problem was not the supply of labor but how to control the flow of colonial produce to Europe.[94]

But changing conditions did not automatically shatter the traditional balance of British politics. Pitt's resignation as prime minister, after nearly eighteen years in office, might conceivably have freed abolitionists from the impasse occasioned by Wilberforce's personal loyalty to Pitt and by Pitt's constitutional scruples over making abolition a government measure. Yet Pitt, in deference to the king and in the interest of national stability, promised to support his successor, Henry Addington, who assumed office in March, 1801, and in whose Cabinet the slave-trading interest gained a stronger voice. By November, 1801, the chief Opposition leader, Charles James Fox, predicted that there would be no hope during the reign of George III of reforming Parliament, of repealing the Test Acts, or of abolishing the slave

[94] The chief exception was the United States, whose citizens continued to defy the law against slave trading to foreign countries. On June 4, 1806, Macaulay wrote the Pennsylvania Abolition Society that the illegal American slave trade posed a serious obstacle to British abolition, since it was argued that American ships, which were governed by no health and tonnage regulations, would simply take up whatever trade England forfeited. Macaulay urged the Pennsylvania Society to press Congress for rigorous enforcement. The English navy, he pointed out, was now in a position to enforce the American law of 1794—an offer which anticipated future negotiations for the right of seizure (Pennsylvania Abolition Society MSS, VI [June 4, 1806], HSP).

trade, and therefore concluded that his Whig followers should feel free to cooperate with Addington on terms of personal expediency. Wilberforce's independence from partisan factions gave him even greater freedom of maneuver and helped him during a succession of administrations to preserve his undisputed title as abolitionist leader. Yet his own hopes sagged when Addington failed, in the peace negotiations at Amiens, to press for international agreement in ending the slave trade. The time had seemed so opportune.[95]

In 1800 and again in 1804, Wilberforce rejoiced over the news that absentee planters from the older colonies favored suspending the slave trade as a means of curtailing sugar production. Though Wilberforce could not publicly compromise his principles, he was more than willing to settle for suspension and forego personal glory. But to his disappoint‑ ment, he discovered that too many of the West Indians feared that a suspended trade could never be revived. And the fate of conventional motions for abolition was even more disheartening. In 1804, the Com‑ mons approved Wilberforce's abolition measure by a three-to-one majority; the following year, as in 1793, the House reversed itself, much to Wilberforce's astonishment. To Pitt, who was once again prime minister and who had urged that the question be postponed, Wilberforce confided that the abolitionists could not sustain another such defeat.[96]

Success would require experiments in political innovation as well as a redefinition of the role of national interest in colonial policy. When Addington assumed office, a group of investors who had the ear of the new administration began pressing for the sale of rich crown properties in Trinidad and St. Vincent, ostensibly for the purpose of increasing government revenue and of encouraging the clearing and cultivation of new lands. Such a move would have given an enormous impetus to the Atlantic slave trade, which was already converging on the new British markets. Patrick C. Lipscomb has recently shown how George Canning seized upon the Trinidad question "as a means of

---

[95] Patrick C. Lipscomb, "Party Politics, 1801–1802: George Canning and the Trinidad Question," *The Historical Journal,* XII (1969), 443, 448–50; Wilber‑ force, *Life of Wilberforce,* III, 31–33. Wilberforce had urged the Abbé Grégoire to help coordinate the pressures on the French and British governments, though by 1802 Grégoire was totally without influence (*Mémoires de Grégoire, ancien évêque de Blois* . . . , ed. by Hippolyte Carnot [2 vols., Paris, 1840], I, 398).

[96] Wilberforce, *Life of Wilberforce,* II, 257–63, 331, 367–68; III, 164–69, 176–82, 212–13; Wilberforce, *Correspondence,* II, 14.

driving William Pitt into opposition to Addington's government and of creating a new opposition party with Pitt as its leader." A shrewd and aspiring young politician, Canning had been exasperated by Pitt's support of a weak administration and searched for any opportunity that might bring both Pitt and himself back into office. And though Canning was a genuine abolitionist who had urged Pitt in 1799 to make abolition a government measure, he was also a close friend and ally of Charles Rose Ellis, an absentee planter who represented the interests of the older West Indian colonies. Canning was thus well-prepared to engineer a political realignment that would drive a wedge between the traditional planter interests and the speculators who were clamoring for a rapid and uncontrolled development of the newer West Indian territories.[97]

Canning saw his chance when Addington casually informed the Commons, in November, 1801, that the government intended to sell the crown properties. After much intrigue and political maneuvering, Canning presented his challenge on May 27, 1802. He warned the Commons of the extreme danger of allowing Trinidad to be settled with slaves, a policy that could only give sanction to later demands for unlimited importations from Africa. In an appeal for broad-based support, he reminded the House not only of its commitment of 1792 but of the Ellis resolutions of 1797, which had looked to a positive policy of encouraging the natural increase of West Indian or "creole" slaves as a means of eliminating the need for African labor. Canning then made a seemingly moderate proposal. He asked that the crown issue regulations that would suspend the slave trade to Trinidad until Parliament had had time to consider the matter. But he also envisioned a far-reaching program of agricultural reform in which Trinidad would become an experimental model for the use of machinery and free labor. Canning failed in his scheme to isolate Addington and to force Pitt into political opposition. Addington simply backed down, and promised that the government would make no land grants that might serve as an excuse for continuing the slave trade or for discouraging the growth in Trinidad of a white or creole population. Yet Canning had succeeded in heading off the possibility of a vastly expanded slave trade stimulated by the unregulated development of Trinidad. He had also discovered a formula for linking abolitionism

[97] Lipscomb, "Party Politics," pp. 442–66.

with the national interest and for weakening the slave trade by closing off its newer and more vulnerable markets.[98]

When the war resumed in 1803, Britain swiftly reconquered the Guianan colonies of Demerara, Berbice, Essequibo, and Surinam, which had been returned to Holland during the brief interim of peace. James Stephen and Wilberforce's other friends demanded an open debate in Parliament on stopping the importation of slaves into Guiana. Wilberforce demurred, since Pitt, who had become prime minister in May, 1804, had assured him this trade would be ended by royal proclamation. Henry Brougham, writing secretly from Holland in 1804, told Stephen that the death warrant of the slave trade depended on a mere dash of Pitt's pen. Yet it was only when Wilberforce threatened to join Opposition leaders in presenting the issue to Parliament that Pitt finally issued an Order-in-Council, on August 15, 1805, cutting off the supply of slaves to captured territories.[99]

This critical measure, which received an enabling order only four months before Pitt died, opened the way for Parliamentary action prohibiting British ships from supplying slaves to any conquered or foreign markets. The Foreign Slave Trade Bill of 1806 eliminated more than half of the total British trade.[100] As Roger Anstey has argued, if policy makers had been swayed by only a narrow conception of national self-interest, they should have been content with this first "abolition." In fact, most of the members of the "Ministry of All the Talents," which succeeded Pitt, were personally favorable to total

[98] *Ibid.; Parliamentary History,* XXXVI, 854 ff. Lipscomb explains why Canning confined his attention to Trinidad. Addington's pledge did not, of course, end the slave trade to Trinidad.

[99] [Stephen], *Crisis of the Sugar Colonies,* pp. 161–92; Wilberforce, *Life of Wilberforce,* III, 38–39, 164, 184, 234; Wilberforce, *Correspondence,* I; 328–31; II, 14; Brougham to Stephen, Sept. 7, 1804, CEW. Brougham was confident that the Dutch would outlaw the African trade in return for the restoration of Guiana. He had doubts, however, about Pitt's "disposition," and asked Stephen to be on watch lest Wilberforce's "unsuspicious nature" prove insufficiently alert. He added that he would begin to suspect Pitt's sincerity if the prime minister let this opportunity pass by. Wilberforce conveyed a rather muted version of Brougham's message to Lord Harrowby, Pitt's Foreign Secretary (Wilberforce, *Correspondence,* I, 328–29).

[100] Macaulay, writing to the Pennsylvania Abolition Society, predicted that the law would abolish between one-half and two-thirds of the total British trade. He hoped that it would allow British and American abolitionists to cooperate in ending the "guilty partnership" between slave-traders of the two countries (Letter of July 4, 1806, Pennsylvania Abolition Society MSS, VI, HSP).

abolition. Lord Grenville, the prime minister, privately expressed the
wish that the Foreign Slave Trade Bill "may be only a prelude to a
much more complete and satisfactory measure"—a measure, one may
add, which he himself was soon to secure.[101]

Yet it must be stressed that abolition was never a foregone conclusion, notwithstanding Ministerial support and the admitted economic weakness of West Indian planters, who were complaining by
early 1807 that the average price of sugar on the British market seldom
equalled the bare costs of production.[102] No administration could easily
break free from the precedents of gradualism, which required that
commitment be balanced with indefinite delay. In order to raise no
suspicions, the Whig leaders presented the Foreign Slave Trade Bill
as merely a supplement to Pitt's Order-in-Council—as a measure
founded on sheer expediency, wholly dissociated from abolitionist
principles or influence. In actuality, there was a virtual conspiracy,
beginning in the spring of 1806, between the abolitionists and such
government leaders as Grenville, Fox, and Lord Henry Petty.[103] At
every point they coordinated strategy, though the abolitionists pretended to be innocent onlookers. It was the knowledgeable Stephen
who helped plug loopholes in the Foreign Slave Trade Bill and who

[101] Anstey, "A Re-Interpretation of the Abolition of the British Slave Trade,"
pp. 319–20, n. 2; William Wyndham Grenville to Wilberforce, May 9, 1806,
Dropmore MSS (again, I am much indebted to Professor Anstey for supplying
me with transcripts, in this case of the Wilberforce-Grenville correspondence in
the Dropmore papers, which he was able to consult on microfilm thanks to the
courtesy of the late Professor W. B. Hamilton).

[102] *Parliamentary Debates* IX (1807), 85–101. Though some ten members of
the Talents Ministry supported abolition, it could not become an official government measure because of the opposition of Sidmouth and Windham.

[103] Wilberforce to Grenville, March 24, 1806; April 23, 1806; May 8, 1806;
June 5, 1806; Nov. 29, 1806; Jan. 31, 1807; Grenville to Wilberforce, April 25,
1806; May 5, 1806; Feb. 2, 1807, Dropmore MSS. Wilberforce initiated the intimate relationship when he wrote Grenville on June 27, 1804, confessing that as
long as he had been in Parliament, he had not realized until then that the success
of a bill from the House of Commons depended in the Lords on some peer
taking personal charge of it (Wilberforce, *Life of Wilberforce*, III, 179–80).
This admission has often been cited as proof of Wilberforce's incredible naïveté.
I suspect, however, that he was simply trying to flatter Grenville, to whom he
wished to entrust the cause in the House of Lords, and to whom he had been
rather hostile until learning that Grenville had become more religious. It was
William Smith, a Unitarian M.P., who was close to Fox and Grey, who
smoothed the way for Wilberforce's alliance with the Grenville Ministry.

played at least a part in drafting the final abolition law. When Grenville developed a plan for introducing the abolition bill in the House
of Lords, he consulted Wilberforce each step of the way, deferring to
the latter's judgment on whether a bill should be simultaneously taken
up in the Commons. The reformers took full advantage of surprise—
as when Fox moved for a resolution in the Commons late in the 1806
session, and when Grenville introduced the bill in the House of Lords
at the very beginning of the 1807 session, in order to provide sufficient
time for possible examining of evidence. But despite the Parliamentary
maneuvering, despite the brilliant stroke of first making sure of the
House of Lords, Grenville found it necessary to exploit all the coercive
powers of his office. Even so, there was barely time for the bill to win
royal assent before the Talents Ministry fell, over the issue of granting
military commissions to Roman Catholics. Wilberforce had no doubts
that a gracious Providence had allowed Grenville to redeem the nation,
just as he was venturing to put the people's happiness "on a popish
foundation," or that the redemption had cleared the way for Wellington's successes in the Iberian Peninsula."[104]

One must not confuse motives with the temporary conditions which
make a political act possible. There is no reason to question the
idealistic motives that helped bring overwhelming final majorities for
abolition—100 to 34 in the Lords, 283 to 16 in the Commons. It was
precisely because abolition had long been defined as a humanitarian
ideal that it had appeal for a political coalition determined to achieve

---

[104] Grenville to Wilberforce, May 5, 1806; July 29, 1806; Nov. 5, 1806; Wilberforce to Grenville, March 24, 1806; June 5, 1806; June 7, 1806; June 10,
1806; Feb. 25, 1807, Dropmore MSS; Wilberforce, *Life of Wilberforce*, III, 304–
5. Stephen convinced Wilberforce that Grenville's plan for stopping the slave
trade by high import duties was "in the highest degree objectionable" (Wilberforce to Grenville, June 2, 1806). But this remained the one point of conflict.
On August 18, 1806, Wilberforce wrote William Smith that he thought Grenville
could be dissuaded from the plan if he received strong written arguments against
it. But the question remained in doubt until September, when Wilberforce seemed
confident of success (Wilberforce to Smith, Aug. 18, 1806; Sept. 5, 1806, Smith
papers, DUL). Roger Anstey credits the General Election of October with
strengthening Grenville's hand against Sidmouth's followers, who might have
forced a compromise measure such as high import duties. By September, Wilberforce was also beginning to worry about the economic hardships which abolition
might bring—a point on which he had previously been far more optimistic than
Stephen and Henry Thornton.

at least one striking reform, even if it were too weak to override the king on such issues as Catholic rights.[105]

But the ideological meaning of a reform is something more than the sum of the reformers' motives and intentions. It was not accidental that the successful abolition law originated in the House of Lords, or that credit for the humanitarian achievement was soon extended to the king himself, in celebration of the jubilee year of his reign.[106] The antislavery movement had originally attracted radicals like Price, Priestley, Walker, and James Martin; it had won the support of liberal reformers like Romilly, Francis, and Fox. By 1815, however, abolitionists were working closely with Castlereagh, Wellington, and Lord Liverpool. The cause gave Clarkson and Allen friendly access to the Emperor of Russia, and allowed the former to address the "Illustrious Potentates!" at the Congress of Vienna. Wilberforce's fears that the abolition act would be repealed by the high Tories proved to be quite unfounded.[107]

The law of 1807 was not a response to petitions, to public clamor, or to threatened boycott. Wilberforce published his "letter" to the freeholders and other inhabitants of Yorkshire because of public ignorance and apathy. The Abolition Committee warned against public meetings or any appearance of organized activity. M.P.'s, they advised, should receive "spontaneous" applications from private individuals. Yet the abolitionist triumph could be advertised as proof that a virtuous government would ultimately confirm, according to its own wisdom, a cause that had expanded the hearts and excited the generous sympathies of the people. The beauty of the act, according to the *Edinburgh Review,* was that the public had pressed the issue upon the government. The abolitionists' success showed that in England a righteous question need only to be fully revealed and understood to

[105] George Macaulay Trevelyan, *Lord Grey of the Reform Bill* (New York, 1920), pp. 142–43, 147, 158.

[106] *Memoirs of Sir Samuel Romilly,* II, 297–98. Romilly was highly indignant over credit being assigned to the king.

[107] Clarkson, MS address to the "Imperial and Royal Potentates," 1814; Grenville to Clarkson, Dec. 31, 1814; Clarkson to Catharine Clarkson, June 28–29, 1814; Clarkson to Castlereagh, Sept. 30, 1818, Clarkson papers, HEH; Clarkson to J. Wadkin, May 1, 1807, Bod. C. 107/156, Rhodes House, Oxford; Add. MS 41267, A, 97–98, British Museum; Clarkson, MS account of his audience with the Emperor of Russia, Gurney MSS, Friends House, London.

be carried. On an issue of pure humanity there could be a mysterious interaction between the government and the governed, implying a unity of sentiment that by-passed questions of representation and consent.[108]

For a didactic age, the achievement presented numerous lessons— not in political action but in what Clarkson termed "practical benevo- lence." The Bishop of London asserted that from the beginning of the world to this hour of triumph, there had never been an act that had exterminated so great a quantity of evil or that had forwarded so great a quantity of good. The British legislature had obtained nothing less than "a total change in the condition of one quarter of the habit- able globe." Writing Wilberforce from Bombay, Sir James Mackintosh predicted that hundreds of thousands would be "animated" by Wil- berforce's encouraging example, which had shown that within the short space of twenty years the exertions of virtue may be crowned by splendid success: "How noble and sacred is human nature, made capable of achieving such truly great exploits!"[109]

Even before success was assured, Clarkson had rapidly been assem- bling materials for his two-volume morality play, *The History of the Rise, Progress and Accomplishment of the Abolition of the African Slave-Trade by the British Parliament*. The history of this "immortal war," which Coleridge compared to the "mean conquests" of Napo- leon, demonstrated the irrelevancy of abstract disputes over theology or ethical systems. It also resolved all the ambiguities of moral judg- ment. The noblest historical achievement of Christianity had also been an infallible test that separated the sheep from the goats "as if," Clark- son wrote, they had been marked by the Divine Being at the Day of Judgment. The cause had unmasked the vicious who pretended to virtue, and had distinguished the moral statesmen from the self-serv- ing politicians. The purpose of the *History*, according to Clarkson, was to provide readers with an informed appreciation of the joy and gratitude they ought to feel when contemplating Britain's most selfless act.[110]

---

[108] Wilberforce, *Correspondence*, II, 112–13; Abolition Committee Minutes, III, 117; *Edinburgh Review*, X (April, 1807), 206.

[109] Porteus MS 2104, 91, 98; Wilberforce, *Life of Wilberforce*, III, 302–3.

[110] William Dillwyn to Samuel and Susannah Emlen, Jan. 25, 1807, Emlen- Dillwyn papers, LCP; *Edinburgh Review*, XII (July, 1808), 355–79; Earl Leslie

The moral of the tale was essentially twofold: no good efforts are ever lost, since Providence brings about an extraordinary "concurrence" of means and circumstances that could neither be foreseen nor contrived. Second, a virtuous cause unites men of all faiths and persuasions, together with men of the humblest and most exalted ranks. The lists of "progenitors" and "coadjutors" furnished a new cast of saints and heroes. William Dillwyn rightly predicted that Clarkson's *History* would offer an opportunity to exhibit "a practical comment on the Principles of 'Quakerism.' " Bishop Porteus recalled with pride that it had been the grandson of an archbishop (Sharp) who had first drawn the public's attention to the iniquities of slavery and the slave trade. Ramsay, an Anglican clergyman, had been the cause's first martyr.[111]

An appreciation of the origins and continuity of antislavery history secured the reputation of Sharp, who as an aging philanthropist was becoming increasingly obsessed with apocalyptic fantasies of "the Black Power" and "the Seven-horned Beast." Soon after his death, in 1813, Sharp was canonized as the first antislavery saint; a monument erected in Westminster Abbey by the African Institution eulogized him as a "model of disinterested virtue." Although Clarkson would be the favorite symbol of abolitionism for poets and liberal reformers, it was Wilberforce who was hailed as God's instrument for preserving the lives of millions, and Wilberforce who was imagined to experience an inward satisfaction that exceeded the temporal rewards of any man in history. In the Age of Revolution, Wilberforce was England's answer to the illustrious Washington, who was after all a slaveholder. Far more to the point—and the comparison hardly needed

---

Griggs, *Thomas Clarkson, the Friend of Slaves* (London, 1936), p. 97; Clarkson, *History of the Abolition of the African Slave-Trade,* I, 1–10; II, 581–83.

[111] Clarkson, *History of the Abolition of the African Slave-Trade,* I, 194–99; Dillwyn to Samuel and Susannah Emlen, Jan. 25, 1807, Emlen-Dillwyn papers; Porteus MS 2104, 92–95. There were, inevitably, hard feelings over Clarkson's omissions and self-glorification that would culminate in his pathetic *Strictures on a Life of William Wilberforce by the Rev. R. T. Wilberforce, and the Rev. S. Wilberforce; With a Correspondence Between Lord Brougham and Mr. Clarkson . . .* (London, 1838). As early as 1814 Clarkson was nettled by criticism that he had omitted mention of James Stephen (Clarkson to Wilberforce, Nov. 20, 1814, CEW). The Emlens complained that an entire "stream" on Clarkson's abolitionist map should have been devoted to Thomas Harrison (Samuel and Susannah Emlen to William Dillwyn, May 9, 1808, Emlen-Dillwyn papers).

elaboration in Romilly's eloquent tribute before the House of Commons—Wilberforce was England's answer to the "common enemy of mankind," who was enslaving Europe while Wilberforce was securing "a Magna Charta for Africa."[112]

The victory inevitably enhanced Britain's self-image at a moment when, as William Allen noted, "the Continent of Europe seems completely at his [Napoleon's] feet, and America is highly inflamed against us." Clarkson spoke for more than the abolitionist community when he wrote:

Nor is it a matter of less pleasing consideration, that, at this awful crisis, when the constitutions of kingdoms are on the point of dissolution, the stain of the blood Africa is no longer upon us, or that we have been freed (alas, if it be not too late!) from a load of guilt, which was hung like a mill-stone about our necks, ready to sink us to perdition.[113]

In 1807, British morale was in need of elevation, and it is understandable that relief from guilt should have been accompanied by extravagant self-congratulation. In the eyes of the Duke of Norfolk, the abolition law was "the most humane and merciful Act which was ever passed by any Legislature in the world." It was no coincidence, he suggested, that the final achievement occurred in Passion Week, when the Son of God displayed "that stupendous instance of Mercy towards Mankind, the redemption of the world by his Death upon the Cross."[114]

Later skeptics, especially those living across the Channel, concluded that Britain's regeneration had been too sudden. During the first quarter-century of antislavery agitation, Britain's share of the slave trade had increased to a virtual monopoly. To expect moral credit from limiting and then ending an escalating trade was rather like

---

[112] *Tenth Report of the Directors of the African Institution* . . . (London, 1816), p. 72; *European Magazine and London Review*, LXX (Dec., 1816), 483–88; *Edinburgh Review*, XXI (July, 1813), 463; *Gentleman's Magazine*, LXXXVIII (Dec., 1818), 489–93; Wilberforce, *Life of Wilberforce*, III, 294–95; Clarkson, *History of the Abolition of the African Slave-Trade*, II, 580; Lady Waldegrave to Wilberforce, March 29, 1807, CEW. Clarkson, however, remained the heroic symbol of abolitionism for American reformers like Henry Clarke Wright, who read the *History* as virtually a sacred revelation (Wright to Mrs. Thomas Clarkson, Oct. 25, 1845, Howard University Library).

[113] William Allen, *Life of William Allen, with Selections from his Correspondence* (3 vols., London, 1846), I, 88; Clarkson, *History of the Abolition of the African Slave-Trade*, II, 583–84.

[114] Porteus MS 2104, 102.

expecting moral credit from limiting or ending unilateral bombing raids. The point applies to the suffering already caused, not to the expected risks of cessation. On the other hand, not every government guilty of ghastly oppression has undergone, for whatever reasons, a change of heart. And from the best modern estimates, it would appear that the British abolition act was not ineffective in reducing the number of slaves transported to the New World. Although it would require more than a half-century of bribes, diplomacy, and coercion for England to realize her objective, the act of 1807 also served as a symbolic precedent that gave courage and sanction to generations of reformers in the United States, France, and Brazil.

For Englishmen, the precedent was all the more meaningful because it had occurred at a time of war and political reaction. Antislavery—at least in its preparatory stage of stopping the African trade—could not be stigmatized as the aberration of a radical era. In some ways the abolition act did signify a radical and fundamental shift in colonial policy—a shift associated, for example, with Stephen's administrative reforms, with his plan for using the crown colony of Trinidad as a model for experiments in free labor, and with his later Registration scheme. But these moves toward social engineering carried the protective coloration of Evangelical religion.

The abolition act was interpreted above all as a triumph of Protestant Christianity and as a moral vindication of the Church of England. And since the cause after 1807 carried the aura of respectable religion, in a way that contrasted sharply with antislavery in the United States, it could serve as a safe vehicle for mobilizing massive public support. In 1814, for example, English leaders were happy to demonstrate to the courts of Europe that the English people, with a single voice, demanded the international suppression of the slave trade. The voice was predominantly middle-class in tone, and to the ears of radicals like Cobbett seemed directly antithetical to the English working class. Yet there is evidence, especially by the 1820s, that abolitionism had filtered down to workingmen who attended Dissenting congregations or the various societies for moral improvement and useful knowledge. It could serve both as an instrument and symbol of upward mobility, or even provide an organizational model for more radical causes.

The West Indian planters, who were still living in an eighteenth-century world, had little comprehension of the changes taking place in

English society. When they harassed and persecuted Nonconformist missionaries, expecting that wild "enthusiasticks" would receive little support from home, they sealed their fate. The social transformations of the first two decades of the nineteenth century made it certain that any attempt to keep the Gospel from slaves would succeed in turning the vast indignation of English Dissent into channels of protest that had won official sanction. The significance of this fact can be underscored by a brief comparison with the United States, where the governing elites had failed to win such national hegemony, and where there was far less religious cleavage between slave-holding and free-labor cultures. Methodists and Baptists scored great successes in the South precisely because they absorbed and reflected the social norms of the southern community. As a result, the national churches tried to accommodate policy to the diverse values of their constituents. And the mediating role of the churches meant, quite literally, that abolitionists would either have to "come out" from the churches or split the churches apart. Yet in England, by the 1820s, a defense of the missionaries and a humbling of the "godless" planters could unite Dissenters and many Anglicans in a great crusading cause.

The domestic implications of the abolition act were somewhat subtler. Stephen and other abolitionists had converted an attack on West Indian slavery into a vindication of the existing social order. This theme ran through the Parliamentary debates of 1807. For example, Walter Fawkes, a new member from Yorkshire, said there was no need to disgust the Commons any further with tales of "floating dungeons" or of the inhuman separation of slave families. What outraged Fawkes was the claim that the West Indian slave would prefer his situation to that of an English peasant. He asked for proof that the slave enjoyed the option of exchanging "the niggardly and parsimonious employer, for the open and generous master; and that he is animated with that proud feeling of country which pervades every British bosom, from the lowest to the highest class of our community."[115] Yorkshire, in the previous year, had been seething with discontent; a Parliamentary committee on the woolen trade had just called for the suppression of the croppers' organization, whose petitions were seen as evidence of Jacobin conspiracy; and "the proud feeling of country" was being turned, by despair, into the violent protest of Luddism.

[115] *Parliamentary Debates*, VIII (1807), 965.

The humanitarian triumph of 1807 coincided, roughly, with the removal of much of the legislation that had protected the traditional customs of trade and the restrictive practices of English workers. By 1809, according to E. P. Thompson, "all the protective legislation in the woolen industry—covering apprenticeship, the gig-mill, and the number of looms—was repealed. The road was now open for the factory, the gig-mill, the shearing-frame, the employment of unskilled and juvenile labour."[116] Clearly there was no causal connection between the two forms of "abolition," although the abolition of the slave trade helped to reinforce the image of England as a land of freedom where proud workers could easily exchange the niggardly employer for the open and generous master. Yet the unrelated acts of abolition did reflect an emerging frame of mind. For it appeared that neither the West Indian planters nor the English workers understood their own true interests. Both groups clung blindly to archaic methods of production, resisting such tools of progress as plows and shearing frames, and issuing portentous warnings that violence and economic ruin would result from any tampering with their obsolete ways. It was necessary, therefore, to apply a negative pressure that would force planters and workers to identify their own interests with those of the nation, as redefined by an emerging hegemony of capitalists and Evangelical reformers. By removing various privileges, monopolies, and protective rules, legislators could at once encourage individual responsibility, strike a blow against slavery, and help to create an undifferentiated labor force as a prime national resource.

How could one later question a cause that had found confirmation in the ancient British constitution, that had won support from the great orators of all parties, and that had finally triumphed in the House of Lords? Regardless of domestic turbulence and scandal, of public doubts and prophecies of doom, England had begun the nineteenth century with an act of sublime nobility. The philanthropists, nobles, peers, and clergy who joined in 1807 to form the African Institution tried, quite literally, to institutionalize that transcendent impulse, to make it a permanent part of national life. Their efforts to redeem Africa, to spread the blessings of British liberty, and to prepare the West Indian slave for ultimate freedom were supported, in the words of the Evangelical organ, by the "spontaneous sentiments of

[116] E. P. Thompson, *The Making of the English Working Class* (New York, 1963), p. 529.

every Christian." And for generations to come, the crusade against slavery and the slave trade would be hailed as unanswerable proof that English humanitarianism outweighed English avarice and class interest. In the famous verdict of W. E. H. Lecky, "the unwearied, unostentatious, and inglorious crusade of England against slavery may probably be regarded as among the three or four perfectly virtuous acts recorded in the history of nations."[117]

The Slave System as a Mirror for English Society

The early antislavery literature shows less concern over arbitrary power per se than over arbitrary power divorced from traditional sanction. It was not simply that the slave owner's "power constitutes right," as James Ramsay said, but that both power and right had been purchased. And what could one say, as Wilberforce asked the House of Commons, of a system that gave such power to any man who could scrape together forty pounds? Virtually any man who could afford a horse in England, Wilberforce said, could afford a slave in the West Indies. Masters included men of all ranks, understandings, and tempers, including, no doubt, the most ignorant and worthless. In 1784, Ramsay had reported:

Slaves chiefly suffer, where they are the property of an ignorant, low-minded, narrow-hearted wretch, or of one indigent and involved, or of a man who makes a figure beyond his income in England, or when they are submitted to some raw lad, or untaught unfeeling manager or overseer.[118]

Because the slave system appeared to be dominated by an unmitigated drive for wealth, it could symbolize all the forces that threatened to

[117] James Stephen, *The Speech of James Stephen, Esq., at the Annual Meeting of the African Institution* . . . (London, 1817), pp. 9–10, 55; *Christian Examiner* (April, 1807), pp. 270–73; MS Account of Thomas Clarkson's labours, 1807 to 1824, pp. 1–3, Clarkson papers, HEH; W.E.H. Lecky, *A History of European Morals: From Augustus to Charlemagne* (2 vols., New York, 1876), I, 161.

[118] *Debate on a Motion for the Abolition of the Slave-Trade*, p. 6; James Ramsay, *An Essay on the Treatment and Conversion of Negro Slaves in the British Sugar Colonies* (London, 1784), p. 92. William Agutter complained that because the activities of slave-traders could not be observed by the "wise and good" of England, there could be no checks against sin (*The Abolition of the Slave Trade Considered in a Religious Point of View* [London, 1788], p. 14). William Dickson reported that in Barbados the slaves on smaller farms were better off than those on large plantations, but that the worst evils resulted from the prejudice and aggression of the poor whites (*Letters on Slavery* . . . [London, 1789], pp. 6, 108).

unravel the fabric of traditional deference, patronage, and hereditary status.

Englishmen were acutely sensitive to such dangers precisely because English society had long been in the vanguard of the march of Western capitalism. It was becoming increasingly clear, by the second half of the eighteenth century, that commercial wealth could provide men with access to social rank and public office. Defenders of the old order, who usually represented earlier stages of commercial success, charged that the purchase of titles or landed estates undermined public respect for authority. Burke complained that the "Nabob" adventurers, who had reaped wealth in India, were inclined to become Jacobins, since they resented the discovery that there were things money could not buy. Although the West Indies were only one source of *nouveaux riches,* popular imagery linked the region with easy money and conspicuous consumption. Richard Pares has called attention to the lack of financial independence of English gentlemen and the younger sons of noblemen, who were forced to look to government patronage as a source of wealth: "Almost the only rich business men with stable fortunes which would look after themselves were the absentee sugar-planters—a fact which goes some way to explain why a somewhat disproportionate number of them sat in the House."[119]

Such absentee planters were not necessarily self-made men, and West Indian fortunes were easily assimilated into English society. Yet in Thomas Day's immensely popular children's book, *Sandford and Merton,* it seemed only natural that a small boy from Jamaica should be a spoiled brat. The author, who had previously won acclaim for his long poem, *The Dying Negro,* also presents Tommy Merton as a little tyrant, arrogant and yet soft. His family lives in ostentatious luxury. The moral of the tale involves Tommy's redemption, at the hands of a simple farmer's son and a masculine clergyman, who teach him the value of hard work and ascetic self-denial. Few Englishmen, no doubt, were prepared to renounce an important source of national wealth or to curtail the privileges that wealth entailed. But in a vague way America, and especially the West Indies, could be identified as the source of avarice and corruption.

[119] Elie Halévy, *The Growth of Philosophic Radicalism,* tr. by Mary Morris (London, 1949), p. 161; Pares, *King George III and the Politicians,* pp. 15–16. Pares also notes that while West Indian incomes were far from regular, "the planters behaved as if they had been."

This is not to say that British attacks on American slaveholding were "merely" a projection of domestic needs and fears. The evils of Negro slavery were no illusion, nor was it unrealistic for Englishmen to see in the slave colonies a paradigm of those forces of plutocracy and unrestrained self-interest which threatened the ordered liberties of the past. Clearly the rise of antislavery sentiment represented a major advance in the moral consciousness of mankind. The abolitionists were among the first protesters to recognize a form of class and institutional exploitation, independent of individual good will; to accuse the government of complicity in such exploitation; and to acknowledge the collective responsibility of all consumers whose luxuries required such heavy human cost. The need to idealize a tradition of domestic liberty may have made it easier to perceive American slavery as a lawless innovation. But it is also probable that the antislavery experience ultimately taught many Englishmen to recognize forms of systematic oppression that were closer to home.

Yet perceptions of oppression often rest on a screening out of subtler species of oppression. As Marx said of an earlier reformer (in words that later critics would adapt to Marx himself), "Luther vanquished servility based upon devotion, because he replaced it by servility based upon conviction. . . . He emancipated the body from chains, because he laid chains upon the heart."[120] I have previously suggested that British antislavery literature mirrored the needs and tensions of a society increasingly absorbed with problems of underemployment and labor discipline. This argument must be developed with considerable care and qualification, in order to avoid the simplistic impression that "industrialists" promoted abolitionist doctrine as a means of distracting attention from their own forms of exploitation. The early British industrialists saw their own innovations as unmistakable agencies of moral progress and human betterment. More to the point, industrialization was only a nascent force during the first decades of the abolitionist movement. On the other hand, British abolitionism coincided with the emerging ideology and societal circumstances which made industrialization possible. The abolitionist movement cannot be detached from its defining social context—from the accelerating pace of enclosures, which augmented a drifting population of rural paupers; from the problem of disposing of convicts,

[120] Quoted in Edmund Wilson, *To the Finland Station: A Study in the Writing and Acting of History* (New York, 1953), pp. 190–91.

who could no longer be shipped to America; from the trade in pauper apprentices, who were being sent by the wagon- or bargeload from London to the mill towns; from the growing desire for utility, efficiency, productivity, and order; or from the industrial employment of small children, which to the generation of the 1790s, as J. R. Poynter has observed, seemed almost a "panacea."[121] If British abolitionists could express horror over the iron chains of the slave trade, their acts of selectivity and definition helped to strengthen the invisible chains being forged at home.

Accusations of "inconsistency" or "hypocrisy" can only obscure the complex relationship between West Indian slavery and the more progressive thought of early industrial England. As reformers grappled with the problems of crime, pauperism, and labor discipline, they seemed to be unconsciously haunted by the image of the slave plantation. Thus Bentham's vision of the model prison, proposed in 1784 as an alternative to deportation to Australia, is a virtual caricature of the planter's ideal:

If it were possible to find a method of becoming master of everything which might happen to a certain number of men, to dispose of everything around them so as to produce on them the desired impression, to make certain of their actions, of their connections, and of all the circumstances of their lives, so that nothing could escape, nor could oppose the desired effect, it cannot be doubted that a method of this kind would be a very powerful and a very useful instrument which governments might apply to various objects of the utmost importance.[122]

Among the various objects for which Bentham recommended his "method" were hospitals, schools, madhouses, and factories. During the 1790s, when British reformers including Bentham were condemning the dehumanization of West Indian slavery, the great Utilitarian circulated grandiose plans for the rational restructuring of English society. The domestic labor problem could be solved, Bentham argued, by building hundreds of great "Houses of Industry," modeled on the Panopticon principles of central surveillance, regimentation, and division of labor. Each House would be managed by a Governor and Governess, assisted by various Foremen and Forewomen, a Chaplain, a Bailiff, a Medical Curator, a Matron–midwife, a School Master, and an

[121] J. R. Poynter, *Society and Pauperism: English Ideas of Poor Relief, 1795–1834* (London, 1969), pp. 22–23.
[122] Quoted in Halévy, *Growth of Philosophic Radicalism,* pp. 82–83.

Organist–clerk—the list reads like a parody of contemporary proposals for reforming the plantation system. The parallel extends to Bentham's ingenious means of guaranteeing a place for each worker, without resorting to the inequitable burdens of the Poor Laws and Laws of Settlement: "But if all infants were branded, painlessly and indelibly, with name, place and date of birth, identification for settlement and a host of other useful purposes would be instantaneous." Each House would be totally self-supporting, as a result of maximizing the output of each worker, including small children. It would be essential, Bentham pointed out, to calculate the net value of children in every age-group. "Was the average child," he asked, in a question that was still disputed in the West Indies, "worth more or less than nothing?"[123]

It is possible to dismiss Bentham's program as the fantasy of an eccentric reformer, though there is still debate over his influence as the creator of an appealing social ideal. If the government failed to construct a network of Panopticons, it did erect the New Union Workhouse, which Poynter aptly describes as a "fortress protecting society from two quite different evils, the starvation and insurrection of unrelieved indigence on the one hand, and the moral depravity and economic ruin of progressively increasing pauperism on the other." The significant point, however, is that Bentham's vision of rational progress suggests an ambivalent response to plantation slavery, a response that embodied, in turn, some of the central contradictions of English society.

In one respect, Bentham's proposals were consistent with the principles of laissez faire. Even the Panopticon prisons would be run without burden to the taxpayer. The government would simply contract with an entrepreneur, who "takes charge of the convicts at so much a head and applies their time and industry to his personal profit, as does a master with his apprentices." The entrepreneur's duties toward his charges would be "so bound up with his interest that he would be forced to do for his own advantage anything that he was not inclined to do for theirs." A system of life insurance, for example, could guarantee that the entrepreneur's profits would decrease if there were a rise in the average rate of mortality.[124] Presumably the same effect could be more easily achieved by converting the convicts into personal property, but this solution would contradict the assumption—or pre-

[123] *Ibid.*, pp. 82–85; Poynter, *Society and Pauperism*, pp. 107–9, 128–38.
[124] Halévy, *Growth of Philosophic Radicalism*, pp. 84–85.

tense—that both entrepreneur and worker were "economic men" in a world of harmonious interests.

In point of fact, there is a striking discrepancy between Bentham's competitive model, based on individual self-interest, and his obsessive concern for social discipline. The same discrepancy is evident in the ideology of the early industrialists, whose ideal of free market conditions gave no justification for attempts to control the behavior and leisure time of their workers. In theory, after all, an employer of free workers, unlike a slave owner, should be interested only in purchasing equal units of labor at the cheapest possible price. Yet entrepreneurs like Richard Arkwright and Josiah Wedgwood had already made practical application of a principle recommended by Bentham: "To be incessantly under the eyes of the inspector is to lose in effect the power to do evil and almost the thought of wanting to do it." Bentham gave the game away not only by proposing a model of prison discipline for schools and factories, but by appealing to the standard of relative happiness: "Call them soldiers, call them monks, call them machines, so they were but happy ones, I should not care."[125]

The alleged happiness of Negro slaves was of course a central argument of American planters. And the alleged happiness of English workers justified new forms of dependence and control that also gave entrepreneurs an exalted role in the production process. While English society increasingly condemned the institution of slavery, it approved experiments in labor discipline which appeared to gravitate toward the plantation model. Paradoxically, planters, especially those in the United States, increasingly followed the industrialists' lead in using incentives to manipulate slave behavior, without fearing, it should be added, that such "amelioration" would be a step toward eventual emancipation.[126] Slaveholders and industrialists shared a growing interest not only in surveillance and control but in modifying the character and habits of their workers.

Long before anyone had dreamed of founding an antislavery society, Daniel Defoe had complained that "there is nothing more frequent than for an Englishman to work till he has got his pockets full of

[125] *Ibid.*, pp. 83–84.

[126] This point is amply documented by Eugene D. Genovese's *Roll, Jordan, Roll* (New York, 1974), and by Robert William Fogel and Stanley L. Engerman's *Time on the Cross: The Economics of American Negro Slavery* (2 vols., Boston, 1974).

money, and then go and be idle or perhaps drunk till 'tis all gone." As early manufacturers soon discovered, the English worker also had a fondness for communal feast days, drunken wakes, and the recuperation of "St. Monday." By the 1780s such habits were no longer tolerable to progressive industrialists.[127] The new generation of entrepreneurs was also discontented over the laxness of the putting-out system, in which a demand for labor could result in higher wages, and higher wages could result in more frequent vacations. As Stephen A. Marglin has pointed out, it was not technology that led irresistibly to the creation of a concentrated and dependent force of wage laborers. In many industries, at least, it was the entrepreneur's new social and managerial role that required continuous supervision of employees and control over the proportions of their work and leisure time.[128]

There was a surface resemblance, to say the least, between the innovations of the new model factories and the contemporary abolitionist portrait of the sugar plantation. James Ramsay, for example, might almost have been describing preindustrial England when he wrote:

Formerly, before we became such accurate planters, and before luxury had rapaciously converted every little nook of land into sugar, the slaves had a field or two of the fallow cane-land yearly divided among them, for a crop of yams, peas, and potatoes; and a field of the best cane-land was annually put in yams, to be reserved for their weekly allowance.

[127] Neil McKendrick, "Josiah Wedgwood and Factory Discipline," *The Historical Journal*, IV (1961), 30–55; Sidney Pollard, "The Adaptation of the Labour Force," *The Genesis of Modern Management* (Cambridge, Mass., 1965), pp. 160–206; E. P. Thompson, "Time, Work-Discipline, and Industrial Capitalism," *Past and Present*, No. 38 (Dec., 1967), 56–97. One should not exaggerate the success of early industrialists in persuading the English worker to abandon his irregular rhythms of work. According to Brian Harrison, as late as the 1830s at least one-third of London's factory employees celebrated "St. Monday"; and in the 1820s there was some truth to the charge that most educated workingmen and self-employed craftsmen were given to regular drunkenness (*Drink and the Victorians: The Temperance Question in England, 1815–1872* [Pittsburgh, 1971], pp. 37–63). Harrison agrees, however, that capitalism required new habits of sobriety among employed workers. For the persistence of "Blue Monday" and other infractions of work discipline in America, see Herbert G. Gutman, "Work, Culture, and Society in Industrializing America, 1815–1919," *American Historical Review*, LXXVIII (June, 1973), 531–88.

[128] I am grateful to Professor Stephen A. Marglin for sending me a copy of his unpublished paper, "What Do Bosses Do? The Origins and Functions of Hierarchy in Capitalist Production."

When the planters became more "accurate," they subordinated every human concern to the single goal of production. At four in the morning a bell called the slaves to the fields or sugar mill, where they worked under close supervision, without rest or moments of leisure, until dark.[129]

Ramsay's words recall Josiah Wedgwood's famed Etruria mill. An ardent abolitionist, Wedgwood was also an "accurate" and autocratic master. A warning bell summoned his employees at 5:45, or one-quarter hour before the men and girl apprentices could see to work. They then toiled until dark, under the constant surveillance of overseers and inspectors. The latter perfected means for eliminating waste or moments of idleness. The mill hands had of course lost all control over the tools of their trade, as well as any claim to "free" time or space for the cultivation of "yams, pease, and potatoes." The use of child labor meant that factory managers displaced parents as the dominant authorities. This was one of the evils of West Indian slavery which aroused the most indignant protest. Like West Indian slaves, Wedgwood's workers resisted the growing pressures for maximized production. But in addition to the threat of blacklisting, they faced grave risks if they contemplated emigrating from the country. In 1783 a riot, brought on by a shortage of wheat, was crushed by military force. One worker was hanged.[130]

Wedgwood's campaign for industrial discipline, cushioned by a benevolent paternalism, drew invaluable support from Evangelical reformers like William Wilberforce. The latter, as Elie Halévy has written, "was at once the mouthpiece of the party of order and of the business world." In his concern for order, Wilberforce combined a nostalgia for the past with a genuine interest in the material and moral well-being of workers. In towns like Sheffield and Manchester, for example, he was distressed to find that apprentices no longer lived with their masters, as part of an extended family; the masters' wives thought themselves too elegant to carry such responsibility. But whatever the causes, Wilberforce knew that the social order was changing and that substitutes would have to be found for the watchful eye of

[129] Ramsay, *Essay on the Treatment and Conversion of African Slaves,* pp. 69, 78.

[130] McKendrick, "Wedgwood and Factory Discipline," pp. 38, 41, 47–52. See also Thompson, "Time, Work-Discipline, and Industrial Capitalism," and Pollard, "Adaptation of the Labour Force."

paternalistic masters. It was his plan, in 1787, which resulted in the Royal Proclamation Against Vice and Immorality and in a special society designed to suppress blasphemy, drunkenness, indecent publications, Sabbath breaking among the poor, village wakes and festivals, and unlicensed places of public amusement. According to Neil McKendrick, even Josiah Wedgwood had been powerless to prevent the work stoppages caused by summer wakes and fairs: "It was only slowly that the passion for wakes died—strangled by the joint efforts of the manufacturers, the methodists, and the Society for the Suppression of Vice."[131]

The "disciplinarians," in E. P. Thompson's words, "won the battle of the Industrial Revolution." Wilberforce's concerns focused on social order and virtue, not on the industrial revolution. Yet his aid to manufacturers was not limited to his leadership in reform movements that helped to destroy preindustrial culture and to create a responsible, predictable, and manipulatable labor force. In 1795, Wilberforce won a major political triumph, again in the cause of order, when he persuaded an immense public meeting in Yorkshire to support Pitt's Sedition Act, which he himself had helped to broaden, and which had aroused storms of protest throughout the land. In 1799 it was Wilberforce who first proposed to Parliament a general Combination Law

---

[131] Halévy, *England in 1815,* pp. 325–26; Wilberforce, *Life of William Wilberforce,* II, 163–64; Coupland, *Wilberforce,* pp. 54–55; McKendrick, "Wedgwood and Factory Discipline," p. 46. Few biographical subjects are so treacherous as William Wilberforce, who has not in general won favor from modern historians. In a future work I hope to explore some of the more attractive contours of his personality. In the meantime, my emphasis on social order should not be confused with the arguments of Ford K. Brown, whose *Fathers of the Victorians* (New York, 1961) portrays Wilberforce as the devious leader of an Evangelical conspiracy to capture control of the Church of England, a conspiracy in which abolitionism served merely as a means for gaining popularity and power. According to Brown, Wilberforce could not have been interested in the actual achievement of abolition, since "no Evangelical principle is more unquestioningly held than that all earthly injustices and oppressions mean nothing" (p. 111). Despite some of Brown's shrewd insights, this is a crude distortion. No one has ever doubted that Wilberforce's interests were more religious than secular, or that his top priorities were reforming English manners and Christianizing Africa. On the other hand, as a young schoolboy, long before his conversion to Evangelical religion, he had denounced the slave trade in a letter to the *York Press.* There is no reason to question the genuineness of his lifelong desire to see a total abolition of the slave trade and an end to the physical barbarities of slavery. A close study of Wilberforce's papers reveals an extraordinarily sensitive and complex mind.

which prohibited workers in any trade from "combining" to protect their interests, which denied the accused a jury trial, and which, in the words of Wilberforce's sympathetic biographer, "killed Trade Unionism for a quarter of a century." In 1817 Wilberforce was a member of the Secret Committee of the House of Commons, investigating domestic dissent, championing a new Seditious Meetings Bill, and approving, in 1818, the suspension of Habeas Corpus.[132]

The Suspension Bill prompted Sir Francis Burdett to ask why Wilberforce should be shocked by African enslavement and not shocked by a law that would allow Englishmen to be seized and treated like African slaves? There would, however, be no reason to admire Wilberforce more if he had consistently supported repressive regimes in both England and the West Indies. The central question involves the relationship between antislavery values and the forces that were shaping a new English working class.

If any abolitionists were unaware of the condition of English laborers or were blind to the parallels with their own indictments of slavery, they had only to read the tracts of their West Indian opponents. As early as 1772 *The Scot's Magazine* reprinted, along with a laudatory review of Anthony Benezet, an essay from a London paper comparing the condition of West Indian slaves to that of English common laborers, who were "more real slaves to necessity, than to Egyptian taskmasters: for necessity makes no allowance for sickness but suffers the sick labourer's wife and children to starve." At least the children of slaves did not fall victim to "unfeeling parish-overseers, who have no private interest in their preservation." To be sure, the English workers were free. They could boast of "the liberty of changing their masters for the same wages. —A mighty boast indeed! to change their masters for the worse, while they still remain slaves to the necessity of constant and hard labour."[133]

By 1789, Gilbert Franklyn could point to the more specific consequences of the early industrial revolution:

[132] Thompson, *Making of the English Working Class, passim;* Paul Mantoux, *The Industrial Revolution in the Eighteenth Century* (rev. ed., tr. by Marjorie Vernon, New York, 1929), pp. 456–60, 476; Wilberforce, *Life of Wilberforce,* II, 125–31, 335; Coupland, *Wilberforce,* 202–3, 413–21.

[133] "Some Observations Upon the Slavery of Negroes," *The Scot's Magazine,* XXXIV (1772), 299–301; William Beckford, *A Descriptive Account of the Island of Jamaica . . .* (2 vols., London, 1790), II, 133–36, 264.

Sure I am, that the labourer in England, who is the *slave* of *necessity*, serves a harder task-master than the African finds in the West-Indies. No severities, there exercised, are equal to the cruelty of enticing poor people, by a small addition of wages, to work in lead, quick-silver, or other metals, or deleterious manufactories, which in a very few months, or years, render the life of the poor victim an unremitting scene of torture and misery, which death alone can relieve him from.

Of course Francklyn drew a preposterously idyllic picture of West Indian slavery. But his response to Clarkson's celebrated prize essay, won at Cambridge, was more on the mark. Why, Francklyn asked, did the two great universities not offer prizes "for the best dissertation on the evil effects which the manufactures of Birmingham, Manchester, and other great manufacturing towns, produce on the health and the lives of the poor people employed therein?" Suppose such a contest uncovered the talents of a Clarkson:

What horror might not an ingenious man excite in the mind of his reader, in describing two or three thousand fine, rosy cheeked children playing in the meads, enamelled with flowers, in all the luxuriance of health and happiness . . . seized on by those baneful fiends, avarice and luxury, and placed together in the hot rooms of different manufactories, till the pestilential vapour, repeatedly enhaled, spreads contagion amongst them.[134]

Note that Francklyn found it necessary to anthropomorphize avarice

---

[134] Gilbert Francklyn, *Observations, Occasioned by the Attempts Made in England to Effect the Abolition of the Slave Trade* . . . (Kingston, Jamaica, 1788; reprinted London, 1789), pp. 10–12, 27–42, 74–75. One encounters interesting paradoxes in the attempts to compare the condition of free and slave workers. Thus a Jamaican clergyman-planter, Dr. Lindsay, insists that it is nonsense to speak of slavery as the "negative of Freedom, and the Reverse of Liberty," and offers the conventional argument that no sharp lines can be drawn between relative states of subordination. He adds that the Negro slave is at least "free in inclinations of heart. . . . Happy fellow, who is so much in favour with the Nymph's of his Colour," and attacks reformers for proposing the "bondage" of monogamous marriage, whose original and only purpose was to avoid confusion in the inheritance of property! On the other hand, William Smith, the abolitionist M.P., took the high ground that the treatment and condition of slaves were irrelevant: "If the Middle Passage were a party of pleasure, and . . . if West Indian slavery were, as far as treatment is concerned, a very tissue of delights—still would my main objections remain in full tone" (Dr. [John?] Lindsay, "A Few Conjectural Considerations Upon the Creation of the Human Race, Occasioned by the Present British Quixottical Rage of Setting the Slaves from Africa at Liberty," MS dated 1788, fols. 9, 11, 15, 189, British Museum Add. MS 12439; William Smith, MS Letter to William Wilberforce, 1807, p. 25, Whitbread papers, County Record Office, Bedford).

and luxury as fiends which "seized" the rosy-cheeked children and "placed" them together in the noxious mills. In the abolitionist view, the recruitment and discipline of a slave labor force depended entirely on physical coercion. Obviously, the lash was not unique to the slave plantation, nor were whippings unfamiliar to English children, wives, apprentices, sailors, or lawbreakers. The six or seven-year-old pauper children in the textile mills knew the meaning of the foreman's strap, or worse still, of the billy roller grabbed from a spinning machine. Yet sensitivities had changed—in England and even in the Caribbean —since the days of cropped ears, bored tongues, and severed bodies. Bentham was not alone in desiring a system of "rational" punishments that would inflict precisely measured pain. And at a time when English industrialists were devising ingenious and more efficient substitutes for physical punishment, the slave system could symbolize a discredited form of authority that seemed to require the personal imposition of continuous pain.[135]

James Stephen thought it sufficient to present a matter-of-fact description of the plantation "driving system," without involving himself in moral judgments. As an experienced witness, he told how slaves prepared the soil for sugar-cane plants, turning up ground with hoes in long, parallel trenches. Blacks of both sexes would be drawn out in line, like troops on parade, and the drivers were required to

[135] Although abolitionists focused attention from the outset on the cruelty of flogging, they also appreciated the importance of the whip as a symbol of authority. In 1823, Zachary Macaulay insisted that even immediate emancipation would be fraught with much less danger than a sudden prohibition of the whip. He complained to Thomas Fowell Buxton that the abolitionists were being blamed for a slave insurrection in Demerara, when it was in fact the Canning administration that had foolishly begun a program of "amelioration" by restricting use of the whip, the most direct interference possible between masters and slaves. The abolitionists, Macaulay pointed out, had always advocated a succession of Parliamentary acts, beginning with the removal of barriers to manumission, which would gradually make the whip less necessary. He himself had no fears over an instant emancipation, if it were not resisted by the masters. But nothing could be more dangerous than a halfway measure that removed the symbol of slavery while trying to preserve the substance (Macaulay to Buxton, Nov. 11, 1823, Macaulay papers, HEH). There can be no doubt about the importance of the whip as a symbol of the planter's authority, but abolitionists exaggerated the frequency of its use, especially by the nineteenth century. The proprietors of the more successful West Indian plantations realized that an ultimate sanction becomes diluted by too frequent use. Like English manufacturers, they relied increasingly on a systematic balance of rewards and deprivations.

keep the lines dressed and moving at equal speed. If one slave hoed slower than the rest, those behind him in line would have to halt work. Only the constant use of a cart whip could ensure that no time would be wasted and that the lines would move without interruption.[136]

Aside from the regimentation of labor, there were crucial differences between the sugar plantation and Wedgwood's Etruria mill (which Edward Radcliffe described as "that paradise"). Wedgwood himself personified the Protestant ethic, and worked as strenuously as his employees. He waged unremitting war on dirt, carelessness, and waste of any kind. It was not the cart whip but incentive that governed his factory discipline. His goal and methods conformed to what recent psychologists have rediscovered as "behavior modification" through positive and negative "reinforcement." To his foremen, Wedgwood issued written rules and instructions describing the common tricks and evasions of workers. He precisely specified the proper methods of approval and reprimand. When workers arrived in the morning, the "Clerk of the Manufactory" let them know their punctuality was on record. Wedgwood also devised what McKendrick terms "a primitive clocking-in system," using tickets to record the exact times of arrival and departure. It is significant that Wedgwood's bell rang on the quarter-hour. The entire factory was synchronized to the clock. Higher wages rewarded superior skill and regularity. Infractions of the rules brought heavy fines.[137]

Like most men of their time, abolitionists refused to accept Francklyn's argument that workers could be slaves "of necessity." Stephen drew the distinction that then seemed self-evident:

Look at the most laborious peasant in Europe, and if you please, the most oppressed: he is toiling it is true from painful necessity; but it is necessity

---

[136] [Stephen], *Crisis of the Sugar Colonies*, pp. 9–13.

[137] McKendrick, "Wedgwood and Factory Discipline," pp. 30–35. At New Lanark, Robert Owen hung colored pieces of wood beside each worker; each day foremen would turn the pieces so that a given color would symbolize the worker's conduct on the previous day. When Owen walked through the mill, he could thus give a stare of disapproval at workers guilty, for example, of "black" conduct. Owen had earlier been shocked by the condition of factory workers in Manchester, who were more degraded and oppressed, he said, "than the house slaves whom I afterwards saw in the West Indies and in the United States" (Wilson, *To the Finland Station*, pp. 88, 91–92).

of a moral kind, acting upon his rational nature; and from which brutal coercion differs as widely, as a nauseous drench in the mouth of an infant, from the medicated milk of its mother.[138]

The imagery is suggestive. The fear of physical punishment is brutalizing, and is as naturally repellent to man as a violent cathartic. But the fear of hunger, prison, or unemployment acts upon man's "rational nature." When coupled with the hope of reward, such fears are a wholesome inducement to labor. Wages suggest the nourishment of a mother's breast. Stephen goes on to compare the Negro slave to a rickety infant whose muscles of voluntary motion have become contracted by unnatural restraint. Just as the infant must be carefully taught to walk, so the slave must gradually learn to work from motives other than blind obedience. Presumably Stephen has in mind "necessity of a moral kind," since he affirms that man is naturally indolent and can only be taught to labor voluntarily as his mind acquires foresight.[139]

The rise of antislavery sentiment in Britain coincided with an urgent domestic problem of labor discipline and labor management. If abolitionists agreed on the necessity of maintaining order and reforming the manners and habits of the working class, they clearly felt some ambivalence, along with many of their countrymen, toward the changes accompanying early industrialization. The immediate problem did not concern an industrial proletariat, but rather an immense rural labor force that had been uprooted, released from traditional restraints and controls, but not yet deprived of the independence of preindustrial village culture. Because the slave system was both distinctive and remote, it could become a subject for experimental fantasies that assimilated traditional values to new economic needs. An attack on the African slave trade could absorb some of the traditionalist's anxieties over the physical uprooting and dislocation of labor. The victims of enclosure were at least not marched in chains to the slave ships, or shipped abroad to unfeeling masters. By picturing the slave plantation as totally dependent upon physical torture, abolitionist writers gave sanction to less barbarous modes of social discipline. For reformers, the plantation offered the prospect of combining the virtues of the old agrarian order with the new ideals of uplift and engineered incentive.

[138] [Stephen], *Crisis of the Sugar Colonies*, pp. 48–49.
[139] *Ibid.*, pp. 53–54, 75.

Abolitionists could contemplate a revolutionary change in status precisely because they were not considering the upward mobility of workers, but rather the rise of distant Negroes to the level of humanity. They could stress the Negroes' capacity for a freer and better life, because such a life depended on an internalized sense of duty. They could repudiate the authority derived from a form of property ownership, but in so doing help to redefine the obligations—or lack of obligations—of legitimate ownership. British antislavery provided a bridge between preindustrial and industrial values; by combining the ideal of emancipation with an insistence on duty and subordination, it helped to smooth the way to the future.

Yet the paradigm of slavery and antislavery also suggested a future of a different kind. Although the abolitionist movement helped to clear an ideological path for British industrialists, it also bred a new sensitivity to social oppression. The concept of slavery is both evocative and elastic. No one sought to prove the debasement of the Negro slave by likening his condition to that of the English worker. When radicals like Cobbett and West Indian apologists like Francklyn tried to divert attention to the plight of English laborers, they automatically talked of "slaves" and "masters." They claimed to be the true "abolitionists," exposing the conflict and oppression masked by a spurious harmony of interests. The metaphors amounted to more than verbal play, since they expanded on the moral vision of the initial abolitionists. When Friedrich Engels later wrote his masterful study of the condition of the working class in England, he echoed one of Cobbett's favorite themes:

A slave is at least assured of his daily bread by the self-interest of his master, while the serf at any rate has a piece of land on the produce of which he can live. . . . The proletarian on the other hand is thrown wholly upon his own resources, and yet at the same time is placed in such a position that he cannot be sure that he can always use those resources to gain a livelihood for himself and his family. Everything that the factory worker can do to try and improve his position vanishes like a drop in the bucket in face of the flood of chance occurrences to which he is exposed and over which he has not the slightest control.

Though Engels wanted to prove that the English factory worker was even more oppressed than the Negro slave, he relied on the conceptual framework of the abolitionists: "The slavery which the middle classes have imposed on the workers can be seen most clearly in the factory system. There, in law and in fact, the operative loses all his rights."[140] The earlier antislavery literature had not only charged Engels's term with moral resonance, but had provided a model for the systematic indictment of social crime. Without debating questions of influence, it is not farfetched to see *The Condition of the Working Class in England* as one of the greatest of antislavery tracts.

[140] Friedrich Engels, *The Condition of the Working Class in England*, tr. and ed. by W. O. Henderson and W. H. Chaloner (Stanford, 1968), pp. 131, 200.

Ten ⁓

Antislavery and the Conflict of Laws

Introduction

The antislavery movement reflected and contributed to a major passage in intellectual history only indirectly related to the political and economic controversies of the Age of Revolution. Disputes over sanction gravitated inevitably toward fundamental principles, as exemplified in Granville Sharp's attempt to prove by the early 1770s that any claim to private property "in the persons of men" violated both divine and human law. Presumably, the following century vindicated Sharp's contention, though not without accompanying transformations in the prevailing views of divine and human law—transformations which Sharp could neither have foreseen nor approved. By appealing to abstract systems of law, precedent, and principle, the critics of slavery offered a covert challenge to some of the more enduring structures of Western culture. In Chapters Ten and Eleven I turn to two testing points of tradition: the conflict of human laws and the changing interpretations of the Word of God.

In 1776, Samuel Hopkins found the illegality of Negro slavery as self-evident as a geometric theorem. If the slave trade was wrong in 1776, it had always been wrong. And if it had always been criminal to capture and enslave innocent Africans, then it was no less criminal to hold them and their descendants in continuing bondage. In 1820, when Elihu Embree submitted a similar argument to the

Tennessee legislature, the slave trade had been outlawed by Britain and declared piracy by the United States. "Of course it follows," Embree wrote, "when this is admitted, that titles obtained to men in this way have no foundation in justice, and can never become just, tho' handed down from father to son, for a thousand generations." This was, essentially, the "higher law" doctrine advanced in 1760 by George Wallace, who felt that judges had the duty to restore Negro slaves to their rightful liberty.[1]

It was one thing, however, to state abstract propositions, which could be countered by other abstract propositions, and quite another to decide how the law applied to a particular case. Judges in both Europe and America recognized claims to slave property even where no municipal law defined a mode of legitimate enslavement or the nature of a master's dominion. Slaves had long been treated in international trade as articles of commerce, and in war as contraband. They were the subjects of international treaties and of conventions for the mutual return of fugitives.[2] Like other chattel property, they could be taxed or seized for debt, and were subject to municipal laws governing wills, estates, and contracts. Slave owners often traveled or changed their place of domicile. They sometimes lived thousands of miles from their slaves, under different or conflicting systems of law. The courts of one country could not deny proprietorship in slaves without raising a web of tangled issues regarding status, contractual rights, jurisdiction, and the comity of states.

By questioning the legality of human property, the antislavery movement evoked significant responses and compromises from the makers and interpreters of law. After the Somerset decision of 1772 it was no longer possible to take for granted the universal legality of slave property. Yet courts of law are not revolutionary tribunals, nor do they often issue sweeping verdicts that ignore the intricacies of property relations. The English common-law courts of the eighteenth century were almost invariably preoccupied with private, not public issues. Parliamentary supremacy, according to Brian Abel-Smith and Robert

[1] Samuel Hopkins, *A Dialogue Concerning the Slavery of the Africans . . .* (New York, 1785), pp. 22–24; E. E. Hoss, *Elihu Embree, Abolitionist* (Nashville, Tenn., 1897), p. 15. Hopkins also demanded that compensation be paid to emancipated slaves for previous work performed.

[2] J. H. W. Verzijl, *International Law in Historical Perspective* (5 vols., Leiden, 1972), V, 247; Robin W. Winks, *The Blacks in Canada: A History* (New Haven, 1971), pp. 24–26.

Stevens, "reduced the common law of England to the status of a delegated system. Not only had constitutional issues to be settled by Parliament, but the logic of the position was that even changes in private law had to be sanctioned by the legislature."[3] Judges ordinarily stuck close to the specific issues at hand and took pains to limit the legal effects of their decisions. There was thus a considerable gap between the enthusiasm of abolitionists and the judicial decisions restricting slavery—a gap that produced both misunderstanding and later judicial confusion.

If slavery was contrary to natural law, were there any constitutional means by which courts could declare it illegal without becoming law-making bodies? Was the institution analagous to polygamy, which was presumed to be illegal except where sanctioned by municipal law? Or was the possession of slaves like the possession of cats or horses, which was presumed to be legal except where explicitly outlawed? Did the slave's status derive from African law, from colonial law, from contract, or from ancient laws of English servitude? Did the comity of states protect the property rights of masters who traveled with their slaves to "free soil" areas? Was the status of a slave or master analagous to the status of a married person whose marriage has been validly performed under the laws of another jurisdiction? If so, how could free countries prevent an influx of slave-owning residents from subverting public policy? Did the principle of comity extend to the return of fugitives, or did the outlawing of slavery create a sanctuary of freedom?

Property versus Legal Personality

The gradual disappearance of slavery from most parts of Europe gave force to the ancient principle of *in favorem libertatis,* which in theory meant that a court might presume any servant was free, subject only to contract, unless his master could prove some hereditary right of ancient dominion. In England the *procedural* devices and presumptions of common law helped to manumit many villeins. In sixteenth-century France, the parlement of Guienne ruled that "la France, mère de la liberté, ne permet aucun esclave."[4] Sergeant-at-law William

[3] Brian Abel-Smith and Robert Stevens, *Lawyers and the Courts: A Sociological Study of the English Legal System, 1850–1965* (London, 1967), pp. 8–9.
[4] R. H. Graveson, *Status in the Common Law* (London, 1953), pp. 15, 26–27; David Brion Davis, *The Problem of Slavery in Western Culture* (Ithaca, N.Y.,

Davy, in the opening argument in behalf of the slave James Somerset, referred to the 1640 impeachment of the judges of the Star Chamber, when the managers of the House of Commons cited the unrecorded case of Cartwright, who had brought a slave from Russia to England. In the eleventh year of Elizabeth's reign, Davy exclaimed, it had been resolved that *"England was too pure an Air for Slaves to breathe in."*[5] In point of fact, Negro slaves were bought and displayed in the courts of Elizabeth and her Stuart successors; they were publicly advertised for sale through most of the eighteenth century; and they were bequeathed in wills as late as the 1820s.[6] Nevertheless, early in the eighteenth century Lord Chief Justice Holt expressed the opinion that "as soon as a negro comes into England, he becomes free." In

---

1966), p. 46; Joseph Story, *Commentaries on the Conflict of Laws, Foreign and Domestic* . . . (8th ed., Boston, 1883), p. 154.

[5] MS transcript of proceedings in the Court of King's Bench, 1772, Sharp papers, New-York Historical Society, p. 43 (hereafter Somerset transcript, NYHS). Sergeant (the title of a senior barrister) Davy kept repeating the stirring phrase about the air of England. Toward the end of the trial, Lord Mansfield, Chief Justice of the Court of King's Bench, asked him "is there any traces there ever existed such a Case as that of the Russian Slave?" Davy replied, "I know nothing more of it than what I told your Lordship" (*ibid.*, p. 131). Davy's citation of Rushworth's *Historical Collections* was repeated in Francis Hargrave's printed pamphlet, *An Argument in the Case of James Sommersett, a Negro, Lately Determined by the Court of the King's Bench* . . . (London, 1772), which was then incorporated into T. B. Howell's *State Trials*.

Although the latter work has generally been thought to provide the only detailed account of the Somerset case, its reliability has been questioned (for example, Jerome Nadelhaft, "The Somersett Case and Slavery: Myth, Reality, and Repercussions," *Journal of Negro History,* LI [July, 1966], 193–208). Yet Howell makes it clear that Hargrave's printed argument was not the one Hargrave presented to the court, and that it had been added in order to round out the skimpy eyewitness report by Capel Lofft. Unfortunately, Lofft, a later abolitionist and a noted Whig man of letters, was the only transcriber of published reports of cases heard between 1772 and 1774 in the Courts of King's Bench and Chancery. It was the youthful Hargrave, however, who made a name for himself with his masterly printed argument, and who subsequently became known as a great historical lawyer (William Holdsworth, *A History of English Law* [12 vols., London, 1938], XII, 139–40, 410). The NYHS transcript contains the long arguments presented by the senior barristers, William Davy and John Glynn, which were apparently unknown to Howell. It is clear that Davy and Glynn developed most of the points, with a few significant exceptions, which formed the substance of Hargrave's printed argument. Indeed, Hargrave sometimes followed Davy almost verbatim. I have found no record of what Hargrave actually said at the trial, though there is a brief indication in *The Scots Magazine,* XXXIV (June, 1772), 297.

[6] James Walvin, *Black and White: The Negro and English Society, 1555–1945* (London, 1973), *passim.* See also, Walvin, *The Black Presence: A Documentary*

1762 the Lord Chancellor laid down the maxim that "as soon as a man puts foot on English ground, he is free: a negro may maintain an action against his master for ill usage, and may have a Habeas Corpus, if restrained of his liberty." Three years later, in the first edition of his *Commentaries on the Laws of England,* Blackstone gloried in the knowledge that

this spirit of liberty is so deeply implanted in our constitution, and rooted even in our very soil, that a slave or negro, the moment he lands in England, falls under the protection of the laws, and with regard to all natural rights becomes *eo instanti* a freeman.[7]

These eloquent opinions, supported by the far more ancient doctrine that slavery was contrary to natural law, seemed to validate Lord Mansfield's reported statement, in the Somerset case, that

the state of slavery is of such a nature, that it is incapable of being introduced on any reasons, moral or political, but only by positive law, which preserves its force long after the reasons, occasion, and time itself from whence it was created is erased from memory. It is so odious, that nothing can be suffered to support it, but positive law.[8]

This judgment raises a number of general problems. Negro slavery had been established in the New World not by positive law but by impromptu decisions, the "reasons, occasion, and time" of which were soon erased from memory. In the Caribbean, Virginia, Maryland, and the Middle Colonies, for example, the law had come after the fact, giving validation by gradual regulation. The early history of New

---

History of the Negro in England, 1555–1860 (New York, 1972); and Edward Fiddes, "Lord Mansfield and the Sommersett Case," *Law Quarterly Review,* L (1934), 509–11.

[7] Smith *v.* Brown and Cooper, 2 *Ld. Raym.* 1274, 91 *Eng. Rep.* 556 (date uncertain); The Case of James Sommersett, a Negro, 20 *How. St. Tr.* 1 at 55 (1772); William Blackstone, *Commentaries on the Laws of England,* I (Oxford, 1765), 123.

[8] 20 *How. St. Tr.* 1 at 82. These were the words later cited in pivotal American decisions (see Story, *Conflict of Laws,* p. 158n.). It has been disputed whether Lord Mansfield actually delivered any general statement on the nature of slavery. There is evidence he did, but probably not precisely in the form reported by Lofft and Howell. It is certain he did not say, as claimed by various nineteenth-century writers, that the "air of England was too pure for a slave to breathe" (Fiddes, "Lord Mansfield and the Sommersett Case," p. 499 n. 2). For a somewhat different interpretation of the questions considered in this chapter, see William M. Wiecek's forthcoming article, in *The University of Chicago Law Review,* "*Somerset:* Lord Mansfield and the Legitimacy of Slavery in the Anglo-American World."

World slavery gave credence to the claim that the institution arose from international trade and custom, and required no other authorization.

Although international law had a belated development in England, Francis Hargrave, one of Somerset's attorneys, acknowledged the opinions of "civilians of great credit," including Hugo Grotius, Samuel Pufendorf, and Ulricus Huberus, who had insisted on the legality of human slavery.[9] According to leading Continental authorities on the law of nations, common practice proved the utility of an institution which natural reason could permit, if not sanction, and which judicial tribunals were therefore bound in some ways to uphold, especially when they turned from private obligations to the larger affairs of state.

Even Somerset's counsel conceded that English courts would have to give effect to a contract for the purchase of slaves abroad; Lord Mansfield affirmed that English law would respect and give effect to such agreements, as it in fact continued to do even after West Indian emancipation.[10] There was thus some logic to Edward Long's contention that a contract sanctioned by English courts and by international

[9] 20 *How. St. Tr.* 1 at 25–28. For views that slavery, even though contrary to the ideal of natural law, was sanctioned by the law of nations, see Davis, *The Problem of Slavery in Western Culture*, pp. 83, 108–10, 114–16, 118. In the preface to his monumental *Conflict of Laws* (1834), Story noted that his was the first treatise to appear on the subject in the English language. He could not comprehend why English lawyers had been "so utterly indifferent to all foreign jurisprudence." No doubt one of the things that made Hargrave's printed *Argument* so learned and novel was its acknowledgement of Continental jurists. It is interesting that the Mosaic code, which served as the model for slavery in seventeenth-century Massachusetts, continued to have some application even in eighteenth-century England. In Smith *v.* Gould (1706) attorneys for the plaintiff appealed to Leviticus in defense of chattel slavery (2 *Salk.* 666, 92 *Eng. Rep.* 338 [1706]; Somerset transcript, NYHS, p. 78).

[10] Somerset transcript, NYHS, pp. 82, 92; 20 *How. St. Tr.* 1 at 79; Graveson, *Status in the Common Law*, p. 29. As late as 1810, the Massachusetts Supreme Court ruled that a contract made in Africa for the sale of slaves could be enforced in the state, even though the law prohibited Massachusetts citizens from engaging in the slave trade. Chief Justice Theophilus Parsons noted that when the contract had been made, in 1802, slave trading was legal in Africa and in South Carolina, the slave ship's destination. He based his decision on the principle of comity. After distinguishing slavery from "marriages incestuous by the law of nature," he contended that enforcement of the contract could not injure the rights or interests of the citizens of Massachusetts. Justice Theodore Sedgwick, a fellow Federalist but a political enemy of Parsons, wrote a vigorous dissent that gave a generously liberal interpretation to the effects of the Somerset decision (Greenwood *v.* Curtis, 6 Mass. [Tyng] 358 [1810]).

custom could not be dissolved by the mere removal of the property to England. The African states, Long also pointed out, had as good a right as any European power to banish their criminals to any part of the world that would receive them. Nor could Englishmen challenge the validity of African justice, unless they were prepared to argue that innocent Englishmen were never banished or executed. Occasional injustices could not be allowed to invalidate the rules required for law and order. Long was by no means the only eighteenth-century British subject who thought of the social compact as

an association of the opulent and the good, for better preserving their acquisitions, against the poor and the wicked. For want, complicated with misery and vice, generally seeks relief by plundering from those who are better provided. An African is as much bound by this supreme power, as the English labourer.[11]

After the Somerset decision it was reassuring to think that slavery had always been repugnant to English law and that ignorance alone had muddied judicial verdicts. Yet both crown and Parliament had given open encouragement to the African slave trade.[12] Prior to the American Revolution, the government had repeatedly disallowed colonial laws restricting slave imports. No one could doubt that positive law subjected colonial slave property to the claims of English creditors. In eighteenth-century England there was nothing faintly resembling

[11] [Edward Long], *The History of Jamaica; or, General Survey of the Ancient and Modern State of that Island* . . . (3 vols., London, 1774), II, 390–93. Ironically, apologists for slavery often found themselves in the position of countering claims that the "savage" customs of Africa deserved no respect. Thus during the Somerset trial, John Dunning contended that Africans were not barbarians and that Europeans must respect their customs, procedures, and judgments, including those that had condemned James Somerset to bondage (20 *How. St. Tr.* 1 at 73). But Sergeant Davy announced the triumphant discovery that under the laws of Virginia (1705), any Negro brought into the colony, who could not prove that he had been free in England or some other Christian country, was deemed to be a slave. Therefore, "having been an African slave had nothing to do with it" (Somerset transcripts, NYHS, pp. 50–52). On the other hand, for Long and many others, the origins of slavery were subordinate to the need for maintaining order. Courts should accept the positive fact that Negroes like Somerset *were* slaves.

[12] In 1791, John Courtenay told the House of Commons that if the slave trade had been sanctioned by twenty-six acts of Parliament, as claimed, he could find twenty-six acts that gave sanction to witchcraft (*Parliamentary History,* XXIX [1791], 333). But this view would seem to have contradicted Mansfield's view that positive law preserves its force long after its original occasions have been forgotten.

judicial review of Parliamentary legislation. Lord Mansfield emphasized that while he had the power to declare the law, as it applied in
the case of Somerset, he could neither make nor create a law to fit
the occasion. He was in fact much concerned about the effects of his
decision on property rights, and suggested that English slaveholders
might seek redress by appealing to Parliament. In what appears to be
the most accurate text of his statement on positive law, he based his
judgment on a doctrine of judicial restraint:

The state of slavery is of such a nature, that it is incapable of being now
introduced by courts of justice upon mere reasoning or inferences from
any principles, natural or political; it *must* take its rise from *positive* law;
the origin of it can in no country or age be traced back to any other
source: immemorial usage preserves the memory of positive law long
after all traces of the occasion, reason, authority, and time of its introduction are lost; and, in a case so odious as the condition of slaves, must be
taken strictly.[13]

[13] *The Scot's Magazine*, XXXIV (1772), 298–99. This report, which legal
historians seem to have missed, gives a fuller and more coherent version of
Mansfield's concluding statement than does the brief and commonly cited
report in *The Annual Register, or a View of the History, and Literature, for
the Year 1772* (6th ed., London, 1800), p. 110. The latter omits any dictum
on the nature of slavery or positive law, a fact which has led Nadelhaft and
others to conclude that Mansfield made no such statement, and that Lofft "put
words, perhaps Hargrave's, into Mansfield's mouth" (Nadelhaft, "Somersett
Case and Slavery," pp. 200–1).

The Sharp papers, NYHS, contain a separate MS transcript of Mansfield's
judgment of June 22, 1772, which includes the following textual variation:
"Slavery has been different in different Ages and States: the exercise of the
power of a Master over his Slave must be supported by the Law of the particular
Countries; but no foreigner can *in England claim* a right *over a Man:* such a
Claim *is not known to the Laws of England.* Immemorial Usage preserves posi-
tive Law after the occasion or accident which gave rise to it has been forgotten.
And *tracing* the subject to natural principles the claim of Slavery never can be
supported. *The power claimed never was in use here, or acknowledged by the
Law.*"

I have already quoted the parallel passage from Howell, who followed Lofft.
The general theme of this "official" version is confirmed by the contemporary
versions in *The Scot's Magazine* and in the above MS. The *Annual Register*
version is clearly an abbreviated and inadequate summary. However, *The Scot's
Magazine* account contains phrases which significantly change the meaning from
that in Howell or the NYHS MS. According to the former text, Mansfield said
that slavery was incapable of being "now introduced by *courts of justice* upon
mere reasoning or inference from any principles, natural or political" (my ital.).
Following this normative judgment, he then stated that as a historical fact the

The earlier judicial cases concerning Negroes had little to do with the law of nations, maritime law, or even the legality of slavery in England. Rather, they involved civil disputes over the ownership of individual slaves, some of whom had obtained *de facto* freedom in England and had been employed for wages. In legal terms, the plaintiff commonly instituted an action of trespass or trover, the latter being a way of recovering the value of personal property wrongly converted by another for his own use.[14] The specific issue raised by such actions was whether English laws protecting personal property could be extended to protect the owners of errant slaves.

The number of slaves in England was relatively small, and the question appeared to raise no conflicts of vital interest. Prior to the Somerset case, the owners of West Indian slaves had little reason either to fear English public policy or to try to universalize slavery by pushing English courts toward a Dred Scott decision. The courts, however, faced a genuine dilemma. During the seventeenth century the juris-

---

origins of slavery could only be traced back to positive law—that is, not to judicial interpretation. And Mansfield's concept of positive law included "immemorial usage," whose original sanction had been lost from memory. Justice Lemuel Shaw later interpreted even the Howell version to mean "that by positive law, in this connection, may be as well, understood customary law, as the enactment of a statute; and the word is used to designate rules established by tacit acquiescence" (Story, *Conflict of Laws*, p. 159n.). If *The Scot's Magazine* report is accurate, Mansfield was not saying, as commonly interpreted, that slavery is so odious that it can only be supported by statutory law. He was simply maintaining that the character of slavery is such that the law must be "taken strictly." Of the various texts, the version in *The Scot's Magazine* is the most detailed and the most consistent with Mansfield's known views (Mansfield, or William Murray, was the son of a Scottish peer; at a time when Scots were less than popular in England, it is conceivable that a Scottish reporter would pay closer attention to the actual words of a countryman who had risen to such an exalted station). In short, the phrases in Howell and in the NYHS MS may be somewhat garbled versions of the text in *The Scot's Magazine*. I shall turn later on to Mansfield's specific ruling.

[14] The tort action of trover provided plantiffs with a wider remedy than trespass, since it embraced the right to possess property without the possession itself. On the other hand, trespass included the slightest interference, if unauthorized, with a plaintiff's goods, even if there was no challenge, as in trover, to the plaintiff's right of possession. There was much debate on the advantages and disadvantages of the two actions, and it appears that some of the judicial cases concerning slaves were decided by procedural technicalities (See C. H. S. Fifoot, *History and Sources of the Common Law: Tort and Contract* [London, 1949], pp. 102–12).

diction of common-law courts, resting on a variety of traditional writs, had steadily encroached upon the domain of the Court of Admiralty. The latter had been attuned to the "custom of merchants" and to the principles of international mercantile law, which drew on Roman and Continental precedents. Since the common law had been shaped by local customs regarding land tenure, status, and contract, it often ran counter to the interests and practices of the merchant community. Lord Mansfield, as Chief Justice of the Court of King's Bench, did much to adapt common law to the needs of merchants—especially by accepting the validity of customs which could not be defined as "immemorial." Yet he could not escape the contradiction between an alien form of commercial property and common-law traditions of domestic liberty.[15]

In eighteenth-century England there was no coherent body of labor law, but rather a hodgepodge of statutes, precedents, and rules of equity. As judges soon realized, there were no rules for regulating the subjects of a labor system totally foreign to the path of English development. Yet judicial decisions on slavery could be a testing ground which might help to define and clarify that path of development. In a nation where labor itself was rapidly becoming a depersonalized commodity, the economy required a consistent and predictable distinction between work discipline and personal rights. The defenders of slavery, pointing to the dependent status of wives and minors, argued that the bondsman received subsistence and protection in return for labor. The analogy between slaves and wives carried some weight, given the legal incapacities of married women. But the notion of absolute dependency could not easily be reconciled with established theories of contract and "legal consideration." It also ran counter to the central doctrine of "legal personality." The new economic man would work not for an individual master but for his own legal personality. It was this abstraction that made him responsible for his contractual obligations, for the support of his family, and for his debts.[16]

[15] Holdsworth, *History of English Law,* XII, 692–93; Harold Potter, *Potter's Historical Introduction to English Law and Its Institutions,* ed. and rev. by A. K. R. Kiralfy (4th ed., London, 1958), pp. 33, 48–49, 58–59.

[16] The point on legal personality is developed by Alexandre Kojève, *Introduction to the Reading of Hegel: Lectures on the "Phenomenology of Spirit,"* assembled by Raymond Queneau, ed. by Allan Bloom, tr. by James H. Nichols, Jr. (New York, 1969), pp. 63–65.

Personal Dominion versus Service

For slaveholding plaintiffs the clearest course was to argue that Negroes were merchandise, commonly bought and sold by European traders in accordance with the recognized law of nations. It was legally more hazardous for a court to acknowledge property rights in a Negro because he was a heathen or infidel. Such discrimination implied that baptism might bring the reward of freedom, as it did in certain jurisdictions under the rules of the East India Company. This question was ostensibly resolved in 1729 by the negative opinions of Sir Philip Yorke, the Attorney General, and Charles Talbot, the Solicitor General. Even Sergeant Davy conceded the point in the Somerset trial, perhaps out of deference to Lord Mansfield's known conviction that baptism could not alter legal status. But the growing consensus on baptism in effect eliminated the plea of religion as an excuse for enslavement.[17]

In 1706, Chief Justice Holt dismissed a trover action involving a "Negro," since the law took no notice of Negroes being different from other men. When Sir Philip Yorke became Lord Chancellor (and Lord Hardwicke), he pointed out that the description presented to Holt in 1706 should have read "Negro slave," since being a Negro did not necessarily imply being a slave. Hardwicke, who did much to fashion the modern system of equity, and who was much revered by Mansfield, his pupil, went beyond the trover issue and twice ruled that a Negro slave remained a slave when brought to England.[18] Yet the word

[17] John Codman Hurd, *The Law of Freedom and Bondage in the United States* (2 vols., Boston, 1858–1862), I, 180–81; Butts *v.* Penny, 2 *Lev.* 201, 83 *Eng. Rep.* 518 (1677); Gelly *v.* Cleve, 1 *Ld. Raym.* 147 (1694); Fiddes, "Lord Mansfield and the Sommersett Case," p. 501; Somerset transcript, NYHS, pp. 88–89. At the conclusion of the case of Lewis against Stapylton (1771), Mansfield asked, "Well am I not right as to my opinion that their being Christians don't take away the right of property?" John Dunning answered, "It does not my Lord." Mansfield added, "I was sure it did not" (MS report of the case of Lewis against Stapylton, Sharp papers, NYHS [hereafter Lewis transcript, NYHS]). The same conclusion had been sanctioned by Blackstone.

[18] Smith *v.* Gould, 2 *Salk.* 666, 92 *Eng. Rep.* 338 (1706); Pearne *v.* Lisle, *Amb.* 75, 27 *Eng. Rep.* 47 (1749); Holdsworth, *History of English Law*, XII, 237, 260. Both Yorke and Talbot were elevated to the office of Lord Chancellor. Their opinions of 1729, given in response to merchants' appeals for security, carried enormous weight, but were by no means equivalent to case law. When Granville and James Sharp employed the attorney of the Lord Mayor's Office to

"slave" carried connotations of personal dominion, discipline, and control which were difficult to assimilate to English law. Samuel Estwick, the assistant agent for Barbados, expressed confidence that the Somerset case would have had a different outcome if Charles Stuart, the master, had claimed Somerset as his "commercial property." This would have conformed with the 1729 opinions of Yorke and Talbot, which were much respected by Lord Mansfield, and would also have prevented irrelevant debates on villeinage. Estwick, who called slavery an "odious word," thought the issues should have been strictly limited to trade and property (as might have been the case in the Court of Admiralty).[19] In a sense, the framers of the United States Constitution later took Estwick's course, and avoided the odious word while giving comfort and protection to the owners of slaves. It was impossible, however, for common-law courts, governed as they were by ancient writs and procedures, to separate property rights from questions of status and dominion.

Personal dominion was the point at issue in Somerset. In 1769, Charles Stuart brought his slave, James Somerset, from Virginia to England. In October, 1771, Somerset deserted his master, and a month later was seized by Stuart's agents and locked in chains aboard a Jamaica-bound ship.[20] In deciding to sell the Negro in Jamaica, Stuart

---

defend them against writs of trespass, in the Jonathan Strong case, the attorney was so intimidated by the 1729 opinions that he told them they could not be defended and advised them to compromise (MS "An Account of the Occasion which compelled Granville Sharp to study Law, and undertake the defence of the Negroe Slaves in England," John A. Woods's transcripts of Sharp papers [hereafter JAW]).

[19] Samuel Estwick, *Considerations on the Negroe Cause, Commonly So Called, Addressed to the Right Honourable Lord Mansfield, Lord Chief Justice of the Court of King's Bench* (2nd ed., London, 1773), pp. xii–xiv, 21, 31, 39 (the 1st ed., 1772, was anonymous, as was a long letter, almost certainly from Estwick's pen, in *Gentleman's Magazine*, XLII [July, 1772], 307–9). Although there were some legal precedents against the position of Yorke and Talbot, both the facts and reporting were often vague, and the cases sometimes turned on faulty declarations. Davy admitted that in Chamberline *v.* Harvey (1696–1697), where the court had supposedly given opinion that no trespass would "lie" for taking away a man generally, the issue of slavery itself had never been decided, since the Attorney General had asked that a decision be withheld until he could be heard, and no judgment had been given (Somerset transcript, NYHS, p. 76).

[20] Stuart, who was cashier and paymaster of customs, actually took Somerset to England by way of Boston. His letters from London to Boston show far less concern over the Somerset case than over the financial panic which hit England at the time of the final court proceedings, a panic which threatened to reduce

acted not only as a property owner, but as a master disciplining a rebellious servant. Before the ship sailed, Lord Mansfield granted a writ of *habeas corpus,* ordering the ship's captain to bring Somerset to court and to file a return showing the cause of detainer. On December 9, Captain John Knowles produced "the body of Somerset," together with a return which appealed to the acknowledged legality of the slave trade and British colonial slavery, and which argued that Somerset had been brought as a slave from Africa to Virginia, whose laws obliged him to serve for life. During his temporary stay in England, Somerset had "without the consent, and against the will of the said Charles Steuart [*sic*], and without any lawful authority whatsoever, departed and absenteed himself from the service of the said Charles Steuart, and absolutely refused to return."[21]

---

many affluent families to a kind of bondage. He wrote James Murray that "the West India Planters and Merchants have taken [the case] off my hands, and I shall be entirely directed by them in the further defence of it" (Massachusetts Historical Society *Proceedings,* XLIII (1890), 451–52).

[21] 20 *How. St. Tr.* 1 at 1–23. Granville Sharp's role in the case is partly described in Prince Hoare, *Memoirs of Granville Sharp, Esq. Composed from His Own Manuscripts* . . . (London, 1820), pp. 70–92, and in Sharp's account, JAW. By April, 1769, Sharp was much afraid of being held in contempt of court, after circulating manuscript arguments to various lawyers. He had also been issuing legal threats to various slaveholders (Sharp to Oliphant, March 8, 1768, Hull Museum). Two years later he wrote a highly critical account of Mansfield's "inexcusable" behavior in the Lewis case, charging that Mansfield's refusal to give judgment was a contempt of the legislature and a breach of law. Sharp wisely refrained from circulating these remarks, saying that he would hold them in "reserve" in the event that the Lewis case were used as a precedent.

Hoare's account is clearly wrong in stating that Somerset was seized by Stuart after January 13, 1772. Sharp claimed that Somerset first came to him on January 13, accompanied by a compositor employed by Sharp, to complain of Stuart's treatment. But Captain Knowles had already given Somerset over to the custody of the court on December 9, 1771, at which time Sergeant Davy had asked for time to prepare his argument against the return. It is certain that Sharp remained cautiously in the background, although he gave Davy the private remarks he had written on Manfield's conduct. Francis Hargrave had communicated with Sharp as early as May, 1769, and had been digesting Sharp's arguments against slavery (Hargrave to Sharp, May 17, 1769, JAW). On January 25, 1772, Hargrave informed Sharp of the impending Somerset case, though he assumed Sharp might already be familiar with it, and offered advice on legal strategy (Sharp papers, NYHS). Six days later Hargrave received a retainer in the case, and assured Sharp that while he feared for his own inexperience, since he had never argued a case publicly before, he would not be lacking in zeal (NYHS). Davy and Glynn presented their first arguments on February 7; Mansfield then postponed further hearings to Easter term, when Hargrave and Alleyne joined

Lord Mansfield had no doubts that the law should enforce obligations of personal service. Moreover, when slaves brought to England had occasionally been impressed into military service, he had used writs of *habeas corpus* to deliver the slaves back to their lawful masters. Though determined to avoid the question of the legality of slavery in England, he was unsure whether the cause on the return was sufficient, or more precisely, whether English law recognized a species of dominion that would allow a master to ship an unruly servant out of the kingdom.[22]

In earlier cases, such as Chamberline *v.* Harvey (1696/1697), plaintiffs had used villeinage as evidence that English law accepted a state of nearly absolute personal dominion. Everyone agreed that no English court had heard a claim of villeinage since the early seventeenth century. Following the lead of Granville Sharp, Sergeants Davy and John Glynn opened the case for Somerset by describing villeinage as the relic of a tyrannical age. Its extinction, said Davy, was "nothing more than a general Assertion of the natural Rights of Mankind, according to the Temper, Disposition, and Spirit of the People of this Country." But English judges were not prepared to agree, along with Condorcet and Granville Sharp, that precedents could be impeached by a "higher law" of reason. If villeinage had disappeared, it was not for that reason illegal. Lord Mansfield expressed the conviction that villeinage *regardant* to a manor had been abolished by statute; yet he and lawyers on both sides acknowledged that in theory a man might still confess himself to be a villein *in gross*—in order to escape, for example, the claims of creditors or other liabilities that legally fell on his master.[23] Moreover, even Francis Hargrave, who joined in the final defense of Somerset, conceded that

---

the antislavery side, and Wallace and Dunning defended Captain Knowles. Meanwhile, Sharp furnished Alleyne with fresh information on how slavery endangered the liberty of whites in America. And he raised funds for the case from wealthy philanthropists like John Fothergill (NYHS). Although Sharp never appeared at the trial, he persuaded Somerset to refuse any compromise offer of manumission.

[22] Lewis transcript, NYHS; 20 *How. St. Tr.* 1 at 70–71, 79–82.

[23] Chamberline *v.* Harvey, 1 *Ld. Raym.* 146, 92 *Eng. Rep.* 603 (1696–1697); Somerset transcript, NYHS, pp. 27–30, 100–7, and *passim;* [Marie Jean Antoine Nicholas de Caritat, Marquis de Condorcet], *Réflexions sur l'esclavage des nègres, par M. Schwartz* (Neufchatel, 1781), pp. 1–2, 13, 29–30; 20 *How. St. Tr.* 1 at 31–34, 40–41, 48, 56–57, 69, 74; *The Scot's Magazine*, XXXIV, 298.

the condition of a villein had most of the incidents which I have before described in giving the idea of slavery in general. His service was uncertain and indeterminate, such as his lord thought fit to require; or, as some of our ancient writers express it, he knew not in the evening what he was to do in the morning, he was bound to do whatever he was commanded. He was liable to beating, imprisonment, and every other chastisement his lord might prescribe, except killing and maiming. He was incapable of acquiring property for his own benefit. . . . He was himself the subject of property; as such saleable and transmissible. . . . Lastly, the slavery extended to the issue.[24]

But it was a serious mistake, as Samuel Estwick realized, for slave-holders to appeal to the precedent or analogy of villeinage. Refining and improving upon the arguments of Davy and Glynn, Hargrave explained that villeinage was always local and prescriptive, extending over a "time whereof no memory runs to the contrary." It was necessary for a lord to prove that villeinage was ancient and immemorial, that the condition had passed without interruption through the blood of a long line of ancestors. If a villain could show that he was a bastard, or in any other way cast doubt on the certainty of his ancestry, he had a legitimate claim to freedom. Obviously, this kind of servitude could not apply to foreigners or to any form of dominion or disability originating outside England. Hargrave's position was both stronger and subtler than Sharp's idealistic view that villeinage had always been illegal and had finally been abolished by a triumphant common law. Hargrave conceded that English law authorized a kind of slavery. Yet the same living law excluded "every slavery not commencing in England, every slavery though commencing there not being antient and immemorial." In other words, the only slavery that could be legal in England was that which had long been extinct.[25]

[24] 20 *How. St. Tr.* 1 at 36–37.

[25] *Ibid.*, 41–48; Hargrave, *Argument*, pp. 35–45; Somerset transcript, NYHS, pp. 20–33, 100–14; Granville Sharp, *A Representation of the Injustice and Dangerous Tendency of Tolerating Slavery; Or of Admitting the Least Claim of Private Property in the Persons of Men, in England* (London, 1769), pp. 107–8; Sharp to Arthur Lee, 1773, Sharp papers, NYHS. The arguments of Davy and Glynn were closer to Sharp's position than was that of Hargrave. All of Somerset's attorneys stressed the mitigation and gradual extinction of villeinage, but whereas Davy and Glynn argued that villeinage was an evil that had at best been tolerated by the courts and that had finally given way to the rule of law, Hargrave held, at least in his published argument, that villeinage was still legal and excluded all other forms of bondage. On the other hand, Hargrave

The precedent of villeinage also made slaveholders vulnerable by confusing the distinction between claims to property and claims to personal service. Though villeins were saleable and transmissible, as Hargrave said, their hereditary obligation to serve a particular family stood out above any theoretical marketability. The terms *in gross* and *regardant* indicated the modes by which a lord could plead his title to a villein, the former referring to a deed or confession and the latter to the manor itself. Hargrave cited a trespass case in which the defendant pleaded that the plaintiff was a villein *regardant* to his manor, but the plaintiff claimed that his great-grandfather had been born in a different county and that the connection between his ancestors and the manor had thus begun "within time of memory." The property element was crucial in establishing title, but was clearly subordinate to the claim of service.[26]

In the trespass case of Chamberline *v.* Harvey, which received lengthy discussion in the Somerset trial, and which involved an action brought by an heir for the recovery of a Negro employed in England as a free worker, the plaintiff's counsel argued that the status of a Barbadian slave was analogous to that of a villein *regardant* to a manor. The court decided that a trespass action could not be sustained for a Negro, who could only be termed a "slavish servant." The master could recover for loss of service, but not for the value of the servant. This precedent seemed important to Stuart's (nominally Captain Knowles's) counsel, who rightly feared that Somerset might be discharged without compensation to Stuart for loss of service. They pointed out that in Chamberline the court would have accepted an action *per quod servitium amisit,* for loss of service; that "if they allowed the means of suing a right, they allowed the right. The opinion cited, to prove the negroes free on coming hither, only declares them not saleable; does not take away their service." Stuart's counsel sought to establish, therefore, that Stuart's claim did not require that either trover or trespass should be admissible for a Negro.[27]

---

borrowed many points from Davy, and according to the report in *The Scot's Magazine,* contended that the law of England "had constantly discountenanced slavery, in the established form of villeinage, until it was totally abolished" (p. 297). Perhaps he altered his position after the trial.

[26] Davis, *Problem of Slavery in Western Culture,* p. 34 n. 8; 20 *How. St. Tr.* 1 at 41–47.

[27] Chamberline *v.* Harvey, 1 *Ld. Raym.* 146, 92 *Eng. Rep.* 603; 20 *How. St. Tr,* 1 at 70, 76. According to *The Scot's Magazine,* James Wallace threw "new

It is conceivable that slaveholders would have fared better in English courts if they had consistently developed this position. As we have seen, Lord Mansfield looked favorably on masters' claims to service; he urged the parties in Somerset and other cases to reach agreement outside of court, much to the dismay and anger of Granville Sharp. Even William Blackstone, to whom Sharp confidently appealed for legal advice, thought that a master's right to service might continue after bringing a slave to England. I have already quoted Blackstone's idealistic view, expressed in the first edition (1765) of his *Commentaries,* that "a slave or negro, the moment he lands in England, falls under the protection of the laws and with regard to all natural rights becomes *eo instanti* a freeman." In the third edition (1768–1769) he revised the sentence as follows: "falls under the protection of the laws, and so far becomes a freeman; though the master's right to his service may probably [possibly] still continue."[28]

On February 20, 1769, Blackstone cautioned Sharp against using the passage from the first edition "as decisive in favour of your Doctrine." Sharp and others had misunderstood Blackstone's position, which should have been clear from a qualification that appeared in the first edition:

Yet, with regard to any right which the master may have acquired, by

---

and interesting light" on the question, after presenting many learned arguments in behalf of Captain Knowles. The "new light" apparently referred to Wallace's argument that it was "a known and allowed practice, in mercantile transactions, if the cause arises abroad, to lay it within the kingdom: therefore the contract in Virginia might be laid to be in London, and would not be traversable. With respect to other cases, the particular mode of action was alone objected to; had it been an action 'per quod servitium amisit,' for loss of service, the Court would have allowed it" (20 *How. St. Tr.* 1 at 70). In *The Scot's Magazine* account, Mansfield interrogated Wallace closely, "particularly on that of contending, that the relation between a negro and his owner might be well maintained on the ground of a contract between master and servant, which was incontrovertibly known to be binding by the established usages and statute laws of the land." But Mansfield then remarked that the nature of the proceedings contradicted this assertion in the strongest terms, and he seemed to reject the very idea of a contract between the parties (p. 297).

[28] In the 4th ed. (Oxford, 1770), Blackstone changed "probably" to "possibly" (Holdsworth, *History of English Law,* X, 658n.). Blackstone's footnote, following "so far becomes a freeman," referred to Holt's famous dictum (*Salk.* 666). I have used the 1st and 5th eds., and the excerpts in 20 *How. St. Tr.* 1 at 28–30n. The textual changes are discussed in Fiddes, "Lord Mansfield and the Sommersett Case," pp. 506–7, but with slight inaccuracies.

contract or the like, to the perpetual service of John or Thomas, this will remain exactly in the same state as before. . . . The slave is entitled to the same liberty [changed to "protection" in later editions] in England before, as after, baptism; and, whatever service the heathen negro owed to his English master, the same is he bound to render when a christian.

Blackstone reportedly told Sharp that a slave's service could be likened to an apprenticeship or implied contract. In a letter he added "that I have never peremptorily said, that 'the Master *hath* acquired any right to the perpetual Service of John or Thomas' . . . I only say that 'if he did, that obligation is not dissolved by his coming to England and turning Christian.' " Hargrave tried to challenge this slippery position by repeating Sharp's arguments on coercion annulling any contract. But the Somerset case left the issue unresolved.[29]

Slaveholders could not really be content with a claim to service alone. To answer their purpose, as Hargrave made clear, "it must be a contract to serve the master here; and when he leaves this country to return with him into America, where the slavery will again attach upon the negro." Such needs virtually precluded compromise. As Davy put it:

Either this man remains upon his Arrival in England in the Condition he was abroad in Virginia or he does not. . . . If he does so remain the Master's Power remains as before—If the Laws having attached upon him abroad are at all to affect him here, it brings them all, either all the Laws of Virginia are to attach upon him here or none—for where will they draw the Line?[30]

[29] Blackstone to Sharp, Oct. 11, 1768; memo to Sharp, Feb. 20, 1769, Sharp papers, NYHS; Blackstone, *Commentaries* (1st ed.), I, 412–13. The text in the 5th ed. reads: "Yet, with regard to any right which the master may have acquired to the perpetual service of John or Thomas, this will remain exactly in the same state as before. . . . The slave is entitled to the same protection in England before, as after, baptism; and, whatever service the heathen negro owed to his American master, the same is he to render when brought to England and made a christian" [Dublin, 1773], I, 424–35). It should be added that on May 25, 1769, Blackstone wished Sharp success "in his humane undertaking" (NYHS).
[30] 20 *How. St. Tr.* 1 at 64–66; Somerset transcript, NYHS, pp. 47–48, 68, 113–14, 118–24. It is important to note, however, that later apologists for slavery in the American South sometimes denied that the *person* of the slave was property. Thus as defined by E. N. Elliott, "Slavery is the duty and obligation of the slave to labor for the mutual benefit of both master and slave, under a warrant to the slave of protection, and a comfortable subsistence, under all circumstances. The person of the slave is not property, no matter what the fictions of the law may say; but the right to his labor is property, and may be

In 1749, Lord Hardwicke had taken the absolutist position that a slave's status was in no way changed by coming to England, and had also asserted that trover could apply to a villein—an opinion later rejected by Estwick and other defenders of slavery, since trover implied unlimited ownership of personal property. Hardwicke's extremism made it easier for Davy to swing to the opposite pole and to claim, in words that would be popularly interpreted as the verdict of the Somerset decision, that the air of England was "too pure for a slave to breathe in."

There was still another way in which discussions of villeinage favored the cause of liberty. Though English lawyers often showed traditional restraint in approaching the subject of progress, the Somerset case provided an irresistible opportunity to review the entire history of civil liberty. "It is the pride of this Country," Davy said, "that it looks upon all other Countries in a bad Light—as this is the only Country where they are free." If Englishmen had once suffered from tyranny, it had been destroyed "by the Genius of the People": "What is most striking in the present Enquiry is that the people themselves—and the Interpreters and Oracles of the Law—who were the Judges—they in all Ages seem to have revolted against Villenage." An infamous law to enslave rogues and vagabonds, under Edward VI, had been repealed by Parliament. For bondage "was a State which an English Mind revolts at—The English Constitution could not bear that any Set of Men under any Circumstances should be put in such a State in this Country." And since the reign of Elizabeth, the laws and air of England had become gradually purer. Sergeant Glynn warned that the issue at hand involved far more than the liberty of an individual: "It would be injurious to [and] affect the General System . . . violating one of the most fundamental Principles of that Constitutional Liberty. . . . It will be productive of Consequences

---

transferred like any other property, or as the right to the services of a minor and apprentice may be transferred. Nor is the labor of the slave solely for the benefit of the master, but for the benefit of all concerned; for himself, to repay the advances made for his support in childhood, for present subsistence, and for guardianship and protection, and to accumulate a fund for sickness, disability, and old age. . . . Such is American slavery, or as Mr. Henry Hughes happily terms it, 'Warranteeism'" (E. N. Elliot, ed., *Cotton is King, and Proslavery Arguments* [Augusta, Ga., 1860], p. vii). One can't help wondering whether Blackstone and Mansfield might not have accepted such an argument.

prejudicial to the Peace and dangerous to the Liberty of the Kingdom if once introduced."[31]

It was one thing, however, to celebrate the disappearance of villeinage and the extension of civil liberty, and quite another to define the proper limits of personal dominion. In Scotland, for example, the case of Knight *v.* Wedderburn (1777–1778) brought a renewed appreciation for a statute of 1701 "for preventing wrongous imprisonment and against undue delays in trials," a law which was said to be far more favorable to liberty than the Habeas Corpus Act of England. Yet even the defenders of Joseph Knight, the Jamaican Negro taken to Scotland, insisted that society required a degree of subordination within certain specified boundaries. If the idea of slavery seemed antithetical to the emerging ideology of contractual relations in a free society, jurists were also reluctant to endorse any far-reaching principles which might encourage insubordination or undermine mercantilist theories of manpower and public policy. As an alternative, they searched for ways to accommodate the ideal of freedom with social utility. Thus, at the conclusion of Lewis *v.* Stapylton (1771), Lord Mansfield expressed the following opinion on the legality of holding men as property in England: "I hope it never will be finally discussed. For I wou'd have all Masters think they were Free and all negroes think they were not because then they wo'd both behave better."[32]

It is naïve to read the judicial cases as clear-cut struggles between the champions of freedom and the self-interested defenders of slavery. Both sides were caught in an internal conflict between utility, as defined by the propertied classes, and an allegiance to the principles of freedom and contract as expounded by Locke, Montesquieu, and Blackstone. The latter sources provided Davy and Hargrave with a strong theoretical indictment of slavery in any form; yet they significantly compromised themselves by admitting the legality of slavery in America: "By an unhappy concurrence of circumstances, the slavery of negroes is thought to have become necessary in America; and therefore in America our legislature has permitted the slavery of negroes. But the slavery of negroes is unnecessary in England." If it had proved

[31] Somerset transcript, NYHS, pp. 20–33, 44–45, 96, 100–2; Hargrave, *Argument,* pp. 23–24. Davy also emphasized economic progress: Villeinage, by denying the incentive of reward, led to the "wretched management" of estates and thus to low returns on investment.

[32] 20 *How. St. Tr.* 1 at 5, 7, 9, 19–20n.; Lewis transcript, NYHS, p. 79.

necessary, Hargrave's libertarian arguments would presumably have lost their force.[33]

Contract and Consent: Toward a Free Labor Ideology

The compromise between utility and principle becomes less mystifying when one examines some further implications of contract and consent. Hargrave held that

the law of England may perhaps give effect to a contract of service for life; but that is the *ne plus ultra* of servitude by contract in England. . . . It will not permit the servant to incorporate into his contract the ingredients of slavery.[34]

Somerset's counsel, following Montesquieu, Blackstone, and Sharp, argued that every sale implies a price, "an equivalent given to the seller in lieu of what he transfers to the buyer"; in the case of slavery, however, "the buyer gives nothing, and the seller receives nothing." Phrased positively, and closer to the famous position of Locke, liberty is a priceless and inalienable possession, essential to self-preservation. In Knight *v.* Wedderburn these principles led to the conclusion that the law of Scotland would not support a voluntary contract for lifetime service without wages; that "the defender had no right to the Negro's service for any space of time."[35]

No doubt the intent of such judgments was to protect the liberty of potential self-sellers, although according to Rousseau, only a madman could truly *consent* to any form of subordination. And in Rousseau's eyes, the myth of consent disguised the fraud and coercion that kept most of mankind in bondage. The justifications for slavery were no more absurd than the justifications for all forms of privilege and inequality.[36] One need not be a Rousseauist to see the ideological

[33] 20 *How. St. Tr.* 1 at 59–60; Somerset transcript, NYHS, 60, 65, 82, 91–92.

[34] 20 *How. St. Tr.* 1 at 50. Davy also admitted that a man might enter into service for life, but insisted that he could not sell himself as a slave (Somerset transcript, NYHS, p. 86).

[35] Somerset transcript, NYHS, pp. 86–87; 20 *How. St. Tr.* 1 at 6, 7 n., 29–30, 49–50; Helen T. Catterall, ed., *Judicial Cases Concerning American Slavery and the Negro* (Washington, 1926–1937), I, 18, F. T. H. Fletcher, "Montesquieu's Influence on Anti-Slavery Opinion in England," *Journal of Negro History,* XVIII (Oct., 1933), 419–20.

[36] Jean-Jacques Rousseau, *The Social Contract and Discourses,* tr. by G. D. H. Cole (London, 1930), pp. 5, 9–13, 215, 227–28.

importance of the no-self-sale doctrine. If English and Scottish courts had admitted that a man might legitimately consent to become a slave, they would have jeopardized all the legal fictions concerning "voluntary labor"—the fictions so essential for separating status from tenure and for redistributing legal liability. No worker, said the courts, could sell himself and then become perpetually dependent. But a worker who accepted token wages could be defined as free, even if in fact he remained perpetually dependent.

Obviously, many men and women have voluntarily degraded themselves for a price. It was not fortuitous, however, that juristic arguments against slavery sometimes included defenses of extreme forms of labor dependency. A remarkable example appears in the memorials or "informations" presented by eminent Scottish jurists in Knight *v.* Wedderburn. Both sides argeed that certain Scottish colliers and salters had been bound for life in the coal mines and salt works where they labored; that such workers were not free to change employment, and were sold by owners along with the property. Although this practice was abolished by statute in 1775, at almost precisely the time when the memorials were written, the jurists did not condemn industrial slavery as a violation of human rights. Rather, they debated whether Marco Polo had seen coal before traveling to China and whether Scotland "was very much covered with wood during the reigns of the Jameses." The purpose of these odd digressions was to prove either that industrial bondage was a fairly recent innovation or that it derived from ancient villeinage.[37]

Judge Allan Maconochie (afterwards, Lord Meadowbank), who supported the cause of Joseph Knight, contended that the binding of miners and salters was of recent origin and could not be used to show the continuation or extension of the laws of villeinage. The condition of colliers and salters was simply the product of economic expediency, and could not be construed as giving general sanction to the principle of slavery. Since Maconochie's defensive arguments were linked with antislavery principles, they are worth quoting at some length:

In the infancy of improvement men are apt to adopt expedients for removing the obstructions it meets with, and other evils which they feel, but the nature and effectual remedies of which they do not comprehend. Thus incorporations and monopolies on the one hand, and on the other

[37] 20 *How. St. Tr.* 1 at 1–12n.

restraints on the members of incorporations and on monopolies have originated. *In the same way it was very natural to seek a curb for the indolence or capriciousness of coalliers, whose high wages, like those of many
other kinds of workmen, disposed them to idleness, faction, or arrogance.*
All regulations, however, framed with such views, are evidently commercial, and never can be construed as either favouring liberty or slavery,
any more than the act of navigation, or any other thing of the same
nature.

By defining such bondage as a "commercial regulation," Maconochie sought to insulate it from moral criticism. The question was
purely one of economic "improvement" and labor discipline, and had
no bearing on personal rights or dominion. Utility alone was the
guide:

The art of working coal successfully requires long practice to attain, *and
is prejudicial to the health of those who are not early accustomed to it.*
It was, therefore, extremely natural, when coal works were begun to be
set on foot, that the proprietors should, in return for the high wages they
gave the workmen, take them bound to continue in their service for a long
term of years, or for life; accordingly we find, that it was at first customary
to take such bonds from coalliers; and, it is known, that the practice continued after the intervention of parliament had superseded the necessity
of it.[38]

Obviously this argument echoed the West Indian planters' claims
that field labor would be "prejudicial to the health" of white men,
that the labor needs of a plantation economy could only be met by
Negro slaves, and that bondage was a necessary curb on indolence,
faction, and arrogance. This was precisely the utilitarian and "commercial" mentality that gave British plantation slavery its shamelessly
exploitive character. In most respects Maconochie's apology for industrial bondage was like a caricature of the proslavery argument.
Indeed, no West Indian could quite match two of Maconochie's
absurdities. He gravely insisted that a Scottish collier—some of whom
wore collars bearing their owners' names—was "capable of being
elected a member of parliament." He also claimed that lawyers were
as much "slaves" as colliers, since lawyers were sometimes obliged to
plead causes whether they wished to or not![39]

The significant point, however, is not Maconochie's insensitivity,

[38] *Ibid.*, 8–10n. (my ital.).
[39] *Ibid.*, 9 n.; Paul Mantoux, *The Industrial Revolution in the Eighteenth
Century,* rev. ed., tr. by Marjorie Vernon (New York, 1929), pp. 74–75.

but his conviction that wages signified freedom. A collier might be sold with the mine to which he was bound for life. But his "high wages" meant that he belonged to "a profession which is voluntarily embraced"—even though, as Maconochie admitted, the profession was "prejudicial to the health of those who are not early accustomed to it," which meant that workers were virtually colliers from birth. A similar conclusion had been advanced in 1771 by John Millar, the brilliant Professor of Civil Law at the University of Glasgow, a social theorist who greatly strengthened the economic argument against West Indian slavery. The Scottish colliers, Millar argued, would not suffer such degradation unless they received more sustenance than they would as free workers. Millar considered this bondage an archaic and expensive system of labor, but he was willing to make allowance for the mine owners' acceptance of inflated labor costs. Such economic waste could be explained by the temporary need for concentrating and supervising labor in one place.[40]

These examples highlight the importance of wages as a symbol of exchange and thus of voluntarism even in a situation of nearly absolute subordination. For antislavery advocates like Millar and Maconochie it was not the slave's subordination or lack of mobility that ran contrary to nature. It was rather the lack of any token of exchange which would make the worker responsible, at least theoretically, for his own destiny. Of course, one might object that the slave received sustenance in exchange for labor; and that according to Millar and his mentor, Adam Smith, this sustenance would probably amount to more than would be paid in wages for the same work performed. The amount of compensation, however, was not the issue. Indeed, for the advocates of laissez faire, any guaranteed compensation, no matter how minimal, was as much a brake on progress as were other economic privileges.

One finds a certain arbitrariness in the antislavery distinction between wages and sustenance. Hargrave, for example, paraphrased Grotius's definition of slavery as "an obligation to serve another for life, in consideration of being supplied with the bare necessaries of life." His own definition, however, totally evaded the question of exchange. And although Hargrave focused on the injustice of absolute

---

[40] John Millar, *The Origin of the Distinction of Ranks; or, An Inquiry into the Circumstances which Give Rise to Influence and Authority in the Different Members of Society* (3rd ed., London, 1781), pp. 341, 354–59.

and hereditary subordination, he dealt cautiously with the prestigious jurists who had argued for the utility of a limited domestic slavery as an antidote for unemployment and domestic disorder.[41]

When one looks closer at the legal arguments against slavery, the "inconsistencies" begin to form a pattern: ideological needs define the meaning and limits of voluntarism. One could begin with Montesquieu, who provided jurists with a basic arsenal of antislavery arguments and who also mapped the routes of compromise. Montesquieu's logic demolished all the classical justifications for slavery and thus weakened appeals to tradition. But when he shifted from abstract syllogisms to specific cases, Montesquieu conceded that slavery might be founded on natural reason in tropical countries, where the heat made men lazy and unwilling to do heavy work except in fear of punishment. In Europe, he said, there were more *effective* inducements to voluntary labor.[42] Blackstone repeated Montesquieu's arguments on consent and contract, but he also held that an American master might have a lawful right to the perpetual service of his slave, a right which would take the form of an implied contract in England. The analogy Blackstone used is of particularly significance: "For this is no more than the same state of subjection for life, which every apprentice submits to for the space of seven years, or sometimes for a longer term."[43]

These rather enigmatic words acquire more meaning when juxtaposed with the remarks of John Dunning, the former Solicitor General who had worked with Granville Sharp in *Lewis v. Stapylton*, who took the opposite side one year later in the Somerset case, and who was, according to William Holdsworth, "universally acknowledged to be at the head of the common law and equity bars."[44] In defending Stuart,

---

[41] 20 *How. St. Tr.* 1 at 25–28.

[42] Davis, *Problem of Slavery in Western Culture*, pp. 394–95, 402–9.

[43] Blackstone, *Commentaries* (1st ed.), I, 413.

[44] Dunning, who became Lord Ashburton in 1782, was dismissed from office in 1770 because of his opposition to the government's American policy. In 1765 he had won a reputation by attacking the legality of general warrants. He also spoke out against the disabilities suffered by Catholics. Holdsworth expresses regret that Dunning never became Lord Chancellor (*History of English Law*, XII, 562–63). Sharp, on the other hand, bitterly noted that Dunning had held Sharp's own *Representation* in hand when declaring in 1771 that there could be no property in men in England; the very next year he appeared on the opposite side: "This is an abominable practice of lawyers to undertake causes diametrically opposite to their own declared opinions of Law and Common Justice" (Lewis transcript, NYHS). Yet Charles Stuart was no more pleased by Dunning's per-

Dunning first elaborated on the distinction, implicit in Montesquieu and Blackstone, between an existing relationship and its origin: "Whichever way it was formed, the consequences, good or ill, follow from the relation, not the manner of producing it." He then turned to the fiction of voluntarism:

I may observe, there is an establishment, by which magistrates compel idle or dissolute persons, of various ranks and denominations, to serve. In the case of apprentices bound out by the parish, neither the trade is left to the choice of those who are to serve, nor the consent of parties necessary; no contract therefore is made in the former instance, none in the latter; the duty remains the same.

He added:

Our legislature, where it finds a relation existing, supports it in all suitable consequences, without using to enquire how it commenced. A man enlists for no specified time; the contract in construction of law, is for a year; the legislature, when once the man is enlisted, interposes annually to continue him in the service, as long as the public has need of him. In times of public danger he is forced into the service . . . as much and as absolutely, as if by contract he had so disposed of himself.[45]

Dunning's examples showed that even in England there were not always sufficient inducements to voluntary labor. The actual status of many British workers could be described "as if by contract" they had accepted perpetual dependency. To condemn Dunning's respect for useful existing relationships, out of a concern for abstract justice, might well lead one to the conclusions of Rousseau. On the other hand, it could always be argued that vagabonds, apprentices, and sailors were much freer than slaves, and that therefore miners and factory workers were, by comparison, truly free men.

The Somerset and Knight cases reinforced Britain's reputation as a free country, and seemed to confirm Blackstone's famous maxim that the spirit of liberty was so deeply rooted in the very soil of Britain that even a Negro, the moment he set foot on the land, came under the protection of British laws. But the domestic implications of "outlawing slavery" extended much further.

The growth of Negro slavery in Britain would clearly have threat-

formance: "Dunning was dull and languid, and would have made a much better figure on the other side" (Massachusetts Historical Society *Proceedings*, XLIII, 451).

[45] 20 *How. St. Tr.* 1 at 75–76.

ened public order as well as the emerging free-labor ideology. Somerset's counsel emphasized the danger of augmenting the existing and free-floating population of some 14,000 to 15,000 blacks, who were termed "foreign superfluous inhabitants . . . a nation of enemies in the heart of the state." When Sergeant Davy exclaimed that the air of England was too pure for a slave to breathe in, he was not inviting more slaves to come and breathe the freedom-giving air. He made it clear that the air of England was also too pure for a Negro to breathe in. He wished to prevent the influx of Negroes, "for now and then we have some Accidents of Children born of an Odd Colour." Unless a law were passed to prevent such immigration, Davy said, "I don't know what our Progeny may be, I mean of what Colour—a Freeman of this country may in the course of time be the grandfather of half a Score of Slaves for what we know." Negroes, in short, should be kept where they belonged—in the West Indies: "There are sufficient Laws in all the Plantations to prevent Slaves being brought over—there can be no danger of a Man's Escaping and so coming into this Country."[46] Davy suggested to Lord Mansfield a highly revealing distinction:

If the Owner of a Slave from Africa or America was to bring him into this Country—if he comes with his Master into this Country, the Master himself Manumits him [i.e., by accepting the effects of the law]. But if he escapes and comes here not being brought by his Master—it should not have that operation.[47]

By the 1770s there was a growing fear of the abandoned and unemployed blacks in London. There was also a distaste for slave auctions and advertisements for runaways and for silver padlocks "for Blacks or Dogs." Arguments of Somerset's counsel anticipated the later official policy of deporting Negroes, whose numbers were swollen by veterans and refugees of the American Revolution, to the new colony of Sierra Leone. It is notable that in 1773 Portugal forbade the entry of Brazilian slaves or free blacks, who were said to constitute unfair competition to domestic labor. In 1777, France issued a royal decree

[46] *Ibid.,* 77; Somerset transcript, NYHS, pp. 57–60, 65.
[47] Somerset transcript, NYHS, p. 64. Davy said the distinction was one he "didn't very much contend for," but proposed it for Mansfield's consideration. His major point was that the master himself manumitted his slave by bringing him to England. In effect, northern American states later adopted the same distinction between fugitives and slaves brought in by their masters.

prohibiting the immigration of Negroes or mulattoes, whether slave or free. This order followed mounting complaints that blacks were causing disorder in French cities, that they were polluting the blood and debasing the culture of France. The French efforts to outlaw intermarriage and to set up detention camps for blacks suggest that by the 1770s the slave-trading nations were approaching common problems with common prejudices. The desire to exclude Negroes often preceded explicit hostility to slavery.[48]

But the Somerset and Knight cases also helped to define and clarify an emerging free-labor ideology. The actual judgments of the courts stopped considerably short of later notions of fundamental liberties. There was great selectivity in identifying the injustices of slavery. No one talked of individual opportunity. No one suggested that servants or workers should be free to be idle or to wander about the countryside. In Knight v. Wedderburn the court held that since the dominion allowed by Jamaican law was unjust, the master had no right whatever to the Negro's service. Some years after the Knight case, however, Lord Mansfield said that his own decision in Somerset went "no further than that the master cannot by force compel him to go out of the kingdom." This interpretation is especially striking in light of Mansfield's maxim on positive law, coupled with his statement that "so high an act of dominion must derive its authority, if any such it has, from the law of the kingdom *where* executed."[49] The question at

[48] *Gentleman's Magazine,* XXXIII (1763), 4; *The Scot's Magazine,* XXVIII, 445; XXXIII, 705; K. L. Little, *Negroes in Britain: A Study of Racial Relations in English Society* (London, 1948), pp. 168–69; Averil Mackenzie-Grieve, *The Last Years of the English Slave Trade: Liverpool, 1750–1807* (London, 1941), pp. 36–37; J. A. Picton, *Memorials of Liverpool, Historical and Topographical* (2 vols., London 1873), I, 224–25; Walvin, *Black and White,* chs. 4–5, 9; José Antonio Saco, *Historia de la esclavitud desde los tiempos mas remotos hasta nuestros dias* (2nd ed., Habana, 1936–1945), III, 345; Charles Verlinden, *L'Esclavage dans l'Europe médiévale; tome premier: Péninsule Ibérique, France* (Brugge, 1955), p. 839; *Le Code noir, ou recueil des reglemens rendus jusqu'à présent; Concernant le gouvernement, l'administration de la justice, la police, la discipline & le commerce des nègres dans les colonies françoises* (Paris, 1742), pp. 192–206, and *passim;* Lucien Peytraud, *L'Esclavage aux Antilles françaises avant 1789* (Paris, 1897), pp. 373–99; Shelby T. McCloy, *The Negro in France* (Lexington, Ky., 1961), pp. 44–49, 54–55.

[49] King v. Inhabitants of Thames Ditton (1785), in Catterall, ed., *Judicial Cases,* I, 20; "Candidus," *A Letter to Philo Africanus, Upon Slavery; in Answer to His of the 22nd November, in the "General Evening Post"* (n.p., 1788), p. 39; *The Scot's Magazine,* XXXIV, 298. Other versions of Mansfield's statement

issue is whether the limitations imposed on a master's authority in England annihilated all the legal incidents of slave status.

Mansfield's own position was less than clear. In the Lewis case of 1771 he endorsed the principle of *in favorem libertatis,* but also accepted the possibility that, even in England, a master *might* prove ownership of a Negro. He refused to make any judgments as to law, leaving it for the jury to decide whether in fact Thomas Lewis was the property of Robert Stapylton, or whether, after being captured by a Spanish ship and after working for wages in various colonies, he had been a free man when seized by Stapylton. As Sharp wrote, in indignation, "it is plain, his Lordship was willing *to presume* . . . that the idea of the *Master's property* in the Boy was sufficient to justify such violent outrages, if it could have been proved." Further, Mansfield confided to Dunning that "ever since that Trial, I have had a great Doubt in my Mind, whether the Negro could prove his own freedom by his own Evidence. . . . Whether a Slave may be a Witness to prove himself Free."[50]

Stuart may have been unwise to claim Somerset as his slave, since this narrowed Mansfield's options. Mansfield could either discharge Somerset, which might result, he feared, in a loss of some £700,000 sterling to the owners of resident slaves; or he could give legal recognition to a form of unrestricted dominion which clearly ran counter to a century or more of political ideology. Mansfield bowed to this ideology when he said that "the meanest Britain would take fire" at the sight of a merchant selling African slaves in England in open market. He affirmed the right of asylum and held that English law would pro-

---

on dominion are as follows: "So high an act of dominion was never in use here; no master ever was allowed here to take a slave by force to be sold abroad, because he had deserted from his service, or for any other reason whatever" (*The Annual Register,* p. 110). "So high an Act of dominion must derive its force from the Laws of the Country, and, if to be justified here, must be justified by the Laws of England" (MS, NYHS). "So high an act of dominion must be recognized by the law of the country where it is used. The power of a master over his slave has been extremely different in different countries" (20 *How. St. Tr.* 1 at 82).

[50] Lewis transcript, NYHS. No one questioned the fact that Stapylton had assaulted, gagged, and forcibly detained Lewis with intent to sell him as a slave in Jamaica. The only point at issue was whether Lewis was Stapylton's slave. The jury found that he was not, an opinion on which Mansfield agreed. The defendants, however, failed to appear to receive judgment for the criminal charges.

tect a galley slave who had escaped from Europe. At first he also seemed to extend the question to "whether any dominion, authority or coercion can be exercised in this country, on a slave according to the American laws?" Yet he paid tribute to Yorke and Talbot, "two of the greatest men of their own or any times," who had "pledged themselves to the British planters for the legal consequences of bringing Negro slaves into this kingdom, or their being baptized." He summarized their opinions, together with Hardwicke's unpublished equity judgment in Pearne *v*. Lisle.[51] Most important, Mansfield's famous words about "so high an act of dominion" referred not to slavery but to the specific question of forcibly confining a slave aboard a ship in order to be sold overseas. The only question adjudicated was whether Captain Knowles's cause was sufficient for the detainer of Somerset, and the cause stated "that he had kept him by order of his Master with an intent to send him abroad to Jamaica, there to be Sold." Mansfield did not deny the legality of "the power of a master over his servant," but simply said that "the exercise of it must always be regulated by the laws of the place where exercised." Despite the eloquent arguments of Somerset's counsel, which even courts soon confused with the decision itself, one must conclude that English "judge-found law" did not totally dissolve the pre-existing relationship between a master and his slave.[52]

---

[51] 20 *How. St. Tr.* 1 at 79–82; MS transcript of Mansfield's judgment, NYHS; *The Scot's Magazine,* XXXIV, 298–99; *The Annual Register,* p. 110. The puisne judges of the Court of King's Bench, Richard Aston, Edward Willes, and William Henry Ashhurst, are not mentioned in Howell and have been supposed to have had no part in the case. However, they did take part in the discussion of precedents, such as Smith *v*. Brown and Cooper (Somerset transcript, NYHS, pp. 81, 85). At one point Mansfield said he would take the opinion of his brother judges, but later declared that since they were all of one opinion on the only question at issue, he would not adjourn the matter to be argued before all the judges, as was usual on a return to a *habeas corpus* (*The Scot's Magazine,* XXXIV, 298; 20 *How. St. Tr.* 1 at 81–82).

[52] The meaning of the "so high an act of dominion" phrase is important, since it was later interpreted as referring to slavery in general. Yet a comparison of the texts clearly shows that it followed and referred to the specific cause on the return. One may also note that Hargrave used the phrase, "that high act of dominion," to describe Stuart's imprisonment of Somerset on Captain Knowles's ship (20 *How. St. Tr.* 1 at 66). Fiddes, in "Lord Mansfield and the Sommersett Case," takes a similar view of the limited scope of the decision, but provides no analysis of the texts. Nadelhaft is right in contending that Mansfield decided no more than that a slave could not be shipped out of England against his will; but

This view was confirmed by Williams *v.* Brown (1802) and received solid substantiation in 1827 in the Court of Admiralty. Lord Stowell, the judge in the latter case, termed himself a "stern Abolitionist" with respect to the slave trade. Yet six years prior to British emancipation, he felt it his duty to clarify the misinterpretations of Somerset. A domestic slave named Grace Jones had been taken to England in 1822 and had been transported back to Antigua the following year. In 1825 a customs official seized her on the ground that she had been free in England and had thus been imported illegally. Lord Stowell, upholding the verdict of the Vice Admiralty Court in Antigua, ruled that she was still a slave.[53]

Somerset's counsel had actually anticipated and tried to refute Lord Stowell's line of reasoning. Sergeant Davy attacked the absurdity of Virginia's law of 1704 which stated that slavery would reattach to any returning Negro who had been temporarily enfranchised as a result of being in England. Hargrave observed that it would have been more "artful" if Stuart had merely cited slavery "as a ground for claiming [Somerset] here, in the relation of a servant bound to follow wherever his master should require his service." In other words, Stuart might have conceded that a Negro brought to England would enjoy certain protections of law, but that unconditional slavery would reattach as soon as the Negro left the jurisdiction of municipal law. Hargrave exposed the illogic of this position. How could English law prohibit the introduction of slavery and yet give effect to even an implicit contract founded on slavery? English law must confer the gift of liberty "entire and unincumbered." The law, said Hargrave, would "not permit slavery suspended for a while, suspended during the pleasure of the master." Yet this was precisely the point Mansfield refused to adjudicate.[54]

Lord Stowell pointed out that transmarine law had never recognized the common-law principle, "once free for an hour, free forever."

Nadelhaft and James Walvin are wrong when they argue that Capel Lofft added an *obiter dictum* which Mansfield never made ("The Somersett Case and Slavery," pp. 193–208; *The Black Presence,* pp. 93–94). Sharp himself was guilty of oversimplification. On July 21, 1772, he wrote Dr. Findlay that Mansfield had decided that, *"tracing the Subject to natural principles . . . the claim of Slavery never can be supported"* (JAW).

[53] Catterall, ed., *Judicial Cases,* I, 23–25, 34–37. In the early nineteenth century the Court of Admiralty began to widen its power and jurisdiction.

[54] Somerset transcript, NYHS, pp. 67–68; 20 *How. St. Tr.* 1 at 64–66.

The maxim had applied only to English villeins. Stowell acknowledged that Grace Jones might have chosen to remain in England as a free woman. Yet the legal rights she possessed there expired with her residence. The Somerset decision, according to Stowell, implied no more than the suspension of colonial slave codes during a temporary residence in England. He complained that Lord Mansfield, after trying to avoid a decision and seeking a compromise settlement out of court, had failed to correct the misinterpretations of law which he had helped introduce. The "limited liberation" conferred upon slaves in England, Stowell wrote, had never altered their status upon returning to the colonies. Joseph Story, the eminent American authority on conflict of law, praised Stowell's decision as "impregnable."[55]

The Grace decision reconciled conflicting domestic and imperial interests in a way that helps to tie together our discussion of dominion. The Somerset case is obviously far better known, for it provided a forum for Sharp and Hargrave and soon became celebrated as a major victory for the humanitarian concience. The 1772 decision proved, reassuringly, that England was a free country; that workers and servants were responsible for their own welfare; and that the principle of voluntarism limited both the dominion and responsibility of masters. If the law itself had adhered closely to this libertarian philosophy, it would have posed a direct challenge to colonial institutions.

The law, therefore, had to balance the needs of domestic ideology against commercial and imperial interests. Within the British empire there was no sharp division, as in the later United States, between a permanent slaveholding class and the owners of other property. The law could gravitate easily toward a pragmatic middle ground. Partly through popular misinterpretations, the Somerset case fulfilled the needs of domestic ideology. In practice, however, a slave's dependency did not cease when he breathed English air. In 1785, Lord Mansfield admitted that when "slaves have been brought here, and have commenced actions for their wages, I have always nonsuited the plaintiff." In the notorious *Zong* case of 1783, Mansfield had no doubt that, so far as insurance claims were concerned, "the case of the slaves was the same as if horses had been thrown overboard."[56] English law was

[55] Catterall, ed., *Judicial Cases*, I, 6–7, 34–37.

[56] *Ibid.*, I, 20; Walvin, *Black and White*, p. 93. There is evidence, however, that some English magistrates immediately interpreted the Somerset verdict to mean there could be no slaves in England. In the case of Cay and Chrichton

flexible enough to recognize the validity of slave property, to uphold contracts for the sale of slaves, and to provide room for a qualified servitude, even a servitude without wages. It simply told masters that they should not repeat Stuart's mistake of locking a slave in irons for forcible shipment out of the country. No doubt the Somerset decision deterred many West Indians from bringing their slaves to England, and those who did were more careful to choose obedient servants or to secure signed indentures.[57] The important point, however, is that regardless of legal forms, English courts endorsed no principles that undermined colonial slave law. For a time, then, the two systems of law could coexist and even interpenetrate within the larger imperial sphere.

Conflicting Jurisdictions

The jurisdictional questions concerning slavery fall into three broad categories: those that involved international law and international relations; those that arose within the French and British imperial systems; and those resulting from the demarcation of free and slave states within the United States. I shall touch on the international conflicts very briefly, observing only that national policy depended on changing circumstance. A few random examples will illustrate this point.

During the late eighteenth century large numbers of Jamaican slaves escaped to Cuba in fishing boats. Partly as a legacy of the earlier Anglo-Spanish wars, Cuban officials held out the offer of freedom to any fugitive who professed the Catholic faith, although Cuban planters

---

(May 11, 1773), the Prerogative Court thought that "Negroes were declared [by the Court of King's Bench] *to be free in England.*" Though the case involved a will of 1769, the court decided that the Somerset decision affected the status of Negroes prior to 1772 as well as afterwards (MS transcript, NYHS). In 1774 London Alderman John Wilkes discharged a Negro from his master, saying that no one could be a slave according to the laws of the country. Wilkes gave the Negro some money, since the case had arisen when the servant's white wife had complained that her husband was unable to support her and their child. Wilkes urged the black to sue his master for recovery of wages (*The Scot's Magazine,* XXXVI [1774], 53).

[57] Walvin, *Black and White,* ch. 8, discusses the use of indentures, which were enforced by courts. See also Catterall, ed., *Judicial Cases,* I, 21–22. As Walvin suggests, few blacks has easy access to the courts, and many were held in virtual slavery. After the abolition of the slave trade in 1808, English courts were more inclined than before to endorse antislavery principles.

were also happy to buy slaves from Jamaica in an illicit trade that the Spanish crown was powerless to stop. Despite the establishment of police patrols, the Jamaican government could not stem the flow of fugitives, which threatened to drain the manpower of plantations along the northern coast. They sent repeated remonstrances and even delegations to the governors of Havana and St. Jago de Cuba, who gravely replied that they had no authority to return fugitives who had come seeking the true faith. In petitions to the English king and council, the Jamaicans denounced this pretext of religion and claimed that the slaves who had been lured to Cuba by false promises of freedom would, if permitted, happily return to their former masters. In 1790, British diplomacy appeared to succeed. Following the Nootka Sound crisis, which brought England and Spain to the brink of war, Spain agreed that henceforth there would be no more harboring of fugitive slaves. Yet by 1792 the Jamaican press reported that the Spanish were smuggling arms to British slaves, telling them that the kings of Spain and England favored their emancipation. The two nations were soon again at war.[58]

The next examples show how quickly British attitudes could be transformed. In 1807, both the governor and the Supreme Court of Michigan Territory refused to return fugitive slaves who had fled from Upper Canada, since the United States Constitution imposed no obligation to surrender runaway slaves to a foreign nation. But by 1829 the Executive Council of Upper Canada had ruled that every slave who entered the Province was free, "whether he has been brought in by violence or has entered . . . of his own accord." Extradition of fugitives could apply only to crimes which were *mala in se,* and which were recognized in Canada and throughout the civilized world. In 1837, John C. Calhoun persuaded the United States Senate to pass a resolution demanding the return of any American slave who claimed freedom as a result of setting foot on foreign soil. Under Article X of the Webster-Ashburton Treaty (1842), the British agreed to extradite persons charged with felonies, including assault, robbery, and forgery—charges which few fugitives could hope to escape. But in 1842 Lord Aberdeen defended the action of Nassau officials who refused to

[58] *Journals of the Assembly of Jamaica,* VI (Jamaica, 1800), 158, 472; VIII (Jamaica, 1804), 457, 458, 462, 528, 538–39, 595–96; clipping from *The Morning Chronicle,* Feb., 1792, Stephen Fuller, Letterpress Book, II, 211, Fuller papers, Duke University Library.

return some American slaves who had seized control of a sloop and had sailed it to the island, after killing one master. A Nassau judge held that blacks could justifiably commit homicide to gain their freedom.[59]

By the time Britain had extinguished slavery in her own Caribbean colonies, she was prepared to take the highest moral ground in refusing to return American slaves who had escaped to Canada or the Bahamas. Yet during the Age of Revolution, it is difficult to think of British armies fighting for the common rights of mankind. One may grant that English generals promised freedom to large numbers of American fugitives, during both the Revolution and the War of 1812 —commitments which led to bitter and prolonged negotiations for restitution. But American loyalists transported substantial numbers of slaves to Canada. And in striking contrast to the Northwest Ordinance of 1787, the British Imperial Act of 1790, intended to encourage immigration to Canada, the Bahamas, and Bermuda, allowed free importation of all "Negroes, household furniture, utensils of husbandry or clothing." It was not an army of liberation that Pitt dispatched to rebellious St. Domingue; nor did the British, when they captured Martinique in 1795, intend to implement the French Convention's recent decree of universal emancipation.[60]

There were no universally accepted principles of international law that provided judges with coherent rules for reconciling conflicts between divergent social and legal systems. On the one hand, the Roman and common-law traditions posited a "supranational body of shared concepts and legal presuppositions" which could resolve conflicts between independent legal systems. On the other hand, in the Netherlands and to some extent in Britain, "the sense of a shared

---

[59] William Wirt Blume, ed., *Transactions of the Supreme Court of the Territory of Michigan, 1805–1814* (Ann Arbor, 1935) I, 87, 99, 321–22; Winks, *The Blacks in Canada*, p. 102; William Renwick Riddell, "An Official Record of Slavery in Upper Canada," *Papers and Records of the Ontario Historical Society,* XXV (1929), 313–14; Betty Fladeland, *Men and Brothers: Anglo-American Antislavery Cooperation* (Urbana, Ill., 1972), pp. 262, 315–16, 330–32.

[60] Arnett G. Lindsay, "Diplomatic Relations between the United States and Great Britain Bearing on the Return of Negro Slaves, 1783–1828," *Journal of Negro History,* V (Oct., 1920), 391–419; Marcel Trudel, *L'Esclavage au Canada français; histoire et conditions de l'esclavage* (Québec, 1960), pp. 54–55; Winks, *The Blacks in Canada*, pp. 24–28; Elsa V. Goveia, *Slave Society in the British Leeward Islands at the End of the Eighteenth Century* (New Haven, 1965), pp. 252–54; Lowell J. Ragatz, *The Fall of the Planter Class in the British Caribbean, 1763–1833* (New York, 1928), pp. 214–93.

universal natural law gave way to an assertion of independent state power and freedom from supranational restraints. . . . In place of supranational obligation, the Dutch developed the notion of comity (*comitas gentium*): each nation, of its own free will, might grant recognition of foreign rights and duties in the interests of harmony and in the expectation of reciprocity."[61]

Britain's continuing involvement with Negro slavery, coupled with the vicissitudes of war and diplomacy, made it difficult to assimilate abolitionist principles to a supranational body of law—as distinct from the municipal law that might grant asylum to fugitives. Moreover, Anglo-American jurists showed increasing respect for a positivistic conception of law as the expression of the legislators' will, and looked to natural law for an orienting set of principles when statutes and case law provided no guidance. Nevertheless, Anglo-American attempts to suppress the slave trade encouraged a few eminent judges to move in a more universalistic direction. In 1812 the English Court of Appeals appeared to recognize a "higher law" that bound all nations. At issue was whether a British warship had the right to seize an American slave ship, in this case the *Amedie*. Noting that both England and the United States had passed municipal laws against the trade, the court admitted that "we cannot legislate for other countries," but concluded that "this is a trade which cannot, abstractly speaking, be said to have a legitimate existence." William Roscoe, the Liverpool abolitionist, rejoiced at the reported dictum that "by the law of nature and nations there can be no property in human beings." In a letter to the Duke of Gloucester, titular head of the prestigious African Institution, Roscoe wrote:

This decision appears to me fully to sanction the opinion in which I observe your Royal Highness concurs, viz. that it can be no breach of the Law of nations to prevent other Countries from a practice which we have ourselves relinquished as contrary to justice & humanity. That this Country ought not to legislate for others I perfectly agree; but the laws & regulations of other states in order to be respected ought to be consistent with the rules of Justice & humanity, or in other words with the common rights of mankind.[62]

[61] "American Slavery and the Conflict of Laws," *Columbia Law Review*, LXXI (Jan., 1971), 80–82.

[62] William Roscoe to the Duke of Gloucester, Aug. 13, 1810, Roscoe papers, item 1767, "British Records Relating to America in Microfilm," introd. by

In the American case of *La Jeune Eugénie* (1822), Justice Joseph Story took similar ground and asserted his right to enforce an antislavery law of nations, "unless it is relaxed or waived by the consent of nations." It thus appeared that both British and American courts were prepared to uphold a universal and supranational law against slave trading, unless the defendants could prove that the practice was legal under the laws of their own countries. Yet both the British and American decisions were soon reversed. In the British case of *Le Louis* (1817), the Court of Admiralty ruled that only French courts could enforce French law, and that it "would have been deemed a most extravagant assumption in any Court of the Law of Nations, to pronounce that this practice, the tolerated, the approved, the encouraged object of law, ever since men became subject to law, was prohibited by that law, and was legally criminal." Chief Justice John Marshall, with Justice Story now concurring, came to a similar judgment in *The Antelope* (1825). Thus, as the *Columbia Law Review* has concluded, "in spite of Story's early attempt to foster a universal and normative law of slavery, American courts arrived at essentially the same conclusions reached by the British courts. The law of nations was, in effect, a neutral force . . . itself subordinate to municipal law."[63]

Within their own imperial system, the French faced jurisdictional problems quite similar to those of the British. If the British were contemptuously amused by pretensions of liberty in Bourbon France, they also found, in the volumes of *Les Causes célèbres,* seeming precedents for the Somerset and Knight decisions. Thus the "Memorials"

Dr. John Rowe. As I have already noted, the judgment in the Massachusetts case of Greenwood *v.* Curtis, also in 1810, implied an almost opposite view from that in the *Amedie.*

[63] "American Slavery and the Conflict of Laws," pp. 83–84, 88–89; Fladeland, *Men and Brothers,* pp. 130–31, 328. I am concerned here, it should be stressed, with a convergence of British and American judicial decisions—not with treaty obligations or later slave-trade diplomacy. Yet Robert N. Cover points out, in his forthcoming study of slavery and the American law, that in 1822 Justice Story was lending judicial support to diplomatic negotiations for suppressing the slave trade. By the time of *The Antelope,* in 1825, the United States Senate had rejected a British proposal for a convention on the limited right of mutual search and seizure. Therefore, the Supreme Court refrained to do what the Senate had refused to do. The backtracking of the Supreme Court illustrates Cover's argument that the authority of international law depends on its being incorporated into the municipal law of actual states and on its reflection of the practice and policy of nations.

filed in the Knight case quoted such stirring maxims as "Il s'est tou-jours regardé comme libre, depuis qu'il a mis le pied en France"; "On ne connoit point d'esclave en France, et quiconque a mis le pied dans ce royaume, est gratifié de la liberté"; and "Nos privilèges ont effacé jusqu'à l'idée de l'esclavage en France."[64] Of course the *Code Noir* of 1685 authorized chattel slavery in the colonies. But numerous slaves won their freedom, for one reason or another, after being taken to the metropolis.

The French crown tried to prevent such actions by an edict of 1716 and a declaration of 1738. Under these laws, masters could bring slaves to the metropolis for the purposes of religious instruction or learning a trade. But the owners were required to post bond and to register each slave with the port authorities; the 1738 declaration prohibited slaves from marrying and required their return to the colonies after a sojourn of three years. Slaves could not be manumitted except by testament, upon a master's death, but could be set free if an owner failed to comply with the regulations. This was apparently the ground for most of the successful freedom suits, although the Parlement of Paris recognized constitutional appeals for freedom within its own jurisdiction. The confusion over grounds for emanci-pation was compounded in 1762 by the celebrated case of Louis, in which appeals to a municipal tradition of freedom were mixed with warnings that an influx of Negroes would disfigure the nation. Louis won his freedom, along with back wages for the work he had per-formed since arriving in France from St. Domingue. But the growing fear of racial intermixture led to ordinances that were designed to keep France not only "free" but racially pure as well.[65]

England never enacted a slave code for her colonies. Consequently, the sanction for slavery was not so explicit as in France, nor was there so formal a recognition of the divergence between metropolitan and colonial institutions. Sergeant William Davy argued that "the King

[64] 20 *How. St. Tr.* 1 at 13–16n. Notwithstanding the attention devoted to French cases in both the Knight and Somerset trials, Thomas Babington Macaulay wrote his father in 1828 that he had discovered a "curious trail" in *Les Causes célèbres:* "A negro—this was before the Somerset cause in England—maintained before the Parliament of Paris that his master had no right to his service in France. And the Court decided in favour of his liberty" (Margaret J. Holland, Viscountess Knutsford, *Life and Letters of Zachary Macaulay* [London, 1900], p. 449).

[65] McCloy, *The Negro in France,* pp. 25–27, 43–49, 54–56.

makes Laws for Virginia, alone if he pleases . . . but he cannot make Laws here without the Consent and Authority of the two Houses of Parliament." Hence the laws of Virginia had no more influence or authority in England "than the Laws of Japan." Yet when the British colonies codified their own slave laws, usually long after slavery had taken root, there was a presumption that the local codes were not repugnant to common law or to the British constitution. Indeed, under William III the government explicitly ruled that colonial legislators could enact no statutes repugnant to the law of England. It was this principle that led Lord Chancellor Hardwicke to conclude that if Negro slaves were free when brought to England (which he denied), then they must also be free in the colonies. By the 1780s a few writers were bold enough to assert that the Somerset decision had proved the illegality of slavery in any British dominion. But since the crown had shown far less interest in slave codes than in disallowing colonial attempts to restrict slave imports, it was no less logical to assume that the institution was legal unless prohibited by positive law.[66]

This view, the precise opposite of Mansfield's supposed dictum, is given some credence by the early attempts to outlaw slavery. In 1652 a rump session of the Rhode Island General Court thought it necessary to prohibit slavery by local statute, but the ruling was never enforced. In 1735 the Trustees of Georgia secured a special law from Parliament which, on grounds of military defense and social utility, made slavery illegal in that colony. The law was soon repealed, a fact that underscores the local and temporal character of slave prohibition.[67] After independence, five northern states adopted laws for gradual emanci-

---

[66] Somerset transcript, NYHS, pp. 54, 116–17; Pearne *v.* Lisle, *Amb.* 75, 27 *Eng. Rep.* 47 (1749); "Shakspeare," *Doubts Concerning the Legality of Slavery in Any Part of the British Dominions* (London, 1789), pp. 4–14; [Thomas Burgess], *Considerations on the Abolition of Slavery and the Slave Trade, Upon Grounds of Natural, Religious, and Political Duty* (Oxford, 1789), pp. 90, 103. Davy did not seem to see the contradiction in arguing that the king alone had allowed slavery in the colonies, but that slaves brought to England were free because they were subjects of the king. "Shakspeare," on the other hand, pointed out that *"if the laws of England are the birthright of the inhabitants of Jamaica,* it is obvious that by the laws of England every man is free, and, whether native or alien, is equally entitled to the protection of those laws" (p. 11); and Burgess maintained that "all the arguments in favour of the Negro's right to liberty in Britain are convertible into proofs of the injustice and illegality of slavery in the British colonies" (p. 103).

[67] Davis, *Problem of Slavery in Western Culture,* pp. 144–50.

pation. These statutes, by their very nature, confirmed the legality of past and continuing enslavement.[68] Of course, many Negroes won individual freedom suits, in the South as well as in the North. In granting such freedom, judges sometimes referred to the natural law principles of the Revolution, although this tendency waned during the early nineteenth century as courts adopted stricter rules in weighing evidence, reputation, and ancestry, and paid greater deference to legislative policy concerning manumission and public liability for the indigent.[69] Vermont stood alone in outlawing slavery by a constitution that embodied principles of "higher law" justice. In Massachusetts, Levi Lincoln's brief for Quock Walker appeared to paraphrase the arguments of Francis Hargrave, and proclaimed that "the air in America is too pure for a slave to breathe in." Chief Justice William Cushing's instructions to the jury, in Commonwealth *v.* Jennison (1783), suggested that "the idea of slavery is inconsistent with our own conduct and Constitution." Yet the issue of constitutionality remained unclear, even if Massachusetts could legitimately claim to be the only state that eradicated slavery by judicial action.[70]

[68] For example, as late as 1833, in Johnson *v.* Tompkins *et al.,* Justice Henry Baldwin charged the jury: "It is not permitted to you or us to indulge our feelings of abstract right . . . the law of the land recognises the right of one man to hold another in bondage. . . . While the abolition act [of Pennsylvania] . . . abolished slavery for life, as to those thereafter born, it did not . . . interfere with those born before, or slaves excepted. . . . Slavery yet exists in Pennsylvania" (Catterall, ed., *Judicial Cases,* IV, 287).

[69] Duncan MacLeod, "Racial Attitudes in Revolutionary and Early National America," pp. 181–210, D. Phil. thesis, Cambridge, 1969. The crucial issue in many freedom suits, as in litigation involving private manumissions, was responsibility for supporting blacks who could not support themselves (see especially Benjamin Joseph Klebaner, "American Manumission Laws and the Responsibility for Supporting Slaves," *The Virginia Magazine of History and Biography,* LXIII [Oct., 1955], 443–53).

[70] "Brief of Levi Lincoln," Belknap Papers, *Collections* of the Massachusetts Historical Society, 5th ser., III (Boston, 1877), 438–42; John D. Cushing, "The Cushing Court and the Abolition of Slavery in Massachusetts: More Notes on the 'Quock Walker Case,'" *American Journal of Legal History,* V (1961), 118–44; Arthur Zilversmit, "Quok Walker, Mumbet, and the Abolition of Slavery in Massachusetts," *William and Mary Quarterly,* 3rd ser., XXV (Oct., 1968), 614–24; Elaine MacEacheren, "Emancipation of Slavery in Massachusetts: A Reexamination, 1770–1790," *Journal of Negro History* (Oct., 1970), 289–306. Levi Lincoln's brief made considerably more appeal to religion than did the arguments of Hargrave and Davy. Lincoln defended Walker in 1781 before the Supreme Court of Judicature. After losing this case, Nathaniel Jennison, the master, fol-

Nevertheless, in both England and America the opinion gradually prevailed that slavery was an exceptional or "artificial" institution that required the sanction of positive law. This view was partly the result of misinterpretations of the Somerset decision. Lord Mansfield had apparently limited himself to the point that "the state of slavery is of such a nature, that it is incapable of being now introduced by courts of justice upon mere reasoning or inferences from any principles, natural or political." It is true that Justice Lemuel Shaw later qualified the positive law doctrine by noting that "positive law, in this connection, may be as well, understood customary law, as the enactment of a statute; and the word is used to designate rules established by tacit acquiescence." Presumably this definition was elastic enough to apply to any territory where slavery had taken root and had not been expressly prohibited. But as generally understood, the positive-law doctrine meant, as interpreted in Michigan Territory, that "as rights of property in persons cannot exist by the common law, but only by statute, the manner of protecting such rights must be regulated by statute. Common-law principles do not apply." Paradoxically, this interpretation also meant that the Northwest Ordinance could not altogether outlaw slavery in Michigan. Augustus B. Woodward, the Chief Judge of the Territorial Supreme Court, pointed out that Jay's Treaty with England guaranteed the property rights of the existing settlers; that "the term property as used in Jay's Treaty includes slaves, as slaves were recognized as property by the countries [France and England] concerned"; and that therefore:

Slaves living on May 31, 1793, and in the possession of settlers in this Territory on July 11, 1796 [the date when the United States finally took possession of Wayne County], continue such for life; children of such slaves born between these dates continue in servitude for twenty-five years [under the provisions of Upper Canada's gradual emancipation act of

------

lowed the route that Lord Mansfield had recommended to British slaveholders: he petitioned the legislature, asking that it either reject the antislavery interpretation of the constitution or relieve him from the duty of supporting a number of Negroes. The state senate failed to approve a bill that would have indemnified masters and provided relief for indigent blacks, and by 1783 Jennison was faced with a criminal trial for assaulting Quock Walker. With respect to constitutional emancipation, an exception might be made for New Hampshire, but the facts are unclear (Isaac W. Hammond, "Slavery in New Hampshire," *Magazine of American History*, XXI [1889], 63–65; Arthur Zilversmit, *The First Emancipation: The Abolition of Slavery in the North* [Chicago, 1967], p. 117).

1793]; children of such children, and all born after July 11, 1796, are free from birth.[71]

Even in the South the positive-law doctrine implied strict territorial limitation. In Rankin *v.* Lydia (1820), to cite only one of numerous examples, the Kentucky Court of Appeals held that slavery was "without foundation in the law of nature, or the . . . common law," but existed by virtue of positive law alone.[72] Moreover, it appeared that once the sanction was removed, slavery could not be restored. Only the French reinstituted slavery after first abolishing it. Yet American states often vacillated on other prohibitions, such as the outlawing of capital punishment or the sale of intoxicating drink. The re-establishment of slavery would have raised serious constitutional debates even in states like Pennsylvania, where the courts refused to give an emancipationist construction to the state constitution's declaration of rights.[73]

Emancipation proposals were debated in the Upper South and were long resisted in New York and New Jersey. But this apparent convergence should not blind us to the momentous implications of drawing "free soil" boundaries. Soon after the adoption of the Constitu-

---

[71] Story, *Conflict of Laws,* pp. 158–59n.; Graveson, *Status in the Common Law,* pp. 28, 32, 34, 64–65; Lemmon *v.* the People, 20 N.Y. 562 (1860). For early American discussions and applications of the Somerset precedent, see Mahoney *v.* Ashton, 4 Md. App. 50 at 196–202, 4 Harris & McHenry 63 at 303–325 (1802); "In the Matter of Richard Pattinson" (1807), in Blume, ed., *Transactions of the Supreme Court of the Territory of Michigan,* I, 415–17. In the latter case, Augustus B. Woodward, Chief Judge of Michigan Territory, essentially agreed with Granville Sharp that Lord Mansfield had declared it an "unquestionable" principle of English law *"that a right of property cannot exist in the human Species,"* but then added that historical circumstances "effectually denied me the privilege of Saying what Lord Mansfield did Say in England." The Maryland Court of Appeals, in the former case, recognized some of the complexities and limitations of Mansfield's judgment.

[72] Catterall, ed., *Judicial Cases,* I, 294.

[73] The point on constitutionality in Pennsylvania is suggested by the report of a legislative committee, Dec. 31, 1792, which found slavery "unlawful in itself" and so repugnant to the state constitution that the legislature had no power "to authorise it under any modification whatsoever" (copy in Friends House, London). However, as Robert N. Cover makes clear in his forthcoming book, American courts generally interpreted the "free and equal" clauses of state constitutions in terms of the framers' presumed intentions, and scrupulously avoided infringing upon the legislatures' prerogatives. In Pennsylvania, particularly, there was great sensitivity to the need to adjust conflicting interests, and to give due weight to the property rights of slaveholders during the process of gradual emancipation.

tion, a "Federalist" complained in the *American Museum* about the unconstitutionality of Pennsylvania's sojourner law which required "foreigners" who resided with their Negro servants at the seat of government (Philadelphia) to leave the state after six months or lose their slaves:

If it be just and right for the law of nations to deprive a foreigner of his property in a slave from principles of conscience and religion, may not a nation, believing in metempsychosis, by the same law deprive a *British friend,* or other good man residing among them, of his ox, or his ass, or any living thing that is his?[74]

Clearly it would be impolitic for a modern nation to invalidate the marriage, divorce, or familial legitimacy of a traveler or resident alien. In general, English law followed Roman precedent and granted that a person's status is defined by the laws of his domicile and accompanies him wherever he goes. In his monumental *Commentaries on the Conflict of Laws,* Story endorsed the maxims of Boullenois and other Continental authorities on the capacity of persons:

Laws purely personal, whether universal or particular, extend themselves everywhere; that is to say, a man is everywhere deemed in the same state . . . by which he is affected by the law of his domicil. . . . Wherever a law is directed to the person, we are to refer to the law of the place to which he is personally subject.[75]

Traditionally, the courts of various nations had upheld certain customs and practices unrecognized by local law. In the United States, moreover, each state was bound to give full faith and credit to the public acts, records, and judicial proceedings of every other state. On the other hand, the principle of extraterritoriality could not be extended indefinitely without subverting public policy and infringing upon state sovereignty. An influx of aliens, carrying their own laws and customs with them, could rapidly transform the institutional structure of any given society. Thus, according to Story, the comity of nations depends entirely on voluntary consent, and "is inadmissible when it is contrary to [a nation's] known policy or prejudicial to its interests." No sovereign state was obliged to recognize laws incompatible with its own interests, and "whatever may be the intrinsic or

[74] *American Museum,* XII (Nov., 1792), 292–93.
[75] Story, *Conflict of Laws,* pp. 35–36, 68–69; Graveson, *Status in the Common Law,* pp. 60–61, 104–5.

obligatory force of such laws upon such persons if they should return to their native country, they can have none in other nations wherein they reside."[76]

In effect, these were the broad principles underlying the Somerset and Knight decisions. It was not necessary to offer convincing evidence that England or Scotland were in danger of becoming slave societies. The courts simply assumed that all residents were under the jurisdiction of municipal law, the principles of which would be violated by granting comity to colonial slave law. Story, who discussed slavery after considering forms of prohibited marriages, asserted that "there is a uniformity of opinion among foreign jurists and foreign tribunals in giving no effect to the state of slavery of a party, whatever it might have been in the country of his birth or that in which he had been previously domiciled, unless it is also recognized by the laws of the country of his actual domicil, and where he is found."[77]

But these general rules left important questions unresolved. Did refusal to "give effect" mean an irreversible change of status and thus a contravening of the laws of the original domicile? Could the status of slavery be "suspended" and then "reattach," as Lord Stowell had said? Was there a grace period before public policy took effect, as the six-month sojourner laws seemed to suggest? Above all, could the law assimilate antislavery principles in one jurisdiction and still provide the means for a mutually acceptable resolution of conflicts with slaveholding jurisdictions?

[76] Story, *Conflict of Laws*, pp. 21–25, 168–69.

[77] 20 *How. St. Tr.* 1 at 71, 74, 77–78; Story, *Conflict of Laws*, pp. 135–54. In *The Scot's Magazine* account, Alleyne laid it down as an "unimpeachable proposition, that all municipal relations which were repugnant to natural laws, ceased to operate the moment the persons affected by them were out of the state in which they were made; that slavery was a municipal relation between master and slave which violated the natural rights of the slave, and therefore, that however it might be established by the laws of Virginia, it could not subsist by force of those laws out of that colony" (p. 297). However, Davy suggested that this principle could not be extended to an ambassador or "a Man coming in a Publick Capacity as the representative of a Prince" (Somerset transcript, NYHS, p. 56).

Robert N. Cover points out that in modern terminology, the "whole law" of a given territory includes the choice-of-law principles that guide a judge in applying the laws of another jurisdiction. Hence questions of extraterritorial effect, which were once discussed in terms of comity, have been absorbed within the concept of a sovereign whole law.

These questions take us far beyond even an elastic "Age of Revolution" and also involve legal complexities manifested in a vast multitude of judicial cases. A brief summary will indicate some of the ways in which antislavery and proslavery principles gradually weakened the conciliatory mechanisms of law. As an initial qualification, it should be emphasized that the deepening controversies over slavery coincided with parallel trends in constitutional theory and in the theory of legal conflict, trends which reinforced the sanctions for particularism and territorial sovereignty.[78]

Thomas R. R. Cobb, a nineteenth-century Georgian and leading authority on the jurisprudence of slavery, acknowledged that public policy must always take precedence over the principle of comity. He contended, however, that the mere transit of a master and slave could in no way infringe upon the rights, liberties, or interests of a non-slaveholding people. Cobb admitted that at the time of the Somerset and Knight cases, colonial slaveholders were abusing the privilege of temporary residence in Britain. John Wedderburn, the owner of Joseph Knight, had been domiciled in Scotland for several years, had allowed Knight to marry, and had furnished no proof of his intent to return to Jamaica. Though Stuart claimed an intent to return to Virginia after completing business transactions, he had resided in England for more than a year when Somerset escaped. Cobb felt that residence should have been the point at issue rather than the irrelevant question of whether British municipal law prohibited the introduction of slavery.[79]

It is difficult to dispute the logic of Cobb's position, so long as one accepts his premise that slavery is analogous to other statuses and contracts which deserve the respect of all nations. He was consistent enough to grant that a slave like Joseph Knight might legitimately be emancipated by the mere fact of acquiring domicile in a free juris-

[78] "American Slavery and the Conflict of Laws," pp. 85–99; Harold W. Horowitz, "Choice-of-Law Decisions Involving Slavery: 'Interest Analysis' in the Early Nineteenth Century," *UCLA Law Review*, XVII (1970), 587–601.

[79] Thomas R. R. Cobb, *An Inquiry into the Law of Negro Slavery in the United States of America* (Philadelphia and Savannah, 1858), pp. 127–35, 151–56, 165–77. Cobb, who was much influenced by the legal positivism of John Austin, was doubtless correct in maintaining that the Somerset and Knight cases focused attention on the conflict between British and colonial laws, and tended to evade the questions of status and residence which preoccupied American courts in the nineteenth century.

diction, and that such a freedman would carry his new status wherever he went. For a time, even southern courts gave support to this position.

Thus in 1833 a slave woman was emancipated in Virginia because her master had taken her to Massachusetts, his original home, with the intention of settling there. Though he returned to Virginia, his residence in Boston had reinstituted his original character as a "man of Massachusetts," and the slave, whose destiny was linked with his, had ceased to "belong" to Virginia. As late as 1850 a South Carolina court freed a Negro who had been taken to Ireland, since his deceased master had consented to his manumission, and the master's widow had brought him back, against his will, to South Carolina. A Louisiana court ruled that it was not in the power of a former owner to re-enslave a Negro woman who had been taken to France to learn hairdressing.[80]

The Northwest Territories presented special problems because of disputes over the Northwest Ordinance, the delay in British military evacuation from Northwest posts, and the wording of later state constitutions. Even Judge Woodward, who in Michigan defended the strongest abolitionist principles, conceded that Canadian law continued to sanction a qualified form of slavery in Michigan. In 1821 the Virginia Court of Appeals, in the case of Lewis v. Fullerton, refused to accept temporary residence in Ohio as a ground for freedom, notwithstanding a *habeas corpus* judgment in Ohio in favor of the slave. In Rankin v. Lydia (1820) the Kentucky Court of Appeals agreed that the Northwest Ordinance applied only to settlers and inhabitants, and not to transients. But since Lydia had lived in Indiana Territory for seven years, had been sold there and brought back to Kentucky,

---

[80] Betty v. Horton (1833), Guillemette v. Harper (1850), Marie Louise v. Marot et al. (1835), in Catterall, ed., *Judicial Cases*, I, 175; II, 418–19; III, 389, 504–5. However, in Mahoney v. Ashton, the Maryland Court of Appeals asserted that slave status should be governed by the laws of Maryland alone, regardless of how a British court might have adjudicated the case. Yet the petition for freedom rested on the claim that a seventeenth-century ancestor had been taken from Barbados to England, and had then been brought to Maryland by Lord Baltimore. The case thus raised the question whether slavery had *always* been illegal in England, as well as the question of territorial jurisdiction (4 Md. App. 50, 4 Harris & McHenry 63 [1802]). In 1846, Louisiana passed an act providing that "no slave shall be entitled to . . . freedom, under the pretence that he or she has been, with or without the consent of his or her owner, in a country where slavery does not exist, or in any of the States where slavery is prohibited" (Catterall, ed., *Judicial Cases*, III, 390).

where she had been sold again, the court ruled that her residence in Indiana had annulled the original sale. The purchaser had no right to Lydia while he remained in Indiana; "and is it to be seriously contended," Justice Benjamin Mills asked, "that so soon as he transported her to the Kentucky shore, the noxious atmosphere of this state, without any express law for the purpose, clamped upon her newly forged chains of slavery, after the old ones were destroyed!" The principle of comity, he concluded, required that Lydia's freedom be as sacred in Kentucky as if it had been her birthright.[81]

Even the famous case of Graham v. Strader (1844), which seemed to reverse the principles of Rankin, did not challenge the view that a slave would acquire permanent freedom if held for more than a temporary sojourn in a free state. Rather, the decision resembled that of Lord Stowell in "the Slave Grace," which was cited as a precedent. Justice Thomas Alexander Marshall, of the Kentucky Court of Appeals, held that a master who took his slave temporarily to a free state, with no intention of residing there, could not be judged as renouncing his right of dominion. In other words, the laws of the nonslaveholding jurisdiction might require the temporary suspension of the master's legal right to enforce dominion, but this suspension was not the same as emancipation. Kentucky was under no obligation to recognize a man as free merely because he could have claimed his freedom while in Ohio. Marshall thought it unnecessary to deal with the more prickly question that would be raised if an Ohio court specifically granted freedom to a transient slave from Kentucky. He implied that a slave state had no duty to recognize the decision of a "foreign tribunal" which disregarded mutual comity. Following Stowell, Marshall further maintained that the master-slave relationship could not be dissolved by the mere fact of temporary residence in an area that had a general prohibition against slavery. In denying an appeal to the United States Supreme Court, Chief Justice Roger Taney held that the laws of Kentucky alone had jurisdiction over a slave who had been in Ohio, and that the laws of Ohio had no peculiar force by virtue of the

---

[81] Lewis v. Fullerton, 22 Va. (1 Rand.) 15 (1821); Rankin v. Lydia, 9 Ky. (2 A. K. Marsh.) 813 (1820). In the former case Judge Roane also invalidated a deed of emancipation executed in Ohio, since the contract "had an eye to the state of Virginia for its operation and effect," and since it did not conform to Virginia law.

Ordinance of 1787, which had been wholly superseded by state and federal constitutions.[82]

These guiding principles were only partially challenged by the ostensibly liberal decisions of New England courts. Thus in Commonwealth *v.* Aves (1836), Justice Lemuel Shaw took pride in the fact that slavery had been abolished in Massachusetts prior to the adoption of the Federal Constitution, "as being contrary to the principles of justice, and of nature, and repugnant to the principles of the declaration of rights, which is a component part of the constitution of the State." All persons coming within the limits of the state were entitled to the privileges of the law. The only Constitutional provision for protecting the interests of slaveholding states, Shaw maintained, was limited to slaves who escaped without the consent of their owners into other states. The comity of nations could not be extended to an institution "entirely inconsistent with our policy and our fundamental principles." Shaw admitted, however, that decisions in both England and America had shown slavery not to be contrary to the law of nations. If slaves became free upon entering Massachusetts, it was "not so much because any alteration is made in their *status, . . .* as because there is no law which will warrant, but there are laws, if they choose to avail themselves of them, which prohibit, their forcible detention of forcible removal." Moreover, the privileges of municipal law did not apply to fugitives or, probably, to bondsmen in transit to a state where slavery was allowed, "where by accident or necessity he is compelled to touch or land therein [in a free state], remaining no longer than necessary."[83]

These maxims were extended and refined in the classic case of

[82] Graham *v.* Strader, 44 Ky. (5 B. Mon.) 173 (1844). In Stanley *v.* Earl (1824), Chief Justice John Boyle had ruled, "no man can, by the law of nature, have dominion over his fellow-man; . . . if the master voluntarily removes the slave to such non-slaveholding state, or if the slave escapes into a foreign country, which does not tolerate slavery, the master's right, so long as the slave remains there, is gone; because he has no remedy to enforce or protect it" (Catterall, ed., *Judicial Cases,* I, 304). Marshall did not dispute this point, but simply observed that it contained no concession that the slave in question was ever free.

[83] Commonwealth *v.* Aves, 35 Mass. (18 Pick.) 193 (1836); Story, *Conflict of Laws,* pp. 155–67n. In the Connecticut case of Nancy Jackson *v.* Bullock (1837), Justice Clark Bissell dissented from a majority opinion which had invoked the Somerset case as well as state laws designed to prohibit slavery, but which had given exemption to travelers passing with their slaves through the state. Bissell denied that the common law of England had any application to slaves in Con-

Polydore *v.* Prince (1837). Judge Ashur Ware, of the Federal District Court of Maine, admitted that the law of nations obliged courts to recognize the validity, at least to some extent, of other communities' statutes regarding persons. This obligation was stronger, however, with respect to statuses founded on "nature," such as marriage or parenthood, than with respect to those resulting from "mere civil institutions." This distinction had been ably questioned by John Dunning in the Somerset trial.

Ware conceded that American and English law determined status by the law of the holder's domicile and the incidents of status by the law of the place where any such incident was exercised. Story, for example, had pointed out that while marital status "accompanies a man everywhere," the rule of universality "does not militate against the law of the country where the consequences of that status are sought to be enforced." But whereas a marriage would not be dissolved simply by denying some of its legal incidents or consequences, Ware could not see how a court could recognize a foreigner's "artificial" status and at the same time refuse "to adopt all those subsidiary laws of his domicile which regulate and protect him in the enjoyment of his personal status." In short, a free state could not acknowledge the relationship between master and slave and then deny all its legal consequences. Davy had made the same point in defending Somerset. Logically, the abstract status of slavery depended on the legal incapacities subsumed under the incidents of status. Yet Ware dealt gingerly with the question of altered status. He interpreted Shaw's dictum, in Commonwealth *v.* Aves, to mean there was no change in the slave's personal state with respect to the laws of the country he had left. Thus Ware confirmed Lord Stowell's judgment that the state of slavery was merely suspended, and might reattach to the Negro if he should return to his former domicile.[84]

Much earlier, English courts had gravitated toward a compromise position that avoided direct challenge to colonial law. The opinions of eminent American jurists like Story, Shaw, and Ware were delivered in much the same spirit, although their emphasis on the terri-

---

necticut, and insisted that the state should give comity to a status recognized by Georgia law (Catterall, ed., *Judicial Cases,* IV, 434–35).

[84] Polydore *v.* Prince, 19 F. Cas. 950 (No. 11, 257) (D. Me., 1837); Graveson, *Status in the Common Law,* pp. 28, 64–67; Story, *Conflict of Laws,* pp. 101–02, 111–15, 168–69.

torial sovereignty of northern states served also to sanction the sovereignty of southern states. There were strong grounds for a national legal consensus: slaves who escaped into the free states, without the consent of their masters, must be returned to their masters; but if a master voluntarily took a slave into a free state, with any intention of residing here, the slave became free. The widening "gray area" concerned the effects of transit or a temporary sojourn and the obligation of slave jurisdictions to respect a change of status as defined by the policy of nonslaveholding jurisdictions. To the sober legal mind it appeared that if slavery itself was unknown to English common law, the triumph of an adapted common law in nineteenth-century America could help reconcile conflicting jurisdictions within an overarching system of consistent, rational, and universal principles. The harmonizing power of reason could offset the impetuous demands of the human "heart."[85]

Thomas Cobb, for example, argued that public feeling had distorted both the issues and judgment in the Somerset case. But Cobb ignored the relevance of public feeling to public policy. When the people had come to see slavery as an "odious" institution, any protection given to transient masters would be interpreted as a complicity in crime and as an infringement upon the liberties of all the people. For Granville Sharp the moral and legal issues would have been the same if Somerset had been the only slave in England and had resided there for only a day. In the Knight case, the master's counsel maintained that one could not presume that the municipal laws of any country were unjust; therefore, on principles of equity the Scottish courts should presume the lawfulness of Jamaican slavery. But this gambit encouraged the court to move beyond Lord Mansfield's position and to decide not only that Jamaican law was without effect in Scotland, but that it violated universal principles of justice and morality.[86]

The Constitution made it far more difficult for American courts to impeach local slave codes in accordance with "higher law" principles. For the supreme law of the land expressly stipulated that "no person held to service of labour in one State under the laws thereof, escaping

[85] For the conflicting expectations regarding the common law in America, within the dialectical framework of "head" and "heart," see Perry Miller, *The Life of the Mind in America: From the Revolution to the Civil War* (New York, 1965), pp. 99–265.
[86] 20 *How. St. Tr.* 1 at 3–6n.

into another, shall, in consequence of any law or regulation therein, be discharged from such service or labour, but shall be delivered up on claim of the party to whom such service or labour may be due." Some northern jurists insisted that if it were not for this clause, a slave would be automatically emancipated, as a result of Mansfield's interpretation of common law, upon fleeing to a free state.[87] But given the force of the Constitution, this view could only be an inducement to noncooperation.

And noncooperation, like "higher law" principles, could work both ways. Missouri courts, for example, had long accepted Sergeant Davy's argument that a master who chose to reside in free territory did, "by such residence, declare his slave to have become a free man." But by 1852, in the portentous case of [Dred] Scott *v.* Emerson, the Missouri Supreme Court reversed an earlier judgment of freedom on the grounds that "no State is bound to carry into effect enactments conceived in a spirit hostile to that which pervades her own laws." Justice William Scott went on to note:

Times now are not as they were when the former decisions on this subject were made. Since then not only individuals but States have been possessed with a dark and fell spirit in relation to slavery, whose gratification is sought in the pursuit of measures, whose inevitable consequence must be the overthrow and destruction of our government. Under such circumstances it does not behoove the State of Missouri to show the least countenance to any measure which might gratify this spirit.[88]

Among those hostile measures, according to Justice Scott's famous upholder, was the Missouri Compromise Act, which deprived a citizen of the United States of his property, without due process, "merely because he . . . brought his property into a particular Territory of the United States."[89]

Here we have an appeal to "higher law" justice of a different kind, and at a time when northern states had moved far toward Granville

[87] Cobb, *Law of Negro Slavery,* p. 203.

[88] Scott (a man of color) *v.* Emerson (1852), Catterall, ed., *Judicial Cases,* V, 185–86; Horowitz, "Choice of Law Decisions," pp. 596–98.

[89] Dred Scott *v.* Sanford (1856), Catterall ed., *Judicial Cases,* V, 200. In a prescient moment, Lord Mansfield had asked, during the Somerset trial, "might not a slave as well be freed by going out of Virginia to the adjacent country, where there are no slaves, if change to a place of contrary custom was sufficient?" (20 *How. St. Tr.* 1 at 70). But in 1772 there was of course no such adjacent country.

Sharp's demand, at the time of Somerset, that courts should enforce common-law principles of liberty and abide by the divine law of Deuteronomy 23:15: "Thou shalt not deliver unto his master the servant which is escaped from his master unto thee." Sharp had succeeded in making England an asylum for a few James Somersets, if not for the Grace Joneses who returned with their masters, prior to 1834, to the West Indies. Partly because of geographic separation, partly because of judicial compromise, Sharp's demand posed no direct threat to colonial slavery, the legality of which Parliament confirmed, in 1833, by generous compensation to the owners of slave property. In the United States, however, "higher law" ideals became something more than goals to be approximated. They became, as it were, transubstantiated into geographic space and national destiny.

Logically, one cannot have two conflicting bodies of "higher law." The effectiveness of a "higher law," like that of any ultimate weapon, depends on its credibility to all concerned. During the early years of the Republic the abolitionists' appeals to "higher law" justice appeared innocently theoretical, since all courts agreed that slavery was legal in many jurisdictions and that the law must ultimately mediate conflicts in accordance with the reciprocal interests of the various states. Hence states like Pennsylvania and New York, when adopting laws for gradual emancipation, specifically allowed for the return of fugitives as well as for the temporary sojourn of southern masters and slaves.

Yet psychologically, at least, the northern abolition laws were acts of self-purification (and let us recall William Roscoe's remark, regarding the British abolition of the slave trade, that "it can be no breach of the Law of Nations to prevent other Countries from a practice which we have ourselves relinquished as contrary to justice & humanity"). These statutes, no matter how qualified, became an affront to slaveholders in neighboring states. As early as the 1790s, masters in Virginia and Maryland bitterly complained that Pennsylvanians were uncooperative in returning fugitives. Frequent attempts to kidnap free blacks, under the pretext of recovering runaways, intensified the spirit of noncooperation. Systematic legal delays led the Maryland legislature to complain, in 1823, that the people were beginning to view Pennsylvania as "a hostile state." Three years later Maryland sent three commissioners to negotiate with the Pennslyvania legislature, much as Jamaica had earlier done with Cuba. The federal law was so ineffective, according to Maryland, that it was necessary for the two states "practically to arrange a treaty."[90] Although the United States Supreme Court finally ruled that Pennsylvania could not interfere in the recovery of fugitives (Prigg *v.* Pennsylvania), by the 1840s the legislature was ready to prohibit any state judge or official from helping to implement the 1793 federal law. Other northern states passed similar personal liberty acts and also repealed the sojourner laws which had allowed, on grounds of comity, a temporary residence of masters and slaves. It appeared that self-purification could not be reconciled with any complicity in the slave system.

Even prior to the Fugitive Slave Law of 1850, bolder assertions of territorial sovereignty were matched by bolder appeals to "higher law" justice. Whereas the Garrisonians condemned the Constitution as a proslavery document, other abolitionists and future Radical Republicans claimed that slavery was itself unconstitutional in any federal jurisdiction. Thus in the relatively moderate view of Senator Salmon P. Chase, the Constitution had "found slavery and left it a State institution—the creature and dependent of State law—wholly local in its existence and character." An institution so directly repugnant to natural right, to the common law, and to the spirit of the Constitution might be tolerated for a time where it had long been entrenched and where it had received the sanction of municipal law. It could not, however, be recognized by the federal government without subverting the character and mission of the American people.[91]

Southern judges had also looked upon slavery as the creature of municipal law, which they had seen as its major shield of defense. Unlike the earlier British defenders of the slave trade, they could not really appeal to the law of nations or to the international custom and practice of merchants. The African slave trade was not yet dead, but it could hardly serve as a touchstone of legitimacy. Indeed, Southerners had often defined Negro slavery as an unfortunate (if neces-

[90] Edward Raymond Turner, *The Negro in Pennsylvania: Slavery-Servitude-Freedom, 1639–1861* (Washington, 1911), pp. 228–35. For a detailed study of legal conflicts over kidnapping and the recovery of fugitive slaves, see Thomas D. Morris, *Free Men All: The Personal Liberty Laws of the North, 1780–1861* (Baltimore, 1974).

[91] Eric Foner, *Free Soil, Free Labor, Free Men: The Ideology of the Republican Party Before the Civil War* (New York, 1970), pp. 76–77. The Constitutional views of antislavery men like Chase and James G. Birney were too complex to be summarized here.

sary) evil bequeathed by British avarice. Thus in terms of law, American slavery had become increasingly circumscribed by the South's own localism and insistence on state sovereignty—both of which, incidentally, justified a refusal to recognize the free status and civil rights of northern or English black seamen who called at southern ports.[92]

Yet the South's legal isolation required mutual comity and respect, which were the only protections against the "higher law" absolutism of the abolitionists. When it became clear that both comity and respect were waning, southern leaders demanded that the federal government protect the rights of slaveholders in the common territories, on the high seas, and in conflicts with free states and nations. For unless such parity could be won, the South would in effect acquiesce to the antislavery view of "higher law" justice, transforming the pretension into a reality. The southern demands were not unprecedented. During most of the eighteenth century the English government had protected the property rights of slaveholders wherever it had jurisdiction. No Southerner could ask for more than Lord Chancellor Hardwicke had granted, in 1749, as a matter of course. But during the following century Anglo-American law increasingly absorbed antislavery doctrine as part of its own continuing self-validation. Southern territorial sovereignty, to legitimize itself, required some external sanction. Yet the external law could no longer legitimize slavery without impairing its own legitimacy. In the words of Chase, which echoed the judgments of Sharp, Davy, and Hargrave, "the very moment a slave passed beyond the jurisdiction of the state . . . he ceases to be a slave; not because any law or regulation of the state which he enters confers freedom upon him, but because he *continues* to be a man and *leaves behind* him the law of force, which made him a slave."[93] Against such a doctrine, it appeared, one could apply only the law of force.

[92] Fladeland, *Men and Brothers,* pp. 187–89, 319–21.
[93] Foner, *Free Soil,* p. 77.

Eleven ∽

The Good Book

The Perversion of Scripture: The Bible's Bondage to Slavery

Whether the Bible was "for" or "against" slavery was a hotly contested issue in ante-bellum America. William Lloyd Garrison, after belatedly discovering Thomas Paine's *The Age of Reason* in 1845, concluded that the Bible must be judged "by its reasonableness and utility, by the probabilities of the case, by historical confirmation, by human experience and observation, by the facts of science, by the intuition of the spirit. Truth is older than any parchment." Garrison's disciple, Henry Clarke Wright, summed up the radical abolitionist view in the title of an essay, "The Bible, if Opposed to Self-Evident Truth, is Self-Evident Falsehood." For Charles Stearns this meant that the Old Testament was a tissue of lies, "no more the work of God than the Koran, or the Book of Mormon." An assault on revealed religion could thus culminate a long history of antislavery challenges to authority.[1]

But George Barrell Cheever, pastor of the Presbyterian Church of the Puritans in Manhattan, took a more compromising and popular position in his detailed antislavery "vindications" of the Bible. Cheever agreed with the Garrisonians that God could never, under any circumstances, sanction slavery. Drawing on German philological scholarship, he tried to prove there was no word for "slave" in Hebrew. Even

[1] Aileen S. Kraditor, *Means and Ends in American Abolitionism: Garrison and His Critics on Strategy and Tactics, 1834–1850* (New York, 1969), p. 93; John Demos, "The Antislavery Movement and the Problem of Violent 'Means,'" *New England Quarterly*, XXXVI (Dec. 1964), 521.

the Greek word, *doulos,* had been transfixed and redeemed by its union, in the New Testament, with *'ebed,* the noble Hebrew word for servant or worker. Thus in Cheever's eyes, corrupt translations had misled both the apologists for slavery and the anti-Bible abolitionists.[2]

Like the Garrisonians, Cheever relied on man's moral sensibility as the ultimate standard of judgment, though for Cheever this standard necessitated a rather strained interpretation of Scripture. For example, if Abraham had owned slaves, it would have been "monstrous" for God to have chosen the patriarch as the exemplar of a righteous society and as the precursor of Christian civilization. According to Cheever's moral logic, it was thus blasphemous to assert that Abraham's servants were slaves.

Unfortunately, Cheever found himself pitted against centuries of Biblical interpretation. He took issue, for example, with an eminent British commentator of the early eighteenth century who had rightly concluded that slavery was an established institution among the ancient Hebrews. Exodus 21:4, which concerns the freeing of Hebrew servants on the sabbatic year, and which probably applied only to defaulting debtors, reads: "If a master have given him a wife, and she have born him sons or daughters; the wife and her children shall be her master's, and he shall go out by himself." Dr. Thomas Pyle, the eighteenth-century commentator, had interpreted this passage to mean that "if a wife were procured him by his master, or appointed him by the magistrate that sold him, *only to breed slaves by,* then, if he leaves his service, he shall leave the wife and children, *as the master's proper goods and possession!* [Cheever's emphasis]." This view is supported by what we know of female slaves in the ancient Near East, who were frequently used as prostitutes or mated with male slaves to increase a master's holdings. But Cheever's outrage focused on the commentator, not the text: "Could there be a manifestation of more profound insensibility, darkness, and consequent perversion of the moral sense, than this?"[3] It was no wonder, he added, that as a result of "such

[2] George Barrell Cheever, *God Against Slavery: and the Freedom and Duty of the Pulpit to Rebuke It, as a Sin Against God* (Cincinnati, 1857), *passim;* Cheever, *The Guilt of Slavery and the Crime of Slaveholding, Demonstrated from the Hebrew and Greek Scriptures* (Boston, 1860), *passim.* Cheever wrote emotional tracts defending the divine justice of capital punishment.

[3] Cheever, *The Guilt of Slavery,* p. 64; Isaac Mendelsohn, *Slavery in the Ancient Near East: A Comparative Study of Slavery in Babylonia, Assyria, Syria*

habits of thinking, and such doctrines of devils, as the supposed water of life," a British sailor like John Newton could have continued in the slave trade even after religious conversion. One may note that Thomas Paine had also complained of religion's brutalizing effects, but had concluded that when we read "the obscene stories, the voluptuous debaucheries, the cruel and torturous executions, the unrelenting vindictiveness, with which more than half the Bible is filled, it would be more consistent that we called it the word of a demon, than the word of God."[4] Cheever assumed, optimistically, that there could have been no dispute over the sinfulness of slavery if men had only been taught the Bible's true meaning.

Apologetics and Latitudinarian Drift

Biblical interpretation had seldom been an important issue in the British controversies over the slave trade. Despite the predominantly religious motivation of British Quakers and Evangelicals, the abolitionists, with a few exceptions like Granville Sharp, made little use of Scriptural argument. Wilberforce, for example, specifically cautioned against introducing such discussion in the House of Commons.[5] The abolitionists' main excursions into Biblical exegesis came as a direct response to experimental probings by the proslavery group. It would be a mistake to conclude, however, that there was little significance to the late-eighteenth-century disputes over the Biblical sanction of slavery.

One may easily explain the relatively secular character of British antislavery arguments. The principal defense of the slave trade lay along lines of national interest and foreign competition. This down-to-earth posture inevitably influenced the strategy of abolitionist attacks. Moreover, the antislavery movement rested, philosophically, on a widely shared set of moral assumptions that allowed active cooperation between Quakers, Unitarians, Methodists, and Evangelicals. There was little need to resort to ultimate and possibly divisive questions of divine authority.

---

and Palestine, from the Middle of the Third Millennium to the End of the First Millennium (New York, 1949), pp. 40, 50–52, 88–89.

[4] Thomas Paine, *The Age of Reason, Being an Investigation of True and of Fabulous Theology* (Paris, 1794–1795), Part I, 17.

[5] William Wilberforce to unknown correspondent, June 17, 1806, autograph MSS, Historical Society of Pennsylvania.

By the 1770s there was a widespread consensus, on the level of moral theory, that slavery not only violated natural law but represented the supreme denial of those benevolent instincts which preserved society from anarchy. The eighteenth-century "man of feeling," the ideal of so much literary, religious, and philosophical writing, had been trained to empathize with human suffering. Convinced that reason and national interest should not require unending misery and slaughter, he would respond automatically to empirical exposures of the slave trade.[6]

Yet the "man of feeling" was also the product of a century's latitudinarian drift away from Biblical legalism. Few Christians were prepared to acknowledge the extent of this drift toward human sentiment as the ultimate arbiter, let alone assert, with Thomas Paine, that God would never choose "such a nation of ruffians and cut-throats as the ancient Jews were."[7] In England, with the exception of a few despised Deists, no one seriously challenged the belief that the Old Testament was the revealed word of God; that its inconsistencies were only apparent and were questioned only by the ignorant (Gilbert Wakefield, on the title page of his refutation of Paine, quoted Pope's "a little learning is a dangerous thing"); that the New Testament was a fulfillment and not a replacement of the Old; and that together they provided a living guide to the present and a key to the future.[8] Sir Isaac Newton had shared his age's passion for deciphering prophecy and for echatological exegesis. Succeeding scholars and mathematicians showed a continuing fascination with the dates and chronology of the Old Testament and made computations based on sabbatic years, jubilees, and astronomical calculations, in an effort to plot the course of things to come. The desire for a scientific system of prophetic

---

[6] David Brion Davis, *The Problem of Slavery in Western Culture* (Ithaca, N.Y., 1966), pp. 333–493.

[7] Paine, *Age of Reason*, Part II, 35.

[8] Gilbert Wakefield, *An Examination of the Age of Reason, by Thomas Paine* (2nd ed., London, 1794); "Philalethes," *Common Sense; or the Plain Man's Answer to the Question, Whether Christianity Be a Religion Worthy of Our Choice in the Age of Reason? In Two Letters to a Deistical Friend* (London, n.d.); Mark Pattison, "Tendencies of Religious Thought in England, 1688–1740," in *Essays and Reviews* (2nd ed., London, 1860), pp. 254–329; G. R. Cragg, *From Puritanism to the Age of Reason; A Study of Changes in Religious Thought within the Church of England, 1660–1700* (Cambridge, England, 1950); Hoxie N. Fairchild, *Religious Trends in English Poetry* (New York, 1939–1949), I (*Protestantism and the Cult of Sentiment, 1700–1740*); II (*Religious Sentimentalism in the Age of Johnson, 1740–1780*).

interpretation was part of the spirit of the Enlightenment. But it also represented a response to deism, which threatened to discredit Biblical chronology and to drive a wedge between Scripture and natural law.

The enlightened world of the mid-eighteenth century, so eager to acclaim a Montesquieu, had little patience for the theories of Jean Astruc, a French physician, who suggested that the discrepancies in Genesis could be explained by studying the book as two separate narratives. A generation later, J. G. Eichhorn met sharp opposition in England as well as in his native Germany when he tried to show that the Pentateuch consisted of interwoven narratives from various epochs. In Britain, the lone figure of Alexander Geddes, a Scottish Catholic, pursued serious critical scholarship on the separate origins of the Pentateuch. But when Geddes published his first outlines of Biblical criticism, in 1792, he was contemptuously denounced by Catholics and Protestants alike. The early Biblical debates over slavery occurred at a time when Protestant literalism still prevailed and when most Englishmen read both Old and New Testaments as a miraculously unified whole.[9]

It is important to add that the early antislavery movement coincided in time with the beginnings of serious Biblical criticism on historical as well as philological grounds. But this scholarship, in the early nineteenth century largely confined to Germany, had a delayed impact in both England and America. On the other hand, the German critical movement drew heavily on British Old Testament apologetics of the mid-eighteenth century, which derived in turn from the earlier deist controversies. The issues aroused by the Deists' challenge gave a new direction to Biblical scholarship; they are also central to an understanding of the later Biblical arguments over slavery.

The English Deists were by no means the first questioners of revelation, and their traumatic impact on British Protestantism cannot be explained by either the originality or popularity of men like Matthew Tindal, Anthony Collins, Thomas Woolston, and Peter Annet. What outraged their supposedly orthodox opponents was that the Deists showed precisely where the growing spirit of rationalism and moralism

---

[9] T. K. Cheyne, *Founders of Old Testament Criticism* (New York, 1893), *passim;* W. Neil, "The Criticism and Theological Use of the Bible, 1700–1950," in *The Cambridge History of the Bible,* ed. by S. L. Greenslade (Cambridge, England, 1963), pp. 238–55. By the eighteenth century, however, there had been a decline in typological and allegorical interpretations.

could lead—namely, to the obliteration of any distinctive notion of sacred history, and hence to the loss of any transcendent, objective standard, independent of man's reason and feelings. Since the orthodox themselves had already absorbed heavy doses of rationalism and moralism, they were particularly vulnerable to arguments that had once been used to demolish Catholic "superstitions" or to prove, contrary to Thomas Hobbes, that nature had endowed man with a spirit of compassion and benevolence. Instead of simply condemning the Deists as heretics, the churchmen felt constrained to defend Scripture against the charges of absurdity, inconsistency, and barbarity. And by accepting the Deists' battleground, the orthodox also accepted the definition of the Bible as a controversial "book." In the words of Leslie Stephen:

To explain a difficulty is to signalise its existence; and even the bare fact that criticism was regarded as applicable to the Bible was at once fatal to the popular conception of its absolute, flawless, and supernatural perfection. To explain that you are only removing the external rust is vain; for who shall say where the rust ends and the true substance begins?[10]

By the 1730s Christian apologists had learned that disputes over textual details could never drain the deepening pools of doubt. As a compromise, it was sufficient to insist on the centrality of the resurrection and the historical fulfillment of Old Testament prophecy. As Stephen sums up the pragmatic resolution, Engishmen could still believe everything in the Bible, "but nothing too vigorously"; if the book was not flawless, it was "true enough for practical purposes."[11]

So far as slavery is concerned, the Deists pointed toward the future position of Paine and Garrison. Thus God, by definition, was good and just. Yet the God of the Bible had authorized slavery as a divine punishment, along with such barbarities as the stoning to death of stubborn children who refused to obey their parents. It followed that the Bible could not be God's word. Tindal specifically compared the Jewish enslavement of Canaanites to the Spanish conquest of Mexico. The claim of divine sanction should not lessen one's outrage over either crime. The Deists held, as a fundamental assumption, that moral laws are as uniform, timeless, and invariable as the laws of Newtonian

[10] Leslie Stephen, *History of English Thought in the Eighteenth Century* (3rd ed., New York, 1949), I, 76–91, 168–73, 202.
[11] *Ibid.*, I, 272–73.

science. Hence there were no special "dispensations"; the truths of Christianity were "as old as creation." One might suppose that this uniformitarianism would be especially congenial to an antislavery philosophy: if enslavement was wrong in the eighteenth century, it had been wrong from the beginning of time.[12]

But this absolutist argument could easily be reversed. If men had enslaved one another throughout history, who was to say that the institution was not part of the natural order of things? As the Deists' critics delighted in pointing out, nature was no less cruel than the God of the Pentateuch. Did not nature, so revered by supposedly enlightened minds, kill thousands of innocent children every day? And if the orthodox felt strained when challenged to justify God's sanction of lying and murder, were not the Deists hard put to explain how nature's seeming evils dissolved in some larger good, that "Whatever is, is right"? Rational criticism might expose the "immorality" of the revealed word, but could reason alone, unaided by revelation, arrive at a knowledge of ultimate right and wrong? Like the Deists, later defenders of the slave trade would appeal to the standards of universality and expediency: no practice could be wrong which had been sanctioned by so many nations in so many ages; the world, moreover, was full of apparent evils which contributed to larger goods.[13]

An answer to this problem—the meaning of evil in a Newtonian universe—emerged from the anti-deist apologies for Christianity. In response to the Deists' insistence on uniform laws, the apologists merged the idea of man's natural benevolence with a theory of moral progress. As R. S. Crane has pointed out, the psychological concepts of association, imitation, and sympathy helped explain the cumulative development of man's moral capacities. Like scientific knowledge, the moral sensibility of the eighteenth century was the product of many centuries of social experience. Accordingly, it was no more reasonable to call the ancient Hebrews "a nation of ruffians and cut-throats" than to expect them to have discovered the laws of planetary motion. This notion of progressive moral development refurbished the ancient theories of Scriptural dispensations in which God had accommodated

[12] *Ibid.*, I, 83–91, 130–34, 171, 259.
[13] *Ibid.*, I, 134, 257–61, 293–307; Gordon Turnbull, *An Apology for Negro Slavery: Or the West-Indian Planters Vindicated from the Charge of Inhumanity* (2nd ed., London, 1786), pp. 34–35; J. Bellon de Saint-Quentin, *Dissertation sur la traite et le commerce des nègres* (Paris, 1764), pp. 18–19.

revelation to man's understanding. As popularized by figures like Edward Law, in the 1740s, and John Taylor, in the 1760s, the idea of continuous progress breathed new meaning into revelation as a concomitant to man's natural advance. God the educator replaced God the engineer. If His truth was eternal, He had timed His revelations to fit man's cultural stages. Thus many of the ordinances of the Old Testament that seemed so barbarous to enlightened critics were simply evidences of the moral limitations of early man. Christianity could not be "as old as creation" precisely because an understanding of Christian obligations required millennia of cultural preparation.[14]

The theory that divine revelation had been adapted to man's changing capacities was part of the intellectual bedrock of the early antislavery movement. Along with the moral philosophies of men like Francis Hutcheson and James Foster, it provided a means for explaining and justifying the historical emergence of an ethic that broke sharply with the religious sanctions of the past. When secularized, the theory of moral progress could lead to the cultural relativism of John Millar, who in 1771 attacked slavery as an obsolete relic which had once been suited to man's political economy but which had disappeared from Europe because of its increasing inutility. Yet most antislavery writers tried to preserve the delicate balance between moral progress and universal moral law. It was treacherous to admit that God had once sanctioned slavery as "suitable" for a more primitive stage of society. Defenders of the slave trade marshaled considerable evidence to prove the present utility of the Atlantic slave system; and if God synchronized His demands with changing human needs, who could say that He disapproved of the unfortunate requirements of Caribbean commerce? The theory of progressive revelation threatened to remove any transcendent standard, and to equate divine justice, so far as it could be known, with man's present capacities and needs.[15]

Thus when slavery's apologists raised the issue of Biblical sanction, they helped expose a quiet but profound transformation in British attitudes toward evil, human nature, and progress. The ideological lines were by no means clear-cut, since abolitionists insisted on their

[14] Ronald S. Crane, "Suggestions toward a Genealogy of the 'Man of Feeling,'" *Journal of English Literary History,* I (1934), 205–30; Crane, "Anglican Apologetics and the Idea of Progress, 1699–1745," *Modern Philology,* XXXI (Feb., 1934), 281–306, 352–79.

[15] Davis, *Problem of Slavery in Western Culture,* chs. 11–13.

own Biblical orthodoxy, and both sides drew on the liberal assumptions of a century of latitudinarian compromise. The apologists could not really deny instances of shocking cruelty and suffering in the African trade, and to some extent they were forced to defer to the catchwords of the Enlightenment, protesting their own concern for human happiness, arguing that isolated abuses should not be allowed to obscure the "realities" of commerce, and calling for calm reason in place of blind "enthusiasm." If antislavery writers conceded that God had not always discountenanced slavery, their adversaries were hardly prepared to call for a reinstitution of the Mosaic code. There were limits and rules, in other words, to the game of textmanship. Yet the abolitionist response to Scriptural authority revealed how far social reform had itself become the ground for faith, supplying fresh symbols for religious emotions and providing a practical test of true divinity.

Initial Salvos

The first skirmish of the Biblical war coincided with the American Revolution and was appropriately transatlantic in character. In 1772, Thomas Thompson, an Anglican missionary who had traveled from the Guinea coast to the West Indies, then to New Jersey, and back to England, took up the theme of abstract lawfulness. Disclaiming any need to prove that the African slave trade was either virtuous or immune from abuse, Thompson limited himself to the central moral issue: if a species of commerce, sanctioned and encouraged by Parliament, could be shown to violate God's law, then England was indeed guilty of a dangerous national sin. Yet in Leviticus 25:39–55 God had made His will manifest, informing Moses that Hebrew servants were not to be treated with rigor and were to be freed every fiftieth year, or jubilee; but that

the children of the strangers that sojourn among you, of them shall ye buy, and of their families that are with you, which they have begotten in your land: and they shall be your possession. And ye shall take them as an inheritance for your children after you, to inherit them for a possession; they shall be your bondmen for ever.[16]

[16] Thomas Thompson, *The African Trade for Negro Slaves, Shewn to Be Consistent with Principles of Humanity, and with the Laws of Revealed Religion* (Canterbury, n.d. [1772 or possibly 1773]), pp. 8–12, 31; Lev. 25:39–55. Isaac Mendelsohn, who has studied Biblical slavery within a wider comparative context, has concluded that the sabbatic year manumission applied only to native

In Thompson's eyes, any practice so clearly and positively sanctioned by God could not be inconsistent with natural law. The enslavement of "strangers" could not in itself be condemned as sin. Moreover, since Paul had sent the fugitive Onesimus back to his master, to serve both as a slave and as "more than a servant, a brother beloved," it appeared that Christian conversion changed a bondsman's spiritual condition, but not his legal obligation.[17]

The relative rarity of such Biblical arguments should not obscure the embarrassment they brought to abolitionist writers who took Scripture seriously and who could never dream of following the later routes of Paine and Garrison. In his own copy of Thompson's pamphlet, Anthony Benezet penned angry marginal comments. What upset him most was the effrontery of raising the question of national sin, and then dismissing it on the ground that Jewish constitutions were consistent with the law of nature. The Jews, after all, had been allowed divorce, even though God had made it clear from the moment of Creation that divorce was contrary to natural law.[18] In 1768, Benezet had been informed by Dr. Daniel Burton that the Society for the Propagation of the Gospel could not condemn slaveholding as unlawful, "finding the contrary very plainly implied in the precepts, given by the Apostles both to masters and servants; which last, were then, for the most part, *slaves.*" Even Granville Sharp, out of respect for the Church of England, had declined Benezet's appeal for public support against Burton. But in two pamphlets Sharp took up cudgels against Thompson, repeating Benezet's objection on divorce and contending

---

debtors, that the Levitical jubilee was designed to protect poor Hebrews who sold themselves into bondage either to fellow Hebrews or strangers, and that such limitations in no way extended to enslaved aliens, whose bondage was hereditary and perpetual (*Slavery in the Ancient Near East,* pp. 32–40, 65, 85–89, 123).

[17] Thompson, *African Trade,* pp. 11–18; Philem. 16. Paul's Epistle to Philemon has aroused endless debate, but modern scholarship casts doubt on earlier antislavery interpretations (see P. R. Coleman-Norton, ed., *Studies in Roman Economic and Social History, in Honor of Allan Chester Johnson* [Princeton, 1951], pp. 164–69; William L. Westermann, *The Slave Systems of Greek and Roman Antiquity* [Philadelphia, 1955], pp. 158–59).

[18] Thompson, *African Trade,* copy annotated by Anthony Benezet, Rutgers University Library. Thompson's arguments were repeated in *A Treatise Upon the Trade from Great Britain to Africa,* by "an African Merchant," a pamphlet which also aroused Benezet and which drew fire from *The Monthly Review,* XLVIII (Jan.–June, 1773), 43–49.

that God had tolerated many practices among the Jews because of their extreme inability, "at that time," to bear a more perfect system of law. The difference between the peculiar Jewish laws and the universal moral laws binding all mankind could be "very easily distinguished by every sincere Christian, who examines them with *a liberal mind*, because the *benevolent purpose* of the Divine Author is *always apparent* in those laws which are to be *eternally binding*." But of course this argument meant that revelation was to be judged by eighteenth-century standards of benevolence.[19]

At the prompting of Benezet, Benjamin Rush wrote an anonymous pamphlet in 1773 which tried, among other things, to show that natural and revealed religion always speak the same truths. He acknowledged that this position aligned him against the recent scholarship of John Millar, who held that the Bible in no place condemned slavery, and that emancipation was a natural outgrowth of later economic progress. Rush also faced the barbs of his colleagues on the faculty of the College of Philadelphia, a "set of free-thinking gentlemen," as he put it, who disparaged all his publications. At the end of his bitter controversy over slavery with Richard Nisbet, Rush privately confessed that "the Negro cause upon this account has suffered through me in Philadelphia." Since he also claimed that three-fourths of the entire province opposed slavery, indicating that Nisbet had taken the unpopular side, the admission was hardly a note of triumph.[20]

[19] Granville Sharp to the Bishop of Llandaff, July 25, 1774, Sharp papers, British and Foreign Bible Society; Prince Hoare, *Memoirs of Granville Sharp, Esq. Composed From His Own Manuscripts* . . . (London, 1820), p. 262; Sharp, *An Essay on Slavery, Proving From Scripture its Inconsistency with Humanity and Religion* (Burlington, West Jersey, 1773; reprinted London, 1776), pp. 19–22; Sharp, *The Just Limitation of Slavery in the Laws of God, Compared with the Unbounded Claims of the African Traders and British American Slaveholders* (London, 1776) pp. 10–11, 14, 26. Sharp, who also attacked the "African Merchant's" *Treatise,* expressed great alarm over the increase in religious infidelity and the "open declarations of Deists, Arians, Socinians, and others, who deny the Divinity of Christ, and of the Holy Ghost" (*Just Limitation,* p. 26n.). It was essential, he felt, to vindicate Scripture and the Christian religion by proving that slavery was contrary to divine law.

[20] [Benjamin Rush], *An Address to the Inhabitants of the British Settlements in America, upon Slave-Keeping* (Philadelphia, 1773), pp. 9–11; Rush to Granville Sharp, May 1, 1773; Rush to William Gordon, Oct. 10, 1773, *Letters of Benjamin Rush,* ed. by L. H. Butterfield (2 vols., Princeton, 1951), I, 80–82. It is unclear whether Rush had religious disputes or personal rivalry in mind.

In the first pamphlet Rush fluctuated between two incompatible positions. Like Sharp, he maintained that the ancient Jews had been "permitted" practices that were clearly condemned by natural law, the telling proof being their allowance of divorce and remarriage for both parties. It is curious that this illustration received such heavy emphasis from early abolitionists, who apparently assumed that the evil of divorce was more self-evident than the evil of slavery, to say nothing of other practices, which they failed to mention, authorized along with divorce, such as the right of a bridegroom to have his bride stoned to death if her father could not produce the "tokens" of her virginity.[21]

Rush's second position represented a retreat from absolutist morality. There was, he found, a mitigating reason for allowing the Jews to enslave the "strangers" in their midst. Only by enslavement could they prevent intermarriage, corruption, and the loss of their mission as a distinct people. White Americans would suggest a similar justification for keeping Negroes enslaved, but Rush advanced the conventional argument that Christ had broken down the barriers between nations, commanding that love be extended to all mankind. He was far too orthodox, however, to suggest that Christ had repealed the Old Testament ("Think not that I am come to destroy the law, or the prophets: I am not come to destroy, but to fulfill"). To be sure, fulfillment could mean drastic tightening of moral requirements, as shown by the succeeding passages of the Sermon on the Mount, which put lust and divorce on the level of adultery, and which exhorted men to love their persecutors. But unless abolitionists like Rush could

---

[21] [Rush], *Address*, pp. 10–11; Deut. 23; 24. The abhorred provisions on divorce, which are part of the Jewish regulations for collective purification, directly follow the most promising antislavery passage in the Bible: "Thou shalt not deliver unto his master a servant that is escaped from his master unto thee: he shall dwell with thee . . . in the place which he shall choose within one of thy gates, where it pleaseth him best (Deut. 23:15–16). Mendelsohn calls the passage "unparalleled in the slave legislation of the Ancient Near East," and suggests that it applied only to Hebrew fugitives escaping from slavery in foreign countries, since otherwise it would have spelled the end to slavery in Palestine (*Slavery in the Ancient Near East*, pp. 63–64). Sharp used the passage to impeach the validity of the fugitive-slave clause in the United States Constitution, and it became a key weapon in the Biblical arsenal of later American abolitionists. Its relatively minor place in early antislavery exegesis may possibly be the result of its proximity to the allowance of divorce, which was offered as the main evidence of the depravity of Jewish law.

show that Christ had specifically condemned slavery, it would appear that the reasons justifying God's earlier authorization might be sufficient under the new dispensation. Here Rush relied on the earlier Quaker view that Christ had attacked theft, murder, pride, intemperance, covetousness, and hate, all of which were ingredients of slavery. But the same could be said for institutions which Rush accepted, such as war. Unlike the Quakers, he seemed insensitive to the implications of identifying individual sins with social institutions.[22]

It was on this point that Nisbet could accuse Rush of blasphemy. Nisbet had been educated at Oxford, had later studied theology and law, and had resided at Nevis and St. Kitts before moving to Philadelphia. His ostensible purpose for writing *Slavery Not Forbidden by Scripture* was to defend his West Indian friends against what he considered Rush's slanders. Nisbet objected to the illogic of inferring an opposition to slavery from Christ's general precepts on charity. So long as men were governed by self-interest, there were no institutions free from abuse and cruelty. Christ and His disciples had boldly denounced a multitude of specific sins. Why not slavery? They had risked persecution by speaking out against the injustices of Roman law, yet Rush "is so wicked as to accuse our Saviour of the meanest dissimulation, by saying, that he forbore to mention any thing that might seem contrary to the Roman or Jewish laws." To suggest that Christ had regarded slavery as a genuine evil was to say that the Saviour had lacked the courage of his convictions.[23]

As for the ancient Hebrews, their foreign or heathen slaves had clearly been regarded as property; unlike Jewish servants, they had been unprotected by any humane code. Nisbet scornfully dismissed Rush's argument that God had permitted the Jews slavery in order to prevent exogamous marriage. During subsequent centuries the Jews had managed to remain a separate people without the benefit of

---

[22] [Rush], *Address*, pp. 10–14; [Rush], *A Vindication of the Address, to the Inhabitants of the British Settlements, on the Slavery of the Negroes in America, in Answer to a Pamphlet Entitled, "Slavery Not Forbidden by Scripture"* . . . (Philadelphia, 1773), pp. 8–9.

[23] [Richard Nisbet], *Slavery Not Forbidden by Scripture; or a Defense of the West-India Planters, from the Aspersions Thrown Out Against Them, by the Author of a Pamphlet, Entitled, "An Address to the Inhabitants of the British Settlements in America, Upon Slave-Keeping"* (Philadelphia, 1773), pp. 1–3, 6–8. Nisbet also reminded his readers that the College of Philadelphia had gratefully accepted a generous donation from the West Indies.

slavery. Besides, was it not denigrating God to explain His command-ments by such petty reasons: "Could an eternal decree of God be overturned by the pitiful revolutions among men? or could not the same omnipotent being, who marked out the descent of the saviour of the world, prevent the race of Abraham from being corrupted?"[24]

Such arguments may have caused merriment among Rush's free-thinking colleagues, but in his *Vindication,* Rush soberly protested that Providence never employs extraordinary means when ordinary ones will do—implying, significantly, that slavery was the normal and natural means for achieving racial purity. He cited the example of Lisbon, where in the absence of legal impediments the white race had been submerged by African blood. This linkage of ideas reveals much about American racial attitudes, even among abolitionists, although Rush quickly added that the Jews were a unique people who had been permitted the evils of slavery and divorce because of the hardness of their hearts. At the time of Creation, as under the later Christian dispensation, neither wrong could be allowed. Rush struggled to reconcile Biblical particularism with universal law. Yet he did not explain why slaveholding should be taken as evidence of a depravity of heart—if at the same time it could be justified as an "ordinary" means of preserving racial purity.[25]

Religious denominationalism had surprisingly little effect on the early abolitionists' approach to the Bible. Rush was a Presbyterian, Sharp an Anglican. John Woolman, as a Quaker, could be expected to minimize the importance of Scriptural authority and to argue, as he did in one of the first antislavery tracts written in America, that men can be held accountable only for their own sins, not for those of their ancestors. Yet even Woolman, the peace-loving Quaker, accepted Israel's enslavement of the Gibeonites as an execution of God's judg-ment against the wicked. He also thought it quite possible that the Jews, despite their degeneracy, had rightfully enslaved the Canaanites as a means of spreading religious truth. By placing Biblical authority

[24] *Ibid.,* pp. 4–7.
[25] [Rush], *Vindication,* pp. 6–8. If Nisbet put Rush in an awkward position, the physician ultimately won his revenge. Nisbet, who was said to be "unstable," was later committed in Rush's barbarous Pennsylvania Hospital. As the modern editor of the doctor's *Autobiography* innocently notes: "Benjamin Rush must often have seen his old pamphleteering adversary there!" (*The Autobiography of Benjamin Rush,* ed. with introduction and notes by George W. Corner [Princeton, 1948], p. 83, n. 12).

above abstract and uniform justice, Woolman left little ground, aside from the claim of historical dispensations, for refuting slaveholders' appeals to precedent.[26]

During the 1770s American and British abolitionist writers developed a common set of arguments to answer the disturbing thesis that Jewish law must be generally consistent with the law of nature. Since none of them was prepared to challenge the authority of divine revelation, the simplest and most consistent position was that taken by naïve writers like James Swan, who held that Christians should look on Negroes as their "brethren," subject to the Jewish protections against manstealing and perpetual servitude. Greater difficulties arose when Samuel Hopkins, the American theologian, advanced the absolutist doctrine that we may be certain, a priori, of the error of any Biblical construction favoring slavery, since slavery is condemned by "the whole of divine revelation." Hopkins, who is best remembered for his thesis that men should be willing to be damned for the glory of God, then added that if God's vengeance had required the enslavement of certain peoples, His human agents were in no way spared from guilt—a view specifically rejected by Granvile Sharp, whose moral absolutism stopped short of questioning the agents of "divine commissions." Hopkins himself was unprepared to condemn *all* enslavement or even to insist that it must always be acompanied by guilt. Thus like Benjamin Rush, he acknowledged that the Jews had received divine permission to enlave the Canaanites as a means of preserving racial and religious purity. He emphasized, of course, that the curses and permissions of the past gave no more warrant for whites enslaving blacks than for blacks enslaving whites. Yet by admitting that the need for racial purity had once justified enslavement, Hopkins and other anti-slavery writers opened the way for a racist theology based on "nature" as well as Scripture.[27]

Moreover, like Rush, Thomas Clarkson, and even Joseph Priestley, Hopkins appealed to sheer expediency in excusing the silence of the

[26] John Woolman, *The Journal and Essays of John Woolman,* ed. by Amelia Mott Gummere (New York, 1922), pp. 354–55, 357–58.

[27] James Swan, *A Dissuasion to Great-Britain and the Colonies from the Slave Trade to Africa* (Boston, 1772), pp. 31–32, 69–70; [Samuel Hopkins], *A Dialogue Concerning the Slavery of the Africans . . .* (Norwich, 1776; reprinted New York, 1785), pp. 26–33. Swan, who had recently arrived in Boston from England, placed particular emphasis on Deut. 24:7, which condemns manstealers to death (but which clearly refers to Jews who kidnapped and sold their brethren).

early Christians. Since slavery was universal in the Roman world, the early Christians could not denounce the institution without exciting a universal prejudice against religious truth. This was precisely the dilemma Wesley's followers would soon face in the southern states, where denominational growth required a tolerance of human bondage. But then why should antislavery be less subversive in the 1770s than in the time of Christ? The answer, more satisfactory to Hopkins and Clarkson than to the Methodists, was that lack of compromise could no longer endanger the survival of Christian truth. Yet this failed to lift the question above the level of expediency. Both Rush and Hopkins made concessions that jeopardized their central thesis that slaveholders could draw no comfort from the Bible. After asserting that slavery was a flagrant violation of divine and natural law, they agreed that exceptions had once been made for special people and that a Christian's duty to denounce the institution depended in large measure on the risks involved.[28]

The same pattern emerges in the early writings of Sharp and Clarkson, both of whom took the Bible as the literal word of God. By 1776, Sharp could indignantly write that he was no longer contending for the cause of liberty alone, but for a much more important issue: "the honour of the holy Scriptures." A decade later Clarkson noted that "the present age would rejoice to find that the scriptures had no foundation, and would anxiously catch at the writings of him, who should mention them in a doubtful manner." If such statements linked antislavery with Protestant orthodoxy, they also forced their authors into awkward corners. Thus Sharp insisted that even under the Jewish dispensation it would have been illegal to enslave Africans, since the Levitical law pertained to a special group of heathens who worshiped devils and who were polluted by unnatural vices.[29] But suppose Sharp's

---

[28] [Hopkins], *Dialogue*, pp. 26–33; Donald G. Mathews, *Slavery and Methodism: A Chapter in American Morality, 1780–1845* (Princeton, 1965), pp. 3–61; Thomas Clarkson, *An Essay on the Slavery and Commerce of the Human Species, Particularly the African* . . . (Philadelphia, 1786), pp. 149–50; Joseph Priestley, *A Sermon on the Subject of the Slave Trade, Delivered to a Society of Protestant Dissenters* . . . (Birmingham, 1788), p. 14.

[29] Sharp, *Just Limitation of Slavery*, pp. 2–3, 6–11, 26; Clarkson, *Essay*, p. 118. As Mendelsohn points out, Leviticus introduced a new distinction between native and foreign slaves, a distinction unknown, for example, in the Hammurabi Code. The provisions allowing redemption by relatives and freedom every fifty years were designed to prevent the poorest classes of Hebrews from becoming per-

opponents could convince their readers that Africans worshiped devils and were polluted by unnatural vices? Clarkson fully accepted the story of a cursed people, and even identified the Carthaginians as "Canaanites" who were righteously punished by the Romans, the supposed descendants of Japheth. He added, of course, that God's vengeance had long since been fulfilled, but this argument almost invited slavery's apologists to demonstrate that Africans were the living descendants of Ham.[30]

The controversy over Ham and the curse of Canaan has been analyzed in a number of recent studies, and requires only the briefest summary here.[31] In the Biblical account it is Ham who stares at the naked body of his drunken father, Noah, and who then informs his brothers, Shem and Japheth, who dutifully cover their father's shame. Afterwards, Noah curses Canaan, Ham's son, saying "a servant of servants shall he be unto his brethren." Although Ham's other sons, Cush, Mizraim, and Put were apparently exempt, the descendants of Canaan were to serve the descendents of Shem and Japheth. According to Gerhard Von Rad, the original Yahwistic narrative had nothing to do with Shem, Ham, and Japheth, but was rather an older story, limited to the Palestinian Shem, Japheth, and Canaan, and was connected with the horror felt by the newly arrived Israelites at the sexual depravity of the Canaanites. Later editors revised the tale in order to include Ham, Canaan's father, in accordance with the subsequent "table of nations." As a result of this confusion, the Babylonian Talmud could point to the Negroes, the supposed children of Ham, as a people cursed with blackness because of their ancestor's disobedience or sexual transgression.[32]

---

petual slaves. According to Mendelsohn, non-Hebrew slaves enjoyed no such protections, for they had no prophetic mission to perform and were not destined to recover ancestral land (*Slavery in the Ancient Near East,* pp. 88–89).

[30] Clarkson, *Essay,* pp. 116–17.

[31] Thomas F. Gossett, *Race: The History of an Idea in America* (Dallas, Texas, 1963), p. 5; Davis, *Problem of Slavery in Western Culture,* pp. 63–64 n. 2, 217, 307, 316–17, 340, 451, 453; Winthrop D. Jordan, *White over Black: American Attitudes toward the Negro, 1550–1812* (Chapel Hill, 1968), pp. 18–19, 35–37, 41–42, 54–56, 60, 62n. 84, 243; H. Shelton Smith, *In His Image, But . . . Racism in Southern Religion, 1780–1910* (Durham, N.C. 1972), *passim.*

[32] Gen. 9:20–25; Gerhard Von Rad, *Genesis, a Commentary,* tr. by John H. Marks (Philadelphia, 1961), pp. 131–33.

Yet as Winthrop D. Jordan has observed, one must distinguish sanctions for slavery from explanations of race. In medieval England the curse of Canaan was used to justify the serfdom of whites. Seventeenth-century writers like Morgan Godwyn, who accepted the possibility that black skin was a mark of the original curse, denied any sanction for enslavement. Jordan contends that the two ideas were seldom linked until Englishmen began searching for an excuse for Negro slavery; and by the time of the American Revolution, Biblical explanations for skin color had largely been supplanted by theories of natural "science."[33]

But the influence of the Biblical account cannot be measured by the relatively few eighteenth-century apologists for Negro slavery who appealed to the curse of Canaan. As early as 1676 William Edmundson felt obliged to attack the argument that Negro slavery was a fulfillment of that curse. There is evidence that even in eighteenth-century Brazil many whites assumed that Negroes were the children of Cain—if not of Canaan—and thus deserved to be slaves. It is clear that early abolitionists felt it necessary to refute both the theory of a Biblical curse and the theory that blacks were a separate and inferior species.[34] Thus in 1772 Granville Sharp wrote in distress to the learned Jacob Bryant, who had shaken Sharp's faith that Africans were descended from Cush: "I am far from having any particular Esteem for the Negroes; but . . . I think myself *obliged* to consider them *as Men.*" Two years later he wrote triumphantly to William Dillwyn, enclosing a letter from Bryant which clearly proved that Negroes were descended from Noah, and were thus of the same common stock as Europeans. In order to vindicate Scripture and to refute David Hume's theory of separate creations, Sharp and Clarkson insisted that Africans were the children of Noah and Ham. But then what of Ham's sin which had brought the fateful curse upon Canaan, his son? The curse, in abolitionist eyes, had never applied to Cush or Ham's other sons. And the posterity of Cain had been exterminated by the flood.[35]

[33] Jordan, *White over Black,* pp. 35–36, 41–42, 243, and *passim;* Davis, *Problem of Slavery in Western Culture,* pp. 97–98, 451, 453.

[34] Davis, *Problem of Slavery in Western Culture,* pp. 307–8; C. R. Boxer, "Negro Slavery in Brazil," *Race* (Jan. 1964), 38–40; Clarkson, *Essay,* pp. 114–17.

[35] Sharp to Bryant, Oct. 19, 1772, reprinted in *Essay on Slavery,* p. 45; Sharp to Dillwyn, July 25, 1774, British and Foreign Bible Society; Hoare, *Memoirs of Granville Sharp,* pp. x–xi; Clarkson, *Essay,* pp. 114–16; review of Jacob

Sharp and Clarkson, like their American counterparts, left little room for maneuver. If Negroes were indeed the descendants of Ham, how could one be certain they were not destined to suffer for Ham's undoubted sins? But apart from their faith in Old Testament genealogy, the early abolitionists built their major case on the transcendent difference between Jewish and Christian dispensations. If Christ's sacrifice had given all men access to saving grace, Sharp argued, it was criminal to reduce to chattel slavery a subject of God's mercy. Clarkson stressed that man's spiritual destiny depends on his moral accountability, for which freedom is an essential condition. Yet for both reformers, freedom was a derivative value, the means to a higher end. Sharp acknowledged that Christianity gave no "express" commission to alter the temporal condition of men. Christian servants, after all, had been instructed to be patient and submissive, since the aim of Christianity was "to draw men from the cares and anxieties of *this present life,* to a better hope in the *life to come.*"[36]

Jesuit Intrigue

In 1708 the Biblical sanction for slavery suddenly became an explosive issue in England. During the earlier 1780s various writers tried to associate antislavery with religious enthusiasm, heterodoxy, and innovation, playing upon traditional prejudice against Quakers and "Puritans" who supposedly searched for innocent-sounding causes that would undermine church and state. Sharp and his friends were accused of omitting important Biblical passages and of twisting others out of context. Perhaps the cleverest charge—and one that would later be

---

Bryant, *A Treatise Upon the Authenticity of the Scriptures, and the Truth of the Christian Religion,* in *Gentleman's Magazine,* LXIII (March, 1793), 245.

[36] Clarkson, *Essay,* pp. 149–52; Sharp, *The Law of Passive Obedience, or Christian Submission to Personal Injuries . . .* (London, 1776), pp. 4–13. Like later abolitionists, Sharp had to come to terms with Eph. 6:5–6: "Servants [translated from the Greek word for slave, *doulos*], be obedient unto them that according to the flesh are your masters, with fear and trembling, in singleness of your heart, as unto Christ, not in the way of eyeservice, as men-pleasers; but as servants of Christ, doing the will of God from the heart." Sharp contended that the duty of slaves to absolute submission "by no means implies the legality of slaveholding ON THE PART OF THEIR MASTERS" (p. 11); but he also hotly attacked the Quaker doctrine of pacifism, arguing that individual duties of patience and submission should not be confused with the "pernicious doctrine of *a national passive obedience*" (p. 41).

repeated with conviction in the American South—was that antislavery agitation made it far less possible for masters to treat their slaves with Christian charity.[37] In general, however, the slave-trading faction maintained a dignified silence, assuming, apparently, that abolitionist writers would hang themselves if given sufficient rope, and that no number of pious tracts could be expected to soften the heads of Parliament.

Then, early in 1788, just as the Privy Council began its investigation of the African slave trade, a new pamphlet circulated among the wealthy and influential gentlemen of London's West End. Purportedly written by a "Reverend Raymond Harris," it was entitled *Scriptural Researches on the Licitness of the Slave Trade, Shewing its Conformity with the Principles of Natural and Revealed Religion, Delineated in the Sacred Writings of the Word of God.*[38]

In February Lord Hawkesbury, president of the Privy Council Committee, had learned that Harris's real name was Don Raymondo Hormaza, that as a Jesuit priest he had been expelled from Spain in 1767, and that after living in various European countries he had finally settled in Liverpool, where he ran a school for young gentlemen. Though Harris had quarreled with the Catholic bishop of Liverpool and had been suspended as a priest, he was widely respected for his charm, learning, and humorous stories. Hawkesbury's informant, William Walton, also reported that Harris had recently spent a month in London, where he was frequently in the company of a Spanish nobleman of high office, who had given the ex-Jesuit a commission that had something to do with the slave trade. Walton had employed an agent to find out the nature of Harris's mission, but without success. He implied that Harris's work might be connected with Spain's desire to develop her own slave trade, thus depriving Britain of a lucrative colonial market.[39]

Spanish officials had no reason to help defend the British slave trade,

---

[37] "Candidus," *A Letter to Philo Africanus, Upon Slavery, in Answer to His of the 22nd of November, in the "General Evening Post"* . . . (London, 1787), pp. 6–8, 20–26; "Some Gentlemen of St. Christopher," *An Answer to the Reverend James Ramsay's Essay on the Treatment and Conversion of Slaves, in the British Sugar Colonies* (Basseterre, 1784), pp. 1–2, 31–36, 38–57.

[38] (London, 1788).

[39] William Walton to Lord Hawkesbury, Feb. 24, 1788, Liverpool papers, Add. MS 38416, fols. 29–31, British Museum.

and it is thus barely conceivable that Harris's pamphlet was calculated to weaken the position of British merchants by intensifying religious controversy and by linking the Biblical defense of slavery with Jesuitical popery. Abolitionists predictably trained their guns on "Jesuitical sophistry," once they learned that their foe was a Catholic. And Harris, unlike his prominent Liverpool adversary, William Roscoe, made no effort to conceal his identity. By late October, James Pemberton could conclude that "poor Raymond Harris" had strengthened the cause he meant to injure.[40] On the other hand, the mysterious Spanish nobleman may simply have asked Harris to furnish information to the Spanish agents sent to study the English trade, and Harris's pamphlet may have been entirely of English inspiration. In June, at any rate, the Liverpool Council formally thanked him for his "excellent publication" and awarded him "the sum of One hundred Pounds as a mark of the high sense this Council entertains of the advantages resulting to the town and trade of Liverpool from the said publication."[41]

Abolitionists took an equally serious view of Harris's influence. Clarkson claimed that the Liverpool faction had distributed copies of the pamphlet among men of weight, and that "many, who ought to have known better, were carried away by it; and we had now absolutely to contend, and almost to degrade ourselves by doing so, against the double argument of the humanity and the holiness of the trade." In July the Abolition Committee eagerly welcomed Roscoe's anonymous "refutation" of Harris's pamphlet, agreeing to pay the printing and advertising costs of the initial edition, and instructing James Phillips to print 2,000 additional copies. At least six replies to Harris appeared within a year.[42]

Since Harris relied on the same texts and Scriptural arguments that had been used before, it is not immediately apparent why his pamph-

[40] James Pemberton to James Phillips, Oct. 21, 1788, Thompson-Clarkson scrapbooks, I, 205, Friends House, London.

[41] Elizabeth Donnan, ed., *Documents Illustrative of the History of the Slave Trade to America* (Washington, 1930–1935), II, 577–78. Donnan also prints part of Walton's letter, above (II, 575–77).

[42] Thomas Clarkson, *The History of the Rise, Progress and Accomplishment of the Abolition of the African Slave-Trade by the British Parliament* (2 vols., London, 1808), I, 483–84; MS Proceedings of the Committee for the Abolition of the Slave Trade, 1787–1819, II, 34, 39–40, British Museum Add. MSS 21254–21256.

let should have caused such a stir. The answer lies partly in the lucidity and logical consistency of his work. It was easy enough for abolitionist writers to expose the special pleading of most merchants and planters, but in Harris they faced a formidable opponent on their own supposedly secure ground of moral philosophy. To make matters more embarrassing, Harris came close to parodying Protestant orthodoxy regarding the primacy of Scripture, and thus forced his opponents to reveal how far they had gone in assuming the primacy of man's moral sense. Finally, Harris went straight to the central issue raised by the Deists—the relation between natural law and "special dispensations"—thereby touching one of the most painful nerves of the Christian Enlightenment.

The main points of his argument can be briefly summarized. He first disarmed his opponents by conceding that oppression can never be vindicated by appeals to tradition or to widespread practice. Nor would any enlightened man wish to justify whatever wrongs were genuinely associated with the slave trade. The only question at issue, Harris emphasized, was whether the slave trade was intrinsically illicit, regardless of incidental circumstances. Obviously, there were abuses and malpractices in many lawful callings, and it would be absurd to infer from the abuses, which could be dealt with separately, that the callings were in themselves illicit.[43]

But how, then, were men to know whether a practice was intrinsically lawful or unlawful? For Harris, speaking to a Protestant audience, the Bible was the only possible guide. Tradition, habits, "mere human reason and sense"—all were fallible. Anyone "with any pretensions to Religion" must immediately assent to the final authority of Scripture. And any person who professed to acknowledge the Bible as the unerring Word of God must assent to every Scriptural decision, without reserve and without questioning God's hidden justice.[44]

Having boxed his readers within this framework of orthodox Protestant assumptions, Harris proceeded to show that slavery had been positively sanctioned by God during the period of natural law, in the time of Abraham and Joseph; during the period of Mosaic law; and during the earliest Christian dispensation. Throughout his argument, Harris adhered to the central premise that intrinsic lawfulness

[43] Harris, *Scriptural Researches,* pp. v–vi, 10–11.
[44] *Ibid.,* pp. 9–11,

is unaffected by changing dispensations. Thus it was immaterial that Mosaic law limited the servitude of Jews to six years. During that time they were slaves, who could be bought or sold; if the practice had been unlawful, God would not have allowed it for one hour. Although Christianity had swept away the ceremonial part of Mosaic law, it could not touch the fundamental principles of righteousness which defined the inherent morality or lawfulnes of human actions. Natural justice, in other words, was perpetual and invariable, which explained why the New Testament in no place condemned slavery. Harris emphasized the universal acceptance of slavery in the time of Christ and the Apostles. He insisted that the first Christians had been expressly allowed to purchase and keep bondsmen. His final and perhaps most telling point was that the use of the Golden Rule against slavery proved nothing by proving too much. If the Golden Rule were to be applied to social position, it would outlaw any subordination of one man to another. Thus the abolitionists' premises were far more subversive than they knew.[45]

The replies to Harris display a sense of shock and apoplectic rage. James Ramsay privately admitted that he had no right to dispute Harris's sincerity, "as far as his own way of thinking is concerned," but feared that few "serious people" could read the extraordinary pamphlet "without having their reverence for their Creator shocked, and their benevolence to their brother affected." The Reverend William Hughes accused Harris of sapping the very foundations of religion by eroding men's belief in the benevolence of God. If the pamphlet's "dangerous and destructive principles were admitted in their full extent," said William Roscoe, it "would shake the foundations of society, and establish, *by the sanction of divine authority,* every variety of oppression, and every species of guilt." The Reverend Henry Dannett agreed with Roscoe that Harris's reasoning could be used to justify murder or incest, and presented his own satirical "Scriptural Researches on the Licitness of PERSECUTION" (and had not the Savior said to his first disciples, "compel them to come in"?).[46]

---

[45] *Ibid.*, pp. 18–20, 39–72.

[46] James Ramsay, MS remarks on Harris, Ramsay papers, Phillipps MS 17780, fols. 29–32, Rhodes House, Oxford; Ramsay, *Examination of the Reverend Mr. Harris's "Scriptural Researches on the Licitness of the Slave Trade"* (London, 1788), *passim;* William Hughes, *An Answer to the Reverend Mr. Harris's "Scriptural Researches on the Licitness of the Slave-Trade"* (London, 1788),

The easiest and perhaps most effective course was to play on native prejudice. Roscoe put the matter bluntly: Harris's "artful and subtle positions" were "totally irreconcilable to the character of an *Englishman,* but are perfectly consistent with that of *a Spanish Jesuit.*" Hughes also appealed to a kind of Protestant populism, disclaiming any desire to imitate Harris's "artificial and scientifick method," since truth could stand by itself, without "the sophistry of learning, the quibbles of metaphysicks, or the dexterous arts of logick." Dannett put Harris in the camp of Spinoza, Hobbes, and Machiavelli, and made the astonishing prediction that the pamphlet would have the unintended benefit of persuading skeptics to see the value of holy Scripture! Harris at least provided Christian apologists with a new occasion for justifying God's ways to man.[47]

The apologists, despite their disclaimers, could not quite escape Harris's "dexterous arts of logick." They could not ignore revelation and simply say that the Christian man of feeling would have an "instinctive abhorrence" for Harris's principles, even if he could not detect the fallacy behind "Jesuitical casuistry." One of the chief fallacies, according to Roscoe, was Harris's trick of deducing general laws from specific permissions. Followed consistently, this method would unravel the moral fabric of society. Yet as Harris had asked, how was one to judge God's specific decisions if their general application violated the universal laws of justice? Roscoe dodged this question by pleading that men could not know God's reasons or purposes from the "external circumstances" of a particular case. Thus it was no doubt consistent with God's wisdom and justice to order Hagar's return to her mistress, even if no human tribunal would be justified in issuing the same verdict.[48]

---

pp. 2–3; [William Roscoe], *A Scriptural Refutation of a Pamphlet, Lately Published by the Rev. Raymund* [sic] *Harris, Intitled "Scriptural Researches on the Licitness of the Slave-Trade"* (2nd ed., London, 1788), pp. 3–4; Henry Dannett, *A Particular Examination of Mr. Harris's "Scriptural Researches on the Licitness of the Slave-Trade"* (London, 1788), pp. 123–41.

[47] [Roscoe], *Scriptural Refutation,* p. 4; Hughes, *Answer to the Reverend Mr. Harris,* p. 3; Dannett, *Particular Examination,* p. ii.

[48] Dannett, *Particular Examination,* p. ix; [Roscoe], *Scriptural Refutation,* pp. 11, 13, 18–20; [Thomas Burgess], *Considerations on the Abolition of Slavery and the Slave Trade, Upon Grounds of Natural, Religious, and Political Duty* (Oxford, 1789), pp. 7, 11, 13, 19, 26–27. Despite its title, the latter work was a specific reply to Harris and appeared within a year after *Scriptural Researches.*

Harris's critics seized a firmer foothold when they attacked his "Jesuitical distinction" between slavery in the abstract and the abuses supposedly "incidental" to slavery. Such distinctions may have satisfied our ancestors, Roscoe wrote (presumably meaning Catholic ancestors), but they were now "out of season." The Saviour himself had taught men to judge a cause by its effects; a proneness to abuse could be taken as strong evidence of wrongness in the principle. The so-called abuses of the slave trade, Ramsay added, were inseparable from its existence.[49] This line of argument promised to undermine Harris's central premise. Yet it also led, if pressed consistently, to a conclusion that would have delighted Thomas Paine. For if moral principles were to be judged by their consequences, without regard for their origin, how could one justify the forms of slavery authorized by the Lord?

This difficulty may explain why Harris's critics were so reluctant to challenge the intrinsic legality of slavery. If cruelty was a necessary and condemning part of the modern slave system, Dannett wrote, this argument could not be extended to the mild servitude described in the Bible. Even a trade in slaves, considered in the abstract, would be lawful if confined to "proper objects," such as criminals, and carried on without abuse. Since West Indian slavery was a special case, there was no reason why the New Testament should have issued a general proscription against slave trading. Burgess showed similar caution when replying to Harris's distinction between abuses and intrinsic justice. He even conceded that abuses do not necessarily prove that a system is bad, but argued that it was expedient to abolish a system whose abuses could not be checked by other means.[50]

It is remarkable how much space these abolitionist writers devoted to apologies for Biblical slavery. And their arguments, like those of Rush and Sharp, evidenced considerable moral confusion. On the one hand, it appeared that the moral ends of Biblical slavery justified its relative evils. Thus according to Hughes, the constant presence of foreign slaves reminded ancient Jews of the abject state from which

[49] [Roscoe], *Scriptural Refutation*, p. 11; Ramsay, *Examination*, pp. 5–6, 29; [Burgess], *Considerations*, pp. 29–31, 66; Robert Robinson, *Slavery Inconsistent with the Spirit of Christianity* (Cambridge, England, 1788), pp. 34–35. Robinson's sermon was apparently delivered just before Harris's pamphlet appeared, and it thus cannot be classed as a reply; yet the arguments paralleled those of the other pamphlets.

[50] Dannett, *Particular Examination*, pp. iii, 3–5, 98–100; [Burgess], *Considerations*, 29.

they had been delivered, and prevented them from forgetting the gratitude and obedience they owed to God. To be effective, this cathartic
mechanism presumably required something harsher than the "mild,
domestic servitude" that apologists usually found in the Bible. The
more the slaves were debased, the more the Jews would be grateful.
Hughes added that if anyone wondered why God would permit vast
numbers of innocents to be subjected to perpetual slavery, in order
to keep the Jews faithful, he should remember that the Lord frequently
uses lesser evils to produce a greater good; and that, unlike British
slave traders, God could ultimately give recompense to innocent
sufferers! But this brand of logic suited the slave trader's purpose
better than the abolitionist's, and it was therefore important to find
ways of delimiting the ends that justified such drastic means. "The
minds of the Jews," Ramsay explained, "had been broken and debased
by the Egyptian bondage; the law was given them as a school-master
to train them up for the perfect religion of the gospel." In other
words, one could not apply modern standards to the Biblical past,
when God "winked at times of ignorance, when men could not receive
a purer law, or be influenced by better motives than those temporary
rewards and punishments which were the sanction of that dispensation."[51]

Harris's critics seemed more comfortable when they shifted attention
to man's improved moral capacity. Christianity, by teaching men to
treat one another as brothers, had gradually abolished slavery, along
with "all oppressive distinctions," and had consequently lifted Europe
far above the world's other civilizations. Why, then, Ramsay asked,
should we look for rules of conduct in the distant past? Dannett cautiously objected to Harris's claim that Scriptural authority is the only
means of surmounting human error. Surely there was nothing infallible
about Scriptural interpretation—witness the Catholics' "discovery" of
such monstrous doctrines as transubstantiation, indulgences, and praying for departed souls. "Now, I have always understood," Dannett
asserted, "that conscience, or the moral sense, is our delegated and
appointed guide in all our judgments and actions." Similarly, Burgess
argued that slavery could not be defended without perverting our

[51] Hughes, *Answer to the Reverend Mr. Harris,* pp. 5, 20–23; Ramsay, *Ex-
amination,* pp. 7, 11–12, 13–14, 22–23; William Agutter, *The Abolition of the
Slave Trade Considered in a Religious Point of View* (London, 1788), p. 9;
Dannett, *Particular Examination,* pp. 3–6.

"common sense of right and wrong": "Whatever appears to the generality of mankind to be intrinsically bad cannot be, I think, essentially good."[52]

It seems likely that these were precisely the appeals that Harris had intended to provoke, in order to show that the abolitionist clergy, like the Deists, relied on conscience or "the generality of mankind" as the ultimate authorities. To be sure, Dannett insisted that Scriptural decisions, when properly understood, could never contradict our ideas of right and wrong. Yet he quickly added that it is "the province of conscience and reason properly to interpret, and justly to limit them." If this was conventional doctrine, it also meant an equation of divine law with eighteenth-century sensibility.[53]

In the Harris controversy one glimpses a transitional moment in the evolution of the modern social conscience. The African slave trade, which had aroused so little protest in earlier decades, was beginning to stand as a symbol of the ultimate injustice. The prime characteristic of the Negro slave, in the imagination of British reformers, was his "innocence." Unlike the Gibeonites, the Canaanites, or the sinners destined for hell, he bore no responsibility for his own suffering. Harris's critics never dreamed of questioning the justice of divine punishment. They would have resisted the argument that the Golden Rule—or man's moral sense—should alter the status of criminals or lighten the obligation of servants and other subordinates. If they had come to believe that cruelty was an inevitable part of the slave trade, they were somewhat less certain about slave keeping itself, which conformed more easily with the traditional ideas of subordination hallowed by Christian charity. Thus Wilberforce, in a private letter expressing his desire to avoid the Biblical question in Parliament, affirmed that there could be no doubt that the principles of the Bible, especially of the New Testament, ran counter to the slave trade, or "even slavery," though on the latter point "explanations" would be required.[54] The

---

[52] Ramsay, *Examination*, p. 7; Dannett, *Particular Examination*, pp. iii–v; [Burgess], *Considerations*, pp. 23–25, 45, 77.

[53] Dannett, *Particular Examination*, p. iii.

[54] Wilberforce to unknown correspondent, June 17, 1806, autograph MSS, Historical Society of Pennsylvania; Robinson, *Slavery Inconsistent*, pp. 30, 34; [Burgess], *Considerations*, p. 37; Ramsay, *Examination*, pp. 13–19; Dannett, *Particular Examination*, pp. 98–105. William Agutter, who in 1788 preached against the slave trade, delivered a sermon in 1792 entitled *Christian Politics; or, the Origin of Power, and the Grounds of Subordination* (London, 1792), in which

slave trade was a highly visible form of oppression, totally lacking in interpersonal subtleties. As such, it could be a test of man's freedom to rely on his own moral judgment while professing to "vindicate" the Bible from charges of immorality.

Early in 1792 there was a curious postscript to the Harris controversy in the letter columns of the *Glasgow Courier*. A writer who adopted the name "Senex" took issue with the Presbytery of Glasgow, which had condemned the slave trade as a violation of every moral and religious obligation. It seems likely that Senex was a shrewd freethinker, adopting the pose of a Biblical literalist in order to embarrass the Presbyterian orthodoxy. After first quoting the usual passages from the Bible giving sanction to slavery, he proclaimed himself an enemy of "these new fangled speculations, by which a vain and presumptuous philosophy is now endeavouring to unhinge the reason and feelings of men, and to set them against good old *Principles,* and sound *Practice*." Among such admirable principles and practice, he cited Moses's wartime order that officers should not spare any enemy males and should kill all women; "but all the women children that have not known a man by lying with him, keep alive for yourselves."[55] What, asked Senex, did the Glasgow Presbytery think of this? "We know what fine things the National Assembly of France have said in *their* Bible, on the subject; and we know what *other* DEISTS, near home, WILL ALSO SAY, IF THEY DARE!"

The Presbytery's defender, "A Friend of Mankind," was suspicious of Senex's purpose. Like Harris, Senex appeared to be arguing that the Bible justified the slave trade, but he then went on to claim that the Bible sanctioned the murder of innocent women and children, and he had the audacity to link all objectors with Deists and French revolutionaries. Whether Senex was a disguised Deist or a hard-boiled traditionalist, his arguments undermined respect for the Word of God. Therefore, the Friend of Mankind felt constrained to deliver a tedious sermon on the depravity of Hebrew customs, the mercy and kindness required by Christ, and the danger of taking Christ's parables too literally. At the outset, the Friend seemed half-amused by the possibility

---

he denounced the absurd notions of a social compact and natural rights, affirming that all power must come from God, not the people.

[55] Numbers, 31:17–18; [Anon.], *Arguments from Scripture, for and Against the African Slave Trade, as Stated in a Series of Letters, Lately Published in "The Glasgow Courier"* (Glasgow, 1792), pp. 4–5.

that Senex really opposed the slave trade. He became less amused, however, when Senex began exploiting his own admissions that bondage had once been ordained by God and that it had been perfectly just to enslave criminal debtors, along with their wives and children. Was this not the very principle, Senex asked, of the African slave trade? Had not the Presbytery decided that a law once given by God was now to be deemed cruel, unjust, and subversive to the rights of mankind?[56]

The Friend's flustered defense showed that Senex's arrow had hit its mark. Although the Friend had wished to restrict the debate to the injustice of the African slave trade, he could not escape the charge of impeaching God's laws. To prove his own orthodoxy, he admitted that "all the rights and sacrifices peculiar to the Mosaic oeconomy, were righteous, good, and necessary observances in Israel." Even the stoning to death of Achan could be justified, whereas the stoning of Stephen could not. The deed was the same, but the Jews who killed the first Christian martyr could not plead the sanction of former law.[57] Once more, the Biblical controversy over slavery had led to a sharper demarcation between Jewish and Christian dispensations, and thus to a weakening of timeless and univeral law.

Come Sound the Jubilee!

The framework of Scriptural arguments over slavery changed very little prior to the radical defiance of the Garrisonians and the gradual influence of German higher criticism. American and English writers tediously repeated the points that had become commonplace by the time of the Harris debate. In America, however, there were a few notable differences.[58]

[56] [Anon.], *Arguments from Scripture,* pp. 6–26.

[57] *Ibid.,* p. 24. For continuing Biblical controversy over slavery, see *The Christian Observer* (June, 1804), 367–68; (Apr., 1807), 519; (May, 1807), 317–18.

[58] [Anon.], *Doubts on the Abolition of the Slave Trade; by an Old Member of Parliament* (London, 1790), p. 4; *Pennsylvania Packet* (Jan. 1, 1780); *Gentleman's Magazine,* LXIX (April, 1799), 300–1; Abraham Booth, *Commerce in the Human Species, and the Enslaving of Innocent Persons, Inimical to the Laws of Moses, and the Gospel of Christ* (London, 1792; reprinted Philadelphia, 1792); Edward D. Griffin, *A Plea for Africa* (New York, 1817); Richard Furman, *Exposition of the Views of the Baptists Relative to the Colored Population of the United States, in a Communication to the Governor of South Carolina* (Charleston, S.C., 1823); [John Gladstone], *Letters Concerning the Abolition of the*

As a result of the Revolution, Americans had moved far toward equating Christianity not only with political liberty but with the rights of mankind. The desire for happiness, according to the Reverend David Barrow, was common to all men, who consequently shared an equal right to its pursuit. This was not to say that Christ had sought to define the personal or civil rights of men. As James Dana admitted, "He left civil distinctions among men as he found them." Yet Dana found an antislavery message in Paul's Epistle to the Galatians which played on the allegorical meaning of Abraham's two sons, Isaac and Ishmael. Paul identified Ishmael, the son of a slave woman, with bondage to the flesh. Isaac symbolized the promise of a new covenant: "Now we, brethern, as Isaac was, are the children of promise. . . . We are not the children of the bondwoman, but of the free" (Gal. 5:22–31). If Paul had meant spiritual freedom only, he had also written: "There is neither Jew nor Greek, there is neither bond nor free, there is neither male nor female: for ye are all one in Christ Jesus" (Gal. 3:28). In Dana's eyes this meant that *all* men were born "not of the bond-woman, but of the free." Christianity was a religion of promise which furthered both the liberty and rights of mankind. And "the *Africans* belong to the families for whom heaven designed a participation in the blessings of Abraham."[59]

In America the natural rights philosophy reinforced the universality of those Biblical laws protecting the person from total degradation. George Bourne merged the rights of man with the more ancient doctrine that "all civil laws which annul the ordinances of God, are a non-entity." He agreed with the English Baptist, Abraham Booth, that manstealing was the sin "most detestable in the sight of God, most pernicious to society and most deserving of death by the sword of the

---

Slave-Trade and Other West-India Affairs; By Mercator (London, 1807); [Anon.], *A Letter, Addressed to Mercator . . .* (London, 1807), pp. 4–5; Alexander Campbell, *A Sermon on the Law* (1816), reprinted in *The Millennial Harbinger*, ser. 3 (1846), 493–521; Caroline L. Shanks, "The Biblical Anti-Slavery Argument, 1830–1840," *Journal of Negro History*, XVI (April, 1931), 132–46.

[59] David Barrow, *Involuntary, Unmerited, Perpetual, Absolute, Hereditary Slavery, Examined; on the Principles of Nature, Reason, Justice, Policy and Scripture* (Lexington, Ky., 1808), pp. 14–15, 19; James Dana, *The African Slave Trade: A Discourse Delivered in the City of New-Haven, September 9, 1790, Before the Connecticut Society for the Promotion of Freedom* (New Haven, 1791), pp. 6–12.

civil magistrate." Although this doctrine occasionally appeared in English pamphlets and sermons, American writers put increasing emphasis on the sin of manstealing, perhaps in part because of their concern over the kidnapping of free Negroes in the North. Yet this was also an instance in which the Bible seemed to confirm a belief in fundamental rights, and thus to prove the illegality of the original act of enslavement.[60]

How, then, did American abolitionists deal with the Biblical authorizations of slavery, which appeared to undercut any notions of unchanging moral law? It is hazardous to generalize from the relatively small number of early pamphlets and sermons that confronted this issue, but it would appear that Americans, far more than Englishmen, were inclined to take allegorical and prophetic views of Scripture. This difference might be explained by the Puritan and Dissenting tradition, filtered through writers like Jonathan Edwards and John Woolman. In any event, American writers tended to draw a sharp distinction between Biblical description and Biblical sanction. The lack of explicit condemnation did not mean divine approval; nor should Biblical prophecies be taken as authorizations. The very fact of textual controversy, Barrow pointed out, proved that many people misunderstood Scripture. Future events would prove which party was right![61]

The question of prophecy centered on the curse of Canaan. The notion that blacks were the descendants of Ham, and therefore destined to be slaves, was by no means confined to America, but American antislavery writers devoted an extraordinary amount of effort to attacking the theory. The curse of Canaan appears to have been the major Biblical precedent to enter popular consciousness. Curiously enough, the attempts at refutation paid little attention to Christ's removing distinctions among men. Rather, the controversy led to

[60] George Bourne, *The Book and Slavery Irreconcilable: With Animadversions Upon Dr. Smith's Philosophy* (Philadelphia, 1816), pp. 24–31, 107, 114; Booth, *Commerce in the Human Species*, p. 6.

[61] Barrow, *Involuntary . . . Slavery*, pp. 14–16, 27, 31; Jonathan Edwards, Jr., *The Injustice and Impolity of the Slave-Trade, and of Slavery of the Africans* . . . (Providence. 1792), pp. 14–17. Dana, *The African Slave Trade*, pp. 6–11, 26–28. One should note that Thomas Burgess and other English writers had also emphasized the distinction between Biblical description and Biblical sanction. While there can be no doubt that Americans increasingly moved away from a literal and legalistic interpretation, nationality may have been less important than theological change.

elaborate exegesis designed to prove that the Canaanites had never
settled in Africa, except in Carthage, and that Negroes were thus the
descendants of Cush. Abolitionists also suggested that the curse must
have expired when the children of Abraham lost their inheritance to
the land of Canaan. Barrow conceded that he could offer no objections
if an American planter could prove himself to be an Israelite, if he
could find some Canaanites for slaves, and if he could then take them
home to the land of Canaan.[62]

Barrow's humor underscored the importance of time and place,
which in America, as Fred Somkin has shown, were acquiring subtle
new meanings.[63] As physical space, America was not simply an extension of the Old World. American land could not be defined or circumscribed by laws that embodied the historical experiences of a different continent. And if American land was free of such feudal
encumbrances as primogeniture, it was no less free of Biblical laws
attached to specific places. Space without entail suggested time without
precedent. Few reformers were prepared to go so far as John Humphrey Noyes, who declared that millennial time had already begun,
removing all obligation to obey external law. Yet from Jonathan
Edwards to Charles Grandison Finney and beyond, there was a tendency to link the millennium with America's infinite capacity for
change. The new dispensation might dawn within a matter of years.
For perfectibilists of varying shades of orthodoxy, the crucial point
was belief in efficacious sanctification. As soon as men strove to live
as if they had been spiritually transformed, or as if the new age had
arrived, then the old law of coercive authority would rapidly disappear.
Clearly, such a setting of spatial and temporal hope had no place for
an institution combining continuous coercion with herditary efface-
ment of hope.[64]

[62] Bourne, *Book and Slavery,* pp. 108–9; Barrow, *Involuntary . . . Slavery,*
pp. 28–29; Griffin, *Plea for Africa,* pp. 4–17; [Frederick Dalcho], *Practical Considerations Founded on the Scriptures Relative to the Slave Population of South
Carolina* (Charleston, 1823), pp. 13–19.

[63] Fred Somkin, *Unquiet Eagle: Memory and Desire in the Idea of American
Freedom* (Ithaca, N.Y., 1967), chs. 2 and 3.

[64] Immediate emancipation, in the words of Amos Phelps, meant "*a yielding
up of the PRINCIPLE of slavery as a practical principle—a basis of action, and
the adoption of its opposite.* This one act is emancipation from slavery. All that
follows is the carrying out of the new principle of action, and is to emancipation
just what sanctification is to conversion," quoted by Anne C. Loveland, "Evan-

Yet America's very uniqueness and openness raised another problem. No doubt antislavery writers strengthened their case when they insisted that the New World had a providential mission, that America should be free of Old World laws, customs, and doctrines which reduced man's spiritual ability. Negro slavery could be presented as the epitome of all the restrictive and brutalizing forces that Americans associated with the Old World past. On the other hand, in order to vindicate Scripture, the abolitionist clergy also underscored the fundamental differences between Biblical and modern slavery. Although English writers made the same distinction, they were more inclined to talk of slavery in the abstract, assuming that historical variations could still be subsumed under the general term. But David Barrow, for example, took pains to qualify "slavery," so far as it existed in America, with five adjectives: unmerited, involuntary, perpetual, absolute, and hereditary. He contended that any form of bondage lacking one or more of these characteristics could not be compared with American slavery. By repeating the five defining adjectives and by arguing that even the bondage of the Canaanites could not have been "perpetual," Barrow severed American slavery from any Biblical precedents.[65]

But this was to say that slavery in the United States was unique in its lack of limitations—that only in America could one find unmerited, involuntary, perpetual, absolute, hereditary servitude. And could it not then be argued that an unprecedented form of slavery was especially suitable for such a grandiose, unprecedented land? Barrow's definition was a mirror image of the American democratic ideal: a form of slavery freed from limits of time or place, unencumbered by ancient custom or common law. And if American democrats wished to rid the land of the last residues of English common law, an English court had declared that the common law knew nothing of slavery. Americans, then, had liberated themselves from the "free soil" of England. They also claimed title to a new Canaan where any prophecy might be fulfilled. Barrow's joke about the American Israelite cut two ways. For the sad fact was that many Americans did consider themselves a chosen people, providentially appointed to rule Ham's children in order to build a new Jerusalem.

gelicalism and 'Immediate Emancipation' in American Antislavery Thought," *Journal of Southern History*, XXXII (May, 1966), 185.

[65] Barrow, *Involuntary . . . Slavery*, pp. 28–33.

Ham's children, however, also dreamed of a new Jerusalem as they flocked to camp meetings or heard their own preachers tell of Moses and Christ, the twin deliverers. If the white dispensers of the Gospel were careful to focus attention on the Christian duties of obedience and submission, the slaves were quick to catch every message of hope. The Scriptural texts, as the controversies had made clear, were filled with latent meaning. There could be no doubt that the children of God had once been slaves, or that God had finally brought them deliverance. "There's a better day a coming," sang the slaves, "There's a better day a coming / Oh, Glory, Hallelujah!" So while the theologians split hairs over the meaning of Hebrew words and the whereabouts of Cush's descendants, blacks like William Wells Brown pondered the refrain from the fields and river boats:

> We are stolen and sold in Georgia,
> Will you go along with me?
> We are stolen, and sold in Georgia,
> Come sound the jubilee![66]

[66] John W. Blassingame, *The Slave Community: Plantation Life in the Antebellum South* (New York, 1972), pp. 70–71. Blassingame provides an excellent account of the slaves' adaptation of Christian doctrine, a subject which is also explored in considerable depth in Eugene D. Genovese's *Roll, Jordan, Roll* (New York, 1974).

Epilogue ⤳

Toussaint L'Ouverture and the Phenomenology of Mind

In 1802, General Charles Leclerc seized Toussaint L'Ouverture by an act of shameless treachery and shipped him off to France, advising the government that "you cannot keep Toussaint at too great a distance from the sea and put him in a position that is too safe. This man has raised the country to such a pitch of fanaticism that his presence would send it up again in flames." But the country continued to burn, and on December 31, 1803, the Haitian leaders issued a formal declaration of independence. On October 4, 1804, before he ordered the massacre of the remaining white residents, General Dessalines was crowned Emperor of Haiti; the crown came from the United States, on the good ship *Connecticut*.[1]

Toussaint's achievements had stunned the world. They had ensured British dominance in the Caribbean, had allowed Americans to expand westward into Louisiana and Missouri, and had tautened the nerves of slaveholders from Maryland to Brazil. The repercussions continued to unfold. Early in 1816, Simón Bolívar made his historic pledge to Alexandre Pétion, then one of the rulers of Haiti, having first tried to win aid from slaveholding Jamaica. In return for the arms and provisions given by Pétion, Bolívar promised that, if his cause were successful, he would free the slaves of Venezuela. Back on South American

[1] C. L. R. James, *The Black Jacobins: Toussaint L'Ouverture and the San Domingo Revolution* (2nd ed., rev., New York, 1963), pp. 332–70.

soil, Bolívar issued his decree to all Negro males from the age of fourteen to sixty: fight or remain in bondage.

Meanwhile, on April 7, 1803, Toussaint had died, at age fifty-seven, in a cold dungeon high in the Jura mountains. Maltreated, humiliated, constantly harassed by his jailers, he had futilely appealed to his new master, who was also the master of Europe:

I have had the misfortune to incur your anger; but as to fidelity and probity, I am strong in my conscience, and I dare to say with truth that among all the servants of the State none is more honest than I. I was one of your soldiers and the first servant of the Republic in San Domingo. I am to-day wretched, ruined, dishonoured, a victim of my own services. Let your sensibility be touched at my position, you are too great in feeling and too just not to pronounce on my destiny.[2]

Napoleon lacked the compassion of William Cowper's evangelical benefactor and did not try to teach Toussaint "what path to shun, and what pursue." But Napoleon apparently assumed that he had broken Toussaint's spirit. When a prisoner himself, at St. Helena, he confessed that he had made a mistake in not governing St. Domingue through Toussaint L'Ouverture. Yet he seems to have thought of the black leader as an ungrateful slave, a bad nigger.

As one might expect of a German philosopher, G. W. F. Hegel was even less suspicious of Napoleon's motives than Touissant had been when leading the resistance in St. Domingue. As the French armies converged on Hegel's university town of Jena, in October, 1806, the philosopher spoke in a letter of the "world-soul" of the messianic emperor. He saw the destruction of the Prussian army—which opened the way for Napoleon's Berlin Decree, for the great commercial struggle with Britain, and for revolution in Latin America—as the culmination and end of human history. Yet with the sound of Napoleon's thundering cannons in his ears, Hegel was completing a work that contained the most profound analysis of slavery ever written.

I began this book by summarizing the historical shifts in Western thought which prepared the way for eighteenth-century antislavery arguments. I have devoted considerable attention to the receptivity and social consequences of those arguments and have examined the issue of slavery as a testing ground for Western culture during a revo-

[2] *Ibid.*, p. 364.

lutionary age. Hegel's analysis leads back to the level of abstract theory and to some of mankind's ultimate questions. A brief summary cannot do justice to the complexities of Hegel's argument. But since it marked the apex of a changing ethical consciousness, an attempt must be made to put it in some historical perspective.[3]

The early modern philosophers had narrowed the ground for any defense of slavery, but in doing so had removed the institution from the supposed protections of an organic and hierarchical social order. Thus Thomas Hobbes gave an original twist to the ancient notion of enslaving prisoners of war. He envisioned a primal struggle between two combatants. The loser, in order to save his life, finally promises absolute obedience to the victor, in return for subsistence and corporal liberty. By terms of the "compact," the slave can only will what his master wills. The master can be guilty of no injustice, since he has spared the slave's life.

For John Locke, on the other hand, slavery could arise only outside the social compact. All men retain, according to Locke, an original and absolute ownership of their own persons, and, by extension, an ownership of their labor and its produce. Hence within the voluntary social compact, every individual should be protected from "the inconstant, uncertain, unknown, Arbitrary Will of another Man." Yet any man may, by an act of violence, forfeit his life to another. Nor can such a criminal complain of injustice if his captor spares his life. For Locke, then, slavery always stood outside the bounds of a peaceful and rational order: "The perfect condition of *Slavery* is nothing else, but *the state of War continued, between a lawful Conqueror, and a*

---

[3] My discussion is based on G. W. F. Hegel, *The Phenomenology of Mind,* tr. by J. B. Baillie (2nd ed., New York, 1964), and on Alexandre Kojève, *Introduction to the Reading of Hegel; Lectures on the "Phenomenology of Spirit,"* assembled by Raymond Queneau, ed. by Allan Bloom, tr. by James H. Nichols, Jr. (New York, 1969). It should be emphasized that Hegel's *Phenomenology* is, in M. H. Abrams's words, "persistently polysemantic, with a sustained inner as well as outer reference, so that the altering master-servant relationship also defines a necessary stage in the cognitive and moral development both of the collective minds of men and of each individual human mind, on the long educative journey toward a consummation of consciousness" (*Natural Supernaturalism: Tradition and Revolution in Romantic Literature* [New York, 1971], p. 363). As Abrams shows, the concepts of mastery and servitude became, during precisely the period we have been studying, central "metaphors of mind" which pervaded romantic literature (see esp. pp. 356–72).

Captive." The elemental struggle between two enemies defined slavery's essential and continuing character.[4]

Primal combat was also Hegel's starting point, but the starting point for man's consciousness of himelf as a fact of experience, and thus of his social identity. Whereas Locke had seen slavery as peripheral to society and history, Hegel saw it as the natal core of man's condition. Let us indulge in a bit of fantasy to introduce Hegel's point. Suppose that Napoleon and Toussaint L'Ouverture are alone in the world, and that each man is convinced he is the emperor of the universe. They are both solipsists, incapable of distinguishing an objective world independent of their own states of consciousness. And since they cannot detect an autonomous object outside themselves, they cannot find an autonomous subject within themselves.[5]

When they first encounter each other, each man perceives the other as an undifferentiated extension of himself—much as young babies, we are told, perceive their parents. The illusion is shattered, however, when both Napoleon and Toussaint begin to discover that the other is an independent consciousness: "They recognize themselves as mutually recognizing one another." This discovery could be negated by murder, but then the murderer would be alone as before, having simply confirmed that the specter of another consciousness was part of the "natural" world. Insofar as each man is "human," his greatest desire is to be recognized as a being of transcendent and unique value —as distinct from a temporary system of repetitive biological functions. When the two men do in fact risk death in an elemental struggle, it is to test the truth of their own self-images of omnipotence and indeterminate existence. But Toussaint finally submits—as he did in history—because he prefers Napoleon's vision of truth to his own death. Napoleon accepts the submission—as he did in history—because it validates his own sense of omnipotence. Indeed, that conviction is no longer purely subjective. Toussaint's bondage is an objective proof that Napoleon's freedom is no illusion.

But the paradigm now becomes more complicated. Aristotle defined

---

[4] Hobbes, *De Cive,* ed. with introd. by Sterling P. Lamprecht (New York, 1949), ii, viii; Hobbes, *Leviathan,* chs. ii, xx; Locke, *Two Treatises of Government, a Critical Edition with an Introduction and Apparatus Criticus,* by Peter Laslett (Cambridge, England, 1960), pp. 297–302, 341.

[5] Hegel, *Phenomenology,* pp. 228–29, 232–33; Kojève, *Introduction,* pp. 7–9.

the slave as a tool or instrument, the mere extension of his master's physical nature. For Aristotle the slave also possessed the rudiments of a soul, allowing him a lower form of virtue if he performed his functions well. The early Christians, drawing on the Cynics, Sophists, and Stoics, also told slaves to be submissive and obedient, but recognized an essential inner freedom that transcended external condition. The world of the flesh did not matter. What mattered was the Christian promise to spare the life of the meanest slave, through all eternity, if he would submit to the greatest Master. Hegel synthesized both the Aristotelean and Christian notions of slavery, and lifted them to a new level.

The master, Hegel argued, sees the slave as an instrument of his own will and demands absolute obedience. Yet every day he must contradict this Aristotelean definition, since he is now dependent on another human life (having spared the life), and since he has found that the "slavish consciousness" is the object "which embodies the truth of his certainty of himself." The act of enslavement has created two opposed forms or modes of consciousness:

The master is the consciousness that exists for *itself;* but no longer merely the general notion of existence for self. Rather, it is a consciousness existing on its own account which is mediated with itself through an other consciousness, i.e. through an other whose very nature implies that it is bound up with an independent being or with thinghood in general.[6]

Hegel developed an intricate dialectic of dependence and independence, of losing and finding one's identity in another consciousness, but his central point is that the master is caught in an "existential impasse," to use Alexander Kojève's phrase, because the master's identity depends on being recognized by a slavish and supposedly unessential consciousness. Even to outsiders, his identity consists of being a master who consumes the produce of his slave's work. Accordingly, the master is incapable of transcending his own position, for which he risked his life and for which he could lose his life, should the slave decide on a second match of strength. The master is trapped by his own power, which he can only seek to maintain. He cannot achieve the true autonomy that can come only from the recognition by another consciousness that he regards as worthy of such recognition.

[6] Hegel, *Phenomenology,* pp. 234–35.

The condition of omnipotent lordship, then, becomes the reverse of what it wants to be: dependent, static, and unessential.

At first the slave is dominated by fear and by the desire for self-preservation. Insofar as he assimilates the master's definition of his slavishness, he has denied his capacity for autonomous consciousness. His life becomes immersed in nature and in his work. Yet the slave's fear and desire for self-preservation necessarily counteract the master's image of a negative and unessential "thing." And the slave's labor, by transforming elements in the natural world, creates an objective reality that confirms and shapes his own consciousness of self:

Thus precisely in labour where there seemed to be merely some outsider's mind and ideas involved, the bondsman becomes aware, through this re-discovery of himself by himself, of having and being a "mind" of his own.[7]

As Kojève has suggested, the product of work becomes for the slave the counterpart of the slave himself for the master. But unlike the master, the slave is not a consumer who looks upon "things" as merely the means of satisfying desires. The products he creates become an objective reality that validates the emerging consciousness of his subjective human reality. Through coerced labor, the slave alone acquires the qualities of fortitude, patience, and endurance. The slave alone has an interest in changing his condition, and thus looks to a future beyond himself. Only the slave, therefore, has the potentiality for escaping an imbalanced reciprocity and for becoming truly free.[8]

It is not fanciful to see in Toussaint's actual deeds a message for later masters and wielders of power, or to see in Hegel's thoughts a message to slaves and the powerless. In their own ways, both men were saying that situations of dominance and submission are not so simple as they seem, and that dominators can never be sure of the future. For a time Hegel perceived the Age of Revolution as the final drama of history, which would terminate the seemingly endless struggle between lords and bondsmen and make the ideal of freedom—which the Stoics had imprisoned within man's subjective soul, and which Christianity had projected to a spiritual afterlife—a worldly reality. What was truly new to the world, however, was not simply

[7] *Ibid.,* pp. 239–40.
[8] Kojève, *Introduction,* pp. 17–19, 22–25, 50, 52.

revolution, but a nation of former slaves who had achieved independence from a master race.

If Hegel was both naïve and visionary in acclaiming Napoleon as the incarnation of man's spirit of freedom, he was right in sensing that the Age of Revolution marked a major watershed, after which things could never be the same. In 1770, to cite the example that has concerned us, antislavery doctrine floated harmlessly in an abstract realm of theory and wishful thinking. By 1823, the black slaves of the New World had completed at least the initial stage of their long ordeal of emancipation. The conclusions of the preceding chapters extend forward in diverging lines of direction. They point, in other words, to struggles for various kinds of emancipation and hegemony, to incomplete definitions and achievements of liberty, and to emerging forms of slavery that went by different names. And apart from Hegel's infatuation with the notion of an all-powerful state, he bequeathed an ideal of freedom which went far beyond the legalistic conceptions of consent, contract, proprietorship, and physical constraint, and which therefore gained added meaning in the "post-historical" age. Hegel's ideal was simply that man can be an autonomous value only as he recognizes other men as autonomous values.

Like the ideal of Christian brotherhood, to which it bears a superficial resemblance, Hegel's ideal seems innocuous in the abstract. Any man might accept it, until he began to think what it really means, and how difficult it is to accept another person's consciousness—with all its distinctness, unknownness, and knowingness—on a parity with one's own. Nor did Hegel entertain any illusions about the difficulty of recognizing a not-me without trying to negate or dominate the threatening presence. This was the point of his paradigm of a primal struggle.

Moreover, the ideal of autonomous interaction helps to expose all the deceptions by which men and women have been re-enslaved. Toussaint, after all, thought that he had won his cause and that he was still a free man; he reminded Napoleon that he had been "the first servant of the Republic in San Domingo"; he thought that he had established his people's independence without dooming their future by a rash and total break with France. Hence his professions of loyalty to France were not without some truth. They were a mark, to be shared by many future black leaders, of his own supreme tragedy.

Beyond such forcible betrayals of faith, Hegel's test of autonomy illuminates the entire history of labor conflict and economic coercion. To cite only one example, it was not accidental in 1867 that when George M. Pullman pondered the need for ideal servants for his elegant railroad palace cars, he turned with inspiration to "what he considered a uniquely appropriate source: the recently freed slaves."[9] And beyond all the overt and self-conscious acts of dominion, such as those that virtually re-enslaved the American blacks after the Civil War, we come to all the subtle stratagems, passive as well as aggressive; to all the interpersonal knots and invisible webs of ensnarement which are so much a part of the psychopathology of our everyday lives that they have been apparent only to a few poets, novelists, and exceptionally perceptive psychiatrists.

Slavery itself has the great virtue, as an ideal model, of being clear-cut. Yet the model is so clear-cut that both abolitionists and later historians often obscured the complexities of actual bondage, whose worst horrors and tragedies did not arise from physical coercion, and whose moments of dignity and humanity can seldom be recognized without ideological risk. Furthermore, as I have tried to suggest in this study, the model was so clear-cut that it tended to set slavery off from other species of barbarity and oppression—except when apologists said, in effect, why should Negro slaves complain when pauper children are starving and sailors are lashed every day?

It was Hegel's genius to endow lordship and bondage with such a rich resonance of meanings that the model could be applied to every form of physical and psychological domination. And the argument precluded the simple and sentimental solution that all bondsmen should become masters, and all masters the bondsmen. Above all, Hegel bequeathed a message that would have a profound impact on future thought, especially as Marx and Freud deepened the meaning of the message: that we can expect nothing from the mercy of God or from the mercy of those who exercise worldly lordship in His or other names; that man's true emancipation, whether physical or spiritual, must always depend on those who have endured and overcome some form of slavery.

[9] Jervis Anderson, *A. Philip Randolph: A Biographical Portrait* (New York, 1972), p. 158. By the 1920s the Pullman Palace Car Company had become the largest single private employer of black labor in the United States (p. 159).

Index